Chicago® magazine's
Guide to Chicago

Chicago magazine's
Guide to Chicago

Allen H. Kelson · Anne Spiselman · David Novick · Don Klimovich

Contemporary Books, Inc.
Chicago

Library of Congress Cataloging in Publication Data

Main entry under title:
Chicago magazine's guide to Chicago.

Includes index.
1. Chicago (Ill.)—Description—1981—Guide-books.
I. Kelson, Allen H.   II. Chicago (WFMT [Radio Station:
Chicago, Ill.])   III. Title: Guide to Chicago.

F548.18.C455   1982   917.73'110443   83-1924
ISBN 0-8092-5893-5 (pbk.)

Photo credits—Cover: Bob Glaze, Artstreet;
71—Chicago Historical Society; 76—Chicago Historical Society;
82—Chicago Historical Society; 107—Museum of Science and Industry;
197—Commission on Chicago Historical and Architectural Landmarks;
207—DePaul University; 245—Chicago Historical Society, Raymond Trowbridge;
258—Chicago Historical Society; 277—Chicago Historical Society; 289—Village of Oak
Park; 322—Chicago Park District; 374—Chicago Historical Society

ISBN: 0-8092-5893-5

First edition

Printed in the United States of America

Staff

Editor and project director—Allen H. Kelson

Principal writers and researchers—Anne Spiselman, David Novick

Staff writer-researcher—Donald Klimovich

Additional writing and research—Beth Jensen, Liane Kleinmann, Susan Watkins, Alan Rosenthal, Laurie Levy

Copy and proof desk—Janet Warner, Tom Yoki, Helen Gordon

Typesetting—Anita Rouse

Layout, assembly, and keylining—Carla Kelson, Pam Macsai-Baumgartner, Joseph Aaron, Pamela Srikantaswamy, Carol Haddon, Penny Pollack, Bonnie Levin

Cartography—Creative Sales Corp.

Light at the end of the tunnel—Janet Visser

Additional support—Heidi Bubel, Jamie Gilson, Constance Hall, Henry Hanson, Gale Kappe, Bill Lowry, Jeff Pilarski, Brenda Shapiro, Charlie Thomas, Richard Warren

Thanks to: Sara G. Bode, Oak Park Village President; Robert White; Beverly Area Planning Assn.; South Shore Historical Society; Fr. George Lane; Albany Park Chamber of Commerce; Richard Marcus; John Dziedzic; Mary Decker, Cindy Mitchell, and other Friends of the Parks; D. Shigley; Roy Forrey, Chicago Commission on Historical and Architectural Landmarks; Eva R. Brown, Coordinator, Interlibrary Cooperation, Chicago Public Library; Sandra Gross, Evanston City Clerk; Irwin Novick; Jean F. Block; Michael Stefanos; Annette Fern; Seymour and Justine Goldstein

Contents

Elsewhere

None of the above, all of the above, and more

Foreword

by Studs Terkel

Janus, the two-faced god, has both blessed and cursed the city-state, Chicago. Though his graven image is not visible to the naked eye, his ambiguous spirit soars atop Sears, Big Stan, and Big John. (Our city is the street-wise and alley-hip of the casually familiar. Thus, the Standard Oil Building and the John Hancock Center are, with tavern gaminess, referred to as Big Stan and Big John. Sears is simply that; never mind Roebuck. Ours is a one-syllable town. Its character has been molded by the muscle rather than the word.)

Our double-vision, double-standard, double-value, and double-cross has been ever since—at least ever since the earliest of our city's fathers took the Potawatomis for all they had. Poetically these dispossessed natives dubbed this piece of turf *Chikagou*. Some say it is Indian lingo for City of the Wild Onion; some say it really means City of the Big Smell. Big is certainly the operative word around these parts.

Nelson Algren's classic, *Chicago: City On the Make,* is the late poet's single-hearted vision of his town's doubleness. "Chicago forever keeps two faces, one for winners and one for losers; one for hustlers and one for squares. One for Go-Getters and one for Go-Get-It-Yourselfers; one for poets and one for promoters. One for the early risers and one for the evening hiders."

It is the city of Jane Addams, a settlement worker, and Al Capone, an entrepreneur; of Clarence Darrow, a lawyer, and Julius Hoffman, a judge; of Louis Sullivan, an architect, and Paddy Bauler, an alderman. (Paddy's the one who some years ago observed: "Chicago ain't ready for reform."). And now, with a new mayor, and the Machine creaking out its last days in the manner of the one-horse shay, all bets are off. It is still the arena of those who dream of the City of Man and those who envision a City of Things. The battle is forever joined. The armies, ignorant and enlightened, clash by day as well as by night. Chicago is America's drama, writ large.

Several years ago the following A-B-C guideline was offered for nonnatives and casual guests. For the most part, it still applies:

Chicago has a North Side, a South Side, and a West Side. There isn't much East Side. If you head too far that way, you're swimming in Lake Michigan—or drowning, as the case may be. Here is the lakefront and the city's beaches. The farther south you travel, the farther the lake recedes. Thus there is more East to the South Side than there is to the North.

Lake Shore Drive, called by most the Outer Drive, is the thoroughfare that extends along the lake through most of the city. The city's fathers are solicitous of the motorist's comforts and time problems. In seeking to serve him, they once chopped down 800 trees in Jackson Park (on the South Side).

7

Much of the South Side and Near West Side comprise the black ghettoes of Chicago, the most expansive in the country. There are smaller such ghettoes in other areas of the city. It is our Soweto.

The Near North Side, along the lake, is an area of high-rise, high-rent apartment buildings, condominiums, nightclubs, and swinging-singles bars. Here is a concentration of bachelors and career girls. It is remarkably convenient, being close to the Loop, the lake, and where the action is.

Old Town, for a time the artsy-craftsy center, had deliquesced into a forlorn shabbiness, with a few oases, such as Second City, hanging on. Now newcomers join them. The Greenwich Village life has moved slightly north and west and diagonally toward Lincoln Avenue. Even so, there's a move toward more dispersed areas, where busy little theaters appear, struggle, and survive.

Further north, New Town came into being. Here weary ex-hippies (how archaic the term sounds today as their younger siblings are observed with *The Wall Street Journal,* neatly folded under their arms) and nomadic artists try to make it. Naturally, the rents in this area have soared. "Wherever I go," an overaged with-it lady informed me, "the rents go up." Thus the commercial nature of vogue.

Urban renewal (new name: gentrification), too, has played its role. Slightly west and north of the "action" areas have lived the less affluent—especially old pensioners. The city fathers have suggested, by means of bulldozer and wrecking ball, that they seek refuge elsewhere. In their place, young career couples have moved into homes and apartments, sudden condominia, in many instances, refurbished, redecorated, and right on. The young wives and live-in mates are modishly hip and the young husbands and lovers may be bangled and bearded, but they're oh, so Establishment straight. The changes have been astonishing. "Gentrification" has worked in many ways its wonders to perform.

Chicago's old established ethnic neighborhoods—those of Poles, Czechs, Yugoslavs, Ukrainians, Germans, Scandinavians, Irish, Italians, Jews—still exist, though they are no longer as homogeneous as once upon a time. The old-timers stay put; their children have taken off toward suburbs called Buffalo Grove, Elk Grove Village, Prospect Heights, Skokie.

Chicago's most cosmopolitan area may be, surprisingly, Uptown, on the city's North Side, close to the lake. Once an exclusively middle-class community, it is now a United Nations compote of have-nots, have-somewhats, and enclaves of haves: transients in rooming houses, Appalachian émigrés, Amerindians, East Indians, American blacks, African blacks, Asiatics, and Hispanics. Faces, languages, cuisines, and lifestyles are infinite in their variety. Halfway houses and nursing homes are here, too. Though the conditions of many are wretched, there are community groups working toward a better way, in face of the ubiquitous developers who are determined to "gentrify" the turf.

Perhaps, with scores of these newly formed community groups at work, tough-minded and proud, there may be a neighborhood resurgence throughout the city. The signs are there. Rehabilitation rather than gentrification is their watchword. The flavor, once European, is now Third World. The ma-and-pa stores, once Italian, Jewish, Greek, Slavic, are now Korean, Japanese, Pakistani, Palestinian, Filipino, Mexican. They and the more adventurous children and grandchildren of the Europeans are digging in. They are not looking toward City Hall, but toward themselves and their neighbors. The suburb is far from their thoughts. As for the Chicago of tradition. . . .

The North Shore suburbs are generally more upper "U" than others, though considerable status differences exist here, too. The largest, Evanston, immediately north of the city, has its own ghetto. The others, despite enormous percentage increases in black-family move-ins, are essentially nearly all white. Though Lake Forest is the uppermost "U," Winnetka and Glencoe are the wealthiest.

The suburbs to the west and south, varying in status, generally are ethnically oriented. A number of southern suburbs have black communities; some are almost wholly black.

Hyde Park, of which the University of Chicago is the core, is one of the few integrated areas in the city. Income is playing an increasing role there, along with the bulldozer. It is becoming more and more middle class. Rather than race, class is the factor in Hyde Park.

Bridgeport, where Mayor Daley lived, is on the Southwest Side of Chicago. As Mike Royko, our city's most perceptive chronicler, pointed out in *Boss,* his superb study of power, it is a neighborhood suspicious of strangers, especially black ones. It is near the former stockyards. (Chicago, for better or for worse, is no longer hog butcher to the world. Carl Sandburg's song is ended, though the melody may linger on. The cattle and swine, no longer shipped on the hoof, are now done in at such places as Greeley, Colorado; Logansport, Indiana; Guyman, Texas; and Clovis, New Mexico. *Sic transit gloria mundi.*) Bridgeport is a lower-middle-class area that was once predominantly Irish. It now includes Slavic peoples, Italians, and Mexicans. No blacks live here; they are on "the other side of the tracks" (the bankrupt Rock Island Line).

The Loop (so called because it is encircled by the elevated tracks that then spin off toward the outskirts) is Chicago's Downtown, its mercantile and financial center.

It is the architecture of Chicago that most impresses visitors. Rightfully and pridefully so. It was here that Louis Sullivan matured the idea of the skyscraper. "It's tall," was his exhilarating observation. It is the symbol, too, of the Big City. The legacies of Sullivan and of his most celebrated disciple, Frank Lloyd Wright, are astonishingly, breathtakingly evident, especially along the lakefront. "It causes the heart to leap," murmured a visitor from a distant continent.

In recent years, the impact of another architectural genius, Ludwig Mies van der Rohe, has made itself felt. His more austere works of steel and glass are reflected in the more modern commercial buildings and high-rises. They are a delight to observe, to work in, and to live in. If you so will. If you dwell in the mercy of the means.

Algren said of Chicago: "It's the city of 'I Will,' but what about those who say 'I Can't'?"

The answer is perhaps provided by Pablo Picasso's statue in the Daley Center Plaza in the Loop—to which we may add Miró's, Oldenburg's, Chagall's, and Calder's. The artist's gift to Chicago is his tribute to its pulse and muscularity. The sculpture's message is a cryptic one. Its strength, hope, or despair—indeed, its beauty, terror, or pity—is in the eye of the beholder. Its rear is as fascinating as its front. To the boast "I Will" and to the plaint "I Can't," it replies, "So What?" Here, too, the spirit of Janus hovers. Here, too, the spirit of Chicago thrusts itself onward and upward.

Introduction

This book celebrates Chicago, piece by piece, by looking at well-known neighborhoods and at obscure ones worth knowing better. It does not seek to be the measure of a city—this multifaceted metropolis has too much breadth and depth to be bound in a single small book. Instead it will give you insight on this sometimes enigmatic town's varied textures and diverse riches. To know Chicago, you must know its neighborhoods. This volume treats each independently.

To make *Chicago* magazine's *Guide to Chicago* work hardest for you,

Get a map. We've prepared up-to-date, street-by-street maps of individual communities, but a map of the entire metropolitan area is helpful.

Buy a Chicago *magazine.* We're not trying to peddle magazines here, but this book and the magazine are designed to work together. Each becomes more useful in the presence of the other. *Chicago* magazine's *Guide to Chicago* paints the broad picture. *Chicago* magazine, on the other hand, carries up-to-the-minute information no book can: programs, plots, persona, and prices of admission for the month's plays, concerts, museum and gallery shows, etc. Restaurant listings in this book are here to give you a choice of alternatives within a given neighborhood. Those in the magazine are critical recommendations made by a staff of professional reviewers on the basis of recent, anonymous visits.

Get a CTA route map (free at Chicago Transit Authority el and subway stations). Most of the neighborhoods in this book can be reached by public transportation, and most are fun to tour on foot. You'll find that some of the neighborhoods lend themselves to biking; in a few, touring by car is most convenient. You should have no difficulty deciding which is right for you when you check the maps or read the descriptions.

Chicago's major attractions—its most important museums, art galleries, theater and dance companies, and so on—are catalogued in chapters that deal exclusively with those subjects. But most of the sections of this book focus on individual neighborhoods, plus Oak Park and Evanston—two cosmopolitan suburbs that grew up with Chicago and have profoundly influenced it (and vice versa).

Here's how community chapters are organized:

The small inset map relates the neighborhood to the city. (The Loop is just east of where the expressways meet.)

The text tells how that neighborhood came to be what it is today—and what evidence of its past remains. It takes you to the major buildings and into the more interesting or important shops, restaurants, and attractions.

Listings include places discussed in the text (they're marked *) and others of more than passing interest. Churches are located by street intersections, not addresses, because many of them traditionally eschew government-prescribed street numbers. (Church addresses in the phone book are often for other buildings associated with the church.)

Neighborhood maps accompany the listings; nearly all have been drawn to the same scale so you will find them as easy to use and to relate to as possible. We compiled the maps as we did our street-by-street research. If you notice discrepancies between our maps and others, trust us; many maps currently on the market are based on outdated data.

As with *Chicago* magazine's editorial content, there is no relationship between advertising and a mention or nonmention in this book. Inclusion depends entirely on our writers' judgement and serendipity.

We sought urban treasures, but one man's meat is another's *poisson,* especially in a place as diverse as Chicago. Criteria of excellence vary from neighborhood to neighborhood, and we picked and chose what to put into the book by applying local standards. The intent has been to show you the best of what's at hand—though in no instance did we list a place we felt wasn't worthwhile. Thus, a shop mentioned on 63rd Street may not necessarily be better than one omitted on State Parkway—but it will be one of the best on 63rd, while the one on State may not be a Gold Coast highlight.

The index has been designed for everyday use. Major categories have been cross-referenced to enable you to find quickly and easily whatever you're looking for. Keep this book handy and use it before wading through metropolitan Chicago's many telephone directories, white and yellow. Our index is a directory with standards of excellence. It's small enough, handy enough, and sufficiently broad ranging to be your first-used reference.

There are no universal parameters, and we make no claims to perfection. So use this volume with an open mind. Feel free to disagree with us, and try to relate your taste to ours. Although we have expended extraordinary effort (and money) to make this book as accurate as possible, we realize that in this imperfect and ever-changing world, there are bound to be errors, and obsolescence is inevitable. We hope you'll pitch in to make the next book about The City That Works, work better. Mail your corrections, comments, and recommendations to us at Three Illinois Center, Chicago 60601. With your help, the next *Chicago* magazine's *Guide to Chicago* can serve you even better.

Getting Around

The nation's transportation hub for more than a century, Chicago carries on as one of the world's major air-travel loci, despite having an airport unequal to the challenge. The city's central location also provides good access to Amtrak and the continent's bus network.

Traveling around metropolitan Chicago is easy. Aptly named Lake Shore Drive extends much of the city's length, and modern expressways radiate from the downtown area. Locals tend to refer to them by name rather than by their interstate highway numbers. The Stevenson (I-55) travels southwest from McCormick Place to Springfield and St. Louis; the Eisenhower (I-290) extends west from the Loop. The major north-south expressway (I-90/94) bears a different name on each side of its "spaghetti bowl" intersection with the Eisenhower just west of downtown. South of this concrete maze, it's the Dan Ryan, one of the country's most confusing and accident-engendering stretches of roadway. North of the juncture, the highway slants northwest as the Kennedy. About eight miles from the Loop, the road forks. The Kennedy (I-90) jogs west past O'Hare (continuing to Rockford as the Northwest Tollway), and the Edens Expressway (I-94) heads to the northern suburbs, ultimately linking with the Tri-State Tollway (I-294 south of this intersection, I-94 to its north), which bypasses Chicago on an Indiana–Wisconsin run. I-57 leads to Champaign/Urbana and to other points south from its beginning at the intersection that marks I-94's name change: Dan Ryan north, Calumet south. Four miles north of that intersection the Chicago Skyway (I-90) branches off the Dan Ryan and forms a direct toll link with the Indiana toll road.

The city is laid out on a grid pattern, acts of nature, engineering, and history excepted. State and Madison Streets mark the address system's zero points, dividing the city into four quadrants, the northeast one severely attenuated by the shoreline's curve. Unlike Washington, D.C., where the quadrants are accurately labeled "northeast," etc., here anything north of downtown is called the North Side and south of downtown is similarly generalized. The West Side begins some vague distance from the Loop; there's no East Side to speak of. This imprecise nomenclature is appended with equally unclear, subjective modifiers, for example, the Far Southwest Side. "Going downtown" means traveling in any direction to the central business district; "Uptown" is a neighborhood, not a vector. Despite the seeming confusion, getting from here to there is simple, once you're used to the Chicago system.

Chicago addresses reveal their distances from one of the base lines because there are normally 800 address divisions to the mile. Thus, 3200 North Halsted Street is exactly four miles north of Madison Street; 842 West Belmont Avenue is just about a mile west of State Street. But unless you know how far east or west of State Street Halsted is, or how far from Madison Street Belmont is, you still haven't the foggiest idea of where to go. The Zip Code & Street Guide in the *Yellow Pages* "B" book gives that other necessary piece of information, locally referred to as a street's "hundred." With that guide, you'll know that Belmont's hundred (as we say) is 3200 north; thus is 842 West Belmont precisely located. On the South Side, "number-name" streets tell more, but somewhat cryptically. Two miles east of State Street you'll find 1600 East 80th Street. It would be great if 80th Street were ten miles south of Madison Street, but it isn't. Roosevelt Road, which used to be 12th Street, isn't a mile and a half from Madison Street, but only a mile. Thus, numbered streets south of there are half a mile closer to the base line than they seem to be: 80th Street is nine and a half miles south of Madison. (Just divide by eight and subtract half a mile.) 80th Place is fractionally further south. Unlike those in New York, Chicago's addresses and street numbers relate to each other. Every building between 80th Street and 81st Street is numbered between 8000 and 8099.

Natives find their way around by memorizing the coordinates of major streets and homing in on destinations by relating them to known intersections. To find 750 West Melrose Street, for instance, one might know that Melrose is a block north of Belmont (3200 North) and that 750 must be just east of Halsted Street (because Halsted is 800 West). This isn't as difficult as it seems: The coordinates of major arteries on the North and West Sides are usually divisible by four, and on the South Side by four minus one. On the Far West Side, a group of north-south streets runs in near-alphabetical order from Keystone through Pueblo; on the Far Southeast Side, Avenues B through O make things easier. Some suburbs use Chicago's base lines; others have their own arcane systems.

Local address systems aren't motorists' only trials. The Tri-State's toll booths every nine miles or so prompt many long-distance truckers to join their local compatriots on the much-burdened inner-city expressways. Negotiating them is demanding much of the day and very difficult during peak periods. Los Angeles and New York-size traffic jams are rare, however, except during temper-straining summertime repair projects. In the central business district, skyscraper construction on nearly every street exacerbates congestion; on-street parking is problematical here and throughout the stylish lakefront neighborhoods. Parking tickets, in recent memory a $3 bargain, now start at $7 for meter violations and skyrocket from there. Winter Snow Route violators aside, usually only the flagrantly foolish are towed by the police from illegal spots outside the Loop.

If you're nabbed for a moving faux pas, assuming an air of obsequious contrition is the best policy—the bribe-taking days are long gone. Walking back to the squad car, rather than awaiting the officer in the comfort of your car, however, is a much-appreciated submissive gesture. An Illinois driver's license, some major auto-club cards, and a few insurance company cards (notably Allstate's) are accepted in lieu of the required bail. Lacking these, you must post a cash bond at the station, a time-consuming operation. Courtroom pleas of innocence that also refrain from impuning police probity are likely to earn dismissals for almost any parking ticket or minor moving violation. A trial date may be missed once with impunity; second dates (notification is automatically mailed) may not be.

Fortunately, viable alternatives to driving abound. The once-unparalleled system of commuter railroads rattles along under the uncertain aegis of the Regional Transportation Authority (RTA), a multicounty agency damned by suburbanites, spurned by Chicagoans, and starved by penny-pinching state legislators. While the commuter trains usually run dependably, schedules of the RTA's stepchildren—suburban bus lines—are so frequently juggled that preembarkation calls to the agency's route information number (800-972-7000) are advisable.

Getting to and around Chicago's suburbs by public transportation is no worse than in many other major metropolitan areas. But getting around the city is far better. The Chicago Transit Authority's (CTA) buses ply almost every major street and run rush-hour express trips via expressways. The fare is about a dollar; seniors and kids enjoy substantial fare reductions systemwide; exact change (no dollar bills) is required on buses. A nominally priced transfer purchased with the fare allows continuous travel on more than one route throughout most of the RTA system without additional charge. (Commuter railroads are the major exception.) Sunday and holiday unlimited-ride Supertransfers are a best buy all year, but from June through October, when the Culture Buses roll, they've an extra use. From a common starting point at the Art Institute, these specials make giant loops through the South, West, and North Sides and are as good for sightseeing as they are for travel to the specific attractions.

Because most streets in the Loop are one-way, many bus routes make return trips on parallel streets. Buses on east-west streets here also travel special contra-flow lanes. This dangerous arrangement was mandated by the Federal government and clearly favors vehicular movement over pedestrian safety. Look both ways before forsaking the curb's safety. Most north-south buses that enter the downtown area (many travel the State Street Mall) make tight circles and then retrace their routes. This makes transferring necessary for bus travel through the Loop, but those route-end circles are very convenient shuttles.

CTA rapid-transit (i.e. elevated and subway train) fares are, with the exception of the Evanston line, the same as those on buses, but ticket agents make change and sell discount-priced tokens good throughout the system. Monthly passes are sold at specified transit terminals and various public-service counters in banks, etc. The trains, known collectively as the el, lead to within striking distance of most places in the city and even extend into the suburbs. From the South Side, the Englewood-Howard and Jackson Park-Howard lines run under the State Street Mall (the continuous platform provides direct access to many major stores), then trace the lakefront north to Howard Street, meeting trains for Evanston and Skokie. The Lake Street-Dan Ryan service races down the Dan Ryan Expressway median (mutely taunting mired motorists), passes through the Loop above Wabash Avenue, then travels to Oak Park above Lake Street. From the Northwest Side, the Congress-Milwaukee line travels the Kennedy Expressway median, crosses the Loop under Dearborn Street, then continues west to Forest Park along the Eisenhower Expressway. The Douglas-Milwaukee service does much the same, but it branches off at the Medical Center District and proceeds to Cicero and Berwyn. Their northern terminus is now the Jefferson Park Terminal, but both lines will ultimately reach O'Hare International Airport. The Ravenswood el zigzags downtown from the Albany Park neighborhood, then circles above the Loop—great for sightseeing. Designated stops allow free intertrain transfers. All trains have route maps.

Sometimes taxis can be a reasonable alternative to public transportation, particularly for several people on a short hop. But too frequently, rude, ill-trained, unknowledgeable drivers pilot unsafe vehicles with seemingly little regard for law, life, and limb. Within the city, meters tick off both distance and waiting-time charges. There's a surcharge for each additional passenger (waived for kids and seniors). Chicago cabs may travel to the 'burbs but must deadhead back to the city, and the suburban cab situation is just the reverse. The fares for these intercity trips usually exceed the straight-meter rate, but not always. Evanston cabs, for instance, go by the meter for trips to most northern suburbs and to Chicago destinations north of Roosevelt Road. Chicago cabs may not exceed the meter for any portion of the ride inside the city limits. From either Midway Airport or O'Hare International, trips to any of the city's contiguous suburbs are "on the meter." There should be a list of qualifying suburbs in the cab. Driver assurances notwithstanding, there are no officially set rates for other trips; it's wisest to negotiate first to avoid later confrontations. Because of these restrictions, chauffeured limousines may actually cost less for some trips. "Super Saver," a voluntary zoned-fare, central business district, shared-ride plan is so unpopular with the cabbies, you'll hardly ever see a taxi sporting the identifying banner except at the airports. For the otherwise very expensive cab trip to or from the airports, Super Saver drivers are free to pick up three like-minded riders. Parties of two or more will save money by insisting on traveling on the meter; singles can save about one third with Super Saver. Don't be filmflammed.

Continental Air Transport's comfortable buses make scheduled, moderately priced trips to O'Hare from major Chicago hotels (at about half the Super Saver cab fare). They also travel from some suburban locations. C.W. Limousine serves the South Side. The *Yellow Pages* lists various additional city and suburban carriers. It's best to prearrange with these nonscheduled services, so a limo awaits your arrival; however, on-the-spot arrangements may be made at the service desks near United's and American's baggage-claim areas at O'Hare. That airport's car-rental set-up isn't bad, and the downtown Chicago locations are very convenient. Travelers who require a car anyway should consider renting at the airport. Budget-watchers can take an express bus from O'Hare to the Jefferson Park Terminal and transfer to the el, but there are no baggage facilities on the trains. Graveyard-shift travelers will find severely limited options. If you're stuck at O'Hare for a while, stroll the underground walkway to the Hilton Hotel, where the amenities and comestibles are significantly better than in the terminal. Courtesy buses will spirit you to nearby hotels for other options. Parking at O'Hare is very expensive.

Midway Airport stands in stark contrast to O'Hare, which replaced it as the world's busiest when big jets demanded long runways. Ignored for years by most commercial carriers, this South Side facility is now home to Midway Airlines, a feisty, no-frills carrier flying DC-9s to major midwestern and eastern cities at fares that are usually much lower than those of other airlines. The airport also serves short-distance commuter lines and private aviation, as does Meigs Field, Chicago's downtown airport-in-the-park, which city administrators are determined to eliminate.

Ground travel: commuting

Continental Air Transport
454-7800

C. W. Limousine Service
493-2700

Regional Transportation Authority (RTA)
836-7000
800-972-7000
TDD 836-4949
Areawide rate, schedule, routing, etc. Mass-transit information.

Chicago and North Western Station
500 W. Madison St.
(Being razed, but service continues.) Chicago and North Western Railroad.

La Salle Street Station
414 S. La Salle St.
(Razed, but service continues.) Rock Island Railroad.

Randolph Street Station
151 N. Michigan Ave.
Illinois Central Gulf, Chicago South Shore & South Bend railroads.

Union Station
210 S. Canal St.
Burlington Northern, Milwaukee Road, Norfolk and Western railroads.

Van Buren Street Station
400 S. Michigan Ave.
Illinois Central Gulf, Chicago South Shore & South Bend railroads.

Ground travel: long distance

Amtrak Ticket Office
505 N. Michigan Ave.
558-1075
Trains leave from Union Station.

Greyhound Bus Lines
74 W. Randolph St.
781-2900

Trailways
20 E. Randolph St.
726-9500

Air travel: short distance

Most flights are from O'Hare International Airport.

Air Illinois
427-9511
Illinois and surrounding states.

Air Wisconsin
686-7424
Wisconsin and surrounding states.

American Central
686-7320
Iowa, Michigan, and Wisconsin.

Britt
686-7445
Illinois and surrounding states.

Direct Air
317-452-4031
Kokomo, Indiana.

Freedom Air
800-321-3342
Michigan.

Midstate
686-7407
Wisconsin, Michigan, and Minnesota.

Mississippi Valley
800-322-6752
Illinois, Iowa, and Wisconsin.

Phillips
686-7452
Northern Indiana.

Simmons
800-338-4842
Michigan.

Air travel: long distance

With the exception of Midway Airlines, major carriers fly only from O'Hare International Airport.

Air Canada 527-3900
Air France 782-6181
Air Jamaica 527-3923
Alitalia 427-4720
American 372-8000
British Airways 332-7744
Capitol 347-0230
Continental 686-6500

Delta 346-5300
Eastern 467-2900
El Al Israel 800-223-6280
Jet America 800-421-7574
KLM 346-3635
Lufthansa 800-645-3880
Mexicana 800-531-7921
Midway 471-4710
Northwest Orient 346-4900
Ozark 726-4680
Pan Am 332-4900
Piedmont 263-3656
Republic 346-9860
Royal Jordanian 236-1702
Sabena 800-645-3790
SAS 800-221-2350
Swissair 800-221-4750
Transamerica 686-7681
Trans World 558-7000
United 569-3000
USAir 726-1201

Sightseeing

American Sightseeing Tours—Chicago
530 S. Michigan Ave.
427-3100
Wide variety of bus tours (more available in summer than winter). The Conrad Hilton is the main starting point; pickups at other hotels by reservation.

Chicago from the Lake
1450 N. Dearborn St.
951-1947
Make reservations to enjoy evening dining, drinking, and dancing aboard the S. S. Betty Jean, which cruises the shoreline between McCormick Place and Navy Pier. Group charters, too.

Coach Horse Livery, Ltd.
1900 S. Prairie Ave.
337-4296
Hansoms await at Chestnut St. and Michigan Ave. seven evenings and weekend days; rides are for 1 to 4 persons; the charge is not cheap.

Crescent Helicopters
Meigs Field
544-9580
Aerial sightseeing.

Gray Line of Chicago
33 E. Monroe St.
346-9506
Services are similar to American; main starting point is near The Palmer House.

Mercury Sightseeing Boats
Michigan Ave. bridge (southwest side)
332-1353
River and lake rides.

Shoreline Marine Sightseeing Co.
Grant Park shoreline
427-2900
Day and evening lake excursions.

Wendella Sightseeing Boats
Michigan Ave. bridge (northwest side)
337-1446
Tours are similar to Mercury's; also runs a bargain-priced rush-hour commuter between the Wrigley Building and the Chicago and North Western Station from late spring through early fall.

The Boonies

Northbrook, Northlake; Park Forest, Forest Park; River Forest, River Grove: Even long-time Chicagoans have trouble keeping the suburbs straight. The following alphabetical listing of nearby suburbs and outlying communities gives the population based on the 1980 census (rounded to the nearest thousand), the municipal-office phone number, and the distance from the Loop. For more detailed mass-transit information, such as for bus links to suburbs without rapid-transit stops, call the Regional Transportation Authority.

The suggested auto routes from the Loop leave by expressway and point toward the destination's center. Interstate-highway directions conform to posted route and guidance signs. For other highways, general compass bearings are used. Chicagoans often refer to major expressways by name, even though many signs use only route numbers.

EXPRESSWAY SYSTEM

I-55 South Stevenson Expressway
I-90 West Kennedy Expressway (becomes Northwest Tollway)

I-90 East Dan Ryan Expressway (becomes Chicago Skyway)
I-94 East Dan Ryan Expressway (becomes Calumet Expressway)

I-94 West Edens Expressway
I-290 West Eisenhower Expressway (formerly Congress)
I-294 Tri-State Tollway
Ill. 5 East-West Tollway

MASS TRANSIT ABBREVIATIONS

BN Burlington Northern
CTA (followed by route name) Chicago Transit Authority

C&NW Chicago and North Western
ICG Illinois Central Gulf
MR Milwaukee Road

N&W Norfolk and Western
RI Rock Island
SS Chicago South Shore & South Bend

Addison (30,000)
543-4100
20 miles (I-290 west, Lake St. exit west)
Alsip (17,000)
385-6902
18 miles (I-94 east, I-57 east, 127th St. exit west)
Arlington Heights (66,000)
253-2340
24 miles (I-90 west, Arlington Heights exit) C&NW
Aurora (81,000)
897-8777
39 miles (I-290 west, Ill. 5 west, Aurora exit) BN
Barrington (9,000)
381-2141 .
36 miles (I-90 west, Ill. 53 north, U.S. 14 west) C&NW

Barrington Hills (4,000)
428-1200
38 miles (I-90 west, Barrington Rd. exit north, Ill. 62 west)
Batavia (13,000)
879-1424
36 miles (I-290 west, Ill. 5 west, Farnsworth Ave./Kirk Rd. exit north, Wilson Rd. west)
Bellwood (20,000)
547-3500
13 miles (I-290 west, 25th St. exit north) C&NW
Bensenville (16,000)
766-8200
21 miles (I-290 west, York Rd. exit north) MR
Berwyn (47,000)
788-2660
9 miles (I-290 west, Austin Ave. exit south) BN, CTA-Congress B

Blue Island (22,000)
597-8600
17 miles (I-94 east, I-57 south, 127th St. exit west) ICG, RI
Bridgeview (14,000)
594-2525
16 miles (Lake Shore Dr. south, I-55 south, Harlem Ave. exit south)
Brookfield (19,000)
485-7344
13 miles (I-290 west, 17th St. exit south) BN
Buffalo Grove (22,000)
459-2525
29 miles (I-90 west, Ill. 53 exit north, Dundee Rd. east)
Calumet City (40,000)
891-8100
23 miles (I-94 east, Sibley Blvd. exit east)

Cary (7,000)
639-0003
*43 miles (I-90 west, Bar-
rington Rd. exit north,
U.S. 14 west) C&NW*

Chicago Heights (37,000)
756-2110
*26 miles (I-94 east, Ill. 394
south, Lincoln Hwy. exit
west) ICG*

Cicero (61,000)
656-3600
*8 miles (I-290 west, Central
Ave. exit south) BN, CTA-
Congress B*

Clarendon Hills (7,000)
323-3500
*19 miles (I-290 west, Ill. 83
exit south) BN*

Country Club Hills
(15,000)
798-2616
*24 miles (I-94 east, I-57
south, 167th St. exit east,
Crawford Ave. south)*

Crete (5,000)
672-5431
*30 miles (I-94 east, Ill. 394
south, Lincoln Hwy. exit
west, State St. south)*

Crystal Lake (19,000)
815-459-2020
*49 miles (I-90 west, Ill. 31
exit north, U.S. 14 west)
C&NW*

Darien (15,000)
852-5000
*21 miles (Lake Shore Dr.
south, I-55 south, Cass Ave.
exit north)*

Deerfield (17,000)
945-5000
*27 miles (I-90 west, I-94
west, Deerfield Rd. exit
west) MR*

Des Plaines (54,000)
391-5300
*20 miles (I-90 west, Mann-
heim Rd. exit north) C&NW*

Dolton (25,000)
849-4000
*19 miles (I-94 east, Dolton
exit west) ICG*

Downers Grove (43,000)
964-0300
*23 miles (I-290 west, Ill. 5
west, Highland Ave. exit
south) BN*

Elgin (64,000)
695-6500
*38 miles (I-90 west, Ill. 25 or
Ill. 31 exit south) MR*

Elk Grove Village (29,000)
439-3900
*26 miles (I-90 west, Elm-
hurst Rd. or Arlington
Heights Rd. exit south) MR*

Elmhurst (44,000)
530-3000
*17 miles (I-290 west, St.
Charles Rd. exit west)
C&NW*

Elmwood Park (24,000)
452-7302
*13 miles (I-290 west, Har-
lem Ave. exit north) MR*

Evanston (74,000)
328-2100
*13 miles (Lake Shore Dr.
north, Sheridan Rd. north)
C&NW, CTA-Evanston*

Evergreen Park (22,000)
422-1551
*13 miles (I-94 east, 95th St.
exit west)*

Flossmoor (8,000)
957-4500
*25 miles (I-94 east, I-57
south, Vollmer Rd. exit east,
Governors Hwy. east) ICG*

Forest Park (15,000)
366-2323
*10 miles (I-290 west, Har-
lem Ave. exit south) CTA-
Congress A*

Franklin Park (18,000)
671-4800
*15 miles (I-290 west, 25th
Ave. exit north) MR*

Geneva (10,000)
232-0854
*36 miles (I-290 west, Ill. 5
west, Kirk Rd. exit north, Ill.
38 west) C&NW*

Glen Ellyn (24,000)
469-5000
*24 miles (I-290 west, Roo-
sevelt Rd. exit west, Park
Blvd. north) C&NW*

Glencoe (9,000)
835-4111
*22 miles (I-90 west, I-94
west, Dundee Rd. exit east)
C&NW*

Glenview (32,000)
724-1700
*20 miles (I-90 west, I-94
west, Lake Ave. exit west)
MR, RTA buses*

Glenwood (11,000)
758-5150
*24 miles (I-94 east, Glen-
wood Dyer Rd. exit west)*

Grayslake (5,000)
223-8515
*42 miles (I-90 west, I-94
west, Ill. 120 exit west) MR*

Gurnee (7,000)
623-7650
*39 miles (I-90 west, I-94
west, Ill. 132 exit east)*

Harvey (36,000)
339-4200
*19 miles (I-94 east, Sibley
Blvd. exit east) ICG*

Hazel Crest (14,000)
335-4600
*22 miles (I-94 east, I-57
south, 159th St. exit east,
Kedzie Ave. south, 170th St.
east) ICG*

Hickory Hills (14,000)
598-4800
*18 miles (Lake Shore Dr.
south, I-55 south, U.S. 45
exit south, U.S. 12 east)*

Highland Park (31,000)
432-0800
*26 miles (I-90 west, I-94
west, U.S. 41 exit north,
Central Ave. east) C&NW*

Hinsdale (17,000)
789-7000
*18 miles (I-290 west, I-294
east, Ogden Ave. exit west)
BN*

Hoffman Estates (37,000)
882-9100
*30 miles (I-90 west, Ill. 53
exit south, Higgins Rd.
west) MR*

Homewood (20,000)
798-3000
*24 miles (I-94 east, I-294
west, Halsted St. exit south)
ICG*

Itasca (7,000)
773-0835
*24 miles (I-290 west, Thorn-
dale Ave. exit west, Old
Rohlwing Rd. south,
U.S. 19 east) MR*

Joliet (78,000)
815-740-2411
*38 miles (Lake Shore Dr.
south, I-55 south, Ill. 53 exit
south) ICG, RI, Amtrak*

Kenilworth (3,000)
251-1666
*17 miles (I-90 west, I-94
west, Lake Ave. exit east,
Green Bay Rd. north)
C&NW*

La Grange (15,000)
579-2300
*14 miles (I-290 west, Mann-
heim Rd. exit south) BN*

La Grange Park (13,000)
354-0225
*15 miles (I-290 west, Mann-
heim Rd. exit south) BN*

Lake Bluff (4,000)
234-0774
*35 miles (I-90 west, I-94
west, Ill. 176 exit east)
C&NW*

Lake Forest (15,000)
234-2600
*31 miles (I-90 west, I-94
west, U.S. 41 exit north,
Deerpath Rd. east) C&NW,
MR*

Libertyville (17,000)
362-2131
*35 miles (I-90 west, I-94
west, Ill. 176 exit west) MR*

Lincolnshire (4,000)
945-8500
*31 miles (I-90 west, I-294
west, Ill. 22 exit west)*

Lincolnwood (12,000)
673-1540
*12 miles (I-90 west, I-94
west, Touhy Ave. exit east)*

Lisle (14,000)
968-1200
*25 miles (I-290 west, Ill. 5
west, Ill. 53 exit south) BN*

Lockport (9,000)
815-838-0549
*33 miles (Lake Shore Dr.
south, I-55 south, Ill. 53 exit
south, Ill. 7 east) ICG*

Lombard (37,000)
620-5700
*22 miles (I-290 west, Ill. 5
west, Highland Ave. exit
north) C&NW*

Lyons (10,000)
447-8886
*12 miles (Lake Shore Dr.
south, I-55 south, Harlem
Ave. exit north, 47th St.
west) BN*

Markham (15,000)
331-4905
*22 miles (I-94 east, I-57
south, 159th St. exit east)*

Matteson (10,000)
748-1559
*29 miles (I-94 east, I-57
south, U.S. 30 exit east) ICG*

Maywood (28,000)
344-1200
*11 miles (I-290 west, 1st or
9th Ave. exit north) C&NW*

Melrose Park (21,000)
343-4000
*13 miles (I-290 west, 25th
Ave. exit north) C&NW*

Midlothian (14,000)
389-0200
*20 miles (I-94 east, I-57
south, 147th St. exit west) RI*

Morton Grove (24,000)
965-4100
*17 miles (I-90 west, I-94
west, Dempster St. exit
west) MR*

Mount Prospect (53,000)
392-6000
*24 miles (I-90 west, Elm-
hurst Rd. exit north) C&NW*

Mundelein (17,000)
566-7070
*37 miles (I-90 west, I-94
west, Ill. 176 exit west)*

Naperville (42,000)
420-6000
*30 miles (I-290 west, Ill. 5
west, Naperville Rd. exit
south) BN*

Niles (30,000)
967-6100
*16 miles (I-90 west, I-94
west, Caldwell St. exit west)*

Norridge (16,000)
453-0800
*14 miles (I-90 west, Har-
lem Ave. exit south)*

North Chicago (39,000)
578-7750
*38 miles (I-90 west, I-94
west, U.S. 41 exit north,
22nd St. east) C&NW*

North Riverside (7,000)
447-4211
*11 miles (I-290 west, 1st
Ave. exit south)*

Northbrook (31,000)
272-5050
*25 miles (I-90 west, I-94
west, Dundee Rd. exit west)
MR*

Northfield (6,000)
441-6113
*20 miles (I-90 west, I-94
west, Willow Rd. exit west)*

Northlake (12,000)
343-8700
*18 miles (I-290 west, Mann-
heim Rd. exit north, North
Ave. west)*

Oak Brook (7,000)
654-2220
*19 miles (I-290 west, Ill. 5
west, Spring Rd. exit north,
22nd St. southwest)*

Oak Forest (26,000)
687-4050
*22 miles (I-94 east, I-57
south, 159th St. exit west) RI*

Oak Lawn (61,000)
636-4400
*14 miles (I-94 east, 95th St.
exit west) N&W*

Oak Park (55,000)
383-6400
*9 miles (I-290 west, Austin
Ave. or Harlem Ave. exit
north) C&NW, CTA-Con-
gress A, CTA-Lake St.*

Olympia Fields (4,000)
748-8246
*28 miles (I-94 east, I-57
south, U.S. 30 exit east) ICG*

Orland Park (23,000)
349-5400
*23 miles (Lake Shore Dr.
south, I-55 south, U.S. 45
exit south) N&W*

Palatine (32,000)
358-7500
*31 miles (I-90 west, Ill. 53
exit north, Palatine Rd.
west) C&NW*

Palos Heights (11,000)
361-1800
*19 miles (I-94 east, I-57
south, 127th St. exit west,
Ill. 83 northwest)*

Palos Hills (17,000)
598-3400
*18 miles (Lake Shore Dr.
south, I-55 south, U.S. 45
exit south, 107th St. east)*

Palos Park (3,000)
448-6150
*22 miles (Lake Shore Dr.
south, I-55 south, U.S. 45
exit south, 123rd St. east)
N&W*

Park Forest (26,000)
748-1112
*30 miles (I-94 east, I-57
south, U.S. 30 exit east) ICG*

Park Forest South (6,000)
534-6451
32 miles (I-94 east, I-57 south, U.S. 30 exit east, Governors Hwy. south) ICG

Park Ridge (39,000)
399-5200
18 miles (I-90 west, Cumberland Rd. exit north) C&NW

Peotone (3,000)
258-3279
43 miles (I-94 east, I-57 south, Peotone Wilmington Rd. exit east)

Richton Park (9,000)
481-8950
31 miles (I-94 east, I-57 south, U.S. 30 exit east, Cicero Ave. south, Sauk Trail Rd. east) ICG

River Forest (12,000)
366-8500
10 miles (I-290 west, Harlem Ave. exit north) C&NW, CTA-Lake St.

River Grove (10,000)
453-8000
12 miles (I-290 west, 1st Ave. exit north) MR

Riverdale (13,000)
841-2200
19 miles (I-94 east, I-57 south, 127th St. exit east, Halsted St. south) ICG

Riverside (9,000)
447-2700
11 miles (I-290 west, Harlem Ave. exit south) BN

Roselle (17,000)
980-2000
28 miles (I-290 west, U.S. 20 exit west, Roselle Rd. north) MR

Rosemont (4,000)
823-1134
13 miles (I-94 west, River Rd. exit north, Ill. 72 west)

St. Charles (17,000)
377-4400
36 miles (I-290 west, Ill. 64 exit west)

Schaumburg (53,000)
894-4500
29 miles (I-290 west, Ill. 72 exit west, Roselle Rd. south)

Schiller Park (11,000)
678-2550
15 miles (I-90 west, River Rd. exit south)

Skokie (60,000)
673-0500
16 miles (I-90 west, I-94 west, Dempster St. exit west) CTA-Skokie Swift

South Holland (25,000)
333-0572
21 miles (I-94 east, 159th St. exit west)

Stickney (6,000)
749-4400
10 miles (Lake Shore Dr. south, I-55 south, Central Ave. exit north)

Summit (10,000)
563-4800
13 miles (Lake Shore Dr. south, I-55 south, Harlem Ave. exit south) ICG

Villa Park (23,000)
834-8500
20 miles (I-290 west, Roosevelt Rd. exit west, Ill. 83 north) C&NW

Waukegan (68,000)
689-7500
40 miles (I-90 west, I-294 west, Ill. 120 exit east) C&NW

West Dundee (4,000)
426-6161
42 miles (I-90 west, Ill. 31 exit north)

Westchester (18,000)
345-0020
14 miles (I-290 west, Mannheim Rd. exit south)

Western Springs (13,000)
246-1820
16 miles (I-290 west, Wolf Rd. exit south) BN

Westmont (17,000)
968-0560
20 miles (Lake Shore Dr. south, I-55 south, Ill. 83 exit north, 55th St. west) BN

Wheaton (43,000)
260-2000
25 miles (I-290 west, Ill. 5 west, Naperville Rd. exit north) C&NW

Wheeling (23,000)
459-2600
26 miles (I-90 west, I-294 west, Willow Rd. exit west, Milwaukee Ave. north)

Willow Springs (4,000)
839-2701
19 miles (Lake Shore Dr. south, I-55 south, U.S. 45 exit south, 87th St. west) ICG

Wilmette (28,000)
251-2700
16 miles (I-90 west, I-94 west, Lake Ave. exit east) C&NW, CTA-Evanston

Winfield (4,000)
665-1778
28 miles (I-290 west, Ill. 5 west, Naperville Rd. exit north, Ill. 38 west, Winfield Rd. north) C&NW

Winnetka (13,000)
446-2500
18 miles (I-90 west, I-94 west, Willow Rd. exit east) C&NW

Woodridge (22,000)
852-7000
25 miles (Lake Shore Dr. south, I-55 south, Ill. 53 exit north, Hobson Rd. east)

Woodstock (12,000)
815-338-4300
55 miles (I-90 west, Ill. 47 exit north) C&NW

Zion (18,000)
872-4546
47 miles (I-90 west, I-94 west, Ill. 173 exit east) C&NW

South of the River

Visitors to Chicago always want to know why locals call this part of the city the "Loop." Usually they are told that the name stems from the elevated tracks encircling the city's center. Actually, the convergence of cable-car lines around the business section formed a loop in the 1890s, but historical niceties aside, the area both within and without the el's circle of steel makes up the Loop: It's Chicago's nucleus, the scene of its start, and the source of its future. City street numbers begin at the intersection of State and Madison Streets; La Salle Street's canyons are the Midwest's financial focus; Clark and Dearborn Streets boast a congress of local, state, and Federal government buildings; department stores and specialty shops line State Street—"that Great Street"—and Wabash Avenue; and Michigan Avenue offers an unmatched cultural com-

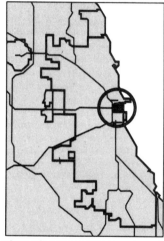

plex. On top of this, the entire downtown is shot through with architectural masterpieces that chronicle Chicago's seminal role in the development of the modern high-rise.

When Indians massacred Fort Dearborn's garrison and some hapless pioneers during the War of 1812, chances looked slim for the fledgling village at the mouth of the Chicago River. By 1816, however, the fort was rebuilt at what is now Michigan Avenue and Wacker Drive, and the Indians were forced west of the Mississippi River in 1825. Canal-building schemes attracted new settlers; about 4,000 celebrated the city's incorporation in 1837.

Early Chicagoans clustered around the fort. In the 1830s, businesses flourished on South Water Street (now Wacker Drive), while manufacturing, warehousing, and shipping spread along the North Branch's banks. By 1850, retailers had moved a block south to Lake Street, leaving South Water to the wholesalers and produce merchants who remained until Wacker Drive was created after World War One. Chicago's political center was fixed in 1853 when the city and county erected a combined office building-courthouse on the site of the present City Hall-Cook County Building, a neoclassical colossus covering a square block at Clark and Randolph Streets. La Salle Street became the financial focus when the Chicago Board of Trade moved there in 1865.

As Lake Street became more congested, sharp operators looked southward. Potter Palmer, a wealthy merchant and Civil War speculator, bought up jerrybuilt frame structures along State Street. By 1870, he had raised a grand hotel bearing his name at Monroe Street and had constructed the forerunner of today's Marshall Field's store at Randolph Street.

The Great Chicago Fire of 1871 turned the thriving downtown to a pile of ashes, leveling elegant new commercial buildings and squalid back-alley housing with egalitarian thoroughness. Hindered only by a nationwide business depression, downtown Chicago, save for the slums, rebounded with a speed that amazed the world. Rebuilding followed the old patterns of activity, but everything was bigger, taller, more assertive. State Street became the center for discriminating shoppers, a distinction it held for almost a century.

Today, the street has lost much of its glamour. Shoppers—especially the carriage trade—have taken their custom to the Magnificent Mile and suburban plazas. The decline began after World War Two and crescendoed in the 1960s when more and more black Chicagoans flocked to the Loop as businesses fled the South and West Sides. Despite police statistics showing downtown to be one of the city's safest areas, whites perceived it as very black and dangerous and stayed away in droves, furthering the self-fulfilling prophecy that afflicts so many of the country's urban centers. Restaurants folded or shortened evening hours and movie palaces booked black exploitation films.

White flight sent waves of panic through State Street's merchants, who responded by supporting the State Street Transit Mall, a dismal, barren misconception that accomplished little more than ridding the strip of remarkably ugly lampposts, legacies of the 1950s modernization flurry. Fast-food outlets and cutrate shops peddling disco duds still dot the west side of the street, interspersed among unprepossessing, low-priced clothing chain stores (bigger versions of those in almost every outlying shopping center) and flagships of just about every budget shoe chain.

But reports of State Street's demise may have been premature. Although some major stores have closed (or are about to), the Great Street's merchants still outsell the Magnificent Mile's, and massive developments on both ends of the Loop promise to restore some of the old glory.

Marshall Field's (111 North) remains everything State Street was and a hopeful sign of what it still can be. One of the world's great department stores, Field's takes the title seriously. Some 450 separate departments filled with everything from the downstairs store's bargains to fine furs, rare books, and antique jewelry surround the store's skylighted central courts. Whether or not the original Marshall Field really commanded "Give the lady what she wants," that's what the company has been doing for more than a century. On the main floor alone, cosmetic counters glisten with enviable selections; the leather-laden luggage department knows few peers; the silver collection shines with 19th-century splendor; and the city's largest candy section overflows not only with the famed Frango mints (mint meltaways, ask for a sample) but also with luxury imported chocolates, delightful *trompe l'oeil* marzipans, and top-quality bonbons turned out by squads of hand-dippers in Field's kitchens.

Equally outstanding merchandise fills the other floors: casual to designer men's, women's, and kids' clothing; lifestyle to fine antique furniture; kitchenware from gourmet gadgets to appliances; an exciting toy selection; an unusually large book department; a liquor section with Frango mint liqueurs and private-label wines; a grocery with everything from truffles, ready-to-eat entrées, and cold cuts to fresh-baked pastries and Field's own ice cream (including Frango mint). Restaurants such as the chic but proper Walnut Room, the oddly named Narcissus Room, and the pink "Victorian" Crystal Palace ice-cream parlor provide sustenance for that Chicago tradition—a day "doing" Field's.

Impressive services range from the expected, such as the Bridal Registry, fur storage, gift wrapping, and Personal Shopping Service, to the rare: interpreters for more than 35 languages, staff-shopping for the handicapped, birthday and anniversary reminders. Coupled with speedy delivery and a liberal return policy, they help explain the store's loyal following.

Marshall Field's was already well-established when **Carson Pirie Scott & Co.** (1 South) moved from Lake Street to the five-year-old, Louis Sullivan-designed Schlesinger and Mayer store in 1904. The buildings say something about the different philosophies of State Street's premier retailers. A model for Daniel Burnham's other great stores—Selfridge's, Gimbel's, Filene's, Wanamaker's, and the May Company—the Field building is almost overwhelming in its classical massiveness and patrician, no-nonsense façade. Carson's anything-but-stuffy lightness and warmth are exemplified by Sullivan's iron ornamentation and wood-paneled rotunda, all lovingly restored under the direction of John Vinci. The two might be called the dowager and the debutante.

Inside, Carson's is basically a middle-class Field's with the high end truncated and the middle ground expanded. Clothing is more likely to be popularly priced and casual; contemporary and Scandinavian furniture get a big play. Special services include cooking demonstrations and guest appearances by big-name chefs in Kitchentech, a fully equipped, seventh-floor classroom; skilled wedding consultants; and a Santa for the hearing-impaired. Promotions (the autumn Import Fairs are the biggest) involve the whole store—special menus in the restaurants, interior decorations, festive window displays, even entertainment—and often spill out onto the sidewalks.

Wieboldt's (1 North), the latest remodeling of Holabird and Roche's Mandel Brothers' block, recalls suburban stores with its decent, a bit trendy, moderately priced, main-line merchandise. For a huge selection of middle-American fare and a touch of history, check out the two firms that made Chicago the country's mass-merchandising mail-order center. **Sears, Roebuck and Co.** (403 South), in Jenney and Mundie's 1891 gem of a building (look up past the modern store windows: It's hard to believe the building's so old), has the work clothes, tools, and appliances that made the company's reputation, plus all the usual department-store stock. **Montgomery Ward & Co.** (140 South) has always lagged behind Sears in retail store operations, and despite a better location, the story's the same in the Loop. "Modernization" has completely obscured the façade of the one-time Fair Store, another William Le Baron Jenney building, which is larger than Sears but doesn't look it. Ward's parent, Mobil Oil, is planning a 60-story office building on the store's site in 1984.

The fashion-conscious may shop the Magnificent Mile, but pickings aren't slim in the Loop, particularly for men. **Lytton's** (235 South) began as The Hub in 1887 and has been on State Street since 1911. Though a women's department was added when the name changed in 1945, men's wear is still the main attraction in this spacious, 1950s-looking store. Besides quality lines such as Bill Blass and Palm Beach, Lytton's offers its own popular Threadneedle Street suits, shirts, and shoes.

The nation's oldest clothing retailer has consistently favored conservative styles, but the "preppy" craze has set the cash registers ringing at the local **Brooks Brothers** (74 East Madison Street). Although the store's nothing special to look at, the racks are crammed with enough Ivy League clothes to outfit several campuses, and expert tailoring has been a trademark since 1818.

The 1982 remodeling of the former Marshall Field's Annex by new owners, with retail space on the first few floors and offices above, brought another purveyor of private-label, traditional clothing to the Loop. **Jos. A. Bank Clothiers** (25 East Washington Street, second floor) carries a huge selection of men's suits, sports coats, slacks, shirts, sportswear, and sundries, as well as a respectable collection of women's wear, at an average of 30 percent below typical retail prices. Owned by Quaker Oats, Bank is so competitive because it manufactures the goods it sells.

Hart Schaffner & Marx, which began as a retailing and tailoring partnership in 1887 and grew into a national brand, produces men's clothing in plants at 728 West Jackson Boulevard and in Des Plaines. Retail outlets include several old-line stores brought under the corporate umbrella. **Baskin** (137 South State Street), for one, is a favorite source for fairly traditional togs with Oleg Cassini, Countess Mara, Christian Dior and, of course, Hickey-Freeman and Austin Reed, both made by the parent company. Gentlemen of distinction shop at **Capper & Capper** (1 North Wabash Avenue), a handsome, old-fashioned store with knowledgeable, almost courtly salesmen offering conservatively styled, expensive clothes. Hickey-Freeman and Oxxford suits top the line, and custom-cut orders can be placed from a library of swatch books. There's also a super selection of appropriate shirts, hats, and accessories.

While both Baskin and Capper & Capper have small women's sections, the Hart Schaffner-owned **Chas. A. Stevens** (25 North State Street) offers seven levels of fashions and services for women, from the bargain-filled budget basement to the sixth-floor Powder Box beauty salon with the Adrien Arpel Spa. The Fashion Shoe Salon shares the main floor with accessory and gift collections. The Designer's Shop, Etienne sport department, a whole floor of junior fashions, and the Executive Place—a boutique featuring dresses, suits, sportswear, sundries, and a Fashion Registry with special services for businesswomen—are among the other attractions. Periodic sales and rapid markdowns make Stevens particularly popular both on State Street and in more than 20 other locations. The almost glitzy Circle restaurant on the sixth floor is a good place to relax over lunch and baked-on-the-premises goodies.

Of an increasing number of shops specializing in hard-to-fit sizes, **Lane Bryant** (9 North Wabash Avenue) may be the oldest and best-known. Moderately priced, mostly Seventh Avenue and California fashions for tall and large women include sportswear by Gloria Vanderbilt, Geoffrey Beene, and Harvé Benard; coats by Pauline Trigère; Bill Tice loungewear; and Catalina swimsuits. These aren't the very trendy, youth-oriented togs that fill many Loop stores, but they are an improvement over the dowdiness that used to be synonymous with clothes for big women.

Evans (36 South State Street) has a fair share of "disco duds" on the jammed-with-racks first floor, but coats, particularly furs, have made the firm famous. Besides raincoats, overcoats, and fine woolens, Evans stocks what may be the city's largest collection of fur, fur-lined, and fur-trimmed coats and accessories that run from inexpensive, fun items to full-length opulence. The store's enormous volume means good values.

Evans is the most visible of scores of furriers crowded into a few downtown blocks. Many are hidden on the upper floors of old buildings, go unnoticed by window-shoppers, and draw their customers by word of mouth. One that does get noticed, because of superb values and a five-year guarantee, is **Mysels** (6 East Monroe Street). Many furs are sold at half the price charged by chic salons at this high-volume operation, which encourages shoppers to try on coats in the elegant showroom, then compare prices. Their like-new used furs (in the twelfth-floor Resale Fur Salon) offer even greater savings.

For bargains on the latest women's fashions (including furs, leathers, and a large assortment of other coats), locals and out-of-towners head to **Handmoor** (300 North Michigan Avenue and 200 West Adams Street). Dresses, suits, separates, sportswear—from practical business clothes to *au courant* casuals to frilly silks—fill a seeming sea of sales racks. New York and California houses are well represented, as are big-name European and American designers. The selection of costume jewelry, belts, handbags, and other accessories is terrific, and fashion coordinators are always handy to help put together the perfect outfit. Best of all, everything is sold for 20 percent or more off the tags' prices. **Loehmann's** (205 West Randolph Street), a similar operation with an almost legendary reputation in New York, has finally opened here and offers equally impressive off-the-rack goodies. For equivalent deals on men's suits, slacks, and shirts, check out the **Clothing Clearance Center** (1006 South Michigan Avenue).

Discounts of 30 to 50 percent on coats by such designers as Benard, Trigère, and Bill Blass are the main attractions at **Coats, Coats, Coats, Inc.** in the **Chicago Garment Center Building** (337 South Franklin Street), where you can browse for buys on everything from maternity clothes to formal wear in two dozen showrooms. Chicago once had a thriving garment district centered on Van Buren Street between Wells Street and Wacker Drive, but soaring land values, new office-tower construction, high labor costs, and the move of manufacturing to the Sun Belt have reduced it to a remnant of its former self. Little else remains except a few manufacturers and fabric outlets, among them **E. M. Bloomberg & Co.** (341 South Franklin Street), **Fraerman Yard Goods & Draperies** (314 West Adams Street), and **White's Fabrics** (226 South Wabash Avenue, second floor).

The Chicago Garment Center is just one of many vintage downtown buildings filled with interesting businesses. The **Stevens Building** (17 North State Street) is the best known, and although it doesn't have the glitter or traffic of Water Tower Place, it has its own, anachronistic, appeal: an elevator starter with castanets; more than a dozen floors of furriers, jewelers, and beauticians; curiosities such as tea-leaf readers; and specialty shops. **Fashionette Swimsuits** (Suite 1412) can fit most sizes from an enormous, year-round collection of beachwear, both discreet and revealing. The shop also carries men's and women's racing suits, goggles, earplugs, and swim caps. The large **Tall Girls Shop** (Suite 1314) stocks everything from uniforms to quality on-the-town togs for women between five feet seven and six feet five, and **Nierman's Tall Girl Shoes** (Suite 1202) has been fitting their feet for more than 50 years with practical to high-fashion shoes in hard-to-find sizes and unusual widths. At the **Capezio Dance Theatre Shop** (Suite 1300), ballet slippers, tap shoes, leotards, calf-warmers, and the like are not only an invitation to dance but also very much in style, even if you don't know a plié from a pliers. **Illinois Theatrical Footwear** (Suite 1533) is a little more performance oriented, right down to a full array of belly-dancing paraphernalia.

Dancers, chorus girls, period-costume designers, Chicago Historical Society clothing conservators, and Saturday seamstresses have been frequenting the **International Importing Bead and Novelty Co.** (Suite 1010) for 60-some years. The wholesale-retail store is stacked floor to ceiling with baubles, bangles, and beads: rhinestones, sequins and sequined patches, intricately carved wood beads, painted porcelain ones, others of faceted crystal, shells, figured stones, jewelry findings, a wall of shoe boxes filled with buttons (don't ask them to match one), trimmings, belt buckles, and jillions of seed beads in a rainbow of colors—sold by the scoop or the piece. **The Hirk Company** (Suite 1130) specializes in monogramming furs and linens. Skilled operators using special machines initial shirt cuffs (very "in"), safeguard sables, and run off emblems for softball teams. The shop will embroider almost anything.

Sam Himoto can personalize pens at **The Universal Pen Hospital** (Suite 1218), but his real fortes are custom-making fountain pens, reshaping points to fit individuals, and doctoring pens with broken points, dried-out pads, and worse. He has been fixing pens for decades, and despite the universality of ball-points, collectors, folks with family heirlooms, and just plain fountain-pen lovers can count on him for help.

Ralph LaBok, self-styled "Mr. Fix-It of Chicago" for more than half a century, plies his trade in the landmark **Reliance Building** (32 North State Street). Designed in 1894 by Charles Atwood of D. H. Burnham and Company, the glass-and-terra-cotta-sheathed building was remarkable for its time and remains a tribute to graceful, turn-of-the-century functionalism. Though hideously disfigured on the lower floors, the interior is virtually unchanged higher up. Notice the striking reliefs on the lobby-level brass elevator doors before having the homey operator take you up to LaBok's **Ace Leather Goods Repair Service** (Suite 1101). He can fix almost anything but traffic tickets: zippers, handbags, jackets, luggage, cases of all sorts. He also specializes in recovering antique umbrellas, cleaning leather and suede, and custom-making leather goods. A wealth of information and everyday philosophy, LaBok peppers the conversation with tidbits about his favorite authors and artists, along with homilies in Yiddish and English. Recycling is planned for the Reliance, so LaBok, who's been a fixture since the 1940s, may have to move soon.

For 64 years, **K. Matsumoto Art Repair Studio** (226 South Wabash Avenue, seventh floor) has been fixing damaged porcelain, glass, ivory, jade, and most other delicate objects except dinnerware and broken hearts, though Matsumoto says he "listens real good." He and several assistants also grind down chipped lips on crystal goblets and do wonders with broken antique lamps. Their museum-quality restorations don't come cheap, nor should you expect overnight service: Many people ride the rickety elevator to the loft shop crammed with a backlog of repairs.

Above Mysels, Jesus Avila at **J & J Silversmith** (6 East Monroe Street, Suite 900) repairs and replates jewelry, restoring pieces for museums, fixing clasps for the city's elite, and creating gigantic trophies for area racetracks. Hard-to-find antique-gold plating is one of the services Avila offers, but his greatest delight is continuing the art he began in Mexico at age eight: designing and making gold, silver, and platinum jewelry.

Like the Stevens Building, the Mallers Building (5 South Wabash Avenue) stacks floors of shopping arcades, but this hive of glass-fronted suites is devoted almost exclusively to the jewelry industry. Diamond merchants and findings sellers share the floors with jewelers, both wholesale and retail. A deviation from the norm, **Jerry Lee Antiques** (Suite 312) not only sells beautiful antique watches and some jewelry but also has a large collection of not-for-sale antiques such as cartoon-character timepieces, old metal toys, and model trains. **Todd's Boots** (Suite 1511), an anomaly for the building, stocks the city's largest selection of men's and women's Frye and Chippewa boots. At lunchtime, you can watch jewelers wheel and deal in the third-floor Coffee Shop, a deli that would be perfectly at home in Manhattan's diamond district.

The Jewelers Club meets in the basement of the 1927 Pittsfield Building (55 East Washington Street), with its handsome lobby arcade and wonderful elevator brasswork. Besides scores of dentists' offices, the Pittsfield is home to **Carteaux, Inc.** (Wabash Avenue entrance), which specializes in gold of a more decorative sort: traditional, classic, and precious jewelry plus top-of-the-line watches. **The Old Jewelry Shop** (Suite 430) is a fine source for Victorian rings, bracelets, brooches, and cameos, as well as some Georgian and Art Nouveau items.

Elijah Peacock sold watches and clocks before Chicago got its charter. Today **C. D. Peacock Jewelers** (101 South State Street) is the city's oldest store. Behind bronze peacock doors, it is the picture of Old World elegance with coffered green-marble ceilings, crystal chandeliers, and polished wood cabinets displaying the big names in crystal and sterling, china and porcelain, lifelike Boehm statuary, top-quality timepieces, stationery, and expensive jewelry.

Peacock's is one of several stores in the **Palmer House's** (17 East Monroe Street) old-fashioned arcade. Among the others are **Pendleton Woolen Mills,** a tiny shop full of the famous, perfect-for-the-country-estate woolen plaids and other men's and women's casual wear, and **Broadstreet's,** a two-story men's store that stocks names like Geoffrey Beene, Oscar de la Renta, and Petrocelli.

Lloyd & Haig Shoes (3 South Wabash Avenue), one of many better shoe salons on Wabash Avenue, carries a wide range of well-crafted, conservatively styled men's shoes, many in hard-to-find extra wide and narrow widths. Frequent sales offer excellent values. The Levine family at **Chicago Trunk & Leather Works** (12 South) has been selling trunks, suitcases and travel accessories in the Loop since 1911. There are good selections of business cases and women's handbags; free monogramming comes with the purchase of luggage by makers like Hartmann, Lark, French, and Skyway.

If you're looking for durable backpacks, rugged field boots, or hunting, fishing, and camping equipment—even a canoe—head up Wabash Avenue to **Eddie Bauer, Inc.** (123 North). Bauer started as an expeditions outfitter and pioneered down-filled clothing, a tradition that continues with an array of down-insulated apparel from Arctic-tested parkas to lightweight pullovers. Two floors of trail equipment, outdoor clothes, and accessories are also appropriate for armchair woodsmen and women. Prices aren't low, but an unconditional guarantee backs everything. The salespeople are helpful, knowledgeable, enthusiastic, and too few, so sign up for a stream of informative catalogues.

Once State Street's rival for retail supremacy, Wabash Avenue was cast into the shadows by construction of the el in the early 1900s. Extending from Lake Street south to Van Buren Street, the intimidating tracks had a chilling effect on commercial life, blocking out the sun, snarling traffic, and gathering armies of pigeons. Building façades are cut off from view above the first-floor level, and pedestrians are in an eerie world punctuated by the ear-shattering squeals and rumbles of trains. Nonetheless, groups dedicated to saving the ironwork relic began forming the moment plans for dismantling it were announced, and along with the shoe and clothing stores, specialty shops survive under the tracks.

A Loop fixture since 1857, **Iwan Ries & Co.** (17 South) is the world's highest-volume tobacco store, renowned for its stock of more than 25,000 pipes and its best-selling Three Star smoking mixture. Catalogues go to 300,000 people; mail orders account for about half the retail business. Cigar smokers flock to the refrigerated walk-in humidor to select house brands that can be warmed in the store's microwave oven. The Pipe Museum has a recorded commentary describing rare and intricately carved pieces, and tools and buffing wheels are on hand for cleaning and polishing your favorite calabash. Pipe prices range from $1.50 to $3,000; advice and encouragement are free.

Cutlery has been the stock in trade at **Otto Pomper** (109 South) since 1890. Knives by Henckels, Case, Chicago Cutlery, Marks, and Wüsthof Trident share the space with a related but odd assortment of devices, both useful and whimsical: straight razors, electric ones, and converters for foreign travel; kitchen gadgets as diverse as silver corncob holders and bean stringers; bird feeders and foot relaxers. Of course, Pomper sharpens knives and scissors.

Of almost two dozen Loop bookstores, many of which are hidden on the upper floors of old buildings, **Kroch's & Brentano's** (29 South and 17 branches) is the biggest and best-known. Carl Kroch, the very active president, has made the 75-year-old K & B a superb full-service bookstore. Astute buyers stock the shelves with all but the most obscure books: best sellers, about-to-be best sellers, cookbooks, foreign-language volumes, delightful children's readers, scientific and technical tomes, and books on art, architecture, business, the professions, religion, travel, and sports. Racks in the basement are packed with an enormous selection of paperbacks. Store services include nominally priced book searches, extensive backlists, autograph parties, one-day delivery to branches, and deliveries anywhere in the world. The salespeople really know—and love—their business. **B. Dalton Bookseller** (129 North), the Chicago flagship of a national chain, is also a good place to find best sellers, and the third floor offers remaindered, special-purchase, and damaged-book bargains.

School supplies and teaching aids are the specialties at **Beckley-Cardy** (324 South), which has the latest in classroom paraphernalia for science, mathematics, and language arts, as well as flash cards and stuff for preschoolers. The friendly staff makes it a good place to go for advice on tutoring your youngsters. Weekend artists and students from nearby schools frequent **Favor Ruhl Co.** (14 South), one of the city's oldest and most prestigious art-supply houses. Prices on oils, brushes, and the like start low; the store carries a full range of materials for commercial artists; and the atmosphere is youthful and exuberant, rather than businesslike.

Parasols, plastic snowflakes, Easter bunnies, piñatas, fishnets, and pink elephants fill **Bregstone Associates, Inc.** (440 South). The imagination-run-wild store supplies "decorative materials" for window displays and advertising sets, but also provides retail customers with the trappings for almost any theme party. Christmas decorations are available year-round; revolving mirrored globes can be rented for home discos.

What Kroch's & Brentano's is to books, **Rose Records** (214 South) is to music. Jim Rose carries on the family business started some 50 years ago by the "Radio Doctors" at Jackson Boulevard and Dearborn Street. The largest record dealer in the Midwest, Rose stocks 40,000 titles—a third more than the Schwann catalogue lists—covering every kind of music. Downstairs bins are divided into classical, soundtracks, nostalgia, jazz, rock, audiophile, women in music, soul, country, folk, and blues—and they're all full. Upstairs, you'll find bargain labels and cut-outs, comedy, ethnic categories, children's, and language-instruction discs along with tapes, cassettes, and a video department. Rose does a huge mail-order business, but be there in person for the winter and summer sales.

Don't be surprised if ghostly music fills your ears at the intersection of Wabash Avenue and Jackson Boulevard. This was once the center of Chicago's music row. The golden days are past—Lyon & Healy is the latest of the giants to leave—but there is still plenty of activity, anchored by **Carl Fischer** (312 South Wabash Avenue), where you'll find the world's largest inventory of published music. The first floor contains vocal music, rock, jazz, and specialty instrumentals—from balalaika to zither; the second floor serves bands and orchestras; and the third is devoted to choral scores, including complete operas. Nothing's ever thrown away at Carl Fischer, so it's a gold mine for collectors; music of the 1920s and '30s is big right now. If you can't remember a title, try humming a few bars; a member of the expert staff—some have been there 50 years—can probably identify it. Fischer also carries topnotch books about music, musical games, and, through its Gamble Music Co. division, musical accessories. The store is such a charmer that many customers drive here from surrounding states rather than use the bustling mail-order department.

Other musical resources jam above-street showrooms. Bill Crowden's **Drums, Ltd.** (218 South, eighth floor) is a hangout for percussionists from symphony orchestras as well as drum-busters from rock groups. Every sort of drum imaginable, cymbals, hand bells, and xylophones are available. Instruments from South America, the Middle East, and Africa give the shop an international flavor. And if you need to rent a one-man band, a San Francisco cable-car gong, a duck call, or a thunder machine, Bill Crowden is the man to see. For something a little less raucous, check out the huge collection of acoustic guitars at **Chicago Guitar Gallery** (216 South, third floor), which also has banjos, mandolins, ukuleles, and, of course, electric guitars and monstrous amplifiers.

Jazz musicians in town for a gig often wind up at **Sid Sherman Musical Instrument Co.** (226 South, third floor) for emergency repairs or just gossip. Sherman carries a full range of brass, reed, string, and percussion instruments—all of professional quality. An equally fine selection at **Kagan & Gaines Music** (228 South, third floor) is geared more to bands and orchestras than to jazz and studio musicians.

Renold Schilke of **Schilke Music Products** (529 South) has been making and repairing brass instruments—mostly trumpets—since 1929. He is one of the few high-quality instrument makers left in America, and back orders run from about six months for trumpets to about a year and a half for piccolos. Horn makers still apprentice with Schilke, but he sees the wave of the future in giant firms like Japan's 4,000-employee Yamaha, for whom he acts as consultant. Not only do **Kenneth Warren and Son** (28 East Jackson Boulevard, eighth floor) make and repair violins, they also operate one of the nation's two violin-making schools. Three generations are involved in this first-class shop that provides instruments for everyone from students to professionals. In the same building, **Douglas Raguse** (Suite 1009) carries on an even more esoteric art: the manufacture of violin, viola, and cello bows. When he began in 1976, Raguse had to make his own specialized tools. Materials are also difficult to get: Pernambuco wood from Brazil is extremely rare; tortoises and elephants that provided ivory and shell are on the endangered-species list; and the secret to laminating tortoiseshell is closely guarded by the London guild of eyeglass makers. No wonder Raguse's waiting list is backlogged several years!

In the **Fine Arts Building** (410 South Michigan Avenue), **Robert Bein & Geoffrey Fushi** (Suite 1014) have one of the city's largest violin-repair facilities and sell rare bowed instruments to an international clientele. **Eugene S. Gordon** (Suite 709) makes and repairs woodwinds. One of a stand of striking Michigan Avenue buildings nourishing the area's artistic life, the Fine Arts Building is an official city landmark designed by Solon S. Beman for the Studebaker brothers' carriage business in 1885 and converted to Chicago's equivalent of Carnegie Hall in 1898. Behind the Romanesque façade with the motto "All passes—ART alone endures" carved inside the entrances, the marble and wood interior is rich with ornament and history. The vaulted-ceiling lobby leads to the **Studebaker Theatre** and **World Playhouse** (*see Theater*), originally music halls, and creaky elevators rise to the tenth floor where skylights illuminate delightful Art Nouveau murals, the work of Joseph C. Leyendecker (known for his Arrow Collar Company drawings) and other artists who once had studios in the building.

Early tenants included Frank Lloyd Wright and Lorado Taft, and gatherings such as the Little Room brought together such luminaries as John McCutcheon, Hamlin Garland, Henry Blake Fuller, Irving and Allen Pond, and Hugh Garden. William W. Denslow and L. Frank Baum collaborated on *The Wizard of Oz;* drama teacher Anna Morgan staged the first American performances of plays by George Bernard Shaw and Henrik Ibsen; the fourth-floor Chicago Little Theater numbered 25 American premières among its 44 productions. Harriet Monroe published *Poetry: A Magazine of Verse* here, introducing sizable audiences to Carl Sandburg, Vachel Lindsay, T. S. Eliot, and Ezra Pound; Margaret Anderson's *The Little Review* was the most avant-garde and controversial literary journal of the time; *The Dial* and the *Saturday Evening Post* were among the many other publications with offices in the building.

Ghosts of the great haunt long corridors lined with practice rooms, recital halls, studios, schools, and related shops and offices. The **Kelmscott Gallery** (Suite 825) mounts fascinating exhibits that focus on British and American architecture (*see Galleries*). At **Scriptorium Benedictine** (Suite 609), Jan Wolkowski and his wife make illuminated books and presentation scrolls on parchment and vellum. And the **Chicago City Theatre Company** carries on the building's little-theater tradition (*see Theater*). Ornate doors, hall clocks, stair railings, and elevator doors remain unchanged, and every floor offers some delightful surprise proving that art does indeed endure.

For all its grandeur, the Fine Arts Building inevitably suffers in comparison to its 1889 next-door neighbor, the Auditorium Building. The first major fruits of a most fortuitous collaboration combined Dankmar Adler's engineering expertise with Louis Sullivan's decorative genius and is deservedly a city landmark. Inside the massive Richardson Romanesque masterpiece, **Roosevelt University** (430 South Michigan Avenue) occupies space that was originally a grand hotel and offices. A private institution dedicated to making higher education available to all on a nondiscriminatory basis since its founding in 1945, Roosevelt has been restoring the building in sections as money permits. Much of the work on the former hotel lobby and grand staircase, laden with mosaic tile, onyx dados, stenciled beams, and gold-leaf ornament, is complete.

The **Auditorium Theatre** (70 East Congress Parkway) is even more magnificent. After the Chicago Opera Company moved to Insull's Civic Opera House in 1929, the theater languished for 30 years, but a more-than-$2-million restoration drive spearheaded by Beatrice Spachner saved it from destruction. Renovated under the direction of Harry Weese, the sweeping 4,000-seat hall, enhanced by gilt, murals, and stained glass, reopened in 1967. The most advanced theater of its day remains one of the world's finest. It was the first "air-conditioned" house and once sported complex hydraulic stage machinery that could lower the entire stage to create an 8,000-person ballroom. Sight lines are excellent (though you have to strain to see from the upper gallery), and the acoustics are near perfect. Just seeing the theater is worth the admission price to one of the many concerts and dance programs sponsored by the Auditorium Theatre Council (*see Music*), but tours are also available. Goldilocks-like logic directs most touring Broadway shows from the too-large Auditorium and Civic theaters, as well as from the too-small Studebaker and World. Musicals play the **Shubert** (22 West Monroe Street), and dramas the slightly smaller and less rococo **Blackstone** (60 East Balbo Avenue).

Theodore Thomas, organizer of the Chicago Symphony Orchestra, complained so vehemently about the Auditorium's size that Orchestral Association trustee Daniel Burnham contributed his design services for a more intimate hall. The 1904, Georgian **Orchestra Hall** (220 South Michigan Avenue) isn't the acoustic equal of Adler's masterpiece, but is one of a spate of World Columbian Exposition-inspired, neoclassical buildings that transformed Michigan Avenue in the early years of this century. The Cliff Dwellers Club, founded in 1907, occupies the city's first penthouse, and the selection of Howard Van Doren Shaw as its designer is said to have caused grumblings from member Frank Lloyd Wright. Most of Chicago's other old-line, exclusive clubs line Michigan Avenue: the University, Illinois Athletic, Chicago Athletic, Chicago; the Union League, the Standard, and the Commercial, sponsor of the Chicago Plan, are nearby.

The Art Institute of Chicago (Michigan Avenue at Adams Street) first occupied a Burnham and Root building on the site of the present Chicago Club, but moved to its ever-expanding quarters in late 1893 (*see Museums*). The newest addition, Skidmore, Owings & Merrill's ultramodern wing, is on the Columbus

Drive side, along with **The Goodman Theatre** (200 South; *see Theater*), an arch salvaged from Adler and Sullivan's demolished Stock Exchange Building, and Isamu Noguchi's playful environmental sculpture, *Celebration.* The new building houses the reconstructed Stock Exchange trading room and the **School of the Art Institute** (208 South), known to most people for its **Film Center.** Public screenings of an extraordinary variety of films, from classic to experimental, keep the auditorium packed; but the school is also an important training ground for aspiring painters, sculptors, and designers. With the fine- and commercial-art students at the **American Academy of Art** (220 South State Street) and at the **Harrington Institute of Interior Design** in the Fine Arts Building, they make Chicago a center for art education and keep the clerks at Favor Ruhl hopping.

Specializations in the arts and media distinguish **Columbia College** (600 South Michigan Avenue), which traces its roots to an 1890 oratory college for women. After some lean years, it's a thriving undergraduate and graduate institution combining liberal arts and technical training. The faculty is heavy with working professionals, and Columbia bought the old **11th Street Theatre** (62 East 11th Street), formerly part of the Chicago Women's Club, for its theatrical and musical programs. The **DePaul University Loop Campus** (Jackson Boulevard and Wabash Avenue) includes colleges of law and commerce and the adult-education School for New Learning in three buildings. Also nearby are the **American Conservatory of Music** (116 South Michigan Avenue) and the **Spertus College of Judaica** (618), which houses the superb **Asher Library** (*see Libraries*) and a peerless **Museum of Judaica** (*see Museums*). In all, more than 40,000 full- and part-time students pursue educations in the area.

Grant Park, with the natural history museum, planetarium, and aquarium clustered at its southern end, faces Michigan Avenue's grand stretch. On the north, the avenue's sweep of public institutions is capped by the **Chicago Public Library Cultural Center** (78 East Washington Street), an Italian Renaissance masterpiece designed by Shepley, Rutan and Coolidge in 1897, five years after they did the Art Institute's central portion. Holabird and Root supervised the outstanding restoration of the lavish marble, mosaic, and Tiffany skylight-graced interior in 1977. The building retains the library system's art and film collections, while operating as a concert hall, art gallery, museum, and, most appropriately, a center for joyous civic celebrations. (*See Museums; Parks and Boulevards; Libraries.*)

Airline offices, travel agencies, consulates, banks, and old-line corporate headquarters also line majestic Michigan Avenue. Behind elegant façades, equally elegant lobbies gleam with highly polished bronze, and uniformed operators man the elevators. In D. H. Burnham and Company's 1911 Peoples Gas Building, the **Chicago Association of Commerce and Industry** (130 South) offers maps and information for tourists and a collection of unabashedly Chicago-proud souvenirs and gifts in a classy shop. Burnham designed the Railway Exchange Building (224 South) seven years earlier and maintained offices there while working on the Chicago Plan. The **Williamsburg Restaurant,** hidden off the white terra-cotta lobby atrium, sports a muraled taproom with a super back-bar. Daily menus feature inexpensive plate lunches, a tradition that is dying in the Loop as fast-food and short-order joints squeeze out old-fashioned lunch spots. **Vitello's Bakery**—enter from the lobby—sells good Italian pastries. Get to **Chas. T. Wilt Company** (232 South) from the street, through a grand bronze entrance. The 120-year-old firm stocks leather goods, attaché cases, and gifts.

Any number of "going out of business" import shops dot the area, but they're outclassed by the gift shops at the Art Institute and Spertus Museum for reproductions, jewelry, books, and prints. Proximity to the Art Institute has attracted several galleries to the avenue, including the excellent **Campanile Galleries** (200 South; *see Galleries*), but some of the best deals on artworks, antiques, jewelry, quality furniture, and furnishings can be had at **Hanzel Galleries'** (1120 South) periodic auctions. Gallery buyers and museum curators from all over the country join antiques dealers and individual collectors for "important" sales with catalogues that may list a Jacobean chest, Georgian silver, or a Picasso print. More frequent "estate" sales offer everything from Chicago's leading families' slightly less imposing possessions to the utilitarian household goods of the comfortably well-off. Suites of pre-World War Two furniture, Oriental rugs, books, paintings, and box lots are worth particular attention. The house's probity is beyond question.

Asian House of Chicago (316 North) may have the Midwest's largest collection of Oriental furniture and furnishings under one roof. Jade and ivory carvings, cloisonné, and vases and urns of porcelain, bronze, and pottery make the first room look like a huge gift shop; but beyond and above spreads a forest of lamps, carved and painted screens and chests, and furniture in a plethora of Oriental genres. The selection is staggering, and although prices are high, decorator discounts are offered. Ironically, antiques (20 percent of the stock) may be cheaper than new pieces because of increased labor costs. Most of the wares are imported from China. Nearby, **The Beautiful Sound, Inc.** (325 North) is the city's exclusive retailer of Yamaha and elite Bösendorfer pianos; Kimball pianos are also available, as are Allen organs.

This strip of North Michigan Avenue languished as a commercial backwater for some years until nearby Illinois Center sparked revitalization, but since the 1920s, it hasn't lacked for architectural wonders. The **Carbide and Carbon Building** (230 North) is a black and dark-green Art Deco gem in the New York tradition, designed by Burnham Bros. in 1929. Holabird and Root's 1928 **333 North Michigan Avenue Building,** based on Eliel Saarinen's second-prize-winning entry in the 1922 Tribune Tower contest, exemplifies a more refined treatment of the style. Alfred S. Alschuler's 1923 **Stone Container Building** (360 North), on the other hand, is a fanciful flurry of neoclassicism.

Most of the temples of commerce forming La Salle Street's financial canyon are also in the classical mode, but the street's focus is the Art Deco **Chicago Board of Trade** (141 West Jackson Boulevard) topped by the statue of Ceres. Visitors can view the action immortalized in Frank Norris's *The Pit* from a fifth-floor visitors' center, or just enjoy the sleek, three-story, marble lobby. From its founding in 1848, the Board of Trade has symbolized Chicago's dominance in commodities trading, and the recently expanded building also houses the **Chicago Board Options Exchange.** Other nearby exchanges include the **Chicago Mercantile Exchange** (444 West), begun in 1874 for perishables trading and presently playing the international-currency-futures game; the **MidAmerica Commodity Exchange** (175 West), a Board of Trade rival since 1868 and recently also trading in gold futures; and the **Midwest Stock Exchange** (120 South La Salle Street). The pace is frantic at all of them.

A decorous calm pervades the stolid La Salle Street headquarters of Chicago's major banks. Certainly the most handsome is the **Continental Illinois National Bank** (231 South), with a marvelous block-long, high-ceilinged banking floor built on the grand scale of a railway station waiting room. The 1924 building is the work of Graham, Anderson, Probst & White, who are also responsible for Union Station, the Civic Opera House, the Merchandise Mart, the Pittsfield Building, and—on the site of Jenney's Home Insurance Building, direct progenitor of modern skyscrapers—the La Salle National Bank Building (135 South), the last Art Deco tower built in Chicago and the last major Loop undertaking before a 20-year hiatus forced by the Depression and World War Two.

Continental maintains a visitors' center in the La Salle Street lobby. Here banking is demystified and you can wheel and deal with a computer. There's a satellite office in the **Rookery** (209 South). The lobby of Burnham and Root's robust 1886 building was designed by Frank Lloyd Wright for a 1905 remodeling. Wrapping around a fanciful iron-and-glass light well, it's one of the most beautiful public spaces in any major Chicago building.

Although the Rookery attracts a steady stream of archibuffs, the city's most magnificent interior goes largely unheralded. The trickle of Amtrak riders passing through **Union Station**'s (210 South Canal Street) splendid waiting room barely notice the ornate, gilt-trimmed capitals atop soaring columns. Few peer into the closed, formerly elegant restaurants or know that the station was once so busy it had its own police detail and jail, inspirations for the 1950, shot-on-location film, *Union Station*.

But at least Union Station survives. The grand concourse building across the street was demolished in 1969, and the **Chicago and North Western Station** fell recently, both victims of a building boom that's transforming the Loop and extending its boundaries. Quickly built office towers are rapidly leased to lawyers and service corporations. Towering over the activity is the monolith that signaled the boom's beginning, the ultimate expression of Skidmore, Owings & Merrill's Miesian modernism: **Sears Tower.** The world's tallest building fills a square block at Jackson Boulevard and Wacker Drive and offers unobstructed views of the entire city from an observation deck.

For a sidewalk-level panorama of Chicago's architectural history, walk down Dearborn Street between the shopping of State and Wabash and the financial activity along La Salle. Modern skyscrapers with monumental-sculpture-adorned plazas are interspersed among buildings from the post-Fire period and the great days of the Chicago School. Don't forget to look up, and inside the lobbies.

Modest post-Fire ambitions show in John Mills Van Osdel's 1872 **McCarthy Building** (32 West Washington Street), and drastic alteration of the lower stories can't hide its Italianate charm. A more ornate treatment of the style marks the **Delaware Building** (36 West Randolph Street), which has been renovated down to the skylighted atrium lobby. Between the two is the **Unity Building** (127 North Dearborn Street), designed by innovative Clinton J. Warren for governor-to-be John Peter Altgeld. Clarence Darrow and Edgar Lee Masters had offices in this building where Rotary International was founded. Across Dearborn, the **Richard J. Daley Center** (Randolph Street between Dearborn and Clark Streets) is a 1965 Cor-ten steel tower designed by C. F. Murphy Associates. The upper reaches house city offices and civil courts; the lobby an information booth loaded with helpful maps and booklets, a changing art display, and lunchtime concerts. In the summer, performances move out into the plaza, where the *Chicago Picasso,* a giant Cor-ten steel sculpture that, it has been shown, resembles both Picasso's last wife and his Russian wolfhound, stares toward the **Brunswick Building**'s (69 West Washington Street) courtyard and Joan Miró's *Chicago,* a surreal woman surmounted by a pitchfork.

Across Clark Street from the Daley Center plaza is the seat of city government. Holabird and Roche's massive, somber, neoclassical **City Hall-Cook County Building** (Randolph to Washington Streets, between Clark and La Salle Streets) was constructed between 1906 and 1911. Mayoral mandates emanate from the fifth floor (La Salle Street side), while the City Council holds forth on the second. The vaulted ceilings of the spacious lobbies are covered with mosaics. If only walls could talk!

A couple of blocks south of the Daley Center, the plaza of the **First National Bank** (Monroe Street between Dearborn and Clark Streets), graced by Marc

Chagall's joyful *The Four Seasons* mosaic, offers more noontime entertainment and a lot of excitement. Beneath the gently tapering curtain wall designed by the Perkins and Will Partnership and C. F. Murphy Associates, there's lots of space, ledges for perching, an outdoor café, popcorn and hot dog vendors—all of which make this the Loop's best summertime people-watching spot.

Bronze reliefs above the entrance and dazzling lobby mosaics depicting scenes from the explorations of Marquette and Joliet relieve the functional austerity of Holabird and Roche's 1894 **Marquette Building** (140 South Dearborn Street), a quintessential Chicago School structure with powerful projecting piers articulating its skeleton. The Marquette shares the block with Helmut Jahn's new **Xerox Centre** (55 West Monroe Street), covered in a sleek baked-polymer skin that curves gracefully around the corner. Jahn's work is a witty example of a younger generation of architects' reaction to the pristine, almost dehumanizing, antiseptic style typified by Mies van der Rohe's **Federal Center and Plaza** (Dearborn and Adams Streets). Even Alexander Calder's *Flamingo,* brightly painted and stylish, doesn't break the chill here, and the low Loop Postal Station punctuating the plaza helps little.

From Jackson Boulevard south to the shell of the Dearborn Street Station, the street seems to narrow under the begrimed, massive weight of the innovative, utilitarian structures that chronicle the Chicago School's struggle to open building façades to daylight. Six-foot-thick walls at the base of Burnham and Root's **Monadnock Building** (53 West Jackson Boulevard) demonstrate the practical limits of load-bearing, masonry walls. The Holabird and Roche addition to the south relies on skeleton construction. In fact, the first tall office building to use iron and steel skeletal construction throughout, the **Manhattan Building** (431 South Dearborn Street), was built in 1890, a year before the Monadnock went up. Burnham embraced the new techniques in the 1896 **Fisher Building** (343 South) and clothed the façade in Gothic ornament, which became popular for skyscrapers a decade later. Holabird and Roche's **Old Colony** (407 South) and **Pontiac** (542 South) can be viewed as practice for the Marquette. Some of these buildings have gotten facelifts in recent years; others have been—or are being—totally rehabbed. While most remain office towers, the Manhattan has been converted to rental apartments with retail space on the first floor. For pamphlets and displays on the area's landmarks, visit the **ArchiCenter** in the Monadnock, and/or sign up for one of the walking tours.

South of Congress Parkway, the sturdy factories that once housed much of Chicago's printing industry are being recycled as **Printing House Row,** a development that is attracting artists and urban pioneers to loft living downtown. The **Dearborn Street Station,** a National Register property designed by Cyrus L. W. Eidlitz and built in the mid-1880s, is being refurbished as offices for the First Federal Savings and Loan Association of Chicago. Behind it, a brand new residential community, **Dearborn Park,** is covering old railroad yards. Bookstores, gallery spaces, related businesses, and a restaurant are beginning to give this small neighborhood some charm; bistros and artsy shops can't be far off.

Basic amenities are a bit harder to come by. **Stop & Shop** (16 West Washington Street), owned by the Levy Organization, is the nearest supermarket of any note. A direct descendant of the 1872 grocery Tebbetts and Garland ran at 18th Street and Wabash Avenue to serve the Prairie Avenue carriage trade, the 1928 ornate brass-and-marble-trimmed store is reminiscent of London's Fortnum and Mason. Cut-to-order prime meats; game and fresh fish; produce of exceptional quality; top-of-the-line imported biscuits, mustards, jams, tinned soups; coffees and teas; and a large candy department with Belgian Neuhaus and other fine chocolates tempt shoppers into defying diets. Vie de France croissants are baked in the store five times a day; delicatessen offerings include fresh caviar, a fine selection of cheeses, and main dishes like game hen; carry-out sandwiches, a fresh-vegetable salad bar, and hot lunches draw noontime crowds; and ice-cream cones are always available. Personal shoppers take phone orders and put them up for delivery or will call; gift baskets and boxes are available on the main floor, in the upstairs wine and liquor department, or by mail or phone order from the colorful catalogue.

Gaper's, which is part of the same corporation, prepares the bakery's cakes and pastries and the deli's salads and entrées. Chicago's oldest caterer feeds countless guests at massive civic banquets and intimate Gold Coast parties. For even a custom-made picnic for four, their retail consultants will arrange local delivery or ship the treat up to Ravinia, where Gaper's directs the food service.

Most Loop delis, fast-food joints, and restaurants are packed at lunch. Department store dining rooms are also crowded, but the waits often aren't as long. The one at Wieboldt's, where the food is adequate but no match for Marshall Field's, can often seat people immediately. Many office buildings, old and new, have restaurants and cafeterias, a number of which are operated by Faber's and offer good value in spotless surroundings.

Magic Miller (210 West Adams Street) represents a recent twist on the cafeteria concept. Several stations sell hot entrées, pizza, burgers, barbecue, baked potatoes with various fixings, salads, bakery goodies, and the like, which patrons can enjoy in a large, bright room. Although at lunchtime **The French Baker** (26 West Madison Street) resembles the Bastille being stormed, a cozy, no-frills, French café atmosphere prevails. The plastic-knife-and-fork-casual downstairs room serves delicious fresh-baked pastries, croissants, imported cheeses, pâtés, and quiches; it's a nice little oasis for a sandwich or dessert break. More formal meals in the upstairs dining room aren't as charming or as good a value.

At the other end of the spectrum, **Nick's Fishmarket** (First National Plaza, Dearborn and Monroe Streets), well known for its flamboyant owner, offers excellent, unusual seafood—including several Hawaiian fishes and fresh abalone prepared four ways—at high prices in clubby, masculine surroundings. It is very popular for business lunches, and reservations are essential for lunch or dinner. They are also advisable elsewhere, whenever possible; lunching late, say after 2 p.m., is an alternative.

Reservations (for fewer than five) aren't taken at **The Berghoff** (17 West Adams Street), and lunch and early-dinner lines often stretch onto the sidewalk. One of the few remaining old-line Loop institutions, the bustling, wood-paneled and gleaming-mirrored Berghoff has been "on Adams and State since 1898." The daily menus, black-jacketed and white-aproned waiters, terrific rye bread, and special-recipe beers and bourbons recall the Loop's German roots, but homemade soups, roasts, steaks, and simply cooked fish are also fine values. For a quick sandwich and brew, check out the handsome stand-up (formerly men's) bar; to avoid the worst crowds, opt for the somewhat plainer basement. The Berghoff is particularly festive around Christmas when roast goose, among other seasonal specialties, is added to the menu. Homemade pastries are a fine finish anytime.

Famous for its turtle soup, **Binyon's** (327 Plymouth Court) also has a German flavor, but reliable steaks and seafood—including sweet, tender, sautéed bay scallops—are among the other choices. The rooms have a no-nonsense plainness and you may have to put up with a lot of cigar-smoking lawyers, but this hideaway is worth discovering.

The large dining room at Don Roth's **Blackhawk** (139 North Wabash Avenue) is decorated with art exhibits of usually good quality and promotional materials, but this Loop standby is cheerful and totally unpretentious. The menu sticks to what the chef does best: fish, steaks, and prime ribs of beef. Portions are ample; prices somewhat high. Only a curmudgeon would interrupt the waiter as he recites, for the zillionth time, the secrets of the Spinning Salad Bowl. **The Cart** (601 South Wabash Avenue) is also justly known for its prime rib but, unfortunately, the dark room is rather cheerless.

Good steaks, chops, and ribs, plus a rather special Greek salad highlight the menu at **Miller's Pub** (23 East Adams Street), a hangout for ballplayers, sportscasters, and fans that serves food until 3 a.m. Another popular wee-hours spot, especially with Lyric Opera-goers and some singers, is the **Italian Village** (71 West Monroe Street). The moderately priced, second-floor Village, one of three restaurants in the complex, offers forgettable Italian specialties in a rustic, Italian hamlet setting complete with tiny blinking lights. You'll find better Italian fare, for both lunch and dinner, at **Café Angelo** in the Oxford House (225 North Wabash Avenue).

Except for plays and concerts, most of the Loop's nighttime action centers around its hotels. At many, cocktail-hour hors d'oeuvres set the scene for dependable, if expensive, dining followed by late-evening lounge entertainment. Refurbished to the tune of $35 million, the Hilton-owned **Palmer House** (17 East Monroe Street) has a grand second-floor lobby with towering ceilings and marble accents; beneath it is a block-long shopping arcade. Besides the expected steak house and a mid-price-range restaurant, dining options here also include a Gaslight Club and the wonderfully garish **Trader Vic's,** which serves flamboyant "Polynesian" fare. The neo-Napoleonic **Empire Room,** where the late Mayor Daley regularly lunched and Chicago's elite dined, danced, and applauded lavish floor shows, is now generally open only for lunch.

Loop hotels suffered as new or elaborately remodeled inns north of the river skimmed the cream of the business travelers. The Morrison, LaSalle, and Sherman House have been demolished; several others barely survive. Two Michigan Avenue landmarks, however, have been renovated in an effort to recapture past glories—and guests. The **Americana Congress** (520 South) was built as an annex to the Auditorium Hotel, and Clinton J. Warren's 1893 façade remains one of the city's most handsome. The Congress served as party headquarters during many national conventions, but it was at the **Blackstone Hotel** (636 South) that the phrase "smoke-filled room" was coined when cigar-puffing politicos masterminded Warren Harding's nomination in 1920. The ballroom and elegant lobby of this Marshall and Fox 1910 Second Empire masterpiece have been restored. **Joe Segal's Jazz Showcase** books the best national and local groups, although the lovely room has a completely different atmosphere than Segal's old Rush Street joint.

Opened in 1927 as the Stevens, **The Conrad Hilton** (720 South) was long the world's largest hotel. It still epitomizes the old-style convention operation with little glamour or glitter, just vast spaces devoted to banquets and meetings. This flagship of the Hilton chain hadn't undergone significant renovation since the 1968 Democratic Convention, when police pushed demonstrators through the windows of the Haymarket Restaurant. But, now that plans for a giant North Loop Hilton have been abandoned, a multimillion-dollar refurbishing is in the works.

The Hilton company's proposed flagship was to have been the keystone of a revitalized area centered at Randolph and Dearborn Streets. A combined hotel-convention center and apartment tower was to have been built on bargain-priced land and exempted from substantial real estate taxes, but the county assessor and the company differed on how much of a giveaway was enough. With this plan on the scrap heap alongside Arthur Rubloff's scorched-earth proposal, North Loop redevelopment will probably be on a more restricted (read: "human") scale. Besides earmarking State Street for retail shops, city guidelines protect some landmarks and encourage saving others.

A citizens' group hopes to weld three of these landmarks into a performing arts center. The **Harris** and **Selwyn Theaters** (170 and 190 North Dearborn Street), now the unused Michael Todd and the Cinestage porn house, would return to their original roles as legitimate stages. They would be linked by a row of cafés, galleries, and shops to the **Chicago Theater** (175 North State Street), where larger shows would play. Called "The Wonder Theater of the World" when it opened in 1921, Rapp and Rapp's baroque fantasy even had lavish, Arc de Triomphe-inspired light displays. Richly ornamented outside and in the grand lobby, it's among the last examples of Chicago's rococo movie-palace architecture.

While North Loop redevelopment drags, an even more ambitious undertaking is already remaking a much larger section of downtown. By the year 2000, a 21st-century city-within-a-city will stretch east of Michigan Avenue from Randolph Street to Wacker Drive. Fujikawa, Conterato, and Lohan's (formerly the office of Mies van der Rohe) **Illinois Center** is planned as a mixed-use complex linked by parkland and local roadways on the elevated "surface," with through streets, parking, and shopping arcades below them (and a network of service roads below that). The specifics of the development are very sensitive to changing economic conditions, but ultimately, towers of hotels, offices, and apartments will punctuate the plazas, with townhouses clustered about them. An underground gauntlet of mercantilism will enable you to spend continuously from Michigan the avenue to Michigan the lake without coming up for air.

Completed portions indicate the shape of things to come. Windy, barren, and sterile, the raised plazas are spurned by pedestrians except on the nicest days. Bustling with people, the subterranean walkways are reminiscent of airports. Unlike similar developments in Canadian cities or at Water Tower Place, most of the arcade shops offer nine-to-five essentials, take-home gifts for travelers, and "I-forgot-to-pack-it" fill-ins, rather than shopping adventures. Except for Arnie Morton's new place, the restaurants tend to be attractively designed, office workers' quick-lunch spots, an increasingly common downtown genre.

Currently, the **Hyatt Regency Chicago** hotel complex (151 East Wacker Drive) is the snazziest part of Illinois Center. Most of the activity is in the East Tower, around the glass atrium lobby's huge fountain. Musicians compete with the rush of water to serenade cocktail-lounge imbibers and diners partaking of moderately priced, domesticated Italian food at **Scampi,** which is open 'round the clock. Off the tamer West Tower lobby, **Mrs. O'Leary's** good onion soup, California-style salads, and homemade potato chips compensate for sometimes disappointing entrées. **Truffles,** the hotel's expense-account, blue-chip restaurant, turns out meals that don't begin to justify the pretensions or extremely high prices.

Although the Prudential and Standard Oil buildings predate Illinois Center, they have been incorporated into the development and will eventually be linked to the underground-arcade network. The 1958 **Prudential Building** (130 East Randolph Street), once the city's tallest, is now dwarfed by Edward Durell Stone's 80-story **Standard Oil Building** (200 East Randolph Street), one of the world's tallest. Despite trees, fountains, and a rather pleasant sunken plaza with a duck-visited reflecting pool and Harry Bertoia's sounding sculpture of slender bronze rods, the 1974 marble-clad monolith seems to stand in isolation, lacking human scale.

Massive developments like Illinois Center look great as architectural models, but only the best invite casual sightseeing and window-shopping: They are usually so awesome that even such "humanizing" attractions as art exhibits, concerts, and special events fail to bring in big crowds. A series of such autonomous enclaves would be the worst realization of plans for downtown's renaissance.

POINTS OF INTEREST xx

1	Carbide & Carbon Bldg.	A-5
2	Chicago Board of Trade	D-3
3	Chicago Bldg.	C-4
4	Chicago Temple	C-4
5	City Hall/County Bldg.	B-4
6	CNA Plaza	D-5
7	Continental Illinois National Bank	D-4
8	Daley Center (Nee Civic Center)	B-4
9	Dearborn Street Station	G-4
10	Delaware Bldg.	B-4
11	Dirksen Federal Bldg.	D-4
12	Federal Reserve Bank	D-3
13	First National Plaza	C-4
14	Fisher Bldg.	E-4
15	Harbor Point	B-8
16	Inland Steel Bldg.	C-4
17	Kluczynski Federal Bldg.	D-4
18	Loop Synagogue	C-4
19	McCarthy Bldg.	B-4
20	Main Post Office	E-2
21	Mallers Bldg.	C-5
22	Manhattan Bldg.	E-4
23	Marquette Bldg.	D-4
24	Metropolitan Correctional Center	E-4
25	Monadnock Bldg.	E-4
26	Old Colony Bldg.	E-4
27	Outer Drive East	B-8
28	Peoples Gas Bldg.	D-5
29	Pittsfield Bldg.	C-5
30	Pontiac Bldg.	E-4
31	Printers Row Printing Museum	F-4
32	Prudential Bldg.	B-6
33	Railway Exchange Bldg.	D-5
34	Reliance Bldg.	C-4
35	Riverside Plaza	C-2
36	Rookery	D-4
37	Sears Tower	D-2
38	Seventeenth Church of Christ, Scientist	A-5
39	Standard Oil Bldg.	B-6
40	State of Illinois Bldg. (Under Const.)	B-4
41	Stone Container Bldg.	A-5
42	Unity Bldg.	B-4
43	Xerox Centre	C-4

TRANSPORTATION Txx

T1	Chicago & North Western Station	C-1
T2	Greyhound Terminal	B-4
T3	LaSalle Street Station	E-3
T4	Randolph Street Station	B-5
T5	Trailways Terminal	B-5
T6	Union Station	D-1
T7	Van Buren Street Station	E-5

SHOPPING Sxx

S1	Asian House	A-5
S2	Baskin's	D-5
S3	Eddie Bauer	B-5
S4	Brooks Bros.	C-5
S5	Capper & Capper	C-5
S6	Carson Pirie Scott & Co.	C-5
S7	Evans Furs	C-4
S8	Marshall Field's	B-5
S9	Kroch's & Brentano's	C-5
S10	Lytton's	D-5
S11	C.D. Peacock Jewelers	C-5
S12	Iwan Ries & Co.	C-5
S13	Rose Records	D-5
S14	Sears, Roebuck & Co.	E-5
S15	Chas. A. Stevens	C-6
S16	Stevens Bldg.	C-5
S17	Stop & Shop	B-4
S18	Wieboldt's	C-5

HOTELS Hxx

H1	Americana Congress	E-5
H2	Ascot House	H-5
H3	Avenue Motel	H-5
H4	Bismarck	B-3
H5	Blackstone	F-5
H6	Essex Inn	G-5
H7	Executive House	A-5
H8	Conrad Hilton	F-5
H9	Hyatt Regency Chicago	A-6
H10	Midland	D-3
H11	Oxford House	A-5
H12	Palmer House	C-5
H13	Travelodge, Downtown	H-5

CULTURAL FACILITIES Cxx

C1	American Conservatory of Music	C-5
C2	ArchiCenter	D-4
C3	AuditoriumTheatre	E-5
C4	Blackstone Theatre	F-5
C5	Chicago Public Library Cultural Center	B-5
C6	Chicago Theater	B-5
C7	Civic Opera House	C-2
C8	Civic Theatre	C-2
C9	Columbia College	F-5
C10	DePaul University Loop Campus	D-5
C11	11th Street Theatre	G-5
C12	Fine Arts Bldg.	E-5
C13	Goodman Theatre	D-6
C14	HOT TIX Booth	C-4
C15	Loop College	A-5
C16	Orchestra Hall	D-5
C17	Roosevelt University	E-5
C18	School of the Art Institute of Chicago	D-6
C19	Shubert Theatre	C-4
C20	Spertus College & Museum of Judaica	F-5
C21	Studebaker Theater	E-5
C22	World Playhouse	E-5

MAP LEGEND

■ Underground road system

● Passage to and from underground road system

▲ One-way passage from underground to street level

▼ One-way passage to underground from street level

Ⓟ underground parking access

Lake Michigan

Chicago Harbor

LAKE SHORE DRIVE

Shedd Aquarium

Adler Planetarium

ACHSAH BOND DR

Field Museum of Natural History

FETRIDGE

Soldier Field

Burnham Park Harbor

Northerly Island

12th Street Beach

To Meigs Field

©1983 WFMT, Inc.

Interesting places

A ▶ *indicates that the building is described in one of the splendid booklets prepared by the Commission on Chicago Historical and Architectural Landmarks and available at the commission's offices, 320 N. Clark St., Room 800, or at the bookstores in the Archi-Center, 330 S. Dearborn St.; the Chicago Historical Society, Clark St. at North Ave.; and the Frank Lloyd Wright Home and Studio, 951 Chicago Ave., Oak Park.*

American Police Center and Museum
1130 S. Wabash Ave.
427-5113
Displays of police uniforms from around the world, Chicago Police Department memorabilia, and crime-prevention information. Some of the photographs may frighten youngsters.

*ArchiCenter
Monadnock Building
330 S. Dearborn St.
782-1776
More than a starting point for tours: exhibits, films, lectures, and an excellent book and gift shop.

*Art Institute of Chicago
Michigan Ave.,at Adams St.
443-3500
Main building designed by Shepley, Rutan and Coolidge in 1892; the East Wing by Walter Netsch for Skidmore, Owings & Merrill in 1974. Vinci/Kenny supervised the 1977 restoration of Louis Sullivan's Chicago Stock Exchange Trading Room. Starting place for Culture Bus routes. (See Museums.)

*Norman Asher and Helen Asher Library
Spertus College of Judaica
618 S. Michigan Ave.
922-9012
(See Libraries)

*Auditorium Theatre
70 E. Congress Pkwy.
922-2110, 922-6634
Tours for groups of ten or more (call in advance).

*Brunswick Building
69 W. Washington St.
The small plaza is home to Joan Miró's Chicago.

*Carbide and Carbon Building
230 N. Michigan Ave.
Burnham Bros.; 1929.

* ▶ Carson Pirie Scott & Co. Building
1 S. State St.
Louis Sullivan; 1899, 1903-4. 1906 addition by D. H. Burnham and Company.

* ▶ Chicago and North Western Station
500 W. Madison St.
454-6000
Wonderful old station was razed to make way for a combination office tower and commuter station designed by Helmut Jahn of Murphy/Jahn.

Chicago Baha'i Center
116 S. Michigan Ave.
236-7771
Information about the religion and its house of worship in Wilmette (see Evanston). Discussion groups meet here.

* ▶ Chicago Board of Trade
141 W. Jackson Blvd.
435-3500

*Chicago Board Options Exchange
141 W. Jackson Blvd.
431-5600
Plans to move into a new building at La Salle and Van Buren Sts. in 1984.

Chicago Coliseum
1513 S. Wabash Ave.
In the 1880s, entrepreneurs reconstructed Richmond's notorious Libby Prison here as a tourist attraction. The Coliseum, completed in 1900 and the scene of several presidential conventions, incorporates some of the wall. Once Chicago's major indoor arena, it's now moldering away.

Chicago Loop Synagogue
16 S. Clark St.
346-7370
Bronze and brass Hands of Peace by Henri Azaz grace the façade; Abraham Rattner's stained-glass windows illuminate the interior. Designed by Loebl, Schlossman and Bennett; opened in 1958.

Chicago Main Post Office
433 W. Van Buren St.
886-2420; tours 886-3360
WPA-lush lobby. Two-hour tours traipse over much of the world's largest P.O., so leave kids under 11 home.

*Chicago Mercantile Exchange
444 W. Jackson Blvd.
648-1000
New CME Center at 30 S. Wacker Dr. scheduled for completion in late 1983.

Chicago Police Department Headquarters
1121 S. State St.
744-4000
The only tour is limited to the Communications Operations Section (the 911 center), and you don't get to see very much.

* ▶ Chicago Public Library Cultural Center
78 E. Washington St.
744-6630
Shepley, Rutan and Coolidge, 1897; Holabird and Root were architects for the 1977 restoration. (See Museums.)

The Chicago Temple (First United Methodist Church of Chicago)
77 W. Washington St.
236-4548
World's tallest church, dedicated in 1924. Chapel in the Sky—400 feet above ground—was opened for worship in 1952. Pilgrimages to the chapel at 2 p.m. daily and after Sunday services. At ground level, stained-glass windows, designed by Giannini and Hilgart and installed in 1965, trace the history of the church.

*Chicago Theater
175 N. State St.
782-7011

Christ the King Lutheran Church
18 S. Michigan, 6th floor
440-1920
Small, liberal church has a congregation of about 100, but serves many more Loop workers and visitors. Chapel sculptures by Egon Weiner.

*City Hall-Cook County Building
Randolph to Washington, Clark to La Salle Sts.
744-4000
Holabird and Roche; completed 1911.

*Continental Illinois National Bank
231 S. La Salle St.
828-2345
In 1924, this Graham, Anderson, Probst & White building was Chicago's tallest.

*Richard J. Daley Center
Randolph St. between Dearborn and Clark Sts.
443-7980
Jacques Brownson, principal designer for C. F. Murphy Associates; completed 1965. Lower level is nexus of underground routes stretching to Wieboldt's and Field's.

*Richard J. Daley Plaza
Washington St. between Dearborn and Clark Sts.
The Chicago Picasso fits the site splendidly. Outdoor café in summer.

*Dearborn Park
Polk St. to Roosevelt Rd., State to Clark Sts.

*Dearborn Street Station
Polk and Dearborn Sts.

*Delaware Building
36 W. Randolph St.
Wheelock and Thomas; 1874.

*Federal Center and Plaza
Dearborn St. between Adams and Jackson

Federal Reserve Bank of Chicago
230 S. La Salle St.
322-5322
Oversees all that frantic La Salle St. finance.

* ► Fine Arts Building
410 S. Michigan Ave.
427-7602
Solon S. Beman; 1885.

*First National Bank of Chicago
Madison St. between Clark and Dearborn Sts.
732-4000

*First National Bank Plaza
Monroe St. between Clark and Dearborn Sts.
732-6204 (Plaza events)

* ► Fisher Building
343 S. Dearborn St.
D. H. Burnham and Company; 1896.

Grace Episcopal Church
33 W. Jackson, 5th floor
922-1426
Not nearly as high as the Chapel in the Sky, but it does have an Atrium Garden Room (3rd floor) for meetings and concerts.

*Harris and Selwyn Theaters
170 and 190 N. Dearborn

Heald Square Monument
Wacker Dr. and Wabash
Lorado Taft's last sculpture (1941; completed by Leonard Crunelle) was the first to be designated a sculptural landmark by the City Council. George Washington is flanked by Revolutionary War financiers Haym Salomon and Robert Morris.

"I Am" Temple
176 W. Washington St.
346-1380
Reading room for the St. Germain Foundation of Schaumburg (882-7400).

Illinois Bell Telephony Museum
225 W. Randolph, Lobby
727-2994
(See Museums)

*Illinois Center
Chicago River to Randolph, Michigan Ave. to the lake
Several new and a few older buildings (Outer Drive East, Standard Oil, Prudential), most connected by underground shopping malls. Additional development scheduled through the decade.

Inland Steel Building
30 W. Monroe St.
The first postwar Loop building, Skidmore, Owings & Merrill's 1957 tower emphasizes the curtain wall by putting supporting members outside the skin. All the mechanical facilities are in a separate shaft.

*McCarthy Building
32 W. Washington St.
Designed by John Mills Van Osdel, Chicago's first architect; erected in 1872 while the ashes were still hot.

* ► Manhattan Building
431 S. Dearborn St.
William Le Baron Jenney; 1890.

*Marquette Building
140 S. Dearborn St.
Holabird and Roche; 1894.

Metropolitan Correctional Center
71 W. Van Buren St.
353-6819
Harry Weese brought all his innovative and humanistic talent to this 1975 Federal jail. The exterior doesn't offend the streetscape; the interior is considerate of inmates' needs.

*MidAmerica Commodity Exchange
175 W. Jackson Blvd.
435-0601

*Midwest Stock Exchange
120 S. La Salle St.
368-2222

* ▸ Monadnock Building
53 W. Jackson Blvd.
Burnham and Root; 1891. South half by Holabird and Roche in 1893.

* ▸ Old Colony Building
407 S. Dearborn St.
Holabird and Roche; 1894.

Old St. Mary's Church
Wabash and Van Buren
922-3444
Fifth location for Chicago's oldest Roman Catholic parish. The original church at Lake and State Sts. was organized in 1833. Veterans of the disbanded Paulist choir—Bing Crosby portrayed its director in The Bells of St. Mary's—*return for the 11:30 a.m. Mass the last Sunday of each month.*

One South Wacker Drive
1 S. Wacker Dr.
Helmut Jahn's eye-catching new building reinforces the street's position as one of the city's most important office-tower rows.

Pacific Garden Mission
646 S. State St.
922-1462
Old-fashioned mission with soup, sermons, and lodging for the down-and-out. Special missions to women, servicemen, and children.

Page Brothers Block
State and Lake Sts.
North wall is the Loop's only remaining cast-iron façade. John Mills Van Osdel; 1872.

*Pontiac Building
542 S. Dearborn St.
Holabird and Roche; 1891.

▸ Prairie Avenue Historic District
Mainly Prairie Ave. between 18th and Cullerton Sts.
After the Chicago Fire, the city's barons built splendid mansions along Prairie Ave. near the site of the Fort Dearborn Massacre, creating Chicago's first Gold Coast. By the turn of the century, the street was passé. Only a few houses remain, including Glessner House, Chicago's only surviving work by H. H. Richardson. The Widow Clarke House, the city's oldest, was moved back near its original location in 1977 and has been beautifully restored. Plaques describe some of the mansions that have been torn down. (See Museums.)

Printers Row Printing Museum
715 S. Dearborn St.
987-1059
(See Museums)

*Printing House Row
Dearborn St. from Congress to Polk St.

*Prudential Building
130 E. Randolph St.

Randolph Street Station
151 N. Michigan Ave.
332-0295
Marked by little more than a decorative kiosk next to the excellent newsstand at the CPL Cultural Center's entrance, this subterranean station serves the Illinois Central Gulf (RTA) and Chicago South Shore & South Bend commuter lines. It's also a link in an underground pathway that connects the Grant Park Garage with the Prudential Building and, by less salubrious but sheltered ways, more of Illinois Center.

* ▸ Reliance Building
32 N. State St.
D. H. Burnham and Company; 1894.

* ▸ Rookery Building
209 S. La Salle St.
Burnham and Root; 1886.

St. Peter's Church
110 W. Madison St.
372-5111
Organized as a German parish in 1846. The present building by Vitzthum and Burns dates to 1951. Now under the Franciscans, the church is popular with politicians.

Sculpture in the Loop
There's lots more than the major plaza works. The Chicago Council on Fine Arts publishes a good guide that's available at its office in the CPL Cultural Center.

*Sears Tower
233 S. Wacker Dr.
875-9696 (Skydeck)
Skidmore, Owings & Merrill's Bruce Graham designed the world's tallest building in 1973. The Skydeck, on the 103rd floor, is 1,353 feet above ground. On a clear day (or night), it's worth the trip. Open 9 a.m. to midnight daily; a visibility indicator at the ticket booth lets you know what to expect. Don't miss Alexander Calder's Universe *mobile in the Wacker Dr. lobby.*

Second Presbyterian Church
Michigan Ave. and 20th St.
225-4951
New Yorker James Renwick designed this 1874 neo-Gothic gem; the interior was redone by Howard Van Doren Shaw in 1901. The cream of Prairie Avenue society—from the Armours to Mrs. Abraham Lincoln—worshiped in light filtered through 14 Tiffany windows and the pair designed by Edward Burne-Jones and William Morris.

Seventeenth Church of Christ, Scientist
Wacker Dr. and Wabash
236-4671
Stunning use of the small site by Harry Weese; 1968.

Shoreline Marine Sightseeing
80 E. Jackson Blvd.
427-2900
Sightseeing boats leave from Shedd Aquarium by day, and a Buckingham Fountain mooring by night.

*Spertus Museum of Judaica
618 S. Michigan Ave.
922-9012
(See Museums)

*Standard Oil Building
200 E. Randolph St.
Developers brought in New York architect Edward Durell Stone in 1974 to design Chicago's second-tallest building.

State of Illinois Building
160 N. La Salle St.
793-3500
Until the new center across the street is finished, this 1924 Burnham Bros. building is the place to get everything from tax forms to hunting licenses.

State of Illinois Center
Randolph to Lake Sts., Clark to La Salle Sts.
Helmut Jahn of Murphy/ Jahn has designed a space-age state office building.

*Stone Container Building
360 N. Michigan Ave.
Originally the London Guarantee Building; Alfred S. Alschuler; 1923.

35 East Wacker Drive Building
35 E. Wacker Dr.
Rococo 1926 building with a fine terra-cotta façade was once the Jewelers Building. Tenants drove from lower Wacker Dr. right into the 22-story central garage.

*333 North Michigan Avenue Building
333 N. Michigan Ave.
Holabird and Root; 1928.

*Union Station
210 S. Canal St.
346-5200
Amtrak trains and commuter runs of the Burlington Northern and Milwaukee Road.

United States Gypsum Building
101 S. Wacker Dr.
Perkins and Will's 1963 steel, marble, and slate building is set at a 45-degree angle to the street and suggests a giant gypsum crystal.

*Unity Building
127 N. Dearborn St.
Clinton J. Warren; 1891.

Victory Center for Servicemen
7 W. Madison, 4th floor
236-2464
Men and women in uniform—mostly sailors-to-be from Great Lakes Naval Training Center—find Ping-Pong, TV, books and magazines, coffee, and a dose of religion, just as they have since W.W. II. In Holabird and Roche's magnificent Chicago Building of 1904.

*Xerox Centre
55 W. Monroe St.
Helmut Jahn; 1980.

Major institutions

*American Academy of Art
220 S. State St.
939-3883

*American Conservatory of Music
116 S. Michigan Ave.
263-4161
Trains students from around the world; offers many free concerts and recitals.

Chicago-Kent College of Law
77 S. Wacker Dr.
567-5000
Illinois Institute of Technology's law school.

*Columbia College
600 S. Michigan Ave.
663-1600

*DePaul University Loop Campus
Jackson Blvd. and Wabash
321-8000

*Harrington Institute of Interior Design
Fine Arts Bldg.
410 S. Michigan Ave.
939-4975

Loop College
30 E. Lake St.
269-8000
One of nine City Colleges of Chicago.

John Marshall Law School
315 S. Plymouth Ct.
427-2737
Chicago's principal unaffiliated law school.

*Roosevelt University
Auditorium Building
430 S. Michigan Ave.
341-3500
Adler and Sullivan; 1889. The handsomely restored lobby contains an exhibit on the history of the building. Other restoration, directed by John Vinci, includes the Louis Sullivan Room, Oscar Fainman Memorial Hall, Rudolph Ganz Memorial Hall, and the south alcove of the 10th-floor reading room.

*School of the Art Institute of Chicago
208 S. Columbus Dr.
443-3700

*Spertus College of Judaica
618 S. Michigan Ave.
922-9012

Hotels

Package deals must be booked in advance, usually require two nights' stay, cost little more for two persons than for one, and are subject to change. Some toll-free "800" numbers cannot be dialed from the Chicago area.

*Americana Congress
520 S. Michigan Ave.
427-3800, 800-228-3278
Modestly priced, room-only, weekend rate.

Ascot House
1100 S. Michigan Ave.
922-2900, 800-621-6909
Bargain bed-and-breakfast weekend deals.

Bismarck Hotel
171 W. Randolph St.
236-0123
The Cook County Regular Democratic Organization's aging home away from home jumps on election nights and offers occasional weekend packages with newspaper coupons.

*Blackstone Hotel
636 S. Michigan Ave.
427-4300
Bargain weekend family rates.

*The Conrad Hilton
720 S. Michigan Ave.
922-4000
800-325-4620 (in Illinois)
Moderately priced weekend packages.

Essex Inn
800 S. Michigan Ave.
939-2800, 800-621-6909
Modest bed-and-breakfast weekend rates.

Executive House
71 E. Wacker Dr.
346-7100, 800-621-4005
Nicely situated, modern, businessman's hotel prices its luxurious weekend packages accordingly.

*Hyatt Regency Chicago
Illinois Center
151 E. Wacker Dr.
565-1000, 800-228-9000
Offers both attractively priced, shoot-the-works packages and inexpensive, weekend, room-only rates.

The Midland Hotel
172 W. Adams St.
332-1200, 800-621-2700
Tastefully refurbished smaller hotel in the financial district has modest, one- and two-day, weekend room rates.

*The Palmer House
17 E. Monroe St.
726-7500
800-325-4620 (In Illinois)
Moderate, weekend room rates.

Quality Inn Oxford House
225 N. Wabash Ave.
346-6585, 800-228-5151
Budget, room-only, weekend rates.

Shopping and services: Department stores

*Carson Pirie Scott & Co.
1 S. State St.
744-2000

*Marshall Field's
111 N. State St.
781-1000

*Montgomery Ward & Co.
140 S. State St.
368-6000
To be replaced by an office building in 1984.

*Sears, Roebuck and Co.
403 S. State St.
875-4900

*Wieboldt's
1 N. State St.
782-1500

Shopping and services: Books

Jane Addams Bookstore
Fine Arts Bldg., 2nd floor
410 S. Michigan Ave.
663-1885
Cheerful shop specializing in new and used books for, by, and about women. Children's books, mysteries, cookbooks, records by women artists, posters. Pastries, coffee, herb teas, cider, all spiced with good conversation.

Bookspace
703 S. Dearborn St.
663-4243
In the heart of Printer's Row, this artist-run bookstore and reference center features books and other publications by artists, as well as notable window displays, exhibitions, and other programs. Shares space with Word City (see Shopping and services: General).

James M. W. Borg, Inc.
8 S. Michigan, Suite 1620
236-5911
A first-rank dealer in rare books from the earliest printed volumes to signed first editions and presentation copies of contemporary authors. Specialties include Dickens, author-related art and artifacts, and women's literature. Borg's catalogues display remarkable scholarship. Appointments suggested.

China Books and Periodicals
174 W. Randolph St.
782-6004
Books, magazines, artworks, and gifts from the People's Republic.

*B. Dalton Bookseller
129 N. Wabash Ave.
236-7615
Other locations.

N. Fagin Books
Stevens Bldg., Suite 1326
17 N. State St.
236-6540
Nancy Fagin got fed up when she couldn't find good anthropology books at any Chicago bookseller. So she opened her own shop where she also offers new and used books about botany, ecology, and zoology. Small selection of Native American prints, too. Free searches for out-of-print books.

I Love a Mystery Bookstore
Stevens Bldg., Suite 810
17 N. State St.
236-1338
City's largest offering of paperback mysteries, domestic and imported. Thrillers and sci-fi share the space.

Illinois Labor History Society
20 E. Jackson, Suite 1005
663-4107
The books here offer labor's side of history and contemporary issues. Buy or rent labor-oriented audio-visual materials. Appointment required.

Jewish Book Mart
127 N. Dearborn, 2nd floor
782-5199
Benjamin Fain sells the books he loves: Hebraica, Judaica, linguistics, and history. New and used, including many recent Israeli publications.

*Kroch's & Brentano's
29 S. Wabash Ave.
332-7500
Other locations.

Kroch's & Brentano's Bargain Book Center
62 E. Randolph St.
263-2681
Remainders and discount editions.

J. Stephan Lawrence Rare Books
230 N. Michigan Ave.
Mezzanine
782-0344
First editions of American and English authors fill the shelves and catalogues of this fine shop, which looks and feels as a rare-book shop should.

London Bookshop & Gallery
79 W. Monroe, Suite 1121
782-2261
Glen Wiche is always ready with tea and conversation about the British Isles. Marvelous browsing: British history, theater, royalty, and culture; autographs, maps, and prints. Some new, but mostly used and out-of-print books.

Marshall Field's Rare Book Department
111 N. State St., 3rd floor
781-4299
In Chicago, only Field's would make room in a department store for this fine antiquarian book operation. All that keeps it from being competitive with the city's best booksellers is the absence of catalogues.

Modern Bookstore
407 S. Dearborn, 2nd floor
663-9076
Politics, history, minority questions, and labor issues, plus some theater and literature. The theoretical stuff follows the Communist Party line.

Kenneth Nebenzahl, Inc.
333 N. Michigan, 28th floor
641-2711
Regarded by many as Chicago's finest rare-book dealer, Nebenzahl sells magnificent maps as well as the finest of books. Prices are not marked. Catalogues updated about twice a year.

Powell's Book Warehouse
1020 S. Wabash, 8th floor
341-0748
Rickety shelves hold remaindered texts, art books, foreign-language volumes. Everything, including paperbacks, 40% off.

Prairie Avenue Bookshop
711 S. Dearborn St.
922-8311
Located in the middle of Printing House Row, Marilyn Hasbrouck's store is devoted to books—new and used—about architecture, design, and urban history and planning. Architectural fragments are sprinkled among the shelves; even some of the furniture has roots in the Chicago School.

Rand McNally Map Store
23 E. Madison St.
267-6868
Maps, atlases, and globes at this outlet of the famous Chicago publisher; also guides and travel books.

St. Paul Catholic Book and Film Center
172 N. Michigan Ave.
346-4228
Good selection of books on Catholicism; some religious articles.

Sandmeyer's Bookstore in Printer's Row
714 S. Dearborn St.
922-2104
Specializes in quality hardbacks (literature, history, biography, etc.) with an emphasis on travel books. Chairs for comfortable thumbing through potential purchases.

Stein's Books and Novelties
526 S. State St.
922-8121
On a seamy stretch of State, the place for how-to books on just about any topic. Many odd finds in this charming, eccentric shop.

U. S. Government Printing Office Bookstore
219 S. Dearborn St.,
Suite 1365
353-5133
Government publications galore: books, pamphlets, brochures, maps, charts, photos. Will order any not in stock.

Shopping and services: Clothing

Bailey's
25 W. Van Buren St.
939-2172
Army-navy surplus, Western wear, some fancy riding duds.

*Jos. A. Bank Clothiers
25 E. Washington St.
782-4432

*Baskin
137 S. State St.
733-4600

*Eddie Bauer, Inc.
123 N. Wabash Ave.
263-6005
Camping equipment, too. Other locations include Water Tower Place.

Besley's Inc.
123 S. Franklin St.
726-4238
17 N. Wabash Ave.
236-8182
Old-time tie manufacturer stocks zillions of ties for men and women, including hand-finished silks.

Brittany Ltd.
29 S. La Salle St.
372-5985
Loop branch of the Michigan Ave. clothier.

*Broadstreet's
Palmer House Arcade
123 S. State St.
726-8902

˙*Brooks Brothers
74 E. Madison St.
263-0100
Also in Northbrook Ct.

*Capezio Dance Theatre Shop
Stevens Bldg., Suite 1300
17 N. State St.
236-1911

*Capper & Capper Ltd.
1 N. Wabash Ave.
236-3800
Also at 909 N. Michigan, in Skokie, and in Oak Brook.

*Chicago Garment Center Building
337 S. Franklin St.

Chiffonnier Rag Salon
980 S. Michigan Ave.
939-9076
Vintage clothing (emphasis on the zoot-suit look) and custom suits for men and women; some women's wear by local designers.

*Clothing Clearance Center
1006 S. Michigan Ave.
663-4170
Several suburban locations.

*Coats, Coats, Coats, Inc.
337 S. Franklin St.
663-1192
Good sportswear, too.

Dance Fashions, Inc.
6 E. Lake St., 2nd floor
726-0661
Ballet slippers, Danskin leotards, and leg warmers.

*Evans, Inc.
36 S. State St.
855-2000
Also 744 N. Michigan Ave. and suburbs.

Fashion Galleries
185 N. Wabash Ave.
726-6072
Airy store with discounted French jeans and tops for men and women.

*Fashionette Swimsuits
Stevens Bldg., Suite 1412
17 N. State St.
332-2802

Gingiss Formalwear
30 W. Lake St.
263-7071
Ben Gingiss rents more tuxedos than anyone, many to prominent Chicagoans. Other locations.

*Handmoor
300 N. Michigan Ave.
726-5600
200 W. Adams, 2nd floor
782-0282
Also in Lake Cook Plaza, Deerfield.

*Illinois Theatrical Footwear
Stevens Bldg., Suite 1533
17 N. State St.
332-7123

Irv's Formalwear Resale
190 N. State St., Suite 542
332-1395
Buying used can be almost as cheap as renting. New ones, too.

*Lane Bryant, Inc.
9 N. Wabash Ave.
621-8700
Other locations.

*Lloyd & Haig Shoes
3 S. Wabash Ave.
263-5352

*Loehmann's
205 W. Randolph, 2nd floor
346-7150
Suburban locations, too.

*Lytton's
235 S. State St.
922-3500
Other locations.

T H Mandy
225 N. Michigan, 2nd floor
938-4300
Wide selection of women's sportswear, discounted.

*Mysels Furs
6 E. Monroe St., 4th floor
372-9513

*Nierman's Tall Girl Shoes
Stevens Bldg., Suite 1202
17 N. State St.
346-9797

*Pendleton Woolen Mills Products Stores, Inc.
Palmer House Arcade
123 S. State St.
372-1699

Lawrence Pucci
333 N. Michigan Ave.
332-3759
Chicago's best-known custom tailor isn't the famous Italian fabric designer, but he does favor a Continental look. Suits, shirts, ties, shoes, for both sexes.

Riddle-McIntyre, Inc.
17 N. Wabash, Suite 605
782-3317
Frank Hee Kong custom makes shirts from your choice of fabrics. $45 and up; 3-shirt minimum initial order.

Sizes Unlimited
16 S. Wabash, 2nd floor
346-4226
Fashions for women in sizes 14½ to 33½ and 38 to 52.

*Chas. A. Stevens
25 N. State St.
630-1500
Other locations.

*Tall Girls Shop
Stevens Bldg., Suite 1314
17 N. State St.
782-9867

*Todd's Boots
5 S. Wabash, Suite 1511
372-1335

Shopping and services: Music

*The Beautiful Sound
325 N. Michigan Ave.
726-7911

*Bein & Fushi, Inc.
Fine Arts Bldg., Suite 1014
410 S. Michigan Ave.
663-0150

Jack Cecchini Guitar Studios
28 E. Jackson, 2nd floor
939-4557
Instruction in classical and modern guitar, including jazz. Instrument repairs and sales.

*Chicago Guitar Gallery
216 S. Wabash, 3rd floor
427-0423, 427-8434

*Drums, Ltd.
218 S. Wabash, 8th floor
427-8480

*Carl Fischer of Chicago
312 S. Wabash Ave.
427-6652

Frank's Drum Shop
226 S. Wabash, 4th floor
922-1300
Fine place for percussion, especially foreign instruments. Rare ones from around the world displayed.

*Eugene S. Gordon Woodwinds
Fine Arts Bldg., Suite 709
410 S. Michigan Ave.
663-0414

Frank R. Graham Music Shop
17 N. Wabash, Suite 601
263-1336
Sells Selmer and Bach band instruments; repair service.

*Kagan & Gaines Music Co.
228 S. Wabash, 3rd floor
939-4083

Musicians' Pawn Shop
424 S. State St.
341-1411
Many musicians stay afloat between gigs by using this service.

*Douglas Raguse
28 E. Jackson, Suite 1009
922-2961

*Schilke Music Products
529 S. Wabash Ave.
922-0230

*Sid Sherman Musical Instrument Co.
226 S. Wabash, 3rd floor
427-1796

*Kenneth Warren and Son, Ltd.
28 E. Jackson, 8th floor
427-7475

Shopping and services: General

AAA Chicago Motor Club
66 E. South Water St.
372-1818
Get an International Drivers License amid Art Deco splendor; free travel info for American Automobile Association members.

Acco Surgical Supply and Manufacturing Co.
21 W. Jackson Blvd.
939-3322
Scalpel, please; also knives from Henckels, Wiss, Case, Sabatier, Puma, and Buck.

*Ace Leather Goods Repair Service
Reliance Bldg., Suite 1101
32 N. State St.
263-3946

American Floral Art School
539 S. Wabash Ave.
922-9328
Learn everything you must to open a flower shop. Visitors welcome.

*Asian House of Chicago
316 N. Michigan Ave.
782-9577
Also in Lake Cook Plaza, Deerfield.

Bachrach, Inc.
104 S. Michigan, Suite 820
236-1991
High-class photoportraits of high-class people.

*Beckley-Cardy Teacher's Store
324 S. Wabash Ave.
922-5507

*E. M. Bloomberg & Co.
341 S. Franklin St.
939-2913
The firm's fine woolens were once in such demand that retail customers were turned away; now they're welcomed.

Boitsov Classical Ballet School
Fine Arts Bldg., Suite 733
410 S. Michigan Ave.
663-0844, 262-1744
Ballet classes in the Russian tradition.

Boy Scouts of America Scout Supply Center
128 S. Franklin St.
263-3492
Uniforms and equipment.

*Bregstone Associates
440 S. Wabash Ave.
939-5130

*Campanile Galleries
200 S. Michigan Ave.
663-3885
(See Galleries)

*Carteaux, Inc.
31 N. Wabash Ave.
782-5375

*Chicago Association of Commerce and Industry
130 S. Michigan Ave.
786-0111

Chicago Bible Society
203 N. Wabash, Suite 1820
236-2169
Publishes and distributes materials in many languages.

*Chicago Trunk & Leather Works, Inc.
12 S. Wabash Ave.
372-0845

ConStruct
101 N. Wacker, Suite 235
853-1125
Maintains sculpture exhibits in the building's lobby and outside. (See Galleries.)

Lou Conte Dance Studio
218 S. Wabash, 3rd floor
461-0892
Learn to dance from creators of the Hubbard Street Dance Company, one of the city's best. (See Dance.)

Corrado Cutlery
26 N. Clark St.
368-8450
Sharpening and selling fine knives and scissors since 1905. Gadgets, too.

Norbert J. Daleiden, Inc.
217 W. Madison St.
332-3893
Retail outlet for makers of religious articles for all denominations. Crucifixes, chalices, vestments . . . and some nice chess sets.

Deak-Perera, Inc.
17 N. Dearborn St.
236-0042
America's oldest dealer in precious metals also handles foreign traveler's checks, currencies, and investments in international monetary, gold, and silver markets.

Downtown Hobby
First National Plaza.
Dearborn St. side
372-2464
Large selection is especially strong on model trains.

*Favor Ruhl Co.
14 S. Wabash Ave.
782-5737
Discount outlet across the street.

The Flax Co.
176 N. Wabash Ave.
346-5100
Art-supply house geared to commercial artists.

*Fraerman Yard Goods & Draperies Co.
314 W. Adams St.
236-6886
Large stock includes imported silks. Few bargains.

Gilbertson Clybourn, Inc.
1307 S. Wabash, 5th floor
427-0650
Topnotch place repairs, replates, refinishes copper, brass, silver, and pewter.

Girl Scout Shop
14 E. Jackson, 13th floor
435-5500
All the official gear.

Guild for the Blind Boutique
180 N. Michigan, Suite 1720
236-8569
Large-type and Braille books, spoken-word records and cassettes, special watches, and other aids for the visually impaired.

*Hanzel Galleries
1120 S. Michigan Ave.
922-6234

*The Hirk Company
Stevens Bldg., Suite 1130
17 N. State St.
346-0194

The House of Hansen
333 S. Franklin St.
372-8750
Memorial chalices, religious statuary, candles, vestments. Replating, too.

House of Williams
37 S. Wabash Ave.
236-6320
Re-tins copperware; repairs, replates, and cleans silver.

Illinois Travel Information Center
208 N. Michigan Ave.
793-2094,
800-252-8987 (events)
Booklets, maps, and other tourist information.

*International Importing Bead and Novelty Co.
Stevens Bldg., Suite 1010
17 N. State St.
332-0061

*J & J Silversmith and Jewelry Repair
6 E. Monroe St., Suite 900
263-0076

Jozef
337 S. Franklin, 2nd floor
939-2463
Jozef Fleischman used to manufacture garments in this building. Now he owns a tiny magic shop filled with gags, gifts, and novelties.

*Kelmscott Gallery
Fine Arts Bldg., Suite 825
410 S. Michigan Ave.
461-9188
(See Galleries)

F. N. Kistner Co.
10 S. Wabash, 10th floor
236-0442
Sells fraternal emblems and supplies.

Kner and Anthony Bookbinders
407 S. Dearborn, Room 345
922-3879
Fine-quality binding and restoration by those whose apprentices have gone on to establish important binderies of their own.

Koro Bags
173 W. Madison, 7th floor
332-4169
Sam Machtinger, in business for more than 40 years, discounts calf, suede, and snakeskin purses; he also makes them from leather or your needlepoint.

Leather Shop on Madison
191 W. Madison St.
782-5448
Expensive, high-quality luggage and accessories.

*Jerry Lee Antiques, Inc.
5 S. Wabash, Suite 312
236-4555

Loop Center YWCA
37 S. Wabash, 3rd floor
372-6600
Open-to-the-public art gallery and inexpensive restaurant. Exercise facilities for members; courses in accounting, assertiveness, the travel business, and more. Workshops on women's topics, fitness classes, and legal counseling, too.

Loop Millinery
6 E. Lake St., 5th floor
346-9665
Funky little shop has everything to make your own wedding gown. Lots of delights such as feathers and fake flowers.

*K. Matsumoto Art Repair Studio
226 S. Wabash, 7th floor
922-4110

Michigan Travel Information Center
55 E. Monroe St.
372-0080
Pick up maps and travel tips on the "shore," berry picking, wine tasting, hunting, fishing, and more.

Near-North Guild, Inc.
215 N. Wells St.
337-2668
*Good general art-supply
store geared to students.*

**Office Furniture
Clearing House**
236 W. Lake St.
332-3456
*Six floors of new and used
office furniture with some
nice antiques as well.*

**Office Furniture
Warehouse**
570 W. Jackson Blvd.
454-1166
*Tons of new office furniture
at deep discounts. Other
locations.*

Jack O'Grady Galleries
333 N. Michigan, 22nd floor
726-9833
(See Galleries)

Old Chicago Smoke Shop
169 N. Clark St.
236-9771
*Cut-rate cigars from the
Canary Islands, Jamaica,
the Philippines, Nicaragua,
and other far-off places.
Generic cigarettes, too.*

*The Old Jewelry Shop
55 E. Washington, Suite 430
263-6764
*Also in Highland Park and
Bloomingdale.*

Out-of-Town Newspapers
Randolph and State Sts.
*The Loop's largest selec-
tion. A smaller assortment at
State and Jackson.*

*C. D. Peacock Jewelers
101 S. State St.
630-5700
Also in several suburbs.

Photo World
20 N. Franklin St.
782-9726
*Excellent pro shop also
rents equipment.*

*Otto Pomper, Inc.
109 S. Wabash Ave.
372-0881

**Rare Coin Company
of America (RARCOA)**
31 N. Clark St.
346-3443
*City's largest dealer in col-
lectors' coins and stamps.*

*Iwan Ries & Co.
17 S. Wabash Ave.
372-1306

*Rose Records
214 S. Wabash Ave.
987-9044
Other locations.

Schultz & Mark
25 E. Washington, Suite 918
236-1156
*Reliable handbag and
luggage repairs; petit-point
and needlepoint mounting.*

***Scriptorium Benedictine
Artistic Lettering**
Fine Arts Bldg., Suite 609
410 S. Michigan Ave.
427-2428

Stebbins Hardware
15 W. Van Buren St.
427-8400
*Last of its kind in the Loop:
reasonably old-fashioned
and very well-stocked.*

*Stevens Building
17 N. State St.

**UNICEF Card and
Gift Shop**
5 N. Wabash, Suite 1502
372-5359
*Fine selection of cards and
note papers; small collection of inexpensive gifts.*

**Universal Bowling
& Golf Corp.**
619 S. Wabash Ave.
922-5255
*Billiard tables and sup-
plies, bowling balls, and
golf clubs at low prices in a
no-nonsense atmosphere.*

*Universal Pen Hospital
Stevens Bldg., Suite 1218
17 N. State St.
332-5373

Valentine & Son
39 W. Van Buren St.
922-6881
*Good prices on barber and
beautician supplies.
Geared to the trade but
open to the public.*

*White's Fabrics
226 S. Wabash, 2nd floor
939-4930
*Moderate selection at rea-
sonable prices. Free sewing
and tailoring advice from
experienced staff.*

*Chas. T. Wilt Company
232 S. Michigan Ave.
922-8347

**Wisconsin Division
of Tourism**
75 E. Wacker Dr.
332-7274
*Everything you need to
know to vacation there.*

Word City
703 S. Dearborn St.
663-4242
*Nonprofit graphic design
and typesetting service is
staffed by artists and does
work for artists and non-
profit groups at about half
commercial rates. Free
consultations, referrals, etc.*

World Antique Mart
1006 S. Michigan, 7th floor
*Half a dozen antiques and
collectibles shops.*

Foodstuffs

*Gaper's Caterers
16 W. Washington St.
332-4935

**Handy Candy
Fruit & Nut Co.**
27 W. Jackson Blvd.
663-1514
*Fresh and dried fruits, raw
and roasted nuts, health
mixes, hard candies, jelly-
beans, and 40 different
kinds of licorice.*

*Stop & Shop
16 W. Washington St.
853-2000
*Other locations. Shop-by-
phone service for city and
suburbs.*

***Vitello's Bakery
and Caterers**
226 S. Michigan Ave.
427-0319

**Zimmerman's Cut-Rate
Liquor Store**
240 W. Randolph St.
332-0012
*Before our taxes went up,
residents of nearby states
would load up their cars
here. Prices are still pretty
low. Many imported wines.*

Dining and drinking

Bacino's on Wacker
75 E. Wacker Dr.
263-0070
*Basically a duplicate of the
Lincoln Ave. spot: thin-crust
and stuffed pizza, salads,
soups, and sandwiches.*

*The Berghoff
17 W. Adams St.
427-3170

*Binyon's
327 S. Plymouth Ct.
341-1155

*Blackhawk
139 N. Wabash Ave.
726-0100

Le Bordeaux
3 W. Madison St.
372-2027
*Old-line basement bistro
with checked tablecloths
and a varied menu remains
a bastion of bourgeois fare
at moderate prices.*

*Café Angelo
Oxford House
225 N. Wabash Ave.
332-3370

*The Cart
601 S. Wabash Ave.
427-0700

Chicago, A Bar & Grill
120 E. Randolph St.
856-1844
*Stouffer-owned place in the
Prudential Building com-
bines Deco and 1950s
décor and serves grilled
fish, steaks, pastas, and
other trendy dishes.*

City Tavern
33 W. Monroe St.
280-2740
*The menu is a grab bag of
items from the Levy Organization's Water Tower Place
restaurants—from daffy-
named sandwiches to nice-
ly grilled seafoods. The
handsome room—rich
woods, Frank Lloyd Wright-
like lighting fixtures,
plants—is packed at lunch
but less hectic during
breakfast and dinner hours.*

Cohasset Punch
207 W. Madison St.
332-0139
*Middling food at lunch and
dinner in this old-line Loop
saloon filled with character—and characters. Good
bar surrounded by pen-
nants and sports pictures.
The only place to get
Cohasset Punch, a cherry-
colored, medicinal-tasting
liqueur (60 proof) served
chilled over a peach half.*

Counselor's Row
102 N. La Salle St.
332-0123
*Watching La Salle Street
lawyers cut deals adds
spice to otherwise un-
distinguished food.*

Bob Elfman's Restaurant
179 N. State St.
332-2807
*Good deli food in a hang-
out for North Loop publications people and Channel
7 staffers.*

*Empire Room
Palmer House
17 E. Monroe St.
726-7500

M. Foley's Printer's Row
550 S. Dearborn St.
461-0780
*Limited selection of creative
nouvelle dishes in snazzy
plum-and-gray room.*

*The French Baker
26 W. Madison St.
346-3532
*Nice wine list; most wines
also available by the glass.
Espresso and cappuccino.*

Fuji Restaurant
76 W. Lake St.
368-0052
*Basic Japanese menu and
table or "teahouse" service
in the Loop's only "formal"
Japanese restaurant.*

Hoe Kow
73 E. Lake St.
332-1223
*Hasn't changed in years.
Loyal following among
those who want to "eat Chinese" without being the
least bit adventuresome.
Noodles in soup aren't bad
for lunch.*

Ingrid's
Goodman Theatre
200 S. Columbus Dr.
443-3820
*Goodman audiences can
indulge themselves with a
pretheater buffet or cocktails and snacks after the
final curtain.*

*Italian Village
71 W. Monroe St.
332-7005

Knossos
180 N. La Salle St.
236-2442
*Good Grecian food from a
limited menu in a modern
room with elegantly spare
furnishings. Busiest at
lunch.*

Kyori Restaurant
316 N. Michigan Ave.
346-2559
*Japanese version of a fast-
food operation with tasty
food that's a bit expensive
for what you get.*

Little Heidelberg
164 N. State St.
263-5732
*Good value if you stick to
the less-complicated Teu-
tonic offerings. German
beers on tap.*

The Loophole
59 E. Randolph St.
236-6242
*Soups, salads, and sand-
wiches in a typically well-
run Don Roth operation.*

***Magic Miller
Bakery Restaurant**
208 W. Adams St.
346-3910
109 W. Madison St.
641-5520

*Miller's Pub
23 E. Adams St.
922-7446

*Mrs. O'Leary's
Hyatt Regency Chicago
Illinois Center
151 E. Wacker Dr.
861-1355

*Nick's Fishmarket
First National Plaza
Dearborn and Monroe Sts.
621-0200

*Scampi
Hyatt Regency Chicago
Illinois Center
151 E. Wacker Dr.
565-1000

Shanghai
406 S. Clark St.
939-3766
*Located in the old China-
town. The menu offers Cantonese, Thai, and Filipino
dishes, though the waiters
may try to convince you that
you won't like the latter.*

A Touch of Italy
171 W. Madison St.
332-4844
*Lots of interesting Sicilian
specialties on the menu, but
their promise outstrips the
chef's performance.*

*Trader Vic's
Palmer House
17 E. Monroe St.
726-7500
*South Seas décor, "Polyne-
sian" food, and a seemingly
year-round parade of kids
on their way back from the
prom. The best of its genre
in Chicago.*

*Truffles
Hyatt Regency Chicago
Illinois Center
151 E. Wacker Dr.
565-1000

Wabash Inn
204 S. Wabash Ave.
427-4259
*Good sandwiches and
lighter fare for lunch from
the Gallios brothers of Miller's Pub. Full dinner menu.*

Walnut Room
Bismarck Hotel
171 W. Randolph St.
236-0123
*The food doesn't get many
votes, but a lunchtime
floor show is provided
by table-hopping pols
whose movements seem
choreographed.*

*Williamsburg Restaurant
224 S. Michigan Ave.
922-7052

Jimmy Wong's
426 S. Wabash Ave.
427-0021
*Classic B-movie décor,
waiters wearing Hawaiian
shirts, and a large menu
that's uncompromisingly
Cantonese.*

Yiannis
3 First National Plaza
443-1000
*Handsome place offers
Greek, Continental, and
American food.*

Entertainment

*Auditorium Theatre
70 E. Congress Pkwy.
922-2110, 922-6634
(See Theater)

*Blackstone Theatre
60 E. Balbo Ave.
977-1700
(See Theater)

***Chicago City
Theatre Company**
Fine Arts Bldg., 3rd floor
410 S. Michigan Ave.
663-3618
(See Theater)

Civic Opera House
20 N. Wacker Dr.
346-0270
*Home of Lyric Opera.
(See Music.)*

Civic Theatre
20 N. Wacker Dr.
346-0270
(See Theater)

**Richard J. Daley
Bicentennial Plaza
Ice-Skating Rink**
337 E. Randolph Dr.
294-4792
*Roller skating in summer.
(See Parks and
Boulevards.)*

*11th Street Theatre
62 E. 11th St.
663-9465
(See Theater)

***Film Center of the
School of the Art Institute**
208 S. Columbus Dr.
443-3737, 443-3733

*The Goodman Theatre
200 S. Columbus Dr.
443-3800
(See Theater)

HOT TIX Booth
West side of State St. between Madison and Monroe
977-1755
*Up-to-date theater infor-
mation by phone; half-price
(plus service charge) tickets
at the booth on the day of
the performance.*

Loop College
30 E. Lake St.
269-8066
*Foreign-language films are
shown weekdays at noon
during the school year.*

*Orchestra Hall
220 S. Michigan Ave.
435-8111
*Home of the Chicago
Symphony Orchestra.
(See Music.)*

RR Ranch
56 W. Randolph St.
263-8207
*A country-Western band,
The Sundowners, keeps
locals and conventioneers
happy. Chili, too.*

***Joe Segal's
Jazz Showcase**
Blackstone Hotel
636 S. Michigan Ave.
427-4300

*Shubert Theatre
27 W. Monroe St.
977-1700
(See Theater)

*Studebaker Theatre
418 S. Michigan Ave.
(See Theater)

*World Playhouse
410 S. Michigan Ave.
922-5101
(See Theater)

Near West Side

Tomorrow's Chicago meets yesterday's Chicago with a bang on the Near West Side. One by one, the old Jewish, Italian, and Greek ghettos have fallen to institutional use, leaving only a few stores and restaurants as feeble reflections of their former life. Once one of Chicago's most densely populated neighborhoods, by day the area bustles with businessmen, University of Illinois students, and Medical Center personnel. At night, except for the tourists in the Greek and Italian restaurants, it's a ghost town.

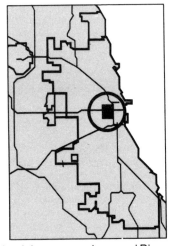

But this is prime real estate, made even more desirable by the Loop's westward-shifting focus. Among the projects proposed or underway are: Wolf Point Landings, a Harry Weese and Jack Wogan residential, shopping, and marina complex; Presidential Towers, a four-building, 49-story residential project; Fulton Court, one of many loft-building condominium conversions; and River City, 12 acres of residences, shopping, light factories, and a marina. The mirrored skin of the **Social Security Administration** building (600 West Madison Street) reflects the area's future, and the Claes Oldenburg *Batcolumn* out front is a toothpick compared to the city clout that's behind the development. In a decade or two, much of Chicago's oldest neighborhood will be little more than an antiseptic extension of downtown.

Chicago's first settlements quickly spread to the Near West Side from the factory-, lumberyard-, and shipyard-lined banks near the mouth of the Chicago River. The city limits reached Ashland Avenue in 1837 and extended to Western Avenue in 1851. Although the far reaches were suburban in the early years, the area close to what is now downtown filled with immigrants. In the 1850s, Germans organized **St. Francis of Assisi** (now at Roosevelt Road and Newberry Avenue), and the Irish **St. Patrick** (Desplaines and Adams Streets)—Chicago's oldest church—and **Holy Family** (Roosevelt Road and May Street). The beautiful brick buildings towered over the meanest of wood shacks. Bohemians followed the early settlers in such numbers that, by 1870, the community centered at Roosevelt Road and Halsted Street was known as Praha (Prague).

The 1871 Chicago Fire, which started at DeKoven and Jefferson Streets, treated the riverside to its first urban-renewal program, but left most of the Near West Side unscathed. Post-Fire refugees swelled the neighborhood's population and, over the next four decades, waves of Italian, Jewish, and Greek immigrants crowded into the already-dilapidated housing stock. Jane Addams and Ellen Gates Starr moved into this milieu of urban desperation and squalor in 1889 with a pioneer concept—the settlement house. For the next 70 years, almost no aspect of life in the neighborhood was divorced from **Hull House** (800 South Halsted Street). By 1907, a square-block complex of buildings serving the community enclosed the 1856 country manor of Charles Hull, which had narrowly escaped the Chicago Fire. The list of Hull House's Chicago firsts is staggering: social settlement; public facilities like baths, a playground, a swimming pool, a gymnasium, and a kitchen; little theater; Boy Scout troop; college extension courses; citizenship classes; art exhibits. Hull House spearheaded investigations into truancy, poor sanitation, infant mortality, and disease control; housing and factory inspections; and fostered the labor-union movement. These activities and more catalogue the social ills largely ignored by the city government.

After the turn of the century, **Maxwell Street** was the center of the Jewish community numbering more than 20,000, most refugees from restrictive Imperial Russian laws. The street scene was lively and festive. Backpack and pushcart peddlers crammed the streets, and clothing stores spilled their wares onto the sidewalks, while women and children did piecework for the nearby sweatshops at home. Fruit stalls overflowed with produce, and heavyweight boxer "Battling" Levinsky, who fought all the greats including Joe Lewis, put in occasional, much-celebrated visits at his sister's fish stand. The ferocity of the local merchants was so notorious that the City Council passed a law in the 1930s outlawing "pullers," men who literally dragged customers into the stores and made getting out without buying almost impossible.

Today, much of the area is vacant lots. Halsted Street houses easy-credit, bad-dude clothing stores, and just a few of the old shops remain on Maxwell Street between Halsted Street and the Dan Ryan Expressway. Six days a week, the scene is remarkable only for its sordidness, but on Sunday the old magic returns. Starting in the wee hours of the morning, a coterie of regulars stakes out favorite spots for the weekly open-air market, a hundred-year-old tradition. By 8 a.m., rain or shine, the blocks west of Halsted Street and south of Roosevelt Road are filled with bargain hunters searching for antiques or used clothing for the kids and loading up on everything from cheap (if overripe) produce to plumbing parts, munching street food, or just listening to the musicians and soaking up the sights.

A spirit of camaraderie draws the sellers together. Many are seniors supplementing meager Social Security checks or bottom-of-the-economic-ladder families augmenting welfare. Others prowl auctions for bargain-priced boxes of old clothes and dishes or spend their weeks in junk stores accumulating stock. One man brings a virtual hardware store in his stake truck; another institutional sinks and toilets in his.

Hardcore antiques buyers arrive by daybreak, each rightfully worried that another will snatch up that undervalued prize. Middle-class tourists and the poor from nearby neighborhoods are on the scene by 9 a.m., when the music is usually going strong. Although a couple of blind street singers wander, the best known, Blind Jim Brewer, is tied down by his electric guitar and the rest of his white-garbed gospel act to a space west of Halsted Street on 14th Street. A block from Brewer, John Henry Davis, Jr. and his family put on a stage show. Davis plays lead guitar, his kids work the drums and bass, his wife and grandfather play and pass the tambourine, and, from time to time, visiting friends sit in for a set. The music—blues, pop, soul—keeps the air festive and requests are honored, if something's dropped in the tambourine.

Strategy is essential for a successful foray to Maxwell Street. If you plan to shop, pay a buck to park at an impromptu central lot so you can dump your treasures before rushing off to find more. If you're just going for fun, park at a distance to avoid the traffic, or come by bus. Prices are best on used stuff: Cheap new clothes can be had at discount stores all over for as little. Of course, it's caveat emptor all the way. Those yarmulke-hatted men with loupes around the jewelry tables know what they're buying; do you?

No trip to Maxwell Street is complete without a nosh. The Polish-sausage and pork-chop-sandwich vendors have their partisans, as do tamale cart, cornhusk-wrapped torpedoes. **Nate's Delicatessen** (807 West Maxwell Street), known to a generation as Lyon's, sells lots of corned beef sandwiches and homemade pickled herring from a grubby basement shop, but one of the city's most famous delis is just across the Dan Ryan Expressway in the Jefferson Street-Roosevelt Road discount district.

Manny's Coffee Shop (1141 South Jefferson Street) may be only a pale reflection of the glossy, flashy Jewish restaurants like Baron's that once lined Roosevelt Road, but the food's not too different. Lamb shanks, prune tzimmes, baked chicken and fish, dairy dishes, and cold plates are served cafeteria-style for about $4. And such corned beef sandwiches! At lunchtime, the place is packed with Jewish businessmen and lawyers from the County Courthouse. Breakfast begins at 5 a.m.: You don't have to shop Maxwell without fortification.

Manny's and the wholesale/retail outlets around it seem very separate from the Maxwell Street market today but, before World War Two, Roosevelt Road was solid with tenements from State Street past Morgan Street and the Halsted-Roosevelt intersection was an exciting jumble of streetcars, wagons, and pushcarts. Halsted Street was filled with high-pressure ladies' clothing stores, and Jefferson Street was the center of the clothing jobber trade. The Dan Ryan Expressway was not built on waste or industrial land but right through a vibrant, if decaying, neighborhood.

Successors of a few of the hundreds of local merchants are still going strong east of the expressway, in factorylike '50s buildings constructed after "slum" clearance. Old-timers remember when the neighborhood giants were just little shops one step ahead of the urban-renewal wrecking ball. **Chernin Shoes** (610 West Roosevelt Road) has grown into what may be the city's largest outlet for name-brand shoes. The pace is hectic and the atmosphere harried in both the men's and women's sections, but the enormous selection and discounted prices make shopping here worthwhile. **Fishman's Fabrics** (1101 South Desplaines Street) boasts bolt after bolt of everything from trendy designer fabrics to funky fake furs, all at reasonable prices. Three levels are filled with sewing supplies.

A forest of double-hung racks fills the football-field-sized sales floor at **Benjamin's Clothing** (1150 South Clinton Street). They are loaded with men's wear from name manufacturers in mostly traditional styles: suits, sports jackets, topcoats, and slacks, all at substantial discounts.

If you want to save even more and can put up with a hodgepodge of styles and incomplete size runs, check out the dozen other, mostly men's clothing outlets in the area for odd lots, samples, store returns, broken sizes, seconds, and factory errors, from Calvin Klein to unlabeled. **Rottapel Clothes** (531 West Roosevelt Road), which has been around for 71 years, sells retail to individuals and wholesales job lots of new clothing, although the used-clothing business that was once a local mainstay has evaporated. (The stuff was collected by pushcarts running down Chicago's alleys, amassed here, then shipped south.) Two more good sources for bargains are **Morris & Sons** and **Meyerson Associated Clothing Co.,** both in the Jeffro Plaza (555 West Roosevelt Road), a lackluster "L" of shops with its own parking lot just south of Roosevelt Road.

The shopping center's most interesting tenant is the **Conte di Savoia,** an international food market. The Italian offerings are exhaustive: pastas of every description, imported tomatoes and oils, a full deli counter with meats and cheeses (Greek, too), olives and artichoke salads, candies, and even espresso pots and spaghetti platters. There are also loads of grains and bulk herbs, spices in bins and barrels, coffee beans, tinned goods, nuts, and candied fruits. The Indian and Oriental sections are also impressive.

Food stores in the teeming Italian ghetto just north of the Jewish one once marked the ethnic dividing line with the heady aroma of garlic, sausages, and cheeses. Construction of the University of Illinois campus truncated this neighborhood, removing Halsted Street's tenements and leaving only the few blocks of neat, turn-of-the-century houses and apartments west of Morgan Street that once represented the good life for the Italians. Of the few groceries, meat markets, and bakeries that remain on Taylor Street, the **Original Ferrara, Inc.** (2210) stands out. This huge bakery may have the largest selection of Italian cookies, pastries, and cakes in the city (no bread, though). Ferrara supplies local restaurants and does a big wedding-cake business. Everything is inexpensive; the cannoli cake (a piece weighs almost three-fourths of a pound) is not to be missed.

With no surviving tradition like the Maxwell Street market, Taylor Street's main draws are restaurants: old-line, Southern Italian spots like **Gennaro's** (1352) and **Mategrano's** (1321) where pizza and pasta are the main fare, the music is likely to be Sinatra, the red wine chilled, and the help gruff. Mategrano's adds a popular, all-you-can-eat Thursday and Saturday buffet with more than a dozen items. The **Vernon Park Restaurant** (1073 West Vernon Park Place) features a nice selection of seafood on Fridays and always has chicken Vesuvio and antipasto, although they are not listed on the blackboard with the dozen daily specials for less than $4. The service in the crummy back room behind the bar is two steps below no-nonsense, but the food's okay and a good value. At the height of the dinner hour, expect to wait here and at the Taylor Street places.

Florence Restaurant (1030 West Taylor Street), opened by Florence Scala and her brother, Mario Giovangelo, where their father had a meat market, provides a charming alternative to mediocre food and indifferent service. With a high tin ceiling, a mural lovingly painted by Giovangelo, and antique woodwork rescued from Hull House buildings, the room is delightful. Although the menu is limited, the food's prepared with a sensitivity usually found only in more expensive spots. Pastas such as linguine in olive oil with walnuts are so good and everyone's so friendly, you probably won't mind the disorganized service. Don't miss the wonderful chocolate-rum torte!

Street food comes into its own on Taylor Street with **Al's Bar-B-Q** (1079), which turns out the Italian beef sandwiches voted number one by *Chicago* magazine's panel; **Rocky's Pan Pizza** (1104), with some of Chicago's best by-the-slice, roof-of-the-mouth scorchers; and Italian-ice stands, which often call the confection Italian lemonade, regardless of the flavor. It's terrific by any name at **Mario's Italian Lemonade** (1070), with more than a dozen varieties, including fresh peach, in 13 sizes of paper cups (15¢ and up).

For a wider choice of restaurants, and to see what the area looked like before urban removal, visit "Little Italy," a section that grew up around the post-Fire McCormick reaper works at Western Avenue and 26th Street. Cermak Road traces the little quarter's northern edge, and the Hispanic shops give no hint of the Italian goodies waiting to the south on Oakley Avenue: half a dozen good, modestly priced restaurants within a couple of blocks.

Basically, the similarities are greater than the differences between these places, so individual favorites are usually the result of a few happy experiences. **Bruna's Ristorante** (2424 South Oakley Avenue) is a classic neighborhood place with a small, aging dining room behind the bar. Everything is cooked to order with great care, and veal dishes and fettuccine stand out. At **La Fontanella** (2414), perhaps the best-known spot, baked and fried chicken Franca are specialties, as are the green noodle casserole and arancini—breaded, meat-filled, deep-fried balls of rice. Considerably cheaper, **Bacchanalia** (2413) is the place for great chicken Vesuvio and veal parmigiana, as well as fine homemade tortellini, not-too-sweet cannoli, and other treats.

For more home cooking, Italian style, check out **Febo** (2501 South Western Avenue), which offers a lengthy menu, friendly service, and generally high-quality food. The many pastas are cooked *al dente*, and the veal's pretty good. The pasta's usually overcooked at **Alfo's** (2512 South Oakley Avenue), but chicken à la Alfo (half a bird pan-fried with sausages, mushrooms, and roast potatoes) and perfectly sautéed spinach are excellent at this place, which bills itself as Northern Italian. Dinners include soup and trips to the small salad bar, which provides sufficient fixings for a fine antipasto. There's a convivial bar in front and a much-needed parking lot in the rear.

Handsomely decorated with restraint—sort of California Italian with stucco-like walls and lots of light wood—**Danilo's** (2435 South Western Avenue) is a bit of a neighborhood anomaly. The atypically short menu features pastas—the homemade tortellini is excellent—and properly prepared veal dishes. The owner-chef makes the rounds when he isn't in back whipping up one of the unusual daily specials.

Restaurants are also the main attractions in "Greektown," another Near West Side ethnic pocket. From 1900 to the onset of World War Two, Greeks settled in the "Delta"—a triangle formed by Halsted Street and Blue Island Avenue—and beyond. They established the country's first, permanent Greek Orthodox parish, Holy Trinity, in 1897 (it has since moved) and purchased Anshe Sholom (Ashland Boulevard and Polk Street) in 1927, rechristening it **St. Basil.** Soon after World War Two, the Eisenhower Expressway cut a huge swath through the community and, in the early 1960s, U. of I.'s Chicago campus claimed the rest after a spirited but futile battle. No homes survived: Two blocks of commercial buildings along Halsted Street north of the expressway are all that remain. (This destruction occasioned the birth of the Lincoln-Lawrence Greektown.)

In spite of the dismantling of the community, or perhaps because of it, the Halsted Street restaurants have become big, main-line businesses. Years ago, **Diana Grocery and Restaurant** (130) was just a little dining room in the back of a Greek grocery. With the original building and all the Greek customers gone, the owners embarked on a promotional campaign to draw in outsiders. Thousands of handkissings, saganaki flamings, and waiting-line ouzos later, the dining room is supermarket size, while the grocery has shrunk to an excuse for the name. Success has even spawned a sanguinal competitor, **Dianna's Opaa** (212).

Most nearby spots offer similar fare in large, noisy rooms decorated with murals (lots of Greek fishermen), hanging plastic grape vines, and the like. Two are a cut above. A whole pig or lamb roasting in the window of **The Parthenon** (314) presages the treats inside. The large menu includes roast, fried, baked, broiled, and barbecued meats; seafood, such as a fine, cold octopus salad and shrimp cooked saganaki style; and the familiar gyros, dolmades, moussaka, and so forth. Portions are generous, everything is well prepared, and watching skilled waiters flambée four saganakis at a time is a free floor show. The darker and often noisier **Greek Islands** (766 West Jackson Boulevard) is a favorite with Chicago authors like Saul Bellow and sells many of the same dishes as "deluxe" choices, about five of which are available daily along with the standards. Egg-lemon soup and spinach-cheese pie are topnotch, as are the desserts. Both places have combination plates for novices (or those who want a bit of everything) and make excellent broiled red snapper.

If you want the fixings for a home-cooked Greek meal, head back to Halsted Street. Greek music and exotic aromas mingle in the air at the large, bright

Athens Grocery (324). In the deli case, half a dozen different types of olives glisten in tubs next to cheeses, mounds of halvah, and jars of fish-roe spread. There are loads more olives in jars, smoked fish, dried herbs, nuts, pastas, grains, and a whole shelf of olive oils. On top of this, Athens is a full American grocery store. The **Mediterranean Pastry Shop** (308) is equally delightful with Greek and French pastries, cookies, and candies in sparkling cases.

Acropolis Hellenic Imports (306) stocks enough decorative accessories to open a dozen Greek restaurants, as well as records, tapes, cards, and books. In-laid backgammon sets, peasant dolls, antique copperware, and costly ancient icons share space with all the usual knickknacks, including Grecian urns.

What did Chicago get when two of its vibrant ethnic neighborhoods were bulldozed for the **University of Illinois at Chicago** (UIC) campus? Skidmore, Owings & Merrill created a complex you either love or hate, but can't fail to notice. Most of the poured-concrete buildings are low and have a suburban industrial-park feel, and the highly touted, towering University Hall may be wider on top than at its base, but so what? The campus probably looked great on the model board, but there's a sterile, unyielding quality to it that's relieved only by the playful Behavioral Sciences and the Science and Engineering Buildings—mad, mul-tileveled boxes stacked at angles, where finding particular classrooms is almost impossible.

A commuter school at the nexus of the expressway system, UIC is well served by public transportation. That may explain why the students have little im-pact on what remains of the neighborhood, parking-space competition except-ed. Although more than 20,000 attend classes each year and undoubtedly bol-ster Taylor Street's business, no collegiate shops herald their presence. What lit-tle campus life there is centers around the student union, Circle Center (750 South Halsted Street), just in back of Hull House. Free concerts (2 p.m. Wednes-days) in the "Inner Circle" (near the food area) feature local rock, country, blues, and jazz groups performing at high volume. (Open to the public: 996-2645.) The Music Department also sponsors free concerts—classical to jazz—most Wednesday afternoons at the Education and Communications Building (996-2977).

Medical schools and hospitals lie just west of the campus in the **Medical Center District.** This unique 365-acre tract was set aside for health-care institu-tions by the legislature in 1941, largely through the efforts of freshman represen-tative Vito Marzullo. In their 1943 annual report, the Medical Center commission-ers compared the center to ". . . a cluster of buildings (at Epidauros) set in a grove of trees and dedicated to the practice and study of the healing arts by an inspired group of men whose leader was the renowned Aesculapius, later to be deified as the god of medicine of the Greeks." Heady stuff for a state report!

The district includes 60 health-care institutions. Some, like Cook County Hospital (built in 1873) and the UIC hospitals, preceded the designation; the Rush-Presbyterian-St. Luke's Medical Center merger and the Veterans Admin-istration Hospital came after 1941. The buildings span a century in styles from baroque to ultramodern.

Homes in the increasingly desirable residential enclave between the univer-sity and the medical center reflect the same diversity. Charles H. Shaw is devel-oping Center Court Gardens, an 18-acre townhouse-style apartment grouping at Ashland Boulevard and Harrison Street. Lexington Street between Lytle and Ada Streets displays well-maintained, Victorian row houses with an Italianate brick house on the corner, showing what middle-class sections of the Near West Side looked like in the 19th century.

The glass-lanterned cupola of **Notre Dame de Chicago** (Flournoy and Ada Streets) overlooks both. Founded in 1864 to serve the local French-Canadian community, Notre Dame outgrew its first building at the corner of Halsted and Congress Streets and built the present church in 1888. Gregoire Vigeant designed the unusual Romanesque, domed structure, which is listed on both the Illinois and National Registers of Historic Places as the only extant example of French church architecture in Chicago. A 1978 fire left the 33 stained-glass windows depicting the lives of Jesus and Mary and the richly painted interior unscathed and damages have been repaired.

The university, Dan Ryan Expressway, and the Roosevelt Road-Jefferson Street urban-renewal project all replaced lower-class communities, but the Near West Side once had an upper crust, too. While the workingmen's hovels were filling in the land along the Chicago River's banks, pioneer real-estate speculator Samuel Walker developed Ashland Boulevard just south of **Union Park** for the gentry. Twice a congressman and five times Chicago's mayor, Carter Henry Harrison, who called the park the "Bois de Boulogne of the West Side," was assassinated in his house at Jackson Boulevard and Ashland Boulevard (demolished) in 1903. The daughter of the home's first owner, Henry H. Honoré, became the arbiter of Chicago society when she married Potter Palmer.

Ashland, Adams, Monroe, and Washington were all fashionable avenues in the second half of the 19th century. Florenz Ziegfeld was raised at 1448 West Adams Street (demolished). Theodore Dreiser lived overlooking Union Park, where his sister Carrie aspired to move. Only one block remains intact today: the **Jackson Boulevard Historic District** (1500 block). The streetscape, a pleasing panoply of Italianate, Queen Anne, and Second Empire styles, evokes a gentler age when men such as Benjamin F. Ferguson, a prominent lumberyard owner and philanthropist, lived there. His house (1501) now overlooks the Whitney M. Young Magnet High School's curtain-walled campus.

After the area fell from favor, its proximity to downtown led to a variety of commercial and institutional uses. Ashland Boulevard north of the expressway is "Union Row," with regional headquarters of the Teamsters, Amalgamated Clothing Workers, and many more. In the early 1900s, the mansions and row houses between Ashland Boulevard and Halsted Street were replaced by massive brick factory buildings that still house publishers, bookbinders, typographers, and printers, making the Near West Side the city's printing center. (Another group lies just east of Greektown, across the expressway.)

Other tenants range from casketmakers to confectioners, and the dour structures provide some of the city's least-known shopping opportunities for those willing to venture off the beaten path. The **Fiesta Mart,** a Mexican bazaar bursting with a border-town's worth of glassware, pottery, clothing, ironworks, rugs, piñatas, bark paintings, and other crafts, is hidden above the huge **Fiesta Restaurant** (1327 West Washington Boulevard), where all-you-can-eat lunches are served from a long steam table. On weekends, the buffet is open evenings, too, fueling revelers in the adjoining disco. Homer Alvarado, who owns the complex, has an extraordinary collection of preconquistador Indian statues, jewelry, and masks, which may some day form the nucleus of a Mexican folk museum.

C & C Florists' Supplies (1245 West Washington Boulevard) maintains a showroom at its warehouse as well as at the Merchandise Mart. One of the country's largest wholesalers of silk and dried flowers, plums and preserved foliage, containers and baskets, C & C welcomes retail customers. Another decorators' resource, **Marble Supply International** (110 North Peoria Street) offers both a design service and discounts "to the trade." In stock are slabs of 50 different marbles and 15 granites for floors, walls, mantels, tables, and furniture tops. The firm also carries marble tiles and designs bathrooms.

Many of Chicago's galleries and major private collectors turn to **Frederic's Frame Studio** (1230 West Jackson Boulevard) for museum-quality framing. This is one of the country's last sources for gold- and silver-leaf work, and the other frames are almost as precious: hand-carved rococo antique reproductions, Art Deco, Art Nouveau, curved corner, Tokyo corner, ribbon corner, and a staggering variety of plainer ones of most woods and finishes in every pattern, shape, and size. Frederic's babies valuable artworks and provides paper and painting conservation services. Fred Baker operates a gallery there, too.

Madison Street, always a commercial thoroughfare, decayed into a skid row after the surrounding neighborhood evolved from residential to industrial use. Missions dotted the street and down-and-outers who couldn't scrape together the flophouses' rates slept in doorways. The city is practicing slum clearance by neglect here, and most of the land stands empty, although a few merchants, notably restaurant-supply houses, remain, offering good selections and prices with no amenities or pleasantries.

Given the area's flux, the **Randolph Street Market's** survival is surprising. Cut off from its former focus, **Haymarket Square,** by the Kennedy Expressway, the mile-long relic of the past stretches to Union Park. In the days of the "Haymarket Riot," this was one of the city's five produce markets, clogged with horse-drawn drays and frenzied activity as farmers hawked their crops to all comers. It's much tamer now. The merchants are small wholesalers who sell to restaurants and little groceries and, often, walk-in customers. With the city-wide proliferation of produce stands, nostalgia is the only reason to make a special shopping trip to the market for such goods, though some bargains can be found, especially if you buy in quantity.

N & G Produce (904 West Randolph Street) always has a good selection ranging from ginger to Mexican peppers, and nothing's prepacked in plastic wrap. **Quality Supermarket Products** (924) is a full-scale wholesale/retail supermarket/butcher. Large sizes of packaged goods and half-case lots of canned ones predominate, some at very attractive savings. Prices are also good at the **Columbus Meat Market** (906) where the wide variety of meats includes goat. The striking, Art Deco Wholesale Florists Building (1313) now houses mostly unrelated businesses, but **Flowers by Villari** (820) sells cut flowers and potted plants for as little as half the prices at this firm's Marina City store or, for that matter, most neighborhood florists.

The city's large wholesale produce jobbers moved out to the **South Water Market** (15th and Morgan Streets) when Wacker Drive cut through its namesake in 1925. Past Lake Street's machinery row, however, Fulton Street is still a meat and fish wholesale center. The meat-packers aren't set up to trim a steak or two from a side of beef for customers but, by its size, fish lends itself to retail sales and several plants on Randolph and Fulton have retail sections. **Pick Fisheries** (702 West Fulton Market), just east of the expressway, sells a wide variety of fresh and frozen fish at low prices in a lovely old building.

For good steaks plus meats not found on Fulton Street, head to **Cafe Bohemia** (138 South Clinton Street). This old-fashioned restaurant is famous for its game—venison, moose, lion, and bear—and by prearrangement runs a limo to and from theaters and sporting events. No exotic treats grace the menu at **Lou Mitchell's** (563 West Jackson Boulevard) but the canny owner has made this big lunchroom a Chicago landmark. The breakfasts—served all day—keep people coming back. Fresh butter and double-yolked eggs, fluffy omelettes served in skillets, and what may well be Chicago's best coffee aren't cheap, but you always feel you've gotten your money's worth. For years, Mitchell has greeted every customer, dubbing the ladies beautiful and dispensing little boxes of Milk Duds. Now a nephew is shouldering more of the load. And the city continues to evolve.

Interesting places

*Jane Addams' Hull House and Dining Hall
800 S. Halsted St.
996-2793
Worth visiting for the restored rooms, exhibits on Jane Addams's life, the library, and a Bicentennial neighborhood display in the dining-hall building.

Amalgamated Clothing and Textile Workers Union
333 S. Ashland Blvd.
738-6100
The union's Midwest headquarters is housed in this 1920s, limestone building.

Chicago Fire Academy
558 W. DeKoven St.
744-4728
Designed by Loebl, Schlossman and Bennett and built on the site where the Chicago Fire allegedly started. The sculptured bronze flame is by Egon Weiner. A tour (by appt.) includes a 30-minute introduction to modern fire-fighting techniques.

Chicago Stadium
1800 W. Madison St.
733-5300
Built in 1929 to accommodate sports and used for everything from Elvis concerts to Democratic Conventions. Mostly basketball and hockey nowadays. Claims to have the world's largest organ.

Church of the Epiphany
Ashland Blvd. and Adams
733-9123
Built in the mid-1880s to plans by Burling & Whitehouse, this ornate brownstone Episcopal church is remarkable for its large nave uninterrupted by columns, the peaked roof supported by a network of massive beams, and superb mosaic altar panels.

Fine Arts Research and Holographic Center Museum
1134 W. Washington Blvd.
226-1007
(See Museums)

First Baptist Congregational Church
Ashland and Washington
243-8047
Built as the First Congregational Church in 1869, facing then-elegant Union Park. Several congregations that shared an aversion to slavery merged and offered the pulpit here to leading abolitionists.

*Haymarket Square
Randolph and Desplaines
Scene of the 1886 riot and first use of a dynamite bomb by U.S. "terrorists." A monument to the 176 policemen (seven of whom were killed) who charged the workers' rally was repeatedly blown up in the 1960s and finally moved to Central Police Headquarters in 1972. A plaque to the four workers who were hanged as a result of the riot was stolen from the side of the Catholic Charities Building: Only the holes remain.

*Holy Family Catholic Church
Roosevelt Rd. and May St.
243-7207
Founded as a "church of all nations" in 1857. John M. Van Osdel was one of the architects involved in building the city's first cathedral-sized church in the 1860s. Gothic with a painted brick façade, a fine tower designed by J. Paul Huber, interior piers stuccoed to imitate stone, Anthony Boucher's statue of St. Patrick, a hand-carved altar railing depicting the three gates to Heaven, nice stained glass, and oak doors. A small statue of the first pastor, Father Arnold Damen, is mounted on a confessional because he wanted "to be near the sinners." Founding place of the First Independent Order of Foresters, Loyola University, and St. Ignatius College Prep, the Jesuit-run school next door.

Illinois Regional Library for the Blind and Physically Handicapped
1055 W. Roosevelt Rd.
738-9200
A bright-colored, whimsical building with an undulating window and curved corridors and counters; Stanley Tigerman was consulting architect. (See Libraries.)

*Jackson Boulevard Historic District
1500 block of Jackson
Designated a city landmark in 1976. A booklet on the district is available from the Commission on Chicago Historical and Architectural Landmarks (744-3200).

*Maxwell Street Market
Center at Peoria and 14th

*Medical Center District
Ashland Blvd. to Oakley, Congress Pkwy. to 13th St.

*Notre Dame de Chicago
Flournoy and Ada Sts.
243-7400

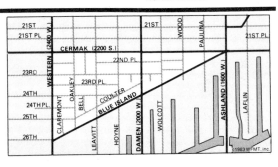

Our Lady of Pompeii
Lexington and Lytle Sts.
421-3757
A handsome, 1923, yellow-brick church on a lovely street.

*Randolph Street Market
From Halsted to Loomis

*St. Basil Greek Orthodox Church
Ashland Blvd. and Polk St.
243-3738

*St. Francis of Assisi Church
Roosevelt and Newberry
226-7575
Founded by German Catholics in 1853, this nice brick church with an unusual vaulted ceiling was moved back 36 feet when Roosevelt Rd. was widened in 1917. The congregation is now predominantly Spanish speaking.

*St. Patrick Church
Desplaines and Adams
782-6171
The brick and stone foundation for Chicago's oldest church was laid in 1852, but a cholera epidemic halted construction; completed 1856. The Romanesque revival building has round arches, narrow windows, and broad, massive walls. The towers—one Gothic, one Byzantine—were added later to symbolize the meeting of East and West in the neighborhood. Celtic serpentine motifs and crosses are incorporated in the beautiful, pastel stained-glass windows; one is of St. Brendan, whom many Irish believe discovered America.

St. Paul Church
Hoyne Ave. and 22nd Pl.
847-7622
Seeing this massive, Henry J. Schlacks-designed Gothic church with great mosaics, stained-glass windows, and statuary is worth a foray into the neighborhood. The soaring steeples are visible for miles around. Drive down the alley to see the original building—little more than a shack.

*Social Security Administration
Great Lakes Program Service Center
600 W. Madison St.
353-4810

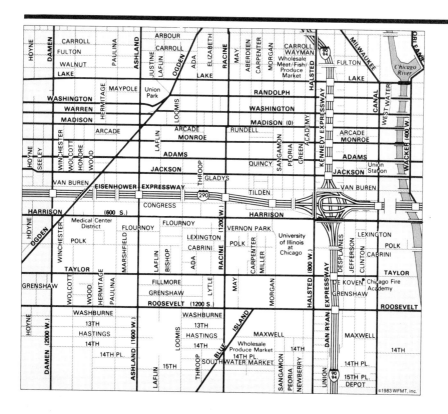

*South Water Market
15th and Morgan Sts.
*Addresses of firms are
space numbers that don't
correspond to the city's
street numbering system.
Because it was built for simpler conditions, the market
is now clogged by 40-foot
trailers and plans are afoot
to move it.*

*Union Park
Ashland and Washington
294-4736
*Once glorious, now
dilapidated: The rustic
bridges and miniature lakes
are long gone.*

United Parcel Service
1400 S. Jefferson St.
920-2900 (Oak Brook no.)
*One of the first post-W. W.
II urban-renewal buildings. A
convenient place to drop off
your packages and save the
two-buck pick-up charge.*

***University of Illinois
at Chicago**
University Hall
601 S. Morgan St.
996-3000

**University of Illinois at
Chicago health services**
(formerly the U. of I.
Medical Center)
1737 W. Polk St.
996-7000
*The Medical Library (1970
W. Polk St.) houses Edwin
Boyd Johnson's nine WPA
frescoes, Great Men of
Medicine, while Edgar Brit-
ton's 1938 fresco Woman
and Child Among Ruins is in
the Pharmacy Building
basement (Rm. 7) and the
WPA mosaic Signs of the
Zodiac graces the archway
at 1819 W. Polk St.*

Shopping
and services

Acme Glass Co.
2215 W. Roosevelt Rd.
226-5454
*Good selection of stained-
glass supplies.*

***Acropolis Hellenic
Imports**
306 S. Halsted St.
332-1182

Athenian Candle Co.
300 S. Halsted St.
332-6988
*Religious candles, incense
including raw frank and
myrrh, medicinal herbs,
wedding and christening
favors in a large store.*

*Benjamin's Clothing
1150 S. Clinton St.
922-1536

Broadway Costumes
932 W. Washington Blvd.
829-6400
*Polar bears, witches, and
Renaissance queens rent
their costumes here. Store
sells make-up, wigs, hats,
and canes. Summer "Dusty
Closet" sale some years.*

*C & C Florists' Supplies
1245 W. Washington Blvd.
421-1500

*Chernin Shoes
610 W. Roosevelt Rd.
922-4545
*Everything from lizard-toe
cowboy boots to sexy
pumps and kiddies'
booties.*

Chiarugi Hardware Store
1449 W. Taylor St.
666-2235
*Great little neighborhood
hardware store with wine-
making supplies.*

**Chicago Christian
Industrial League
Halsted Resale Store**
112 S. Halsted St.
421-2553
*If you can't get it on Maxwell
St., it's probably here, but
not as cheap. A room of
books, a floor of furniture,
and lots of old clothes,
housewares, etc.*

Joseph Cinofsky, Inc.
210 S. Clinton St.
782-4684
*Discount men's wear. The
real deals are irregular
Arrow, Enro, and Excello
shirts for $4, guaranteed
against major defects.*

*Fiesta Mart
1327 W. Washington Blvd.
421-7862

*Fishman's Fabrics
1101 S. Desplaines St.
922-7250

*Flowers by Villari
820 W. Randolph St.
738-1600

*Frederic's Frame Studio
1230 W. Jackson Blvd.
243-2950

**Gingiss Formalwear
Center**
555 W. 14th Pl.
829-0001
*Discounts on new and used
formal wear and accesso-
ries. Discontinued rentals
sold for one-time rental fee.*

Gold Brothers
1140 W. Madison St.
666-1520
*Restaurant stoves, tables,
chairs, and other fixtures.
No dishes or pots and pans.*

**Grand Stage
Lighting Co., Inc.**
630 W. Lake St.
332-5611
*Everything to start a little
theater. Building was Zepf's
Hall, a union meeting place.
The hall is intact and the Illinois Labor History Society
hopes to preserve and
restore the building, perhaps as a labor museum.*

S. Hirsh & Sons
621-23 W. Randolph St.
263-5213
*Huge stock of used clothing
and shoes, Army and Navy
surplus, and some beauti-
ful costume and period
things. Hirsh really knows
clothing and isn't giving
anything away; he also rents
to photographers. Call
ahead.*

**Krispy Kist Korn
Machine Co.**
120 S. Halsted St.
733-0900
*Manufacturing, wholesal-
ing, and retailing commercial popcorn machines
since 1925. Replica antique
nut roasters, too.*

H. L. Latt
118 N. Clinton St.
346-7988
Big store in an old loft building is jammed to the rafters with repros of antique oak and brass, lifestyle furniture, and accessories. Not top quality, but some priced very low.

McIntosh Stereopticon Co.
132 N. Clinton St.
876-0939
This 90-year-old company started by a pioneer in medical optics had a booth at the World's Columbian Exposition. Since there's little demand for stereopticons nowadays, it now makes 2-inch projection slides for industrial, medical, and educational uses.

*Marble Supply International
110 N. Peoria St.
226-3010

*Meyerson Associated Clothing Co.
555 W. Roosevelt Rd.
421-5580
Clothing for tall and short men. Lots of designer stuff. Discounted prices; free alterations.

*Morris & Sons Co.
555 W. Roosevelt, 2nd floor
243-5635
Complex pricing system but lots of good values on a stock of quality men's wear that changes continually.

Plum Tree Shop Goodwill Industries
120 S. Ashland Blvd.
738-3860
Store-within-a-store carries nice glassware, linens, jewelry, other collectibles.

Richie's
560 W. Roosevelt Rd.
427-3565
Leather jackets, coats—most made in Korea and not too expertly—and shoes discounted.

*Rottapel Clothes
531 W. Roosevelt Rd.
942-0816

I. Sachs Inc.
637 W. Roosevelt Rd.
666-0091
Every conceivable shoe part and lots of shoe polish (some decades old and in outlandish colors) piled ceiling high in Dickensian disorder, but the wholesale prices (sometimes arrived at informally for retail customers) make up for the time it takes to find what you want. Second floor filled with leather and hides sold by the square foot.

Salvage One
1524 S. Peoria St.
733-0098
Fourteen floors of salvaged architectural artifacts: doors, mantels, mirrors, moldings, stairs, railings and spindles, stained glass, terra-cotta tiles, wrought iron, and more. Choice items hidden away. Prices can be outlandishly high.

N. Turek & Sons Supply Co.
333 S. Halsted St.
263-3560
A neighborhood fixture (in various locations dictated by urban renewal) for more than a half century. Supplies contractors with industrial hardware, paints, and plumbing equipment. Huge and not self-service, there are catalogues to identify what you want.

Twillby's
568 W. Roosevelt Rd.
431-9840
Seconds of jeans, tops, slacks, and Hawaiian shirts.

Foodstuffs

Alpen's Cheese Barn
1246 W. Randolph St.
421-1535
Limited selection of cheeses, including hard-to-find Hungarian ones, at fair prices.

*Al's Bar-B-Q
1079 W. Taylor St.
733-8896

*Athens Grocery
324 S. Halsted St.
332-6737

Borsini's Food Mart
2359 S. Western Ave.
847-6698
Old-fashioned ma-and-pa grocery has great carry-out submarine sandwiches.

*Columbus Meat Market
906 W. Randolph St.
829-2480

*Conte di Savoia
555 W. Roosevelt Rd.
666-3471

Fontana Bros. Bakery
2404 S. Oakley Ave.
847-6697
Little Italian bakery sells excellent bread and superb rye breadsticks. Cookies, too.

Gourmet Frozen Foods
97 South Water Market
226-1849
Seafood by the bag and box (usually 3 lbs. or more) at very reasonable prices. "Special consideration for church groups."

L. Isaacson and Stein Fish Co.
800 W. Fulton Market
421-2444
Sells retail, accepts food stamps.

Lucca Packing
1138-40 W. Randolph St.
421-4699
Wholesale and retail, imported and domestic Italian foods at good prices.

Mama Tish's Old Fashioned Italian Ices
1459 W. Taylor St.
733-5911
Italian ices and ice cream.

*Mario's Italian Lemonade
1070 W. Taylor St.
No phone
Bags of nuts and seeds, too.

*Mediterranean Pastry Shop
308 S. Halsted St.
332-1771
Sells own brand of filo leaves.

*N & G Produce
904 W. Randolph St.
942-9432

*Nate's Delicatessen
807 W. Maxwell St.
421-9396

Nea Agora Packing Co.
1056 W. Taylor St.
421-5130
*Good buys on lamb, a half
leg or more.*

*Original Ferrara, Inc.
2210 W. Taylor St.
666-2200

Pan Hellenic Pastry Shop
322 S. Halsted St.
454-1886
*Two tables and coffee so
you can enjoy the goodies
on the spot, but pastries are
better at the Mediterranean
Pastry Shop.*

*Pick Fisheries
702 W. Fulton Market
226-4700

***Quality Supermarket
Products**
924 W. Randolph St.
421-1887

**R. C. Philippine
Trading Corp.**
1132-34 W. Fulton Market
829-1600
*Large, complete Filipino
food store, wholesale and
retail.*

Randolph Fish Inc.
837 W. Randolph St.
666-3202
*Some smoked fish at good
prices; smaller selection of
raw seafood than Isaacson
and Stein at about the same
reasonable prices.*

Restauranic, Inc.
1122 W. Randolph St.
226-0643
*Charles and Wylie Mok
make fancy canapés for
hotels, country clubs, Marshall Field's—and you.
Great-for-parties works of
art at $35 for a box of 100
frozen; $50 fresh with one-
day notice.*

*Rocky's Pan Pizza
1104 W. Taylor St.
738-0452
Try a slice of sausage pizza.

Scafuri Bakery
1337 W. Taylor St.
733-8881
*Call in the morning for a
deluxe, medium-thick pizza
at noon. In case you forget
to call, cheese ones are
usually available on the
spot. Breads and other
bakery stuff, too.*

Vogt's Wine Shop
1100 W. Adams St.
421-2875
*Dump of a warehouse with
loads of wine, beer, and
pop at good prices by the
case. A block off skid row:
Lots of winos stop in daily.*

Zachary Confections Inc.
855 W. Washington Blvd.
226-3070
*The "Easter-Bunny head-
quarters": 27 different kinds
of bunnies, Valentine's Day
chocolates, and other candies are made in the factory
and sold by the case. Call to
make sure it's in stock.*

Dining and drinking

*Alfo's Italian Restaurant
2512 S. Oakley Ave.
523-6994

*Bacchanalia
2413 S. Oakley Ave.
254-6555

*Bruna's Ristorante
2424 S. Oakley Ave.
847-8875

*Cafe Bohemia
138 S. Clinton St.
782-1826

**The Courtyards
of Plaka Restaurant**
340 S. Halsted St.
263-0767
*Chicly modern compared to
most Greektown spots,
Plaka serves some unusu-
al dishes as well as the familiar specialties. Special
menus can be arranged for
parties. Live music.*

*Danilo's
2435 S. Western Ave.
847-6375

***Diana Grocery
and Restaurant**
130 S. Halsted St.
263-1848
*Smells good, but better
food can be had elsewhere.*

***Dianna's Opaa
Restaurant**
212 S. Halsted St.
332-1225
*The owner is a compulsive
hand-kisser.*

*Febo Restaurant
2501 S. Western Ave.
523-0839

*Fiesta Restaurant
1327 W. Washington Blvd.
421-7862

*Florence Restaurant
1030 W. Taylor St.
829-1857

*La Fontanella
2414 S. Oakley Ave.
927-5249

*Gennaro's
1352 W. Taylor St.
243-1035

*Greek Islands
766 W. Jackson Blvd.
782-9855

*Manny's Coffee Shop
1141 S. Jefferson St.
939-2855

Market Club Restaurant
69 South Water Market
421-6796
*Breakfasts, generous sand-
wiches, and steam-table
blue-plate lunches for
about $3. Opens 3 a.m.*

*Mategrano's
1321 W. Taylor St.
243-8441

*Lou Mitchell's
563 W. Jackson Blvd.
939-3111

*The Parthenon
314 S. Halsted St.
726-2407

Red's Place
2200 W. Cermak Rd.
847-8874
*Super burger at lunch in an
old-fashioned, red-
checked-tablecloth saloon.*

Roditys Restaurant
222 S. Halsted St.
454-0800
*A favorite with local author
Harry Mark Petrakis.*

Rosebud Café
1500 W. Taylor St.
942-1117
*Sleek-looking restaurant-
bar. Serves steaks, sea-
food, and ribs (a specialty)
at higher prices in more
handsome surroundings
than most nearby spots.*

*Vernon Park Restaurant
1073 W. Vernon Park Pl.
226-9878

Pilsen

Of all the 19th-century South and West Side residential neighborhoods that once ringed the Loop, only Pilsen has survived. Industrial development in the '20s claimed some; Depression-era public housing replaced others. Highway and institutional construction continued neighborhood destruction in the 1950s and '60s and, finally, misguided HUD policies finished what neglect had missed. Like a patch of ground that remains dry during a storm, Pilsen, though surrounded by railroad tracks, edged by industry, and a bit run down, somehow endures, providing housing to recent immigrants as it has throughout its history.

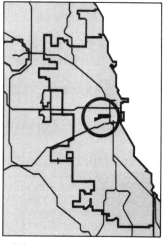

English has been the second language here for a hundred years. By the 1890s, Pilsen's side streets were filled with frame houses as well as two-, three-, and four-story brick buildings housing as many Czech families as there were floors. Lined with small commercial buildings and with grander flats-over-storefront graystones, 18th Street catered to the area's stockyard and factory workers.

Travel the side streets: Every block harbors fanciful, bright-hued façades. Lintels, elaborate cornices, cast-iron storefronts, and hammered-tin-covered bays are painted in contrasting colors, highlighting their ornamental patterns. Mansard roofs, turreted towers, and neoclassic friezes all vie for attention. Reminders of the past are everywhere, including an old-time photographer's studio at 1439 West 18th Street. The two-story, stone-fronted building houses a barbershop behind the unaltered vintage storefront, and the slanted north wall of the second story is all glass to admit the light necessary for pioneer photography. There may be no architectural masterpieces, but there's plenty to see.

Of course, most of the Czechs have moved away and today Spanish is the predominant language. The neighborhood feels a bit "tough," but an adolescent wearing the wrong gang's jacket has more worries than does the reasonably prudent visitor.

The shopping streets—Ashland and Blue Island Avenues and 18th Street—have all the familiar Mexican-neighborhood fare: *bodegas* crammed with tropical imports, little old-fashioned department stores, outlets for imported pottery and religious artifacts, butcher shops with real butchers and real meat (heavy on pork), record stores spilling music out into the street, countless taco stands, lots of seedy taverns, and lovely bakeries. Half a dozen bake shops offer characteristic unfilled sweetened bread or puff-dough pastries topped with glazes or granulated sugar. Popular, too, are giant cookies, fried doughnuts, and loaves of dense, crusty bread, also sold by the buttered-and-sugared slice. **Nuevo Leon** (1634 West 18th Street) displays them all in handsome wood cabinets and, like many, is set up for self-service. Grab a tray and load up. Prices average 20 cents, and you can't find a better sidewalk munchie or morning-coffee accompaniment.

For more substantial fare, check out the taco places that offer much more than the familiar Tex-Mex ground-beef tacos. Soft or crisp-fried corn or wheat tortillas filled with pork, chicken, beef, tripe, and al pastor (a sort of Mexican gyros) are among the possibilities. The repertoire at **Birria Tepatitlan** (1834 South Blue Island Avenue), a white-tiled, fresh-scrubbed, open-kitchen place, includes goat, liver, and tongue tacos, as well as tortas (Mexican sandwiches in the style of Mexico City), menudo (tripe soup), braised-goat dinners, fresh fruit juices, lemonade, and squimos (fresh fruit blended with ice and vanilla, also called licuados)—the Mexican answer to Orange Julius.

Modest restaurants serving enchiladas, flautas, eggs ranchero, bistec, and tacos are common in Pilsen, and they also titillate the adventurous with unusual dishes. Another **Nuevo Leon** (1515 West 18th Street) has authentic treats like breaded fried brains, while the rustic, exposed-brick **Cuernavaca** (1160 West 18th Street) features a braised-goat dinner that has earned a strong local following. **Sabinas** (2022 South Ashland Avenue) offers a weekend Mexican barbecue as well as half a dozen fish dishes in a clean bright storefront, while the menu at **Ostioneria Playa Azul** (1514 West 18th Street), a plastic and Formica place enlivened by a few nautical accents, lists only seafood.

Café Casa Blanco (1609 West 18th Street) is the neighborhood's grandest restaurant: The menu combines seafood, conventional Mexican entrées, and American-style steaks, chops, and roast beef. The Blancos spent four years turning the second floor over their grocery store at 18th Street and Ashland Avenue into an attractive, if flamboyant, family dining spot with brick-and-stone walls, mosaic stained-plastic windows depicting Indian gods, hand-tooled leather menu covers, and the family crest emblazoned on every plate. Prices are modest, a combo plays dance music (not rock) on weekends, and if you have a party in the third floor banquet room, the cake is on the house!

If your taste for Mexican food goes only as far as chili, head to **Chicago's Original Bishop's Famous Chili** (18th Street and Damen Avenue), which for more than 50 years has been serving what many Chicagoans consider to be the world's finest. A bowl of the tomatoless, soupy blend, with plenty of sauces around to spice it up, goes for about $1.60 in a clean, no-nonsense storefront. The chili is also packed to go.

Although Bishop's is closed on Sunday, impressive, local Catholic churches are most accessible then. Immigrant neighborhoods expressed their pride through parish churches and Pilsen was no exception. Designed by Paul Huber and dedicated in 1883, **St. Procopius** (18th and Allport Streets) is one of the city's oldest and has a traditional, Gothic vaulted interior. The South Side's oldest Polish parish, founded in the mid-1870s, built **St. Adalbert** (17th and Paulina Streets), a white-brick, Beaux-Arts masterpiece with clock towers and pink marble Corinthian columns, in 1914. Two blocks south, at 18th Place, the Victorian **St. Vitus** sports handsome, figural stained-glass windows. Equally exciting stained glass adorns the Shrine of St. Jude, **St. Pius V Church** (19th Street and Ashland Avenue), which also has an unusually horizontal-feeling nave with a ceiling supported by inlaid wood beams.

Also dedicated to St. Jude, the mural across the street may well represent the modern outlet for the impulses that inspired churches. There are more than 20 major wall murals in Pilsen, created in the past ten years by such artists as Aurelio Díaz and Ray Patlan, often with itinerant local assistants. The paintings make strong contemporary comments in the Mexican tradition of Rivera (to whom one is dedicated). Colors are bold; perspective is distorted; decorative elements draw heavily on Aztecan and Mayan themes; and subjects range from the socio-political ("Wall of Brotherhood") and religious ("Mi Religion") to pop culture ("Plastic Fantastic Lover"). The Chicago Council on Fine Arts publishes an excellent guide to Chicago's murals that wisely singles out Pilsen (and Hyde Park) for walking tours.

Pilsen muralists flaunt their work, but the presence of another group of artists is barely evident from the street. Although more than 200 painters, sculptors, potters, weavers, etc., have studios in the vicinity of Halsted and 18th Streets, no sign heralds the "Pilsen Artists' Colony"; no chic little restaurants serve crêpes in plant-filled dining rooms; and no galleries host Friday-night openings.

Yet there is a "colony," the brainchild of John Podmajersky, a second-generation Pilsenite who wanted to arrest the neighborhood's decline. Finding no takers for a tavern he had renovated, Podmajersky converted the space to studios and the complex was born in the early '60s. Over the years, the colony spread to form a "U" around a central courtyard hidden between 18th and 19th Streets on Halsted's east side. For a glimpse of this artily landscaped patio complete with goldfish pond, stroll up the alley between 18th and 19th Streets off Union Avenue or attend the autumn Pilsen Artists' Open House and see the insides of the studios, too. (*See Annual Events.*)

Weathered wood facing and bubble windows across Halsted Street from the original compound testify to the success of Podmajersky's private urban-renewal project. Although his renovations and those of individual artists presently affect only a corner of Pilsen east of the railroad tracks at Sangamon Street, several local Latino groups fear gentrification and hotly contested a plan to develop the old **Schoenhofen Brewery** (18th and Canal Streets) into a combined residential, institutional, and commercial complex. The city's decision to tear down most of the buildings squelched the idea, and the chances of Pilsen becoming the South Side's Old Town look increasingly slim.

Interesting places

Holy Trinity Croatian Church
Throop St. between 18th and 19th Sts.
226-2736
Built in 1914, this small brick church and school blend in with the surrounding homes. The congregation was originally Croatian and Mass is still said in that language, as well as in Spanish and English.

Providence of God Church
Union Ave. and 18th St.
226-2929
Built in 1915 to serve a growing Lithuanian community, this handsome brick church has beautiful stained-glass windows from Bavaria, was visited by Pope John Paul II, and virtually abuts the expressway splitting the neighborhood.

*St. Adalbert Church
17th and Paulina Sts.
226-0340

*St. Pius V Church
19th St. and Ashland Ave.
226-0074

*St. Procopius Church
18th and Allport Sts.
226-7887

*St. Vitus Church
18th Pl. and Paulina St.
226-0380

*Schoenhofen Brewery
18th and Canal Sts.
Richard E. Schmidt was the commissioned architect for the 1902 main brewery, but the design of the nicely accented building was probably by Hugh Garden.

Shopping and services

Blanco Bakery
1540 W. 18th St.
733-9293
This place is a grocery store and meat market as well as a Mexican bakery.

Butcher Block & More
1600 S. Clinton St.
421-1138
Factory outlet sells butcher-block furniture the company makes, as well as a few Danish-modern pieces— mostly tables, chairs, and a few wall units. The company's retail stores in Glenview and Downers Grove have even more stuff.

La Casa del Pueblo
1810 S. Blue Island Ave.
421-4640
Like many large Mexican-neighborhood grocery stores, this one has a luncheonette serving tacos and steam-table dishes.

Diana's Bakery
1720 W. 18th St.
226-1443
Nice assortment of Mexican goodies.

Libreria Giron
1335 W. 18th St.
829-2697
One of several locations (the other Pilsen store is at 1443 W. 18th St.). Carries a general range of Spanish-language books, records, and lots of tapes.

**Libreria y
Discoteca Novedades**
1219 W. 18th St.
243-4775
Another of the many Spanish book and record stores in Pilsen, this one has loads of paperback novels for about 70¢. Fewer records and tapes than Giron.

La Mexicana Bakery
1339 W. 18th St.
666-3395
Fancy wedding cakes are the specialty. Pastries are kept in glass cabinets.

M. L. Morgan & Co.
1907 S. Blue Island Ave.
421-3080
A restaurant-supply place that retails to the public.

*Nuevo Leon Bakery
1634 W. 18th St.
243-5977

Plaza Blanco
1609 W. 18th St.
666-7845
A large grocery store with ceramics and other imported gifts, too.

Stark's Warehouse Store
1601 S. Canal St.
733-4300
This huge place in the former KC Baking Powder plant has a bit of everything at discounted prices: jeans, jackets, other sportswear and work clothes (mostly men's); boots and shoes; automotive supplies; camping equipment; and an enormous fishing department with forests of rods and even aluminum dinghies. Some is surplus, some cut-outs and seconds, some first-quality stuff, some schlock.

**Zemsky Bros.
Department Store**
1700 W. 18th St.
226-6230
An old-style neighborhood department store with flowers painted on the building. Other locations.

Dining and drinking

*Birria Tepatítlan
1834 S. Blue Island Ave.
942-9592

*Café Casa Blanco
1609 W. 18th St.
666-7845

*Chicago's Original Bishop's Famous Chili
1958 W. 18th St.
829-6345

*Cuernavaca Restaurant
1160 W. 18th St.
421-9632
The menu is fairly broad. This place also has its own parking lot.

*Nuevo Leon Restaurant and Taqueria
1515 W. 18th St.
421-1517

*Ostioneria Playa Azul
1514 W. 18th St.
733-9091
One of three locations.

Sabas Vega Market
1808 S. Ashland Ave.
666-5180
A clean, friendly market that doubles as a restaurant on weekends and specializes in Mexican barbecue— beef, pork, goat, tripe— which is also available to take out. (Weekdays, pork only.) Very inexpensive.

*Sabinas Restaurant
2022 S. Ashland Ave.
829-9256

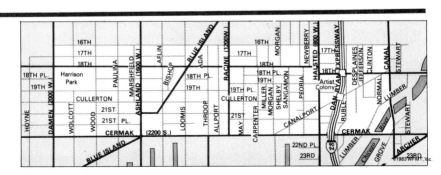

Chinatown

Chinatown—images of almond-eyed women in thigh-high slit skirts fluttering into dark doorways; sinister youths in leather jackets menacing tourists with sullen glares; bent old women hobbling through a tangled maze of narrow, foodstall-filled lanes; wizened merchants presiding over precious gems and antiquities in hole-in-the-wall shops; opium dens, Mah-Jongg parlors, and a hundred other forbidden pleasures lurking behind inscrutable storefronts; atonal music, temple bells, wind chimes saturating the exotic-spice-thickened air—the mysteries of the Orient.

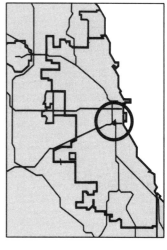

This florid collage is a haphazard, Hollywood-style distillation of San Francisco's Barbary Coast, New York's Chinese enclave, and Macau. But Chicago's Chinatown is just another ethnic neighborhood, if a little more removed from the mainstream than most by the barriers of language, race, and geography.

The city's first Chinatown was centered at Clark and Van Buren Streets until shortly before World War I, when the On Leong Tong, one of two fraternal organizations in the area, created the settlement at Cermak Road and Wentworth Avenue in a complicated series of real-estate deals. While this tong built the fanciful chinoiserie **On Leong Merchants Association** building on South Wentworth Avenue, its long-time rival, the Hip Sing Association, remained in the South Loop until the Federal Detention Center replaced its building in 1970. The Hip Sing, under the guidance of restaurateur Jimmy Wong, has embarked on creating another Chinatown at Broadway and Argyle, a venture which has proceeded more slowly than planned, although the North Side lakefront location is promising.

The Chinese who moved to South Wentworth Avenue joined an Italian community of 20 years' standing. **St. Therese Chinese Catholic Mission** (218 West Alexander Street), an intimate, yellow-brick church with handsome stained-glass windows, was built in 1904 as Madonna Incoronata and it served an Italian congregation until 1964. Even today, the Italian enclave in Bridgeport reaches as far north as West 24th Street, so Chicago's Chinatown, like New York's and San Francisco's, abuts a Little Italy, yielding a rich cultural mélange.

Although Chinatown's roots stretch back 70 years, the community has remained fairly isolated from the city at large. Assimilation has been difficult for the Chinese, and even those who don't enter the mainstream often leave Chinatown's crowded, deteriorating housing, returning to join their less fortunate cousins only for shopping and religious festivals. Out of touch with the city's political processes—for years, business disagreements were adjudicated in the Merchants Association's private courtroom—Chinatown has been forced to depend on privately funded revitalization, such as G. H. Wang's Appleville Condominiums at South Canal Street and West 24th Place.

An ever-increasing flow of new arrivals keeps Chinese not just the first language but, in many cases, the only language of a significant proportion of the area's 7,000 residents. Even many long-time store owners catering to Occidentals are uncomfortable with English. The unassimilated, whether recent immigrants or long-term residents, may involuntarily subsidize local restaurants' low prices by working long hours at substandard wages.

Despite abuses of capitalism, the neighborhood remains staunchly Nationalistic. The **ornamental gate,** built in 1975 over South Wentworth Avenue at West Cermak Road, is inscribed with quotations from Chiang Kai-Shek and Sun Yat-Sen. The tongs were supporters of Chiang's struggles, and the Kuomintang (Chiang's political party) owns local real estate. Mainland China's presence is limited to a few shops, such as **Roxy Books and Gifts** (2310 South Wentworth Avenue), which stocks prints, silk screens, and colorful stamps; English, Chinese, and bilingual books including lots on cooking; delicate papercuts; embroidery supplies and Oriental patterns; other art supplies; and recordings.

The Wentworth strip is crammed with stores peddling trade goods to tourists. Several stand out. The **Chinese Trading Company** (2263) is a huge, wholesale noodle company with an attached, spacious store cluttered with gifts. Specialties include quality dishes, small vulgar statues, jardinières and patio statuary, baskets, and those fanciful lanterns so popular in Chinese restaurants. The atmosphere at the **House of Ming** (2237) is more like that of a gallery. Expensive cloisonné and enamel vases, sets of dinnerware, gold and jade jewelry, carved jade and ivory, and handsome lacquerware fill most of the store, although the front is devoted to cheaper stuff like painted eggs and ornaments. For the Suzy Wong look, head to **Far East Fashions** (2219) where elaborately embroidered silk kimonos and pajamas are displayed in a small rear showroom behind a wide selection of less opulent, mostly rayon and cotton clothing for adults and kids. The **Oriental Boutique** (2262) mixes much of the same with slippers, decorative combs, other accessories, and kung-fu supplies.

Only a sign on the chinoiserie façade of the **Ling Long Museum** (2238) alerts passersby that this is more than just another gift shop. Above cases filled with for-sale objects in the back of the store, however, are massive, gilt-framed dioramas depicting legendary and historical figures and events from China's past. A miniature Chinese wedding procession stretches above them along one wall; a funeral procession graces the other. Most of the displays were left in this country following the 1933-34 Century of Progress Exhibition. Don't miss the huge portrait on silk dating from the 1650s.

Yick Wing (2226), a musty-feeling store, is full of 1950s five-and-dime novelties like finger traps and other tricks, harmonicas, back scratchers, plastic fans, and Chinese yo-yos—at 1950s prices. It also offers surprisingly inexpensive carved ivory and cinnabar. But for a microcosm of the quintessential, old-line Chinatown, spend some time in the pagoda-roofed On Leong Merchants Association building's ground floor shops. (The "temple" is reserved for members.) **Chinatown Books and Gifts** (2214) bursts with cheap jewelry, cookbooks—including one with 400 miso recipes—paper lanterns, coolie hats and other tourist favorites, cassettes and records, and a Chinese newspaper and magazine section ironically adorned with an English "no reading" sign. The **Golden Gate Restaurant** (2212), one of the building's two lunch-counter spots, serves standard Cantonese food on nifty, old-fashioned green-line dishes, as well as always hot, ready-to-eat dim sum, which make great street nibblies. The stock and the wooden store fixtures at **Sun Chong Lung** (2220), a food store catering to Orientals, look like they haven't changed since the building was erected.

Although several local shops are always "closed" to Occidentals and many of the smaller food stores make no concessions to them, three large, very well-stocked groceries are easy to shop in. **New Quon Wah** (2215) entices shoppers with a window display of roast ducks (as do a number of other places), carries a wide line of canned and packaged goods including a Filipino section and rarities like dried tangerine peels, and is close to Chinatown's free parking lot on the northeast corner of Wentworth and Cermak. At the other end of the strip, **Golden Country** (2422) is a multi-room maze of noodles, canned goods, condiments, spices, dried fish, and other delicacies, Thai and Filipino specialties, as well as frozen, prepared Chinese dim sum (tea-lunch goodies such as filled, steamed buns). Prices on roast duck, roast pork, Chinese sausage, and woks are quite good, and the overall selection is unsurpassed in Chinatown. **Wah May** (2403) is a slightly smaller copy of Golden Country, without the roast pork and duck. Most of the food stores also carry some produce but, on weekends, locals stock up on bok choy, snow peas, Chinese celery cabbage, and the like from the produce truck at the corner of Wentworth Avenue and 22nd Place.

For baked goods, check out **Happy Garden Bakery** (2358), which has a full line of filled rolls, cookies, and sweets, or **Dong Kee** (2252), where the more limited selection includes excellent fortune cookies and unequalled almond cookies. When available, overbaked almond cookies are sold at reduced prices and are, if anything, more flavorful than regular ones. The shop also stocks lots of teas, dinnerware, woks and other cooking implements, plus some canned goods and Chinese vegetable seeds—all at reasonable prices.

Chinatown's shops draw a fair share of visitors, but the restaurants are the

A Chinese prince and his commissioners visit Chinatown, 1904

main attraction for most people. In keeping with the conservative, slow-to-change bent of the area, the majority of them feature Cantonese food, while trendier cuisines sweep the North Side. Nevertheless, several of the Cantonese spots are outstanding, and Chinatown remains the city's main source for dim sum. Choosing a restaurant can be difficult, but *Chicago* magazine reviewers have consistently singled out three bargains.

The **Chinese Deli** (225 West Cermak Road) serves unique won tons, noodles—fried or in soups—and seafood specialties to a knowing, mostly Oriental clientele in modest surroundings. **Hong Min** (221 West Cermak Road), well known for its wide selection of excellent dim sum, has an extensive, first-rate menu. Eschew the mundane chop suey/chow mein offerings for treats like West Lake duck, hong sue scallops, and other seafood. At the tiny, original location of **Three Happiness** (209 West Cermak Road), the lunch-counter décor is short on amenities, but the multipage menu provides an opportunity to sample a wide range of dishes including several casseroles and noodles (try the Singapore fried rice ones), and preparations are generally excellent. The restaurant's spacious third location (2130 South Wentworth Avenue) has tablecloths and a liquor license, but the food and service aren't always up to snuff.

Perhaps a notch below these, **Lee's Canton Cafe** (2300 South Wentworth Avenue) is an old-line broad-menu place that not only serves dim sum lunches, but also will pack ready-to-cook dim sum throughout business hours—an unusual service. To satisfy the late-evening munchies, chow down with cops, cabbies, and other night people at **Chinatown Chop Suey** (207 West Cermak Road), where egg foo young, chop suey, chow mein, and a few other standards are served in desultory surroundings until the wee hours of the morning.

Of the Northern Chinese options, **Moon Palace** (2206 South Wentworth Avenue) is the largest, but the small street-level dining room is more cheerful than the big upstairs one and has the added attraction of a take-out counter full of delicacies. **Three Happiness II** (216 West 22nd Place), which used to be Cantonese, now specializes in Szechwanese food. The menu is as long and varied as its sister restaurants', although portions seem a bit smaller and prices are higher. Old favorites and unusual offerings are very good here and at **ManDar-Inn** (2249 South Wentworth Avenue), which moved from a larger location in late 1982. Decorated in gray and maroon, with beautiful Oriental artifacts, fresh flowers, and white-clothed tables, it is the neighborhood's most elegant dining spot.

Whatever your reason for visiting Chinatown, keep in mind that the neighborhood just to the east is definitely insalubrious and, at night, unsafe. Discretion dictates traveling to Chinatown by car.

Interesting places

*Chinatown Gate
Wentworth Ave. and Cermak Rd.

*Ling Long Museum
2238 S. Wentworth Ave.
225-6181

*On Leong Merchants Association
2216 S. Wentworth Ave.
225-5751

*St. Therese Chinese Catholic Mission
218 W. Alexander St.
842-6777

Shopping and services

Cathay Gifts
2235 S. Wentworth Ave.
326-5921
Lots of jewelry and carved ivory (which, we are told, was imported before the recent ban), including Chinese chess sets for about $100.

*Chinatown Books and Gifts
2214 S. Wentworth Ave.
326-1761

*Chinese Trading Company
2263 S. Wentworth Ave.
842-2820

Chung Wah Cultural Inc.
2247 S. Wentworth Ave.
842-3659
Another outlet for Chinese books, records, and tapes.

*Dong Kee
2252 S. Wentworth Ave.
225-6340

D-Sun Hardware
2245 S. Wentworth Ave.
225-9794
*A good source for in-
expensive woks (especial-
ly large ones) and Chinese
knives and cleavers.*

*Far East Fashions
2219 S. Wentworth Ave.
326-2076

Ken Genghis Gifts
2227 S. Wentworth Ave.
225-6519
*A nice selection of parasols
(about $5) from Mainland
China, as well as dishes,
jewelry, and other decorative items.*

*Golden Country
2422 S. Wentworth Ave.
842-4111

*Happy Garden Bakery
2358 S. Wentworth Ave.
225-2730

*House of Ming
2237 S. Wentworth Ave.
326-5921
*The sign says House of
Buddha, which is actually
an alternate name for
Cathay Gifts next door.*

*New Quon Wah
2215 S. Wentworth Ave.
225-8285

*Oriental Boutique
2262 S. Wentworth Ave.
842-3798
*Quilted jackets are
a specialty.*

Palace Court
2317 S. Wentworth Ave.
225-1115
*Prices on Chinese handi-
crafts, etc. aren't low, but
the place will write your Chinese name on a bookmark
for a mere 50¢.*

*Roxy Books and Gifts
2310 S. Wentworth Ave.
225-6683

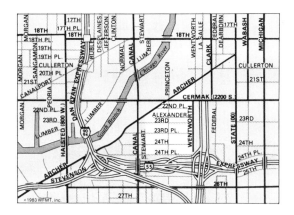

© 1983 WFMT, inc.

*Sun Chong Lung
2220 S. Wentworth Ave.
225-6050

Sun Sun Tong
2260 S. Wentworth Ave.
842-6398
*One of the few places fea-
turing Chinese herbs and
ginseng, as well as other
foods and gifts.*

*Wah May
2403 S. Wentworth Ave.
225-9119

*Yick Wing
2226 S. Wentworth Ave.
225-7992

Dining and drinking

Bertucci's
300 W. 24th St.
225-6398
*At this neighborhood bar
and restaurant, Theresa
Bertucci cooks up a couple
of home-style Italian
specials every weekday.
The biggest selection, including excellent beans and
greens, is on Friday. Prices
are very low.*

*Chinatown Chop Suey
207 W. Cermak Rd.
326-2265

*Chinese Deli
225 W. Cermak Rd.
326-3171

*Golden Gate Restaurant
2212 S. Wentworth Ave.
842-5242

*Hong Min
221 W. Cermak Rd.
842-5026
Dim sum 9 am-4 pm daily

*Lee's Canton Cafe
2300 S. Wentworth Ave.
225-4838
Dim sum 11 am-2 pm daily

*ManDar-Inn
2249 S. Wentworth Ave.
842-4014
Buffet and dim sum at lunch

*Moon Palace
2206 S. Wentworth Ave.
842-2390

*Three Happiness I
209 W. Cermak Rd.
842-1964
Dim sum during lunch

*Three Happiness II
216 W. 22nd Pl.
225-7393

*Three Happiness III
2130 S. Wentworth Ave.
791-1228
*Dim sum served from roll-
ing carts during lunch*

Bridgeport/Canaryville

Many Chicagoans envision Bridgeport as an almost legendary land where neat, political-poster-festooned bungalows line very, very clean streets and hard-working Hibernians alternate between their city jobs and Democratic Organization obligations. That Bridgeport isn't entirely mythical. The streets and homes *are* tidy, most residents *are* Democrats, and for 46 years Chicago's mayors *did* live in Bridgeport. But the myth, like all myths, is misleading. It obscures a rich, 100-year, multiethnic history that has made Bridgeport and adjoining Canaryville quintessential working-class Chicago neighborhoods.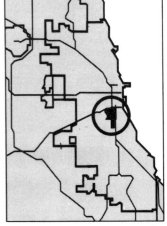

Lithuanians, Germans, Italians, and Poles have long outnumbered the Irish here. Many are second- and third-generation Bridgeporters. They work all over—less than 15 percent have government jobs—but often live their entire lives in the community, owning small houses or renting flats within shouting distance of relatives, maintaining strong church and family ties, and sending their children to nearby parochial schools.

Bridgeport began as Hardscrabble (named for the first resident's farm), a shantytown for workers on the Illinois-Michigan Canal in the 1830s and '40s. The completion of the canal in 1848 brought new industries, notably meat slaughtering and packing. Following the 1865 consolidation of South Side slaughterhouses into the Union Stock Yards, successive waves of Eastern Europeans poured in. Each group clustered in a small section and built its own church and school where classes and services were held in the immigrants' native tongue. Seen from the Stevenson Expressway, Bridgeport looks Old Worldly, with dozens of spires towering above low houses.

While **Holy Cross Lutheran Church** (31st Place and Racine Avenue), which still has services in German, is a smallish, single-steeple, German-style church, **All Saints St. Anthony Padua** (Wallace Street and 28th Place), formerly St. Anthony of Padua, is much grander. In 1913, construction was underwritten by the Western Indiana Railroad, which had expanded its yards onto the congregation's original church property at 24th and Canal Streets. With all the bills paid, the parish lavished the building with mosaics and stained glass imported from Munich. The opulent interior also houses an excellent organ.

Equally impressive, especially for its beautifully painted interior, magnificent dome, towers, and stained-glass windows, **St. Mary of Perpetual Help** (32nd

Street between Morgan and Aberdeen Streets) was founded in 1889 as an off-shoot of St. Adalbert in Pilsen, the South Side's first Polish parish. The octagonal **St. Barbara** (Throop Street between Archer Avenue and Lyman Street) was built two decades later to handle the overflow of an expanding Polish population. It rests on a floating base, which protected it from blasting at the nearby quarry. (Long inoperative, the quarry is now being filled in with construction debris.) Chicago's first Lithuanian church, **St. George** (33rd Street and Lituanica Avenue), was built in 1886 and is a handsome Gothic structure with a stonework bas-relief of St. George slaying the dragon over the entrance. The narrow surrounding streets are reminiscent of Europe.

St. Gabriel (45th Street and Lowe Avenue), built a year later, testifies to the affluence of the Irish parishioners in Canaryville, which originally attracted packinghouse managers, as well as lower-paid workers. They were wealthy enough to afford architect John Root's services, and his Romanesque brick church with its low, steep roof, massive bell tower, Tiffany-style dome and figural windows, marble altar and floors, and geometric wall decorations, is outstanding. Poet Harriet Monroe, Root's sister-in-law, called it "as personal as the clasp of (the architect's) hand."

Nativity of Our Lord's(37th Street and Union Avenue) plain exterior gives no hint of the lovely pastel and gold-trimmed interior with intricate arches setting off the three aisles and fine stained glass. On Sundays, Mayor Daley used to stroll here from his house at 3536 South Lowe Avenue. The politically faithful can still be found at the nearby 11th Ward Democratic headquarters (3659 South Halsted Street). **Schaller's Pump** (3714), the slightly seedy bar across the street, is also a favorite with 11th Ward regulars, and the juke box is loaded with old standards like "Chicago," Irish tunes bulleted with shamrocks, and, appropriately enough, Doris Day's "Sentimental Journey."

Almost a century old, Schaller's is a survivor from the days when taverns lined Halsted Street. "Big Jim" O'Leary, son of Mrs. O'Leary of the apocryphally pyrotechnic cow, ran a big gambling spot and a separate saloon on the 4100 block, which once boasted more than 40 bars. O'Leary's and most of the others are long gone. Of the present bars on the strip, **The Fifth Wheel** (4439) is the place to hear one of the sweetest pedal steels around.

Between 1890 and 1933, the stockyards processed about thirteen million animals a year, but marketing and technological advances and the increased use of trucks instead of railroads closed them in 1971. Today, only a few firms and the Burnham and Root **Union Stock Yard Gate** (Exchange Avenue and Peoria Street) remain as landmarks to the teeming activity immortalized by Carl Sandburg and Upton Sinclair. The limestone head over the gate's central arch is thought to be Sherman, a prize-winning bull named for stockyard magnate—and Burnham's father-in-law—John B. Sherman.

The stockyard real estate has been incorporated into the Central Manufacturing District, a pioneer industrial park that opened at the northern edge of the yards in 1903 and expanded west over the years. Chicago's first "Miracle Mile" was not Michigan Avenue north of the river, but the stretch of 35th Street between Ashland and Western Avenues with its monolithic blocks of industrial buildings.

The **International Amphitheatre** (Halsted and 42nd Streets), built in 1934 to house livestock shows after its predecessor burned in a huge stockyard fire, lingers on. Remodeled after the decline of the cattle trade, it was used for the 1952 Democratic and Republican Presidential Conventions, as well as the strife-torn 1968 Democratic one. Although it has been eclipsed by McCormick Place, the Amphitheatre still hosts a circus and other special shows.

Terra-cotta cowboys and cattle adorning its north entrance recall former glories, but today this section of the Amphitheatre accommodates **Morris Men's Store,** Chicago's largest outlet for Western wear. Here, urban cowboys can find an immense selection of all the big-name men's and women's cowboy boots (from plain to snakeskin), jeans, shirts, vests, leather jackets (fringed or not), Western-style suits with slash pockets and triangular corner reinforcements, tons of hats and fanciful feather hatbands, and even complete rodeo gear. Many items are modestly discounted, and sale prices can be very attractive.

For jeans and khakis of every description, mosey over to **The Pants Shop** (3513 South Halsted Street) on what may be the most interesting block of the neighborhood shopping strip along Halsted Street from 30th to 36th Streets. The Pants Shop claims to have the lowest prices in the city and cuffs your purchases free while you wait. Across the street is the **Ramova Theater** (3518), a handsome little third-run house with a striking stained-glass window over the marquee. Buy a copy of the *Bridgeport News* at the newspaper's office (3506), take it to the **Ramova Grill** (3510), and join the locals for a very thin, freshly ground hamburger or a bowl of chili in this archetypal greasy spoon. The **Granata Bakery** (3520) offers breads, including an unusual pork-crackling loaf, homemade Italian beef and sausage sandwiches, as well as terrible pizza by the slice.

Walk a few blocks north to Halsted and 32nd Streets for a taste of Lithuanian Bridgeport. The **Healthy Food Restaurant** (3236) serves breakfasts, sandwiches, and about two dozen Lithuanian/American entrées with Lithuanian side dishes, as well as first-rate breads, blynai (blintzes), koldūnai (dumplings), and kugelis (fried potato-pudding slices) in a pleasant, wood-paneled room. **The Continental** (3139) has a smaller selection of much the same fare at slightly higher prices in trendier surroundings. To enjoy some of these treats at home, load up at **Ace Bakeries** (3202) where kugelis, soft Lithuanian rye bread, cookies, and pies are very reasonably priced.

The northeast quadrant of Bridgeport, an Italian bailiwick for generations, is heaven for Italian street-food fans. Locals and cops from the station down the block hang out at **Bruno's** (525 West 31st Street), a combination produce store and sandwich joint with only two tables. The food makes up for the lack of ambiance. Inexpensive Italian beef, sausage, meatball, and breaded-steak sandwiches are joined by less familiar poor boys—pepper and egg, fried eggplant, asparagus or squash with eggs. Lines of cars double-parked in front of **Ricobene's Pizzeria** (250 West 26th Street) attest to the popularity of this take-out spot's Italian beef and terrific breaded-steak sandwiches.

Rosie's Snack Shop (2600 South Wallace Street) also does a brisk take-out business but adds an unusual feature for the area: a slick, exposed-brick dining area. Prices are moderate, and homemade giardiniera is conveniently bottled to

O'Leary's saloon and gambling house, Halsted Street, 1906

take home. At **Connie's Pizza** (481 West 26th Street), a modern, woody, checked-cloth restaurant, the pizza, pasta, and sandwiches are such favorites that hour-long waits for tables are not uncommon. Fortunately, Connie's take-out counter always has freshly baked, excellent cheese and sausage pizzas ready to pick up. Savvy locals even flag down the many Connie's delivery vans to buy pizza.

For pizza by the slice, head to **La Milanese Pizza** (3156 South May Street), one of several commercial ventures flourishing on residential side streets. The pizza has a superb crust and very sweet sausage; sandwiches are big, cheap, and good; and the homemade peperoncini and giardiniera are great.

A Bridgeport tradition is a day—any day—at **Comiskey Park** (35th Street and Wentworth Avenue), the nation's oldest major league ball field. An athletic field since the 1860s, the land purchased for the park from "Long John" Wentworth's estate just barely fulfilled an agreement with the Cubs that the White Sox never play north of 35th Street.

The 35th Street exit from the Dan Ryan Expressway puts you right at the ball park, and the rest of Bridgeport is only a few blocks west. Just to the east are the **Illinois Institute of Technology** campus and **De La Salle Institute** (3455 South Wabash Avenue), training ground for generations of local politicians. The Dan Ryan Expressway and Halsted Street are the best routes to the neighborhood from the North Side or downtown. Some might feel unsafe making the trip west from Lake Shore Drive.

Interesting places

*All Saints St. Anthony Padua
Wallace St. and 28th Pl.
842-2744

*Comiskey Park
324 W. 35th St.
924-1000

*De La Salle Institute
3455 S. Wabash Ave.
842-7355
Mayors Kennelly, Daley, and Bilandic are among the famous graduates of this parochial school, which opened in 1892.

Fuller Park Field House
331 W. 45th St.
268-0062
Designed by Edward H. Bennett and built in 1915, this concrete complex displays interesting textures and patterns. Murals are by John Norton.

*Holy Cross Lutheran Church
31st Pl. and Racine Ave.
523-3838

*Illinois Institute of Technology
Main office: 3300 S. Federal
567-3000
Several of the interestingly grouped buildings were designed by Mies van der Rohe.

Immaculate Conception Church
Aberdeen and 31st Sts.
927-1078
Note the 1892 church to the east, now the Knights of Columbus Bridgeport Community Center, with its dominant roof and external buttresses.

*International Amphitheatre
42nd and Halsted Sts.
927-5580

Livestock National Bank Building
4150 S. Halsted St.
The bank is no more, but the building, a replica of Independence Hall, remains.

*Nativity of Our Lord
37th St. and Union Ave.
927-6263

*Ramova Theater
3518 S. Halsted St.
927-5957

*St. Barbara
Throop St. between Archer Ave. and Lyman St.
842-7979

St. Bridget
Archer Ave. and Arch St.
523-4130
Built in 1905, this handsome, large, barrel-vaulted church is the home of an Irish parish established in the late 1840s.

*St. Gabriel
45th St. and Lowe Ave.
268-9595

*St. George
33rd St. and Lituanica
376-2141

St. Jerome
Princeton Ave. between 28th and 29th Sts.
842-1871
In 1912, Chicago's largest Croatian parish bought this church from a Swedish congregation. Most of the Croatians came from Sinj, scene of a famous victory over the Turks, and Croatians still celebrate the battle with a feast August 15.

***St. Mary of
Perpetual Help**
32nd St. between Morgan
and Aberdeen Sts.
927-6646

**Union Ave. United
Methodist Church**
Union Ave. and 43rd St.
268-3900
Built in 1877, this charming
red-brick church was funded by meat magnate Gus-
tavus Swift and is still known
as "Swift's Church."

***Union Stock Yard
Gate**
Exchange Ave. and Peoria

**Valentine Chicago
Boys Club**
3400 S. Emerald Ave.
927-7373
The colorful totem poles
flanking the Deco-like entrance to this '40s factory-
looking building were
carved in Seattle out of
Alaskan logs; they depict
Pacific Northwest Indian
tribal history.

Shopping and services

*Ace Bakeries
3202 S. Halsted St.
225-4973

Cicero Rye Bread Bakery
3500 S. Union Ave.
927-7351
A "penny" candy store, too!

Decorators Supply Corp.
3610 S. Morgan St.
847-6300
Started in 1893 to supply
ornamental trim for
buildings at the World's
Columbian Exposition, this
firm still makes the same
plaster and wood moldings,
capitals, and wood-fiber
carvings that were used at
the turn of the century.
Catalogues of available
fireplace mantels, orna-
ments for woodwork fur-
niture, decorative plaster,
etc., are a valuable resource
for rehabbers.

Diana Farms
3233 S. Halsted St.
326-6966
A good source for fresh
poultry.

Filbert's
3033 S. Archer Ave.
847-1520
This soda bottling plant has
been making old-fash-
ioned, rather sweet root
beer (and other flavors) for
more than half a century. It
is also a South Side outlet
for Lasser's pop and Vess, a
mediocre St. Louis brand.

*Granata Bakery
3520 S. Halsted St.
847-8306

Greifenstein's Pharmacy
3659 S. Union Ave.
847-5656
Turn-of-the-century dis-
plays in the windows of this
drugstore, which moved
from 25th and Wentworth
when the expressway came
through, hint at the won-
derful stuff inside: antique
oak cabinets, brass fixtures,
old ceiling fans, and oodles
of apothecary jars filled with
mysterious medicines.

**Henry's Sports
and Bait Shop**
3130 S. Canal St.
225-8538
One of the city's largest bait
and tackle stores has general sporting goods, too.
Open long hours and all
night on weekends during
the fishing season. Adjoining marine store—boats,
motors, water-skiing gear,
etc.—is open regular
business hours.

Michalski Bakery
3236 S. Racine Ave.
523-0978
Bills itself as "the oldest
bakery in Bridgeport," and
the building could be the
oldest, too. Very good,
mace-and-cardamom-
flavored egg twist.

*Morris Men's Store
4200 S. Halsted St.
927-3887

*The Pants Shop
3513 S. Halsted St.
247-4364

Spiegel Outlet Store
1105 W. 35th St.
523-9519
Lots of fairly trendy clothing—some schlocky, some
nice—at low prices. Bed-
ding, toys, etc., too.

Veteran Tamale Foods
3133 S. Archer Ave.
927-1282
This place supplies restaurants with those tamales you
used to get at the high-
school hangouts and on
street corners. You can buy
them here for less than a
quarter, but you have to
heat them at home.

Dining and drinking

***Bruno's Famous
Italian Sandwiches**
525 W. 31st St.
842-9406

*Connie's Pizza
481 W. 26th St.
326-3443

*The Continental
3139 S. Halsted St.
326-1183

*The Fifth Wheel
4439 S. Halsted St.
536-9497
Good for dancing. No cover
or minimum.

Glass Dome Hickory Pit
2801 S. Halsted St.
842-7600
Chicago *magazine gave the
ribs at this large, suburbanlike place a three-and-a-
half-bone (out of four)
rating.*

*Healthy Food Restaurant
3236 S. Halsted St.
326-2724

*La Milanese Pizza
3156 S. May St.
254-9543

*Ramova Grill
3510 S. Halsted St.
847-9058

*Ricobene's Pizzeria
250 W. 26th St.
225-9811

*Rosie's Snack Shop
2600 S. Wallace St.
225-5425

*Schaller's Pump
3714 S. Halsted St.
847-9378
*Home-cooked meals are
served on white-clothed
tables in this plain neighborhood bar, but the noise
precludes pleasant dining.*

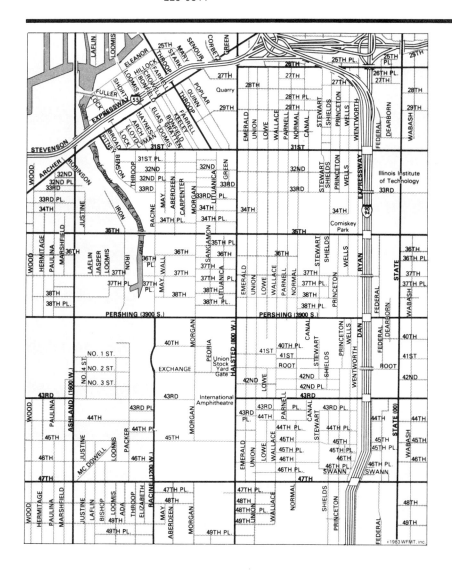

Back of the Yards

The faint stench lingering over Back of the Yards is a reminder of the conditions Upton Sinclair depicted, but now that the Union Stock Yards are gone, the neighborhood is no longer *The Jungle*. Ma-and-Pa groceries, bakeries, taverns, and Old Worldly churches nestle quietly on side streets among small, frame houses—as in other older, inner-city, ethnic communities. On the main shopping streets, "*se habla Español*" increasingly replaces "*mowimy po Polsku*" in shop windows. Kids are everywhere: This is the kind of family neighborhood where any holiday brings window decorations to homes and stores.

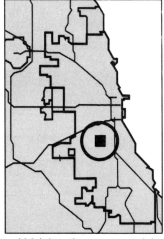

Back of the Yards was a by-product of the livestock industry, which dominated every aspect of the residents' lives—even the foul air they breathed. Although Sinclair may have exaggerated, life was brutal for the Poles, Lithuanians, and Slovaks who followed the Germans and Irish into the area to work in the stockyards. Violence flared during the Knights of Labor's unsuccessful organizing efforts in the packinghouses in 1886 and at a 1921 mass meeting in Davis Square Park; martial law was imposed during the 1894 railroad strikes and the 1919 race riots.

Workers had more than job conditions to protest. Tiny homes and sordid boarding houses were woefully overcrowded. In 1900, 10 years after its annexation to Chicago, Back of the Yards had no electric lights and only a few paved streets. Inadequate sewer and water systems, an open dump along 47th Street, and stockyard effluents resulted in staggering infant-mortality and tuberculosis rates. The situation was so bad that bureaucrats excluded the neighborhood from a 1901 housing survey to avoid dragging down city-wide averages!

While the city slowly improved Back of the Yards physically, private groups attacked social ills. In 1895, the University of Chicago opened a settlement house which served the community for 80 years. Mary McDowell, its first director, was a fervent women's-movement and union supporter who is remembered with a local street name. In 1904, she helped establish **Davis Square Park** (44th Street and Marshfield Avenue). The Burnham Company-designed field house provided some recreational respite from the surrounding squalor. The area's three Polish parishes organized the Guardian Angel Day Nursery and Home for Working Women (4600 South McDowell Avenue) in 1912, on a corner of the notorious, saloon-laden "Whiskey Point." Back of the Yards leaders and Hyde Park liberals joined forces in 1939 when Saul Alinsky, Joseph Meegan, and Bishop Bernard J. Sheil created the Back of the Yards Neighborhood Council, an umbrella organization to direct attacks on juvenile delinquency and sub-standard housing. Community self-help groups across the country have been fundamentally influenced by Alinsky's initial effort; the council presently numbers more than 160 member organizations.

Back of the Yards continues to attract recent immigrants as it has for more than a century, and services in many tongues fill turn-of-the-century churches, though some Eastern European congregations are dwindling. Polish masses are still celebrated at **St. Joseph** (48th Street and Hermitage Avenue), which was built by the neighborhood's oldest parish in 1913. The ornate, Romanesque building has many trompe l'oeil "marble" and "mosaics" inside, heavily carved confessionals, and impressive statuary; the towers loom large over the surrounding streets. You can also hear Polish masses at **St. John of God** (52nd Street and Throop Street), a 1905 graystone, Beaux-Arts monolith facing Sherman Park. Elaborately painted ribbing sets off the complex, airy interior space which is adorned with lots of gilt and unusual painted Stations of the Cross. Behind metal doors enhanced by carved stonework, the Lithuanian **Holy Cross** (46th Street and Hermitage Avenue), built the same year as St. Joseph, reveals green marble Corinthian columns, "rock" grotto shrines, high-relief Stations of the Cross, stained-glass portraits of the saints, and outstanding transept windows.

With **Nativity of the Blessed Virgin Mary** (Paulina and 50th Streets), Back of the Yards Ukrainians and Croatians re-created the onion-domed churches of their homeland in miniature, and the Byzantine rite is still followed in the beautiful, intricately painted church dominated by a central dome. There's also an Oriental air about **St. Basil** (Garfield Boulevard and Honore Street), a big, barrel-vaulted, domed, elaborate basilica with intricate rose windows and marble trim, but it was built by an Irish congregation in 1904. The German **St. Augustine** (Laflin Street between 50th and 51st Streets) is a stark, vertical, Gothic church enlivened by fine stained glass and surrounded by a block of related institutions, including a convent, a school, an auditorium, a social center, and a credit union. Built in 1896, the charming, modest, red-brick **St. Martini Lutheran Church** (51st Street and Marshfield Avenue) still has masses in German, while Spanish and English masses alternate at **Immaculate Heart of Mary Vicariate** (Ashland Avenue and 45th Street), a cleverly remodeled storefront with a California-Spanish, yellow-brick façade.

This church is at the quiet north end of Back of the Yards' bustling shopping section. Stores radiate in four directions from the Goldblatt's at Ashland Avenue and 47th Street. They include branches of almost all the lower-priced clothing and shoe chains, furniture outlets, and some surprises. Two large, local department stores survive; tiny to huge super mercados abound; bridal salons and photographers' studios flourish; and the record shops stock discs not found in the big stores downtown.

A branch of the city's largest Spanish record chain, **Casa Pan-Americana** (4830 South Ashland Avenue) carries Spanish translations of popular rock 'n' roll and disco, every kind of music from almost every Hispanic country, and records by local Mexican groups. Representing a recent immigrant group to Back of the Yards, **Hassan's** (4819 South Ashland Avenue) has Islamic records and tapes as well as an enormous selection of Islamic books and a few gift items. Owned by polka-band leader and weekend radio personality Eddie Blazoncyk, the **Bel-Aire Music Studio** (1740 West 47th Street) pays tribute to the old guard with Polish records and tapes, including, naturally, lots of polkas. If square dancing's more your speed, swing over to the **Gibson Music Store** (1956 West 51st Street). With more than 100,000 different 45-rpm titles in stock, thousands of

LPs, and guitars and other paraphernalia, it may be the nation's largest country-and-Western music store.

As in most ethnic neighborhoods, exotic foodstuffs beckon from groceries, meat markets, bakeries, and delis. At the heavily Hispanic northern end of South Ashland Avenue, the **Central Bakery** (4523) prepares an unusually wide selection of Mexican pastries. Behind a wedding cake-filled window, **Raiger's Bakery** (1657 West 47th Street) offers an intriguing mix of Mexican, Polish, and American goodies. No display heralds the **Baltic Bakery's** retail outlet (4627 South Hermitage Avenue) adjoining the wholesale operation, but the wonderfully disorganized shop is worth a special trip. Besides fresh breads and discounted store returns, there are pastries, topnotch pierogi, great Polish sausage straight from the bakery's ovens, sauerkraut, pickles, spices, grains, apples, and Polish and Lithuanian newspapers! Almost as eclectic, a branch of **Bobak's** (1658 West 47th Street) sells its own excellent sausages made in a nearby factory, as well as pastries from a few North Side bakeries.

For even more sausages, head to **Krystyna's** (4729 South Ashland Avenue). You can take them home, along with homemade lunchmeats and bottled imported delicacies, or enjoy them at the little lunch counter along with great soups and a few hot dishes at very modest prices. More substantial fare can be had at **Cafe Chicago** (1825 West 47th Street). The sophisticated name and neon sign are foolers. This large, simply decorated spot is totally unpretentious. Complete Polish dinners, from duck-blood soup to coffee and dessert, start at $4.25. American steaks, roast beef, and ribs are just a few dollars more. On Fridays, there's lots of fish.

Aquatic window decals, a sea-blue marbleized-Formica décor, and an aquarium herald the exclusively piscatorial offerings at **Ostioneria Playa Azul** (1632 West 47th Street). Pan-fried red snapper and several other fish are served either plain or sauced in typical Mexican styles, like a la Veracruz with onions, tomatoes, and green olives. Shrimp grilled with lots of garlic are quite good, and spicy crab or fish ceviche is a specialty.

The friendly staff makes **Elvia's** (1738 West 47th Street) one of the neighborhood's more inviting, little Mexican restaurants. The menu offers conventional

Frank Leslie's Illustrated Newspaper *on Chicago's best-known industry, 1878*

tacos, burritos, tostadas, and flautas, as well as a few dinners, breakfast plates, and token American sandwiches like a B.L.T. club. For Mexican sandwiches and tacos with unusual fillings, try the local branch of **Birria Tepatitlan** (4537 South Ashland Avenue). Translating the menu on the wall is difficult, but worth the trouble *(see Pilsen for more).* You'll also find several other full-menu, modestly priced Mexican spots along Ashland.

Interesting places

Berean Memorial Baptist Church
44th and Paulina Sts.
376-0637
Now mostly Spanish, this tiny, red brick church was Russian Orthodox until about a decade ago, and numbered many gypsies among its varied congregation.

*Davis Square Park
4430 S. Marshfield Ave.
927-1983
Men in early sports costumes and women in ethnic ones flank allegorical figures in the field house's mural entitled Constructive Recreation—The Vital Force in Character Building. *Though rather dull, the small park was laid out by the Olmsted firm.*

*Holy Cross
46th St. and Hermitage Ave.
376-3900

*Immaculate Heart of Mary Vicariate
Ashland Ave. and 45th St.
247-2344.

*Nativity of the Blessed Virgin Mary
Paulina and 50th Sts.
737-0733

Sacred Heart
Wolcott Ave. and Honore
523-5112
Located on the second floor of a school, this church still has masses in Polish.

*St. Augustine
Laflin St. between 50th and 51st Sts.
254-4455

*St. Basil
Garfield Blvd. and Honore
925-6311

St. Cyril and St. Methodius
Hermitage Ave. and 50th St.
778-4044
Extraordinarily well-executed, figural stained-glass windows adorn this plain church.

*St. John of God
52nd and Throop Sts.
285-6008

*St. Joseph
48th St. and Hermitage Ave.
254-2366

*St. Martini Lutheran Church
51st St. and Marshfield Ave.
776-7610

St. Mary's Byzantine Catholic Church
Seeley Ave. and 50th St.
434-1710
Built in 1926, this large church is relatively plain inside.

Sherman Park
1301 W. 52nd St.
268-8436
Named for its benefactor, stockyard magnate and Park District Commissioner John B. Sherman, this park—a miniature of the large parks in the system, complete with boating lagoon and little bridges— has fallen on hard times. The 1904, Burnham Company-designed field house sports classical murals of famous North American historical figures and events painted by Art Institute students in 1912.

Shopping and services

Archer Tinning & Re-tinning
1019 W. 47th St.
927-7240
Owner Arjen Byvoets, whose grandfather was a coppersmith in England, is re-tinner to the stars: Jean Banchet of Le Français brings his pots here, and so can you. Average pot: $10.

*Baltic Bakery
4627 S. Hermitage Ave.
523-1510

*Bel-Aire Music Studio
1740 W. 47th St.
847-0658

*Bobak's
1658 W. 47th St.
847-4845.

*Casa Pan-Americana
4830 S. Ashland Ave.
254-1717

*Central Bakery
4523 S. Ashland Ave.
no phone

Farmers' Market
S. Justine and W. 47th Sts.
744-6426
In season, this parking lot becomes a city-sponsored market for locally grown produce once a week.

Felix's Bakery
5201 S. Wood St.
476-3756

Owner Alex Dziedzic makes two special treats: huge strawberry cream puffs on Tuesdays and enormous Bavarian cream (custard and whipped cream)- filled puffs on Wednesdays. Call ahead to reserve them because they go fast!

*Gibson Music Store
1956 W. 51st St.
776-0700

*Hassan's
4819 S. Ashland Ave.
247-2666

*Krystyna's
4729 S. Ashland Ave.
376-2658

Miller's Bakery
4803 S. Seeley Ave.
523-4760
This Polish bakery with white tile up to the ceiling and beautiful, old oak cabinets sells goodies that look like they were made by someone's grandma—kolacky, wonderful strudels, pierogi, etc.

*Raiger's Bakery
1657 W. 47th St.
927-4167

Schwab Liquors
4831 S. Ashland Ave.
247-8073
Many brands of tequila and other Mexican specialties have replaced most of the Polish wines and beers.

South Side Knitting Mills
5036 S. Ashland Ave.
776-7949
Manufactures and retails high-school letter sweaters and leather-sleeved, zippered school jackets. Out-of-date colors are half price. Main-line sportswear is nothing special.

Sula Supplies
2034 W. 51st St.
776-1737
The public is welcome at this restaurant-supply store.

Universal Candies
5056 S. Ashland Ave.
778-9580
Chester Laciak not only makes the candies for this crowded shop (lots of stuffed animals, too!); he also wholesales all over the city.

Dining and drinking

*Birria Tepatitlan
4537 S. Ashland Ave.
847-9843

*Cafe Chicago
1825 W. 47th St.
847-2024

*Elvia's
1738 W. 47th St.
376-4513

*Ostioneria Playa Azul
1632 W. 47th St.
847-8293
One of three locations.

Paradise Hall
1758 W. 48th St.
247-6775
Stepping into this bar/restaurant/banquet hall (popular for Polish weddings) is like entering a foreign country or old Chicago. No one speaks any English—not even the youths playing pool in the back room. So, if you want to order from the menu on the wall, bring someone along who speaks Polish.

McKinley Park/Brighton

In the days when Chicago's reputation rested on industrial output, stockyards, and gangsters; when State Street was unchallenged as "that great street"; before black and Hispanic migration and white flight changed the complexion of many neighborhoods, much of the city was like McKinley Park and Brighton— Eastern European, blue collar, staid. Somehow, the changes of the last 30 years have missed large parts of the Southwest Side, an anomaly that is nowhere more apparent than in these two communities where the slickest stores are fast-food outlets along Archer Avenue. McKinley Park and Brighton are *so* ordinary that they are special.

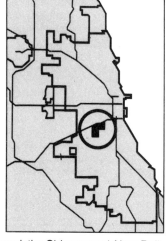

Like so many of the 19th-century villages surrounding Chicago in its infancy, they owed their growth to fortuitous geographic accidents. Located along the first routes into the city from the southwest—the Illinois–Michigan Canal, the Chicago and Alton Railroad, and Archer Road—McKinley Park and Brighton were natural sites for early development until surpassed by areas closer to the city's center. The Brighton Park Race Track, for example, flourished in the 1850s and '60s only to be supplanted by the Dexter Park Race Track in Canaryville. By 1870, former mayor "Long John" Wentworth had no better use for this portion of his estate than to lease it to farmers as a cabbage patch; for 30 years, it produced raw material for the sauerkraut industry. The land was absorbed into the Chicago park system and named **McKinley Park** in honor of the recently assassinated president. The surrounding neighborhood eventually took on the same name.

Similarly, the consolidation of the Union Stock Yards in 1865 killed the livestock business at the Brighton Stock Yards just north of the racetrack. Other industries, however, quickly filled the gap: steel mills, brickworks, explosives factories, and a cotton mill, opened in 1871 by one of Brighton's original incorporators, John McCaffery. These are gone now too, but the Central Manufacturing District, Crane Manufacturing Company's giant Corwith Works on Kedzie Avenue, and industrial development along 47th Street established the present character of the area before World War One.

Naturally, residential growth hastened on the heels of industrial expansion. The Poles and Lithuanians who followed the first Irish and German settlers into McKinley Park after the turn of the century built the brick bungalows and two-flats that today line the side streets with rarely relieved monotony. The streetscape is more varied in Brighton, particularly between Western Avenue and Kedzie Avenue, where frame houses predominate.

A significant exception to the modest scale of the neighborhoods is an 1860s mansion standing forlornly at 3558 South Artesian Avenue. Built by John Dolese, a contractor whose firm paved the major South Side boulevards, it was purchased in 1890 by McCaffery, who was then a member of the firm. Originally set in formal gardens along Western Avenue, the house was moved to its present location in the 1920s. Another antique edifice molders on Campbell Avenue's dead end, just north of the intersection of Archer Avenue and 38th Street. At the other end of the spectrum, the squalid tenement row houses on the 3500 block of South Honore Street, built in 1886 to house industrial workers, were known as "Outhouse Alley" because of the line of outdoor privies that once stood behind them.

Brighton's most handsome church is **St. Joseph and St. Anne** (38th Place and California Avenue). Erected by a small local French colony in 1891, it is the National Shrine to St. Anne, a center of French Catholic religious life in this country. The plain exterior gives little hint of the Gothic interior, done in "French" blue and gilt with a highly ornate apse enlivened by striking paintings; rich stained glass; *trompe l'oeil* marble Corinthian columns; and beautifully executed, surprisingly naturalistic, bas-relief Stations of the Cross.

Take the area's pulse with a shopping excursion on Archer Avenue, the former cattle route that skewers Brighton and McKinley Park as it slants toward the Loop. Gary "Snake" Martin and Mike "Doc" Duggan run the **Southwest Tattoo Emporium** (4390), one of Chicago's few remaining body-art studios. Martin looks like, and is, a biker, but his hands are talented. Modern single-needle technique means fine lines and surprisingly complex designs, so there's more to tattooing than anchors on biceps. Martin stocks thousands of designs, many of his own invention, and he can also transfer a customer's design to a cartoon and then to skin. The parlor attracts a wide range of customers, including many women (who typically leave with a butterfly or flower in a semiprivate place).

Santo Sport Store (4270) has all the paraphernalia to get your body in shape (avoid distortions: exercise first, tatoo second). Unlike at North Side shops, racquet sports are of secondary importance here. Santo does a big business in trophies, custom-drilled bowling balls, and fishing equipment.

For a totally sedentary approach to sports, head to the **Trading Card Company** (4220) where shelves, bins, tables, counters, and boxes in storage overflow with more than 12 million cardboard tributes to athletic greats. Patrick Quinn and his partners combined their collections a few years ago to start what they claim is the world's largest such store. Besides baseball cards, they stock football, basketball, and hockey cards, autographed balls, caps, posters, plaques, baseball books, and all sorts of other sports memorabilia. Prices range from pennies to thousands of dollars.

Nothing goes better with baseball than hot dogs. You can get old-fashioned weiners at **Sliz's Delicatessen** (3116 West Pope John Paul II Drive), just off Archer Avenue, as well as sausages, potato dumplings, blintzes, Polish baked beans, and salads. Sliz's and **Mathew's** (4328 South Archer Avenue) are just two of the many Polish sausage shops in the neighborhood. Three or four outstanding soups, including duck's blood, are available daily at **Anna's Home Cooking** (4100 South Archer Avenue), a quaint, lunch-counter spot with only three tables. Handwritten signs indicate each day's Polish-style offerings— pierogi, oxtail stew, chicken—and full meals, served with homey touches, are real bargains at $3 to $3.50.

The **Archer Fish Mart**'s (4160) fish-shaped business card says "If it swims we will get it." The store stocks a variety of fresh and smoked fish, and also sells fish-and-chips to go. The Friday all-you-can-eat fish fry at **Blake's Alley** (3623) is bargain priced, but the food at this neighborhood restaurant recalls college-commons fare. Eating here on Mondays or Thursdays can be unsettling: That's when the piranha in the aquarium dine on live goldfish.

For everything from a tuna sandwich to dessert, check out **Gertie's Candies** (4231), next to the Brighton Theatre. What may well be the city's finest hot fudge and butterscotch sundae toppings are two of the joys at this 1930s luncheon-ette/ice-cream parlor/candy store. Owner Ted Zaffer makes all the toppings, ice cream, and candy. He also sells his book on candymaking. Before you leave, be sure to call someone from the old-fashioned, wooden telephone booth: There aren't many left.

All the usual clothing and shoe stores also dot this strip of Archer Avenue, as do fast-food stops and car showrooms. The storefront **Balzekas Museum of Lithuanian Culture** (4012), next to Balzekas's auto dealership, is the only real surprise *(see Museums)*, especially since most of the area's Lithuanians have moved to Marquette Park. Brighton is the most solidly Polish neighborhood in Chicago, still often called the second-largest Polish city in the world.

Interesting places

*Balzekas Museum of Lithuanian Culture
4012 S. Archer Ave.
847-2441
(See Museums)

Five Holy Martyrs
Richmond St. and
Pope John Paul II Dr.
254-3636
When he was in Chicago, Pope John Paul II celebrated Mass at this unpretentious, rambling church, the seat of one of the city's two auxiliary bishops.

*McKinley Park
Pershing and Western
523-3811
The statue of President McKinley, dedicated in 1905, was recast from the bronze of Columbus, which once stood in Grant Park.

St. Agnes
Pershing and Washtenaw
247-5356
A 1905 yellow-brick church with good stained glass, asymmetrical towers, and a handsome parish house.

St. Andrew's Lutheran Church
Honore and 37th Sts.
523-0130
German-style Gothic church, home of the Wisconsin synod.

*St. Joseph and St. Anne
38th Pl. and California Ave.
927-2421

Sts. Peter and Paul
Paulina and 38th Sts.
523-3410
A Renaissance-style façade and excellent, pictorial stained glass distinguish this 1906 church.

Trilla Steel Drum Corp.
2959 W. 47th St.
847-7588
Art mirrors life: The façade is decorated with brightly painted 55-gallon drums.

Shopping and services

*Archer Fish Mart
4160 S. Archer Ave.
523-3429

Archer-35th Recreation
2051 W. 35th St.
254-1363
Funky spot that's the home of the Petersen Classic, a nine-month-long bowling tourney with almost $750,000 in prizes.

Avalon Galleries
4243 S. Archer Ave.
247-6969
A nice gift store with carved Polish plates and boxes, bisque dolls, porcelain figurines, music boxes, etc.

Brighton Park Art & Hobby Centre
4238 S. Archer Ave.
523-3334
It's crowded with model kits and craft supplies.

Hal's Bakery
2025 W 35th St.
847-2121
The sign on the cream-and-green, 1930s façade says "Strauss." Good white bread.

Kozy's Cyclery
1610 W. 35th St.
523-8576
This Schwinn dealer carries high-riders, unicycles, ex-ercycles, and more. There's another branch on the North Side.

*Mathew's Supreme Homemade Sausage
4328 S. Archer Ave.
523-2809

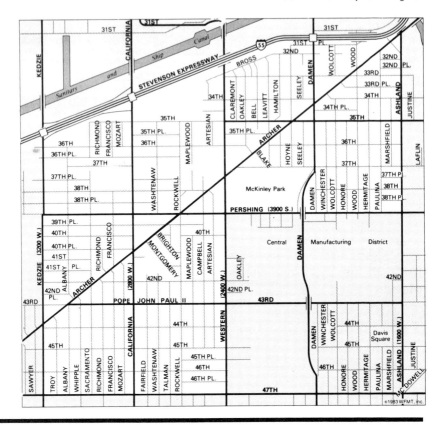

Mr. Newport Beverages
3430 S. Ashland Ave.
523-0020
Enter the warehouse in front of this soda bottling plant to buy Mr. Newport's own pop, less expensive than name brands. The logo, a man in formal attire, probably dates to the company's beginning early in the century.

*Santo Sport Store
4270 S. Archer Ave.
927-1125

*Sliz's Delicatessen
3116 W. Pope John
Paul II Dr.
523-9533

***Southwest Tattoo
Emporium**
4390 S. Archer Ave.
376-8119

*Trading Card Company
4220 S. Archer Ave.
927-8883

Tropicana Living Things
3879 S. Archer Ave.
254-2131
Wide selection of tropical fish.

Windy City Poultry
4601 S. Kedzie Ave.
847-7368
One of the few live-poultry places left in the city. Chickens, ducks, geese, turkeys, etc., are slaughtered on the premises and sold by "hanging" weight. Fresh eggs, frozen pheasants, and rabbits are also available.

Dining
and drinking

*Anna's Home Cooking
4100 S. Archer Ave.
927-7181

*Blake's Alley
3623 S. Archer Ave.
254-4080
Small but attractive salad bar; mediocre food.

*Gertie's Candies
4231 S. Archer Ave.
247-4076

Julia's Restaurant
4440 S. Western Ave.
523-4922
The trucks parked outside this plain, no-nonsense place are a clue to the hearty, inexpensive fare within. Most dinners, which include soup and ample bread and butter, are less than $3. The menu changes daily and offers dishes like roast pig, pot roast, stuffed cabbage, and homemade sausage, as well as sandwiches.

Gage Park/Marquette Park

Gage Park and Marquette Park were the last of the pre-World War II neighborhoods to grow organically from the stockyards. Unlike, say, Bridgeport with its grand old churches and political hegemony, they have few institutions to attract outsiders' attention. Instead, lurid newspaper accounts of racial confrontations mold the area's reputation. While integration was far from smooth at Gage Park High and the ravings of a few nuts in Nazi regalia may articulate widely held fears, these communities behind Western Avenue's Maginot Line of car lots have an evocative texture apart from their occasional notoriety.

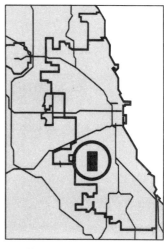

This is a Chicago where fast-food franchises haven't replaced 1950s-style hamburger grills, where corner taverns have '40s glass-brick fronts suffused with the glow of colored fluorescent tubes, where second-run movie houses still draw family crowds from surrounding 1920s bungalows and two-flats. This is a Chicago often neglected by the rest of the city and City Hall: no expressways, no rapid transit, few civic improvements.

First settled by German farmers in the 1840s, Gage Park experienced a speculative real-estate boom in the 1870s in anticipation of a railroad along Central Park Avenue and the South Park Commission's land purchase for its boulevard and park system. Development didn't really take off, however, until the 20th century. During the first three decades, the Kenwood Manufacturing District opened; industries spread along Western Avenue; German, Irish, Polish, Czech, and Balkan workers, escaping the congestion of the stockyards communities and attracted by the new factories, moved into bungalows and two-flats very similar to those in Brighton. Homes on the eastern edge of Gage Park are mostly frame; further west, the somewhat newer houses are usually brick, but none are grand.

The neighborhood's ethnic diversity is unusual for the older Southwest Side. While each ethnic group had its own churches in nearby communities, **St. Gall,** Gage Park's oldest parish, has always served a multilingual congregation. Founded in the fledgling settlement of Elsdon near 51st Street and Kedzie Avenue, St. Gall moved to the present location at 55th Street and Kedzie Avenue in 1916. Church membership soon included 16 nationalities. Volunteers helped build what is known as a crypt church: Foundations for a large structure were laid, then covered with a low roof as a temporary expedient until a traditional soaring church could be raised. Temporary can be a long time. Not until 1958 was the present structure finally built, and it is quite different than originally planned. Radislav Kovacevic designed a stark, pie-wedge-shaped building with a front almost totally given over to modernistic stained-glass windows. The massive, low-relief, bronze Stations of the Cross by Peter Recker are well worth a look. Across the street is another institution central to Gage Park, the home office of **Talman Home Federal** (5501 South Kedzie Avenue), Illinois's largest savings and loan.

With the busy shopping strips on Archer Avenue in Brighton to the north and on West 63rd Street in Marquette Park to the south, Gage Park never developed a major commercial center, but a few inviting shops are scattered through the neighborhood. Perhaps the best known is **Gertie's Own Ice Cream** (5858 South Kedzie Avenue), an old-fashioned, wood-paneled-and-boothed, corner shop. Started in 1901, the city's oldest ice-cream parlor serves good, homemade, 14 percent butterfat ice cream in sodas and sundaes with evocative names like "Tin Roof" and "Lover's Delight." On summer nights, when the show lets out at the Colony Theater next door, lines frequently stretch out Gertie's door.

Just steps from Gertie's, **Silvery Moon** (5838 South Kedzie Avenue) stocks high-quality, exceptionally imaginative, handmade goods. Besides quilts, pillows, table accessories, ceramics, and dried-flower arrangements, this shop has some fine soft sculptures and mosaic and stained glass. (The owner also does restorations.) The real treasures, however, are the toys, including wonderful thick wooden jigsaw-cut puzzles made by a Bridgeport artist. Be it dinosaurs in a tropical forest, a chicken with a baby chick in an egg inside its body, or custom-cut names, the puzzles are great for young kids to play with and aesthetically pleasing to adults.

The instruments at **Imperial Accordion/Star Concertina Company** (2618 West 59th Street) are definitely not toys: They average about $3,000. Imperial, the country's largest manufacturer and national distributor of accordions, has been hand-crafting polka pumps since 1935. Although the custom-made accordions cost 20 percent more than equivalent imported ones, professionals gladly wait six months for delivery. Imperial bought Star Concertina in 1976 and merged the Milwaukee Avenue company with its Gage Park factory. The move was sensible because both squeeze boxes are constructed similarly. Imperial is also the American distributor for Elka electronic keyboard instruments from Italy.

The **Italo-American Accordion Company** (3137 West 51st Street) has been building accordions since 1905 and sells only its own. Here, too, the instruments are custom-made, and a particularly fancy electronic one can cost as much as $8,000, although prices start at about $2,000. Both firms do repairs.

If you want to repair an instrument—any instrument—yourself, **Pro-Master Music** (3044 West 59th Street) should be your first stop. Tom Zydron has more parts for more kinds of music makers than anyone else in the city. They fill loads of file cabinets in the deep, double store, which is packed to the rafters with guitar cases (2,000), guitar strings (1,200 different sets), strings for everything from sitars to zithers, sheet music (22,000 titles): The list is endless. On top of all this, Pro-Master sells acoustic and electronic instruments, makes electronic sound cables, and builds speaker systems.

For electronic sounds of a different sort, head to **Don Lindy Enterprises** (2808 West 55th Street), where used juke boxes start at about $400 and pinball machines are $500 and up. Then peer through the windows into Stanley's Barber Shop (2812)—Lindy rarely has jukes old enough to fit in with the décor here—and stock up on good homestyle doughnuts at **Kof-E-Brake** (2822).

Across the street at **John's Delicatessen** (2811), John Gadomski smokes his own mild ham and makes super sausages, both Polish and blood and tongue. In autumn, he also gathers wild mushrooms in Indiana that his wife pickles and sells for about half the price of imported jars. (They are gone by Christmas.)

Of several bakeries in Gage Park, **Sixta's** (5405 South Kedzie Avenue) may be the most popular. This cheerful, friendly shop sells Polish, Bohemian, Hungarian, French, and Danish pastries, as well as cakes and breads. The sublime Babcia's rye (large, round, light, chewy loaves) is available only on Thursdays and Saturdays. Get to Sixta's early because the goodies go fast.

Many Gage Park restaurants cater to factory workers, are closed by dinnertime, and have little to offer visitors. Three Polish ones are exceptions. While **Polonia Inn** (2735 West 55th Street) serves all the old favorites in comfortable surroundings at reasonable prices, for a couple of dollars more, you can taste them all in one meal at the **Olympic Inn** (5111 South Kedzie Avenue). The all-you-can-eat buffet offers good salads, stuffed cabbage, pierogi, sauerkraut-and-meat casseroles, sliced-to-order baked ham and roast beef, and daily specials such as roast duck (Thursdays). Dinner includes a bowl of soup, decent desserts, and coffee. The **Europejska Lounge** (2524 West 51st Street) serves Polish dinners and à la carte specialties, also at low prices, in a huge banquet-hall-like room. Unlike many ethnic places, it has a liquor license and stays open late. The real treat is live entertainment on weekends: The sign advertises "modern music," which means acts such as a "hot" combo-backed chanteuse belting out '60s-style rock 'n' roll in Polish—not polka bands. There's even a large dance floor highlighted by a revolving mirrored ball.

The neighborhood of Marquette Park appears, at first glance, to be an extension of Gage Park—perhaps because the section between 59th and 63rd Streets is just that. But a solidly Lithuanian enclave surrounding the park and the 63rd Street–Kedzie Avenue area, which evolved from a 19th-century suburb, is quite different.

John E. Eberhart subdivided Chicago Lawn, which is still the official designation of the entire Marquette Park neighborhood, in 1873. Eberhart, who was Cook County's first superintendent of education and is said to have introduced Stephen Douglas to Abraham Lincoln, built his large brick house at **3415 West 64th Street,** where it stands today—the oldest for miles around. More homes from the pioneer period are nearby, mixed in with brick bungalows and small apartment buildings. Although none are mansions, a drive down the east-west streets between 63rd and the park takes you past most of the older houses and other curiosities such as the Prairie School-inspired cottages at 64th Place and Spaulding Avenue. To the east of California Avenue, streets lined with octagonal-fronted, leaded-windowed brick houses are reminiscent of Rogers Park.

Chicago's Lithuanian population is the country's largest. South of Marquette Road (67th Street), Lithuanians moving from Bridgeport, Back of the Yards, and Brighton early in the century formed a tight little village now served by a massive complex of Lithuanian institutions. The first of these, the **Sisters of St. Casimir Mother House** (2601 West Marquette Road), was built in 1911 and maintains a Lithuanian museum that rivals the Balzekas Museum of Lithuanian Culture in Brighton (*see Museums*). In addition to their other activities throughout the city, the more than 350 Sisters of St. Casimir staff the nearby Holy Cross Hospital, built in 1928; Maria High School, where very polished performances of grand opera, in Lithuanian, are mounted in the spring; and the Nativity of the Blessed Virgin Mary School. Nativity of the B.V.M. parish was established in the late 1920s, and services were held on the first floor of the school until the present church was built in 1957. A striking Lithuanian baroque structure recalling Old World churches, **Nativity of the Blessed Virgin Mary** (Lithuanian Plaza Court and Washtenaw Avenue) incorporates both Christian and pagan themes in the dramatic bell towers and detailing. Exterior mosaic murals by noted Lithuanian artist Adomas Varnas depict scenes from Lithuanian history, while the murals and centuries-old artifacts inside are also inspired by a combination of religious, military, and pagan traditions.

Mayor Daley proclaimed the area "Lithuanian Plaza" in 1966. In 1980, the city renamed 69th Street between California and Western Avenues "Lithuanian Plaza Court" (L.P.C.), inaugurated a Lithuanian festival here, and widened and landscaped the sidewalks. The physical changes are similar to those at Lincoln Square, but this is no crowded commercial strip with stores jostling each other for attention. Instead, finds have to be eked out in shops that maintain Old World traditions and often conduct business in Lithuanian. **Baltic Blossoms** (2451 L.P.C.) is a good example. Baltic is, of course, a florist—and a nice one. But an employee is related to East Coast artist Vytautas Ignas, and the shop is also a gallery for his limited-edition woodblocks. The same strong designs are reproduced on stationery and cards sold in the store. **Talman Grocery and Deli** (2624) stocks ingredients for Lithuanian cuisine and wonderful ready-to-eat food. The little corner shop is crammed with sausages (Lithuanian sausage is like Polish sausage with onions instead of garlic), fresh sour cream guaranteed not to curdle in hot soup, salads, meats in aspic, whole roast duck, and prune-stuffed duck rolls. Unique Lithuanian napoléons and nut tortes are sold at very attractive prices.

Nearby Lithuanian restaurants differ subtly from equally inexpensive Polish ones. Besides rye, the bread baskets offer eggy, raisin-studded bread; soup choices always include lightly spiced sauerkraut, which, like all the nonstarchy broths, is served with boiled potato on the side. More sauerkraut and boiled potatoes accompany many entrées, which range from the familiar roast duck, pork, and chicken, dumplings and potato pancakes, and other stick-to-the-ribs fare to lighter selections such as fruit-filled pancakes. Greenery and ethnic handicrafts enliven the places, most of which change their menus daily and close early.

Ramune's Restaurant (2547) retails many of the same delicacies as Talman in its deli section, or you can do as presidential candidate Ronald Reagan did and enjoy complete meals in the dining room for about four dollars. Having one of the superb torte slices for dessert adds 75 cents to the tab. **Tulpé** (2447) is a smaller, less festive, and less Americanized version of Ramune's, without the deli counter. The dozen or so daily offerings on the signboard over the tiny lunch counter and three tables may include fine dumplings or pancakes and gira, a fermented-rye-bread beverage.

At **Nida Delicatessen and Restaurant** (2617 West 71st Street), stuffed cabbage, dumplings, and excellent filled pancakes are always on the menu in the cozy, seven-table dining room. The deli selection is much smaller than Ramune's, and the tortes are more costly. **Neringa Restaurant** (2632 West 71st Street) may well be the area's largest and busiest. The quality and bounty of the food easily explain the restaurant's popularity. Bread baskets sport three or four varieties, duck usually isn't overroasted—a rarity—and the potato pancakes are crisp delights. Although there are no tortes, stewed fruits make an appropriate ending to a very inexpensive meal. Unfortunately, none of these restaurants has a liquor license and some idea of morality, timidity, or business considerations prohibit bringing your own.

Besides restaurants, West 71st Street harbors a few surprises. The stock at **Gifts International** (2501) runs the gamut from folk art (straw Christmas ornaments, locally made pottery, Polish carved boxes, and wood-marquetry plaques) to the sophisticated (European flashed glassware, cut crystal, and lots of amber jewelry). Many of the books, records, and tapes are in Lithuanian.

Even without the two guard dogs, **Eagle Sales** (2443) would be singularly off-putting. "Military collectibles" are the stated stock-in-trade of this small store, but the Nazi helmets, insignia, ephemera, and modern T-shirts emblazoned with Nazi emblems are likely to appeal only to those types who frequent **Lincoln Rockwell Hall** (2519), the Nazi headquarters, dedicated to the "memory of our fallen commander." The boarded-up façade makes the place look like a fortress. From time to time, the boys lift a few in the bar next door.

The 63rd Street shopping strip, on the other hand, may be the South Side's most inviting. A broad, bustling business area, brightened by some fanciful, '20s-style terra-cotta façades, it offers the usual panoply of neighborhood shops as well as the unexpected: two motorcycle customizing houses, an Arab enclave, and a tavern run by an ex-Munchkin.

Recent arrivals to the community, the Arabs are bringing a vitality to 63rd Street's eastern section. One of the more established of the restaurants and grocery stores that are springing up, **Al-Ahram** (2509) serves a limited selection of modestly priced, tasty, Middle Eastern favorites in very casual surroundings. An adjoining bakery (2513) retails Syrian pastries by the pound, as well as hot-from-the-oven pita, grains, Turkish coffee, etc. More Near Eastern goodies can be found at **Eastern Bakery and Grocery** (2639), a much smaller operation.

Marquette Park's Teutons (and others) keep **Hoeffken's Bakery** (3044) hopping. The sign says THE BUSY BAKERY, and no billing was ever more true. As many as six women work the counters of this 40-year-old institution. Standard sweet rolls are nothing special, but the pound cake is terrific and the German and Eastern European pastries are quite good, as are the breads. (Try the whole-wheat-raisin.)

Driftstone Wedding Cake-A-Rama (3135) offers only made-to-order nuptial creations: plain or chocolate, all-butter, pound cakes frosted with white butter cream. Neither time nor changing fashions can induce Sy and Ben Kopersmith to vary their mother's 50-year-old recipe. Samples are available during the wedding season.

You might get the ice cream to go with your cake at **Cupid Candies** (3143). Cupid's window and counter displays are beautifully tempting, and the store looks like a 1940s movie set: You almost expect to see Mickey Rooney and Judy Garland splitting a soda at the fountain. Although the candy for this small chain is made in a large factory further south on Western Avenue, all the ice cream is produced in the rear of this shop. Virtually Gertie's equal, Cupid is, for some reason, not nearly as popular—or as crowded.

Emil's Delicatessen (6238 South Kedzie Avenue), just around the corner, also carries candy, most imported from Germany. This festive store, reminiscent of New York's East Side delis, is crammed full of German delicacies, newspapers, magazines, mugs, and gifts. Hand-sliced Nova Scotia salmon and Koenemann's nitrite-free bacon are just two of the treats at the sausage/cheese counter. Emil's also makes sandwiches and gives big spenders colorful, German-language calendars printed in Germany.

Active locals—and there are lots of them, including the members of the Lithuanian soccer club—head to **Marquette Sports** (3206 West 63rd Street) for football, bowling, golf, and fishing supplies, as well as a smattering of other sports equipment, trophies, and team jackets. **Trost Hobby Shop** (3111) stocks everything for the armchair athlete. Model trains are big here (repairs, too), as are slot cars and plastic scale models. Although mostly male-oriented, hobby supplies of almost every kind can be found in this huge store. **Something from Knotting** (6405 South Kedzie Avenue) is devoted to—naturally—macramé supplies. At **Gowdy Leather Works** (2849 West 63rd Street), a very low-key place, Vida and Tom Marshall will teach you leather crafting or sell you finished, hand-tooled purses, belts, wallets, photo album covers, and more, as well as commercially manufactured deerskin accessories.

Since winning *Chicago* magazine's pizza taster's palates, **Giordano's** (3214 West 63rd Street) has come into its own. Having abandoned a smaller place across the street, this local institution now deep-dishes up terrific double-crusted monsters in a slick, subterranean spot in a strikingly renovated vintage building. Outlets have spread all over, but devotées swear that the original is always more satisfying.

Imagining a less likely location for a decent bargain-priced French restaurant is difficult, but **The French Kitchen** (3437) is just that. Owner/chef Lorraine Hooker brings her individual style to the eclectic, limited menu at this storefront. You can bring your own wine and enjoy an interesting, though not haute cuisine, meal for about $10—on the patio in the summer.

There's plenty to do in the area after dinner, particularly on weekends. Live entertainment at taverns ranges from go-go girls (remember them?) to Las Vegas lounge-type shows. Loud rock or disco blares from more than half a dozen bars, some of which charge a minimal cover and have dance floors.

For a relatively slick look and a softer sound, check out **Tommy Kraw's Lounge** (6459 South Kedzie Avenue) on Wednesdays, Fridays, and Saturdays. A horseshoe bar and banquettes face the tiny stage where pop combos play to a straight, older crowd. There's no cover, but a sign on the door warns that three I.D.s are required. **Pepe's Show Lounge** (4142 West 63rd Street), a full-scale nightclub, books middle-of-the-road acts—Elvis impressionists, Donny and Marie sound-alikes, '50s bands—for Tuesday through Sunday weeks and charges a $2 to $4 cover. At the **6511 Club** (6511 South Kedzie Avenue), a pleasant, North Side-looking Irish pub, a young crowd gathers on Friday nights to play pool in the back, drink Guinness, and listen to traditional Hibernian folk music.

Any night of the week is a good time to stop at **Dove Candies and Ice Cream** (6000 South Pulaski Road) for what may be the city's largest sundaes and sodas. Owner Mike Stefanos, scion of a confection-making family whose stores once blanketed the South Side (his uncle owns Cupid), is a C.P.A., but portions at Dove show no signs of cost control. The '50s-looking place is a find: Whipped cream is the real stuff, mint meltaways rival you-know-who's Frango mints and are far cheaper, and the sublime ice-cream bars could make Good Humor grouchy.

Dove is on a strip of Pulaski Road which, though technically not in Gage Park or Marquette Park, is worth exploring. **Izzy Rizzy's House of Tricks** (6034) is probably the largest store of its kind in Chicago, with loads of magic tricks, gag items, adult novelties, Halloween masks, and more. **Irish Treasures and Imports** (5926) stocks a nice selection of goods from the Emerald Isle, including wool ties, men's caps and hats, and reasonably priced fisherman's-knit sweaters (dress right for the 6511 Club!), as well as kitsch bumper stickers and pottery. Other noteworthy spots range from the highly visible, first **Jewel Grand Bazaar** (5320) to the small **Krakus Delicatessen** (5754½), which smokes its own ham and makes excellent sausages.

Interesting places

Darius Girenas Monument
California and Marquette
Erected in 1935 to honor fliers Stephanas Darius and Stasys Girenas, who were killed on a goodwill flight to Lithuania.

*John E. Eberhart House
3415 W. 64th St.

Elsdon Station
3601 W. 51st St.
Built as a commuter railroad station to serve the little community of the same name in the northwest corner of Gage Park in the turn of the century.

*Nativity of the Blessed Virgin Mary
Lithuanian Plaza Ct. and Washtenaw Ave.
776-4600

*Lincoln Rockwell Hall
2519 W. 71st St.

"Roots," mural
3541 W. 63rd St.
This abstract mural by C. Yasko, L. Radycki, and local residents celebrates Chicago Lawn's centennial (1876-1976).

*St. Gall
55th St. and Kedzie Ave.
737-3113

St. Nicholas of Tolentine
Lawndale Ave. and 62nd St.
735-1121
Built in 1937, this large church appears conventional from the outside, but the interior's low ribbing treats traditional church architecture with typical '30s massiveness. Rich, figural, deep-blue, stained-glass windows.

St. Peter and St. Paul Eastern Orthodox Church
53rd St. and Western Ave.
778-9353
An onion-domed church built in 1931.

Map of Gage Park/Marquette Park area showing the street grid. Major labels include: Central Manufacturing District, Kenwood Manufacturing District, ARCHER, Central Park, Gage Park, Marquette Park, Mann, Redfield, Hollett, Kanst, Lithuanian Plaza, Marquette (6700 S.).

North-south streets (west to east): Komensky (4000 W.), Pulaski (4000 W.), Harding, Springfield, Avers, Hamlin, Ridgeway, Lawndale, Millard, St. Louis, Trumbull, Homan, Christiana, Spaulding, Sawyer, Kedzie (3200 W.), Troy, Albany, Whipple, Sacramento, Richmond, Francisco, Mozart, California (2800 W.), Fairfield, Washtenaw, Talman, Rockwell, Maplewood, Campbell, Artesian, Western (2400 W.), Claremont.

East-west streets (north to south): 48TH PL., 49TH, 50TH, 51ST, 52ND, 53RD, 54TH, 54TH PL., 55TH, 55TH PL., 56TH, 56TH PL., 57TH, 57TH PL., 58TH, 58TH PL., 59TH, 59TH PL., 60TH, 60TH PL., 61ST, 61ST PL., 62ND, 62ND PL., 63RD, 63RD PL., 64TH, 64TH PL., 65TH, 65TH PL., 66TH, 66TH PL., MARQUETTE (6700 S.), 67TH PL., 68TH, 68TH PL., 69TH, 69TH PL., 70TH, 70TH PL., 71ST, 71ST PL.

©1983 WFMT, inc.

St. Rita
63rd St. and Fairfield Ave.
434-9600
Dominating an entire block, this huge Byzantine church with massive transepts is completely marble lined, has a sweeping, barrel-vaulted nave, a fanciful altar, and fine stained glass.

*Sisters of St. Casimir Mother House
2601 W. Marquette Rd.
776-1324
The museum is open only by appointment.

Southtown Club of the Deaf
5832 S. Western Ave.
TDD 776-0089
Established in 1945 in Englewood, this 150-member club—essentially a place where members can enjoy a drink without feeling awkward—is one of four such organizations in the city. Open Friday-Sunday evenings.

*Talman Home Federal
5501 S. Kedzie Ave.
434-3322

Shopping and services

*Baltic Blossoms
2451 Lithuanian Plaza Ct.
434-2036

The Best for Less Resale Shop
2423 W. 71st St.
925-2919
New and used men's and women's clothing in good condition. Lots of furs at reasonable prices in winter.

*Eagle Sales
2443 W. 71st St.
436-5544 (after 4 p.m.)

*Gifts International
2501 W. 71st St.
471-1424

*Gowdy Leather Works
2849 W. 63rd St.
434-4822

*Imperial Accordion/Star Concertina Company
2618 W. 59th St.
476-3401

*Irish Treasures and Imports
5926 S. Pulaski Rd.
581-5911

*Italo-American Accordion Company
3137 W. 51st St.
776-2992

*Izzy Rizzy's House of Tricks
6034 S. Pulaski Rd.
735-7370

*Don Lindy Enterprises
2808 W. 55th St.
247-4444

*Marquette Sports Equipment
3206 W. 63rd St.
436-3311
Another in Oak Lawn.

Marzano's Miami Bowl
5023 S. Archer Ave.
585-8787
80 lanes! Open 24 hours, 365 days a year!

Nate's Leather and Suede Salon
2950 W. 63rd St.
925-1973
This store manufactures and retails police leather jackets and other leather goods.

*Pro-Master Music
3044 W. 59th St.
476-6660

*Silvery Moon
5838 S. Kedzie Ave.
776-9717

*Something from Knotting
6405 S. Kedzie Ave.
778-0661

Standard Law Book Co.
4814 S. Pulaski Rd.
376-1711
Specializes exclusively in books for lawyers, paralegals, law students, and policemen.

*Trost Hobby Shop
3111 W. 63rd St.
925-1000

Windy City Music
3919 W. 63rd St.
735-2027
Loads of drums, guitars, mixers, amps, speakers, and other electronic music paraphernalia, discounted.

Foodstuffs

*Al-Ahram Bakery
2513 W. 63rd St.
737-2333

Baltic Bakery
2616 Lithuanian Plaza Ct.
737-6784
A branch of the great bakery in Back of the Yards.

Carmen's Italian Foods
3629 W. 63rd St.
581-4395
Probably the largest Italian grocery-deli for miles around.

Peter Cora Coffee
4304 W. 63rd St.
767-7154
In the espresso business for 25 years, Cora is the U.S. distributor for excellent Elli espresso machines and imports his own V.I.P. espresso coffee used in many Chicago restaurants. He sells wholesale or retail, carries pasta makers, and does repairs, too.

*Cupid Candies
3143 W. 63rd St.
737-6277

*Dove Candies and Ice Cream
6000 S. Pulaski Rd.
582-3119

*Driftstone Wedding Cake-A-Rama
3135 W. 63rd St.
737-3331

*Eastern Bakery and Grocery
2639 W. 63rd St.
925-4857

*Emil's Delicatessen
6238 S. Kedzie Ave.
776-1918

*Gertie's Own Ice Cream
5858 S. Kedzie Ave.
737-7634
Also at 7600 S. Pulaski Rd.

*Hoeffken's Bakery
3044 W. 63rd St.
737-0390

International Meat Market
2913 W. 63rd St.
436-4337
Petras Burkauskas smokes
his own Canadian bacon
and makes his own
salami—a rarity.

*Jewel Grand Bazaar
5320 S. Pulaski Rd.
284-7700

*John's Delicatessen
2811 W. 55th St.
776-5200

Kobal's Meat Market
5225 S. Kedzie Ave.
778-5433
A nice butcher shop—
and the largest one in the
neighborhood.

*Krakus Delicatessen
5754½ S. Pulaski Rd.
735-1959
Also at 4772 N. Milwaukee.

Marquette Delicatessen
2553 W. 71st St.
776-2717
Another excellent deli.

Parama Food and Liquors
2534 Lithuanian Plaza Ct.
737-3332
This Lithuanian grocery has
an unusually large selection
of imported chocolates.

*Sixta's Bakery
5405 S. Kedzie Ave.
737-2113

*Talman Grocery and Deli
2624 Lithuanian Plaza Ct.
434-9766

Tuzik Bakeries
5311 S. Kedzie Ave.
776-4283
A small Polish bakery
selling cakes, pastries, and
good whole-wheat bread.

Dining
and drinking

*Al-Ahram Restaurant
2509 W. 63rd St.
436-2111

Club El Bianco
2747 W. 63rd St.
471-9700
Bountiful Italian meals
served in spacious, festive
surroundings. The fiesta
dinners are famous at this
old-line place.

*The French Kitchen
3437 W. 63rd St.
776-6715

*Giordano's
3214 W. 63rd St.
436-2969

Ingeborg Lounge
6361 S. Kedzie Ave.
778-9224
A seedy bar that's been
serving a home-cooked
dinner for a buck after
4 p.m. for years.

*Kof-E-Brake Donut Shop
2822 W. 55th St.
778-3826
Hamburgers, too.

**Little Joe's Pizzeria
and Restaurant**
2921 W. 63rd St.
476-5233
Big, crowded place with a
huge menu: thin-crust,
deep-dish, and stuffed
pizza; pasta; veal and all the
usuals. Take-out, too.

The Midget Club
4016 W. 63rd St.
284-9191
Former Munchkin Parnell S.
Aubin and his equally tiny
wife serve short beers and
strong drinks to mostly full-
sized customers amid
diminutive surroundings in
this neighborhood bar.

*Neringa Restaurant
2632 W. 71st St.
476-9026

***Nida Delicatessen
and Restaurant**
2617 W. 71st St.
476-7675

*Olympic Inn
5111 S. Kedzie Ave.
776-0795

*Polonia Inn
2735 W. 55th St.
737-3044

*Ramune's Restaurant
2547 Lithuanian Plaza Ct.
925-4254

Ruta Restaurant
6812 S. Western Ave.
778-3493
Yet another inexpensive
Lithuanian spot.

*Tulpé
2447 Lithuanian Plaza Ct.
925-1123

Entertainment

*Europejska Lounge
2524 W. 51st St.
434-1350

*Tommy Kraw's Lounge
6459 S. Kedzie Ave.
778-9598

*Pepe's Show Lounge
4142 W. 63rd St.
585-1770

Sheldon's Pub
3334 W. 63rd St.
No phone
Very dumpy place with a
go-go dancer almost every
night. Rather sad.

*6511 Club
6511 S. Kedzie Ave.
778-9434

Hyde Park/Kenwood

"Live Among Giants" was the lure of a locally celebrated ad trumpeting Hyde Park housing. It conjured up intellectual colossi like Enrico Fermi, Saul Bellow, and 40 other Nobel laureates who have made this neighborhood their home. The massive, steel-strapped oak door pictured in the ad also evokes Hyde Park's formidable stock of institutions: the University of Chicago, half a dozen theological and professional schools, the Museum of Science and Industry, the Oriental Institute, the David and Alfred Smart Gallery, the DuSable Museum of African American History, and the Morton B. Weiss Museum of Judaica (*see Museums*).

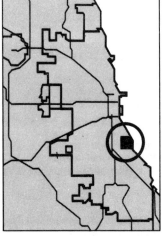

But contrary to popular misconceptions, Hyde Park isn't merely an academic fortress surrounded by slums. It's true that nearby depressed areas make prudence necessary, particularly at night, but crime statistics there are well below the city average. Hyde Park is Chicago's most successfully integrated community and an increasingly affluent one at that. The only independent ward during the Daley years, it maintains a reputation for political activism. Denim has long been a common uniform, but trendy designer jeans are few and far between. Birthplace of an intellectual comedic style which Mike Nichols, Elaine May, and other Compass Players honed into the Second City, the neighborhood remains an artistic stronghold with many fine classical music groups, such as Music of the Baroque and the Chicago Children's Choir (*see Music*), and crowd-pleasing events like the 57th Street Art Fair and the University of Chicago Folk Festival (*see Annual Events*).

The pastoral, middle-class, residential suburb Paul Cornell envisioned when he bought 300 acres of South Side lakefront land in 1853 so flourished that, 36 years later, when Hyde Park was annexed by Chicago, it was called the Evanston of the South Side. (Cornell was even related by marriage to John Evans and Orrington Lunt, the founders of Evanston and Northwestern University, respectively.) The predominance of large, older homes and the presence of major universities in both communities make the epithet equally apt today.

Founded in 1892 by John D. Rockefeller as a Baptist bastion, the University of Chicago is well worth seeing. Free daily walking tours begin at the **Administration Building** (5801 South Ellis Avenue). Or make up a tour using the map, fact book, and pamphlets available in Room 104.

The first building on campus, **Cobb Hall** (5811 South Ellis Avenue), opened two weeks before the adjacent World's Columbian Exposition in 1893 and, like the other early Gothic/Tudor halls, illustrates the school planners' desire to imitate the great English universities. While **Hitchcock Hall** (1009 East 57th Street) combines neo-Gothic architecture with indigenous "prairie" detailing—stonework ears of corn, grapes, and sunflowers, the **Mandel Hall/Mitchell Tower/ Reynolds Club** complex (57th Street and University Avenue) demonstrates real Anglomania. The exterior was modeled on the Great Hall of Crosby Place; the tower, which houses the Alice Truman Palmer bells (the only Midwestern change-ringing society practices on them), was copied from Magdalen College; and Hutchinson Commons, the wood-paneled dining hall, is a Christ Church Commons replica. (Avoid the food!)

Jousting scenes from *Ivanhoe,* gleaming in the magnificent stained-glass window over the entrance to **Bartlett Gymnasium** (5640 South University Avenue), are best seen from the building's interior in the morning. Frederic Bartlett's (the building donor's son) giant mural on the opposing wall, dedicated to the "Advancement of Physical Education and the Glory of Manly Sports in Memory of Frank Bartlett" (the painter's brother), depicts single stick and broadsword exercises which, like jousting, were presumed to be the sports popular in the period of the building's architecture. The walls of the third-floor theater in **Ida Noyes Hall** (1212 East 59th Street) are covered with Jessie Arms Botke's murals of the student/faculty *Masque of Youth,* performed in 1916 to celebrate the dedication of what was then the Women's Union. Now a student center, the building is full of splendid antiques, and has a *Konditorei,* too.

Carved bosses, vibrant stained-glass windows, dark woodwork, and a copper strip bearing Biblical quotations in a Gothic script so ornate that deciphering it often distracts frequenters of medieval-music concerts, decorate tiny **Bond Chapel** (1025 East 58th Street), hidden inside the quadrangle behind the Divinity School's Swift Hall. **Rockefeller Memorial Chapel** (5850 South Woodlawn Avenue) hosts free weekly noontime concerts on one of the country's finest concert organs during the school year and performances on the world's second-largest carillon almost year round. The chapel also maintains a choir and orchestra which give several annual concerts, including a Christmastime *Messiah,* and the chancel is used for occasional, appropriate plays such as *Murder in the Cathedral.* Elaborate woodwork carved *in situ,* vaulted ceilings, and Norman Laliberté's liturgical banners created for the Vatican Pavilion at the 1965 World's Fair adorn the interior. The more than 70 exterior stone sculptures by Lee Lawrie and Ulric Ellerhusen, friends of chapel architect Bertram Grosvenor Goodhue, are a hodge-podge of allegorical figures with music represented by J. S. Bach and architecture by Goodhue!

Traditional and modern sculptures dot the campus. Henry Moore's *Nuclear Energy,* on the old Stagg Field next to Regenstein Library, marks the site of man's first controlled, self-sustaining chain reaction, while Ruth Duckworth's ceramic mural *Earth, Water, and Sky* enlivens the lobby of the striking, modern Geophysical Sciences Building. A statue of celebrated Swedish botanist *Carl von Linné,* holding one of the books he wrote and a flower he discovered and named, graces the Midway just south of Harper Library. The *Tomáš Masaryk Monument,* a tribute to Czechoslovakia's first president, who once taught at the university, stands at the east end, and Lorado Taft's famous *Fountain of Time*—with the sculptor and his assistant included in the line-up on the back—is on the west end where the Midway flows into Washington Park.

Midway Studios (6016 South Ingleside Avenue), Taft's workplace and home until his death in 1936 and now home to the university's fine-arts department, is one of four National Historic Landmarks on campus. Another is Frank

Lloyd Wright's 1909 **Robie House** (5757 South Woodlawn Avenue), the ultimate Prairie School statement.

Homes on the residential streets to the north and east of the campus represent an unusually wide variety of styles from pre-Fire Italianate villas (5630 South Kimbark Avenue and 5714 South Dorchester Avenue) to urban renewal townhouses by Harry Weese, E. M. Pei, and others. Pullman architect Solon Beman designed Rosalie Villas (Harper Avenue between 57th and 59th Streets) as a planned community in the mid-1880s, and the Victorian and Queen Anne houses form an evocative streetscape free from modern intrusions. The list of architects who designed turn-of-the-century homes on University Avenue—many of them restrained, spacious brick dwellings built for academics—reads like a Who's Who of American architecture: Henry Ives Cobb (5855), Hugh Garden (5735), Arthur Maher (5629), Howard Van Doren Shaw (5533), Borst & Hetherington (5327). Those on Woodlawn Avenue complete the picture: Rapp and Rapp (5725), Dwight Perkins (5711), Holabird and Roche (5637), Tallmadge and Watson (5605-9), J. M. Van Osdel (5548), Pond & Pond (5533), W. F. Shattuck (5127), and, of course, Wright's Robie House (5757) and the 1897 Heller House (5137).

Many of these architects were also at work designing revival Elizabethan, Romanesque, Georgian, and colonial residences in adjoining **Kenwood,** which became the choice of Chicago's elite after Prairie Avenue fell from grace. Woodlawn, Greenwood, and Ellis Avenues, between Hyde Park Boulevard and 47th Street, boast one of the city's highest concentrations of grand mansions uninterrupted by high-rises or commercial development. Meat-packers T. E. Wilson (4815 South Woodlawn Avenue) and Gustavus Swift (4848 South Ellis Avenue); lumber merchants Martin Ryerson (4845 South Drexel Boulevard) and William Goodman (5026 South Greenwood Avenue), benefactors of the Art Institute and its theater; Sears, Roebuck executive Julius Rosenwald (4901 South Ellis Avenue) and Marshall Field's president John Shedd (4515 South Drexel Boulevard, demolished), who endowed the Museum of Science and Industry and the aquarium, all moved to Kenwood within ten years of 1900. They spared no expense, and the houses, set on huge lots, are palatially equipped with ballrooms, walk-in safes, greenhouses, coach houses, and more.

Although most don't have ballrooms or coach houses, Chicago's finest collection of Queen Anne villas lines Kimbark Avenue between 48th and 49th Streets. Wright's 1892 McArthur and Blossom houses (4856 and 58 South Kenwood Avenue) give few hints of the architect to come, but the Blossom coach house, designed by Wright 15 years later, is archetypal Prairie School. Other streets sport an engaging mix of Edwardian townhouses, apartment buildings, and medium-sized homes, while charming, tranquil Madison Park, a private, landscaped drive between Woodlawn and Dorchester Avenues, is a virtual microcosm of local architecture. (Mind the speed bumps if you drive through.)

Both Hyde Park and Kenwood are on the National Register of Historic Places, and the latter has been designated a Chicago Landmark District. The Commission on Chicago Historical and Architectural Landmarks' Kenwood pamphlet is an excellent guide to the area's riches, and Jean Block's profusely illustrated *Hyde Park Houses* (U. of C. Press, 1978) thoroughly covers Hyde Park and Kenwood through 1910. To get inside some of the Kenwood homes, take the Ancona Montessori School's spring house walk (*see Annual Events*). You can get a free, poster-sized map of the neighborhood from Urban Search (337-2400), the area's biggest residential broker.

Tall buildings dominate the area east of the Illinois Central Railroad tracks. **The Powhatan** (1648 East 50th Street), a towering luxury co-op designed by Robert De Golyer and built in 1928, is the neighborhood's, if not the city's, Art

Deco *pièce de résistance.* Lavishly ornamented inside and out with sculpted terra cotta, multicolored ceramic tile, and handsome metalwork, the Powhatan and its slightly plainer neighbor, the Narragansett, led to the label "Indian Village" for the triangle of East Hyde Park north of Hyde Park Boulevard.

Fanciful ornamentation adorns many of East Hyde Park's buildings. The Barclay (4940 East End) wears its florid Hispano-Moorish entrance modestly, and pairs of flamingos bow sedately to each other on the parapet of the Flamingo Apartments (5500 S. South Shore Drive). Magnificent Indian braves in full regalia decorate the Del Prado Hotel at the corner of 53rd Street and Hyde Park Boulevard and, surrounded by sculpted ears of corn, tobacco leaves, and other native plants, are echoed in plaster on the lobby's ceiling. Like most of the area's famous hotels—the Shoreland, the Broadview, the Sherry—the Del Prado has been converted into apartments.

Mies van der Rohe's first important Chicago commission, the Promontory Apartments (5530 S. South Shore Drive), stands in stark contrast to the older skyscrapers, as do groups of three-story flats. East View Park, a private street off 54th Street, presents a homogeneous crescent of vaguely Prairie School façades facing the lake.

If you've a taste for monumental architecture, tour Hyde Park's churches. Ten of them form a compact group centered around 57th Street and Woodlawn Avenue. Aside from Rockefeller and Bond chapels, don't miss the **First Unitarian Church** (5650 South Woodlawn Avenue), with its grand nave and wood-paneled chapel, and **St. Thomas the Apostle** (5472 South Kimbark Avenue), a neo-Moorish building designed in 1922 by Barry Byrne, with a terra-cotta exterior by Alfonso Iannelli and G. Faggi's interior bas-reliefs depicting the Stations of the Cross. The Victorian graystone **United Church of Hyde Park** (1448 East 53rd Street) offers a fan-shaped sanctuary with a striking dome and outstanding stained-glass windows. The interior stonework is all *trompe l'oeil,* but the adjoining community house's woodwork is all real. The home of the Midwest's oldest Jewish congregation, **K.A.M. Isaiah Israel** (1100 East Hyde Park Boulevard), is an official city landmark. Alfred S. Alschuler designed the Byzantine tile-and-stone building in 1924 with recently excavated Mesopotamian temples in mind. The Morton B. Weiss Museum of Judaica is concealed behind the domed sanctuary, and Alschuler's son designed the temple's modern addition.

The pioneer Hyde Park/Kenwood Urban Renewal Plan of the mid-'50s changed the neighborhood substantially. Not only were scores of "deteriorating" homes demolished to be replaced by townhouses and the streets turned into a maze of one-ways and dead ends to reduce traffic flow, but the major commercial strips—Lake Park Avenue and 55th Street—were almost totally dismantled. An additional casualty was the 57th Street "Artists' Colony." This collection of clapboard shacks left over from the World's Columbian Exposition was a hangout for Theodore Dreiser, Edgar Lee Masters, Carl Sandburg, Sherwood Anderson, and other greats early in this century. In 1965, a few of the colony's tenants moved into **Harper Court,** a unique urban-renewal complex built to house artists' workshops with rent subsidized by adjoining conventional stores. Unfortunately, most of the artists languished in the court's commercial atmosphere, and today the cluster of bilevel buildings around a sunken plaza on Harper Avenue between 52nd and 53rd Streets hosts only two survivors—Plants Alive and the Fret Shop.

Artisans 21, a group of local artists and craftsmen who banded together to sell their paintings, graphics, pottery, jewelry, and other items, moved to Harper Court in 1979 and restored some of the intended ambiance, as did **Contemporary Craftsman,** another outlet for hand-made goods. On the other hand, most of the shops offer the usual cross section of middle-class wares. Their names tell the story: Harper Lights, Freehling Pot and Pan, the Sewing Circle, Art Directions, Jack's Book Center, Harper Court Sports, J's Pipe Shop, and Sunflower Seed Health Foods. Owned by the Hyde Park Co-operative Society, **Scan,** an early importer of Scandinavian furniture and housewares, occupies a whole building.

Just north of the court, **Toys Et Cetera** (5206 South Harper Avenue) is crammed full of all the toys and games anyone ever wanted, and owner Nancy Stanek offers expert advice on choosing just the right ones. Modeled on continental salons, **Odom's Cosmetique** (5200) next door is all pale blue and maroon plush. Facials, manicures, pedicures, nail sculpturing, and body wraps are done in private rooms, and the shop sells its own line of cosmetics as well as select European ones. Odom's doesn't do hair, but Roger Bob at the **Rustic Continental Studio** (1375½ East 53rd Street) is famous for his creative scissors work. Named "best colorful hairdresser" by *Chicago* magazine in 1979, Bob also provides livery service from O'Hare and the suburbs in his Jaguar XKE and treats his clients to periodic fashion shows, jazz concerts, dinners, and barbecues. The shop overflows with collectibles, many of which are for sale—to his beauty-parlor customers only.

For chic duds, head to **The Source,** in the Village Center at Lake Park Avenue and Hyde Park Boulevard. The trendy accessories, designer sportswear, silks, and sultry evening things attract savvy shoppers from all over the city. The Hyde Park Shopping Center (Lake Park Avenue and 55th Street), another urban renewal legacy, houses **Fritz on 55th,** which sells conservative evening wear, dresses, sportswear, and jewelry, and **Cohn & Stern,** purveyors of designer and college looks for men. **The Co-op** grocery, Hyde Park's answer to Treasure Island, dominates the center, which has several other clothing stores and the usual neighborhood supply and service-type shops.

Three excellent bookstores share the 57th Street strip between Kimbark and Harper Avenues with an unimpressive assortment of groceries, cleaners, and restaurants. Browsing at **Powell's** (1501 East 57th Street) can easily occupy several days. Perhaps the largest used-books store in the city, it is bursting with books: shelves of literary criticism, foreign language, ancient history, modern poetry, drama, fiction, scholarly, and children's books; thousands of paperbacks; bargain-table clearances; stacks on the floor; and occasionally even boxes of freebies outside. Most used books still in print go for about half price; many are reviewers' or sample copies of works just published. Since Powell's often buys entire collections, lots of rare and out-of-print volumes can be found. Prices vary with market conditions. **O'Gara's** (1311 East 57th Street) also has an extensive, excellent selection of used hardbacks and paperbacks, especially in history, the arts, philosophy, and theology. Well-lit and orderly (unlike Powell's), the store looks like a movie version of a second-hand-books shop. **Staver's** (1301 East 57th Street), the strip's new paperback outlet, is in an English basement, appropriately enough, stocks lots of Penguin and other imported editions with a nonfiction concentration—history, arts-and-crafts, Americana, mathematics. Books are plastic-wrapped to protect them from grubby hands, but patrons may unwrap them to browse.

The Green Door bookstore used to be in front of the **Medici Gallery and Coffee House** (1450 East 57th Street) but, years ago, the Medici expanded to specialize in pan pizza. The restaurant also serves excellent hamburgers and a variety of hot chocolate and coffee drinks. Art on the walls and some of the old coffee-house atmosphere remain, making it a popular local hang-out. A branch of **Edwardo's** down the block (1321 East 57th Street), a white-wash-and-planty sort of place, serves deep-dish and stuffed pizza.

Several Hyde Park restaurants look much better than the food tastes. Most try to keep their prices within student range. Even The Court House, long the neighborhood's most serious fine-dining contender, has switched gears to become **Casa Segunda,** a moderately priced Mexican place serving fresh fish and some unusual dishes, as well as the basics. At the least expensive end of the spectrum, **Valois,** a cafeteria at 1518 East 53rd Street, has been dishing up hearty, just-like-Mom-used-to-make, all-American grub at rock-bottom prices for about 60 years. Cops and cabbies eat here (no one "dines"); the Hopperesque place looks grubby but really isn't; and the motto is "See your food"!

Everyone complains about Hyde Park's lack of night life, but there are adequate diversions for those in the know. **Court Theatre** offers quality productions almost year round (*see Theater*); there are always loads of classical-music concerts; and the university sponsors film series and other special events. Although the Compass and other 55th Street bars which spawned the Second City are gone, a couple of local spots—**Chances R** (in Harper Court), and the **Valhalla Pub** (1515 East 53rd Street)—have live jazz at times. The juke box at **The Cove** (1750 East 55th Street) was rated one of the five best in the city by *Chicago* magazine and boasts more than 100 jazz discs ranging from Duke Ellington to Deodato.

The Woodlawn Tap (1172 East 55th Street), known by everyone as **"Jimmy's,"** is the last of the great university watering holes on 55th. University types and regulars hang out at this squalid, noisy place, playing chess or backgammon and arguing with the notoriously erudite bartenders who have on hand an *Encyclopaedia Britannica* and a Webster's *Second International* to settle disputes. More refined sorts used to frequent The Eagle (5311 South Blackstone Avenue), which was as much a museum of 1930s memorabilia as it was a bar. The Eagle closed in the fall of 1981 and was replaced by a **Giordano's** stuffed-pizza place. The loss can be blamed on *Chicago* magazine, which helped make Giordano's the big deal it is today!

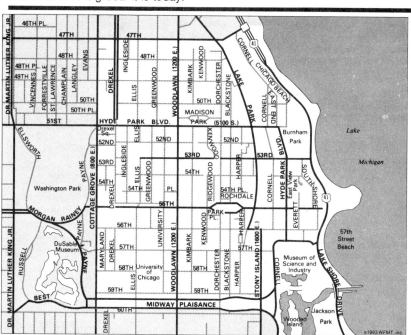

Interesting places

Augustana Lutheran Church
55th St. and Woodlawn Ave.
493-6451
Designed by Edward Dart in 1968, this smallish building translates classical church architecture into modern form. Occasional concerts.

Blackstone Branch Library
4904 S. Lake Park Ave.
624-0511
Chicago's oldest branch library was built in 1904. Oliver D. Grover's allegorical murals encircle the grand rotunda.

DuSable Museum of African American History
740 E. 56th Pl.
947-0600
(See Museums)

*First Unitarian Church
5650 S. Woodlawn Ave.
324-4100

Hyde Park Art Center
1701 E. 53rd St.
947-9656
Renowned in the '60s for its innovative exhibits of works by artists like the Hairy Who and the Nonplussed Some, this community art center mounts regular shows and has classes for adults and kids.

Hyde Park Bank and Trust Company
1525 E. 53rd St.
752-4600
Built in 1929 from a design by K. M. Vitzthum, the 11 stories house a restaurant on the top floor and the grand, gilt-ceilinged banking hall on the second and third. Marble floors and walls, immense bronze chandeliers, grates and grills, and a playful clock over the front entrance.

Hyde Park Historical Society Headquarters
5529 S. Lake Park Ave.
493-1893
The tiny building was once a cable-car ticket office and a comfort station for conductors. Open weekends.

Hyde Park Union Church
56th St. and Woodlawn
363-6063
The striking stained-glass windows in this Romanesque, red-brick building, dedicated in 1906, are foolers. Four modern-looking panels from the Tiffany studios predate the traditional, European-style ones and the rose window. The broad, shallow-peaked roof is supported by a system of beams, rather than by pillars, creating a very unusual space. Originally the Hyde Park Baptist Church, of which University of Chicago President William Rainey Harper was a member, the church still maintains close ties with the university.

*K.A.M. Isaiah Israel Congregation
1100 E. Hyde Park Blvd.
924-1234

*Kenwood District
Bounded roughly by 48th St., Blackstone Ave., Hyde Park Blvd., and Ellis Ave.

Museum of Science and Industry
57th St. and Lake Shore Dr.
684-1414
(See Museums)

*The Powhatan
1648 E. 50th St.

*St. Thomas the Apostle Church
Kimbark Ave. and 55th St.
324-2626

"Spirit of Hyde Park," mural
South wall, Illinois Central viaduct
57th St. at Lake Park Ave.
Astrid Fuller's 1973 wall painting of Hyde Parkers working and playing together is one of more than a dozen murals on I.C. viaducts and around the neighborhood. Several of the others also by Fuller.

*United Church of Hyde Park
1448 E. 53rd St.
363-1620
Music of the Baroque concerts take place here.

Interesting places: University of Chicago

*Administration Building
5801 S. Ellis Ave.
962-8369 (tours)

*Bartlett Gymnasium
5640 S. University Ave.

*Bond Chapel
1025 E. 58th St.

*Cobb Hall
5811 S. Ellis Ave.

*Hitchcock Hall
1009 E. 57th St.

*Mandel Hall/Mitchell Tower/Reynolds Club
57th St. and University Ave.
Lots of concerts and other activities here.

*Midway Studios
6016 S. Ingleside Ave.

*Ida Noyes Hall
1212 E. 59th St.

Oriental Institute
1155 E. 58th St.
753-2474
(See Museums)

**Renaissance Society
at the University of
Chicago**
Cobb Hall, 4th floor
5811 S. Ellis Ave.
962-8670
*The name is misleading:
This gallery, known for its
pioneering modern art ex-
hibits, mounted some of the
earliest Midwestern shows
of works by artists like Miró,
Klee, Matisse, and Kandin-
ski. The annual November
"Art for Young Collectors
Sale" is a must.*

*Robie House
5757 S. Woodlawn Ave.
962-8369 (tours)

***Rockefeller Memorial
Chapel**
5850 S. Woodlawn Ave.
753-3381 (tours)

**David and Alfred Smart
Gallery**
5550 S. Greenwood Ave.
753-2121
(See Museums)

Shopping
and services

Bob's Newsstand
5100 S. Lake Park Ave.
684-5100
*One of the largest selections
of periodicals in the city—
thousands.*

Boyajian's Bazaar
1305 E. 53rd St.
324-2020
*Asian, African, and Near
Eastern handicrafts and
giftware in a pleasant store.*

**Breslauer's
Department Store**
1236 E. 53rd St.
493-5395
*An old-line department
store that's been a neighborhood fixture for more
than half a century. A bit of
everything at reasonable
prices, including a good
selection of old-fashioned
cotton print fabrics.*

*Cohn & Stern
1502 E. 55th St.
752-8100

***Contemporary
Craftsman**
Hyde Park Hilton
4900 S. Lake Shore Dr.
493-6900
*Moved from Harper Court in
May 1981, after being a
long-time fixture there.*

*Co-op Super Mart
1526 E. 55th St.
667-1444
*This cooperative grocery
store started in a Quonset
hut, but now rivals the snazziest North Side places.*

For U Service Center
1608 E. 53rd St.
667-2800
*One of the few places where
you rent space to fix your
car. You can rent-a-wreck,
too.*

*Fritz on 55th
1500 E. 55th St.
288-5454

House of Gandhi
1457 E. 53rd St.
643-1100
*Natural-foods store with a
sit-down juice bar.*

*O'Gara's
1311 E. 57th St.
363-0993

The Pinocchio
1517 E. 53rd St.
241-5512
Another good toy store.

*Powell's
1501 E. 57th St.
955-7780

***Rustic Continental
Studio**
1375½ E. 53rd St.
288-7080
Appointments are essential!

Seminary Co-op
5757 S. University Ave.
752-4381
*This co-op bookstore (there
are about 8,000 share-
holding members) carries
academic books on every-
thing except the physical
sciences, and has very
good sections on philoso-
phy, theology, political science, and art history.*

**The Singular Group
Creative Arts
Cooperative/
VOV Gallery**
First Unitarian Church
57th St. and Woodlawn
324-4100
*Artisans 21 members who
chose not to move to Harper
Court formed the nucleus of
this group that sells its
wares—paintings,
ceramics, jewelry, etc.
Closed July and August.*

*The Source
1509 E. Hyde Park Blvd.
667-5366

*Staver Book Sellers
1301 E. 57th St.
667-3227
*Also carries Tintin and
Asterix comics.*

**University of Chicago
Bookstore**
970 E. 58th St.
753-3311, 962-8729
*The best university book-
store in town. Managed by
Stuart Brent, the general
books department has
excellent psychology, en-
gineering, physics, eco-
nomics, and fiction sections
with lots of interesting, offbeat titles.*

University of Chicago Continuing Education Program
1307 E. 60th St.
753-3137
Offers all sorts of general interest and scholarly courses—from Chicago Neighborhoods to Modern Astronomy—at three locations: on campus, at Spertus College (618 S. Michigan Ave.), and at 190 E. Delaware Pl. Also sponsors forums, at various locations, and study tours to places like the Stratford, Ontario, Shakespeare Festival and Russia.

Shopping and services: *Harper Court

Art Directions
5211 S. Harper Ave.
493-6158
Supplies for all sorts of arts and crafts from painting and calligraphy to woodworking and basket weaving.

*Artisans 21
5225 S. Harper Ave.
288-7450

Cooley's Corner
5211 S. Harper Ave.
363-4477
Paraphernalia for every room in the house: mugs, dishes, place mats, gadgets, scented soaps, bedroom accessories— a good place for gifts.

Freehling Pot and Pan
5210 S. Harper Ave.
643-8080
An extremely well-stocked kitchenware store with everything from appliances to tiny gadgets. Lots of quality pots and pans, too.

Fret Shop
5210 S. Harper Ave.
667-6310
This is the local source for old and new stringed instruments, books, classes, repairs—and advice.

Harper Court Sports
5225 S. Harper Ave.
363-3748
Excellent prices on custom-strung racquets and speedy repair services, as well as sports clothing and running shoes.

Harper Lights
5210 S. Harper Ave.
667-6228
A very up-to-date, though cluttered, lamp store.

Hobby Cellar
5210 S. Harper Ave.
643-4777
This outgrowth of Toys Et Cetera packs a lot into a little space. Big, expensive, "G" gauge, L.G.B. model trains (engines can weigh 20 lbs. and cost $400; tracks are solid brass) and smooth-sailing Seifert model boats from Germany are for a grown-up budget, but kids will find more affordable versions, along with kites, plastic-model kits, and role-playing and fantasy games. Classes in balsa plane building and Dungeons & Dragons.

Jack's Book Center
5211 S. Harper Ave.
643-1900
Strong on new and hard-to-find fiction, mysteries, science fiction, home improvement, and cook-books, and they're all arranged alphabetically to make finding things easy.

J's Pipe Shop
5225 S. Harper Ave.
288-5151
This small pipe and tobacco shop has a walk-in humidor to keep your cigars fresh as . . . well, not exactly a daisy.

*Odom's Cosmetique
5200 S. Harper Ave.
752-3600

Plants Alive
5210 S. Harper Ave.
667-2036
Crammed full of lush greenery. Even the weeds outside look cared for.

*Scan
5201 S. Harper Ave.
324-9010
Hyde Park's only new-furniture store has two huge floors full of Danish modern teak, rosewood, and oak, as well as upholstered sofas and chairs, rugs, designer housewares, etc.

The Sewing Circle
5225 S. Harper Ave.
363-5237
Prices of fabrics are more reasonable and the stock is broader than one might expect at a store this size. Classes, too.

Sunflower Seed Health Foods
5210 S. Harper Ave.
363-1600
All the usual.

*Toys Et Cetera
5206 S. Harper Ave.
324-6039
Probably one of the best, most thoughtfully stocked, toy stores in the city.

Dining and drinking

*Casa Segunda
5211 S. Harper Ave.
667-4008
The former Court House's teak floor and tables go well with the new image.

*Edwardo's
1321 E. 57th St.
241-7960
Stuffed pizza is the specialty here, but it is rather bland and uninteresting.

*Giordano's
5311 S. Blackstone Ave.
947-0200

Harper Square
1501 E. 53rd St.
241-6592
A few fresh-fish dishes and Greek specials make this handsome place more appealing than the average coffee shop, but the food has a bad local reputation.

House of Eng
1701 E. 53rd St.
324-6200
Take a drink out onto the balcony for a great view of the city. The food is run-of-the-mill Chinese at higher-than-average prices.

Mallory's
1525 E. 53rd St.
241-5600
The high-ceilinged room is a knockout, but the culinary pretensions far exceed the quality of the food in this penthouse restaurant.

*Medici Pan Pizza
1450 E. 57th St.
667-7394
The deep-dish pizza has its fans.

Mellow Yellow
1508 E. 53rd St.
667-2000
The warm, "North Side" décor would be a delight, were it not for the disco music. Machine-made crêpes are often filled with unappetizing glop. A favorite meeting place for early-morning coffee.

Morry's Deli
5500 S. Cornell Ave.
363-3800
Popular full-service deli serves good sandwiches and hot dogs (ice-cream cones, too) to eat in or to take out. Morry's also has a branch in the University of Chicago Bookstore and a fried-fish take-out spot at 1603 E. 55th St.

Orly's
1660 E. 55th St.
643-5500
Fun food came to Hyde Park in mid-1981 and was greeted with open arms.

Ribs 'n' Bibs
5300 S. Dorchester Ave.
493-0400
This joint sells some of the best take-out ribs around. The spicy sauce is liquid fire!

Seafruit
1461 E. Hyde Park Blvd.
493-0972
Sample fried fish, soul-food style, in the safety of Hyde Park. Small salad bar offers a few good relishes. Adjoining fish store.

T.J.'s Restaurant
5500 S. South Shore Dr.
643-3600
Steaks and seafood with some interesting specials.

*Valois
1518 E. 53rd St.
667-0647
Standing rib roast is an outstanding buy, and home-made biscuits and dumplings are excellent. Don't be put off by the atmosphere.

*The Woodlawn Tap
1172 E. 55th St.
643-5516

Entertainment

Blue Gargoyle
5655 S. University Ave.
955-4108
Occasional entertainment runs the gamut from folk concerts to multimedia "performances." A health-food snack shop is open for lunch. The Gargoyle sponsors various youth-oriented, community-service programs and is located in the handsome University Church-Disciples of Christ.

*Chances R
5225 S. Harper Ave.
363-1550
Hamburgers are okay, but Saturday-night jazz parties are the main attractions.

*Court Theatre
5535 S. Ellis Ave.
753-4472, 962-7005
(See Theater)

*The Cove
1750 E. 55th St.
684-1013
Quiet bar catering to university students. Very infrequent big-band performances; excellent jazz juke box.

University of Chicago Student Activities Office
Ida Noyes Hall
1212 E. 59th St.
753-3591
753-2150 (events)

*Valhalla Pub
1515 E. 53rd St.
241-6827
Disco music blares at this neighborhood bar, except on weekends when there's live jazz.

Rebuilding the Columbian's Palace of Fine Art for the new Museum of Science and Industry, 1932

South Shore

In South Shore's heyday, when the South Shore Country Club was the private playground of the privileged, the future promised unending prosperity. No one could prophesy the ravages that racial change and white flight would bring. Enviably situated along the lakefront and served by rapid transportation to the Loop, the neighborhood developed strong community organizations and a healthy commercial base. By 1930, it had experienced three decades of astonishing growth. Not even the Depression dampened local boosters' spirits. While Chicago's population doubled between 1900 and 1940, South Shore's increased eightfold to 80,000.

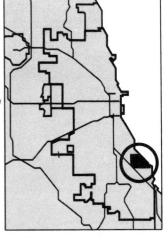

South Shore's early development paralleled much of Chicago's. The Illinois Central Railroad station at 71st Street and Jeffery Boulevard was opened in 1881 to accommodate the hamlet of Bryn Mawr's 30-odd homes. A few years later, pioneer developer Frank Bennett bought the Ferdinand Rohn farm and built the first subdivision, which he called South Kenwood. Many of his houses still stand on Euclid Avenue between 71st and 73rd Streets. At the turn of the century, most of South Shore was still rural. The Windsor Park Country Club occupied an 80-acre tract from South Colfax to South Yates Avenues between East 75th and 79th Streets, an amusement pier brought day-trippers to the sandy beach at East 75th Street, and East 79th Street remained farm land.

By 1930, however, South Shore was one of the South Side's most desirable upper-middle-class communities. Although the population was cosmopolitan, a country-wide mania for things Tudor dictated subdivision names like Chatham Field, Avalon Highlands, and Cheltingham—originally called Hoboken! Many of the homes were English-style cottages. The grandest legacies of the feverish construction activity are the **Jackson Highlands** and the lakefront high-rises (7321 S. South Shore Drive, designed by De Golyer, is the city's only residential tower on the National Register of Historic Places).

The Highlands is an ironically named plot between Jeffery Boulevard and Stony Island Avenue overlooking Jackson Park, a low-lying marsh until early in the century. The first residents were a diverse lot, ranging from successful businessmen to acclaimed artists. Edward Kemeys sculpted the lions which guard the Art Institute's portals in a studio behind his house at **7209 South Euclid Ave-**

nue. Today, the same sorts of people live in these large, elegant homes lining South Euclid, Constance, and Bennett Avenues, between 67th and 71st Streets. Though built a bit later and on smaller lots, many of the houses rival Kenwood's, and are South Shore's most valued properties.

Four local institutions testify to South Shore's meteoric rise, even more rapid decline, and present arduous stabilization. The **South Shore Country Club** (7059 S. South Shore Drive), organized in 1906 by Prairie Avenue resident Lawrence Huyworth, quickly became the center of activity for South Shore's, if not the South Side's, social set. The main structure of the handsome neo-Spanish, stucco-covered complex designed by Marshall and Fox dates from 1916. Suffering from declining membership throughout the 1960s, the club folded in 1974. Now everyone can play the links and wander in awe through the clubhouse, although the opulent furnishings were auctioned off before the property was purchased by the Chicago Park District. The city's Mounted Police Patrol is headquartered in the club's stables, but plans for the rest of this National-Register facility are in flux and the subject of much neighborhood controversy. The renovated gates may look forbidding, but drive on in: It's all ours.

The **Bryn Mawr Community Church** (Jeffery Boulevard and 70th Street) attracted many of the same local luminaries as the country club. Because of his connection with the English Sunday School Movement, an English churchman, Albert Gardner, was asked to organize the church, which had begun as a children's Bible-story center. The first church building, patterned after a Northern Italian Protestant one, was built in 1916. For the next decade, Bryn Mawr was South Shore's non-denominational Protestant church, attracting a very affluent congregation including the chairman of the board of Standard Oil and many Illinois Central executives. In 1926, the original building was moved back on the lot and the present, beautiful, English Gothic church was erected. The church had difficulty weathering the Depression, but enjoyed a resurgence after the war when young families used their G.I. Bill money to buy hundreds of homes in the area. The congregation numbered 3,000 by 1960, and more building plans were afoot when racial panic hit. Today, 400 local members, half white and half black, are approaching real social integration. Pastor Jim Shiflett is returning the church to its roots, incorporating Bible-story dramatizations and—recalling the days of the Bryn Mawr Players—a theater.

The **Church of St. Philip Neri** (72nd Street and Merrill Avenue) was completed in 1926 to open for the International Eucharistic Congress held in Chicago that year. The magnificent structure, styled on the grand English cathedrals, can seat more than 1,500. The Stations of the Cross are exquisite mosaics executed in Rome by P. Dachiardi in 1920; the clerestory stained-glass windows above the oak wainscotting pair male and female saints; the ornate altar and painted, beamed ceiling are masterpieces. The lavish building attests to the affluence of the lace-curtain Irish who were central to South Shore's life through 1950. Unfortunately, the congregation has dwindled to 600, and the Irish have, for the most part, scattered throughout the city.

For years, South Shore (like Hyde Park) was mistakenly considered to be a "Jewish" neighborhood. It has, in fact, always been predominantly Christian, although the Jewish population was substantial until the 1960s. The South Shore Congregation was established in the early 1920s and held services in a small, wooden house at Jeffery Boulevard and 72nd Street until 1928, when the temple was built on the site. The huge, adjoining auditorium was added about 20 years later. The congregation continued to swell through the 1950s, fed, in part, by immigrants from racially changing Englewood. But the 1960s and early '70s brought a virtual exodus from South Shore: Younger families moved to the suburbs—typically Skokie—and older residents with stronger South Side loyalties moved to Hyde Park. The temple building is now the **Old Landmark Church Holiness in Christ.**

Postwar population shifts on the South Side also increased South Shore's Greek community, which built the magnificent Byzantine SS. Constantine and Helen in 1946. Twenty-six years later, the church followed its congregation to Palos Hills and the church became **Masjid Honorable Elijah Muhammad** (Stony Island Avenue and 73rd Street). The Black Muslims also own the neighborhood's former **Swedish Club** (Ridgeland Avenue at 73rd Place), a rambling Tudor structure behind the mosque, which is used as a community house. During the 1920s, '30s, and '40s, the building was the social center for a substantial Swedish community. Businessmen made deals over lunch; the halls housed social events; and many of South Shore's civic clubs met here weekly.

Unlike some Chicago neighborhoods that have experienced drastic racial resegregation, South Shore isn't filled with burned-out hulks and empty HUD houses awaiting the arsonist's torch. Although claims that the community is on its way back up are best taken with a dash of salt, decay has probably been arrested. The South Shore Bank's commitment of energy and assets to revitalization has helped. Several blocks of three-story apartment buildings near Stony Island Avenue have been renovated, and most of the cottages and two-flats on the side streets are well maintained. Business areas remain the biggest problems.

The South Side's most elegant stores once embraced both sides of the railroad tracks running along East 71st Street, but the specialty shops, restaurants, and professional offices that attracted shoppers from miles around are all gone. In their place (behind iron grates) are bars, wiggeries, record shops, and neighborhood service places. Always a notch below East 71st Street, East 75th Street and East 79th Street host the same kinds of stores, as well as grubby take-out joints, readers and advisors, childcare and tutoring facilities, and garages.

There is, however, some wheat mixed in with the chaff. At **The Workbench** (7048 South Stony Island Avenue), Kiyoshi Tanouye has been custom-crafting hardwood bookcases, dining room tables, desks, kitchen counters, and cabinetry for twenty years. Although most of the costly furniture is contemporary in style, Tanouye is dedicated to building things people can't find elsewhere. The **A & A Boutique** (2106 East 71st Street) is crowded with nice sportswear, some disco sleaze, and some silk. **Creative Fashions** (1949 East 71st Street) has a strong local following for its smart women's clothes, and the sparsely stocked **Rochon's Store for Men** (2100 East 71st Street) carries designer men's wear. **Shirley's Hallmark** (1944 East 71st Street), a landmark of sorts, was the first black-owned Hallmark franchise in the country. **Drew Sales** (1964 East 73rd Street) is the only store outside the Loop to specialize in Masonic lodge regalia. African masks, baskets, and other artworks can be found at **The Native Shop** (2606 East 79th Street), along with some incongruous head-shop ephemera.

Dining in South Shore is problematical. Restaurants like the Kickapoo (formerly at Stony Island Avenue and 79th Street), a low, stucco-covered steak-and-chop house that attracted everyone from mobsters to the carriage trade, are only a fond memory. **Alexander's** (3010 East 79th Street) is the last of the old-line places. The large room, with a handsome 1950s bar stretching along one wall, is crammed with overstuffed vinyl banquettes. Steaks and seafood are the staples here, and standing rib roast is the specialty. Although nothing to write home about, adequate dinners are in the $10 range.

The Essex Restaurant (1652 East 79th Street) is the soul-food equivalent of the little Lithuanian spots a few miles west in Marquette Park. Smothered chicken, ham hocks and greens, and chicken and dumplings are casually served at this faded, luncheonette-type place for less than $4.

Take-out rib joints dot the neighborhood. **Thomas Bar-B-Q** (2347 East 75th

Street) may well be the best. The owner minds the pit while supervising his young crew, which is kept busy passing the smoky, meaty ribs and topnotch fried chicken to hungry crowds on the other side of the bullet-proof partition. Phoning ahead will reduce the wait. Ask for the sauce on the side or your french fries will be reduced to a soggy mess.

Interesting places

*Bryn Mawr Community Church
Jeffery Blvd. and 70th St.
324-2403

*Church of St. Philip Neri
72nd St. and Merrill Ave.
363-1700

Haven of Rest Missionary Baptist Church
7901 S. Stony Island Ave.
375-4489
Broadcasts gospel services on Sundays, 8-9 a.m. (WMPP) and 3-4 p.m. (WBEE). The rococo-Moorish building, a reflection in miniature of the Miracle Temple Church, has been everything from a dance hall to an American Legion post.

**Lawrence Huyworth House
South Shore Historical Society Museum**
7651 S. South Shore Dr.
375-5397
Headquarters of the South Shore Historical Society. When Huyworth, founder of the South Shore Country Club, bought the house, it had been barged from Hyde Park to one block east of its present location. He moved the house west after it was almost swept into the lake by a storm. The historical society plans to restore the house for adaptive re-use with community meeting rooms, a library, and display galleries.

*Jackson Highlands
S. Constance, Bennett, and Euclid Aves. between E. 67th and 71st Sts. are lined with beautiful old homes. More are scattered east of Jeffery as far south as 75th and on South Shore Dr. down to 79th.

*Edward Kemeys House
7209 S. Euclid Ave.
A private home. Furniture designer George Clingman lived at 7210.

*Masjid Honorable Elijah Muhammad
7351 S. Stony Island Ave.
667-7200

Miracle Temple Church
1645 E. 79th St.
768-8955
Formerly the Avalon Theater, this grand, rococo-Moorish building was one of the smaller Balaban & Katz neighborhood theaters—hard as that is to believe.

Oak Woods Cemetery
1035 E. 67th St.
288-3800
A beautiful cemetery founded in 1853. A large monument honors the Confederate prisoners who perished at Camp Douglas. Paul Cornell, William Hale "Big Bill" Thompson, Enrico Fermi, and Jesse Owens are among the notables buried here.

*Old Landmark Church Holiness in Christ
Jeffery Blvd. and 72nd St.
955-1409

Our Lady of Peace
79th St. and Jeffery Blvd.
768-0105
A grand, Beaux-Arts, graystone Catholic church built in 1933.

Charles Ringer Company
7915 S. Exchange Ave.
This delightful building has a grand, bank-lobby-style main floor with English oak paneling and a Tudor beamed ceiling. Built soon after Ringer subdivided the Windsor Park Country Club in 1923, it hasn't changed much since then.

*South Shore Country Club
7059 S. South Shore Dr.
363-2255
Officially Park No. 429 and currently undergoing renovation. The pergola is in danger, however, because the Park District doesn't have a half million dollars to restore a "decorative element."

*Swedish Club
Ridgeland Ave. at 73rd Pl.

Frederick Wilkinson House
7660 S. South Shore Dr.
This private home was built by the founder of the Hyde Park Herald, *Chicago's oldest community newspaper, in 1880; it joined five other houses on a sandy wasteland. Wilkinson's daughter, Elia, literary editor of the* Chicago Tribune, *married Robert Peattie, who became a Chicago correspondent for the* New York Times. *Their son, Donald Culross, was a well-known natural-history writer. The façade has been much modernized.*

Shopping and services

*A & A Boutique
2106 E. 71st St.
493-7272

*Creative Fashions
1949 E. 71st St.
684-8773

*Drew Sales
1964 E. 73rd St.
752-1700

Mr. T and Company
1922 E. 71st St.
643-4900
Thomas Hayden, the owner of this beauty salon, is a nationally known hairstylist. Movie stars, such as Cecily Tyson, and other luminaries visit the shop when they're in town.

*The Native Shop
2606 E. 79th St.
221-3577

*Rochon's Store for Men
2100 E. 71st St.
363-9678

*Shirley's Hallmark
1944 E. 71st St.
363-1944

Sportsman Seafood
2158 E. 71st St.
684-7930
The neighborhood's most salubrious fresh and deep-fried seafood take-out place: catfish, buffalo, jack salmon.

WGN Flag and Decorating Co.
7984 S. South Chicago
768-8076
A 56-year-old institution with four buildings of flags, flagpoles, pennants, and banners for every business and occasion. Bring in a design and WGN will make a flag for you. The company also builds floats and sells float materials.

*The Workbench
7048 S. Stony Island Ave.
363-1957

Dining and drinking

*Alexander's Steak House
3010 E. 79th St.
768-6555

*The Essex Restaurant
1652 E. 79th St.
734-0032

Leon's Bar-B-Q
1640 E. 79th St.
731-1454
One of Leon Finney's several places. Good barbecue.

*Thomas Bar-B-Q
2347 E. 75th St.
221-4265
Many prefer it to Leon's.

Southeast Side

From the Chicago Skyway's antiseptic heights, the city's southeast section—part of the country's largest concentration of steelworks—is a miasma-covered wasteland akin to murky hinterlands like Gary. It is cut off from Chicago's heartland by distance, railroad tracks, waterways, and huge industrial tracts. People in the communities clustered along the Calumet River's despoiled banks have adjusted to their isolation. They take a certain pride in 10th Ward Alderman "Fast Eddie" Vrdolyak's antics; support their own newspaper, the *Daily Calumet;* and live the American work ethic, sustained by their churches on Sundays and the steelworkers' union during the week.

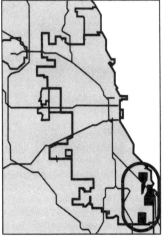

But for an historical accident, the remote-seeming Southeast Side might have been Chicago's center. In its natural state, the mouth of the Calumet River was very similar to the Chicago River's. The Federal government survey party sent to select a fortification site at Lake Michigan's edge in the early 1800s considered both locations and observed that the Calumet region even offered an interior harbor—Lake Calumet. Legend has it that one of the team's army officer's love for an Indian maiden determined Fort Dearborn's Chicago River location.

The 1833 Lake Michigan–Mississippi River canal route survey chose the Calumet River, but the Chicago won again. The party was led by a man with a penchant for lost causes—Jefferson Davis. While Chicago grew, the Calumet region stagnated. George Ewing bought a huge chunk of it from an Indian woman for $1,000 in 1851 but by 1860 only five houses had been built. Development didn't take off until the Federal government dredged the harbor in 1870. Railroads crisscrossed the area by 1873, and James Bowen's Calumet and Chicago Canal and Dock Company platted the land to the west of the river's mouth (the river runs north and south, taking a dogleg east at 91st Street to drain into the lake) in 1875.

The first steelworks opened at 109th Street and the river the following year, a harbinger of the heavy industry that would eventually span thousands of acres all the way to Indiana. Sparked by the destruction the Chicago Fire caused and spurred by the Illinois Central's commuter line reaching 91st Street in 1883, the neighborhood of South Chicago and the 91st Street–Commercial Avenue shopping area were firmly established by the turn of the century.

The years have taken their toll on "Millgate" and "The Bush," the oldest sections of South Chicago. The Poles who flocked to work at what is now the **U.S. Steel South Works** in the 1890s built inexpensive homes—mostly two- and three-story frame houses and apartment flats. The community's creative energies seem to have been lavished on **St. Michael** (83rd Street and South Shore Drive). The common-brick façade of this former bishopric belies a magnificent, European-style cathedral interior. St. Michael's lush stained glass, carved altars, intricate ribbing, and detailed ceiling frescos all command attention. The **Immaculate Conception B.V.M. Church** (Commercial Avenue and 88th Street) is also worth a visit. The oval-shaped nave's walls, arches, and ceiling are richly polychromed in pastels, and the arcades are lined with figural stained glass. At both churches, memorial services for the dead are likely to be for those with Polish surnames, while wedding bans list Spanish ones.

South Chicago's main business strip, which begins at 87th Street and continues along Commercial Avenue to 92nd Street, reflects the same sweeping ethnic change and is a bit run down. The **Polka Home Style Sausage Company** (8753) is a good place to stock up on homemade sausages, cold cuts, and the raw ingredients for duck-blood soup. (A long-time neighborhood fixture, Polka has a second store in East Chicago.) Naturally, there are lots of taco restaurants, and the nicest is **Cocula Restaurant** (8911). A huge, naïve mural above the door hints at the selection, which includes goat, brains, tripe, tongue, and al pastor (Mexican gyros). Licuados, blended fresh-fruit coolers, are good here, too. The **San Luis Restaurant and Bar** (9141 South Houston Avenue) has a full menu and boasts a live dance band on weekends (as do a couple of less appealing places). The music is loud, and the scene may appear slightly menacing, but entire families make an evening of it here.

Sonny's Inn (3102 East 91st Street) is the neighborhood's last Polish-style restaurant. The former railroad station is divided into two rooms: a bright, crowded diner and a warmer-feeling, memorabilia-filled, taproom. The menu's the same in both: a couple of inexpensive plate lunches; a few sandwiches; and enormous (half-pound-plus), freshly ground burgers—a treat and a best buy. Locals from all walks of life stop in on weekdays (closed weekends).

For dessert and an instant trip to the past, check out **Gayety Candy and Ice Cream** (9211 South Commercial Avenue). The low butterfat ice cream is only fair (and the candy's worse, except for hard-to-find dark chocolate turtles), but freshly whipped cream and fresh fruit-salad topping make a vanilla sundae bearable while you drink in the shop's charming old-fashioned ambiance. Good hot chocolate served in wonderfully thick cups is a winter warmer.

Foodstuffs are really the most exciting buys along Commercial Avenue. The clothing, shoe, and neighborhood service shops are ordinary, as is the little Goldblatt's, save for its '30s façade.

"Slag Valley," part of South Chicago's original subdivision, is cut off from the area north of 95th Street by railroad embankments and the Skyway. This Yugoslavian enclave backs on **Wisconsin Steel's** slag-processing land and faces the American Shipbuilding Co. The setting isn't salubrious, but Slag Valleyites experience the beautiful sunsets only pollutant-rich air can provide.

St. Archangel Michael (Commercial Avenue and 98th Street), an onion-domed, Serbian Orthodox church, rises above the industrial squalor and overlooks a few taverns right out of the Old Country. On Saturdays after 9 p.m., tamburitza music—occasionally by the famous Popovich Brothers—passionate singing, and dancing fill **The Rafters** (9757). Entertainment at **Casino Liquors** (9706) is usually confined to the television set, but the huge portions of well-prepared Serbian specialties at ridiculously low prices are diverting enough. This is strictly a no-frills operation catering to locals, but the long-time owners (who are selling) are comfortably bilingual, so the menu's mysteries can be explained.

Croatian Hall (9618), once the scene of some mighty parties, now houses one of the Democratic Party's mighties. Edward Vrdolyak's law firm occupies part of the building and the 10th Ward Democratic Club some of the rest. Very cozy. Across the street is one of several private picnic grounds. The wood-roofed patches of open space were treasured before the park system reached this far south; they are still used.

More than the Calumet River separates the East Side from her sister mill communities. Although early German and Swedish settlers built large houses in the late 1800s (some can be seen on the east side of Avenue H between 97th and 98th Streets) and one of the oldest sections (100th to 106th Streets west of Ewing) resembles other 19th-century, working-class areas, much of the neighborhood could be part of Hammond, Indiana, which it abuts. There's a Hoosier quality about the ethnically diverse, neat subdivisions.

In 1880, about 1,000 hardy souls lived on the East Side, where the land east of Ewing Avenue was mostly swamp. During the first two decades of this century, several small developments replaced farms south of 106th Street on Avenues H and J. The largest development, however, was Frank Lewis's Fair Elms Estates, a multiacre tract from Buffalo Avenue to the Indiana state line between 108th and 114th Streets. Fair Elms was conceived as a community of typical Chicago-style, brick three-flats, but the plan was changed with the post-World War One demand for single-family houses. Two three-flats on 113th Street at Avenues G and L stand out like sore thumbs amid the hundreds of brick bungalows. With reduced population density, the planned commercial strip never came off, and the intersection of 106th Street and Ewing Avenue remains the entire neighborhood's primary shopping area.

For years, East Siders did their serious shopping in neighboring Hammond, but now suburban shopping malls such as River Oaks get their big bucks. Local shopping is lean, confined to a few clothing stores, gift shops, music outlets, and neighborhood service places, without any big chain-store anchor. Specialty sports stores reflect popular athletic activities. For example, **Branko's Sports World** (10411 South Ewing Avenue) specializes in soccer clothing and equipment, while **East Side Archery** (3711 East 106th Street) caters to hunting bowmen and also has a small indoor range.

Taverns, pizza joints, and restaurants outnumber the other businesses. The best-known eatery is the **Golden Shell** (10063 South Avenue N), in an old, rambling frame building with several dining rooms and a bar. The extremely wide-ranging menu includes Croatian, American, and Italian entrées, out-of-the-ordinary offerings like wild duck and rabbit, and a dozen fish choices. Except for good bread and real mashed potatoes, the food isn't exceptional, but large portions, moderate prices, weekend entertainment, and long serving hours make this place very popular with locals. **Giappo's** (4000 East 106th Street), formerly a branch of Giordano's, continues to serve stuffed pizza and sandwiches in a California-fast-food-style building that's slick by East Side norms.

To duplicate or surpass a Golden Shell meal at home, stock up at **D & M Foods and Liquors** (10500 South Ewing Avenue). This small store has a bit of everything: smoked meats, sausages, and Yugoslavian-style bacon; imported beers, wines, and liquors; ajvar (Balkan pepper relish); jams, grains, bargain-priced fruit syrups; Turkish coffee; and Yugoslavian newspapers. A visit to **Banner Liquor and Tap** (10606) provides a good selection of Yugoslavian wines and spirits.

There are several Mexican spots in the area; the best is the **Mexican Inn** (9510 South Ewing Avenue), a small but bustling restaurant that does a land-office take-out business with inexpensive, well-prepared tacos, tostadas, and enchiladas. Italian outlets include **La Bella Sorrento** (9485), a relaxing place with a full Italian menu, as well as all-you-can-eat specials Tuesday through Thursday. The **Continental Bakery** (3522 East 95th Street) half a block away roasts whole lambs and pigs on Sundays; ordering ahead is a good idea. Their koláčky and thick-crusted Italian bread are good, too.

To get the feel of the neighborhood on a warm summer weekend, stop at **Calumet Fisheries** (3259 East 95th Street) on the bridge leading to the East Side from South Chicago. Load up on topnotch fried shellfish, frog legs, and fish and chips; excellent smoked trout, sable, and chubs. Then, head east to hard-to-find **Calumet Park,** the only patch of public lakefront south of Rainbow Park. The large park's beach will be jammed and the drives clogged with youths showing off their cars. Join the families picnicking on the grass and reflect on the incongruities of urban life. The park's lakefront is hemmed in on both sides by ugly industrial tracts, but the land for the park was reclaimed from the lake, using slag as landfill. The 1924 field house, hailed as "the finest in the country, if not the world" at its dedication, was built with "popcorn" slag. The park also harbors a U.S. Coast Guard station and a yacht club.

"Where the Hell is Hegewisch?" asks a local T-shirt. To find out, take Avenue O south past the **Republic Steel** works to 130th Street. Highlights of Hegewisch include neat bungalows with huge TV antennas to pull in distant signals; 14 industrial waste dumps; Chicago's only sawmill; Wolf Lake, where Leopold and Loeb dumped Bobby Frank's body and Leopold inadvertently dropped his glasses—the clue to the crime's solution; Baltimore Street, a desultory shopping strip six blocks west of Avenue O; **Island Homes** (132nd Street and South Avenue F), the city's only trailer park; and the **Kolo Club** (13537 South Avenue O), the southeasternmost restaurant in the city. Serbian barbecue is king in this ramshackle building. Lamb and pork—sandwiches or dinners—are piquantly sauced and served with homemade sweet-and-sour peppers. A family-style combo includes lamb and pork, chicken, stuffed cabbage, and terrific homemade strudel.

After dinner, the easiest way to return to the city's center is to continue south to Brainard Avenue, make a hard right and travel northwest past the South Shore Railroad's little station at 135th Street to 130th Street, and take 130th west to the Calumet Expressway (I-94).

Interesting places

Calumet Harbor Lumber Co.
13651 S. Buffalo Ave.
646-1444
Started in 1922, this is Chicago's only sawmill.

*Calumet Park
9801 S. Ave. G
721-3925

Church of the Annunciata
111th St. and Ave. G
221-1040
A modern, semicircular church built in 1968. The parish's original church was built in the 1940s about a block away on land donated by Frank Lewis, developer of the surrounding area.

*Croatian Hall
9618 S. Commercial Ave.
374-8181

*Immaculate Conception B.V.M. Church
Commercial and 88th St.
768-0214

*Island Homes, Inc.
13240 S. Ave. F
646-2200

*Republic Steel Corp.
11600 S. Burley Ave.
933-4000
U.S. Steel signed a contract with the fledgling Steel Workers' Organization Committee in 1937, but Republic resisted for six years, leading to much local strife, including the 1937 Memorial Day "Massacre."

Sacred Heart Croatian Church
96th St. and Escanaba Ave.
768-1423
Modern church with a striking, stained-glass window was built by Croatians who split from St. George's congregation.

*St. Archangel Michael Serbian Orthodox Church
Commercial and 98th St.
375-3848
Built in 1926.

St. Francis de Sales
102nd St. between Ave. J
and Ewing Ave.
734-1383
*The East Side's oldest
Catholic parish. The present church was incorporated into the school building
after its magnificent predecessor burned in 1925. The
5,500-lb. bell, which had
been sitting in the priest's
yard for years, was then
mounted in the school's
tower.*

St. George Church
Ewing Ave. and 96th St.
734-0554
*A handsome brick church
built in 1903 by Slovenes
and Croatians.*

*St. Michael Church
83rd St. and South Shore
734-4921

St. Patrick's Church
Commercial and 95th St.
768-0721
*Although the present
church and school were
built in 1889, South Chi-
cago's oldest parish was
established in 1857.*

**St. Simeon Mirotocivi
Serbian Orthodox Church**
114th St. and Ave. G
375-8334
*This Eastern-style church,
covered with yellow and red
bricks forming intricate patterns, was built in 1968. The
congregation split from St.
Archangel Michael over political differences.*

*U.S. Steel South Works
3426 E. 89th St.
933-3000
*One of the country's largest
steelworks.*

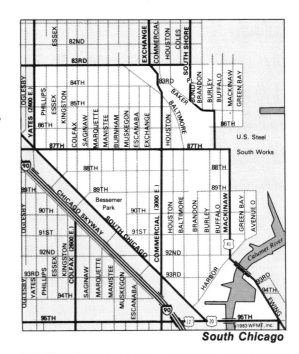

South Chicago

**United Steel Workers of
America Local 1033**
Memorial Hall
11731 S. Ave. O
646-0800
*Across from scene of 1937
Memorial Day march. A
small plaque on the
adjoining flagpole com-
memorates the "martyrs—
heroes—unionists shot
down May 30, 1937. . . ." A
small annual ceremony
honors them. The union hall
is used for social gatherings
as well as business.*

*Wisconsin Steel
2800 E. 106th St.
933-7000
*This is your best chance to
see a steel mill up close:
The fences around it are low
and there are none where
100th St. cuts through the
slag heap. Very surrealistic!*

Shopping
and services

*Banner Liquor and Tap
10606 S. Ewing Ave.
721-9393

*Branko's Sports World
10411 S. Ewing Ave.
375-2800

*Calumet Fisheries Inc.
3259 E. 95th St.
933-9855

The Clip Joint
3837 E. 106th St.
768-6806
*Surprise! As many men as
women get their hair styled
in this friendly, planty place.*

*Continental Bakery
3522 E. 95th St.
721-5940

***D & M Foods
and Liquors, Inc.**
10500 S. Ewing Ave.
374-5086

*East Side Archery
3711 E. 106th St.
721-0115

***Gayety Candy and
Ice Cream**
9211 S. Commercial Ave.
933-9867

***Polka Home Style
Sausage Company**
8753 S. Commercial Ave.
221-0395
10528 S. Ewing Ave.
768-5209
Also in Calumet City.

Dining
and drinking

*La Bella Sorrento
9485 S. Ewing Ave.
374-0030

*Casino Liquors
9706 S. Commercial Ave.
221-5189

*Cocula Restaurant
8911 S. Commercial Ave.
374-3214

The Cottage
525 S. Torrence Ave.,
Calumet City
891-3900
*A touch of class in the wil-
derness! The décor imitates
a French-countryside res-
taurant and the food is well-
prepared and rather ele-
gant. Limited blackboard
menu; dinners about $20.
The owners are a friendly
couple.*

*Giappo's Pizza
4000 E. 106th St.
734-4700

***Golden Shell
Restaurant & Bar**
10063 S. Ave. N
221-9876

*Kolo Club
13537 S. Ave. O
646-3052
*The paper place mats say
"If you're satisfied—tell
everyone—If you're not—
tell us." A satisfying place.*

*Mexican Inn
9510 S. Ewing Ave.
734-8957

Rupcich Restaurant
4040 E. 106th St.
375-7575
*Popular spot with local
business types.*

**Salvino's Restaurant
& Pizzeria**
10063 S. Ewing Ave.
375-7539
*A popular place that does a
big take-out business and
offers a full Italian menu in
comfortable surroundings.
Mediocre food; all-you-
can-eat weekday specials.*

Phil Smidt & Son
1205 N. Calumet Ave.,
Hammond, Ind.
219-659-0025
*Straightforward, old-line
place serving filling, decent
meals. Pan-fried perch is a
specialty.*

*Sonny's Inn
3102 E. 91st St.
221-0261

Entertainment

Avala Restaurant
9966 S. Commercial Ave.
375-3232
*Occasional Yugoslavian-
style entertainment: bands,
singing, kolo dancing.*

*The Rafters
9757 S. Commercial Ave.
731-0288

***San Luis Restaurant
and Bar**
9139-41 S. Houston Ave.
374-0734

Hegewisch

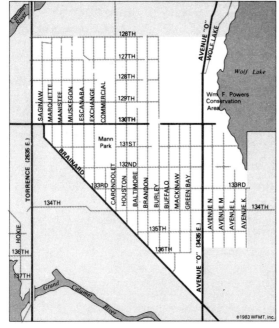

©1983 WFMT, Inc.

Pullman

Pullman, on the far Southeast Side, was voted the "most perfect" town in the world at the Prague International Hygienic and Pharmaceutical Exposition of 1896. Visiting the Pullman Historic District vividly recalls 19th-century political and social history. Designed in the 1880s by architect Solon S. Beman and landscaper Nathan Barrett for George Pullman around his Pullman Palace Car Works, this company town was unique in its attention to the workers' health and comfort. More than 80 percent of the original 1,800 buildings stand today, providing a lasting model of what was then Solomon-like community planning.

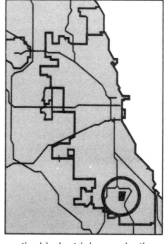

The town and its amenities were not a philanthropic venture. Not only did Pullman believe that well-housed workers would be more productive long before social scientists "proved" it, he also intended the development to produce a modest profit as part of a pioneer vertical industrial organization. (The brass and other raw materials for the railroad cars were manufactured at the works, as were the very bricks for the factory buildings and town.)

All did not go well in this would-be utopia. In 1889, dissatisfied residents voted for annexation to Chicago over Pullman's objections. The company reacted to the depression of 1893 with wage cuts and layoffs but didn't lower rents or utility charges. Intolerably burdened, many workers joined Eugene Debs's American Railway Union, which struck in 1894. After Pullman refused arbitration, the strike spread nationwide and became brutal. It was ultimately broken by Federal troops; Debs was jailed and the ARU immeasurably weakened. Shortly afterward, however, public outrage led to a court order forcing the company to divest itself of all nonindustrial property (and streets were renamed to expunge Pullman family names).

The company no longer manufactures railroad cars, but social history is still being forged in Pullman. The Historic Pullman Foundation has acquired major historic sites for restoration, is spearheading adaptive reuse of dilapidated factory buildings, is aiding in the rehabilitation of adjoining North Pullman, maintains a community center, publishes a quarterly newspaper, runs a monthly antiques fair, and conducts monthly walking tours as well as an annual house tour.

The foundation also owns and is restoring the **Florence Hotel** (11111 South Forrestville Avenue), the best place to begin a neighborhood tour. Opened in

1881, the four-story, 51-room, Queen Anne masterpiece boasted elegant public rooms, as well as a palatial owner's suite, and had many unusual features for its day: a servant call/fire-alarm bell system, indoor plumbing, gas lights, and central heating supplied by the town's Corliss steam engine (which had earlier supplied power to Philadelphia's Centennial Exposition, where Queen Anne architecture was first introduced to the United States). Volunteers give guided tours of the public areas and refurbished Pullman suite daily, from 11 a.m. to 2 p.m. The beautifully appointed dining room makes a delightful spot for lunch.

Armed with a walking-tour map, take to the streets to see Pullman. Not surprisingly, the company-town's housing was stratified by corporate position. The grandest homes are the free-standing duplexes built for executives on East 111th Street, behind the hotel. Foremen lived in the largest row houses along South St. Lawrence Avenue between the hotel and the **Greenstone Church** (St. Lawrence Avenue and 112th Street), built as a nondenominational meeting house in a country-English Tudor style and named for the mineral cast of its serpentine rock. Housing for skilled craftsmen lines the street for a block south of the Greenstone, which is now a Methodist church. With the exception of the executives' houses, the differences between the homes of the select and humbler workers are less important than their similarities. They are all muted Queen Anne, two-story, attached row houses with little applied ornament, although the larger, better ones are faced with Indiana red pressed brick and the simpler ones with brown, common brick. (Common clay for the common clay, one might say.) With few modern intrusions, the streets present unified patterns of entranceways, windows, and gentle decorative peaks.

Farther from the amenities of the hotel and the long-gone shopping arcade building, the mass of workers lived in the smallest houses south of East 113th Street and along South Champlain Avenue. Only a few of the tenements that housed the lowest echelons and single men remain along Langley Avenue, and several modern apartment buildings, which some misguided architect undoubtedly claimed were sympathetic to the streetscape, have been built here.

While most of Pullman's domestic architecture has a New England mill-town flavor, the **Market Hall** (112th Street and Champlain Avenue) and surrounding Romanesque Colonnade Apartments evoke Savannah or New Orleans. Originally a one-story structure for food stalls with a central second-story and tower meeting room, the building burned in 1882 and was rebuilt by Beman with an additional story. The four, curved-front, Colonnade buildings were constructed at this time. Interrupted only by the intersecting streets, they circle the market, forming a handsome group. In 1932, another fire destroyed the upper floors of the market, but the deteriorating building remained in use until a final fire gutted it in 1973. The Historic Pullman Foundation, which had at first hoped to rebuild along the original plans for commercial use, now intends to adapt Market Hall for condominiums and offices.

The foundation's tour covers about 30 percent of South Pullman, including all the important attractions, but the area's so small it's easy, and sensible after the long trip to the neighborhood, to see the whole thing. Don't forget North Pullman, either. Built about ten years after the designated Chicago Landmark District, North Pullman is included in the national Pullman Historic District and, although a bit run down and less intact, is worth a look.

Pullman also owned a large tract of land west of the Illinois Central tracks, although his vision of industrial perfection wasn't imposed with as much ferocity here. When Presbyterians rented the Greenstone Church, the only house of worship allowed in Pullman proper, Catholics and Swedish Lutherans petitioned Pullman for permission to build their own churches. He eventually leased them land and made a similar arrangement with Swedish Methodists. The towers of

Holy Rosary Catholic Church (King Drive and 113th Street), a handsome, red brick, 1890 Romanesque church; **Reformation Lutheran Church** (113th Street and Forest Avenue), built in 1888 as Elim Lutheran Church; and the **New Pasadena Mission Baptist Church** (Indiana Avenue and 113th Street), originally the 1892 Swedish Methodist Church, form a line along the south side of Palmer Park. Many other churches also dot the neighborhood west of the I.C. tracks.

Like many other city parks, **Palmer** (111th Street and Indiana Avenue) was landscaped by the Olmsted firm and the 1904 field house was built by D. H. Burnham and Company. The auditorium sports three idealized, colorful murals done in 1934 by J. E. McBurney. They depict indigenous Indians, explorer Père Marquette, and wooden-shoed farmers. The **George M. Pullman Branch Library** (11001 South Indiana Avenue), a fine, 1927 neoclassical building, nestles in one corner of the park. The town's library was in the magnificent Pullman Arcade Building east of the tracks until that was demolished in 1926. The collection of Pullman historical material is outstanding.

Mendel Catholic High School (250 East 111th Street), north of the park, opened as the Pullman Free Trade School in 1917. The campus, which incorporated now widely accepted educational concepts, provided free technical training for the children of Pullman company workers until it closed in 1945. The Augustinians reopened it in 1951 as a boys' Catholic college prep.

Joseph Schlitz built a mini beer empire on a plot of land just west of the I.C. tracks that escaped Pullman. The taverns did a land-office business because Pullman wouldn't allow workers' bars inside his town. Schlitz imitated Pullman's paternalism by building homes for his employees along South King Drive and a commercial block on East 111th Street. Wander into a couple of the Schlitz tavern buildings that remain on Front Avenue between 114th and 115th Streets to see beautiful tiled floors and tin ceilings, Victorian and 1930s backbars, and colorful 1950s murals.

A few vestiges of a thriving, turn-of-the-century Italian community remain on 115th Street across from the **Schlitz Block,** a Germanic, copper-turreted building. Nearby Michigan Avenue, once Roseland's bustling shopping strip, is sadly deteriorated and has little more than clothing stores selling shoddy, trendy goods. Lots of new, government institutional buildings are filling in the wasteland between Pullman and the Calumet Expressway.

Interesting places

Administration Building and Clock Tower
11101 S. Cottage Grove
Former Pullman corporate offices. During the 1894 strike, there were rumors that workers were going to blow up the wonderful, Gothic clock tower, and troops were stationed near it day and night.

*Florence Hotel
11111. S. Forrestville Ave.
785-8181
Named for Pullman's favorite daughter. Books on the town are at the front desk.

*Greenstone Church (Pullman United Methodist Church)
St. Lawrence and 112th St.
785-1492

Historic Pullman Center
614 E. 113th St.
785-8181
Originally a rooming house, then a Masonic lodge, now a community center owned by the Historic Pullman Foundation, which conducts guided tours of the neighborhood the first Sunday of the month, May to October ($2 donation). Tours begin here at 1:30 p.m. Audio-visual presentation and photo exhibit, too.

*Holy Rosary Catholic Church
King Dr. and 113th St.
568-4455

*Market Hall
112th St. and Champlain

*Mendel Catholic High School
250 E. 111th St.
995-3700
Rigorous academic program: 95% of the all-black student body goes on to college.

*New Pasadena Mission Baptist Church
Indiana Ave. and 113th St.
995-9774
Fine brick church with excellent stained glass.

Pabst Milwaukee Building
116th St. and Front Ave.
A real rarity.

*Palmer Park
111th St. and Indiana Ave.
785-4277

***George M. Pullman
Branch Library**
11001 S. Indiana Ave.
995-0110

Pullman Stables
112th St. and Cottage
Grove Ave.
*A town rule stipulated that
all horses had to be kept
here—there was room for
60. The building also
housed a volunteer fire
company. A service station
now occupies it, but carved
horses' heads remain over
the garage entrance.*

***Reformation
Lutheran Church**
113th St. and Forest Ave.
785-4570

St. Anthony's Church
Kensington and Indiana
468-1200
*A large brick church with
terrific mosaic panels. Built
in 1960.*

St. Salomea
Indiana Ave. and 118th St.
785-0273
*The clockless clock towers
of this massive, 1912 brick
church are the tallest things
for miles around.*

*Schlitz Block
115th St. between Front
Ave. and King Dr.

Shopping
and services

Cheryl's Boutique
11125 S. Michigan Ave.
928-9774
*For an average price of $60
(polyester; wool more), this
place will custom make a
woman's suit the same day.
Choose from Vogue and
Simplicity pattern books,
scrapbooks full of Frederick's of Hollywood clip-
pings, or bring in a picture.*

**Pullman Wine & Liquor
and Italian Cheese Co.**
305 E. 115th St.
785-6527
*Italian deli meats, cheeses,
and salads. Mega-heroes,
made with their best, run
about $7 per ft.*

Sam's Foods
249 E. 115th St.
928-7744
*Eight vaguely Italian
luncheon meats and four
cheeses go into their super-
long heroes, which cost
about $8 per ft. and can be
as long as 8 ft.*

Dining
and drinking

***Florence Hotel
Dining Room**
11111 S. Forrestville Ave.
785-8900
*Homemade soups, sand-
wiches, burgers, salads,
and all-American daily
specials are served in
charming Victorian sur-
roundings.*

Landmark Inn
11112 S. Langley Ave.
821-9468
*Schlitz installed the wonder-
fully ornate bar after
Prohibition.*

Pesavento's
11500 S. Front Ave.
468-3156
*Faded place that's been
around for most of this century. Handsome 1940s
backbar, old-line lunch
counter, great murals in the
rear dining room.*

© 1983 WFMT, Inc.

Beverly Hills/Morgan Park

Twelve thousand years ago, Lake Michigan's waters surrounded the Blue Island Ridge. A hundred years ago, a developer's promotion boasted that Beverly Hills/Morgan Park, centered on the northern half of the ridge, "claims among its residents some of the best businessmen of Chicago, and is blessed with having, generally, the right kind of citizens." Today, buffeted by waves of radical racial change on the north and east, the area has more-or-less stabilized as an integrated community. Residents think of it as a "village in the city" and work hard to maintain the tranquil, suburban ambiance. Young families are renovating the grand houses on the ridge and fine Victorian homes that line curved, tree-shaded streets in and around the 2.9-square-mile **Ridge Historic District.**

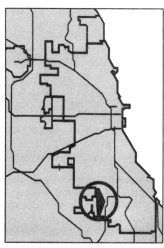

The **Beverly Area Planning Association,** a pioneer community self-help organization, carries on a century-old tradition of internally motivated neighborhood improvement. Early settlers underwrote the cost of the first railway stations, built the many churches that are still local mainstays, and even started their own art group, the John H. Vanderpoel Association, named for a prominent local artist. The story of how this association helped spawn a full-fledged community art center provides a good picture of the Beverly spirit.

Two years after the popular portraitist and long-time head of the Art Institute's instruction department died in 1911, a defunct North Side club offered one of Vanderpoel's paintings—*The Butter Makers*—to local residents. They raised $600 for the purchase from $1 door-to-door solicitations, and the association was born. Additional purchases and contributions from the artist's friends and students augmented the collection, which includes the world's largest group of Vanderpoel's portraits. When the $1-million holdings outgrew the Ridge Park Field House, local banker Arthur Baer and his wife spearheaded a fund drive to build the **Beverly Art Center** (2153 West 111th Street) on the grounds of the Morgan Park Academy in the late 1960s. Within three years, the community had paid off the mortgage. In addition to housing most of the **Vanderpoel collection** (a small portion still hangs, somewhat inaccessible, in the field house), the Art Center offers a full range of classes and hosts many cultural activities, including an annual juried art fair, theater productions in the 460-seat auditorium, lectures, concerts, and gallery exhibits.

The Center is also the starting point for the Beverly Hills/Morgan Park house tour (see *Annual Events*), but if you haven't the patience for guided tours or the heart for the annual 10,000-meter marathon, which covers much of the nation's largest historic district on a grueling, hilly course, the following circular driving/biking tour hits the highlights. Start at the Art Center and note the small, wood-frame house across the street (2204 West 111th Street). Built in 1872 for the Rev. Justin A. Smith, one of the founders of the Chicago Baptist Theological Union, it was the scene of conferences between representatives of John D. Rockefeller, William Rainey Harper, Thomas Goodspeed, and others, leading to the founding of the University of Chicago, which absorbed the Theological Union. Smith's descendants formed a 60-year dynasty at the *Chicago Daily News*.

Drive east past the Norman revival **Walker Branch Library** (11071 South Hoyne Avenue) and turn left onto Longwood Drive—the area's most imposing homes are perched on its heights—and go north past the **Morgan Park United Methodist Church** (Longwood Drive and 110th Place), a rambling Prairie School building with handsome stained-glass windows, designed in 1912 by Perkins, Fellows, and Hamilton. Howard L. Cheney designed the yellow brick, neoclassical **Thirteenth Church of Christ, Scientist** (Longwood Drive and 103rd Street). Nearby the limestone hulk that now serves as the **Beverly Unitarian Church** is an 1886 replica of an Irish castle on the River Dee and perhaps the best-known local landmark.

Louis Sullivan designed the 20-room Horton House (10200) in 1887 for the founder of the Chicago Bridge and Iron Co., a fitting commission given Sullivan's affection for decorative ironwork. Frank Lloyd Wright executed the Prairie School Evans House (9914) in 1909, but seeing a style tailored for the flat prairie on some of the highest land for miles around is disconcerting. Local architect Murray Hetherington, who designed 30 buildings in the area and revamped the **Ridge Park Field House** (off 96th Street), which has the usual Park District gym, swimming pool, arts and crafts shops, and auditorium, is represented at 9765 Longwood. Tallmadge and Watson, who built many of Oak Park's and Hyde Park's grand homes, designed 9640.

Travel west on 95th Street to Damen Avenue, then north to 92nd Street. Proceed east to Winchester Avenue, then north to 91st Street, and turn right. The boulder just before Pleasant Avenue marks the old Vincennes Trail. The red brick, Arts and Craft Movement-inspired mansion designed by John Hetherington is the parish house for the **Church of the Holy Nativity** (Pleasant Avenue and 93rd Street). The Belding House (9167 South Pleasant Avenue) incorporates stones from the sheepcote of early settler Thomas Morgan's farm. (Speaking of stones, a chair-shaped granite rock in the yard of the Victorian-frame Inglehart House, 11118 South Artesian Avenue, is said to have been the council seat for a Potawatomi Indian chief.) W. M. R. French, one of the Art Institute's first directors, lived at 9203 South Pleasant Avenue. His brother, Daniel Chester French, who designed the Lincoln Memorial, contributed a frieze to the home. John Vanderpoel lived at 9319 South Pleasant Avenue until 1910.

Turn left at 95th Street and right onto Prospect Avenue and proceed to **Walter Burley Griffin Place** (104th). Of the more than 30 Prairie School houses in the area, 12 were designed by this Wright disciple who also planned Canberra, Australia's capital. Off-center peaked roofs, pointed windows, and almost Japanese wood-and-stucco façades make his work easily recognizable.

Return to Prospect Avenue on 105th Street and continue south past some of the community's oldest houses. The Tudor-revival Dickey House (10900) is on a four-acre lot—the largest in the district. The impressive Victorian Blackwelder House (10910), built in 1866, was the home of the neighborhood's sixth resident. The houses at 10924, 10929, and 10934 are also quite early. As you head back towards the tour's starting point along 111th Street, detour south on Hoyne Avenue to the **Morgan Park Congregational Church** (at 112th Street). The Prairie School-influenced building was constructed in 1915. The Masonic Hall across the street was the church's original building.

Other local landmarks include the 1871 Platt House (10821 South Drew Street) with an 800-year-old council oak in the yard; the Driscoll House (10621 South Seeley Avenue), home of the **Ridge Historical Society,** and **Sacred Heart Church** (Church between 116th and 117th Streets). Slated for demolition until purchased by the city for adaptive reuse, the humble church built by early French settlers was closed by the Archdiocese over congregants' spirited objections. Although not as architecturally significant as the houses in Hyde Park/Kenwood or Oak Park/River Forest, the diverse, well-designed, mostly brick homes in Beverly Hills/Morgan Park are so pleasantly situated and free from modern intrusions that they capture a glimpse of the past.

Unfortunately, noise and exhaust fumes from heavy traffic make the area's main commercial strips—95th Street and Western Avenue—less salubrious than the residential sections. **Evergreen Plaza,** where the two come together, was an urban-shopping-center pioneer when it opened in 1952, but today affluent locals prefer distant suburban centers, and owner Arthur Rubloff's forty Western American bronzes on display there are more noteworthy than the scores of standard clothing and shoe stores. Like Daniel Chester French's seated Lincoln, most are working models for monumental public sculptures.

South of the mall, Western offers a discouraging mixture of auto shops, nursery and garden centers, professional-office complexes, neighborhood service stores, and fast-food outlets. Only a hidden tennis shop, a few barely promising restaurants, and two furniture refinishers are of interest. East of the mall on 95th Street, stores for the home abound: large furniture outlets featuring garish Mediterranean and French provincial, kitchen-remodeling places, tile shops, carpet emporiums. With its fine array of Oriental carpets, the **Eastern Oriental Rug Co.** (1814—marked by a wonderful neon sign of an Arab on a camel) is one of the few stores that attracts shoppers from all over. Others are the **Guitar Center** (2215) with 15,000 square feet of guitars, basses, drums, keyboards, speakers, and amps, and **Tejay** (1931), which bills itself as having the largest selection of lamp shades in Illinois—the kind you see in the living room windows of Southwest Side homes. Staid, main-line clothing shops also line the strip. From the outside, **For Men, Jr.** (1712) looks like the rest, but it is actually the city's largest outlet for boy's designer clothing, has a men's college shop evocative of the 1960s, a ceiling painted like a cloud-filled sky, and a 10-foot-tall stuffed polar bear guarding the entrance—perhaps a tribute to the store's large selection of "husky" sizes.

A few stores are clustered around each of the neighborhood's four Victorian railroad stations. The 99th Street group includes a furniture restoration and refinishing service, **Oddlie Ltd.** (1743). **Toadstool Studios** (1739) specializes in needlework and painting supplies and offers classes, but dollhouse construction materials are also a big attraction. Besides little windows, doors, and other basics, Ron Drynan and his wife retail the architecturally accurate, 1-inch-to-the-foot construction plans that Drynan has created and wholesales throughout the world. Even a novice can follow the templates and careful, step-by-step instructions to build anything from a Cape Cod cottage to a high-rise featuring "four elegant street-level shops combined with luxurious, spacious one-bedroom apartments, each with a balcony."

To indulge other creative passions, head to **Skyway Studios** (10705 South Hale Avenue) near the 107th Street station, where Lelde Kalmite designs stained-glass windows, repairs old ones, and offers workshops. At **The Writer's Desk** next door, Elizabeth-Anne Vanek gives creative-writing classes, rents desk space (complete with filing cabinets and reference materials) to writers, and operates a writers' support group, which sponsors literary readings and provides an information exchange for writing skills.

If you want a memento of your trip to Beverly Hills/Morgan Park or one of Chicago, stop in at **The Heritage Gallery** (1915 West 103rd Street). Owner Jack Simmerling has cornered the Beverly-landmark sketch market, and the store is filled with his and other artists' drawings and paintings of the city's houses and streetscapes—many now gone. Not-for-sale memorabilia from razed mansions, such as the iron entrance gates to the Everleigh Club and a section of the mahogany mantelpiece from Cyrus McCormick's Rush Street mansion, are displayed in the "Chicago Room." Simmerling also appraises, frames, and restores paintings, including those in the Vanderpoel collection.

Many locals dine at the area's three country clubs, which may explain the dearth of exciting restaurants. A cozy, tree-shaded beer garden with lawn chairs and a small play area for kids is the main attraction at the **Maple Tree Inn** (10730 South Western Avenue). New Orleans-style seafood is the specialty in the spare, antiques-accented dining rooms, but the owner-chef's presentations don't measure up to the place's culinary pretensions or exalted local reputation. At **Svea's** (11160 South Western Avenue), an old-line Swedish place with no-nonsense service and décor, the fish (it comes from **DiCola's** market nearby) is often better and always cheaper. Complete dinners, including appetizer or soup, salad, entrée (the meat dishes can be like cafeteria fare), coffee, and dessert (good homemade pies), are in the $6 range. For a trip down memory lane, don't miss **Top Notch Beefburgers** (1822 West 95th Street), where you can dig into those flat, juicy burgers with grilled onions that take you back to your 1950s high-school hang out days.

Interesting places

*Beverly Area Planning Association
9730 S. Western Ave.
233-3100
Pick up free pamphlets about the community.

*Beverly Art Center
2153 W. 111th St.
445-3838

*Beverly Unitarian Church
103rd St. and Longwood
233-7080
Limestone to complete real-estate developer Robert C. Givins's $80,000 Irish castle had to be hauled by oxcart from the Joliet area.

*Church of the Holy Nativity
Pleasant Ave. and 93rd St.
445-4427

*Walter Burley Griffin Place
104th Pl. between Prospect Ave. and Wood St.
Griffin designed 1666, 1712, 1724, 1727, 1731, 1736, and 1741.

*Morgan Park Congregational Church
Hoyne Ave. and 112th St.
238-8020

*Morgan Park United Methodist Church
Longwood and 110th Pl.
238-2600

*Ridge Historical Society
10621 S. Seeley Ave.
881-1675
Open Sun., Thu. 2-5 p.m. Exhibits confined to upstairs room and scattered display cases in this somewhat modernized house.

*Ridge Historic District
Bounded by 87th and 114th Sts. and irregularly by Prospect and Hoyne Aves.
Two sections—Walter Burley Griffin Pl. and Longwood Dr.—of the nation's largest historic district are city landmarks.

*Ridge Park Field House
96th St. and Longwood Dr.
238-1655

*Sacred Heart Church
Church between 116th and 117th Sts.
Locals advocate city landmark status for the building.

*Thirteenth Church of Christ, Scientist
Longwood and 103rd St.
238-2378

*Walker Branch Library
11071 S. Hoyne Ave.
233-1920
Local land developer George C. Walker donated the land for this 1890 building, designed by Charles S. Frost.

*John H. Vanderpoel Memorial Art Gallery
Beverly Art Center
2153 W. 111th St.
445-9616

Shopping and services

Beverly Paperback Exchange
2057 W. 95th St.
239-0163
Good selection of well-organized books (lots of mysteries and romances). Friendly owner; complex trade-in arrangement.

Croydon China Co. Inc.
9321 S. Western Ave.
445-7000
Huge store with row upon row of tables set with quality ironstone and china. Registration service for brides. Others: Lincoln and Touhy; Woodfield Mall.

*DiCola's Seafood
10754 S. Western Ave.
238-7071
Because much of the fish at this local institution has been frozen, the main virtues are late hours and the wide variety of fish that's fried up to take out.

*Eastern Oriental Rug Co.
1814 W. 95th St.
233-4295

*Evergreen Plaza
95th St. and Western Ave.
445-8900 (office)

*For Men, Jr.
1712 W. 95th St.
233-7111

Fortino & Dutton Tennis
10912 S. Western Ave.
779-0334
Good selection of rackets, clothes, shoes, and string materials at discount prices. Stringing on the premises.

Green Things
1751 W. 95th St.
No phone
Lots of lush plants in this crowded shop.

*Guitar Center
2215 W. 95th St.
881-8800

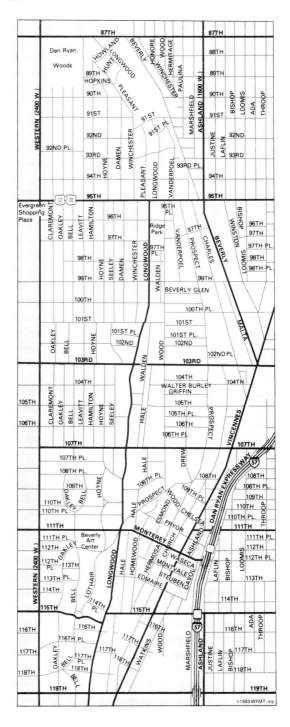

c 1983 WFMT, inc.

*The Heritage Gallery
1915 W. 103rd St.
233-0084

Himmel Furs
2201 W. 95th St.
779-7000
Three generations of Himmels run this more than a century-old business, one of the largest exclusive furriers in America. Customfitted furs of top-quality pelts are made on the premises.

Jerome Fabrics
1750 W. 95th St.
238-5560
Huge selection of silks, woolens, cottons, polyesters, and more in several rooms.

*Oddlie Ltd.
1743 W. 99th St.
233-0525

Osis & Carter
9045 S. Western Ave.
881-7157
Furniture refinishing and interior decorating.

*Skyway Studios
10705 S. Hale Ave.
238-5200

Sunshine Unlimited
1937 W. 95th St.
239-0107
Handicrafts and other gift items. Monogramming, too.

*Tejay Lamp Shoppe
1931 W. 95th St.
881-9417

Three's Company
10107 S. Western Ave.
238-1551
Trendier than most of the many furniture stores in the area.

*Toadstool Studios
1739 W. 99th St.
445-1010

The Wood Corp.
2745 W. 111th St.
238-9663
Furniture repair and refinishing, mirror resilvering, chair recaning, reveneering, and other services. Custom-made novelties, too.

*The Writer's Desk
10703 S. Hale Ave.
779-7464, 238-3130

Dining and drinking

Karson's Restaurant
11060 S. Western Ave.
238-9260
It calls itself "the place for steaks," but the real deals are complete dinners for $4-$5 in this large, bright, Greek-American restaurant. The food is decent, and the place is open all night on weekends.

*Maple Tree Inn
10730 S. Western Ave.
239-3688

Paul's Swiss Chalet
10854 S. Western Ave.
881-9622
It looks more like a roadhouse than a Swiss chalet. Joining older locals for a drink at the bar provides a taste of history. Owner Paul Bergamini, whose father was maître d' at famous spots, is full of stories about the good old days, and photos of him with visiting celebs fill a bulletin board over the fireplace.

The Purple Cow
10409 S. Western Ave.
239-4044
Everything is purple at this snack shop/ice-cream parlor, even the Bresler's vanilla ice cream. Vala's and Bicyea ice creams, too.

Rainbow Cone
9233 S. Western Ave.
No phone
Looks like Atlantic City circa 1929 and serves five-flavor cones—orange sherbet, pistachio, vanilla with fruits and nuts, strawberry, chocolate—for about a buck.

*Svea's Restaurant
11160 S. Western Ave.
881-9246

*Top Notch Beefburgers
1822 W. 95th St.
445-7218

Touch of Green
11044 S. Western Ave.
239-2992
Simply designed by Phil Rowe, this barnlike bar is the local hangout for young singles who arrive in droves in their daddys' big cars. Early in the evening, it resembles a high-school dance with guys clustering around the electronic games, girls at tables on the other side of a central bar, and couples in the booths.

Entertainment

Drury Lane South
2500 W. 95th St.,
Evergreen Park
779-4000
Shows usually feature a name star. (See Theater.)

Erik the Red
11050 S. Spaulding Ave.
779-3033
Southwest Side singles dance to loud disco and rock 'n' roll in this large bar that was once an auto body shop. The place is a real trip with lots of dark wood, antique light fixtures casting an orange glow, mirrors, a movie screen showing slides of dancers and sometimes movies, and a Viking-boat-shaped bar with serpent's eyes that pulsate to the music.

The Keye's
9936 S. Western Ave.
233-3211
Former classical pianist Bill Morris plays pop and jazz on his 9-ft. Steinway grand Sun.-Thu. A band plays Fri. and Sat., and there's dancing. The square, 1960s-style, dimly lit bar is the kind of place where your attire and appearance must pass muster before you're buzzed in.

Ryan's
2531 W. 95th St.,
Evergreen Park
423-3046
This 1940s-looking club books everything from pop and country to blues and R & B. Dancing, too. Cover.

North of the River

The Magnificent Mile, the Miracle Mile, Boul Mich, Avenue M: The names for Michigan Avenue from the river to Oak Street are many, but they all mean ten miles' worth of elegance, opulence, and excitement on the more-than-magnificent, though less than a mile long, strip. Most of the city's ritziest hotels, finest restaurants, classiest shops, and highest night life are on the avenue and on neighboring streets. The area hosts the media (both daily newspapers' headquarters, two television networks' facilities, many radio stations, numerous periodical publishers, plus a welter of ad agencies) and is also the home of a huge educational-medical complex; two major cathedrals; the Midwest's wholesale apparel, furniture, and furnishings center; and an unparalleled collection of art galleries and fine antiques dealers. New and coming attractions, such as

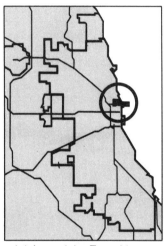

One Magnificent Mile, Neiman-Marcus, Bloomingdale's, and the Terra Museum of American Art, all reflect and reaffirm the avenue's importance. No city in the country offers such a compact concentration of activities.

Michigan Avenue's present fame rests on a bedrock of peerless shops, but the environs have been prime residential real estate for two hundred years. Jean Baptiste Point Du Sable probably built the city's first home here around 1779, and John Kinzie, Chicago's first big-time trader, purchased it in 1803. The site is marked by **Pioneer Court,** in the Equitable Building Plaza just north of the Michigan Avenue Bridge. By 1840, homes of such luminaries as William B. Ogden, Chicago's first mayor, dotted the fashionable neighborhood. The immensely profitable McCormick Reaper Works dominated the Chicago River's north bank, and so many McCormicks built mansions on Rush Street that the area eventually was called "McCormickville."

The 1871 Chicago Fire wiped out forty years' work. The old **Water Tower** (Chicago and Michigan Avenues), designed by W. W. Boyington and completed in 1869, was one of the few buildings to survive. Oscar Wilde may have called the Gothic limestone tower a "castellated monstrosity with pepper boxes stuck all over it," but Chicago's unofficial symbol endured the widening of Michigan Avenue and today stands anachronistically surrounded by modern glitter. A **Visitors Information Center** on the first floor dispenses advice, leaflets, and maps. Across the avenue, the still-in-use machinery of Chicago's oldest pumping station, a squat cousin to the tower, can be viewed through internal glass walls.

After the fire, other local landmarks were rebuilt in similar styles. Only the tower of the Edward Burling-designed St. James Episcopal Church, now the **Cathedral of St. James** (Wabash Avenue and Huron Street), survived, but in 1874 the church was rebuilt along its original lines. Bertram G. Goodhue's Chapel of St. Andrew was added in 1913. Modeled on an ancient Scottish abbey, it honors the place where the Brotherhood of St. Andrew was founded. The beautiful cathedral serves the city's oldest Episcopal parish—the roster of early members reads like "Who's Who" of Old Chicago—and is the scene of many concerts and of a Noontime Summerfest held in the plaza.

Holy Name Cathedral (State and Superior Streets), another Burling-designed fire casualty, was rebuilt the same year as St. James and remodeled by Henry J. Schlacks in 1915. Eight Masses are celebrated daily in the lovely, intricately arched cathedral, which, along with Catholic schools, a convent, and the rectory, takes up an entire city block. The gray limestone **Fourth Presbyterian Church** (Michigan Avenue and Chestnut Street) is distinguished by larger-than-life muses of the Psalms mounted on massive pillars, an unusual patterned ceiling painted by Frederic C. Bartlett, and an Aeolian-Skinner organ. Designed by Ralph Adams Cram, a prominent ecclesiastical architect and Gothic revivalist, it was completed in 1914. The congregants included the cream of society, such as the McCormicks and Howard Van Doren Shaw, who designed the parish house and the fountain in the tranquil garden.

Edward Burling was also responsible for the 1883 **Samuel M. Nickerson House** (40 East Erie Street), known for years as the "marble palace." This official city landmark is the grandest reminder of the imposing mansions that blanketed the area after the fire. Henry Ives Cobb, the University of Chicago's first architect, designed three Richardson Romanesque buildings in the highly desirable neighborhood, including the rugged granite-façaded, turreted second home of the **Chicago Historical Society** (632 North Dearborn Street). His even larger **Newberry Library** (60 West Walton Street) faces **Washington Square,** the city's oldest park. The **John Carroll Sons Funeral Home** (25 East Erie Street) was built by Cobb in 1878 for Ransom Cable and later occupied by a McCormick. To see the interior of a typical mansion, dine at one of half a dozen restaurants in more-or-less similar, more-or-less faithfully maintained houses on the surrounding streets.

Two events doomed the elegant, ante-bellum enclave. During World War One, "Captain" Streeter was evicted from his impromptu landfill empire, which encompassed much of the real estate from Ohio to Oak Streets east of Michigan Avenue. Streeter's scow had run aground in 1886, and he encouraged dumping to augment natural sand accretion, proclaiming the new land the independent "District of Lake Michigan." He defended the claim in court and at the battlements, but ended his life selling fish from a shack. When the **Michigan Avenue Bridge,** a key provision in the Chicago Plan, opened in 1920, development of "Streeterville" and the avenue took off. Throughout the 1920s, high-rise apartments and institutions, including the sprawling Northwestern University professional schools/hospitals complex, filled Streeter's empty land.

The first Michigan Avenue skyscraper sparked by the new access to the south bank and the Loop was the gleaming white, terra-cotta-covered **Wrigley Building** (400), designed by Graham, Anderson, Probst & White in a French Renaissance style. The clock-tower-topped building was completed in 1921; the Greek-temple-capped annex in 1924. The brightly illuminated Wrigley was one of Chicago's most beautiful sights until it became partially obscured by new buildings.

The tale of the competition that led to Hood & Howells's 1925 Gothic **Tribune Tower** (435), studded with stones from famous buildings around the world, is oft repeated. The marble-clad lobby, inscribed with freedom-of-the-press quotations, is well worth a look, or take the tour. The old Mandel Brothers Warehouse (425), behind the Equitable Insurance Building, has inconveniently housed the **Chicago Public Library** since its former building was converted to the Cultural Center. Walter W. Ahlschlager designed the Moorish, dome-and-minaret-topped Medinah Club of Chicago for the Shriners. Now part of the **Radisson Chicago Hotel** (505), the $10-million building completed in 1928 has housed various hotels for years. The lavish polychromed ceilings in the old lobby, the opulent banquet room up the grand steps, and the 16th-floor Olympic-size swimming spa worthy of Roman baths go largely unnoticed by many of the businessmen and conventioneers the hotel hosts.

Marshall and Fox's 1920 **Drake Hotel** (140 East Walton Street) boasts even grander public spaces, including an English Great Hall lobby and a shopping concourse. A few steps down East Lake Shore Drive, the **Mayfair Regent** (181) is riding the crest of a demand for luxury that has transformed many of the area's smaller hotels into chic, European-style inns. With attentive staffs lavishing personal attention and amenities—afternoon tea, handmilled soaps, complimentary Perrier, bedtime Cognac or chocolates, in-room refrigerators and bars, and in-building libraries—the Mayfair Regent, Tremont, Whitehall, Park Hyatt, and Knickerbocker offer megabuck lodgings to elite business travelers. On weekends, the suites and restaurants are almost empty, so attractive discount packages are available.

Weekend deals are also the rule at the new, big, conventioneer-oriented hostels built between the Radisson and The Drake in the 1970s. Although the architecture of most is forgettable and the services of the smaller hotels can't be duplicated, these giants are very serviceable and weekend prices are real bargains. Costs and availability change often, and most require reservations.

For out-of-towners or escaping-the-kids suburbanites, staying at the hotels is an easy introduction to Michigan Avenue's riches. They have glitzy or clubby bars, usually with cocktail-hour hors d'oeuvres and evening entertainment; at least two restaurants, one a casual pricey affair, the other a lushly decorated, even more pricey "gourmet" room; and a few exclusive shops. Of course, the zenith of the complete hotel genre is the **Ritz-Carlton** at Water Tower Place, the ultimate never-leave-the-building complex.

Water Tower Place (845) opened in 1976 to accolades mitigated only by some controversy over its architecture. Michigan Avenue's $200-million marble-clad monolith houses not only the 22-story hotel, but also luxury condominiums, indoor parking, offices, theaters, restaurants, and the seven-level Atrium Shopping Mall. It offers sufficient diversions to fill weeks.

Faced in Italian travertine marble, with *ficus benjamina* trees flanking the Michigan Avenue entrance waterfall and with dramatic, glass-walled elevators, the Atrium Shopping Mall has been hailed as a model of modern beauty. Such praise provokes some healthy skepticism. Lacking places to sit down and people-watch, the mall is rather hard-edged and austere. Many shops are on corridors off the central area, and there are no checking or locker facilities: The place seems set up to maximize schlepping.

Nonetheless, the more than a hundred shops, which account for almost half of the Magnificent Mile's business, are among Chicago's main attractions. They range from Vidal Sassoon's giant hair salon to the stall-in-the-wall Lighterworks, and include institutions like Kroch's & Brentano's. You can outfit your kitchen at a branch of Cook's Mart, decorate your bedroom and bath from other specialty shops, brighten your whole house with beautiful textiles from Clothworks, buy gifts from all over the world, indulge in a fabulous facial and make-up lessons at Georgette Klinger or half a dozen other beauty-care centers, adorn yourself with baubles from as many jewelers, find practical shoes for trekking around the mall or fancy ones for stepping out, and dress yourself at a score of boutiques. Women's clothing stores outnumber men's by more than two to one. Several—August Max, Casual Corner, Limited Express—are trendy, more-or-less affordable places specializing in Seventh Avenue and California fashions. **Chas. A. Stevens,** a long-time Loop firm, has three shops in the mall: the main store (6th level) features better designer fashions and accessories; **Chas** (5th level) has *au courant* sportswear, dresses, and suits in misses and junior sizes; and the **Petite Store** (7th level) carries traditional, fairly conservative clothing for shorter women. **Enchanté** (4th level), with its sexy window displays, offers a unique collection of sensuous underthings from designers like Sami, Sanchez, and Loré: silk-satin camisoles, slips, and nightgowns; lacy silk teddies, briefs, and 1930s-style panties; and almost equally slinky nylon lingerie.

What makes the mall really shine, however, are the very chic, expensive outlets for haute couture houses, for example, Courrèges and Rodier of Paris (3rd level). At **Dana Côte d'Azur** (3rd level), you can find the classic suits and separates that a conservative Frenchwoman would wear: gabardines, tweeds, linens, silk blends, and lovely silk shirts. **Jaeger** (3rd level), an English firm, has a fine selection of well-made women's suits as well as men's wear for everything from business to boating. While the women's clothing is all made in England, some of the men's fashions are designed in England and produced in Italy. Women who shop at **Matthews** (3rd level) can put together a whole wardrobe with the help of the expert staff. Based in Beverly Hills, Ruth Matthews designs her suits, dresses, and separates in natural fabrics and wonderful colors to be coordinated and to look good on women of most sizes and shapes. From cashmere-silk-blend sweaters to shoes, scarves, and jewelry, there are also individual pieces that will fit in well with already developed wardrobes. **Caché** (6th level) is a terrific place to splurge on evening things, such as ultra-high-fashion silk gowns or more casual, but equally chic, lounging outfits. The shop has an impressive selection of impeccably tailored silk blouses, slacks, exquisite sweaters, and other beautifully designed clothing and accessories—all at prices to match the quality.

Charles Jourdan (3rd level) may be the mall's designer salon *par excellence*. Although Jourdan's superb footwear is available elsewhere, the knowledgeable staff makes shopping here a delight. The boutique also features the Paris designer's clothes (whimsical silks, beautiful beachwear, and butter-soft leathers) and accessories (jewelry, ties, hats, umbrellas, pens, perfume, scarves, gloves, handbags, small leather goods, and luggage)—in short, almost everything. Here, as at the other shops, styles change with the seasons, so there's always something new to covet.

Avventura (4th level) has the finest men's French, Italian, and American handmade, leather shoes (from Lucchese Western boots to super-soft moccasins), but when it comes down to cases, **I Santi** (7th level) is the place to go. The shop smells of fine leathers, from luggage and calfskin attaché cases to belts, gloves, and even lizard bracelets. This Italian company is the only source in the world for naturally patterned suede bags made from wild African goatskin; it also offers unique purses made from ostrich, iguana, and unusual species of crocodile, as well as popular pastel lizard and snakeskin ones. Elegant Lucite and Lucite-accented evening bags in eye-catching colors are another specialty. Like Charles Jourdan, I Santi may be another Gucci in the making.

Some of the leathers at **North Beach Leather** (3rd level) have a Western flair: snakeskin cowboy boots, sheepskin jackets, rawhide and suede hats. Decorated with polished oak and beveled-glass fixtures, the spacious shop feels a bit like a movie-set Western saloon. Other clothes are the outrageously theatrical kind found, say, in *Playboy*—elaborately fringed and feathered women's dresses and tops, ultratight spandex swimsuits—with sexy *Playboy* posters on the wall to prove it. But there are also more conservative coats, suits, and skirts for women, as well as men's jackets and coats, including the latest in down-filled leather. Featured in everything from *Vogue* to *Movie Mirror,* much of the clothing comes from California designers, is handsome but not superbly made, and is not as outlandishly priced as one might expect from the ambiance.

If you're looking for a bit of English countryside, **Laura Ashley** (6th level) stocks wonderful, soft-colored print cottons by the yard, as well as charming Victorian-looking dresses, table linens, bedspreads, pillows, quilts, and lamp shades. Lovely floral wallpapers, dinnerware, and other accessories coordinate with the fabrics. There's even Laura Ashley eau de toilette. Started in London in 1953, the company moved to Wales in 1961; it now has 10 factories and 80 shops worldwide.

Caswell-Massey (7th level) looks like an 18th-century apothecary shop and is a fabulous source of scents. Founded in 1752, the country's oldest chemist and perfumer still makes George Washington's favorite cologne and carries tons of soaps, lotions, perfume oils, toilet waters, and herbs and spices (from pizza to lily of the valley) to make sachets and potpourris. Here you can find hard-to-come-by straight razors, shaving accessories, complexion brushes, barrettes and clips, and various imported and domestic sundries. Similar delights are also available at **Crabtree & Evelyn** (5th level), and **Rare 'n' Fair** (7th level) offers fine French perfumes, as well as jewelry (pearls, South Seas coral, opals), crystal, and "rare and fair" gifts.

Glassware from **The Crystal Suite** (7th level) makes a beautiful gift. All the biggies—Orrefors, Kosta, Baccarat, Lalique, Daum—are well represented by figurines, vases, bowls, ashtrays, paperweights, and the like. There's even a small selection of art glass from Lotton A. G. Studio, and prices range from less than $10 for glimmering trinkets to thousands of dollars. Blue carpeting and wall coverings accented by mirrors set off the crystal well.

A handsome store with green marble floors and huge plate-glass windows, **Top Brass** (7th level) shines with (you guessed it) brass, from high-fashion brass tableware and bath accessories to door knockers and a brass abacus, highlighted by gorgeous dinnerware from Fitz and Floyd. **Et Cetera** (2nd level) is crammed full of brass side tables from Thailand, antique copper pots, a fair amount of junk, and handmade goodies: ceramic automobile cookie jars, wood-and-cloth marionettes, ceramic-framed mirrors, enamel fun jewelry, soft sculptures. Oodles of soft sculptures run the gamut from people to parrots to piggies at **Fantasies** (7th level), another crafts shop with some fascinating items, such as neon sculptures and ceramic face and eye masks.

International gifts abound at **Primitive Arts, Ltd.** (2nd level): African bags, baskets, and odd items like monkey-bone combs; marble boxes from Ireland; lots of handicrafts from Central and South America; Chinese cloisonné. There's so much that separating the good stuff from the schlock is difficult. All the beautiful antique and new pieces at the **Chinese Friendship Store** (7th level) come from Mainland China: porcelain dinner and tea sets, embroidered jackets and kimonos, purses, Ming vases, fans, cinnabar, old and new cloisonné, embroidered mats, jewelry, carved ivory, scenic hand-carved cork pictures, and much more.

With paper models of the Water Tower, reproduction Riverview and gangster maps, and charms of city landmarks, **Accent Chicago** (7th level) provides just the right touch for visitors who want to take home a bit of Chicago. It also has T-shirts, stationery, glasses etched with the city's skyline, and lots of the usual touristy stuff—most at touristy prices.

Attractions for kids include the well-stocked toy store, **F.A.O. Schwarz** (4th level); **Beagle & Company** (7th level), devoted to, as the neon sign says, "Snoopy and Friends" with everything from stuffed Snoopys to Snoopy T-shirts and overalls; and, best of all, **Beauty & the Beast** (7th level). Unicorns, Benji in several sizes, Persian cats and kittens, leopards, and even armadillos are among the wonderful stuffed beasties at this shop; the beauties include childlike dolls and incredibly delicate porcelain-faced ones, such as a jester with the comedy and tragedy masks. Clever cardboard carriers for your docile new pets and classical music in the background make Beauty & the Beast a perfect delight.

Classical music, classical décor (complete with Greek columns), and contemporary art exhibits in a separate gallery make the **Rizzoli International Bookstore** (3rd level) great for browsers. One of Chicago's better bookstores, Rizzoli is particularly strong on art, architecture, art history, the performing arts, foreign languages (notably Italian and French), and travel. Daily newspapers from Italy, France, Germany, and England are available, and there is a well-chosen music and spoken-word recordings department.

Settle down with your foreign newspaper or new book at the **Vie de France Boulangerie & Carry-Out** (mezzanine) for a Continental breakfast, country French snacks, salads, and sandwiches. Or get warm bread and croissants to take home. There are lots of other food options in the mall. **De Brucio's Pizzeria** (4th level) sells decent deep-dish pizzas whole or by the slice (a pricey $1.95). The **Theatre Café** (2nd level) offers fancy coffee-shop fare and the added attraction of its Kron Chocolatier. (Have a chocofest: Compare the candies here with those at Marshall Field's and at Godiva Chocolatier on the 7th level.) One of the most popular eating places, **D. B. Kaplan's** (7th level) may have the longest menu in town. More than 150 sandwiches vie with lots of other deli fare and ice-cream delights. Warning: This is one of those crowded, convivial spots where dishes have names like "Studs Turkey," "Latke Mountain High," "When You Knish Upon a Star," and "Saul Food." For fresh fish charcoal-grilled over mesquite, California-style, check out the turn-of-the-century-looking **Chestnut Street Grill** (mezzanine), which is also well known for its excellent selection of California white wines and cappuccino ice cream. The lunch and dinner menus are the same, so plan on spending about $20 to $25 a person. Most of the other restaurants aren't particularly cheap, either. For one of the best lunch deals in the mall, stop at the deli counter on the seventh floor of **Marshall Field's.** Here sandwiches are sold basically for the cost of the ingredients (50¢ to $2 or so). The ample selection is indeed proof that, as one of the store's promotions boasts, "Field's is Chicago."

The State Street Field's is certainly one of the world's great department stores, and the Atrium Shopping Mall branch would do most cities proud as the best shop in town. From cosmetics and a men's department on the first level to gourmet foods and kitchenware on the seventh, with everything—a fine cross section of women's wear, a super kids' section, a good book nook, furniture (even antiques), and more—in between, Field's tradition of quality and service has been successfully transplanted to the Magnificent Mile.

Lord & Taylor shares equal billing with Field's at the Michigan Avenue entrance to the mall, but a cunning set of mezzanines leads you up and back by small seductive steps until you're at the mall's east end. The flagship of a seven-shop Chicago-area chain offers men's wear, housewares, linens, and all the usual department-store fare (little furniture), but it concentrates on high-quality women's clothing. American designers such as Bill Blass, Calvin Klein, and Ralph Lauren are featured, along with European names, less expensive knock-offs, casuals, and fun clothes.

Many of the same labels crop up at the three-floor **Bonwit Teller** (875 North Michigan Avenue), across the street in the Hancock Center. They're joined by Albert Nipon, Koos van den Akker, Laura Biagiotti, and others, all set up in boutiques that make Bonwit's a specialty store filled with specialty stores. The Designer Salon, the trendier S'fari, the designer sportswear section, and a Missoni boutique are particularly notable. Space near the elegant cosmetics and perfume department is leased to **Hermès,** saddler to royalty for centuries, which also manufactures superb leather bags and accessories. Whatever's in fashion may be found at Bonwit's—the store's a class act.

I. Magnin (830), in a handsome building constructed for Bonwit's in 1958, is equally exciting. In-store boutiques here include Rive Gauche with Yves Saint Laurent's chic fashions, Louis Vuitton luggage and bags, Les Must de Cartier personal accessories, Laykin et Cie fine jewelry, and Godiva chocolates. The famous Carol and Irwin Ware Fur Collection is probably the city's largest and best, with the latest fashions and colors from major couture houses as well as their own. Magnin's is a bustling but personal store where saleswomen phone regulars when something special comes in.

Elevator operators in the oldest of the three buildings that make up **Saks Fifth Avenue** (669) still call out the time-honored litany "First floor, cosmetics; third floor, designer salon" that sets the tone for this long-established store. Sure, all the big designers are on hand, but there's also a comfortable, calming air about Saks, and praise for the sales help is frequently extravagant. The peerless children's department, traditional men's clothing, jewelry selection, and beauty parlor are also much touted. Bonwit's and Magnin's aggressively crowd the cutting edge of fashion, but ask any chicly dressed Chicagoan where she shops and Saks is always high on the list. In the elegant Regency Room, salespeople "dress" their customers in everything from lithe day dresses to svelte evening wear beautifully made from superb fabrics. The clothes are the work of the best American and European designers: Pauline Trigère, André Laug, Chloé, Yves Saint Laurent, Emanuel Ungaro, Valentino. Regency prices are top drawer, but shopping at Saks need not cost a fortune, and as at all the Michigan Avenue department stores, sales are big money savers.

Dollar signs are figuratively written over everything at **Gucci** (713), while the famous "G" is literally imprinted on many of the exquisite leather goods. Gucci's shoes, handbags, and accessories have won plaudits for years, and this handsome, mini department store also stocks men's and women's clothing, gorgeous gifts, and scents, in the grand-couture-house fashion. The store doesn't observe the Rome-New York custom of closing for lunch, and it eschews the reputation for hautiness that has made the New York Gucci infamous.

Stylish versions of the famous coat Thomas Burberry designed for trench warfare are available in all their permutations for men and women at the bilevel **Burberrys** (633), along with other outerwear, tailored slacks and skirts, sports jackets and blazers, Shetland and cashmere sweaters, shirts and sundries. Such high quality doesn't come cheaply, but the traditional look, popularized as "preppy," will probably never be out-of-date. It can also be found in abundance at the huge, more competitively priced **Mark Shale** (919). The main floor has scads of men's suits, slacks, jackets, shirts, and sweaters (both designer and privately labeled); the second floor is devoted to similar women's clothing; and the lower level offers rugged, but fashionable, sportswear and outdoor gear.

Once staid, **Stanley Korshak** (912) has shed a dour image and has flowered into one of Chicago's premier fashion sources. Visually diverting, the soft-colored shop would be comfortable around the corner on Oak Street with the other pacesetting boutiques. Look here for the Barry Bricken complete line of separates; dresses from Trigère, Krizia, and Halston; lovely silk blouses; furs by Maple of Oak Park; and a fabulous, fanciful jewelry and body adornment selection. There's not a poorly chosen item in the place.

Brightly lit and decorated with wood trellises, **The Seasons Best** (645) is aptly named. Trendy sportswear from main-line houses is jammed into every corner. The names are American, but many of the clothes are made in Hong Kong, so racks of silk shirts, slacks, and separates in natural fabrics don't cost an arm and a leg. Chic footwear comes from everywhere—Spain, Italy, Denmark, Brazil, Argentina—and the bag collection is equally outstanding. The store is crowded and short on amenities, but selection and affordability make it an office-girl's dream.

Naturally, Michigan Avenue has its share of big-ticket men's apparel shops, but traditional looks tend to be favored over the flamboyant. The spacious **Morry's** (645) offers one of the city's most comprehensive collections, and one of the most expensive. Successful types, perhaps a bit thick around the middle, shop here for Louis Roth, Hickey-Freeman, St. Croix knits, and other famous-name suits and quality sportswear. **Brittany Ltd.** (642) has traditional styles from Southwick and Norman Hilton, as well as Alan Paine sweaters, Izod knits, Burberry coats, and Ralph Lauren's Polo line. The shop feels a bit like a men's club and also has a downstairs women's annex. For a league's worth of Polo, check out **Polo Ralph Lauren** (906), an airy space adjoining Stanley Korshak, which also carries some of the line's women's goodies in an upstairs loft.

There are probably as many shops selling $10,000 watches as there are those selling designer jeans on the Magnificent Mile. The department stores have respectable jewelry counters, and those megabuck timepieces featured in full-page magazine ads around the holidays can be had at almost any purveyor of the precious, but several jewelry boutiques stand out.

Lester Lampert (701) is a talented designer whose glittering showroom is kept well stocked in the $50 to $50,000 price range with the production of his workroom. Susan Berman, a rising light in design circles, works in a Michigan Avenue studio and retails at one prestigious store per city. In Chicago, that store is **Trabert & Hoeffer** (738). The original shop duplicated the firm's New York base, and some of the striking Art Deco fixtures were incorporated into the present elegant, gray showroom where customers are seated at little tables to be shown the works of various designers. Private rooms in back are available for discreet transactions.

The Loop has Chicago's oldest commercial establishment, Peacock Jewelers, founded in 1837, but the Magnificent Mile boasts a branch of **Tiffany & Co.** (715), started in New York the same year. You won't find breakfast behind the august portals, but you will find exquisite, made-in-the-New York-shop jewelry from famous designers such as Elsa Peretti and Paloma Picasso—Tiffany exclusives and *très cher*. The walls are lined with many representative patterns of luxury crystal and hand-painted china (including Tiffany's Private Stock), and with Tiffany's own sterling hollow and flatware. Mixed in with it all are surprisingly affordable gifts and sundries.

Spaulding & Co. (959, in The Drake) is no newcomer, either. Founded in 1855, the firm takes a more conservative approach to the carriage trade, although it had a hand in popularizing gold as an alternative to platinum precious-jewel settings in the 1930s. Unheralded craftsmen produce the traditional jewelry in house and out. Sterling is from the "guild" manufacturers—Gorham, Reed & Barton, Towle, Kirk, and so forth—while, as at Tiffany, tableware is made by such fine old houses as Spode, Wedgwood, Waterford, and Baccarat. Spaulding's also sells an exclusive line of stationery and maintains a bridal registry, but luxury watches, privately labeled at Tiffany, bear the makers' names' later.

The crummy block that is **Levinson's** (739 North Clark Street) setting is a vivid reminder of Chicago's largest diamond dealer's turn-of-the-century pawnshop roots. Levinson's still eschews the standard channels of trade, preferring instead auctions, estate sales, and other alternative sources to keep prices low. Your money will be refunded on any diamond that doesn't appraise for 50 percent more than its price. The store handled Henry Ford's estate, and the Russian Imperial crown, and holds the 70.20-karat Idol's Eye, valued at $5 million. There's also a full-time designer and plenty of flashy nondiamond jewelry and watches.

The jade collection at **Jade House** (Barclay Chicago Hotel, 166 East Superior Street), hidden on the fourth floor, is unique to the city, if not the country. About 300 pieces are on display from a motherlode of more than 5,000 that run the gamut from centuries-old Chinese sculpture to jewelry in every color from all over the world. There are Burmese jade pendants, bracelets, earrings, and rings; figurines in all sizes; vases, plaques, screens, and other objêts d'art to satisfy any collector.

Oriental virtu is just the tip of the area's art iceberg. Michigan Avenue and Ontario Street have long been centers of Chicago's gallery scene. Two basic types of galleries prevail: those devoted to coherent shows (*see Galleries*) and those that merchandise mixed collections of everything from old masters to new junk (and may also mount shows). Together they canvass almost every kind of art and offer opportunities aplenty for investment, both aesthetic and monetary.

For example, French Impressionist and Postimpressionist masters are the specialty at the huge **Wally Findlay Galleries** (814 North Michigan Avenue), and **R. H. Love** (100 East Ohio Street) is strong on 19th-century American art. **Richard Gray** (620 North Michigan Avenue) not only stocks the work of European and American painters and sculptors, but also mounts shows of Chicago artists and carries artifacts from ancient and primitive cultures. Local artists are the forte of the lively and influential **Phyllis Kind Gallery** (226 East Ontario Street), which has brought the word to the nation by opening a branch in New York. **Douglas Kenyon, Inc.** (155 East Ohio Street) focuses on photography and has the Midwest's largest gallery collection of 19th-century shots to new works, as well as a large Audubon selection. Look for big-name prints at **Joseph Faulkner-Main Street** (620 North Michigan Avenue), which does much of its selling by catalogue to collectors and museums.

The **Museum of Contemporary Art's** shop (237 East Ontario Street), a wonderful place to find lots of imaginative modern jewelry and gifts, also stocks a few original prints, some posters, and a super collection of modern-art books and catalogues. Head to **Aiko's Art Materials Import** (714 North Wabash Avenue) for Japanese watercolors and ceramics, Oriental and Occidental artists' supplies, art books, bookbinding materials including an enormous selection of lovely marbleized end papers and subtle mulberry papers (great as wall decorations), as well as hand-painted stationery and cards.

Art books are just the beginning at Michigan Avenue's major bookstores. **Kroch's & Brentano's,** the city's finest chain, started as a little shop in the Loop in 1907. Like the many other locations, the Magnificent Mile's K & B (516) offers an excellent selection of hard- and soft-cover books, cards and party goods, maps and periodicals. There's only one **Stuart Brent Book Store** (670) and only one Stuart Brent. Modeled on Oxford's Blackwell's, the carpeted shop looks like a library and has a stock tailored to serious readers; the owner has a reputation for loving books more than people. But he must like kids because he writes children's books, and the lower-level kids' books and toys section is charming. At **Hamill & Barker** (400 North Michigan Avenue, Room 1210), one of the city's best antiquarian book dealers, books are art. Specialties include rare and first editions, incunabula (books printed before 1500), literature, natural history, and early Chicago material.

Museum-quality 17th- and 18th-century English furniture is sold by Chicago's premier antiquarian, **Malcolm Franklin Inc.** (126 East Delaware Place). The stunning case pieces, tables, and chairs are dated by monarchial reign and segregated into separate rooms by the variety of wood. A few paintings and Staffordshire porcelains accent this Anglophile gallery. Prices reflect rarity, but browsing's free. **Nahigian Brothers** (645 North Michigan Avenue) offers an equally auspicious collection of Oriental carpets: 5,000 examples from Chinese to Romanian, antique and new. Fashions in these handmade artworks change with the times and Nahigian has them all: 1920s and '30s Sarouks; Kermans, including huge antique $65,000 ones; intricate, colorful hunting-scene Tabriz; Nain rugs with 1,000 knots to the inch; silk Quom hangings; and more.

Besides Oriental rugs, **Colby's** (129 East Chestnut Street) has three floors over Michigan Avenue filled with main-line furniture from Drexel, Heritage, Henredon, and John Widdicomb, and with furnishings in every style from traditional to modern. At **Scandinavian Design** (920 North Michigan Avenue), a giftware department highlighted by Svend Jensen crystal and Royal Copenhagen porcelain leads to a block-long second-story labyrinth of room settings with that natural, Danish-modern look. This multiunit chain imports some of the finest teak and rosewood sofas, chairs, wall units, and dining- and living-room sets from Scandinavian manufacturers such as Cado, Bruksbo, and Interform. Rugs, lamps, and accessories; a design service; and a separate department handling stylish, functional office furniture round out the picture.

With your office and almost every room in the house outfitted for modern living, the next natural step is to **Crate & Barrel** (850 North Michigan Avenue). Like the chain's other Chicago-area locations, the bright, woody store is a colorful riot of kitchen chic. Much of the sleek glassware and tableware is Scandinavian, and Crate & Barrel stocks tons of heavy, enamel-clad cookware, as well as bargain-priced seconds in the basement. Endless bins of kitchen gadgets, food processors and other appliances, high-tech storage units, baskets, and other delights compete for attention, while the impulse to buy a yard or two of bright, naive Marimekko fabric for a tablecloth is almost irresistible.

For more conventional table linens, bedding, and bath wares, shop at **Shaxted** (900 North Michigan Avenue). The store stocks a very good selection of the best brands and innovative accessories and will special order extravagant silk sheets and Swiss-embroidered tablecloths; it will also make up towels, placemats, napkins, tablecloths, and more to match your wallpaper or décor.

Luxury in linens is the byword at **Franklin-Bayer** (630 North Michigan Avenue). Irish linen, Italian silk, and Egyptian long-staple cotton sheets; Madeira openwork and Swiss-embroidered table linens; silk-satin peignoirs; custom-made kimonos of antique Oriental fabrics; and cashmere bathrobes are every bit as expensive as they sound, but if you've got it. . . . Highly personalized and service-oriented, the shop will monogram anything, make bed linens from your materials, and counsel on decorating. It also offers discounts to designers.

Until late 1950s zoning changes, Oak was essentially a quiet residential street around the corner from nightclub row, but now the block between Michigan Avenue and Rush Street is Chicago's ultrachic boutique bailiwick. Most buildings have been radically remodeled—from English basements up—to accommodate shops. Stainless steel, dull anodized aluminum, and masonry storefronts punctuated by glittering display windows climb as high as five stories, beckoning stylish, daytime passersby. In the evenings, the street is busy with the overflow from Rush Street's singles and music bars and patrons of the Art Deco **Esquire Theatre** (58). So strong is the glamour's lure that One Magnificent Mile, a new high-rise on the southwest corner of Oak Street and Michigan Avenue, includes a multilevel shopping mall, an astute departure from many modern towers' sterile, purposeless lobbies.

The shops on Oak and nearby Walton and Rush Streets tend to be more offbeat and adventurous than those on Michigan Avenue. The fashionable offerings change with the seasons and trends, and regular customers—who are frequently contacted when new shipments come in—rely on the taste of savvy owners. If you have plenty to spend and crave the latest, or what is about to become the latest, this is *the* place to shop.

Start at **Ultimo** (114 East Oak Street), generally agreed·to be Chicago's ultimate haute couture spot, largely because of owner Joan Weinstein's superlative sense of style. First to ride the crest of the Italian designers—Armani, Basile, Missoni—now found in department stores, Ultimo boasts men's and women's sportswear and evening clothes designed by the stars and soon-to-be-stars of American and European fashion. The accessories—hats, belts, scarves, bags, jewelry—are equally distinctive, and the bilevel boutique is itself a visual treat.

Barbara Glass combs Paris and New York for the ultratrendy, sophisticated women's (and some children's) clothes that fill the upper level of the dramatic-looking **Bottega Glaseia** (106 East Oak Street). The shop combines classics with the newest creations by up-and-coming designers, be they as basic as sweat shirts and jeans or as fancy as evening attire. Many prices are within reason, and the collection of inexpensive accessories makes browsing fun. Downstairs is a striking fashion-related gallery with limited-edition photographs, magazines, and more. At **Pompian** (57 East Oak Street), you'll find wonderful sweaters from England and Italy, loads of silk blouses, exquisite quilted silk jackets, and lots of European sportswear, as well as dresses, suits, and coats by designers from all over the world.

From Colette Nievel's one-of-a-kind sweaters tufted with glitzy fabric to Marie Pierre Tattarachi's sexy dresses and flashy outfits that look like costumes from *Flash Gordon,* the women's clothes at **Jean Charles** (1003 North Rush Street) are mostly French and lean toward the avant-garde. Not everyone is ready for such extraordinary sophistication, so Jean and Nancy Kevorkian also buy more traditional, highly wearable clothing like soft suedes and Italian-style men's suits. The shoe salon offers an excellent selection of high-fashion footwear.

Most of the clothes at **Kontessa II** (53 East Walton Street) are designed by Kontessa and made by seamstresses at the shop. Here are sultry silk blouses that would be daring in any disco, décolletage chiffon gowns studded with rhinestones, hand-painted and hand-embroidered silk dresses, sensuous velvet-flocked jump suits, and unconventional cottons. Kontessa also custom designs for her clients. Her prices reflect the workmanship—plus amenities like limousine service, Champagne, and parties for regulars. Outfits can easily run into the thousands.

Of the more affordable shops, the large, two-story **Ann Taylor** (103 East Oak Street) offers an appealing mix of casual and business wear ranging from sporty khakis to silk blouses by Nora Noh, John Henry, and others. The informal, tailored look predominates, and the upstairs shoe department (mostly Joan and David shoes) is a fine place to round out an outfit with low-heeled walking shoes or attractive pumps.

Jackie Renwick (65 East Oak Street) specializes in clothes for the businesswoman—conservatively tailored, natural-fabric suits and separates in the mid-price range—and stays open late on week nights to facilitate after-work shopping. **Barbara Weed** (66 East Walton Street), done up in soft grays, carries lots of frilly things, such as silk print dresses and dressy and casual wear by Bill Blass, Halston, and Helga Howie, as well as imports. Irish designers prevail in **Ireland House** (120 East Delaware Place), tucked away on two small floors of an old house. Here you can find lovely Hibernian tweeds, rustic casual suits, business wear, loads of pricey Aran fishermen's sweaters, and accessories such as tams, ties, and scarves.

Inviting and diverting, **My Sister's Circus** (101 East Oak Street) is, quite simply, fun. Trendy dresses, slacks, blouses, and outlandish sweaters crowd each other on the racks. Upstairs, sexy swimwear ("a bikini zoo") covers the walls, and a whole room is devoted to very feminine silk and cotton evening dresses. **Sugar Magnolia** (110 East Oak Street), formerly a hit on a second floor in Lincoln Park with its combination of vintage and fresh fashions, moved to a lower level on Oak Street in 1980. Sit at the tiled espresso bar and survey a sea of stylish, affordable delights: Hawaiian floral jump suits and blazers, flouncy blue-denim skirts, billowy harem pants, bright Mexican jackets, gauzy cotton sundresses, funky T-shirts, and a few vintage kimonos. New and old handbags and other accessories (lots of whimsical plastic pins and combs) fill display cases and are decorative additions to any outfit.

If you want your feet to be as fashionable as the rest of you, head to **Via Lusso** (106 East Oak Street) for the latest women's haute couture French and Italian footwear. The shop also has *très* chic lizard and leather bags and fabulous, bold jewelry by various New York artists. The busy **Smyth Bros.** (33 East Oak Street) offers an enormous selection of moderately priced to expensive shoes and boots for any occasion, from walking your dog to hobnobbing with celebrities. The designers include Charles Jourdan, Joan and David, Geoffrey Beene, Adriano Fosi, and Anne Klein. **Shoes etc. etc. etc.** (51 East Walton Street) is crammed full of often stylish footwear (much of it Italian and South American) at reasonable prices; there's always a sale on.

Shop for the best in traditional and contemporary men's wear at **Davis for Men** (41 East Oak Street). The comfortable two-story store is filled with top-quality business and casual clothing. Downstairs are the expected fine slacks and shirts; upstairs are the finds for up-scale fashion-conscious customers with money to spare. Besides suits from such designers as Jean-Paul Germain, Giorgio Armani, and Corneliani, the shop, which was a Chicago leader in carrying Yves Saint Laurent and Pierre Cardin for men, scored another triumph with the Chester Barrie label. Totally handmade in the United States by Hickey-Freeman from Italian patterns and yard goods, the $600-and-up suits (made to measure for $25 more) resemble Brioni's $1,100 ones. Davis is also a source for smart leathers.

Burdi (68 East Walton Street) and **M. J. Carr** (104 East Oak Street) are among the other men's boutiques that feature the contemporary (nowadays, Italian) look. **Stuart/Chicago** (102 East Oak Street) stocks several lines including a comparatively traditional private-label one, middle-of-the-road Dimitri, and a more expensive, highly styled one typified by Benvenuto Cellini suits. **Jeraz** (51 East Oak Street) is a source for European ultrachic that is priced to match. Suits and casual wear come mainly from France, Italy, and Spain; such handmade items as one-of-a-kind sweaters are gorgeous, as are fur and leather coats and jackets.

The colorful, cluttered **Clown** (72 East Oak Street) probably has the city's finest selection of designer clothes for children, with everything from delicate party dresses by Petit-Bateau and Liberty of London to practical overalls from Oshkosh. The clothes, accessories, and shoes—including baby moccasins and embroidered Chinese slippers that look like they're made for dolls—make this an enjoyable place for kids to shop for themselves. In fact, it's not unknown for a cab to deliver a ten-year-old clutching mom's American Express card (the helpful staff prefers mom to call ahead).

One of the best ways to round out a new image, or to acquire one if your pocketbook can't accommodate a new wardrobe, is to spring for a chic haircut. Although clients follow their favorite hairdressers (each of whom has his own "look") from salon to salon, several places can be counted upon to provide top-notch coiffures, as well as permanents, hair coloring, facials, make-up instruction, manicures, and pedicures, for both sexes.

At **Charles Ifergan** (106 East Oak Street), **Robert Bracken & Company** (57 East Oak Street), **Marc Benaim Coiffures, Ltd.** (49 East Oak Street), and **Paul Glick Inc.** (701 North Michigan Avenue), the cost of a haircut starts at from $25 to $45. The chief honcho is usually around, but you pay a premium to have him do the honors. All the shops offer amenities like free coffee. The sleek Ifergan puts out an informative hair-and-skin-care booklet, and a facial, including make-up application using Ifergan's own line of products, costs about $30. **Marilyn Miglin** (112 East Oak Street), in an elegant little Beaux-Arts building dwarfed by Ifergan's modernistic one, is another good place to go for make-up help. Sessions cost from about $35 for basic make-up to $200 for the works. The cosmetics are manufactured in a spotless upstairs laboratory (ask to see it) and sold, along with brushes and applicators of all sorts, in the charmingly feminine salon and at select stores.

Parfumerie (946 North Rush Street) carries some theatrical make-up, but hundreds of perfumes, eaux de toilette, body lotions, and powders line the shelves in the small, elegant shop. Their mingled fragrances permeate the air. The heady collection runs the gamut from the popular Chloé, Halston, and Bal à Versailles to perfumes in rare collectors' bottles, such as Joy in Baccarat crystal ($350) and Molinard in Lalique; oddities like Gravel, a men's cologne made in a New Jersey garage; and scents not found elsewhere in Chicago.

While Parisian perfumes are famous worldwide, **La Provence de Pierre Deux** (113 East Oak Street) has brought another kind of French artistry to the United States. When x-ray consultant Pierre Moulin and F.B.I. agent Pierre LeVec opened a country-French antiques store on New York's Bleeker Street in the late 1960s, they little knew that the colorful fabrics used to highlight the pieces would become the hottest items. Now they have more than a dozen shops throughout the country selling Charles Demery's "Souleiado" ("sunny day") fabrics. Many of the 300-odd patterns are hundreds of years old. Walk into the Chicago store and you're likely to be greeted by managers Gus and Connie Pentek's miniature gray poodle and overwhelmed by the array of color. The cottons are available by the yard and are also made up into women's and children's peasant dresses, bed and table linens, pillows, bags, accessories—almost anything that can be sewn or covered. A line of faience dinnerware made for Pierre Deux in France complements the fabrics. No wonder the place is popular with designers.

The **Alaska Shop** (104 East Oak Street) is as muted as Pierre Deux is bright. Here you'll find Eskimo handicrafts in a gallerylike setting: soapstone carvings, a bit of scrimshaw, and naive lithos. Prices, unlike the art, are bendable. **Lee Benkendorf Antique Clocks** (67 East Oak Street) is a gallery full of museum pieces. Benkendorf specializes in 17th- and 18th-century long-case, wall, bracket, and table timepieces. Rare clocks by great artists may include an enamel French lyre table clock by Kinable of Paris (*circa* 1800), an English mahogany striking regulator by John Holmes (*circa* 1770), or a 1715 arch-dial longcase clock by John Knib, a famous clockmaker who was twice mayor of Oxford. Prices can easily run into five figures, but the collection is worth seeing, even if you can't afford to buy.

Prices aren't low at **J.B.L. Antiques, Inc.** (941 North State Street), either. This high-ceilinged, exposed-brick store has a bit of everything, especially some nice Empire and Oriental furniture. **La Bourse** (45 East Walton Street) carries mostly smaller items: silver, fine porcelain, crystal, decorators' accessories. Some are antique, some new, but what makes this shop special is that many are donated. The Woman's Board of The Chicago Medical School runs the shop to raise funds. The board also holds sales of reasonably priced estate furniture on the first Sunday of the month at 225 West Huron Street.

Many furniture, interior-design, and house-beautiful showrooms mark a path to the **Merchandise Mart.** With seven-and-a-half miles of corridors on 97 acres of floor space (which would cover the entire Loop, if spread out), the Midwest's home-furnishing foundation and once world's largest building occupies a square block at Wells and Kinzie Streets. It stands on Wolf Point at the confluence of the Chicago River's branches. Hallowed ground as the city's cradle (and site of one of the first taverns in the 1830s), the area was covered by railroad yards and wharves by the time of the Chicago Fire. A decade later, the Chicago and North Western Railway built a Victorian pile of a station that was demolished (its stations must be star-crossed) to make way for Graham, Anderson, Probst & White's 1930 Mart monolith.

Built as Marshall Field's wholesale division warehouse, the debt-ridden building was snapped up by Joseph Kennedy after World War Two to create the country's first mega wholesale center. Eight larger-than-life bronze busts facing the Mart honor the giants of American merchandising, including Chicagoans Marshall Field and Julius Rosenwald. Fifteen muted murals of romanticized foreign-market scenes by Jules Guerin grace the Art Deco lobby.

Devoted mainly to four industries—home furnishings, contract (commercial) furnishings, floor coverings, and giftwares—the Mart hosts more than 20 "markets" a year to introduce new products and to promote old ones to hordes of accredited retailers and interior decorators from throughout the Midwest. Between these deal-making, acquaintance-renewing, partying orgies of order writing, the Mart's exhibitors do a brisk, if somewhat more subdued, business. They sell only "to the trade" and can be divided into two very different types. Manufacturers—from broad-based giants like Knoll to smaller, specialized firms such as Thonet—maintain factory display rooms devoted solely to their own products. Designer showrooms, each the exclusive area representative for as many as a hundred different lines, or antiques and art specialists, take up the balance of the 1,000-plus spaces. Some handle a department store's breadth of wares, while others are known for the depth of their collections and for their special services.

An interior designer is the key to unlocking the Mart's treasures. Although nothing prevents you from peering through the showrooms' windows, almost all require a "Mart Card" to consummate a deal. In addition, savvy designers can zero in on sought-after objects that might take the uninitiated months to find, and they enjoy hefty discounts—around 40 percent on furniture, 30 percent on carpeting, 20 percent on accessories, and varying amounts on fabrics. Remember, however, that almost everything except an antique is a sample. Purchases are delivered after the irritating three-, six-, or nine-month wait that is the plague of the furniture industry, and cartage can add amply to the bill.

The Mart's success spawned the adjoining 1977 Skidmore, Owings & Merrill **Apparel Center** (350 North Orleans Street), which is topped by the **Holiday Inn Mart Plaza** (the bar is a nice place for a drink), with a dramatic atrium, and houses **Expocenter/Chicago,** the world's largest privately owned exposition facility. Showrooms catering to interior designers also spill over into the surrounding neighborhood. A few are open to the public, for example, the stunning **Roche Bobois** (333 North Wells Street), which carries contemporary European furnishings, lighting, and accessories (showroom only; purchases must be made at the retail outlet in Winnetka or by catalogue). But at most, a "Mart Card" is either required or commands a substantial discount. Get your Aunt Gertie, the one who dabbles in decorating, to take you exploring at places like **Design Connection, Inc.** (404 North Wells Street) for wonderful accessories: Oriental antiques and ceramics, lacquered and goatskin tables, and Fitz and Floyd dishes.

When the old Bowman Milk distribution building, with its potentially magnificent trussed roof and massive skylight, came on the market several years ago, interior designer Richard Himmel and his son John decided to buy it. Innumerable gallons of white paint later, the fabulous **Richard Himmel Design Pavilion** (219 West Erie Street) was ready with exclusive lines: massive, rustic furniture from London Marquis, a West Coast company turning out pine and cedar log pieces that would fit right into a hunting lodge; astonishing glass limited editions from Farallon Studios of Sausalito, combining molded, carved, and colored crystal to produce functional sculptures; and dozens more. Himmel also has luxurious upholstered furniture, distributes the output of individual fabric artists, carries antiques, and builds his own line of historic reproductions. A dazzling variety of pieces, unified only by their beauty and obvious quality, makes a dramatic design statement, and open-to-the-public sales draw huge crowds.

January and July sales have been attracting crowds to **Keevan Sadock** (412 North Orleans Street) for decades, and the huge, upper-floor operation offers bargains all year long. A complete cross section of traditional and contemporary middle-of-the-road furniture, upholstery and drapery fabrics, lamps, and other furnishings are sold to the public at 20 percent off list price. The same discount applies if one of their decorators takes you through the Mart.

At **Workbench** (154 West Hubbard Street), the design statement is one track: high-tech. This wildly successful chain, with 35 East Coast locations, opened its first Chicago store in 1981. The huge loft, with exposed masonry, wood beams, pipes, and track lights, perfectly sets off two floors of affordable high-tech and contemporary furniture and accessories. Bright-colored modular foam furniture, butcher-block tables, wood or laminate wall units, and plastic storage units create a panoply of color shouting, "Buy me."

City (213 West Institute Place), formerly Granfalloon on Huron Street (which made Gladys the Goose lamp famous in Chicago), caters to the sophisticated tastes of the times with a total design look. In addition to fine lines of German-designed upholstered furniture and Italian lighting fixtures, the store has sections devoted to the most fashionable furnishings and accessories, for example, imported bath wares, high-tech storage systems, and color-coordinated sundries such as clothespins and telephone patch cords. The conception is so comprehensive that it even includes a collection of high-style casual clothes and a European-style café.

If you crave the latest in kitchen chic, head to **Cook's Mart** (609 North La Salle Street). This main store stocks more than the Atrium Shopping Mall branch of the large commercial and professional supplies that fit in so well with high-tech, as well as dishes, glassware, gadgets, and home-gourmet musts such as food processors and pasta machines. It also offers gourmet foods and cooking classes. To upgrade your culinary facilities to match the new pots, check out the **Kitchen & Bath Mart** (746 North Wells Street), where several complete kitchens and bathrooms are displayed and design services are available. **Bathwares** (740 North Wells Street) specializes in highly styled Italian fixtures and other bathroom paraphernalia: Box, Bogart, and I Balocchi faucets; Erion and Maki modular wall systems; Quadrarco and QT 70 vitreous-china pedestal sinks, toilets, and bidets; and Bagno accessories that won the 1979 Compasso d'Oro prize for design excellence.

Tech may be trendy and functional, but decorators are always searching for that special antique to highlight a room, too. The huge first floor of **Jay Robert's Antique Warehouse** (149 West Kinzie Street) is filled mostly with European imports—furniture, ceramics, clocks, some of everything; the second floor has architectural pieces and brass beds. The three floors of **Donrose Galleries** (751 North Wells Street) are an incredible jumble of rococo furniture, artworks, and antique accessories. Both places have so much that a decorator is a big help sorting it out; he also enjoys a trade discount.

Between these two giants, Wells Street houses more specialized antiques stores. At **Georgian House Antiques** (739), the name says all: 18th- and 19th-century English furniture is displayed in an airy, bright setting. **Fly-By-Nite Gallery** (714), on the other hand, is anything but what the name suggests. This dim, crowded shop overflows with carefully researched Art Nouveau, Art Deco, and other late 19th- and early 20th-century pieces. Sculpture, pottery, glassware, and paper ephemera—all bearing scholarly annotations—cram every corner of every case. It's like a museum where everything's for sale.

O'Hara's Connoisseur Gallery (707) is a 1950s-style, confused antiques store with everything askew. The barking guard dogs don't make shopping any easier; however, O'Hara's is a complete restoration center for every type of art and artifact. The perfect, pre-1840 objects at **Tom Menaugh Antique Furnishings** (442) don't need restoration, but your bankroll will after paying the tariff that the museum-quality stock commands. This is probably the city's second-best source (Malcolm Franklin is first) for early 19th-century European furniture.

At the turn of the century, loft buildings, warehouses, and tenements filled this neighborhood. It was an Italian ghetto, and life centered around the city's first Italian parish, **Assumption Church** (Illinois and Orleans Streets), built by Servite fathers between 1884 and 1886 to resemble their mother church in Rome, only much smaller. Later the area became a tough red-light district that endured through the 1950s. Hardly a week passed that a newspaper headline failed to trumpet a tale of a visiting fireman rolled by a B-girl.

Now all the stories are about a SoHo-style renaissance, and the real estate is some of the city's hottest. Artists, photographers, designers, musicians, and filmmakers have lived and worked in the old manufacturing spaces for years (carrying on a neighborhood tradition dating back to the garret conversions of Rush Street's mansions in the 1930s and '40s), but more conventional urban pioneers are swelling their ranks. People who can afford $200,000 condominiums in completely renovated buildings with 12-foot ceilings, four-foot-thick walls, and newly glistening wood floors are gladly trading suburban amenities for downtown convenience and the ever-changing, hip streetscape.

The area is an intriguing patchwork of shops, galleries, lounges, and restaurants. A growing number of trendy, house-proud stores augments the mart's train of antiques and furniture places along Wells Street. The revitalization got its start with the innovative West Hubbard Street galleries. The first to open here, **N.A.M.E. Gallery** (9), is a cooperative, but shows by artists other than the founders have drawn national attention. Two feminist galleries—**ARC** (6) and **Artemisia** (9)—share the street with half a dozen spaces, both cooperative and commercial (*see Galleries*), and with the offices of **Harry Weese & Associates** (10), without whom there probably wouldn't have been much of a loft-conversion movement. Now it's so established that main-line galleries seek the dramatic environments around Huron, Superior, and Franklin Streets, while the gay bars and used-periodical stores that lined Clark Street's once-dismal stretch dwindle in number. Fortunately, the **Jazz Record Mart** (11 West Grand Avenue) remains, stocking the largest and finest selection of used and new jazz and blues discs—everything from rare old collectors' items to hard-to-find little labels. The cut-out bins sometimes yield real finds and are always a bargain. Occasionally, owner Bob Koester shows clips from his jazz-film collection to all comers, free. After closing, he frequently takes apprehensive aficionados on tours of South Side blues bars at no charge except the sightseers' bar bill. Koester is also a founder of the Jazz Institute, which coordinates the summer Grant Park Jazz Festival and sponsors a big winter Jazz Fair at the Blackstone Hotel (*see Annual Events*).

The façade of the **Off Center Shopping Mall** (300 West Grand Avenue) picks up the neighborhood's artsy ambiance with Richard Haas's *trompe l'oeil* cutaway mural of a possible inside view of the old spaghetti factory. Inside, six floors of stores give the art of merchandising a few new twists. One of the country's largest importers of Afghan Kilims and carpets, **Caravans Awry** (6th level) manufactures Oriental rugs and sells new and used ones by the square foot. The selection's good and there's plenty of space to spread out the carpets. **Royal Knitting Mills** (1st level) offers casual, on-the-playing-field sweaters and tops produced by the Chicago factory.

Some of the other noteworthy Off Center shops are discount outlets for chic stores. **Lady Madonna Maternity Outlet** (3rd level) features better prices than the chain's Atrium Shopping Mall shop, as does **Shepherd-Scott, Ltd.** (2nd level), which carries out-of-season wear from the Atrium Mall's Robert Vance: conservative, well-made, men's clothing in natural fabrics at discounts up to 50 percent. **Stefano** (4th level) is no longer a Stanley Korshak sale outlet, but still stocks top-of-the-line women's wear from designers like Pierre Cardin and Perry Ellis at good prices; it also has women's shoes. Saving money is in the bag at **That's Our Bag** (1st level), where leather purses, briefcases, luggage, and accessories spill over onto the floor from walls of shelves. The really cheap stuff is just that, but the medium price range offers a huge selection of fine values.

The neighborhood's rebirth touches the inner man, too. **One Fish Plaza** (745 North La Salle Street) is a mini comestibles complex shared by **Burhop's Seafood** and the **La Salle Street Market,** with free parking to boot. The venerable fish firm continues to purvey one of the city's best, most expensive selections and now also has wine. The market sells the usual assortment of gourmet goodies—cheeses, pastas, bulk coffees, smoked fish and meat, exotic tinned goods—and prepared foods, such as pâtés, quiches, salads, and desserts. Pick up the fixings here for an elegant party or a beach box lunch. Another source of *au courant* nibbles is the California/SoHo deli **Delish** (544 North Wells Street). Have a fancy sandwich or salad in the little whitewashed dining room, or order to go.

Ready-to-eat, extravagant, French-style entrées are a specialty of **Mitchell Cobey Cuisine** (100 East Walton Street). Fancy salad and sweet choices are abundant, the cheese counter offers lots of hard-to-find varieties, and the pâtés include several from the beatific kitchen of Le Français. Cobey is one of Chicago's premier caterers and also packs a wide range of surprisingly affordable box lunches.

No area of the city or suburbs boasts more restaurants, both boffo and blah, per square mile. New ones seem to open weekly; old ones redecorate and/or redo their menus to hold or recapture the limelight. Stay abreast of the best by picking up a current *Chicago* magazine. Fancier restaurants require reservations; they help at many of the others, too. Remember that police tow trucks vigilantly cruise the neighborhood throughout the evening.

Le Français, generally recognized as one of the country's great restaurants, flourishes in the wilds of Wheeling, but the Art Deco **La Mer** (1 West Maple Street), owner-chef Jean Banchet's in-town collaboration with Arnie Morton, provides much the same sublime excess. The nouvelle cuisine influenced menu may offer the best seafood between the coasts, and daily specials often include fish flown in from France. Rich sauces, divine mousses, diet-defying pastries, and artful presentations all combine to make this a must for any gourmet. A subaltern guards the elevator to **Le Perroquet** (70 East Walton Street), another temple to gastronomy. Five-course prix fixe dinners (about $40) and less expensive prix fixe lunches are impeccably served in the elegantly understated dining room. Though the nouvelle cuisine here may appear austere compared to La Mer's, everything from pâtés and other creative openers to simply sauced entrées, seductive specials, and scrumptious desserts (the soufflés are favorites) is deftly prepared.

Swank dining rooms are the rule in Magnificent Mile hotels. They do a brisk weekday trade with expense-account businessmen, but the food lives up to the menus' promises and prices at only a few. The opulent **Ritz-Carlton Dining Room** is one of these. Delicate appetizers (try a vegetable mousse), well-made soups, nouvelle-inspired entrées, seasonal specials, and luxurious desserts all show more imagination than the room's name. The wine list is one of the country's largest. **La Tour,** in the Park Hyatt, also has an impressive wine list (including about forty Champagnes), but the menu is limited, and the chef hasn't really gotten his act together yet. On the other hand, the room overlooks the old Water Tower and is beautifully decorated with Rousseau-like murals, tilework, and Oriental carpets.

L'Escargot, a pleasant, friendly spot in the Allerton Hotel, offers a hearty bourgeois alternative to haute and nouvelle cuisine. Complete, table d'hôte dinners run about $20, half the price of posher places, and the five-course petit dinner, early and late on week nights, is an even better bargain. The Tremont Hotel's popular **Cricket's** couples clubbiness with generally fine Continental food in a beamed, stuccoed room carefully hung with scads of collectibles. The broad menu takes chances, as with crème Senegalaise soup, and the kitchen usually brings them off.

Chicago's European-style bistros, with bustling, open-to-the-sidewalk cafés in front of more formal, yet still convivial, dining rooms, are booming. Bright and noisy, **Le Relais Chicago** (50 East Oak Street) typifies the genre, and the menu keeps pace with a good cross section of inventive dishes, both light and more substantial. **Yvette** (1206 North State Street) was an instant hit when it opened in 1982—and with good reason. The Art Deco café is stunning, the dining room (done in grays) is stylishly soothing, and the menu is varied, inviting, and reasonably priced.

Unconventional menu twists and extraordinary décors characterize other trend-setting restaurants that strongly reflect their owners' visions. **Gordon** (512 North Clark Street), the Jean Cocteau-like renovation of the old St. Regis Hotel coffee shop, was, like Yvette, an immediate success and remains a reliable and rather romantic option. Lightly sauced fresh fish are among the bright stars of the ever-changing menu. Gordon Sinclair and his chef John Terczak also opened **Lexander** (508 North Clark Street), a bilevel, slightly bizarre, bemuraled spot with an innovative menu that might best be described as "nouvelle American." In addition to the fashionable Tango in New Town, George Badonsky has to his credit the handsome, French-poster-adorned **Bastille** (21 West Superior Street). Wine bar selections are impressive, and the brasserie's simply grilled meats and seafoods are usually good. Even more striking in a 1940s streamlined style, Badonsky's **George's** (230 West Kinzie Street) is an extremely popular and congenial place to sample a wide range of Northern Italian dishes.

For classic Northern Italian meals, head to **Doro's** (871 North Rush Street) in the heart of Chicago's night-life action. The overblown décor recalls the 1950s, the food has a French accent, and the help a Latino one, but it all works. **House of Bertini** (535 North Wells Street), an old-line Italian place in a nearby, charming, terra-cotta-fronted building, leans more toward steaks, is usually quite good, and is reasonably priced. Some of the best steaks in town (and very expensive, especially with à la carte extras) are found at **Morton's** (1050 North State Street) and at the ostentatious **Arnie's,** both located in the same building and owned by Arnie Morton, scion of an old Chicago family of restaurateurs. At **Carson's—The Place for Ribs** (612 North Wells Street) and **Lawry's—The Prime Rib** (100 East Ontario Street), the name's the game. Carson's, the *Chicago* rib-tasting-panel winner, also has highly rated steaks, but Lawry's serves nothing but prime rib at dinner (with a Simpson's-on-the-Strand flair) in a former McCormick mansion, once the site of the Kungsholm Swedish restaurant and puppet-opera theater.

The Palm, in the Mayfair Regent, is as bumptious as Lawry's is sedate. The playful décor—giant comics on the walls, sawdust on the floor—creates an intriguing ambiance for ultra-expensive steaks and huge, equally dear lobsters, but the waiters can make a meal, and the check, a rude experience. Try instead the **Cape Cod Room** in The Drake. Some (Gael Greene included) have faulted the waiters, but the dependable seafood served in a New England tavern setting is justly touted. Another reliable piscatorial source is the **Chestnut Street Grill** in Water Tower Place, although here the atmosphere is San Francisco.

The seafood at **Hatsuhana** (160 East Ontario Street) is of a different school. Sampling 35 varieties of the finest sushi in town or combination dinners (such as half a lobster, tempura, sushi, sashimi, custard with fish, and grilled seafood) in the spare, angular, natural-wood place is utterly authentic. Prices are high by run-of-the-mill Oriental-restaurant standards, but Hatsuhana's trips to O'Hare for fresh seafood aren't typical. If absolute dollars are important, a more limited selection of similar goodies can be had at the much smaller **Yanase Japanese Restaurant** (818 North State Street). The convivial sushi bar may be full, but there's also a pleasant upstairs dining room. Between these two, in every way, is **Shino** (18 East Huron Street), a Japanese surprise in a period brownstone. The Japanese piano bar above the dining rooms is accessible to Occidentals. George Kuan and Austin Koo have three outposts of their Chinese empire in the area, all topnotch places offering exciting selections: **Hunan Palace** (1050 North State Street), **House of Hunan** (535 North Michigan Avenue), and **Szechwan House** (600 North Michigan Avenue).

The fun-food burger in all its permutations flourishes at **Hamburger Hamlet** (44 East Walton Street), but the whole funky bag—fried zucchini, chili, nachos, avocado this, sprouts that—is served up in a richly paneled, determinedly turn-of-the-century-looking room. Two million dollars worth of décor at this busy lunchtime spot may prove that the medium really is the message: The food is mediocre. Ironically, the area's best burger may be at the **Acorn on Oak** (116 East Oak Street), a small, clubby neighborhood tap with Chicago's much-lauded piano-bar artist, Buddy Charles. At the other end of class is **The ? Mark** (439 North Wells Street), an old-line workingmen's bar in the shadow of the Merchandise Mart, which proudly and congenially serves the "world famous helluva burger." It is: big, juicy, properly cooked, inexpensive, and wonderful with grilled onions (though available only through lunchtime).

Even the American mainstay-on-a-bun is greasy at the **Billy Goat Tavern** (430 North Michigan Avenue, lower level), but the squalid dump (said by some to have inspired *Saturday Night Live*'s "cheeseburger, cheeseburger, Pepsi, Pepsi" routine) attracts newspaper types as diverse as pressmen, mailers, and Mike Royko, who called the original owner "the city's greatest tavern keeper." It's an institution, but there's no accounting for tastes.

Newsmen with somewhat more sensitive palates gather at **Riccardo's** (437 North Rush Street), an atmospheric bistro with a huge palette-shaped bar, palette-shaped door windows, and wall murals—legacies of the original owner, artist Ric Riccardo. Lunch and after work are the times to be seen at this famous celebrity hangout. Journalists also favor **The Wrigley Building Restaurant** (410 North Michigan Avenue) for reliable, solidly prepared American standards in an archetypal 1950s room and, of course, the private Chicago Press Club downstairs, with its own, less dependable kitchen.

The humble pizza, raised to Olympian heights, may be Chicago's claim to culinary fame: This is deep-dish pizza's cradle. Join the line at **Pizzeria Uno** (29 East Ohio Street) or the slightly slicker **Pizzeria Due** (619 North Wabash Avenue) for the classic example. The rich, pastrylike crust is topped with lots of fresh, uncased sausage, cheeses, and whole tomatoes; and a small pizza (about $5.50) serves two, especially when preceded by the delicious Italian salad. The help can be brusque. Revisionists praise the pies at **Giordano's** (747 North Rush Street), and *Chicago* magazine's panel rated them number one after being seduced by the unique, double-crust version served here. The pizza's really good but looks like a manhole cover and doesn't travel or reheat well.

Andy's (11 East Hubbard Street) serves thin-crust pizza by the pie or slice and hamburgers, but live jazz is the real draw at this cavernous, wood-paneled bar. After work, crowds from the IBM Plaza and other nearby office towers jam the room for the traditional jazz and Dixieland sets that start at 5 p.m. and last for three to four hours. Topnotch Chicago studio musicians, joined by old-timers like Louis Armstrong's drummer Barret Deems and sometimes by out-of-town guests, keep the joint jumping with some of the city's best sounds. The $2 cover charge is waived at the bar. Later in the evening after the button-down types make their trains, Andy's is a hangout for local loft dwellers.

Smoke-filled and woody, **The Backroom** (1007 North Rush Street) is everything a jazz club should be. Devotees in both denim and evening clothes tramp down a narrow causeway to this former stable seven nights a week, frequently to hear name groups. The names are even bigger at **Rick's Café Americain** (Holiday Inn, 644 North Lake Shore Drive), one of the city's premier jazz rooms. Done

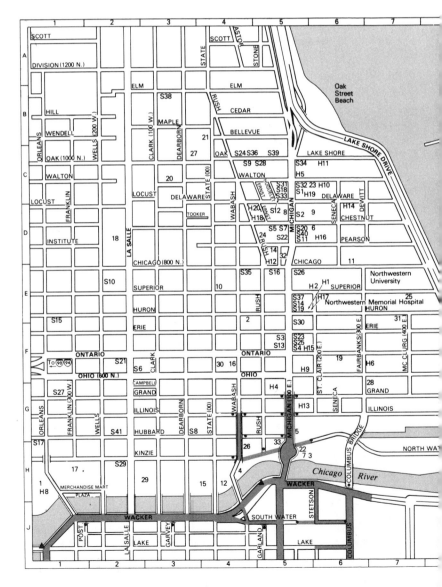

up in Casablanca style, this is a likely, though expensive, place to catch an all-time-great's set.

Tourists and regulars also frequent **Milt Trenier's** (901 North Rush Street), but the house trio's sounds are a tamer, nightclubby blend of old favorites and show tunes with dancing between sets. Dancing to a combo's jazzed-up versions of pop songs is on the bill at **Billy's** (936 North Rush Street), however, the bar area is sometimes so jammed that even moving is difficult. A very expensive renovation of a former strip joint, this is a gathering spot for Chicago's well-healed, over-35, gold-chain types and their frequently younger companions.

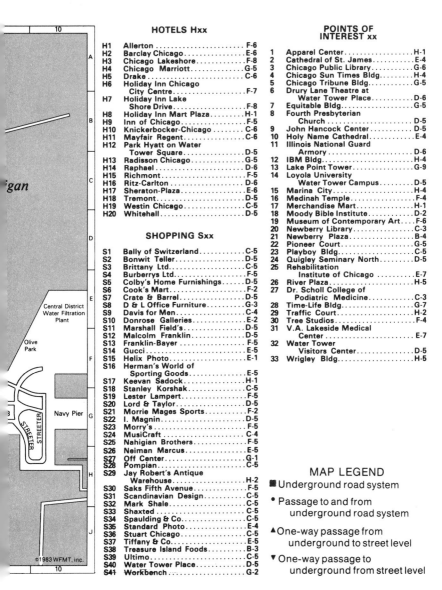

HOTELS Hxx

H1	Allerton	F-6
H2	Barclay Chicago	E-6
H3	Chicago Lakeshore	F-8
H4	Chicago Marriott	G-5
H5	Drake	C-6
H6	Holiday Inn Chicago City Centre	F-7
H7	Holiday Inn Lake Shore Drive	F-8
H8	Holiday Inn Mart Plaza	H-1
H9	Inn of Chicago	F-5
H10	Knickerbocker-Chicago	C-6
H11	Mayfair Regent	C-6
H12	Park Hyatt on Water Tower Square	D-5
H13	Radisson Chicago	G-5
H14	Raphael	D-6
H15	Richmont	F-5
H16	Ritz-Carlton	D-6
H17	Sheraton-Plaza	E-6
H18	Tremont	D-5
H19	Westin Chicago	C-5
H20	Whitehall	D-5

SHOPPING Sxx

S1	Bally of Switzerland	C-5
S2	Bonwit Teller	D-5
S3	Brittany Ltd.	C-5
S4	Burberrys Ltd.	F-5
S5	Colby's Home Furnishings	D-5
S6	Cook's Mart	F-2
S7	Crate & Barrel	D-5
S8	D & L Office Furniture	G-3
S9	Davis for Men	C-4
S10	Donrose Galleries	E-2
S11	Marshall Field's	D-5
S12	Malcolm Franklin	D-5
S13	Franklin-Bayer	F-5
S14	Gucci	E-5
S15	Helix Photo	E-1
S16	Herman's World of Sporting Goods	E-5
S17	Keevan Sadock	H-1
S18	Stanley Korshak	C-5
S19	Lester Lampert	F-5
S20	Lord & Taylor	D-5
S21	Morrie Mages Sports	F-2
S22	I. Magnin	D-5
S23	Morry's	F-5
S24	MusiCraft	C-4
S25	Nahigian Brothers	F-5
S26	Neiman Marcus	E-5
S27	Off Center	G-1
S28	Pompian	C-5
S29	Jay Robert's Antique Warehouse	H-2
S30	Saks Fifth Avenue	F-5
S31	Scandinavian Design	C-5
S32	Mark Shale	C-5
S33	Shaxted	C-5
S34	Spaulding & Co.	C-5
S35	Standard Photo	E-4
S36	Stuart Chicago	C-5
S37	Tiffany & Co.	E-5
S38	Treasure Island Foods	B-3
S39	Ultimo	C-5
S40	Water Tower Place	D-5
S41	Workbench	G-2

POINTS OF INTEREST xx

1	Apparel Center	H-1
2	Cathedral of St. James	E-4
3	Chicago Public Library	G-6
4	Chicago Sun Times Bldg.	H-4
5	Chicago Tribune Bldg.	G-5
6	Drury Lane Theatre at Water Tower Place	D-6
7	Equitable Bldg.	G-5
8	Fourth Presbyterian Church	D-5
9	John Hancock Center	D-5
10	Holy Name Cathedral	E-4
11	Illinois National Guard Armory	D-6
12	IBM Bldg.	H-4
13	Lake Point Tower	G-9
14	Loyola University Water Tower Campus	D-5
15	Marina City	H-4
16	Medinah Temple	F-4
17	Merchandise Mart	H-1
18	Moody Bible Institute	D-2
19	Museum of Contemporary Art	F-6
20	Newberry Library	C-3
21	Newberry Plaza	B-4
22	Pioneer Court	G-5
23	Playboy Bldg.	C-5
24	Quigley Seminary North	D-5
25	Rehabilitation Institute of Chicago	E-7
26	River Plaza	H-5
27	Dr. Scholl College of Podiatric Medicine	C-3
28	Time-Life Bldg.	G-7
29	Traffic Court	H-2
30	Tree Studios	F-4
31	V.A. Lakeside Medical Center	E-7
32	Water Tower Visitors Center	D-5
33	Wrigley Bldg.	H-5

MAP LEGEND

■ Underground road system

• Passage to and from underground road system

▲ One-way passage from underground to street level

▼ One-way passage to underground from street level

© 1983 WFMT, inc.

The Backroom, Trenier's, and Billy's are in the heart of Chicago's singles-bar row, which extends along Rush Street and rounds the corner onto Division Street. Live music is the magnet in some spots; at others, dancing while a deejay spins the discs is the draw. The crowd itself often exerts such a synergistic force that sidewalk lines of revelers wait, with I.D.s in hand, to cram into an already-packed bar. The action peaks on Friday and Saturday nights, but weekday cocktail-hour specials and nice weather anytime also bring out hordes of hopefuls.

They flock to places like the bilevel, glass-fronted **Snuggery** (15 West Division Street), where two dance floors, a deejay, trendy fun food, and nicely dressed masses promise an evening's diversion in plant- and brass-filled surroundings. Of a dozen similar spots nearby, **Houlihan's Old Place** (1207 North Dearborn Street) is a front-runner in the overblown-décor department. Part of a Kansas City-based chain that claims to own the country's largest collection of antiques, it's filled with stained glass, old posters, and gewgaws of all sizes and sorts. A magnificent backbar highlights the meeting-and-phone-number-exchanging front room, and mediocre fun food is artlessly served in the equally ornate dining room.

Once a popular singles meat market, the basement **Mother's** (26 West Division Street) isn't "decorated" with such determination, but it aims for an environment pleasing to a variety of tastes. Special promotions, such as boxing and ladies' nights, and video tapes to amuse nondancers provide some of the diversity. For the most part, though, a young, informal set boogies to digestible music—rock, salsa, reggae, anything that's "in."

The older-line saloons thrive without live music, dancing, or gimmicks. **Butch McGuire's** (20 West Division Street), a Prohibition speakeasy and the area's original singles bar, is always packed, and you see as many suits as jeans. Antiques and Irish memorabilia hang from the ceilings, and the waiters are famous for wending their way through the press of bodies without spilling a drop of the required social lubricants. As at the other Irish bars, St. Patrick's Day occasions more hoopla than you can shake a shillelagh at.

Next door on the singles-scene main drag is **She-Nannigans** (16). Slicker than McGuire's and just as jammed, this big, pine-walled, stained-glass-and-antiques-accented spot draws a somewhat more sophisticated-looking group. The height of coupling chic, however, is **Harry's Café** (1035 North Rush Street). Designer Phil Rowe's classic creation, filled with oak, beveled glass, antiques, and plants, is Chicago's answer to Maxwell's Plum. This is *the* place for the Gold Coast's and Near North Side's affluent, stylish, under-35s who always look like they're posing for a festive magazine layout. Fun food, steaks, and seafood are served in windowside galleries, and the crowded room makes for a fine floor show.

There are easily a hundred more watering holes in the immediate neighborhood, not to mention the hotel bars, almost all of which offer cocktail-hour treats and evening entertainment to while away lonely hours away from home. Find out who's performing where by picking up a copy of *Chicago* or the *Reader*. If you just want to watch the game rather than play it, line up for an outdoor table at **Café de Melvins!** (1116 North State Street). This local landmark (with matchbooks that say "Melvin's Truck Stop") is also a great place to see morning-after couples stumble back to the scene of their meeting for Sunday brunch.

GUIDE TO LISTINGS

Interesting places

**Annunciation Greek
Orthodox Cathedral**
La Salle and Oak Sts.
664-5485
*Erected in 1910; the lovely
little church's mural-rich interior has been restored.*

*The Apparel Center
350 N. Orleans St.
527-4210

*Assumption Church
Illinois and Orleans Sts.
644-0036
*First Italian parish estab-
lished in 1881; Mother
Cabrini opened the church
school in 1899.*

***John Carroll Sons
Funeral Home**
25 E. Erie St.
944-6060

*Cathedral of St. James
Wabash Ave. and Huron St.
787-7360

CBS Inc.
630 N. McClurg Ct.
944-6000
*WBBM television and radio
come to you from a former
ice-skating rink and horse
arena.*

***Chicago Public Library
(Central)**
425 N. Michigan Ave.
269-2900
(See Libraries)

Chicago Sun-Times
401 N. Wabash Ave.
321-3000; tours 321-2032
*See the presses in opera-
tion from the hallways or
take one of the hour-long
tours at 9:30 or 10:30 a.m.
weekdays. Built in 1957 to
also house the defunct Chicago Daily News, the plant
has a pleasant riverfront
plaza.*

Church of the Ascension
Elm and La Salle Sts.
664-1271
*Started from a schism in St.
James Episcopal Church,
this was a poor congrega-
tion until the 1940s when a
rector donated his personal
fortune. Built in the 1880s,
the limestone church, with
nice stained glass and a
64-rank organ, has mostly
1950s decorations. Main-
tains a high liturgy.*

**City of Chicago Central
Office Building**
320 N. Clark St.
*Designed by George C.
Nimmons and built for
Reid, Murdoch and Com-
pany in 1913. Brick with
terra-cotta accents. Most
people visit at one time or
another: Traffic Court con-
venes here.*

**860-80 Lake Shore Drive
Apartments**
860-80 N. Lake Shore Dr.
*Built in 1952, the first apart-
ment towers to embrace the
commercial glass-wall style
spawned myriad imitators.
Astonishingly, Mies van der
Rohe did the basic design
in the '20s.*

*Expocenter/Chicago
350 N. Orleans St.
527-4141

**54 W. Hubbard St.
Building**
54 W. Hubbard St.
*Designed by Otto Matz, the
Romanesque, granite,
1892 Cook County Criminal
Court now houses various
Chicago police units and
other city departments.*

***Fourth Presbyterian
Church**
Michigan and Chestnut
787-4570

**John Hancock
Observatory**
875 N. Michigan Ave.
751-3681
*94th floor; adults $2.50,
kids $1.50. Grownups
might spend their money
better on drinks at Images,
the 96th-floor bar. It's quieter and has the same view.*

*Holy Name Cathedral
State and Superior Sts.
787-8040

IBM Building
Wabash Ave. and Kinzie St.
*This is the last building de-
signed by Mies van der
Rohe, and the sleek tower
typifies his life's work.*

Lake Point Tower
505 N. Lake Shore Dr.
*The tallest apartment build-
ing in the world is also one
of the most handsome.
The bronzed-glass-and-
anodized-aluminum, three-
lobed tower was adapted
by Schipporeit-Heinrich
Associates from a 1921
Mies van der Rohe
proposal.*

Lake Shore Drive Bridge
Crossing the Chicago
River
*One of the world's biggest
bascule bridges and scene
of the infamous, soon-to-go
"S" curve. FDR gave the
dedication speech in 1937
chastising "aggressor
nations."*

Lake Shore Park
Field House
808 N. Lake Shore Dr.
294-4720
*One gym, indoor and out-
door team sports, yoga and
exercises; no crafts or
drama.*

La Salle Street Church
La Salle and Elm Sts.
944-2488
*Built as an English Lutheran
church in the early 1880s;
now an independent
nondenominational church.
Small Gothic building with
crumbling limestone
façade.*

Marina City
300 N. State St.
222-1111
*Architect Bertrand Gold-
berg's cylindrical,
balconied towers (with
pie-shaped rooms inside)
won raves when they were
constructed in the 1960s
and are an unofficial Chicago symbol (often pic-
tured in photo books). The
model of a modern city has
everything: apartments, an
office building, garages,
restaurants, a bank, a bowling alley and health club, a
few shops—even a marina.*

Medinah Temple
600 N. Wabash Ave.
944-4266
*Hoehl and Schmid's 1912
Moorish temple built for the
Shriners of Chicago has a
central cupola flanked by
two smaller ones, small
arches with delicate floral
stained glass, and a dra-
matic entrance. See the
auditorium during the an-
nual Shrine Circus in the
spring; occasionally used
to record the Chicago
Symphony.*

*Merchandise Mart
Merchandise Mart Plaza
Wells and Kinzie Sts.
527-4141
*On The Scene (661-1440)
arranges group tours for
Thurs., 10 a.m. and 1:30
p.m. Reserve on Wed.*

Mercury
Sightseeing Boats
Michigan Ave. Bridge
(southwest side)
332-1353, 381-5192
*1-, 1½-, and 2-hour lake
and river tours.*

*Michigan Avenue Bridge
Michigan Ave. and the
Chicago River
*Double-decked bascule
bridge built in 1920. J. E.
Fraser's bas reliefs, The
Pioneers and The Dis-
coverers, grace the north
pylons. Father Marquette, a
Jesuit, wears Franciscan
robes. Site of Ft. Dearborn
marked at south end.*

John B. Murphy Memorial
50 E. Erie St.
*Fanciful, rococo-façaded,
1926 auditorium designed
by Marshall and Fox was
dedicated to an early 20th-
century surgeon and is
owned by the American
College of Surgeons. Pan-
els in massive doors show
the history of medicine.*

*Museum of
Contemporary Art
237 E. Ontario St.
280-2660
(See Museums)

Navy Pier
Grand Ave. and the lake
*Built in 1916 for com-
mercial shipping but has
had many uses. In 1976,
the east end of the 3,000-
foot-long pier, with its wonderful domed auditorium,
was renovated by the city,
and murals were painted
along the north walkway.
Since then, it has hosted a
variety of events from ethnic
fairs to ChicagoFest (see
Annual Events). Plans are
afoot to turn it into a giant
complex with a hotel, restaurants, shops, entertainment, and more. Great
place to catch a summer
breeze. You can tour the
U.S.S. Silversides, part of
The Great Lakes Naval and
Maritime Museum (see
Museums), and the S.S.
Clipper, which operates as
a bar/restaurant with dancing, as well as a museum
(admission charge).*

*Newberry Library
60 W. Walton St.
943-9090
*Adult-education program,
too. Don't forget to check
out the bookshop. (See
Libraries.)*

*Samuel M. Nickerson
House
40 E. Erie St.

Oak Street Beach
Oak St. and Michigan Ave.
*Chicago's the only northern
city where you can buy a
designer swimsuit on the
grand boulevard, put it on,
and walk to the beach.*

Olive Harvey Park
Lake Shore Dr. and Ohio
*A bit of grass, rabbits hiding
in the bushes, a small
beach, and limited metered
parking. Bicycle rentals.*

*Pioneer Court
Equitable Building Plaza
401 N. Michigan Ave.
*Summer lunchtime con-
certs. Lower-level shops
and riverside restaurant
with a patio.*

Quigley Preparatory
Seminary North
103 E. Chestnut St.
787-9343
*Constructed between 1910
and 1920, the seminary
and chapel are modeled on
medieval French Gothic
buildings.*

Scottish Rite Cathedral
Dearborn and Walton Sts.
787-7605
*Originally the Second Uni-
tarian Church and rebuilt as
such after the Chicago Fire.
The Shriners bought the
building in 1902 and used it
until the Medinah Temple
was constructed, then sold
it to this Masonic order.*

*Second Chicago
Historical Society
Building
632 N. Dearborn St.

Time-Life Building
541 N. Fairbanks Ct.
Designed by Harry Weese in 1970. The effect of the daylight on the gold-tinted reflecting windows is ever-changing. The lobby's unusual set up results from the dictates of double-decker, odd-even elevators, a visually successful innovation that has some drawbacks.

Tree Studios
6 E. Ohio St.
Judge Lambert Tree commissioned Brooklyn's Parfitt Brothers to re-create their studio complex in his backyard in 1894, hoping to keep some of the World's Columbian Exposition's artists in town. Over the years, several architects were involved, and another generation of artists still work in the bright, high-ceilinged studios surrounding a hidden-from-the-street garden.

*Tribune Tower
435 N. Michigan Ave.
222-3232; tours 222-3993
One-hour-and-15-minute tours six days a week.

*Washington Square Park
Dearborn and Walton Sts.
The city's oldest park was known as Bughouse Square for its open forum in the 1930s.

*Water Tower
806 N. Michigan Ave.

*Water Tower Visitors Information Center
806 N. Michigan Ave.
225-5000, ext. 276
Open daily, 9 a.m. to 5 p.m., except Thanksgiving and Christmas. Direct phone lines to restaurants, Chicago Hotel and Motel Association, activity lines, CTA.

Wendella Sightseeing Boats
Michigan Ave. Bridge
(northwest side)
337-1446
Chicago River and Lake Michigan trips in good weather leave from the foot of the Wrigley Building. Regular commuter runs to and from Chicago and North Western Station. Charters, too.

*Wrigley Building
400 N. Michigan Ave.
558-8080

Major institutions

Access Living
505 N. La Salle St.
649-7404, TDD 649-8593
Helps the handicapped help themselves: financial-benefit counseling, housing and personal-care aid, workshops. Monitors legislation relating to the disabled. Funded by the government and the Rehabilitation Institute of Chicago.

American College of Surgeons
55 E. Erie St.
664-4050
Association serving surgeons from the U.S., Canada, and some foreign countries.

American Dental Association
211 E. Chicago Ave.
440-2500
Organization for dental practitioners. Pick up free booklets on current trends in dentistry.

American Library Association
50 E. Huron St.
944-6780
World's oldest and largest organization dedicated to improving library service. Nonprofit; publishes reference books, too.

American Medical Association
535 N. Dearborn St.
751-6000
Professional organization of physicians.

American Red Cross Mid-America Chapter
43 E. Ohio St.
440-2050
Disaster relief, blood bank, community services, classes, and free literature.

Catholic Charities Near North Center
721 N. La Salle St.
266-6100
Alternative-education services, addiction counseling, alcohol safety program, senior-community and social-development services.

Dr. William M. Scholl College of Podiatric Medicine
1001 N. Dearborn St.
280-2880
280-2900 (foot clinic)
Founded in 1912; four-year and postgraduate programs. Not-for-profit, inexpensive foot clinics are open to the public.

Henrotin Health and Fitness Testing Center
920 N. Clark St.
440-7790
Comprehensive physical evaluation and training using lifestyle modification to alter diet and exercise. In a lovely little building with a multicolored brick-and-terra-cotta façade.

**Loyola University
Water Tower Campus**
820 N. Michigan Ave.
670-3000
Loyola's downtown branch.

Moody Bible Institute
820 N. La Salle St.
329-4000
*Started by Dwight L. Moody
in 1886 to train lay leaders
in the church. Large com-
plex offers three-year program teaching general
Christianity and the Bible to
turn out Christian leaders.*

**Northwestern Memorial
Hospital**
Superior and Fairbanks Ct.
649-2000
*Enormous conglomeration
of Northwestern Univer-
sity's hospitals.*

**Northwestern University
Chicago Campus**
339 E. Chicago Ave.
649-8649
*Includes this Evanston uni-
versity's medical, dental,
and law schools, and the
evening undergraduate
and extension classes.
Some handsome Gothic
buildings.*

**George and Anna Portes
Cancer Prevention
Center**
33 W. Huron St.
440-7100
*Complete cancer screening
takes three hours and costs
$140. The Midwest's oldest
cancer-prevention center
can see 120 people a day:
Computers do part of the
work.*

**Rehabilitation Institute
of Chicago**
345 E. Superior St.
649-6000
*"Twenty-seven years of put-
ting lives back together."
In- and out-patient
services.*

**Salvation Army
Central States
Territorial Headquarters**
860 N. Dearborn St.
440-4600
*Administrative offices.
Those for the Northern Illinois Unified Command are
in an older limestone building across the street.*

**University of Chicago
Graduate School
of Business**
190 E. Delaware Pl.
266-3430
*Downtown branch is home
of the "190" and "ex-
ecutive" business-school
programs.*

**Veterans Administration
Lakeside Medical Center**
333 E. Huron St.
943-6600

Hotels

*Weekend packages are
subject to availability and
change. Advance reserva-
tions are normally required.*

Allerton Hotel
701 N. Michigan Ave.
440-1500
*Weekend deals reduce
rates slightly at this budget
business hotel.*

Barclay Chicago Hotel
166 E. Superior St.
787-6000, 800-621-8004
*Luxury suites are radically
reduced on weekends.*

Chicago Lakeshore Hotel
600 N. Lake Shore Dr.
787-4700, 800-528-1234
*Substantially reduced rates
on weekends at this Best
Western hotel.*

Chicago Marriott Hotel
540 N. Michigan Ave.
836-0100, 800-228-9290
*Weekend package includes
some meals. The hotel
boasts the Marquis, an upper-floor deluxe hotel-
within-a-hotel, and a shopping mall that has yet to
catch on.*

*The Drake Hotel
140 E. Walton St.
787-2200
*Room rates are reduced
modestly on weekends.*

**Holiday Inn
Chicago City Centre**
300 E. Ohio St.
787-6100, 800-238-8000
*Packages include dining
coupons and parking. As
always, kids under 18 sleep
free; and those under 12
also may eat free from a
special menu.*

**Holiday Inn
Lake Shore Drive**
644 N. Lake Shore Dr.
943-9200, 800-238-8000
*Great lakefront views from
some rooms, and from the
bar and a revolving rooftop
restaurant. Big-name jazz at
Rick's Café Americain.
Deals same as above.*

***Holiday Inn
Mart Plaza**
350 N. Orleans St.
836-5000, 800-238-8000
*Same weekend packages
as at other Holiday Inns.*

Inn of Chicago
162 E. Ohio St.
787-3100, 800-621-4028
*Substantially reduced
weekend rates at this Best
Western hotel.*

**Knickerbocker-Chicago
Hotel**
163 E. Walton St.
751-8100, 800-621-8140
*Weekend rates at this lux-
ury operation are virtually
half price.*

*Mayfair Regent Hotel
181 E. Lake Shore Dr.
787-8500, 800-621-8135
Superb Old World lounge-tearoom and some magnificent views. You save almost 50% on weekends.

**Park Hyatt on
Water Tower Square**
800 N. Michigan Ave.
280-2222, 800-228-9000
Opulent renovation of a modern hotel cost $10 million! Weekend single-night discounts are substantial. Or book the $2,000 per night penthouse with Steinway-graced music room, library, dining room, kitchen, and valet.

*Radisson Chicago Hotel
505 N. Michigan Ave.
944-4100, 800-228-9822
Room-only weekend rate is a best buy.

Raphael Hotel
201 E. Delaware Pl.
943-5000
Less expensive than the other little, deluxe hotels. Weekend suite package includes some food.

Richmont Hotel
162 E. Ontario St.
787-3580, 800-621-8055
This budget operation cuts rates and tosses in a few frills on rooms or suites on weekends.

*Ritz-Carlton Hotel
160 E. Pearson St.
266-1000, 800-621-6906
A shoot-the-works package includes theater tickets and dinner at the posh Dining Room for little more than the normal up-scale room rate.

Sheraton-Plaza Hotel
160 E. Huron St.
787-2900, 800-325-3535
Both one- and two-day packages are offered at this busy convention hotel.

Tremont Hotel
100 E. Chestnut St.
751-1900, 800-621-8133
Classy packages feature room service from Cricket's and big savings at a little luxury inn.

Westin Hotel Chicago
909 N. Michigan Ave.
943-7200, 800-223-3000
This bustling convention hotel offers a variety of packages.

Whitehall Hotel
105 E. Delaware Pl.
944-6300, 800-621-8133
Several weekend deals add up to big savings at this smaller, deluxe spot that is popular with celebrities. Guests may dine in the private club.

Water Tower Place

Shopping
and services

*Accent Chicago, Inc.
7th level
944-1354
Also in Hyatt Regency Chicago.

*Laura Ashley
6th level
951-8004
Also in Oakbrook Center and Northbrook Court.

August Max
6th level
266-6416
Skillful sales people help you put stylish, moderately priced outfits together quickly. Several suburban locations.

*Avventura
4th level
337-3700

Baskin
2nd level
943-3000
Quality, conservative men's wear. Outlets all over.

*Beagle & Company
7th level
337-8002

*Beauty & the Beast
7th level
944-7570

Christian Bernard
6th level
664-7562
Specializes in gemstone jewelry with a French flair. Also, watches with nicely designed bands, some art glass, pottery, and handicrafts in a lovely shop. Other stores on Michigan Ave. and in Stratford Square in Bloomingdale.

Bigsby & Kruthers
7th level
944-6955
One of several stores for all the latest, big-name men's wear: Giorgio Armani, Yves Saint Laurent, Calvin Klein, and so forth.

*Caché
6th level
951-8230

Casual Corner
5th level
642-4100
More trendy, lighthearted women's wear. Good sale prices; very nice staff. Many other locations.

*Caswell-Massey
7th level
664-1752

*Chas
5th level
787-5769

Merrill Chase Galleries
2nd level
337-6600
The subject of several brouhahas, the gallery displays everything from bar art to old masters and publishes a helpful pamphlet defining art terms. Other locations.

*Chinese Friendship Store
7th level
642-3707

Clothworks
7th level
266-0282
Loads of colorful fabrics and all sorts of goodies— drapes, bedspreads, kimonos, rag dolls, pillows, marionettes, and trapuntos (stuffed, quilted pictures)— made from them. Part of a chain.

Cook's Mart
4th level
280-0929
A bit smaller than La Salle St. store but has tons of professional and decorator cookware. Copper, brass, and kitchen gadgets galore; 50¢ espresso, too. Several suburban locations.

Courrèges
3rd level
337-0606
Replica of main Paris salon and exclusive Chicago outlet for André Courrèges-designed, elegant, very expensive women's clothing.

*Crabtree & Evelyn
5th level
787-0188

*The Crystal Suite
7th level
944-1320
Also in Old Orchard and Oakbrook Center.

*Dana Côte d'Azur
3rd level
787-8611

Alfred Dunhill
2nd level
467-4455
Pipes, tobacco, and cigars (of course); gentlemen's accessories; opulent chess sets and other decorative luxuries. Only Dunhill in Illinois.

*Enchanté
4th level
951-7290

*Et Cetera
2nd level
944-0405

*Fantasies
7th level
642-0381

Gia
9th floor
944-5263
Beautifully designed, hand-constructed gold and platinum jewelry. Custom designs, remakes passé pieces, sets stones—everything from delicate wire work to massive stuff. One of several jewelers tucked away on the 9th floor, which is mostly offices.

Godiva Chocolatier
7th level
280-1133
Gorgeous molded chocolates with true-fruit-flavored fillings taste as good as they look. Priced accordingly. Fancy velvet boxes et al.

The Goldsmith Ltd.
2nd level
751-1986
Don Lawrence and Cathy Starr custom design contemporary gold jewelry. You can watch them at work behind a counter that looks like the entrance to a Century of Progress pavilion. Their pieces and commercially produced ones are displayed handsomely in suede-lined shadow boxes. Also in Woodfield Mall.

Hollands Jewelers
5th level
944-4300
Rogers and Hollands, the Chicago area's largest jewelry chain, has two stores, but only this one carries estate jewelry, as well as a full range of new watches, baubles, bangles, etc.

H. Horwitz Co.
9th floor
337-3500
Traditionally styled jewelry is beautifully displayed in this more-than-80-year-old firm's handsome, well-lit showroom. Lots of diamond rings. Prices are lower than retail. The knowledgeable staff and out-of-the-way location make shopping here pleasant.

M. Hyman & Son
4th level
266-0061
Chain store specializes in clothes for "big men, tall men."

*Jaeger International Shop
3rd level
642-6665
Also in Northbrook Court.

*Charles Jourdan
3rd level
280-8133

Joyce-Selby Shoes
6th level
664-8281
Wide variety of styles and sizes; two brands—Joyce and Selby. Elsewhere, too.

Georgette Klinger
3rd level
787-4300
Many swear by the facials at this seafoam-blue salon with more than two dozen private rooms. Make-up application, manicure, pedicure, massage, etc., too. Klinger cosmetics used. At-home guide available to help you maintain the glow.

Kroch's & Brentano's
4th level
943-2452
*The usual good selection,
particularly strong on fine
and performing arts.*

**Lady Madonna
Maternity Boutique**
6th level
266-2420
*Fashionable clothes for
mothers-to-be and babies.
Other locations.*

Limited Express
6th level
943-0344
*The outrageous Fiorucci
failed in this space. Jeans
and inexpensive sports-
wear are now peddled in
the glitzy surroundings.
Other locations.*

*Lord & Taylor
Levels 1 to 7
787-7400
Other stores.

*Marshall Field's
Levels 1 to 7
781-1234
Other stores.

*Matthews
3rd level
664-1203

*North Beach Leather
3rd level
280-9292

Over the Rainbow
6th level
943-2050
*Nice selection of designer
clothing for children.*

Pam's Young Folks
4th level
951-0292
*More fashionable kids' stuff
here and at several
suburban locations.*

Pennington's du Canada
4th level
664-6164
*Trendy women's clothes in
large sizes. Other locations.*

*Primitive Arts, Ltd.
2nd level
337-2011

Quintessence
7th level
944-7781
*Small shop with a nice se-
lection of chic women's
clothing.*

*Rare 'n' Fair
7th level
266-9571

***Rizzoli International
Bookstore**
3rd level
642-3500

Rodier of Paris
3rd level
337-0178
*Classic and contemporary
women's clothing. Also at
Northbrook Court and Oak-
brook Center.*

*I Santi
7th level
280-8398

Vidal Sassoon
3rd level
751-2216
*They call it "sassoooon-
ing." We call it big business. Don't expect to see
Vidal himself at this giant
salon.*

*F.A.O. Schwarz
4th level
787-8894
*Toys, dolls, toys, games,
more toys. Some you can
play with right in the store.*

LeSportsac
7th level
266-9635
*High-tech store with loads
of sporty bags, some dis-
played on a conveyor belt
that keeps going even when
the place is closed.*

*Chas. A. Stevens
6th level
787-6800
Other locations.

***Chas. A. Stevens
Petite Store**
7th level
943-6313

Tennis Lady
3rd level
649-1110
*One of the best selections
of tennis wear outside of a
pro shop by Fila, Ellesse,
and other designers. Not
cheap. Also in Old Orchard
and Northbrook Court.*

Thorpe Furs
6th level
337-1750
*Ninety-three-year-old
Evanston firm stocks
women's, men's, and chil-
dren's fur jackets, coats,
capes, mittens, hats, and
other accessories by all the
major designers. Also in
Northbrook Court.*

*Top Brass
7th level
280-7709
*Also in Northbrook Court
and Glencoe.*

Robert Vance, Ltd.
3rd level
280-0534
*Traditional American
clothing, mostly for men.
Ladies' shop on 3, too. Also
at Hawthorn Center.*

Louis Vuitton
3rd level
944-2010
*Complete line of luggage
and accessories from the
prestigious French firm.*

Dining
and drinking

*Chestnut Street Grill
Mezzanine
280-2720

*De Brucio's Pizzeria
4th level
951-6777

Dos Hermanos Cantina
6th level
280-2780
*Decent Mexican food.
Drinking the 27-ounce
margarita can occupy a
whole afternoon.*

Hillary's
Mezzanine
280-2710
*Handsome place with a
central octagonal bar and
lots of mirrors, brass,
greenery, and glass. So-
phisticated fun food is on
the pricey side. Good
burger.*

*D. B. Kaplan's
Delicatessen
7th level
280-2700

*The Theatre Café
2nd level
943-8443

*Vie de France
Mezzanine
266-7633
Other locations.

Shopping and services

On and near Michigan Ave.: Clothing

Avenue Five-Forty
540 N. Michigan Ave.
321-9540
Verne Castress carries unique and almost unique clothes by up-and-coming designers. Hand-crocheted sweaters, cotton dresses, patchwork suede jackets, and unusual handbags are a few of the goodies you may find here, even though the shop doesn't look like much at first glance.

Bally of Switzerland
919 N. Michigan Ave.
787-8110
Known for fine, handmade, leather footwear for men, this firm also carries men's suede and leather jackets, attaché cases, women's shoes and handbags, and small accessories for both sexes. Also in Northbrook Court and Oakbrook Center.

*Bonwit Teller
875 N. Michigan Ave.
751-1800
Also in Oakbrook Center.

*Brittany Ltd.
642 N. Michigan Ave.
642-6550
Also in the Loop and Northbrook Court.

*Burberrys Limited
633 N. Michigan Ave.
787-2500

Evans, Inc.
744 N. Michigan Ave.
855-0333
More elegant than the Loop store, but carries similar clothing and furs. (See South of the River.)

Giovanni
920 N. Michigan Ave.
787-6500
Designer clothing that tends toward the frilly and feminine: silk chiffon dresses, Victorian-looking silk and lace blouses, pretty silk prints.

*Gucci
713 N. Michigan Ave.
664-5504

Hanig's
660 N. Michigan Ave.
642-5330
Source for Johnston & Murphy good-quality, main-line men's shoes. Shoes by Wright and Bruno Magli, too. Loop locations.

*Hermès
875 N. Michigan Ave.
787-8175

*Ireland House
120 E. Delaware Pl.
337-2711

Joseph
679 N. Michigan Ave.
944-1111
Shoes and boots by Anne Klein, Beene Bag, Joan and David, Frye, Salvatore Ferragamo, Charles Jourdan, and many others; also designer fashions, Judith Leiber handbags, jewelry, and other accessories. Five others.

*Stanley Korshak
912 N. Michigan Ave.
280-0520
Also in Northbrook Court.

*I. Magnin
830 N. Michigan Ave.
751-0500
Also in Northbrook Court and Oakbrook Center.

Hy Miller's
524 N. Michigan Ave.
329-9290
Women's footwear from all over the world in the $40 range. Also in Loop.

*Morry's
645 N. Michigan Ave.
642-1610
Also in Northbrook Court.

**New Wineskins
Leather Gallery**
832 N. State St.
951-0315
Rustic sheepskin coats, butter-soft tennis racquet cases, bags, cases, wineskins, and other leather goods. Custom work, alterations, repairs, and cleaning, too. Gregarious owner.

*Polo Ralph Lauren
906 N. Michigan Ave.
280-0550

N. H. Rosenthal Furs
666 N. Michigan, 2nd floor
943-1365
One of the first and best furriers on Michigan Ave. Designers include Givenchy, Yves Saint Laurent, Chloé. Family run, with a reputation for good quality and service.

*Saks Fifth Avenue
669 N. Michigan Ave.
944-6500
Also in Old Orchard and Oakbrook Center.

*The Seasons Best
645 N. Michigan Ave.
943-6161

*Mark Shale
919 N. Michigan Ave.
440-0720
Other locations.

On and near Michigan Ave.: Jewelry

Gallai Ltd.
666 N. Michigan Ave.
321-1360
Good selection of antique jewelry and watches. Some modern, too. Business card lists London hallmarks. Owner can be abrupt.

Sidney Garber Jewelers
902 N. Michigan Ave.
944-5225
Jewelry designed by Garber and others; some is ornate or garish, some Art Deco looking.

*Jewels by Stephanie
540 N. Michigan Ave.
782-6300
Largish, full-range, designer jewelry salon with everything from Van Cleef & Arpel to basic gold pieces; lots of crystal and brass; china by Minton, Royal Doulton, and Limoges; silver by Georg Jensen and Reed & Barton; other gifts, too.

*Lester Lampert Inc.
701 N. Michigan Ave.
944-6888

P. D. Rocca
840 N. Michigan, Suite 714
944-0300
Carries wonderful antique jewelry, porcelain, silver, and other objèts d'art; designs new jewelry and settings for old stones.

*Spaulding & Co.
959 N. Michigan Ave.
337-4800
Also in Northbrook Court.

*Tiffany & Co.
715 N. Michigan Ave.
944-7500

*Trabert & Hoeffer
738 N. Michigan Ave.
787-1654

Wellington Jewels
540 N. Michigan Ave.,
Mezzanine
321-1044
Mme. Wellington has turned her simulated diamonds, which started as a mail-order business, into a multimillion-dollar fortune. Settings are real gold, often with real stones as trim. Priced in the hundreds rather than in the thousands. Shop is elegant enough to show off the real thing. Several stores on East Coast.

On and near Michigan Ave.: Art and antiques

*Aiko's Art Materials Import
714 N. Wabash Ave.
943-0745

Arts Club of Chicago
109 E. Ontario St.
787-3997
(See Galleries)

Brudno Art Supply Co.
601 N. State St.
787-0030
Large, well-stocked store; personable service.

Desire Art & Antiques
607 N. State St.
664-8966
Small shop specializes in Art Deco: jewelry, cigarette cases, chrome cocktail shakers, ceramics, 1940s kitchenware.

*Joseph Faulkner-Main Street Galleries
620 N. Michigan, 3rd floor
787-3301

*Wally Findlay Galleries
814 N. Michigan Ave.
649-1500

*Malcolm Franklin, Inc.
126 E. Delaware Pl.
337-0202

*Richard Gray Gallery
620 N. Michigan, 2nd floor
642-8877

*Jade House
Barclay Chicago Hotel
166 E. Superior, 4th floor
266-0911

*Douglas Kenyon, Inc.
155 E. Ohio St.
642-5300
Restoration lab for conservation of artworks on paper, too.

*Phyllis Kind Gallery
226 E. Ontario St.
642-6302

*R. H. Love Galleries, Inc.
100 E. Ohio St.
664-9620

*Nahigian Brothers, Inc.
645 N. Michigan, Suite 225
943-8300
Not to be confused with competitors in Skokie, H.C. Nahigian & Sons.

Oriental Mart
210 E. Ohio St.
944-0711
Extensive stock of new and antique pieces from China, Japan, and Korea: carved and inlaid chests, tables, and screens; cloisonné; porcelain; ivory carvings; jewelry; and more. Discounts "to the trade." By appointment.

Ray-Vogue College of Design
664 N. Michigan Ave.
280-3500
Professional fashion/commercial art school has a second-floor gallery displaying student and professional work.

Romano Gallery
613 N. State St.
337-7541
Small antiques shop with assorted pottery, glass, oil paintings, jewelry, and an occasional fine piece, such as a Tiffany cigarette case. Not cheap.

Sotheby Parke Bernet
840 N. Michigan, 4th floor
280-0185
Chicago branch of the world's largest art and antiques auction house. Auctions held at large hotels.

On and near Michigan Ave.: Books

*Stuart Brent Book Store
670 N. Michigan Ave.
337-6357

*Hamill & Barker
400 N. Michigan Ave.,
Room 1210
644-5933
Closed July and Aug.

*Kroch's & Brentano's
516 N. Michigan Ave.
321-0989
Eighteen locations.

Abraham Lincoln Book Shop
18 E. Chestnut St.
944-3085
U.S. political history with an emphasis on Lincoln and the Civil War. Books about presidents, Chicago and Illinois material, rare books, imprints, autograph letters and documents. When he was head of the Chicago Library Board, Ralph G. Newman earned notoriety by backdating documents for President Nixon.

Harry L. Stern Ltd.
620 N. Michigan, 5th floor
787-4433
Antiquarian book and map dealer specializes in early Americana, travels and voyages of exploration, and early printed books. Publishes book and map catalogues.

Walton Books
172 E. Walton St.
787-7635
Mary Mills Dunea, who designs and replenishes libraries for fine hotels, specializes in books about England and the British royal family and also has bestsellers at this cozy shop.

On and near Michigan Ave.: General

Alliance Française-Maison Française de Chicago
218 E. Ontario St.
337-1070
Decades-old cultural institution offers a wide range of classes in conversational French, literature, wine, and more; maintains a library; and sponsors all sorts of programs and events including an annual Bastille Day celebration.

Amtrak Ticket Office
505 N. Michigan Ave.
558-1075
You can buy tickets here for trains that leave from Union Station.

Elizabeth Arden
717 N. Michigan Ave.
266-5750
Enter the red door a mess and come out a new woman: massages, facials, haircuts, shampoos, sets, manicures, the famous cosmetics, high-fashion clothes, and accessories. Some of the dresses on the sale rack look like '50s haute couture.

Bee Discount Co.
839 N. State St.
266-1810
Wholesale to beauticians and retail. Name-brand shampoos, conditioners, and setting lotions by the gallon, as well as standard sizes. Make-up and brushes, too. Other locations.

Carnegie Printers
837 N. State St.
337-7022
Specializes in stationery and wedding and social invitations, with more than a dozen binders of samples.

Coach Horse Livery, Ltd.
Chestnut and Michigan
337-4296
Rent a horse and carriage for a romantic evening ride. It costs a not-so-romantic $15 per half hour.

*Colby's Home Furnishings
129 E. Chestnut St.
266-2222
Suburban locations, too.

*Crate & Barrel
850 N. Michigan Ave.
787-5900
Other locations.

Mark Cross
909 N. Michigan Ave.
440-1072
Elegant, classic leather goods made by the firm.

Downtown Court Club
441 N. Wabash Ave.
644-4880
A good, full-service, reasonably priced facility.

Drake Hotel Barber Shop
140 E. Walton St.
787-2200
Popular place for a good haircut.

*Franklin-Bayer Inc.
630 N. Michigan Ave.
944-4737

*Paul Glick Inc.
701 N. Michigan Ave.
751-2300

Herman's World of Sporting Goods
111 E. Chicago Ave.
951-8282
Good selection for all sports at reasonable prices in this multilevel store. Suburban locations, too.

Hoffritz Cutlery
634 N. Michigan Ave.
664-4473
New York-based firm carries fine knives as well as hip flasks, German beer mugs, and other paraphernalia. Other locations.

Jason-Richards Ltd. Florist
42 E. Chicago Ave.
664-0605
Pretty shop in a fine old building. Especially nice selection of cut flowers. Does contract work for Park Hyatt, among others. Very competitive prices.

Old Wells Record Shop
664 N. State St.
943-4068
Hundreds of thousands of LPs and 45s are stacked precariously on furniture, fill the bathroom, line the walls, and spill out of bins and boxes in this run-down-looking store. Jazz—from current releases on small labels and of little-known artists to out-of-print discs—is the specialty, and prices are reasonable. Owner Bill Chavers has as many yarns to spin as there are records.

Outside In
500 N. Michigan Ave.
644-3083
Handsome L-shaped shop with a little Japanese bridge and teahouse, loads of potting materials in back, planters of all sorts, dozens of potpourris, silk flowers, and gifts. Cut flowers, including unusual varieties, are half price on Fri.

Rena, Inc.
920 N. Michigan, 7th floor
944-6663
Get into shape with total fitness exercise classes at this salon. No fancy equipment.

*Scandinavian Design
920 N. Michigan Ave.
664-9232
Other outlets all over.

*Shaxted, Inc.
900 N. Michigan Ave.
337-0855
Also in Plaza del Lago, Wilmette.

Spencer's Marina City Bowl
300 N. State St.
527-0747
Slightly seedy, but the only downtown bowling alley open to the public; 38 lanes.

Standard Photo Supply
43 E. Chicago Ave.
440-4920
One of the country's oldest and largest photographic suppliers. Also at 132 N. Wells St.

Victor's Stereo
8 E. Erie St.
787-0750
Top-of-the-line audio equipment and consulting. Also in Morton Grove.

*Water Tower Place Atrium Shopping Mall
845 N. Michigan Ave.
440-3460
See separate heading.

Write Impressions
42 E. Chicago Ave.
943-3306
One of Chicago's widest selections of customized stationery and desk accessories plus lots of fun and casual notes, cards, etc. Barbara Ruben also does individual designs. In a converted apartment in a lovely post-Fire building where Hemingway is said to have lived.

Zuverink
724 N. Wabash Ave.
751-2290
Full of colorful silk and other cloth flowers, many from West Germany, artfully arranged in your pot or theirs.

Oak-Rush-Walton area: Clothing

*Bottega Glaseia
106 E. Oak St.
337-0777

Boutique Caprice
47 W. Division St.
943-6993
Pleasant women's boutique with some nice silks, etc.— and some not so nice.

The Brass Boot
55 E. Oak St.
266-2731
Woodsy, chic little shop owned by Nunn Bush sells well-made, expensive shoes and boots.

*Burdi
68 E. Walton St.
642-9166
Sleek men's boutique with marble floors and track lighting.

*M. J. Carr Ltd.
104 E. Oak St.
787-3739

*Jean Charles
1003 N. Rush St.
787-3535

*Clown
72 E. Oak St.
642-6636

Dance Centre of Chicago Ltd.
59 E. Oak St.
787-9600
Loads of colorful dance wear and other active leisure clothing. Upstairs there's a "body fitness" studio with classes to help you get in shape. Also in Highwood.

*Davis for Men
41 E. Oak St.
751-2582
Also in Water Tower Place and at 1547 N. Wells St.

Fila Italia Sport
49 E. Oak St.
787-6782
Carries the entire line of sleek, boldly colored Italian sportswear favored by pros and duffers alike. Also in Glenview.

*Jeraz
51 E. Oak St.
266-7300

Jerolds on Oak
106 E. Oak St., 2nd floor
337-6300
Designer wedding gowns for sophisticated women. Suburban locations have gowns in all price ranges. Appointments advised.

Jerolds II
106 E. Oak St., 2nd floor
280-0800
Men's formal wear to buy or to rent.

*Kontessa II
53 E. Walton St.
951-0530

*My Sister's Circus
101 E. Oak St.
664-7074

*Pompian
57 E. Oak St.
337-6604

*Jackie Renwick Clothes for the Businesswoman
65 E. Oak St., 2nd floor
266-8269
Also in Loop.

Schwartz's Intimate Apparel
945 N. Rush St.
787-2976
Everything in lingerie from cotton flannel gowns to slinky polyester. Some silk (such as hand-embroidered camisoles), swimwear, large selection of bras including hard-to-find sizes. Also in Skokie.

*Shoes etc. etc. etc.
51 E. Walton St.
642-2261

*Smyth Bros. Shoe Parlor
33 E. Oak St.
664-9508
Also in Water Tower Place. Other locations.

*Stuart/Chicago
102 E. Oak St.
266-9881

*Sugar Magnolia
110 E. Oak St.
944-0885

*Ann Taylor
103 E. Oak St.
943-5411
*Also at 1750 N. Clark St.
and in several suburban
locations.*

**Thanks For The
Memories**
1154 N. Dearborn St.
337-0744
*Vintage and new clothing
with an emphasis on Vic-
torian whites.*

*Ultimo
114 E. Oak St.
787-0906

*Via Lusso
106 E. Oak St.
280-9161

*Barbara Weed
66 E. Walton St.
649-0223

Oak-Rush-
Walton area:
General

*Alaska Shop
104 E. Oak St.
943-3393
Also in Lake Forest.

***Marc Benaim
Coiffures, Ltd.**
49 E. Oak St.
644-3010

***Lee Benkendorf
Antique Clocks**
67 E. Oak St.
951-1903

The Book Market
6 E. Cedar St.
944-3358
*Good place to find the latest
paperback fiction. Some
hardbacks and nonfiction,
too. Lots of periodicals.
Other locations.*

*La Bourse
45 E. Walton St.
787-3925

***Robert Bracken
& Company**
57 E. Oak St.
944-7557

Deutsch Luggage
111 E. Oak St.
337-2937
*Quality luggage and ac-
cessories; repairs. Also at
56 W. Van Buren St. and in
Oak Brook.*

The Face Boutique
100 E. Walton St.
440-1195
*Large shop devoted to cos-
metics, perfumes, and
toiletries. Make-up demonstrations, facials, man-
icures, and pedicures, too.*

Garrett Galleries Ltd.
1010 N. Rush St.
944-6325
*People walk by this small
shop hundreds of times
and wonder what's inside:
antique ivory, silver, Orientalia; new and antique jewelry. Prices commensurate
with location.*

Great Lakes Jewelry
104 E. Oak St.
266-2211
*Basement shop with good
selection of charms and
chains, as well as other
jewelry.*

*Charles Ifergan
106 E. Oak St.
642-4484

**International
Eyewear Boutique**
67 E. Oak St.
440-1055
*All the latest frames,
including leather ones.*

*J.B.L. Antiques, Inc.
941 N. State St.
787-0603

*Marilyn Miglin
112 E. Oak St.
943-1120

MusiCraft
48 E. Oak St.
337-4150
*The first location of Chi-
cago's only chain to carry
only name brands has been
dwarfed by suburban
outlets it spawned, but is
still the only one to have
"pro" and disco systems
besides a full range of popular and audiophile equipment. Always price-com-
petitive; guarantee-repair
policy shines.*

NeedleMania
66 E. Walton St.
664-3511
*Lots of patterns, canvases,
and yarns.*

Oak Street Bookshop
54 E. Oak St.
642-3070
*An Oak St. fixture for almost
two decades, the store
stocks a good selection of
hardcovers and paper-
backs. The cozy back room
has one of the city's best
theater and film collections,
making it an occasional
hangout for theater types.*

**Ruth Page Foundation
School of Dance**
1016 N. Dearborn St.
337-6543
*Full range of ballet and
modern-dance classes for
all ages at school started in
1971 by one of the big
names in Chicago dance.
The auditorium, used for
the annual student
performances, is also
rented to theater groups.*

*Parfumerie
946 N. Rush St.
944-1432

***La Provence
de Pierre Deux**
113 E. Oak St.
642-9657

Robert's
41 E. Walton St.
944-7870
*Designer tableware glitters
on mirrored tables in this
steel-blue shop. Rueven's
modern, dishwasher-safe,
Art Nouveau glasswear and
other delights.*

Rustic Revival
672 N. Dearborn St.
337-5932
*Reproduction, mostly
made-in-the-South
baskets, toys, quilts, other
folk art, and furniture make
this a charming store.*

A Show of Hands
43 E. Walton St.
943-3413
*Handcrafted delights for
kids and adults: papier-
mâché vegetables, baskets,
baby batik T-shirts, and
loads of ceramics including
sophisticated porcelains.*

Tratt & Tratt Interiors
1110 N. State St.
664-3133
Specializes in custom-made sofa beds, drapes, bedspreads, etc. Show-room has mostly smaller items: brass, woods, decorator accessories. Interior-design firm provides Mart services, too.

Universal Recording Studios
46 E. Walton St.
642-6465
One of the country's largest state-of-the-art, full-service audio studios occupies a huge second floor and part of the first. Studio A is famous for its 24-ft. ceilings and sound ambiance. Blues Brothers movie and lots of records produced here.

We'll Keep You in Stitches
67 E. Oak St., 2nd floor
642-2540
More than 200 yarns and free knitting instruction if you buy some. Needlepoint patterns and supplies; embroidery threads, too. Colorful shop with finished pieces displayed to provide inspiration.

Around the Mart: Furniture and furnishings

Barrett Freiwald
701 N. Wells St.
642-1722
Interior-design studio with a small, striking retail show-room. Sixty percent of their business is residential, but you can see a sample of their stunning commercial work at Trabert & Hoeffer on Michigan Ave.

*Bathwares
740 N. Wells St.
642-9420

The Carpet Place
222 W. Ontario St.
664-6818
Loads of regular and commercial carpeting. If you don't see what you want, Harry Schiffman will take you to the Mart and order it at his usual low markups. Parquet or tile floors; refinishing, too. You can bargain.

Casa Vago International
501 N. Wells St.
222-0600
Handsome antiques shop specializes in 18th- and 19th-century French and English furniture.

China Clipper
445 N. Clark St.
645-1133
Furniture and objèts d'art (both antique and new) from the Orient are beautifully displayed in this spacious shop.

*City
213 W. Institute Pl.
664-9581

*Cook's Mart
609 N. La Salle St.
642-3526

D & L Office Furniture
30 W. Hubbard St.
527-3636
Five stories of office furniture and furnishings are, for the most part, available for immediate delivery from here or from the huge warehouse. Most of the important lines are carried; there are custom, designer, and contract services. C.O.D. purchasers can negotiate for discounts. To save even more, visit the subterranean sale showroom for discounts of as much as 80% on returns, cut-outs, and retired rentals. Other locations.

*Design Connection, Inc.
404 N. Wells St.
836-0073

*Donrose Galleries
751 N. Wells St.
337-4052

The Down Shoppe: Continental Quilt
500 N. Wells St.
822-0200
Mostly custom-made, excellent quality goosedown comforters; some in stock. Prices average in the hundreds but go as high as $3,000 for a king-sized eiderdown quilt. Pillows and quilt covers, too.

*Fly-By-Nite Gallery
714 N. Wells St.
664-8136

*Georgian House Antiques
739 N. Wells St.
266-9777

Great Lakes Hot Tubs Inc.
15 W. Hubbard St.
527-1311
Sells and installs hot tubs, Fiberglas spas, and whirlpool baths. Retail and wholesale. Sample the wares by renting a hot tub in a private room (reservations essential). Bring your own towel and rubber duckie.

Hendricks Music Co.
755 N. Wells St.
664-5522
Started by Lyon & Healy employees when that store closed. Steinway and other pianos.

*Richard Himmel Design Pavilion
219 W. Erie St.
266-0002

Kinzie Square Furniture Co.
220 W. Kinzie, 5th floor
822-9329
Essentially a buying club accessible to everyone, with no membership charges. The benefits are 40% discounts, F.O.B. factory, on almost any furniture and furnishings. Mart and designer services are offered, but if you know what you want, just phone the order in and send a check.

*Kitchen & Bath Mart
746 N. Wells St.
943-7060
Also in suburbs.

Littman Bros.
738 N. Wells St.
943-2660
Old-style, heavy-duty ceiling fans in several finishes. Also in suburbs.

***Tom Menaugh
Antique Furnishings**
442 N. Wells St.
664-9321

Mr. Rents
222 W. Hubbard St.
943-4500
A loft full of lifestyle rental furniture. Sells, too.

New Metal Crafts
812 N. Wells St.
787-6991
Custom-designed, imported, and antique lighting fixtures. Manufactures brass ones, too.

Off the Wall Beds
208 W. Kinzie St.
527-1212
Lifestyle wall units that include regular, retractable beds—a far cry from the old Murphy beds. Not cheap.

***O'Hara's
Connoisseur Gallery**
707 N. Wells St.
751-1286
Mostly ornate, pricey.

Phoenix Design Ltd.
733 N. Wells St.
951-7945
Rattan and lifestyle furniture in a brick-and-planty store.

***Jay Robert's
Antique Warehouse**
149 W. Kinzie St.
222-0167

*Roche Bobois
333 N. Wells St.
951-9080

Roman Marble Company
120 W. Kinzie St.
337-2217
Old firm sells antique mantels, alabaster tables, and marble slabs and fabrications, retail and to the trade.

*Keevan Sadock
412 N. Orleans, 4th floor
642-2800

Scandia Down Shop
607 N. Wells St.
787-6720
Goose-down quilts, covers, sheet sets, and pillows in a little shop accented by illuminated geese.

Studio 502
502 N. Wells St.
337-0452
Mark Malinowsky translates your ideas into acrylic.

Tiffany Stained Glass Ltd.
549 N. Wells St.
828-0680
Supplies, classes, books, and a studio, which makes most of the panels, lamps, and windows they sell. Also restorations.

Wooden Gallery
502 N. Wells St.
828-0333
Naïve furniture and sculptures by Jerzy and Maria Kenar.

*Workbench
154 W. Hubbard St.
661-1150

Yesterday's Party, Ltd.
361 W. Superior, 5th floor
642-6400
Locates, restores, refinishes, and redesigns gorgeous, antique backbars, front bars, and other case pieces for business or home use. Consulting services; rentals; impressive guarantee.

Around the Mart: General

**Adco Display
Material Co.**
713 N. Wells St.
943-5080
Paper fold-outs, pinwheels, chains, and plastic and fabric flowers for parties and holidays.

Anti-Cruelty Society
157 W. Grand Ave.
644-8338
Get your cat or dog from the Ritz of animal shelters. Stanley Tigerman's new building allows pets-to-be to see the world (they were in the basement of the old building) and passersby to see them. Who could resist taking one home?

*ARC Gallery (Artists, Residents of Chicago)
6 W. Hubbard St.
266-7607
(See Galleries)

*Artemisia Gallery
9 W. Hubbard St.
751-2016
(See Galleries)

The Center for New Television
11 E. Hubbard St., 5th floor
565-1787
Video workshops, guest exhibits and lectures, and special events. Members can rent video equipment (particularly for editing) at reasonable rates.

Chicago Camera Hospital
15 W. Hubbard, 2nd floor
329-9229
Repairs camera and strobes; rents studio and darkroom space to experienced amateurs or professionals.

Costumes Unlimited
814 N. Franklin St.
642-0200
Costume house set up like a salon. Custom designs for chic parties and does lots of commercial work. Rent complete ready-made costumes.

East Bank Club
500 N. Kingsbury St.
527-5800
Crème de la crème of health clubs, the world's largest, has every imaginable facility and attracts a stylish, moneyed set. Very posh and expensive.

Flite Luggage and Repair
230 W. Superior St.,
3rd floor
664-2142
*Large selection of better
name-brand business
cases, luggage, and some
accessories at significant
discounts.*

Gamma Photo Labs, Inc.
314 W. Superior St.
337-0022
*The biggest. Offers complete services and enjoys a
good reputation with pros.*

Gold Coast Divers
215 W. Chicago Ave.
751-1130
*Essentially a factory store
for a company that produces diving and other
training films, designs
product lines, etc. Offers
diving lessons and carries
video equipment and
cassettes.*

**Golden Age
Nostalgia Shop**
534 N. Clark St.
527-0079
*The shop is a motherlode
for magazines and old comics and a bewildering jungle
of other memorabilia, such
as advertising premiums,
movie stills, and model
trains.*

Helix Ltd.
325 W. Huron St.
944-4400
*Where the pros shop for an
unbeatable selection of
photographic equipment at
good prices.*

*Jazz Record Mart
11 W. Grand Ave.
222-1467
Also at 4243 N. Lincoln.

Lawson YMCA
30 W. Chicago Ave.
944-6211
*Complete exercise and racquet facilities (no tennis),
loads of classes, and a hotel. The usual, somewhat
seedy, YMCA atmosphere.*

*Levinson's Inc.
739 N. Clark St.
337-3720

Morrie Mages Sports
620 N. La Salle St.
337-6151
*Huge selection of sportswear. Master of marketing
boasts about low prices,
but they aren't always the
best. Famous all-night
sales.*

Male Hide Leathers
66 W. Illinois St.
321-1536
*In addition to erotic leather
accessories, this shop
stocks American-made
bomber and motorcycle
jackets (harder to find than
Korean imports), Western
wear, etc. Open late on
weekends.*

*N.A.M.E. Gallery
9 W. Hubbard St.
467-6550
(See Galleries)

***Off Center
Shopping Mall**
300 W. Grand Ave.
321-9500
Shops include ***Caravans
Awry** *(222-0144),* ***Lady
Madonna Maternity
Outlet** *(329-0771),* ***Royal
Knitting Mills** *(329-1433),*
*Shepherd-Scott, Ltd.
(280-0532), ***Stefano**
(943-5330), ***That's Our
Bag** *(527-0091), and a few
others.*

Ronsley
363 W. Ontario St.
427-1948
*Bills itself as "the total design center and probably
the finest florist in the
world." Bright, white, high-tech display floor full of
flowers, plants, and decorator accessories. Specializes
in floral arrangements that
run the gamut from bud
vases to installations at
Navy Pier. Mike Leventhal
and Frank Rosenberg employ 40 people to design
and construct sets for
theme parties, etc. Clients
include biggies such as the
city government. Arrangements are among the most
imaginative around.*

Saldi
233 W. Huron St.
787-3237
*Leather handbags, cases,
and more by Battaglia, plus
some imported clothing, at
discounts of 40% to 60%
off retail.*

Seedhoff
600 N. Wells St.
943-2311
*Eclectic selection of mostly
tropical plants and succulents (some quite large);
also pretty accessories.*

Tuscany Studios
601 N. Wells St.
664-7680
*Outdoor statuary stand—
simulated Pompeiian stone
pagodas, cherubs, owls,
urns, fountains, all seven
dwarfs, and more—
is a local landmark.*

Weddings, Inc.
223 W. Erie St.
787-2280
Convention Consultants
787-2284
*Plans private, corporate,
and municipal parties, from
finding locations and sending invitations to supplying
orchestras and flowers. Coordinates conventions.*

***Harry Weese
& Associates**
10 W. Hubbard, 4th floor
467-7030
*Enfant terrible of Chicago
architects and steady
gadfly to dull development.*

Foodstuffs

Bragno World Wines Ltd.
40 E. Walton St.
337-5000
Very good selection of wines; rather high prices. Lots of miniatures. Cellar— with sometimes less than ideal storage conditions— occupies catacombs built for an ill-fated restaurant.

*Burhop's Seafood
One Fish Plaza
745 N. La Salle St.
644-7825
Other locations.

Cafe Croissant
72 E. Walton St.
280-7783
Striking white-and-brass bakery sells good (and expensive) croissants, French bread, pastries, sherbets, chocolates, sandwiches (a few), espresso and cappuccino. Stand-up tables.

*Mitchell Cobey Cuisine
100 E. Walton St.
944-3411
Catering, too.

Connoisseur Wines, Ltd.
77 W. Chestnut St.
642-2375
Elegant little shop with a carefully chosen, small stock—strong on Rhônes, Burgundies, and Champagnes—and some unusual French brandies.

*Delish
544 N. Wells St.
670-2600

Häagen-Dazs
70 E. Oak St.
266-6252
Get hand-packed pints, cones, and sundaes made with New York's famous ice cream from the counter at this bright, high-tech parlor, the firm's first Illinois retail outlet. Others.

*La Salle Street Market
One Fish Plaza
745 N. La Salle St.
943-7450

Let Them Eat Cake
948 N. Rush St.
951-7383
Fair pastries and cakes at this popular place and always some samples to nibble. Famous for fancy fun cakes. Petits fours and wedding cakes with notice. Other locations.

Mr. Beef on Orleans
666 N. Orleans St.
337-8500
The Italian beef sandwich was a Chicago magazine winner. Other sandwiches, such as steak, are American style. Beef sold by the pound, too. Nothing high-toned about the ambiance.

*One Fish Plaza
745 N. La Salle St.

Ricci & Co.
162 W. Superior St.
787-7660
Nuts to you! This half-century-old company has all sorts—raw or roasted and salted—at decent prices.

Rocky's Live Bait
138 N. Streeter Dr.
664-2792
Fried seafood also served from this shack by the lake.

3 Little Bakers, Inc.
550 N. Wells St.
644-9581
Bright, nifty-looking place sells okay sweets at good prices. Lots of whipped-cream pastries.

Treasure Island Foods
75 W. Elm St.
440-1144
Gourmet supermarket with free indoor parking—a real boon in this neighborhood.

Under the "El" Deli
233 W. Superior St.
664-6354
Jewish-Italian deli with hot dogs, corned beef, mortadella, poor boys, other sandwiches, and breakfast omelettes.

Dining

French and near French

*Bastille
21 W. Superior St.
787-2050
Two very different rooms in this brasserie offer completely different ambiances—muted gray-and-green modern or French subway-car intimate—but the food's the same: simply grilled meats and fish, excellent wines by the glass.

La Cheminée
1161 N. Dearborn St.
642-6654
Wine-cellar décor in an old row house is the setting for expensive meals.

Chez Paul
660 N. Rush St.
944-6680
A former McCormick mansion is a more than suitable background for so-so haute cuisine meals. The wine cellar shines.

Ciel Bleu
Mayfair Regent Hotel
181 E. Lake Shore Dr.
951-2864
Great views from this striking penthouse, but the fancy food doesn't measure up.

The Consort
Westin Hotel Chicago
909 N. Michigan Ave.
943-7200
Franz Benteler, his Stradivarius, and the "Royal Strings" play suitable selections for this florid, purple-accented room. An $8 cover charge

for the schmaltz pushes the tab for the ordinary fare to unconscionable levels. The experience recalls a courtesan more than a consort.

*L'Escargot
Allerton Hotel
701 N. Michigan Ave.
337-1717
Good onion soup plus other bourgeois dishes, somewhat low prices, and increasingly competent service makes this New Town expatriate a winner. Table d'hôte, breakfast, lunch, early- and late-dinner menus.

Jacques Garden
900 N. Michigan Ave.
944-4795
If you want to be transported to a New Orleans "courtyard" and don't care that the food is mediocre, try it. Lunch only.

Jovan
545 N. State St.
944-7766
One of the city's pioneer prix fixe restaurants remains a reliable favorite. Fine dessert soufflés.

The Magic Pan
60 E. Walton St.
943-2456
Crêpes, crêpes, crêpes, palacsintas, a few other entrées, and sandwiches in this cheery, country-French outlet of the Quaker Oats-owned chain. Kids menu; moderate prices. Other locations.

*La Mer
1 W. Maple St.
266-4810

*Le Perroquet
70 E. Walton St.
944-7990
One of the more expensive prix fixe meals (about $40) but well worth the tariff. This is one of the country's great restaurants, with innovation and superb service justifying the reputation.

*Le Relais Chicago
50 E. Oak St.
944-3300
Noisy, convivial bistro serves decent dinners and light meals. Watch the crowds go by while you sip a drink at the sidewalk café.

*Ritz-Carlton Dining Room
Water Tower Place
160 E. Pearson St.
266-1000
One of Chicago's most expensive restaurants is most often worth it. Outstanding wine list.

Toulouse
51 W. Division St.
944-2606
This small dim, elegant spot just west of singles-bar row has a well-chosen, limited menu; intimate piano bar, late-night menu, and well-stocked bar.

*La Tour
Park Hyatt Hotel
800 N. Michigan Ave.
280-2230
This beautiful room may develop into a world-class restaurant, but for the moment, the nouvelle cuisine may not justify the haute prices.

*Yvette
1206 N. State St.
280-1700
Smashing Art Deco bistro serves appealing, mostly light fare at reasonable prices. Attracts a chic crowd. Gourmet take-out.

Italian

Agostino's
7 E. Delaware Pl.
642-8540
Okay Italian dishes—the pasta's best—in a red dining room that gives little hint of the old-mansion setting. Moderate prices.

Avanzare
161 E. Huron St.
337-8056
Rich Melman's first foray into Northern Italian food is in a striking high-rise lobby and is a kind of stylistic cross between his Ambria and Un Grand Café.

*Billy's
936 N. Rush St.
943-7080
Noise from the band in the popular, over-35 singles bar spills into the slick dining room. Expensive food doesn't live up to the extensive menu's promises.

Club Lago
331 W. Superior St.
337-9444
Right out of a 1940s movie, this old neighborhood spot is untouched by the area's new sophistication. Food and prices are just like at the Taylor St. joints.

Corona Cafe
501 N. Rush St.
527-5456
Old-line place is popular with press types. The back room offers a similar menu with lower prices.

*Doro's
871 N. Rush St.
266-1414
The décor is 1950s swank, but the Northern Italian dinners overcome it. The pasta's superb, but so, too, are subtly sauced, complex entrées. Such greatness doesn't come cheap, but the wine list includes many sensibly priced selections.

Edwardo's
1212 N. Dearborn St.
337-4490
In addition to thin-crust and stuffed pizza, this attractive room serves pastas and salads. Take-out pasta shop, too.

Gene & Georgetti's Club
500 N. Franklin St.
527-3718
An old-line spot in the shadow of the el serves the usual Southern Italian fare, but is celebrated for charred prime steaks. All you need is money, reservations, and kinship with the maître d'!

*George's
230 W. Kinzie St.
644-2290
Stunning décor, convivial atmosphere, good Northern Italian food (especially seafood-adorned pastas). Occasional entertainment.

Gino's East
160 E. Superior St.
943-1124
Chicago pizza in the plush upstairs or collegiate basement of an old row house that often has a line stretching out the door.

Gino's on Rush
932 N. Rush St.
337-7726
Deep-dish pizzas with a loyal following, and a few Southern Italian entrées in a subterranean, wood and stained-glass room at fair prices.

*Giordano's
747 N. Rush St.
951-0747
This is the downtown source for the double-crust pizza that swept the city after rating number one in a Chicago magazine tasting. Prices seem high at first, but two slices are a meal and a half. The spinach or special are sure winners. Order ahead by phone to cut down on waiting time.

*House of Bertini
535 N. Wells St.
644-1397
Another old-line, moderate, Italian steak house that's straight out of a Raymond Chandler novel, save for the owner's better-than-average artwork.

Mama Mia! Pasta
711 N. State St.
787-5606
Fresh pastas and sauces, salads, and desserts to take out or to eat in a green-and-white, high-tech setting. Counter service means plastic trays, plates, and forks, but beer and wine are available, and prices are reasonable.

*Pizzeria Due
619 N. Wabash Ave.
943-2400
Many claim the deep-dish pie is archetypal in this often crowded, multiroom, vaguely cantinalike basement place. Prices are low.

*Pizzeria Uno
29 E. Ohio St.
321-1000
The same pies are served at the same prices as at Due's, but the surroundings are scruffier and the hours are shorter. If one is closed or too crowded, check out the other: They're just a block apart.

Pronto Ristorante
200 E. Chestnut St.
664-6181
The place is simply gorgeous—white walls and brass trim—high-tech lights, and an open kitchen. Unfortunately, the ambitious Northern Italian menu delivers too many disappointments for the prices.

*Riccardo's
437 N. Rush St.
944-8815
Relive the 1950s and hobnob with celebs while you eat pretty good traditional Italian fare, some with a Greek accent. Sidewalk café (drinks only).

Sogni Dorati
660 N. Wells St.
337-6500
Very expensive food from many regions of Italy can be had in a lush renovation of the old Erie Café. This is the di Pinto family's attempt to break into the city after operating several suburban locations.

Continental and near Continental

*Arnie's
1030 N. State St.
266-4800
High-hopes, lower-performance (except for the steak) food is served in an overdone Deco dining room with a glassed-in garden. The bar is a pleasant place for a drink when not mobbed, there's a trio for dancing, and the enclosed "outdoor" sidewalk café is great for people-watching.

Artists & Writers
919 N. Michigan Ave.
(entrance on Walton St.)
337-4100
The décor at this Gene Sage spot is fairly sedate Art Deco; the menu is rather staid. High-quality beef and veal; seafood and other entrées are disappointing.

Biggs
1150 N. Dearborn St.
787-0900
Disappointing prix fixe meals are indifferently served in a beautiful 1874 mansion, designed by Edward Burling for a prominent banker; was later the home of a society caterer, Joseph H. Biggs.

Le Coq Rouge
Holiday Inn Chicago
City Centre
300 E. Ohio St.
787-6100
Standard hotel menu augmented by a best-buy dinner buffet.

*Cricket's
Tremont Hotel
100 E. Chestnut St.
280-2100
The casual atmosphere belies an ambitious, expensive menu, both in range and depth. Onion soup is one of the best in town. Usually crowded.

Gentleman Jim's Grill & Parlour
720 N. Rush St.
787-7711
The décor in this 19th-century mansion (formerly Jasands) is ersatz 1890s; the menu includes some modern variations on old-time Western dishes, as well as steaks, grilled fish, pastas, etc. Affordable prices; entertainment in the piano bar.

*Gordon
512 N. Clark St.
467-9780
A Chicago *magazine Dining Poll winner.*

*Lexander
508 N. Clark St.
467-1800
The surrealistic murals are beautiful, but the loft dining area is noisy and encourages service problems.

Manhattan Tavern & Grill
1045 N. Rush St.
751-2001
Glitzy Deco bar (complete with cocktail waitresses in bellhop outfits) features live jazz; the dining room serves steaks, seafood, duck, and other Continental standards at fairly high prices.

The 95th
John Hancock Center
875 N. Michigan Ave.
787-9596
The food may yet approach the view.

Oak Terrace Dining Room
The Drake Hotel
140 E. Walton St.
787-2200
The old Raleigh Room, updated, provides a garden-like setting for steaks, seafood, and other hotel favorites. Wine bar; on-premise baking.

The Pinnacle
Holiday Inn
644 N. Lake Shore Dr.
943-9200
Revolve while you revel in mediocre, overpriced meals and super views.

The Raphael Restaurant
Raphael Hotel
201 E. Delaware Pl.
943-5000
Good versions of hotel standards at fairly reasonable prices in a cozy room.

The Ritz-Carlton Café
Water Tower Place
160 E. Pearson St.
266-1000
Nice hotel/coffee-shop fare is served in this fairly elegant, open room off the hotel's 12th-floor lobby, 24 hours a day. More ambitious menu during conventional eating hours.

The Signature
Holiday Inn Mart Plaza
350 N. Orleans St.
836-5000
There's nothing exceptional about the Continental menu (priced for those on expense accounts), but during the Lyric Opera season, well-orchestrated packages feature dinner selections from that evening's opera's country of origin, a plot summary and commentary, free parking, and transportation to the performance. (You supply the tickets.)

Oriental

Benihana of Tokyo
166 E. Superior St.
664-9643
The first and cheapest of the city's teppanyaki spots.

Hana East Japanese Steak House
210 E. Ohio St.
751-2100
This mid-price-range teppanyaki operation boasts several teahouse rooms, with traditional menus, too.

*Hatsuhana
160 E. Ontario St.
280-8287
More than 35 varieties of utterly fresh raw seafood are crafted into sushi and sashimi. Cooked food, too. Clean, attractive décor.

*House of Hunan
535 N. Michigan Ave.
329-9494
Prices are a bit high, but this is one of the best spots in town for Hunanese cuisine, and the choice is impressive.

*Hunan Palace
1050 N. State St.
642-1800
More Hunanese specialties, including game, exotica, and Peking duck (without advance notice), in more opulent settings, hidden on the second floor of Newberry Plaza near Arnie's and Morton's.

Kon Tiki Ports
Radisson Chicago Hotel
505 N. Michigan Ave.
527-4286
Fabulous wooden-ship setting just makes the second-rate Polynesian food more disappointing. Have a drink instead.

Ron of Japan
230 E. Ontario St.
644-6500
The menu choices are more limited and the prices higher here than at Benihana or Hana East, but the portions are huge, and the sirloin steak meets the menu's boast.

*Shino
18 E. Huron St.
944-1321
The cozy rooms of an old row house make a delightfully different setting for some excellent Japanese meals.

*Szechwan House
600 N. Michigan Ave.
642-3900
The area's only serious source for this potent provincial cuisine. Luncheon buffet.

*Yanase Japanese Restaurant
818 N. State St.
664-1371
Your needs are attended to with more alacrity at the sushi bar than in the upstairs dining room. The inexpensive sushi's always great.

Steaks and/or seafood

Blackhawk on Pearson
110 E. Pearson St.
943-3300
Spanish décor and a salad bar replace the Loop location's old-line ambiance and "spinning salad bowl," but the beef and scrod are the same.

*Cape Cod Room
The Drake Hotel
140 E. Walton St.
787-2200
This old-fashioned fine-dining seafood room offers the unusual—pompano and lobster in paper—as well as the expected.

***Carson's—
The Place for Ribs**
612 N. Wells St.
280-9200
The place for ribs. Steak, too. Other locations.

*Chestnut Street Grill
Water Tower Place
845 N. Michigan Ave.
280-2720
One of the city's pre-eminent seafood sources with prices to match.

Eli's—The Place for Steak
215 E. Chicago Ave.
642-1393
Haven for celebs and expense-accounters. The calf's liver is highly touted.

Hy's of Canada
100 E. Walton St.
649-9555
Expensive steaks and seafood are served in a clubby dining room; no Canadian specialties.

Ireland's
500 N. La Salle St.
337-2020
Salad bar and big fresh-seafood selection in a trendy, woody atmosphere. Stick to the simple fare.

*Lawry's—The Prime Rib
100 E. Ontario St.
787-5000
If you can afford it, this is the place to take an indecisive date. The only choices are the cut, temperature, and peas of creamed spinach.

*Morton's
1050 N. State St.
266-4820
This is the place to stuff yourself with enormous cuts of great steaks, but remember, everything is à la carte, and nothing this good is cheap. Big lobsters, great potatoes.

*The Palm
Mayfair Regent Hotel
181 E. Lake Shore Dr.
944-0135
Bring your credit cards—all of them. And try the onions.

Don Roth's River Plaza
405 N. Wabash Ave.
527-3100
The menu and décor are more contemporary than at Roth's other spots, but the kitchen just can't get it together, yet.

Shuckers
150 E. Ontario St.
266-6057
More informal and intimate than many other nearby spots. Mostly seafood, mostly fresh. Good oysters.

The Waterfront
1015 N. Rush St.
943-7494
Raw brick and wood décor with nautical accents and the decent seafood make this smallish place pleasant. So does the help. Nice salad bar at night.

Burgers and fun food

*Acorn on Oak
116 E. Oak St.
944-6835
Some of the best burgers in town are served in what is essentially an upper-crust neighborhood bar. Buddy Charles, Chicago's most touted ivories artist, is a late-evening bonus.

Bagel Nosh
1135 N. State St.
266-6369
Fun food with a Yiddish accent is served cafeteria-style in a very handsome Santa Monica/Sausalito pine-walled, plant-filled room.

Billy Goat Tavern
430 N. Michigan Ave.
(Lower level)
222-1525
The name comes from the official mascot. No kidding.

*Hamburger Hamlet
44 E. Walton St.
649-6601
If only you could eat the décor: It's certainly four-star.

Meriwether's
1160 N. Dearborn St.
337-6617
Seafood and stir-fry dishes are specialties on the fun-food menu at this very handsome spot with a multiroom lounge and a clubby dining room.

*The ? Mark
439 N. Wells St.
644-3146
It looks like a dump from the outside, but isn't.

Riverside Pub
400 N. Clark St.
329-9344
This pub serves good grub, including freshly ground burgers.

Sherlock's Home
900 N. Michigan Ave.
787-0545
The clubby bar is a popular after-work watering hole for razzle-dazzle refugees, and there are the usual burgers et al., too. Nice salad bar.

Sweetwater
1028 N. Rush St.
787-5552
This lush restaurant/bar is a place to be seen or to make connections. The menu keeps up with the latest trends, but the food could, and should, be better.

Tamborine
200 E. Chestnut St.
944-4367
Brass, mirrors, and dark blue walls make the bar area a snazzy place for a tryst, and the weekend cabaret makes it even better.

Farrago

The Bon Ton
1153 N. State St.
943-0538
This homey Hungarian institution serves full meals, but only the pastries shine.

Boudin Bakery
63 E. Chicago Ave.
329-1580
Try a sandwich on the famous San Francisco sourdough bread.

Cafe Jasper
105 E. Ontario St.
642-5404
Très chic European-style, gray-and-black brasserie plays classical music and displays original art. Pricey sandwiches at lunch; stuffed puffs and daily specials at dinner when a wine bar operates. Considering the place's attractiveness and homemade cuisine, the food should be better. Bargain breakfasts.

Chapman Sisters Calorie Counter
444 N. Michigan Ave.
329-9690
High ceilings, bright and airy atmosphere, and an outdoor café in warm weather make this a lovely lunch spot even if you aren't counting calories. There's an informal, we're-all-in-it-together mood about the place.

Gaylord India
678 N. Clark St.
664-1700
Check out the tandoori chef through the kitchen's glass walls on the way to the stark, modern dining room. His wares are the usual Indian fare. Lunch buffet.

La Gruta
19 E. Chestnut St.
944-2928
Sure, it's just one more middle-of-the-road Mexican restaurant, but the Dino's Grotto legacy means you can get pan pizza, too.

GuadalaHarry's
1043 N. Rush St.
337-0800
General Foods-owned chain outlet follows an accepted recipe for success: chic surroundings, cutesy menu, corporate Mexican food.

Khyber India
50 E. Walton St.
649-9060
Elegant setting highlights a full menu from the subcontinent, and there's a popular lunch buffet.

Meson del Lago
158 E. Ontario St.
649-9215
Live music, pretty south-of-the-border décor, and affordable prices makes this a nice family spot that's neat for dates on a budget, too. The food—cliché Mexican—is okay, and there's an all-you-can-eat taco bar for lunch and dinner.

Out To Lunch
200 E. Chestnut St.
(Lower level arcade)
642-4649
Hidden in the Seneca Hotel, this is a pleasant source for broodjes (little Dutch sandwiches). A big eater could spend a fortune. They're great picnic goodies, too.

San Francisco Bar & Grill
400 N. State St.
644-0606
Inviting West Coast décor makes this a nice place to sample fresh seafood and such Bay area delights as "Joe's Special."

Sayat Nova
157 E. Ohio St.
644-9159
Decent Armenian food in this atmospheric basement, but no exciting culinary stunts.

Su Casa
49 E. Ontario St.
943-4041
More main-line Mexican food in somewhat intimate Latin surroundings.

The Taberna
303 E. Ohio St.
329-0262
Sample Greektown food within walking distance of the hotels, in the lower level of the Time-Life Building.

Terrace Garden Cafe
Sheraton-Plaza Hotel
160 E. Huron St.
787-2900
Lunch alfresco or have a drink beside the 40th-floor pool in good weather.

Ting-a-Ling Chocolate Shop
42 W. Division St.
751-0825
Once one of Chicago's nicest ice-cream parlors, but cheap meals have all but displaced the candy and fountain creations. A visit to the little Art Deco shop is worthwhile; it opened in the days when singles were suspect, not big business.

*The Wrigley Building Restaurant
410 N. Michigan Ave.
944-7600

If you wonder what the better restaurants your parents used to frequent were like, check out this one. Good *meats from steak tartare to sweetbreads. Fine bay scallops, too. Menu changes daily.*

Entertainment

Bars: Music

*Andy's
11 E. Hubbard St.
642-6805
Live jazz many weekdays at noon, too. Fri. evening cover: $2 at door.

*The Backroom
1007 N. Rush St.
751-2433
Minimum on weekends; occasional cover.

Baton Show Lounge
436 N. Clark St.
644-5269
Female-impersonator review, Wed. to Sun. Cover and minimum.

Blondies
936½ N. Rush St.
280-0963
This dim, modern spot decorated with photos of famous blondes features sophisticated jazz. Cover varies; two-drink minimum.

La Cage Chicago
50 E. Oak St.
944-3293
Late-night, mostly gay club above Le Relais features female impersonators and disco dancing. Cover weekends; no minimum.

The Candy Store
874 N. Wabash Ave.
642-3100
Maybe you call it dancing. A $10 temporary membership buys you all the near-beer and pop you can drink while a stripper does her thing. This, and a few other similar spots, recalls Rush Street's bad old days.

Emerald Isle Pub
21 E. Pearson St.
944-9030
This huge barn of a place has traditional Irish music five days a week. The weekend-only cover's low and the atmosphere is pub.

Gaslight Club
13 E. Huron St.
440-7040
Italian lights on a quiet side street draw you to the old Tudor mansion. Inside, someone is always playing a piano, singing, or leading a band in each of three performance spaces. The first-floor dining room, decorated with lighting fixtures from the Vanderbilts' Kingsbury estate, serves decent steaks. The original Theodora statue from the Everleigh Club graces the bar, but you can't touch the girls here. You can, however, arrange a temporary membership at the door.

Joann
730 N. Wells St.
951-9779
A mixed neighborhood audience in the piano bar, where almost anyone may drop by.

The Lion Bar
Westin Hotel Chicago
909 N. Michigan Ave.
943-7200
Comfortable, librarylike room is a fine place to catch live jazz five nights a week. No cover or minimum. Seafood bar; limited dinner menu, but the food is decent.

Razzles
Chicago Lakeshore Hotel
600 N. Lake Shore Dr.
787-4700
Local Dixieland band plays Tues. to Sat.

*Rick's Café Americain
Holiday Inn
644 N. Lake Shore Dr.
943-9200

*Milt Trenier's
901 N. Rush St.,
Lower level
266-6226
Modest cover and minimum.

Bars: Social

B.B.C.
9 W. Division St.
664-7012
Once a society disco; now caters to only a semidressy crowd. Cover weekends.

Brehon Pub
731 N. Wells St.
642-1071
Probably the "cleanest" bar in town. It was the famous Mirage.

*Cafe de Melvins!
1116 N. State St.
664-0356

Finley's
17 W. Elm St.
664-8452
An antiques-and-stained-glass singles spot down an alley.

Flapjaws Saloon
810 N. Wabash Ave.
642-4848
This Loyola college bar serves a good burger.

The Gold Coast
501 N. Clark St.
329-0565
Full-length feature films on Sun.; Tues. is leather night, Wed. is uniform night. Women will feel uncomfortable here.

The Hangge Uppe
14 W. Elm St.
337-0561
Disco madness with a dee-jay on the main floor and oldies on the juke box downstairs. No cover or minimum.

*Harry's Café
1035 N. Rush St.
266-0167
The ultimate slick singles bar.

Hogan's
1 W. Erie St.
944-6998
Popular lunch and after-work spot for good beers and muffalettas—a New Or-leans round hoagie.

The Hotsie Totsie Yacht Club and Bait Shop
8 E. Division St.
337-9128
A neat nautical place with a great name and no sailors.

*Houlihan's Old Place
1207 N. Dearborn St.
642-9647
Antiques overkill. Several in suburbs.

Images
John Hancock Center
875 N. Michigan Ave.
280-5487
Splendid views from the 96th floor make the pricey drinks endurable.

Loading Zone
46 E. Oak St.
266-2244
One of the area's more pleasant gay bars draws a fairly prosperous group. Video room shows x-rated films, often months before they hit the theaters.

The Lodge
21 W. Division St.
642-4406
A very popular meat rack.

*Butch McGuire's
20 W. Division St.
337-9080
The boast is how many married couples meet here, but that's not really the prime aim of the patrons.

Marina City Restaurant
300 N. State St.
321-0786
Deejay and dancing daily, but the real draw may be watching the river from the lower-level, boaty bistro.

*Mother's
26 W. Division St.
642-7251
Cover for special events.

Pippin's Tavern
806 N. Rush St.
787-5435
Convivial, collegiate bar near Loyola University.

P.O.E.T.S.
5 W. Division St.
951-9350
A young crowd favors this subterranean disco.

P.S. Chicago
8 W. Division St.
649-9093
Is it a disco with a big bar, or a singles bar with a jammed dance floor? Whatever it is, it sure is popular.

Puck's Pub
676 N. La Salle St.
642-6531
This cozy brew-and-burger spot in a recycled factory building with lots of arty ten-ants is decorated with strik-ing photos, many done by locals, and serves good cinnamon coffee, too.

Remington's
1007 N. Rush St.
951-6522
Popular singles spot, deco-rated with antiques and American Indian artifacts, has one of the strip's long-est weekday happy hours: 11 a.m. to 7 p.m. Young crowd sports mostly jeans.

*She-Nannigans
16 W. Division St.
642-2344

*Snuggery Saloon & Dining Room
15 W. Division St.
337-4349
Band plays some nights.

Theaters

Carnegie Theatre
1026 N. Rush St.
944-2966
A first-run and art-film house that has experi-mented with live performances.

Chicago Filmmakers
6 W. Hubbard St.
329-0854
This center for independent filmmakers provides facili-ties for members and has public showings on week-ends. Lots of arty hand-held stuff.

Drury Lane Theatre at Water Tower Place
175 E. Chestnut St.
266-0500
(See Theater)

*Esquire Theatre
58 E. Oak St.
337-1117
One of the city's important first-run houses.

McClurg Court Theatre
330 E. Ohio St.
642-0723
The technical facilities at this 1,250-seat, first-run house with a glitzy subterra-nean lobby are topnotch. Why doesn't anyone come?

Sandburg Theatre
1024 N. Dearborn St.
944-4430
Currently an art house.

Water Tower Theatres
845 N. Michigan Ave.
649-5790
This four-screen Plitt opera-tion is probably the most important first-run house in town. It's got the glamour.

Gold Coast

Chicago's most desirable residential neighborhood stretches along the lakefront between the Magnificent Mile's glitter and Lincoln Park's greenery. The Gold Coast is aptly named—it costs a fortune to live here and the lifestyle has a special, rarified air. High-rises shoulder each other along Lake Shore Drive, giving some fortunate Chicagoans superb lake and beach views. Behind them, more luxury apartments and elegant townhouses designed by architectural greats in a rich variety of styles grace charming tree-lined streets. The famous hotels and restaurants, even the school and tot lot, speak in carefully modulated tones of Chicagoans who have arrived. Mixed in are apartment-sharing professionals, stewardesses between flights, and assorted young hopefuls attracted by the adjoining Rush Street and Division Street action, keeping the Gold Coast from being stuffy.

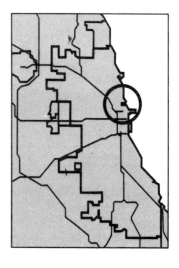

Part of Chicago when the city was incorporated, the neighborhood has always suggested wealth. "Astor's Addition"—named for John Jacob Astor—was an area between Division and Schiller Streets. The "Catholic Bishop of Chicago's Addition" stretched to North Avenue. The **Archbishop's Residence** (1555 North State Parkway) set the tone for the first wave of mansions built here in the 1880s. The guest list of the 1880 Alfred F. Pashley Queen Anne gem bristling with turrets, gables, and 19 chimneys has included two popes and a president. Lavish parties presided over by the arbiter of Chicago society brought fame to another trend setter. Potter Palmer erected his fairyland Tudor "mansion-to-end-all-mansions" on the lakefront in 1882, signaling the end of Prairie Avenue's hegemony over the super-rich. Demolished in 1950, the house had no doorknobs on the outside. Even the Palmers had to be admitted into the incredibly lush interior by servants.

By 1890, the upper crust flocking to the Gold Coast turned from flamboyance toward the massive Romanesque style popularized by Boston architect H. H. Richardson. Of the many examples on Astor Street, perhaps the best are the houses at 1316-22 designed by Charles Palmer (no relation) for Potter Palmer. Howard Van Doren Shaw, on the other hand, used English Tudor inspirations for the restrained residence at 1451. When *Chicago Tribune* publisher Joseph Medill had New York's ill-fated society architect Stanford White design a wedding present for his daughter Nellie and son-in-law Robert Patterson, they got a replica of a Renaissance palace. In 1927, David Adler expanded the already huge house for Cyrus McCormick II. The **Patterson-McCormick House** (1500, entrance at 20 East Burton Place) later housed the private Bateman school, and is now broken up into condominiums.

In 1892, lumber merchant James Charnley hired the prestigious firm of Adler and Sullivan to design his residence; chief designer Frank Lloyd Wright got the assignment. The **Charnley House** (1365) must have stopped people in their tracks when it was built. Today, it doesn't look that odd, and the future according to Wright is obvious in the strong horizontal thrust overlaid with Sullivan's ornament. Ten years later, Hugh Garden, working in the offices of Richard E. Schmidt, gave a Chicago twist to the **Madlener House** (4 West Burton Place). The emphasis here also is on the horizontal—a harbinger of the emerging Prairie School style. The **Graham Foundation for Advanced Studies in the Fine Arts** restored the house and makes it their headquarters.

Georgian revivals appeared after 1910, but they blended into the streetscape quite nicely. So do even more modern forms such as Art Deco, adopted by Holabird and Root for the house at 1444 North Astor Street. The **Astor Street District** includes all the old homes on Astor and guarantees their protection, but don't limit a stroll just to this street. The **Frank Fisher Apartments** (1207 North State Parkway), the work of Andrew Rebori—one of Chicago's overlooked masters—is a small, curved-front, white-brick-and-glass-block Art Moderne building wrapped around a lovely court. You'll also want to see the outside—visitors are not welcome—of the **Playboy Mansion** (1340), once home of the big bunny and retinue. Nearby, the **Three Arts Club** (1300 North Dearborn Street), in a fine Holabird and Root building, provides a more wholesome environment for young women studying at Chicago's art schools and conservatories.

With several exceptions, such as the **International College of Surgeons** (1516) and the **Polish Consulate General** (1530), the mansions that once lined Lake Shore Drive have disappeared. In their stead are apartment towers intended for a clientele demanding great spaces and lavish appointments. The Palmers, Wrigleys, and Insulls lived in co-ops of 20 or more rooms with separate servants' quarters on lower floors. Some have 20-foot-high ceilings, parquet floors inlaid with pewter, and organ lofts. One of the most elegant of these buildings, 1550 North State Parkway, overlooks Lincoln Park rather than the lake. Benjamin Marshall, architect of the Blackstone Hotel and The Drake, created 9,000-square-foot residences on each of ten floors. Today, each apartment is subdivided into four. The Depression and World War Two temporarily halted construction of mighty towers such as these, but more recent buildings have virtually finished a solid wall along the lakefront.

Neighborhood amenities on the Gold Coast are few but first class. Nannies hover over kids playing in the Goudy Square Tot Lot (Astor and Goethe Streets), and many of the toddlers' older siblings attend the exclusive **Latin School of Chicago** (59 West North Boulevard), housed in a Harry Weese-designed building. A branch of **Stop & Shop** (1313 North Ritchie Court) caters to grocery needs in style. Women who pass the doorman's muster and climb the marble stairs to the spacious, subdued **Kane's** (1325 North State Parkway) enter a carriage-trade world that has almost disappeared elsewhere. After browsing through the sportswear boutique in the rococo-accented salon with its crystal chandeliers, they relax on comfortable sofas while skilled saleswomen display Alfred Bosand formals and cocktail outfits; Sansappelle hand-painted silk dresses; Becky Bisoulis laces and suedes; Roberta and Brenda knits; sportswear by Dana, Tiktiner, and Anne Klein; Hanae Mori silks; and finery by Emanuel Ungaro, Oscar de la Renta, Geoffrey Beene, Bill Blass, and Pauline Trigère, as well as other American and European designers.

Gold Coast restaurants are equally classy. In the days when stars of stage and screen paused in Chicago on their journeys between New York and Hollywood, they spent time between the Twentieth Century Limited and the Super Chief at **The Pump Room** (Ambassador East Hotel, 1301 North State Parkway). The city's most famous, flashiest restaurant, its Booth Number One was always reserved for the most celebrated celebrities. Under Lettuce Entertain You Enterprises' ownership, waiters in knee breeches and tights serving flaming delights have given way to more subdued elegance, but the Continental menu often promises more than it delivers. Nonetheless, there are highs as well as lows, and the staff's willingness to accept food returns mitigates some of the risk. A harpist plays in the dining room; the bar provides a fine selection of drinks, one of the city's most lavish, free cocktail-hour buffets, and a torch singer. And The Pump Room remains a place to be seen.

Gene Sage's **Eugene's** and **Sage's on State** (Churchill Hotel, 1255 North State Parkway) are reliable sources for better-than-average, though not particularly innovative, meals in opulent, clubby surroundings. Steaks and seafood are mainstays of large menus, which also offer standards such as ribs, rack of lamb, veal, duck, and lots of shellfish appetizers. Extensive wine lists include an impressive assortment of fine Cognacs. With three small "Victorian" rooms arranged around a popular bar, a blazing fireplace, and a menu written in vintage *Guys and Dolls* New Yorkese, Eugene's is the more ornate of the two. But both are good places to bring business associates or relatives, and they have evening entertainment, too.

If the food at **Enzio's** (21 West Goethe Street) tasted as good as the huge menu makes it sound, this would be a great Northern Italian restaurant. Lots of openers from antipasto to mussels marinara, almost a dozen pastas, and loads of veal and seafood dishes make your mouth water in anticipation. But despite occasional triumphs, the kitchen seldom measures up to the tab. Formerly L'Epuisette, the handsome wood-paneled room has undergone little Italianization and is marred by aqua vinyl banquettes and taped Frank Sinatra hits.

The same owners completely revamped the old Café de Paris, once one of Chicago's big-name French restaurants, and opened **Trumpets** (1260 North Dearborn Street) in mid-1981, a no-more-successful effort at a cuisine that has yet to do well in Chicago: regional American.

Only a few blocks away but worlds apart, the **Germania Inn** (1540 North Clark Street) is essentially a neighborhood bar-restaurant with Teutonic knick-knacks and travel posters for decoration and waitresses in dirndls serving down-to-earth, hearty German fare, including daily specials. The food goes down easily with beer but doesn't send you running to the chef for recipes.

Although the Inn is of fairly recent vintage, the **Germania Club** (108 West Germania Place) around the corner dates to the time when Chicago's German elite lived in elegant townhouses along La Salle Street. August Fiedler's 1889 building contains a rich baroque interior—occasionally accessible for public events—that reflects the community's turn-of-the-century wealth. The bold blue-and-yellow **Swedish Club of Chicago** (1258 North La Salle Street), opened in 1896, is a legacy of a powerful Swedish community.

By World War One, many of the elegant mansions along La Salle Street were converted to rooming houses. When the city widened the street in the 1930s, making it a major Loop-bound artery, decay accelerated as transient hotels multiplied. Today, however, the street is enjoying a renaissance, with the remaining townhouses being converted to condominiums and shabby apartments restored to elegance. The delightfully eclectic, privately funded, individual rehabilitations of Burton Place's townhouses are tangible symbols of the revival that was recognized by the city when the block was turned into a cul-de-sac at Wells Street. So, too, are Richard Haas's *trompe l'oeil* façades on 1211 North La Salle Street, which give a *fin de siècle* rebirth to a '20s high-rise.

Developments along Clark Street explain much of La Salle's decline and revival. By the end of the First World War, Clark Street was lined with cheap hotels, dance halls, and saloons. By the end of the next war, the street had become such a civic embarrassment that a massive residential development was scheduled to replace the honky-tonks. Interestingly, some of the antiques stores that gave Clark Street what little class it had moved west to Wells Street, sparking upgrading there.

Developers competed frantically for the chance to build on the multiacre site stretching from North Avenue to Division Street between Clark and La Salle Streets. When the dust settled, Arthur Rubloff's mixed high- and low-rise scheme, designed by Louis Solomon and John Cordwell, prevailed, and the first phase was completed in 1965. Planned as a middle-income, integrated "city within a city," **Carl Sandburg Village** was never more than tokenly integrated, and most singles could afford the rents only by doubling up.

Expense notwithstanding, Sandburg Village quickly became the choice of young, unmarried Chicagoans. Proximity to Rush Street and Division Street bars, in-complex swimming pools and tennis courts, and the sheer number of like-minded fellow residents proved powerful draws. Everything in the "Village" seems to revolve around sociability. The **Sandburg Super Mart** (1525 North Clark Street) has a surprising wine department; **First St. Paul's Evangelical Lutheran Church** (Goethe and La Salle Streets) offers a number of outreach programs and singles activities; and the Sandburg Village Art Fair feels like a neighborhood craft show. Serious art lovers do somewhat better at the Gold Coast Art Fair, and the setting is prettier. (*See Annual Events.*)

Interesting places

*Archbishop's Residence
1555 N. State Pkwy.

*Astor Street District
Astor St. from North Blvd. to Division St.
The Commission on Chicago Historical and Architectural Landmarks publishes an informative booklet.

*Charnley House
1365 N. Astor St.
John Vinci is guiding the restoration.

*First St. Paul's Evangelical Lutheran Church
Goethe and La Salle Sts.
642-7172, 664-9466
Old German church established in 1846 at Ohio and La Salle Sts. Moved to the present location in 1910; the old structure was razed in 1970 and replaced with a design by Edward Dart.

*Frank Fisher Apartments
1207 N. State Pkwy.

*Germania Club
108 W. Germania Pl.
664-0740

*Graham Foundation for Advanced Studies in the Fine Arts
4 W. Burton Pl.
787-4071
Especially strong in its support of architecture. Excellent lecture series open to the public. Located in Madlener House.

*International College of Surgeons
1516 N. Lake Shore Dr.
642-3555
Its museum next door (1524) is devoted to the history of surgery. (See Museums.)

*The Latin School of Chicago
59 W. North Blvd.
787-0820

*Madlener House
4 W. Burton Pl.

Merchandise National Bank
1536 N. Clark St.
280-8008
Located in the Germania Club building, the bank has been remodeled to provide an 1890s feeling.

*Patterson-McCormick House
20 E. Burton Pl.

*Playboy Mansion
1340 N. State Pkwy.
Originally the George S. Isham House, designed in 1889 by James Gamble Rogers of Paris. The French influence is clearly evident in the mansard roof and the lavish Beaux-Arts detail.

*Polish Consulate General
1530 N. Lake Shore Dr.
337-8166

St. Chrysostom's Episcopal Church
Dearborn and Schiller Sts.
944-1083
Fine English Gothic church erected in 1925. On Sundays, Robert Lodine plays the organ and carillon wonderfully. Standing-room-only Easter service.

*Carl Sandburg Village
Bounded roughly by La Salle and Clark Sts., North Ave., and Division St.

*Swedish Club of Chicago
1258 N. La Salle St.
664-4270

*Three Arts Club
1300 N. Dearborn St.
944-6250

Shopping and services

Ambassador East Hotel
1301 N. State Pkwy.
787-7200
Home of The Pump Room, this remains one of Chicago's première hotels. Special weekend rates— two people, two nights— begin at $136 and include breakfast in The Pump Room. Dinner in The Pump Room is extra.

Ambassador West Hotel
1300 N. State Pkwy.
787-7900
Some of Chicago society's most glittering events are held in the West's Guildhall. "Golden Escape Weekend" for two runs $125 and includes a suite, free parking, cocktails, and Continental breakfasts.

*Kane's
1325 N. State Pkwy.
787-0700

Mid-Town Court House
1235 N. La Salle St.
787-8400
Racquetball and exercise facilities. People get their bodies in shape to meet other bodies.

The Perfect Touch
1538 N. Clark St.
664-0130
Claims to be the Midwest's largest importer of "antique" 17th-, 18th-, and 19th-century paintings. The paintings may be antiques but they are merely decorative. Pretty frames.

Racquet Club of Chicago
1363 N. Dearborn St.
787-3200
Very exclusive private club; the sort of place to meet mother for lunch before shopping at Magnin's.

*Sandburg Super Mart
1525 N. Clark St.
337-7537
Convenience grocery for Sandburg dwellers gets a big plus for its outstanding wine room, with one of the country's best selections of German wines and one of the city's best collections of red Bordeaux. Tasting bar; knowledgeable, personable service; above-average storage conditions.

*Stop & Shop
1313 N. Ritchie Ct.
853-2150

Dining and drinking

Arturo's Le Coq au Vin
1400 N. Lake Shore Dr.
280-8800
Old-line French restaurant with an unremarkable menu; the atmosphere is nice but a little matronly.

*Enzio's
21 W. Goethe St.
280-1010

*Eugene's
1255 N. State Pkwy.
944-1445

*Germania Inn
1540 N. Clark St.
642-9394

Métro
1300 N. Astor St.
943-1111
Maxim's de Paris, Chicago's bastion of Art Nouveau opulence and haute cuisine for two decades, closed in 1982. The new owners retained the décor (a close copy of the Maxim's in Paris, France) but opted for simpler fare: grilled items, fresh fish, lighter sauces, and the like. The menu has an international flair; entrées average $10 to $15.

*The Pump Room
Ambassador East Hotel
1301 N. State Pkwy.
266-0360

*Sage's on State
1255 N. State Pkwy.
944-1383

*Trumpets
1260 N. Dearborn St.
266-8000

Entertainment

Byfield's
Ambassador East Hotel
1301 N. State Pkwy.
787-6433
Small, elegant cabaret showcases local talent and, occasionally, big-name music and comedy acts. Cover varies. Inexpensive dinner buffet week nights.

Village Theater
1548 N. Clark St.
642-2403
Sandburg Village's neighborhood movie house with good second-run films and midnight specials for cultists of various kinds.

Old Town

In the 1960s, "Old Town" and "Wells Street" were synonymous to the crowds that jammed the stretch from North Avenue to Division Street, making walking a challenge and parking almost impossible. From city and suburbs, people were drawn to places like the College of Complexes, Big John's, Piper's Alley, the Quiet Knight, and Mother Blues to eat, drink, shop, and—if they were really lucky—rub elbows with the artists and hippies who were the reputed denizens of the neighborhood.

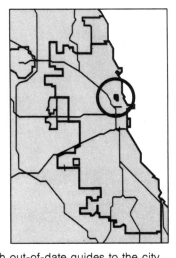

But in the '70s the crowds waned. Whether due to sophistication or saturation, the fickle masses abandoned Old Town for the newer attractions of Lincoln Avenue and New Town. Ersatz-antique street lamps, installed in a vain attempt to lure customers back to Wells Street, showed that mere light couldn't do the job; their eerie amber glow shone on muggers, moribund shops, and a handful of tourists with out-of-date guides to the city.

The dawn of a new decade, however, has bestowed on Wells Street the beneficent fallout from a Near North Side residential renaissance. Carl Sandburg Village has been transformed into an in-town, high-rise suburb of condominium owners. The Atrium Village townhouses sprang up on Division Street and, across from them, the bold, glazed-brick façade of a huge, new YMCA recreational complex heralds further activity. A growing number of shopkeepers and restaurateurs are betting on continued gentrification, joining the few who held on during the lean years.

Two stores that witnessed two decades of changes still thrive by astutely tailoring their stock to shifting fashions. **The Emporium** (1551 North Wells Street), cleverly decorated with white woodwork and architectural trappings to suggest a surrealistic gazebo, is aglow with a garden of soft sculptures, candles, soaps, pillows, hanging lamps, baskets, fancy wrapping papers, kites, and fabric flowers. **The Town Shop** (1561) packs in much of the same, plus an entire room of baskets and lots of Orientalia, including stoneware mugs, tea sets, and Chinatown-like lacquerware collectibles.

In a charming courtyard nearby, Jim Nowik's **Old Print Store** (1407) carries a varied and affordable collection of 18th- and 19th-century, old and rare prints and specializes in Early American lithographs and engravings—artworks executed during the period of Old Town's very first flowering. Although its trailblazing owner and namesake, Barbara Siegel, has moved on, **Barbara's Bookstore** (1434) remains an attractive store and a fertile ground for browsers with a fine selection of periodicals, paperbacks, and hardcovers, including hard-to-find books from little presses. The literature, cookbook, and children's sections are particularly good.

One of Chicago's merchandising success stories began on Wells Street at **Crate & Barrel** (1510). After launching a fleet of chic kitchen- and housewares stores, the original has re-embraced the warehouse-outlet concept. Discontinued patterns, overstocks, and seconds of elegant tableware and gourmet cookware at bargain prices fill the brick-and-wood main floor. Linens and fabrics, including sought-after Marimekko yard goods, are in the loft. The low prices mean no fancy gift wrapping and precious little sales help.

The flashiest remnant of the P. T. Barnum, honky-tonk days is **Ripley's Believe It or Not Museum** (1500), but sleazy headshops, such as one in a tawdry mall, still hang on. On the other hand, the **Up Down Tobacco Shop** (1550) has moved from a subterranean cranny to a virtual smokers' supermarket by catering to addicts of a more respectable weed. An impressive collection of luxury pipes includes many meerschaums; cigar humidors are filled with quality smokes from around the world; and the selection of imported cigarettes is extraordinary. If none of the standard pipe tobaccos please, the knowledgeable staff will mix a custom blend.

Your nostalgia for Old Town's recent past may run rampant at **Piper's Alley** (1620). Once Wells Street's focus, the original twisty rabbit warren of boutiques, studio cinemas, headshops, and poster stores was demolished in 1975. The antiseptic "theme park" replacement designed by Stanley Tigerman (but restrained by money problems) reuses the old mall's rescued-from-mansions architectural ephemera, but re-creates little of the old excitement. Mundane tenants—a supermarket, a savings and loan, a telephone company store—loom large, but a few shops are worth noting. **R.S.V.P.** glitters with hundreds of brass items, including reproductions of Victoriana and Pullman-style overhead racks (useful in closets and johns). **Yeast Works** is one of the city's few remaining sources for wine- and beer-making supplies. While **Paper-Party-Funalia,** a happy little place with clever cards, posters, and party supplies, is reminiscent of the original mall's shops, **Material Matters,** one of the newest tenants, aims to recapture the heyday ambiance. The bilevel, low-tech shop with graphics painted on the floor stocks a continually changing array of natural-fiber fabrics, as well as a few funky, versatile clothes, some of which are by local designers. Custom-design services are available, too. On the second level, Horse of a Different Color, a new incarnation of a late-1960s Wells Street shop, specializes in yarns and threads for fiber art and offers classes. **My Sister's Shoes** sells a thoughtfully chosen selection of women's shoes, hats, purses, and other accessories.

North of Piper's Alley, Wells Street saw less of the circuslike frenzy typical of the strip further south. Here, on the "front porch" of the Old Town Triangle District, the shops have a comfortable, settled feel that comes from catering to a prosperous neighborhood trade, rather than to tourists. **Handle With Care** (1706) is one of those lovely little stores that reflects an enthusiastic owner's love of the beautiful. Finds like Margarita Sosa-Vásquez's pillows and blouses of Victorian lace, June's beaded body adornments, and Suzanne Bucher's imaginative jewelry share space with trendy clothing and accessories, vintage Japanese kimonos, luscious soaps, and clever furnishings, all at reasonable prices.

Interior designers Robert and Gloria Turner collect furniture and objèts d'art from all over the world for their **Design Source** (1710). The emphasis is on the unusual and the handmade, such as rustic furniture fashioned from willow limbs, a restored and reupholstered 1930s living-room suite, or a custom cabinet-maker's *trompe l'oeil*-parchment table. The Turners introduced Tarahumara pottery—Stone Age-like clayworks from an isolated Mexican Indian tribe—to Chicago, and the shop's other primitive-to-modern accessories are equally fascinating. The adjoining **Light Source** has a forest of ultramodern lamps and track lighting to go with the furniture. The huge, forestlike **Green** (1716) down the block stocks an excellent selection of big plants for big apartments, succulents, small plants, cut flowers, and even flats for planting.

Bigsby & Kruthers On The Park (1750 North Clark Street) epitomizes the prosperity of the area. Formerly the Warehouse, a minimall of diverse shops that failed, the huge, multilevel space has been turned into a dozen B & K boutiques. They cater to well-heeled men seeking Italian and British suits, more conservative business clothes, avant-garde sportswear, duds by top designers, and luxurious accessories such as leather suspenders and cashmere socks. They also stock an extensive collection of clothing for short men. To complete the chic shopping concept envisioned by the owners, there's a small Ann Taylor shop with *au courant* women's attire, a men's hair salon, a florist, and a restaurant.

With its curious façade and unabashed celebration of those who give it ink, **Treasure Island** (1639) may be Old Town's best-known store. The readable community bulletin board may have provided much of the source material for its temporary immortalization in Bob Greene's and Paul Galloway's newspaper serial (then book, then musical play) *Bagtime,* the saga of bagboy Mike Holiday and his cat Helen. More important, T.I.'s collection of esoteric and imported foodstuffs, produce, and gourmet delicacies may be unsurpassed in Chicago.

Gourmet pickings can also be had at a number of specialty shops. **Coffee Corner** (1700) stocks a good selection of whole beans, teas, spices, and related paraphernalia and serves espresso at a stand-up counter. For a classic *petit déjeuner,* try a flaky fruit tart or croissant from **Maison Barusseau** (1446). Skilled *pâtissier* Guy Barusseau also turns out fine tortes at this homey spot, but no bread. Get that at **Mangia Italiano** (1557), which specializes in freshly made pastas, sauces, and heat-and-serve entrées. Other offerings include delicious ice creams plus imported deli meats and cheeses, both by the pound and in built-to-your-specifications subs. To round out a picnic in the park or at the beach, head to **The House of Glunz** (1206), where Louis Glunz's family has sold wine and beer since the 1880s, surviving Prohibition by selling sacramental and medicinal libations. Now the Midwest's largest distributor of altar wines, the shop is better known for excellent table wines and highly regarded *vins ordinaires* sold under its own label. A collection of memorabilia dates back to the days when it was a tavern catering to neighbors Oscar Mayer and Dr. Scholl.

Though countless new and established restaurants have gone belly up in Old Town, still you can stroll up Wells Street from Glunz's and pass dozens of eateries, from odd to opulent. Find a limited choice of competent, inexpensive Middle Eastern specialties at the plain **Old Jerusalem** (1411) or good soups and simple meals at **Bowl and Roll** (1339), a cavelike place decorated by owner Marshall Kobata's brother-in-law, The Bakery's Louis Szathmáry. **Ciao** (1516) has an airy, austerely modern dining room but, in clement weather, the cognoscenti enjoy some unusual, moderately priced Italian dishes and pricey but top-rated Italian beef sandwiches on the patio. Try kamoosh—"Mexican pizza"—in the fruit-tree-shaded garden of **Cafe Azteca** (215 West North Avenue), one of Chicago's oldest Mexican-American restaurants. The bucolic charms and strolling musicians may add a bit to the tab for standards here, but they're still better than the Spanish choices.

Kamehachi of Tokyo (1617 North Wells Street), one of the city's first sushi bars, also serves a full menu of cooked foods. While the fish still shines, the staff ranges from condescending to surly. If oysters or clams satisfy your raw cravings, sidle up to the picture-perfect oyster bar behind **A Restaurant Named Desire** in Piper's Alley and wash the shellfish down with appropriate libations like Hurricanes and Ramos gin fizzes. The warm, woody restaurant serves such New Orleans goodies as duck-and-sausage gumbo and pecan pie to the strains of good taped jazz. At the elegant **Chef Eduardo's** (1640), the fare is Northern Italian—sometimes good, sometimes not, but always with classical background music. This is a nice place for lovers who can forgive occasional flaws in food and service for intimate surroundings.

For moderately priced steaks and ribs, consider the jointly owned **Fireplace Inn** (1448) and **Courtyard Inn** (1531), casual Old Town standbys with identical menus. The prime steaks don't measure up to the prices at **O'Brien's Sirloin Inn** (1528), which has dinner-jacketed waiters and drips beveled glass—incongruous notes for the neighborhood. More in keeping, perhaps, is **That Steak Joynt** (1610), which packs in conventioneers and locals seeking beef in Victorian-brothel surroundings. The dining experience may be iffy, but there's a dinner-theater package with the **Second City** (1616) next door.

Behind a façade salvaged from Louis Sullivan's Garrick Theatre, the umpteenth Second City cast performs the current irreverent revue. On week nights, free improvisations that first made the place such a joy follow the set piece. For roughly a quarter of a century, this Chicago institution has nurtured artists who've gone on to shape the nature of theater and comedy all over the world.

What Second City is to comedy fans, Earl Pionke's **Earl of Old Town** (1615) is to folkies. Though crowded and noisy, this is the place to catch as-yet-undiscovered talents and name acts. When they're in town, alumni Steve Goodman, Bonnie Koloc, John Prine, and others still share the Earl's spotlights.

For people-watching and just plain drinking, Old Town has two near-legendary taverns. The **Old Town Ale House** (219 West North Avenue) attracts interesting crowds, as it did when Eric Van Gelder first drew a beer here in 1958. Though many customers can no longer afford to live nearby, they return to play the eclectic juke box, converse in a sort of near-shout, and watch other people watching them. **O'Rourke's Pub** (319) is plastered with photos of Irish writers, IRA graffiti, and plastered Chicago journalists who wander in after becoming bored drinking at Riccardo's. Afternoons and early evenings, it's a pleasant neighborhood bar.

Although commercial glitter draws most visitors, the neighborhood has another, quieter, side: the **Old Town Triangle District,** bounded by North Avenue, Wells Street, and the imaginary extension of Ogden Avenue to Lincoln Park. The **Old Town Triangle Association** (1816 North Wells Street), one of the city's most active community organizations, watches over the well-being of this official city landmark district and coordinates activities as diverse as tree-planting, the Old Town Art Fair, crime prevention, and architectural preservation.

The earliest settlers—German truck farmers, brewers, and factory workers—could afford only the classic balloon-frame Chicago cottage, and these sprang up on cramped lots along the narrow, meandering streets. **St. Michael's Church,** erected in 1852 for $750 on land donated by brewer Michael Diversey, was the community's pride. When the parish grew, a new church was constructed at Eugenie Street and Cleveland Avenue. The eclectic but elegant structure, completed in 1869, cost $131,000, an eloquent statement about the parishioners' improved circumstances.

The Great Fire of 1871 left only three walls standing. Residents immediately began rebuilding, and while shoveling ashes into the basement, they discovered, undamaged, a picture of Our Lady of Perpetual Help entrusted to the church in 1865 by Pope Pius IX. The picture occupies a special place at one of the altars. (Bottled ashes from the fire are still sold to raise money for the church.) The rebuilt structure was dedicated a year and three days after the fire. Five huge bells, still heard throughout the neighborhood, were blessed in 1876. The same energy that went into the reconstruction of St. Michael's went into rebuilding the surrounding area. Wooden cottages, cheap and easy to construct, sprang out of the rubble. Many still exist. At the same time, with the creation of Lincoln Park on the site of the old municipal cemetery, the area became an attractive place to live. More elegant, substantial masonry buildings in Italianate or Queen Anne style lined many streets. Behind several, the older frame buildings, moved there during construction and later used by in-laws or rented out, still stand. By the end of the 19th century, the area was completely built up.

The parish became more affluent and St. Michael's became more beautiful. In 1902, five altars, including the 56-foot-tall main altar, were installed, as were 16 stained-glass windows from Munich. Stations of the Cross, carved in Austria, were added in 1920, and a year later frescoes were painted on the interior walls. The splendid interior of this church is awesome.

But just as the church reached full flower, the community began to experience problems. The old German settlement was breaking up as many residents moved north along Lincoln Avenue. Housing, especially the frame buildings, began to deteriorate. With the onset of the Depression, complete decay of the area seemed assured. But some people saw this as an opportunity. Many were artists, eking out a living on WPA stipends, attracted by the Old World feeling of the neighborhood. Barely able to afford the prices, they were precursors of today's urban pioneers. They stabilized the community and gave it the Bohemian reputation it retains to this day. Old Town's arty ambiance flourished in the 1940s and '50s, with its name coming from the Old Town Holiday, now the Old Town Art Fair and still a highlight of the city's ever-growing summer street fair scene. A charming garden walk is part of the celebration. (*See Annual Events.*) Many prominent Chicago artists and architects still call the area home.

Their best efforts were needed when a 1960s urban-renewal scheme threatened to destroy much of Old Town's charm. Happily, organization and concerted pressure won out over the bulldozers, and the neighborhood was kept pretty much intact. The only realization of the plan is the **Ogden Mall,** a pedestrian walk and greenway stretching diagonally through the community. It replaces a wide, underused street that had divided the neighborhood.

Walking the mall is one way to get a feel of today's Old Town. Begin at St. Michael's and walk northeast past Willow Street and Fern Court to the **Midwest Buddhist Temple** (Menomonee Street and Hudson Avenue), built in 1972 to the design of Hideaki Arao. Even though Old Town's once-sizable Japanese population is dispersed, many return for the Obon and Ginza festivals (*see Annual Events*). The old temple, in what was the Armour family's carriage house (1763 N. North Park Avenue), now serves as a community center and judo academy. A short distance east, on Sedgwick Street between Wisconsin and Menomonee, the present hits you with a jolt. Ten new townhouses by nine of Chicago's major architects (South from the southeast corner of Wisconsin and Sedgwick: Stanley Tigerman; Booth/Hansen & Associates; Will Rueter; Joseph Boggs/Studio of Dewberry, Nealon & Davis; James E. Economos and Joseph J. Anselmo for Urban Six Associates, Inc.; Booth/Hansen again; Mits Otsuji; Wayne Hanson; Robert Erdmann and Keith Youngquist for Jerome Cerny Associates, Inc.; Thomas E. Greene) stretch out like a life-size museum exhibit. Whether or not it works as cityscape is up to you. Continuing northeast, past the new **Church of the Three Crosses** (Wisconsin and Orleans Streets), across Lincoln Avenue, you come to the site of an as yet unrealized community center and the vista of Lincoln Park.

Another pleasant walk begins at Lincoln Avenue and Lincoln Park West.

Head south on Lincoln Park West to the **Louis Sullivan Townhouses** (1826-34), designed in 1885 and in splendid condition. The **Wacker House** (1838) is modeled on a Swiss chalet and boldly displays its gingerbread; next to it is the old carriage house, brought to the front by Charles Wacker of the Chicago Plan Commission and author of *Wacker's Guide,* all too familiar to generations of Chicago high-school students who were forced to study it. The **Tonk House** (1817) was designed by an unknown French architect and is now noted for its carved doors, advertisements for woodcrafter Max Tonk, son of the first owner. At the southwest corner, unpretentious but handsome, is a beautifully maintained old farmhouse. Be sure to visit Lincoln Park West in the spring, when the flowering crab apple trees heighten the pleasure of this already delightful street.

Perhaps the best idea of all is to walk around without any plan. You might discover the delights of the **Crilly Court** buildings around St. Paul and North Park Avenues, stumble into the mewslike Concord Place, or catch a whiff of the ribs at the **Twin Anchors** (1655 North Sedgwick Street). You might, in fact, concur with architect John Holabird, Jr.: "The houses in Old Town look well by themselves and they look well in groups; they produce neighborhood and street façades. In absolute fact, they make a city—and in half a hundred years we have not done so well." Explore. The bells of St. Michael's will make you feel at home.

Interesting places

*Church of the Three Crosses
Wisconsin and Orleans
751-7916

*Crilly Court Properties
Wells St. to North Park Ave.,
Eugenie St. to St. Paul Ave.
Daniel F. Crilly began this development in 1885. It grew to include a row of single-family residences, Georgian apartment buildings, and the storefronts on Wells St. They remain in excellent condition. Be sure to walk down the alleys to see the gardens.

*Midwest Buddhist Temple
Menomonee and Hudson
943-7801

Moody Memorial Church
Clark St. and North Ave.
943-0466
Dedicated to evangelist Dwight L. Moody, the 1925 building was designed by Fugard & Knapp. One of the largest churches in America; the main floor seats 2,300 and the balcony 1,700. The exterior is a mix of Italian Romanesque and elements of St. Sophia in Istanbul, but the congregation is solidly fundamentalist.

*Ogden Mall
Runs southwest from Clark and Armitage to North and Larrabee

*Old Town Triangle District
Bounded by North Ave., Wells St., and the imaginary extension of Ogden Ave. to Lincoln Park

*Ripley's Believe It or Not Museum
1500 N. Wells St.
337-6077

*St. Michael's Church
Eugenie St. and Cleveland
642-2498

*Louis Sullivan Townhouses
1826-34 N. Lincoln Park West

*Tonk House
1817 N. Lincoln Park West

*Wacker House
1838 N. Lincoln Park West

Shopping and services

*Barbara's Bookstore
1434 N. Wells St.
642-5044

*Bigsby & Kruthers On The Park
1750 N. Clark St.
440-1750

Collectors Nook
1714 N. Wells St.
642-4734
Eclectic antiques store specializes in Primitives, Early American, and country English. Prices tend to run high, but a few small victories have been won through haggling.

*Crate & Barrel Warehouse Store
1510 N. Wells St.
787-4775

*Design Source, Inc.
1710 N. Wells St.
751-2113

Adrienne Edwards Studio
1720 N. Sedgwick St.
549-6622
Fine vintage clothing; wedding gowns are a specialty. Adrienne also revamps old pieces and makes new ones (often from antique fabrics). By appointment; occasional fashion shows.

*The Emporium
1551 N. Wells St.
337-7126

Feline Inn
1445 N. Wells St.
943-2230
On Wells since the street's salad days, the Inn boards cats on a daily basis and sells litter to luxuries. The nominal admission fee is refundable with purchases.

*Green
1716 N. Wells St.
266-2806

*Handle With Care
1706 N. Wells St.
751-2929

Hatfield's Miniatures
1422 N. Wells St.
266-8119
Small shop with a smallish selection of small objects including acrylic dollhouse furniture, nifty dollhouse accessories like pool tables, and cityscape dioramas.

Hoosin Ltd.
Studio & Gallery
1543 N. Wells St.
337-4230
Seashells for collectors plus objects made from them, for example, nautilus-shell lamps. Call ahead.

Imports of Sorts, Ltd.
1660 N. Wells St.
280-1988
Importers of gold chains and charms, rings, diamonds, watches, and some cheaper stuff. Guarantees its prices as the lowest in the city with a 30-day return period if you find the equivalent item for less elsewhere. Design and repair services, too.

*Light Source, Inc.
1712 N. Wells St.
944-6967

*Material Matters
Piper's Alley
1608 N. Wells St.
787-4058

*My Sister's Shoes
Piper's Alley
218 W. North Ave.
642-3427

A New Leaf
1645 N. Wells St.
642-1576
Pleasant plant store specializes in cut flowers and seasonal decorations.

*Old Print Store
1407 N. Wells St.
266-8631

*Old Town
Triangle Association
1816 N. Wells St.
337-1938
Stop in for literature on the neighborhood, especially the pamphlet published by the Commission on Chicago Historical and Architectural Landmarks.

*Paper-Party-Funalia
Piper's Alley
1620 N. Wells St.
642-3052

Philrowe Studios
1416 N. Wells St.
266-0860
Interior-design studio of the man who popularized the wood-brass-antiques-stained-glass-plants look found at Harry's Cafe and other singles bars. By appointment only.

*Piper's Alley
1620 N. Wells St.
Mall of shops and restaurants.

*R.S.V.P.
Piper's Alley
1620 N. Wells St.
664-4760

Sandler's
1549 N. Wells St.
642-9246
Nice selection of trendy women's clothes. Small fur salon in back.

*The Town Shop
1561 N. Wells St.
337-3844

*Up Down
Tobacco Shop
1550 N. Wells St.
337-8025

*Yeast Works
Piper's Alley
1620 N. Wells St.
280-8992

Foodstuffs

*Coffee Corner
1700 N. Wells St.
951-7638

The Fudge Pot
1532 N. Wells St.
943-1777
One of the treats of a visit to Old Town in its heyday was freshly made fudge. It's a treat you can recapture.

*The House of Glunz
1206 N. Wells St.
642-3000

*Maison Barusseau
1446 N. Wells St.
337-8130

*Mangia Italiano
1557 N. Wells St.
951-0652

*Treasure Island
1639 N. Wells St.
642-1105
Other locations.

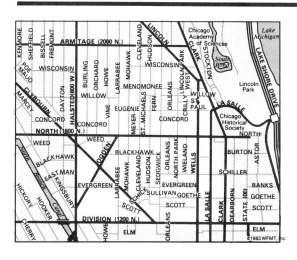

Dining and drinking

*Bowl and Roll
1339 N. Wells St.
944-5361

*Cafe Azteca
215 W. North Ave.
944-9854

*Chef Eduardo's Ristorante
1640 N. Wells St.
266-2021

*Ciao
1516 N. Wells St.
266-0048

*Courtyard Inn
1531 N. Wells St.
664-7387

*Fireplace Inn
1448 N. Wells St.
664-5264

Hemingway's Movable Feast
1825 N. Lincoln Ave.
943-6225
Zillions of sandwiches and Vala's ice cream.

Jeff's Laugh Inn
1800 N. Lincoln Ave.
751-0434
Coffee shop open 'round the clock sometimes has all-you-can-eat specials.

*Kamehachi of Tokyo
1617 N. Wells St.
664-3663

*O'Brien's Sirloin Inn
1528 N. Wells St.
787-3131

*Old Jerusalem
1411 N. Wells St.
944-0459

*Old Town Ale House
219 W. North Ave.
944-7020

*O'Rourke's Pub
319 W. North Ave.
944-1030

Redamak's
1530 N. Wells St.
787-9866
Sample the freshly ground burgers that "made New Buffalo, Mich., famous" in stylish Old Town surroundings.

*A Restaurant Named Desire
Piper's Alley
1620 N. Wells St.
664-4158

Rush Inn
1920 N. Lincoln Park West
787-7874
Bright, bemuraled spot sells fast-food health food to take out or to eat at the counter. Closed in winter.

Tap Root Pub
636 W. Willow St.
642-5235, 642-5293
Harley Budd became a neighborhood folk hero when he tried to prevent urban-renewal bulldozers from leveling the old Tap Root. He lost that battle and now features relatively in-expensive lobster and "all you can eat" fish dinners at this newer spot in a neigh-borhood that's beginning to take off.

*That Steak Joynt
1610 N. Wells St.
943-5091

*Twin Anchors
1655 N. Sedgwick St.
944-2258
An Old Town landmark where great ribs are mostly a legend.

Entertainment

Bijou Theatre
1349 N. Wells St.
943-5397
X-rated gay movies in storefront surroundings.

Carol's Speakeasy
1355 N. Wells St.
944-4226
One of Chicago's biggest gay nightclubs, with four bars. Screens Hollywood movies on Sundays with free buffet.

Cave of the Duke of Alba
Toledo Restaurant
1935 N. Sedgwick St.
266-2049
On Friday and Saturday nights, a full flamenco troupe performs down-stairs at this Spanish res-taurant. $5 cover; no mini-mum.

*The Earl of Old Town
1615 N. Wells St.
642-5206
Cover and minimum vary.

Old Town Players
645-0145
Chicago's oldest commu-nity theater (started in 1933) lost its lease in 1981 and is looking for a new home in the neighborhood. (See Theater.)

*Second City
1616 N. Wells St.
337-3992
(See Theater)

Zanies
1548 N. Wells St.
337-4027
Club hosts stand-up and improvisational comedians and full-blown satirical shows like the long-playing Byrne, Baby, Byrne. Cover varies; two-drink minimum.

Lincoln Park

Lincoln Park represents the good life—Chicago style. The neighborhood is a sampler of the city's best: fashion boutiques à la Oak Street, restaurants that would do the Magnificent Mile proud, charming streetscapes that rival Old Town's, architecture that challenges the Gold Coast. Yet, with all the 24-hour-a-day glamour, Lincoln Park retains a human scale. The side streets are tranquil, tree-shaded wonders of urban revitalization; the mass of highrises east of Clark Street is softened by the neighborhood's front yard—the stretch of Lincoln Park with zoo, conservatory, and boating lagoon.

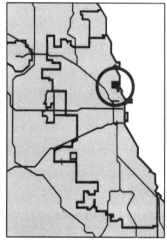

The model for the social changes that remade DePaul and New Town, Lincoln Park has a gentility that parvenu communities can only emulate, not duplicate. The singles scene is more refined, independent politics—the only acceptable kind—less boisterous, designer sportswear drapes with a certain élan, lovely living spaces are generally accented, rather than overwhelmed, by plants and antiques. A focus of the "action," Lincoln Park nonetheless remains a family neighborhood, although kids are likely to attend the exclusive Francis Parker or Latin schools.

The mold for Lincoln Park fashionability was cast a century ago. Middle-class merchants and skilled craftsmen built their homes amid the early farms that edged Clark Street's forerunner—Green Bay Road—an old Indian trail and pioneer route to Wisconsin. As Chicago grew, travelers on the road skirted the swampland on its east, known as the Ten Mile Ditch, on their way to the picnic groves and resorts of Lakeview. By the end of the Civil War, the area was heavy with balloon-frame cottages—perfect fuel for the Fire of 1871.

Strict post-Fire building codes coaxed brick and stone structures from the ashes. After the old city burial ground was transformed into parkland, the area grew into an even more attractive German and Scotch-Irish neighborhood.

Three handsome churches on Fullerton Parkway—Lincoln Park's grand boulevard and Chicago's northern border until 1893—attest to its relative affluence. Prominent hotel architect Clinton J. Warren designed the Norman-Romanesque **Church of Our Saviour** (Fullerton Parkway and Cambridge Avenue) in the late 1880s. The limestone-faced, red-brick Episcopal church is graced with Victorian decoration, including striking oak woodwork, beautiful stained glass (especially the Tiffany altar window), and exquisite terra-cotta tile. The Michigan sandstone **Lincoln Park Presbyterian Church** (Fullerton Parkway and Geneva Terrace), built as the Fullerton Avenue Presbyterian Church, dates from the same period, although its copper spire has been removed. Red oak pews radiate from the altar in semicircular aisles, and the sanctuary windows are outstanding. The Johnson & Son tracker organ, the only one of its kind still heard in Chicago, was originally water powered. The present congregation is the result of several mergers and supports a warm, involved ministry.

St. Pauls United Church of Christ (Fullerton Parkway and Orchard Street), one of the city's oldest congregations, has been twice tried by fire. The sanctuary that replaced the original log-cabin meetinghouse at La Salle and Ohio Streets was consumed by the 1871 conflagration. The German Evangelical congregation rebuilt downtown but split in 1898, with a faction erecting a magnificent structure at the present location. Faulty wiring in the newly installed organ probably started the 1955 Christmas Day fire, which destroyed the building. Benjamin Franklin Olson, who had designed the 1950 chapel and parish house of the block-long complex, harmonized the replacement church with his earlier efforts. The 1957 building houses one of Chicago's few Aeolian-Skinner organs.

A strong institutional base—Children's Memorial, Grant, Columbus, and Augustana hospitals; DePaul University; Francis Parker School—added stability, and the neighborhood prospered, with some ups and downs, through World War Two. The doldrums that infected so many urban areas as the country's focus shifted to the suburbs increased rooming-house conversions of the spacious old houses and brought a down-at-the-heels look to Clark Street's shops. But the sixties saw an influx of newcomers eager to restore and renovate. So successful was the concerted community cooperation that, in 1977, the Commission on Chicago Historical and Architectural Landmarks designated much of the neighborhood the **Mid-North District,** asserting that it "vividly portrays the character of the typical Chicago residential neighborhood at the end of the 19th century."

This is a neighborhood for strolling. Not only are the narrow streets a congested maze of frustrating one-ways, but parking borders on impossible. In any case, you'll want to let its subtly shifting moods envelop you. On warm evenings, fashionably attired office types head home, jackets slung over their shoulders; the side streets evoke Paris's Left Bank. Weekend afternoons, weather permitting, Clark Street's sidewalks are jammed with shoppers and browsers. In spring, summer, and fall, joggers and picnickers stream to park and beach.

Almost every street is a visual treat. Cleveland Avenue, from Fullerton Parkway to Dickens Avenue, parades a pastiche of styles. The two-story houses (2239 and 2243) that survived the Fire are said to mark the conflagration's northern limits. A beautifully maintained Italianate townhouse (2234-36) splendidly plays off the row of shared-wall masonry townhouses across the street. A Greek Revival cottage (2208) stands next to a new concrete home designed by Lawrence Booth in 1980; Bruce Graham, who designed the John Hancock Center, is responsible for 2215. The façade of an older building at 2150 was replaced with striking Art Deco, diamond-shaped leaded glass in the 1930s; across the street, the unusual brick cottage with a triangular bay (2147) is sometimes attributed to Louis Sullivan. A mansard-roofed, Queen Anne-influenced château (2114-16) provides a graceful contrast to Booth and Nagle's modern 1970 house of brick, glass, steel, and wood on the corner. Turn here onto Lincoln Avenue to see a delightful red-brick Victorian mansion that withstood the blandishments of the urban-renewal project that cleared the rest of the block for modern, modified-A-frame townhouses.

Other rewarding walks include Hudson Avenue (delightful differences in detailing), Belden Avenue (the elegant residences were rooming houses 20 years ago), Cambridge Avenue's cul-de-sac (the little mewslike court's buildings were carriage houses for the homes on Belden Avenue), and Fullerton Parkway (the grandest townhouses and churches). The Park West Antiques Fair is held annually in the alley just to the north (see *Annual Events*). Don't overlook the side streets north of Fullerton Parkway, either.

The lakefront attracted the wealthy, and some of their residences remain, separated from the shore by the park's landfill. Two of particular interest are the **Theurer/Wrigley House** (2466 North Lake View Avenue) and the **Francis J. Dewes House** (503 West Wrightwood Avenue). Built in 1896 for German brewers, both are official city landmarks. The Theurer mansion was the work of Richard E. Schmidt who, with Hugh Garden, later designed the powerhouse for Theurer's Schoenhofen Brewery. Splendid details, such as terra-cotta ornamentation and the copper cornice, add distinction to this Italian Renaissance gem. The Dewes house is even more spectacular. European architects Adolph Cudell and Arthur Hercz created a baroque fantasy, complete with caryatids supporting the wrought-iron balcony. For many years, the building housed the Swedish Engineers Society; it is again a private residence.

A spate of high-rise building in the teens left a legacy of a gracious bygone age. Peer through the windows of 451 West Wrightwood Avenue to see a medieval cloister in pink marble. The lobby of the less ornate building next door (443) resembles a more restrained cloister. The **Belden Stratford Hotel** (2300 North Lincoln Park West), the northern link in a chain of three grand hotels built a block apart facing the park, has a magnificent, two-story, marble-clad lobby and a photo gallery of luminaries who made the hotel their home. Check it out while going to one of the hotel's three restaurants or to hidden shops, such as the little florist/gift shop/antiques store.

Lincoln Park's largest housewares source is also a bit hard to find. **The House Store** (620 West Schubert Avenue) is a supermarket for high-tech fans. This is the place to shop for hardwood-and-metal storage units that cover whole walls, bright nylon-covered foam sofas and chairs that fold out into beds, more substantial upholstered couches, butcher-block tables, kitchen chairs and stools of all sorts, lighting, bins, baskets, dishes, and all the little things that make for efficient living. Everything for the apartment can be color coordinated, right down to coat hooks, garbage cans, ashtrays, and telephone cords. Furniture is rated with the level of assembly difficulty; most pieces need only a screwdriver or pliers.

Gothic Craft (2701 North Clark Street) specializes in simply designed, well-crafted, utilitarian furniture in a variety of woods—pine, birch, oak, teak, maple, walnut—or in Formica. Beds, wall units, cabinets, and desks are stocked unfinished. Gothic Craft will finish them for a charge; they build to order, too.

The turn-of-the-century oak dressers, hallstands, and buffets at **Paul James Antiques** (2727 North Clark Street) are beautifully refinished, as are most of the stunning mahogany and walnut European pieces. In addition to massive wood furniture, the store has marble-topped tables and lots of brass: hall trees, beds, dictionary stands, candlesticks, door knockers, and novelties, such as ice tongs made into a paper-towel holder.

A forest of brass chandeliers with fancy, frosted- and etched-glass globes casts a warm glow in **Stanley Galleries Antiques** (2118 North Clark Street). Ken Stanley specializes in American lighting fixtures from 1850 to 1925. All the brass lamps and chandeliers have been disassembled, buffed with a succession of polishes, washed in solvent, sprayed with lacquer, baked to fuse the lacquer so it won't need to be polished for years (Stanley claims to be the only one in Chicago doing this), and reassembled. The prices—far more than a brass farthing—reflect the gleam of the results. Russell Tarver's handsomely refinished American furniture, dating from the 18th century to 1920, complements the lighting fixtures perfectly. Some terra-cotta ornaments, architectural hardware, and stained glass are also on hand.

Countertop-to-ceiling shelves lined with Wedgwood and Rosenthal china in scores of patterns fill the tiny **Distinctive Interior Designs** (2322 North Clark Street). Dan Korbelak sells more Wedgwood dinnerware than anyone in the city except Marshall Field's; he also carries Galway and Rosenthal crystal, candle holders, and pewter.

If you're looking for handcrafted pottery, the **Craft Connection** (2415 North Clark Street) has an art fair's worth. About 20 local artisans are represented by their ceramics, which run the gamut from hand-thrown mugs with names on them, tea sets, stoneware casseroles in earth tones, and nicely glazed porcelain to offbeat slab vases with incised decorations and frames highlighted by colorful flowers. Clever soft sculptures by owner Marcia Fensin and other artists, handmade jewelry, quilts, and macramé at reasonable prices are among the other offerings. Cluttered but comfortable, **The Merchant of Venice** (2260 North Lincoln Avenue) stocks some handmade goods (toys, dolls, jewelry) as well as children's and women's clothing.

Lacy Mexican wedding gowns, embroidered dresses and tops, and colorful ponchos are a few of the attractions at **Mexican Folk Arts** (2433 North Clark Street), an airy shop that looks as south-of-the-border as its stock. Household items and gifts include wall hangings, pottery, tinware, and other Mexican and Latin American goods that range from inexpensive trinkets to pricey masks.

Fearsome masks from Papua New Guinea are among the objèts d'art at **Les Primitifs** (2038 North Clark Street), a fascinating store that specializes in African and Oceanic "ethnographic art." Working with African specialists and shopping the South Seas villages themselves, Keith and Irene Barton hand-pick all the items for this shop and for their much larger space on Ontario Street (see North of the River). Intricate weavings and other textiles, basketry from Botswana and South Africa, woodcarvings, Javanese puppets, and ethnic jewelry are a few of the things at the Clark Street store, where the stock is always changing. Some items, such as fragments of pre-Columbian fabric and magnificent beaded marriage skirts, are museum quality at accessible prices.

Affordable gifts abound at **Tivoli Gardens** (2262 North Clark Street), a lovely shop with inviting display windows and a charming central gazebo (where you can sip free espresso or cappuccino). Sprawling arrays of scents, soaps, jewelry, dolls, cards and other paper goods, little baskets, and boxes of all sorts make browsing a joy. Don't miss the upstairs, which has some space-age-looking casual clothing, handwoven rugs, glassware, ceramics, and more baskets and boxes.

Nonpareil (2300 North Clark Street) is wonderfully eclectic, with everything from baskets of fun plastics, such as fish pens and Star Wars masks, to Turkish, Iranian, and Zapotec Indian rugs and exquisite Chinese silk embroidery. The almost matchless selection of handcrafted items includes Peruvian textiles, Bolivian dolls, Thai flutes, colorful soft-sculpture parrots, woodcarvings (by a Southern minister), beautiful jewelry by Suzanne Bucher and other artists, and ceramics such as Nancy Funk's "hands" bathroom fixtures. There's also Henry Grethel sportswear, offbeat clothing by several young designers, and more.

Clothes by local designers such as Maria Rodriguez and Hino & Malee are featured at **Jácher** (2419 North Clark Street), a women's boutique that aims at being high-fashion while avoiding outrageous prices. For the most part, it succeeds with au courant silks, cottons, gabardines, soft leathers, and slightly outrageous jewelry made of beads and feathers. Some things are always marked down 20 percent, which really makes stopping in worthwhile. The equally sophisticated **Dégagé** (2252) specializes in mixing and matching clothes, mostly by

American designers (Berek, Perry Ellis, Norman Todd, Irka, Willi Wear) in unexpected ways to outfit its enthusiastic clientele. With a predominant theme and color and carefully chosen stock, the small shop is itself a model of coordination.

Chicago designer **Billy Falcon** (Belden Stratford Hotel, 2300 North Lincoln Park West) creates haute couture dresses and gowns that are youthful, whimsical, and unique. Falcon interviews his clients and makes muslin body patterns (initial fee: $300) to keep on file so he can tailor his designs to their individual needs. Once on file, you can simply call up to explain what you want and, if you're not providing the fabric, choose from swatches he sends you. Evening gowns run about $1,000, suits about $450. Falcon's customers include Mayor Byrne, Peggy Lee, and arts patron Muriel Newman, who contributed two of his pieces to a show at New York's Metropolitan Museum of Art. His sportswear is available throughout the country—in Chicago at I. Magnin and Ultimo. If you can't afford Falcon, loads of fashionable clothes—in silks, linens, gabardines, cottons, wools—are not unreasonable at **Luv Boutique** (2110 North Clark Street). Three rooms are full of separates, dresses, sportswear, suits, lingerie, and lots of accessories, such as zippy shoes. There's a "Career Women's Corner" with 9-to-5 duds, and pleasant salespeople make shopping here a delight. The even larger **Sir Real** (2204) carries trendy clothes for fashion-conscious men. Silk shirts and suits, fine woolens, and more are by Jean-Paul Germain, Yves Saint Laurent, and various Italian designers.

Presence (2501 North Clark Street) offers bargains aplenty on women's clothing from places like India and China. All of it's casual, trendy, and fun: colorful overalls and jumpsuits, simple jumpers, gauzy cotton dresses, outlandish socks, Chinese rayon jackets, cotton and pure silk blouses for about $30, tons of light-hearted jewelry and accessories. The frequent sales are legendary; the salespeople are helpful but not intrusive.

At **Clark Street Waltz** (2360 North Lincoln Avenue), you'll find stylishly funky frocks from the late 1900s through the '40s and the accessories to go with them: outrageous feathered hats, beaded bags, old silk scarves, Deco clips, and other jewelry. There are fun furs in winter, some elegant silk and velvet dresses from the 1920s and '30s, Oriental kimonos, Victorian underthings, and some new imported clothing with an ethnic flair.

While Clark Street Waltz stocks some Art Deco, **Steve Starr Studios** (2654 North Clark Street) is the place to go for chrome cocktail shakers, highly stylized statuary, etched mirrors, sleek cigarette cases, fabulous perfume bottles, and other terrific stuff from the 1920s and early '30s. Old and new photos in classy Deco frames cover the walls, but they are not for sale. In fact, convincing Starr to part with anything in the small, crowded shop may be difficult, despite the very high prices. High pressure he's not; abrasive he can be.

If Starr won't sell you that carnelian brooch, check out **McCaffrey Metalsmiths** (2210 North Clark Street), where jewelry from the early 1800s to the 1920s accounts for about 30 percent of the stock. Tom McCaffrey, who learned his trade in Ireland, also restores antique jewelry and takes on repairs most other jewelers won't touch. He and his wife Judy custom design gold and precious-stone pieces and stock some of their own classic-looking jewelry, as well as high-quality, contemporary items from other suppliers. Excellent craftsmanship makes the prices seem more than fair.

Jan Dee (2304-08 North Clark Street), who quit her job as a psychiatrist's secretary to apprentice herself to a metalsmith in Italy, also designs the kind of gold and silver jewelry that looks timeless. Her specialties are unusual diamond rings and wedding-band sets, but she and her apprentice produce just about everything: earrings, bracelets, watchbands, necklaces, and so forth. Half of Dee's business is custom making pieces based on customers' ideas or sketches.

Many of Lincoln Park's artists work in a medium even more malleable than gold, though no less valued by locals. Twenty years ago, **The Bakery** (2218 North Lincoln Avenue) was *the* fine dining spot outside the Loop, but scores of innovative restaurants have changed that.

The Art Nouveau **Ambria** (Belden Stratford Hotel, 2300 North Lincoln Park West) is at the top, one of the city's best restaurant's. Nouvelle cuisine here means sophisticated entrées, unusual combinations of ingredients, ethereal sauces, beautiful presentations, and great style, matched only by the prices and the difficulty of getting reservations. Owners Rich Melman and Gabino Sotelino also run **Un Grand Café**, a less formal bistro across the lobby. At **Gitanes** (2350 North Clark Street), adventurous dishes are not always executed successfully but, behind an elegant awning and lace curtains, the place is a knockout with Oriental carpets, colorful paintings, Art Deco cushions, and huge potted plants softening the cream-wall-and-light-wood austerity. Free cocktail-hour snacks in the wine bar and sometimes terrific service help compensate for other failings and, along with the décor, make this a popular spot.

The offerings at **La Fontaine** (2442 North Clark Street)—a *Better Homes and Gardens* country-French-looking restaurant with a fountain in a nicely restored townhouse—are more traditional. Dishes such as vichyssoise, veal normande, paupiette of salmon, and chateaubriand are well prepared, if expensive; the cozy surroundings and formal service make for romantic dining. The décor at **L'Auberge** (2324) is determinedly rustic, and the middle-of-the-road provincial fare is often made with a heavy hand. Pretending you were at dockside in Marseilles at Ismet Deletioglu's **French Port** (2585) was easier before it expanded. Now the ambiance is only vaguely nautical. The seafood—with provençal accents—isn't always up to snuff.

Geja's Café (340 West Armitage Avenue), John Davis's dark, smoky, usually crowded basement café, is about as French as fondue—cheese for openers; beef, chicken, seafood, and/or vegetables for entrées; fresh fruit dipped in chocolate for dessert—and has live classical guitar and flamenco music. An impressive wine list, tastings, and classes have made it a gathering place for oenophiles. On Friday and Saturday nights, when it's first come, first served, couples who find enforced togetherness (fondues are served only for two or more) romantic and don't mind the brusque-to-crummy service might wait hours for the tiny tables.

The other ethnic choices are staggering: Japanese, Mexican, Middle Eastern, Indo-Pakistani, Jewish deli, Greek, Chinese, Czech, and Italian. The chic, expensive **Salvatore's** (525 West Arlington Place), for example, is one of the city's better Northern Italian restaurants with excellent appetizers, properly prepared though smallish pasta dishes, and mostly veal and seafood entrées. The tiny, sometimes crowded **Dragon Seed** (2300 North Lincoln Park West) is among the top of its genre—Mandarin, Hunan, Szechwan cooking. The old standbys—spring rolls, fried dumplings, moo shu pork—are deftly prepared, but more unusual dishes, such as Hunan lamb sauté and Szechwan diced chicken, are also rewarding.

This neighborhood nurtured the fun-food movement in its infancy and is still a stronghold for restaurants with outrageously worded menus, improbable drinks, offbeat food, and young, enthusiastic help. **R. J. Grunts** (2056 North Lincoln Park West) was the first, and remains the busiest, of the Lettuce Entertain You ventures that have spread throughout town. A top-of-the-line salad bar, solid burgers, plenty of food for the money, and a totally informal atmosphere keep bringing people back for more. Grunts also risks some more difficult preparations and sometimes brings them off. A bountiful salad bar and the "Motherlode" (a landmark in hamburger technology with a mind-boggling number of bread and trimming combinations) are the main attractions at the **Chicago Claim Company** (2314 North Clark Street). The décor is, naturally, early Gold Rush, and menus are printed on huge mining pans—reminders that the "experience" may take precedence over the food.

Tastefully designed and cheerful, **Mel Markon's** (2150 North Lincoln Park West) stays open late (3:45 a.m. week nights, 4:45 a.m. Saturdays) and offers everything from breakfast omelettes and pancakes to dinner entrées and late-evening snacks and sandwiches, from Jewish deli to health foods—and elaborate tropical drinks. Quality is fair, but portions are ample and prices very low.

All these spots tend to be crowded, especially on weekends, as does **Jerome's** (2450 North Clark Street), a brick-and-bamboo place where the healthy fun food has a distinct California flair. Jerome's is really a cross between fun and Continental, with entrées like veal Marsala, chicken supreme, and sautéed scallops in the $8-$12 price range, as well as the cheaper California (curried chicken) salad, tostadas, and burgers; wine-bar selections; and fresh-baked wheat bread and pastries, which are also available at a retail counter. The Sunday brunch has a loyal following and, in summer, the outdoor terrace is Lincoln Park's best spot for people watching.

The food at the **Clark Street Café** (2260 North Clark Street) is also California influenced—lots of salads, lots of avocados. Lincoln Park's most elegant, trendiest singles bar is sort of San Francisco-style with lots of hardwood and antiques, high ceilings, beveled mirrors, and plants. It draws a crowd as attractive as the surroundings and has come a long way since the days when it was Hayes's Tavern, a dumpy neighborhood bar whose only claim to fame was a picture of FDR, reminding everyone who was in the White House when the Volstead Act was repealed.

Laid-back and relaxing, with tin ceilings, nautical paintings, and a flotilla of miniature ships, the **John Barleycorn Memorial Pub** (658 West Belden Avenue) is not exactly a singles bar, but has long attracted hip, intellectual sorts with classical music, free silent movies, and one of the best bar burgers in town. At the **Wise Fools Pub** (2270 North Lincoln Avenue), one of the older music bars west of Clark Street, some of Chicago's best jazz and blues acts—Mighty Joe Young, Son Seals, Vanessa Davis—draw a good mix of neighborhood people and fans. The crowd often spills over from the music room into the bar, but no one seems to mind. The cover charge varies; a two-drink minimum is usually waived on Sundays. Jazz and jazz-pop groups—the Ghalib Ghallab Quartet to the Eldee Young Ensemble—perform at **The Bulls** (1916 North Lincoln Park West), a small cave of a club with a tiny stage and a catacomblike ceiling that successive owners have left intact, despite complaints from just about everybody. Cover is reasonable, and there's never a minimum.

Park West (322 West Armitage Avenue) is the antithesis of The Bulls. A large, glitzy, modern version of the old-style nightclub, it has a very sophisticated sound system, brings in top jazz and folk-music acts (among others), and charges accordingly ($7.50-and-up cover, two-drink minimum). Good-looking waitresses in slinky Danskin outfits add to the ambiance.

Two other bars feature gimmicks to attract women, who will attract men, and so forth. After riding out the Western craze as Rodeo, **Juke Box Saturday Night** (2251 North Lincoln Avenue) changed its image in late 1981. Decorated with for-sale, 1950s and '60s paraphernalia, the place offers a live disc jockey, a large dance floor, malt-shop munchies, and an old Riverview dunking machine to replace the once-popular mechanical bull. At **The Ultimate Sports Bar and Grill** (354 West Armitage Avenue), sports memorabilia cover the walls, some of the tables are in a boxing ring, and patrons can show off their foulability at the basketball hoop next to the bar.

You don't have to frequent the bars to find entertainment in Lincoln Park. The **Body Politic** (2261 North Lincoln Avenue), a pioneer off-Loop theater, mounts its own shows and shares space with the innovative **Victory Gardens Theater** (2257; *see Theater*). The **Parkway Theatre** (2736 North Clark Street) shows computer-selected—but wildly successful—film revivals with a different double feature daily. And, of course, there's all the marvelous entertainment in the park for which the neighborhood is named (*see Parks and Boulevards*).

Interesting places

*Belden Stratford Hotel
2300 N. Lincoln Park West
348-6610

Chicago Academy of Sciences
2001 N. Clark St.
549-0606
(See Museums)

Chicago Historical Society
Clark St. at North Ave.
642-4600
(See Museums)

*Church of Our Saviour
Fullerton and Cambridge
549-3832

*Francis J. Dewes House
503 W. Wrightwood Ave.

Elks National Memorial Building
2750 N. Lake View Ave.
477-2750
Built in 1926 as a memorial to members who died in W.W. I. Egerton Swartwout designed a monumental structure with a 100-ft.-high rotunda. Inside are marble columns, classical sculpture, heroic murals, and a lavish reception room.

Ann Halsted House
440 W. Belden Ave.
Built in 1883, this is one of the earliest examples of the Adler and Sullivan partnership.

Lincoln Park Conservatory
Fullerton and Stockton Dr.
294-4770
(See Parks and Boulevards)

*Lincoln Park Presbyterian Church
Fullerton and Geneva Ter.
248-8288

Lincoln Park Zoological Gardens
2200 N. Cannon Dr.
294-4660
(See Parks and Boulevards)

*Mid-North District
Bounded roughly by Armitage, Lincoln, Fullerton, and Clark
A fuller discussion of this historic neighborhood appears in the Commission on Chicago Historical and Architectural Landmarks' booklet, Landmark Neighborhoods in Chicago, available at the Chicago Historical Society or at the Archi-Center, 330 S. Dearborn St.

Policeman Bellinger's Cottage
2121 N. Hudson Ave.
Bellinger and friends worked mightily to save this charming house from the Fire of 1871, but it's probably not true that they used cider to wet down the roof after the water ran out. The architect was W. W. Boyington, who designed the Water Tower.

Reebie Storage and Moving Co.
2325 N. Clark St.
549-0120
One of the finest examples of neoclassical Egyptian architecture in the country. George Kingsley was the architect, but the real artist was Fritz Albert of the North Western Terra Cotta Co. who designed the multi-colored decoration and hieroglyphics. The pharaohs at the entrance represent William and John Reebie, the firm's founders, and the hieroglyphics on the statue at the right read "I give protection to your furniture." Be sure to take a peek inside.

*St. Pauls United Church of Christ
Fullerton and Orchard St.
348-3829

*Theurer/Wrigley House
2466 N. Lake View Ave.

Shopping and services

Affordable Portables
2608 N. Clark St.
935-6160
Large, cluttered store with the kinds of lifestyle furnishings that would fit into a low-budget studio apartment. They'll also make cubes, tables, and so forth from Formica. Another at 222 W. Kinzie.

Aspidistra Bookshop
2630 N. Clark St.
549-3129
Excellent array of used books in 40 sections. Selection is one of the best, with new arrivals in a special area. Prices are fair; don't expect under-priced treasures.

Chrome Yellow
2312 N. Lincoln Ave.
929-6220
Furniture store with a fairly good selection of the better lines of lifestyle and high-tech items. Lots of lamps— including George Kovacs— and seating.

The City Child
2413 N. Clark St.
935-0266
Designer children's clothes and accessories in a shop run by people who really care about kids.

*Clark Street Waltz
2360 N. Lincoln Ave.
472-5559

Contemporary Art Workshop
542 W. Grant Pl.
525-9624, 472-4004
Organized in 1950 by John Kearney, Cosmo Campoli, Leon Golub, Ray Fink, and Al Kwitz as an artist-run alternative gallery. Offers studio space to promising artists; classes, shows. (See Galleries.)

*Craft Connection
2415 N. Clark St.
248-8885

Cycle Smithy
2468½ N. Clark St.
281-0444
Good bike shop, but the real treat is a 150-ft. slot-car track in the cool months. Bring your car or rent one.

*Jan Dee Jewelry
2304-08 N. Clark St.
871-2222

*Dégagé
2252 N. Clark St.
935-7737
A place to go on Monday to buy the frock you saw in the New York Times Magazine on Sunday.

*Distinctive Interior Designs
2322 N. Clark St.
248-0738
Semiannual 20% discount Wedgwood sales.

*Billy Falcon
Belden Stratford Hotel
2300 N. Lincoln Park West
281-5898
By appointment only.

Floral Designs, Inc.
2353 N. Clark St.
528-9800
Sam Bezanis creates some of the most imaginative floral arrangements in the city. Prices start at $15 and soar from there.

For Eyes Optical Co.
2562 N. Clark St.
929-5553
Pleasantly kooky assortment of frames at bargain prices.

The Furniture Factory
2534 N. Clark St.
248-5291
Decently constructed, unfinished wood tables, dressers, chairs, bookcases, and the like for first apartments.

Ginkgo
Belden Stratford Hotel
2300 N. Lincoln Park West
348-1418
A spare, Oriental-feeling popular shop for flowers, plants, antiques, and gifts.

Dei Giovani
2421 N. Clark St.
549-4116
Men's fashions that will make you look like an Italian movie star if you're built for them, or like an extra in The Godfather *if you're not.*

*Gothic Craft
2701 N. Clark St.
248-5551

Paul Heath Audio, Ltd.
2036 N. Clark St.
549-8100
One of Chicago's premier audio consultants offers "audio for the perfectionist," such as amplifiers with Teflon-insulated gold wiring. Wear a suit to get the respect a $5,000 purchase entitles you to.

*The House Store
620 W. Schubert Ave.
525-7771

Raymond Hudd
2545 N. Clark St.
477-1159
Hudd creates fine feathered and flowered fantasies at one of the city's few millinery shops.

*Jácher
2419 N. Clark St.
327-7711

*Paul James Antiques
2727 N. Clark St.
549-0898

Juke Box Saturday Night
2251 N. Lincoln Ave.
327-4333
Steve Schussler's showroom (upstairs from the namesake bar he designed) features Art Deco and futuristic pieces that he uses for interior design, party planning, and rental as stage and photo props. By appointment.

The Kitchen Store
744 W. Fullerton Pkwy.
472-1597
Large, crowded store with a
very nice selection of
kitchen gear—pots, pans,
cutlery, gadgets—as well as
gourmet foods, fresh pas-
ta, and an espresso bar.

**Lehmann Courts
Racquet Ball Club**
2700 N. Lehmann Ct.
871-8300
Thirteen racquet and handball courts, indoor run-
ning track, Nautilus fitness
center, universal exercise
room, saunas, steam
rooms, juice bar and
lounge, plus low fees attract
young singles who want to
work out as they make out.

Logos of Chicago
2423 N. Clark St.
935-4540
The emphasis at this bookshop is on religion, but the
general collection is good.
Fine selection of books
about Chicago.

*Luv Boutique
2110 N. Clark St.
929-2330

*McCaffrey Metalsmiths
2210 N. Clark St.
871-0288

*The Merchant of Venice
2260 N. Lincoln Ave.
477-5005

*Mexican Folk Arts
2433 N. Clark St.
871-1511

R. A. Nantus Gallery
2355 N. Clark St.
248-6660
Good selection of prints, including some 17th- and
18th-century items, as well
as contemporary graphics.

*Nonpareil
2300 N. Clark St.
477-2933

Park View Pet Shop
2222 N. Clark St.
549-2031
The Marshall Field's of pet
stores offers gourmet foods,
high-fashion dog sweaters,
and sensible advice. Oc-
casional Sunday brunches
and a Halloween dress-up
party for furry friends.
Carries fish, birds, and
small mammals.

Francis W. Parker School
330 W. Webster Ave.
549-5904
Lincoln Park's famous
private school offers community classes for adults
and children in 99 subjects
ranging from opera appre-
ciation to Swedish
massage.

*Presence
2501 N. Clark St.
248-1761

*Les Primitifs
2038 N. Clark St.
528-5200

Recess
2248 N. Clark St.
935-5554
"With-it" duds for tots and
pre-teens by Calvin Klein,
Bonjour, and the like.

Reflections on Clark
2236 N. Clark St.
327-8340
Eclectic, modest stock of
antiques plus caning, re-
finishing, and restoring.

*Sir Real
2204 N. Clark St.
528-5130

***Stanley Galleries
Antiques**
2118 N. Clark St.
281-1614

*Steve Starr Studios
2654 N. Clark St.
525-6530

Studio 23
2358 N. Lincoln Ave.
327-8099
Workshop and gallery with
displays of jewelry, ceramics, metal sculptures, prints,
watercolors, wood con-
structions, fabric creations,
and more by owners
Charlotte Newfeld and
Robert Pierron.

Take a Walk
2112 N. Clark St.
528-8510
Shoes by Timberland,
Kalso Earth Shoes, Frye
boots, and Birkenstock sandals are designed for comfort; form takes a back seat
to function. Also, stylish
casuals.

*Tivoli Gardens
2262 N. Clark St.
477-7710

Whispers
2441 N. Clark St.
327-4422
Ladies' undergarments that
are imaginative but on the
proper side of Frederick's of
Hollywood.

Dining and drinking

The Abacus
2619 N. Clark St.
477-5251
Innovative Chinese restaurant offers Cantonese, Mandarin, Shanghai, and
Szechwan selections, but
quality doesn't always
match expectations.

*Ambria
Belden Stratford Hotel
2300 N. Lincoln Park West
472-5959

Anything Goes
2256 N. Clark St.
327-7788
New York-chic, lower-level
spot that's half dining room
and half gourmet shop with
anything on the menu to go.

*L'Auberge
2324 N. Clark St.
248-4408

Bacino's on Lincoln
2204 N. Lincoln Ave.
472-7400
One-time outpost of Gior-
dano's still has people
flocking in for its stuffed
pizza.

*The Bakery
2218 N. Lincoln Ave.
472-6942
Once the restaurant in Lincoln Park, it now rates either raves or howls. Chef Louis Szathmáry steams on, undaunted.

***John Barleycorn
Memorial Pub**
658 W. Belden Ave.
348-8899

**Belden Corned Beef
Center**
2315 N. Clark St.
935-2752
Unofficial headquarters for lakefront liberals with soups, sandwiches, and heartier fare 24 hours a day. Also in Rogers Park.

Bengal Lancers
2324 N. Clark St.
929-0500
Americanized Indian cuisine in a fairly pleasant room on the second floor of a row house.

Bratislava
2525 N. Clark St.
348-6938
Roast duck, svickova, and other Czech specialties that are costlier and less satisfying than those you'll find on Cermak Road.

Café Figaro
2242 N. Lincoln Ave.
549-5755
This tiny spot on the ground floor and front patio of an older house started as a pastry/espresso spot but has evolved into a satisfying, expensive, nouvelle cuisine restaurant. Popular Sunday brunch.

***Chicago
Claim Company**
2314 N. Clark St.
871-1770

**Chicago Pizza and
Oven Grinder Co.**
2121 N. Clark St.
248-2570
You don't have to go to Philly to get a "grinder"—a hot hero sandwich—since it shares the bill with so-so pizza at this youth-oriented bar and restaurant.

*Clark Street Café
2260 N. Clark St.
549-4037

*Dragon Seed
Belden Stratford Hotel
2300 N. Lincoln Park West
528-5542

Francis J. Dewes House, Wrightwood Avenue, circa 1923

*La Fontaine
2442 N. Clark St.
525-1800

Frances' Food Shop
2453 N. Clark St.
248-4580
The steam table at this neighborhood institution is still one of the best food bargains in the city, but don't try it unless you're ready to have someone order "So eat!" after you've already loosened your belt a notch.

*French Port
2585 N. Clark St.
528-6644
Every Thanksgiving Ismet Deletioglu serves free dinners to 1,000 needy people—a generous gesture that makes up for some of the restaurant's shortcomings.

*Geja's Café
340 W. Armitage Ave.
281-9101

*Gitanes
2350 N. Clark St.
929-5500

*Un Grand Café
Belden Stratford Hotel
2300 N. Lincoln Park West
348-8886
Sophisticated bistro serves light fare, country-French specials, and rich desserts. Good place to linger over cappuccino—and to watch people.

*R. J. Grunts
2056 N Lincoln Park West
929-5363

Hashikin
2338 N. Clark St.
935-6474
Classy Japanese spot. The standard selections—including a sushi bar—are good, but prices are high.

*Jerome's
2450 N. Clark St.
327-2207

Lan's
346 W. Armitage Ave.
871-8461
Good Mandarin and Szechwan food in fairly handsome surroundings. Try the moo shu pork.

*Mel Markon's
2150 N. Lincoln Park West
525-5550

Middle Eastern Gardens
2621 N. Clark St.
935-3100
Middle Eastern fare in a pleasantly dark room. Good kebabs and lamb dishes. The offerings have a distinctly healthy quality, with whole-wheat pita, vegetarian kibbe, and fresh-squeezed juices.

Olympos Naoussa
2665 N. Clark St.
871-2810
Small, cramped, friendly Greek restaurant where the lamb and beef are grilled in front. The crockery looks like it came from your aunt's attic and is perfect for the food, which is good and cheap.

Oxford Pub
2263 N. Lincoln Ave.
477-5146
A singles bar that is the scruffy Lincoln Ave. equivalent to the elegant Clark Street Café.

Ranalli's Pizzeria
1925 N. Lincoln Ave.
642-4700
Better-than-average pizza—deep-dish, thin crust, and unusual stuffed-and-deep-fried—in an always-crowded neighborhood bar.

*Salvatore's
525 W. Arlington Pl.
528-1200

Shalimar
2560 N. Clark St.
248-3515
Indo-Pakistani—they offer some beef dishes—in a pleasant storefront. Meat dishes tend to be tough.

2350 Pub
2249 N. Lincoln Ave.
929-9027, 281-9859
Neighborhood tavern with a big dining area and an even bigger menu offering interesting specialties and good salads, as well as bar fare.

***Ultimate Sports
Bar and Grill**
354 W. Armitage Ave.
477-6787

Entertainment

*Body Politic
2261 N. Lincoln Ave.
871-3000, 348-7901
(See Theater)

*The Bulls
1916 N. Lincoln Park West
337-3000

Japanese Cinema
Francis Parker School
330 W. Webster Ave.
549-5904
Sunday-afternoon screenings of Japanese-language films at various times.

***Juke Box
Saturday Night**
2251 N. Lincoln Ave.
525-5000

Neo
2350 N. Clark St.
929-5501
Crowded New Wave disco. The rockers turn into accountants and copywriters at 9 a.m.

*Park West
322 W. Armitage Ave.
929-5959

*Parkway Theatre
2736 N. Clark St.
929-9555

*Victory Gardens Theater
2257 N. Lincoln Ave.
871-3000, 549-5788
(See Theater)

*Wise Fools Pub
2270 N. Lincoln Ave.
929-1510

DePaul

Old frame cottages suddenly sport angled cedar siding, solariums, or skylights. "For Sale" signs beckon from scores of dilapidated buildings. New townhouses pop up everywhere. DePaul is the model neighborhood-on-the-make, with a solid core of securely renovated, fancifully fronted, turn-of-the-century brick two- and three-flats and newfound activity on streets that seemed lost just a few years ago. Halsted Street and Armitage Avenue house almost as many realtors as trendy shops and bars. Fortunately, for all the feverish construction, the area hasn't turned into a singles' pressure cooker à la New Town, but remains a friendly, low-key sort of place with lots of old-timers sticking it out in carefully maintained, ungentrified homes next to those rehabbed by young families.

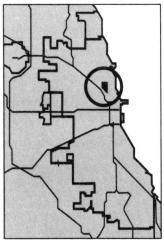

The very name DePaul rankles some of the long-time residents who think of minineighborhoods like Wrightwood or Sheffield as part of the Lincoln Park community. They have a point. While the lakefront truck farms of German immigrants were being subdivided to accommodate the gentry at the end of the 19th century, laborers who worked in the factories and lumberyards rising along the North Branch of the Chicago River settled west of Halsted Street. Economic necessity forced some of the Irish, Italians, and Eastern Europeans to evade the post-Fire building ordinances, so they threw up frame cottages, creating a distaff side to the lakefront's affluence.

The area was as hard hit by the post-World War Two doldrums as the rest of Lincoln Park, and it didn't share in the revitalization of the 1960s. Later, as developers traveled west for dessert after the lakefront feast, "DePaul" was "discovered." But, with Federal funds dried up and community organizations more cautious about social shocks, the change here has been more understated and thoughtful than in other real-estate hot spots.

DePaul University, the community's namesake, began as St. Vincent's College and grew around the lovely **St. Vincent de Paul Church** (Webster and Sheffield Avenues). Lush stained glass, including a deep-blue rose window, pierces the gray stone walls of the 1895 Romanesque building, which has a striking coffered ceiling and superb marble altars. Campus and community are strongly linked, with locals attending lectures, concerts, and theater performances, and supporting a plethora of lifestyle adult-education courses. Although the school is presently best known for its basketball team, its less transitory reputation stems in large part from its Loop-campus law program. The alma mater of many judges, lawyers, and politicians, it's considered something of a prep school for Chicago's power brokers.

When McCormick Theological Seminary moved to Hyde Park in 1977, DePaul acquired the property, expanding to encompass much of the area between Fullerton and Webster Avenues, from Halsted Street to Racine Avenue. Among the new holdings are a chapel (now a musical arts center) and a residential complex, the fruit of a late 19th-century revenue-earning scheme. Deservedly protected by city landmark status, the **McCormick Row House District**'s charming Queen Anne houses along Fullerton and Belden Avenues, and on Chalmers Place inside the quadrangle, are the perfect starting point of a random tour of the neighborhood's quiet residential streets. Architectural history wasn't written here, but many of the Victorian buildings between the campus and Webster Avenue east of Sheffield Avenue are lovely.

Adaptive reuse is the present rage in DePaul. The 1886, red-brick St. Augustine's Home (Sheffield and Fullerton Avenues) couldn't meet modern nursing-home safety standards, but the Little Sisters of the Poor didn't want to tear the building down or move their facility for the indigent elderly out of the area. Instead, they shifted operations to the old Alexian Brothers Hospital complex at Belden and Racine Avenues and sold their building to condominium converters. Adaptive reuse is also turning the former Dietzgen Drafting Supplies factory across the street into offices and shops, and the same fate awaits other nearby commercial structures.

It's already happened at the **Lill Street Studios** (1021 West Lill Avenue), an old horsecar stable where the Robbins Clay Company produces modeling clay for schools and clay for ceramists. The studio also houses 17 potters whose work is displayed in a common gallery. Brides who eschew Tiffany's can develop a pattern with a potter and set up a gift registry. The **Chicago Center for the Print, Ltd.** (1509 West Fullerton Avenue) occupies space vacated by Atomic Auto Parts. The complex includes facilities for intaglio, relief, and lithographic printing; a gallery and slide registry; lecture space; and a library. There are also tours and demonstrations to encourage artists, inform the public, and, it is hoped, tempt collectors.

Bold paintings by such artists as Fritz Scholder and Len Agrella cover the walls of **American West** (2110 North Halsted Street). Devoted to contemporary art of the Southwest, this gallery also carries posters from major exhibitions of Western art, ceremonial artifacts, pottery, and some personal adornments. **Maya Imports** (2044, rear) ranges further south with high-quality arts and crafts from Latin America, including a unique-to-Chicago collection of Amazonian Indian objects such as masks and tapa-cloth wall hangings. There are handwoven Peruvian rugs, primitive bark paintings, replicas of Mayan statues, and other decorative items, plus clothes that range from embroidered Mexican shirts and dresses to handknit Peruvian sweaters.

Aran sweaters, handwoven scarves, unisex caps, tweed jackets, and fuzzy lap robes are among the fine woolens at Mary Dugan's **Erinisle** (1959 North Halsted Street). Women's coats, suits, and dresses tend to be wool in winter, cotton and linen in summer. The cheerful shop, scented with potpourri and herb tea, also sells rustic thrown stoneware, handsome heavy glassware that's the antithesis of fine Irish crystal, and an ever-changing display of handicrafts and gifts, all to the strains of Irish folk music.

City sophistication is the message at **Port of Entry** (2032), a chic, track-lit, light-plum-colored shop on the first floor of an old row house. Trendy separates by Fenn Wright & Manson and Cathy Hardwick, sexy silks, and Hanky Panky's intimate frivolities are just right for the up-scale woman. Let the California girl in you go at **Geneva Convention** (1128 West Armitage Avenue), which sells playful sample sportswear in smaller sizes at very attractive prices. Or indulge a taste for the slightly bizarre at **Indulgence** (2451 North Lincoln Avenue). Many of the feather boas, satiny capes, sequined caps, and other frilly clothes are made at owner Mary Hickey's Chicago Costume Co., Inc. in Lincoln Park; a private line of cosmetics provides the finishing touches.

Vintage glad rags are the business of **Kitsch** (1007 West Webster Avenue), a spacious, seductive shop where Joan Crawford jackets, slinky dresses, silk lingerie, Hawaiian shirts, and funky men's suits await the fashion conscious who want to make a statement. Art Deco accessories, jewelry, objêts d'art, and a smattering of furniture highlight the collection.

Nearby Halsted Street's antiques stores cover every collectible period. **Old World Antiques** (2040) features post-Civil War American and European furniture (including many large case pieces), Art Nouveau, bronzes, and wonderful French advertising broadsheets by Mucha and other artists. A complete design service and discounts "to the trade" are offered. **Quercus Antiques** (2148) sells expensive, very well refinished oak and walnut furniture from an airy showroom, and mixes in a few smaller items. A beautiful store carved out of an old stable, the **Antiquery Warehouse** (2050) is rich with European and American period furniture and some fine dinnerware. The owner's handsomely appointed quarters in the rear are worth seeing. Here, too, decorators get discounts, as they do on the restored lighting fixtures and hardware at **Brass Works** (2142).

The stretch of Armitage Avenue from Halsted Street to Sheffield Avenue is a delightful stroll past renovated cottages and steep-stooped brick row houses with shops on the high first floors. Lovely 19th-century flats-over-storefront buildings, with decorated bays overhanging the sidewalk, cluster around the el. The antiques shops fit right in. In a ramshackle old building, **Katherine's Antiques** (826) offers two floors of mostly as-is jumble, but lots of the stuff is super. Look especially for old advertising paraphernalia, fixtures, and accessories. The white-washed **Turtle Creek Country Store** (850) is a perfect setting for white wicker furniture and oodles of antique patchwork quilts, as well as various textiles, both old and new. Pricey, nicely refinished, turn-of-the-century oak and other furniture can be found at the crowded **Collectables Antiques** (845), the spare **Elf Shoppe** (846), and at **Century Clocks** (844) along with a few nice case clocks and pocket watches.

Antiques accent both locations of **Something Different.** The newer one (837) carries crystal, silk and dried flowers, cut flowers, and blooming plants, while the original (816, rear), a charming add-on behind an old house, has rag rugs, ceramics, and other goodies that lean toward kitsch, plus a dollhouse of a greenhouse that perfumes the whole place. The small, hidden **Greenhouse Unlimited** (849) is another of the many planteries satisfying the plants-and-antiques interior-decorating treatment Victorian buildings seem to cry for.

The huge **Fertile Delta** (2760 North Lincoln Avenue) grows an excellent selection of greenery in high-ceilinged rooms and has a complete outdoor-gardening center. **Village Green** (1952 North Halsted Street) stocks more of the same. Planters, starters, tools, bags of soil and fertilizer: Everything for the perfect patio fills the big store and the rear yard—a touch of the suburbs in the city.

The presence of a university may contribute to the wealth of bookstores in DePaul. Douglas McDonald's **Stone Circle** (2050 North Halsted Street) maintains a commitment to poetry and poets with a poetry library, as well as a good selection of books and little magazines for sale. Chat with the staff about the poetry scene, sign up for the newsletter, or get the latest information on poetry readings here. **Women and Children First** (922 West Armitage Avenue) is devoted to feminist issues and children. All the fiction and poetry is by women; some of the kids' books aim specifically at debunking cultural stereotypes. A play area and meetings on women's topics make this more than just a bookstore.

Of the area's other advocacy bookshops, **Guild Books** (2456 North Lincoln Avenue) not only stocks loads of liberal-minded books and periodicals on social issues, the social sciences, history, politics, and the like, but also features books from little presses, general literature, and works on the arts. Special programs and autographing parties for authors like Kurt Vonnegut Jr., Studs Terkel, and Calvin Trillin make it particularly exciting. Book discussions are also on the bill at **Revolution Books** (2525), which carries a broad range of rhetoric from the Left, mostly Marxist style. One of the city's better general-interest used-books shops, **Booksellers Row** (2445), replenishes its racks often and is great for browsing.

To browse instead through racks of lamb, head to **Gepperth's Meat Market** (1970 North Halsted Street), a sawdust-on-the-floor neighborhood institution with fancy cuts and a good variety of homemade sausage. Some items require preordering, but you always get free advice and see surgical precision. Toscana Bakery, another standby, is no more, but the Chiappa family's ovens and secrets live on at the **Chicago Baking Company** (1003 West Armitage Avenue). The shop stocks fancy pastries and croissants, but aficionados claim the bread's not the same.

The **John Lasser Co.** (2452 North Sheffield Avenue), the oldest pop manufacturer in the city, has been doing business at the same location since 1879. The ginger ale you enjoy at the Berghoff was delivered in Lasser's 1949 Dodge, the oldest pop truck in the city. Greg Lasser, representing the fourth generation, runs the shop under the eyes of his father and experiments with new and offbeat flavors (watermelon, pine); he could probably whip up a batch of soda to your specs if you placed a big enough order. If you're looking for harder stuff, Lasser's carries two dozen beers from imported and domestic breweries, large and small. Prices are rock bottom.

Gourmet goodies pepper the exposed-brick, natural-woodwork Gourmet-To-Go-Shop at **Bentley's Wine Bar-Cafe** (801 West Willow Street), but the imported jams and coffees are just the frosting on the cake. Most of the pastas, baked goods, and cheeses, to say nothing of the intriguing selection of wines, are grist for the attached restaurant's mill. The stark, white café, strikingly accented with natural oak, serves a limited nouvelle cuisine menu and offers almost 50 wines by the glass. There's an equally handsome bar and a room for regularly scheduled wine tastings, too. Fresh seafood is the show at the **Halsted Street Fish Market** (2048 North Halsted Street), where it's sold raw or cooked—to go, or to eat in the rear dining room. This cunningly targeted spot opened with a splash, but because of mediocre cooking, it's just drifting along now.

Nouvelle-inspired fresh fish dishes often have Oriental overtones at **Jackie's** (2478 North Lincoln Avenue), and everything from appetizers to desserts on the small but varied and exciting menu is expertly prepared and beautifully served on exquisite dinnerware. Decorated in soft grays accented by dark wood and etched glass, the room is elegant in its simplicity. The considerate staff observes amenities of service sometimes ignored elsewhere.

Mexican and occasional Cuban specialties are very well prepared at **Tacos & Things** (1119 West Webster Avenue), a small restaurant at the back of a Hispanic grocery. The tasteful, spare décor and pleasant service make you forget you're dining in what was once a meat cooler. **Café Bernard** (2100 North Halsted Street) is a handsome modern spot in a neat, late 19th-century building. Chef Bernard LeCoq (who also has ownership interest in Chicago Baking, Halsted Street Fishmarket, and a restaurant in Northbrook) may have his finger in too many pies: The country-French food has never lived up to its early promise. The place is worth a try if charm and low prices are enough to placate your palate.

You wouldn't call **The Beaumont** (2020 North Halsted Street) charming, but this bar comes close to capturing the surface DePaul—young, affluent, fashionable. The owners did a good job creating a tavern that looks as if it has been in the 1896 graystone block since the beginning. A new tin ceiling, lots of polished wood, and old Chicago photographs evoke earlier times; but the juke box—carefully programmed for the latest fads—and the crush of people force you to the present. Afternoons, when classical music replaces pop and there's no crowd, are a good time to soak up atmosphere and inspect the walls for newer pictures by top Chicago photographers like P. Michael O'Sullivan and Jonas Dovydenas.

Kelly's Pub (949 West Webster Avenue) shows another side of DePaul's bar scene. Part old-time Irish saloon, part college hangout, it's always noisy, always crowded—except during finals week—and always fun—except when DePaul loses a basketball game. In good weather, there's horseshoe pitching in the back.

In fact, most of DePaul's bars share a congenial, unhassled feeling you won't find on Rush Street. People sometimes get drunk and sometimes get lucky, but good moves often take a back seat to good music. Several of the city's premier clubs are conveniently located within a few chords of each other.

B.L.U.E.S. (2519 North Halsted Street) is Hollywood-set perfect: crowded, noisy, smoky, and dumpy looking. It's also a great place to hear hard-driving, Chicago-style urban blues by the masters: Sunnyland Slim, Lefty Dizz, Jimmy Walker, Jimmy Johnson, and Erwin Helfer, among others. There's music nightly, and even the juke box keeps the faith. Many of the same performers also hold forth at **Kingston Mines** (2548), a peripatetic club that's finally come home. With friends sitting in between the featured band's sets, the music's continual, and the two-room place really hops "after-hours," when musicians wander in from their gigs to jam and enjoy good barbecue.

Blues share the bill at **Orphan's** (2462 North Lincoln Avenue) with a smattering of rock and folk and a fair amount of jazz. Because of the imaginative booking policy, this is a good place to catch budding stars. Next door, **Holsteins** (2464) became an instant star when the eponymous brothers—folksinger Fred, bartender Alan, impresario and shamelessly corny emcee Ed—opened it in 1981. A comfortable music room with a fine sound system makes this Chicago's best place to hear local, national, and international folk musicians. Fred, happily, spends lots of time on stage, and barn dancing is a Monday tradition.

On Thursdays after 10:30 p.m., folkies from the Old Town School of Folk Music drop by **The Roxy** (1157 West Wrightwood Avenue) after class for impromptu hootenannies. Movie stills and posters plastering the walls of this cozy bar set the stage for 8 p.m. Tuesday showings of Hollywood classics, while variety acts and occasional cabaret shows enliven the weekends.

More than a quarter of a century old, the **Old Town School of Folk Music** (909 West Armitage Avenue) is a DePaul institution. Step inside and you'll hear the echoes of Win Stracke, Fleming Brown, Jo Mapes, Ella Jenkins, and Bob Gibson. Many still come back, and classes, workshops, concerts, kids' programs, and several all-night folk-music parties a year keep the flame burning.

Exciting programs of new films and retrospectives seven days a week have made **Facets Multimedia Center** (1517 West Fullerton Avenue), an old loft building with two screening rooms, nationally famous. Milos Stehlik and company put together events ranging from science-fiction and rock-and-roll film festivals to workshops with distinguished directors, such as Louis Malle, Werner Herzog, and Costa-Gavras. Saturday and Sunday afternoons are given over to the best in children's films. The screens are small and the seats less than luxurious, but that just adds to the arty camaraderie.

The **Biograph Theatre** (2433 North Lincoln Avenue) is DePaul's most infamous landmark. Neighborhood residents insist on dragging visitors to the spot where G-men gunned down John Dillinger, whether they're interested or not. (The film was *Manhattan Melodrama* and nobody knows if he enjoyed it.) For a long time the Biograph lived on its notoriety and a string of B movies, but now it shows high-quality foreign and American films too chancy for general distribution. A Vie de France café in the building adds to the urbanity. On the other hand, the same DePaul nurtured the weekend *Rocky Horror Picture Show* cult—costumed veterans of countless screenings lining up for hours to shout dialogue, throw rice, and squirt water pistols in amusing synchronization with this incredibly campy film—that made the Biograph notorious again.

Interesting places

*DePaul University
Bounded by Fullerton,
Halsted, Webster, and
Racine
321-8000

*McCormick Row Houses
From the el tracks to about
830 West between Fullerton and Belden Aves.
*A fine descriptive pamphlet
is available from the Commission on Chicago
Historical and Architectural
Landmarks.*

***St. Vincent
de Paul Church**
Webster and Sheffield
327-1113

Shopping and services

*American West Gallery
2110 N. Halsted St.
871-0400
(See Galleries)

**. . . and Feathers
Bird Studio**
1015 W. Webster Ave.
549-6944
*Say "how-do" to
a cockatoo.*

Apple Rhodes
951 W. Armitage Ave.
348-1291
*A SoHo-like little shop with
handcrafted jewelry (including neat sterling
charms), art glass,
and prints by local
photographers.*

Balloons to You Ltd.
961 W. Webster Ave.
327-0909
Sold at store or delivered.

Beyond Design
1005 W. Webster Ave.
248-7647
*Bright, high-tech accessories, storage systems,
and furnishings.*

*Booksellers Row
2445 N. Lincoln Ave.
348-1170

***Chicago Center
for the Print, Ltd.**
1509-13 W. Fullerton Ave.
477-1585

**Chicago Yachting &
Navigation, Ltd.**
1661 N. Elston Ave.
822-0797
*Probably the city's largest
boating-accessories store.
Lots of appropriate
clothing, too.*

DePaul Mini Courses
Stuart Center
2324 N. Seminary Ave.
321-7977
*Classes in everything from
Chinese cooking, conversational French, art, and
crafts to dance and house
rehabbing; mostly in the
evenings.*

Distinctive Dimensions
1964 N. Halsted St.
549-6692
*Lots of lamps and "pottery
by Donovan."*

*Erinisle
1959 N. Halsted St.
280-0082

*Fertile Delta
2760 N. Lincoln Ave.
929-5350

Fiber Works
2457 N. Lincoln Ave.
327-0444
*Knitting, spinning, natural
dyeing, basketry, weaving,
and fiber sculpture—supplies and classes.*

*Geneva Convention
1128 W. Armitage Ave.
975-6280

**Grant Hospital
Wellness Center**
550 W. Webster Ave.
883-2119
Very inexpensive health-oriented classes and stop-smoking clinic.

*Greenhouse Unlimited
849 W. Armitage Ave., rear
281-7484

*Guild Books
2456 N. Lincoln Ave.
525-3667

Habitat Interiors
1804 N. Halsted St.
664-6888
*You know a neighborhood
has arrived when an
interior-design studio
opens.*

**John Healy's Wilderness
Outfitters Inc.**
907 W. Montana St.
477-9271
*Sells top-quality outdoor
equipment; manufactures
some items.*

Home Amusement Co.
952 W. Webster Ave.
327-0350
*Buy a pinball machine, juke
box, pool table (bar size),
foosball machine, or arcade
game.*

*Indulgence
2451 N. Lincoln Ave.
935-7903

Lakeshore Centre
1320 W. Fullerton Ave.
477-9888
Open around the clock, this glitzy health and sports complex is the Illinois Athletic Club of the singles-bar set. Indoor and outdoor tennis, Nautilus equipment, steam rooms, whirlpools, racquetball, track, and more provide excuses for socializing. Jock's Nouvelle Bar & Grill serves "healthy" food.

Lands' End
2317 N. Elston Ave.
384-4170
This sailing accouterments firm has grown into a major supplier of clothes and accessories for the outdoorsy; it emphasizes quality workmanship and enduring styles. The catalogue is a treat, the store stocks many essentials, and the warehouse outlet down the block has out-of-season goods at very reasonable prices. Out of the way but worth the trip.

*Lill Street Studios
1021 W. Lill Ave.
248-4414
Classes, too. Groups can arrange tours of this complete ceramics center.

Marks Ltd.
2756 N. Racine Ave.
883-4477
A huge selection of "clothes for the shorter man," including outerwear, by Givenchy, Lanvin, Giorgio Sant' Angelo, and Kilgour, French & Stanbury. Even the ties are shorter.

*Maya Imports
2044 N. Halsted St., rear
281-2176

New City YMCA
1515 N. Halsted St.
266-1242
Gleaming new Y covered with a rainbow of bright glazed bricks has swimming, exercise equipment, whirlpools, etc., at low prices. Community programs include day care.

Omiyage Ltd.
2482 N. Lincoln Ave.
477-1428
Small shop crammed with small delights that make nice gifts, even if only for yourself. Imaginative selection; some pre-W.W. II Oriental items.

Park West Books
2430 N. Lincoln Ave.
327-1166
Large, general bookstore with a Rudolph Steiner section also sells posters and does framing.

Petals
1964 N. Halsted St.
549-6692
Large selection of cards plus flowers, baskets, and pottery.

*Port of Entry
2032 N. Halsted St.
348-4550

*Revolution Books
2525 N. Lincoln Ave.
528-5353

Roy's Furniture
2455 N. Sheffield Ave.
248-8522
Roy buys discontinued or slightly flawed furnishings by the truckload. Some of it is pretty tacky, but you can find real bargains.

Saturday's Child
2146 N. Halsted St.
525-8697
Lovely toy store specializes in creative and educational playthings, many made of wood and imported from Northern Europe, for infants to 10-year-olds. Good selection of kids' books.

Sheffield Gallery
1970 N. Dayton St.
883-8848
(See Galleries)

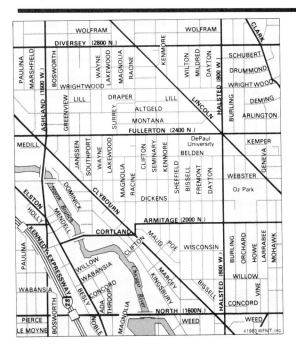

Skandia Interiors
2130 N. Halsted St.
281-8203
Frequent sales are worth waiting for at this expensive Scandinavian-furniture mart.

*Something Different
816 and 837 W. Armitage
871-6810
Custom glazes pottery.

Speedy Strippers
2546 N. Halsted St.
528-9550
Using their own furniture-stripping formula, they are speedy. Rather cheap, too.

*Stone Circle Inc.
2050 N. Halsted St.
248-4484

Underthings
804 W. Webster Ave.
472-9291
Embroidered cotton frillies from China, some silk knits; it's all so pretty you'll want to show somebody.

*Village Green
1952 N. Halsted St.
472-2800
Firewood and Christmas trees in winter.

Wax Trax
2449 N. Lincoln Ave.
929-0221
Headquarters for domestic and imported punk and New Wave records. Old-ies-but-goodies bins are worth browsing through.

*Women and Children First
922 W. Armitage Ave.
871-7417

Shopping and services: Antiques

Aged Experience
2034 N. Halsted St.
975-9790
Lots of 20th-century antiques as well as new, old-fashioned, handmade goods such as quilts.

*Antiquery Warehouse
2050 N. Halsted St.
528-3121

B. H. Ltd.
843 W. Armitage Ave.
528-5145
Once a major force on the city's vintage-clothing scene, this peripatetic little shop always has some-thing nice.

*Brass Works
2142 N. Halsted St.
935-1800

*Century Clocks
844 W. Armitage Ave.
549-5727

*Collectables Antiques
845 W. Armitage Ave.
929-6266
Architectural pieces, too.

Cosmopolitan Galleries
2476 N. Lincoln Ave.
935-5773
A large shop crammed with antique tableware and mostly uninteresting fur-niture. Decorating service.

*The Elf Shoppe
846 W. Armitage Ave.
935-4110

Endangered Species
940 W. Webster Ave.
929-6500
Nicely refinished golden oak at fairly high prices.

*Katherine's Antiques
826 W. Armitage Ave.
525-1133

*Kitsch
1007 W. Webster Ave.
327-9665

Lulu's Antiques
825 W. Armitage Ave.
975-1403
A nice eclectic shop.

*Old World Antiques
2040 N. Halsted St.
871-5500

Pier W Antiques
1221 W. Diversey Pkwy.
327-7621
Always looks as if a new shipment has just arrived— maybe so: The varied selections are ever chang-ing. Several other small an-tiques shops are on the block.

*Quercus Antiques
2148 N. Halsted St.
281-2616

John Turner of Penn-Draagon
2010 N. Halsted St.
871-0568
Stained-glass windows restored and designed. Fine workmanship.

*Turtle Creek Country Store
850 W. Armitage Ave.
327-2630
Country furniture instead of wicker in winter.

Foodstuffs

*Chicago Baking Co.
1003 W. Armitage Ave.
549-5800

Clearwater Fisheries
2461 N. Lincoln Ave.
929-1017
Good neighborhood fish house with limited variety but high quality. Deep-fried fish and shrimp to go.

Farmers' Market
Armitage Ave. and Halsted
744-6426
Farm-grown fruits and veg-etables; Saturdays, late June through mid-October. City sponsored.

*Gepperth's Meat Market
1970 N. Halsted St.
549-3883

*John Lasser Co.
2452 N. Sheffield Ave.
549-0400

Romano's Italian Lemonade
1136 W. Armitage Ave.
281-7031
Some of the city's best Ital-ian ices dispensed from an old-fashioned storefront.

Sam's Wine Warehouse
756 W. North Ave.
664-4394
Disreputable-looking store on a disreputable corner, but the basement contains one of the city's best selections of fine wines.

Schmeissing Bakery
2679 N. Lincoln Ave.
525-3753
Reliable German bakery performs wonders with party cakes. Very slow serv-ice when crowded.

Dining and drinking

Athenian Room
807 W. Webster Ave.
348-5155
Started as a gyros joint, this bustling spot now serves a limited Greek menu that's better than average.

The B.A.R. Association
1224 W. Webster Ave.
871-1440
Basic bar chow with some Persian specialties (lamb, shish kebab) in comfortable surroundings; summer dining and drinking in the trellised garden.

*The Beaumont
2020 N. Halsted St.
281-0177
Try a bargain-priced burger. Outdoor beer garden.

*Bentley's Wine Bar-Cafe
801 W. Willow St.
280-9126
Catering, too.

Buster Crab Seafood
1008 W. Armitage Ave.
525-1080
Popular, cozy spot for seafood and Italian fare offers inexpensive early-dinner specials.

*Café Bernard
2100 N. Halsted St.
871-2100

La Canasta
1007 W. Armitage Ave.
975-9667
Inexpensive, carefully prepared Mexican dishes in a small storefront that neighborhood people wish hadn't been discovered. Also at 3511 N. Clark St.

Cocina Mexicana
948½ W. Webster Ave.
525-9793
Just as good as La Canasta, but not as many people have discovered this one.

Diddles
2520 N. Lincoln Ave.
975-8558
A hangout for dart players, this small bar sometimes has live folk music on weekends.

Everleigh Club
2447 N. Halsted St.
477-4631
Neighborhood tavern evokes memories of Chicago's most famous brothel in name only. Raw bar.

Fernando's Restaurant
1800 N. Halsted St.
664-1801
Handsome décor and intriguing menu, but the Mexican food doesn't live up to the prices.

The French Peasant Restaurant
2748 N. Lincoln Ave.
281-0997
The kind of place you used to go to after seeing an "art film." Still a cheap date, but don't expect too much from the food. Jazz piano some nights.

Gare St. Lazare
858 W. Armitage Ave.
871-0062
French bourgeois cooking varies widely in quality.

Glascott's Groggery
2158 N. Halsted St.
281-1205
Old Irish saloon metamorphosed into a singles bar.

*Halsted Street Fish Market
2048 N. Halsted St.
525-6228

Site of new St. Vincent's College (now DePaul University, around 1906)

Harry and the Bear
2150 N. Halsted St.
248-1295
Chicago *magazine*
researchers liked the rib
tips. The high ceiling,
mirrored walls, and old bar
give the place a somewhat
New Orleans feel.

*Jackie's
2478 N. Lincoln Ave.
880-0003

Jock's Nouvelle
Bar & Grill
Lakeshore Centre
1320 W. Fullerton Ave.
477-9888
Zippy high-tech place sur-
rounded by running track
and tennis courts serves
more-or-less healthy fun
food. Menu indicates how
much exercise is required
to burn off the calories in
each dish.

*Kelly's Pub
949 W. Webster Ave.
549-9150

Mr. McGiddie's
2423 N. Lincoln Ave.
472-7037
Ordinary food (burgers,
omelettes, etc.), but the ice-
cream drinks are made with
Petersen's ice cream.
Alfresco dining in summer.

Nick's
1973 N. Halsted St.
664-7383
Drinking and dating to
sounds from a broadly
stocked juke box.

Periwinkle
2511 N. Lincoln Ave.
883-9797
An outdoor terrace and
classical music make this a
particularly charming place
to enjoy salads, sandwich-
es, and other light fare, as
well as pastries, sorbets,
teas, and coffees.

Roma's Pizzeria
1001 W. Webster Ave.
327-2121
University hangout with very
good thin-crust pizza and
run-of-the-mill sand-
wiches. The modern
equivalent to a malt shop.

Seminary Restaurant
2402 N. Lincoln Ave.
549-5193
Cops, DePaul basketball
players, organization pols,
folk singers, and ordinary
folk rave about the butt
steaks. Bar open until 4 a.m.

Southport City Saloon
2548 N. Southport Ave.
975-6110
Trendy bar and nice beer
garden in an up-and-
coming part of the neigh-
borhood. Combo plays
weekends.

Stefani's
1418 W. Fullerton Ave.
348-0111
Northern Italian dining at
prices that won't break you.

Suzy Wong's
901 W. Armitage Ave.
348-7360
Regional Chinese food in
glitzy surroundings; piano
bar, too.

*Tacos & Things
1119 W. Webster Ave.
348-3493

Tastebuds
746 W. Webster Ave.
348-0333
Handsome in its simplicity,
this small café serves
sandwiches and salads and
is a perfect place to have
dessert and cappuccino.

Entertainment

Apollo Theater Center
2540 N. Lincoln Ave.
935-6100
(See Theater)

*Biograph Theatre
2433 N. Lincoln Ave.
348-4123

*B.L.U.E.S.
2519 N. Halsted St.
528-1012
Cover varies.

Chicago Chess Center
2666 N. Halsted St.
929-7010
Tournaments and open
play; mostly evenings.

Chicago Comedy
Showcase
1055 W. Diversey Pkwy.
348-1101
A full stage and profes-
sional lighting make this
spot unique among Chi-
cago comedy clubs. Sam
Glick Memorial Players ap-
pear often. (See Theater.)

Chicago Dance Center
2433 N. Lincoln Ave.
929-7416
(See Dance)

*Facets Multimedia
Center
1517 W. Fullerton Ave.
281-4114, 929-KIDS

*Holsteins
2464 N. Lincoln Ave.
327-3331
Cover and minimum vary.

Irish Eyes
2519 N. Lincoln Ave.
348-9548
Neighborhood tavern has
Irish music Fri. and Sat. No
cover or minimum.

*Kingston Mines
2548 N. Halsted St.
549-1250
Music nightly. Cover varies.

*Old Town School
of Folk Music
909 W. Armitage Ave.
525-7793

*Orphan's
2462 N. Lincoln Ave.
929-2677
Cover varies.

*The Roxy
1157 W. Wrightwood Ave.
472-8100
Burgers, chili, salads. Cover
weekends.

Single File
934 W. Webster Ave.
525-1558
Even the rock acts struggle
to be heard over the din of
the young crowd that hangs
out here. Music weekends;
sometimes jazz or blues. $1
cover.

Three Penny Theatre
2424 N. Lincoln Ave.
281-7200
Nondescript movie house
features first-run films and
some sleepers.

New Town

The neighborhood surrounding Belmont Avenue and Broadway's intersection is a little like a flat San Francisco. Eclectic shops sell essentials for the good life; stylish boutiques and jeans spots compete with fast-food joints for space; restaurants form a gastronomic United Nations; bars cater to every taste. Young on-the-make singles and upscale families share the streets with the city's largest gay concentration, and there are Hispanic and Oriental enclaves as well. Rents are high and parking is impossible.

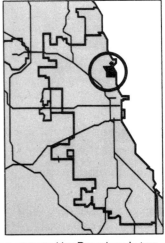

Chicago's Babylon-on-the-lake is so fluid, so varied, residents can't even agree on a name. Affluent professionals in chichi lakefront apartments know *they* live in Belmont Harbor, even if the harbor's a mile away. Jammed into low-rises and execrable four-plus-ones built when developers dubbed the area "New Town," members of the me-generation attracted by Broadway's tawdry glitter don't stay long, but their ranks are continually replenished, and the name sticks. Artsy sorts, community organizers, and local businessmen opt for the East Lakeview label. To old-timers, it's just plain Lakeview, and what's all the fuss about anyway?

Whatever the community's name, the shoreline has been a magnet for development ever since the Lake View Inn opened at Byron Street and the lake in 1853. After the completion of a plank road—now Broadway—stately houses rose along the lakefront, homes of owners of greenhouses and clay pits to the west. Construction of the Lake View Town Hall (site of the present Town Hall District police station) at Halsted and Addison Streets reflected the importance of the township's eastern half.

By 1889, when Lake View Township was annexed to Chicago, the English, Irish, and others were pouring in, diluting the heavily German and Scandinavian presence (although the Swedes maintained an enclave around Belmont and Wilton Avenues until the 1940s) and creating a housing demand that resulted in the subdivision of large estates. Towering apartment buildings shot up closest to the lake; smaller multifamily houses were built to the west.

Churches took root to serve the diverse influx of new residents. The foundation stone for the oldest surviving structure, **St. Peter's Episcopal Church** (Belmont Avenue and Broadway), was laid in 1893. **Lake View Presbyterian**

Church's (Addison Street and Broadway) charming frame building was designed in 1897 by the famed John Wellborn Root; subsequent alterations haven't diminished its simple dignity. Broadway had a different name in 1901 when the Evanston Avenue Methodist Episcopal Church was built; you can still see the old name on the façade of today's **Broadway United Methodist Church** (Broadway and Buckingham Place).

Jewish residents worshipped at **Temple Sholom's** old building (now **Anshe Emet Synagogue,** Pine Grove Avenue and Grace Street) when the North Side's oldest Reform congregation—established in 1867—moved from its Gold Coast location in 1911. Their present Byzantine-inspired 1930 temple (Lake Shore Drive and Stratford Place) was the only synagogue built in Chicago between the Depression and the end of World War Two. Irish Catholics organized a parish as early as 1886, but it was not until 1913 that they laid the cornerstone of **Our Lady of Mt. Carmel Church** (Belmont Avenue and Orchard Street), a beautiful Tudor Gothic structure.

Churches remain, but lakefront mansions and other reminders of early wealth are hard to find. A few are tucked between Lake Shore Drive and Sheridan Road; others dignify the streetscape off Pine Grove Avenue south of Barry Avenue. Spacious homes line both sides of Hawthorne Place (3412 North) between Broadway and Sheridan Road. And **Alta Vista Terrace** (1054 West between Grace and Byron Streets) is a treasure. Hidden away on this London-like street, facing rows of townhouses take you into another time as you walk between them. Built between 1900 and 1904 by Samuel Eberly Gross, self-proclaimed "World's Greatest Real Estate Promoter," the houses remain virtually unchanged; landmark protection will keep them that way. None of them is particularly dramatic on its own, but taken together they make a stunning streetscape and, close up, a parade of all the fashionable detail and decoration of their time. This is one street that's more fun to walk on a foggy day.

Many Chicagoan's flirt with deep depression every time they pass the corner of Clark and Addison Streets. **Wrigley Field,** one of the few wonderful ball parks left in America, should stir feelings of joy, even in the dead of winter; instead it recalls decades of disappointment. Since 1916, it's been the home of the Chicago Cubs, for whom some of America's greatest ballplayers have labored, mostly in vain. Because the late Philip Wrigley, long-time owner, looked at innovation with a jaundiced eye, it remained the only park without lights, had scoreboard numbers manipulated by hand, and required that gentlemen wear shirts in box seats. The players also seemed tradition bound, usually folding in August. However, in 1981 the Tribune Company bought the Cubs and came up with the slogan "building new traditions"; changes are on the way.

"Wrigleyville" used to be typical, earthy, blue-collar Lakeview, except for the vistas from the roofs of turn-of-the-century flats overlooking right field, but the wind of change has swept down Clark Street. Ball fans may be as likely to follow the Tokyo Giants as they do the Cubs in the string of Oriental restaurants and shops that have sprung up almost overnight around Roscoe Street. Community growth and gentrification have the Hispanic enclave around Belmont Avenue and Clark Street caught in a squeeze play.

Change is what New Town is all about. Twenty years ago there wasn't a duller neighborhood. Then Broadway became a singles mecca, and developers couldn't build studio and one-bedroom apartments fast enough. Tacky four-plus-ones replaced single-family houses on side streets, and modern high-rises the vintage lakefront low-rises. The churches, once withering as members died or moved away, now actively serve growing congregations made up of the young, gays, minorities, affluent lakefronters, and pensioned seniors.

New Town's birth also meant renewal for some old buildings. The **Brewster**

Apartments (2800 North Pine Grove Avenue), designed by E. H. Turnock in 1893, exude Gay Nineties robustness and were lovingly restored by Mieki Hayano in 1970. The interior of the buildings proves that Hyatt Hotels' John Portman didn't invent central elevators and skylit atria. In the **Brewster Antiques Mall** (500 West Diversey Parkway), more than a dozen dealers display wares ranging from expensive furniture to cheaper collectibles in a perfect setting.

Less sensitively restored, **The Century** (2828 North Clark Street) was once a jewel in the Balaban & Katz movie-house chain. The announcement in the early 1970s that it was to be recycled as a shopping mall brought hope to conservationists. Chicago would have an exciting mall with shops built into the ornate lobby, behind a preserved terra-cotta façade. Too bad it didn't happen that way! The marquee was ripped off, the façade pierced by superfluous windows, and the interior gutted. Millions were spent creating the glitzy, hard-edged, six-story mall, but the result is basically cut-rate Water Tower Place. Even the Christmas caroling, ethnic fairs, and variety shows that the management stages to beef up business aren't quite up to snuff.

Of the 70-odd shops—jeans stores, an Indian bazaar with wares spilling out into the hall, furniture stores, stereo outlets, a general book store, a cosmetics salon, an instant-tan place, a bath shop—only a few are really exciting. After parking in the garage (reduced rates with merchant validation), the best way to see the mall is to take one of the hydraulic elevators ("Look, Ma: no cables!") to the top and work down, Guggenheim Museum fashion.

Something's Brewing (sixth level) may be Chicago's best coffee-and-tea store. Besides roasting beans on the premises, it stocks about 20 coffees, including rare Indonesian ones, dozens of teas, and pots, such as sought-after cappuccino makers at discount prices. A tiny high-tech café at the rear of the store serves topnotch espresso and cappuccino, coffee of the day, and pastries baked by amateur entrepreneurs.

More than a dozen apparel shops dress up the mall, but the **Chicago Ltd.** stores (first level) are the only really distinctive ones. Both the men's and women's locations sell quality, traditional suits and sportswear in silks, tweedy wools, and other natural fabrics by designers like Calvin Klein and Ralph Lauren. Accessories such as Coach leather goods are also on hand. The shops offer complimentary beverages and free tailoring—a real rarity in women's wear.

Lots of clothing stores featuring everything from jeans to popularly priced Seventh Avenue and California fashions line the neighborhood shopping strips, but a few stand out. Natural-fiber separates and casual wear are among the attractions at **Apropos** (3315 North Broadway), a whitewashed and track-lit women's store that's always abreast of the times. Sexy lingerie, a complete line of Danskin, and trendy accessories round out the collection. A charming, English-basement boutique, **Elle** (3435) goes a step further with highly styled women's fashions and accouterments, many from France. Though not for everyone, they're perfect for women who want to make a dramatic statement. Vibrant Micheline Sassoon cosmetics complete the picture. Frequently featured in newspaper and magazine fashion sections, **Jovanna Ltd.** (3441) carries equally dramatic separates, sportswear, and accessories. Chicago designers are well represented: Here you may find handpainted tote bags by Harriet Hanson and Judy Lichtenstein, handwoven and handloomed silk and cotton outfits by Maria Rodriguez, stunning belts by Suzanne Bucher and Robin, and lots of other unique pieces. A real trend setter, Jovanna Ltd. also tries to remain affordable.

The **Weaving Workshop** (3352 North Halsted Street) is a good place to go for a one-of-a-kind sweater or shawl. Besides custom knitting and weaving, the shop offers classes, looms, yarns, dyes, and sales space for handicrafters who would rather make their own fabrics than buy them. The large assortment of ready-made quilts for sale at **The Contemporary Quilt** (2863 North Clark Street) may inspire aspiring quilt makers, while kits, supplies, and lessons provide the wherewithal to realize their needlework fantasies.

While such tranquil pastimes appeal to dyed-in-the-wool artistic types, the huge **Sportmart** (3134 North Clark Street) probably better reflects the New Town lifestyle. Racks of running shoes, jogging shorts, and down parkas share space with row upon row of athletic gear. In the winter, the ski section is the hottest spot but, when the weather warms, everything from bicycles to tennis racquets tempts the energetic bent on a workout.

For those who would rather explore the uncharted paths of the mind than the jogging track in Lincoln Park, the **Occult Bookstore** (3230 North Clark Street) offers classes in the occult arts; a resident astrologer casts horoscopes and reads tarot cards. The city's oldest bookstore specializing in witchcraft, astrology, cabala, and other spooky stuff has an extensive line of new and used books on the occult, Oriental philosophy, yoga, magic, and mysticism, as well as candles, crystals, and incense to create the proper atmosphere. **East West Books** (506 West Diversey Parkway), a branch center of the Himalayan Institute, carries books on Oriental philosophies, works on yoga and meditation, holistic medicine, cooking, psychology, and just about anything else concerned with mysteries of mind and body. Classes in yoga and vegetarian cooking, too.

Europa Bookstore (3229 North Clark Street) stocks an enormous selection of books in German, French, and Spanish, including general culture and history, reference works, technical tomes, and kids' stuff. Foreign-language Monopoly and Scrabble round out the picture.

A good general bookshop, **Barbara's Bookstore** (2907 North Broadway) concentrates on high-quality paperbacks, including many from small university presses, as well as some self-published works by local poets. The annex is devoted to theater, dance, art, and film, reflecting community interests. An informal meeting place, as its sister store on Wells Street once was, Barbara's offers poetry and play readings some Sunday afternoons.

While Barbara's stocks some posters, **Poster Plus** (2906 North Broadway) has one of the city's largest collections of 19th- and 20th-century posters, ones from art and cultural exhibitions, World War One propaganda pieces, and just plain pretty posters. Prices are high, but you can save some money by taking your find across the street to **The Great Frame Up** (2905), where the helpful staff will teach you how to frame it yourself after you've chosen the materials.

Shops specializing in gifts and decorative accessories to spiff up an apartment dot the neighborhood. **Kiyo's Oriental Gifts** (2831 North Clark Street), possibly the city's largest store devoted to Japanese crafts, is filled with high-quality, traditional porcelain, lacquerware, bamboo and wicker furniture, and jewelry. It's expensive, but there are some small, affordable pieces such as delightful china chopstick holders. Nothing is traditional at the striking **Traffick** (3313 North Broadway). Barry Graffagna stocks the store with things he likes—carefully arranged papier-mâché fruits, colorful moiré pillows, jardinières, pullovers, Crabtree & Evelyn preserves—but the oddball selection always manages to keep pace with, or anticipate, changing tastes. Assorted imported wares are the fare at the charming **Natural Selection** (711 West Belmont Avenue): jams, salt-free mustard from London, stone carvings from the Urals, toys and decorative pieces from China. The annex contains fabrics and more folk arts.

Scandinavian Design (548 West Diversey Parkway) has well-made, clean-lined, rosewood and teak furniture. Prices are high, though there are frequent and meaningful sales. Weekly sales (plastered across the pages of the *Reader*) offer significant discounts on already fair prices at **The Great Ace** (2818 North Broadway). Only the basement of this three-floor neighborhood institution, which serves as a kind of Crate and Barrel-plus for people living in studio apartments,, bears any resemblance to a traditional hardware store. Inexpensive do-it-yourself furniture, security locks, kitchenware, china, linen, and plants bring in the crowds, especially in the traditional moving months (May and October).

An excellent selection of plants is sold at extremely reasonable prices in **Hammock House** (3201 North Halsted Street), a miniconservatorylike place whose windows are almost always steamy. Albert Corrales and Jon Wood started by selling hammocks a decade ago and still stock the all-cotton, Pawleys Island rope hammocks from South Carolina, as well as baskets, pottery, and gifts. In summer, they open the yard and sell garden stakes, seeds, and bulbs.

The Greenhouse on Buckingham (745 West Buckingham Place) recaptures the elegant past. Geo. Witbold Florists, established in 1857, lost the location during the Depression. Witbold's legacy includes a tropical greenhouse for plants and flowers, replete with pools and fountains at the back of the shop, lovely woodcarvings above the coolers, and lots of stained glass.

The stained- and beveled-glass windows of **Victorian House Antiques** (806 West Belmont Avenue) have made this freestanding townhouse almost a local landmark. Three floors crammed with ornate furniture, fine antiques, glassware and porcelain, and some stuff sold "as is" in the basement offer few bargains, but browsing is fun. Lots more exquisite stained glass adorns the **Victorian House Restaurant** next door (800), and the interior has been lavished with opulent antiques that far outshine the food.

Roan Galleries (3457 North Halsted Street), the kind of shop you'd expect to find on Oak Street, has big-ticket, elegant items (including some oil paintings) suited to a Gold Coast apartment. **Chicago Fine Arts** (3521 North Halsted Street) specializes in French furniture, Japanese woodblock prints, European graphics, and Chinese porcelains.

Josie's (3323 North Broadway) is a wonderful place to go for smaller items: sterling curios, signed pottery, glassware, old perfume bottles, lots of Art Deco, cigarette cases, beaded handbags, and precious-metal and Celluloid antique jewelry. The shop also carries vintage clothing—Victorian to the '40s—at reasonable prices, and does a bustling business. **Blake** (614 West Belmont Avenue) is the crème de la crème of several vintage clothing stores in the neighborhood. Two beautiful items—a different two every few days—grace the plate-glass windows. The sparsely stocked shop sells chic, mint-condition garments ranging from stylish suits to silk lingerie, Oriental kimonos, Victorian dresses, and elaborately embroidered shawls. Marilyn Blaszka and Dominic Marcheschi have completely restored some of them.

If you're into leather, Anthony Ozog whips up cowboy hats, belts, and handbags at **Conrads Leather House** (3147 North Broadway), while **The Great Showing Machine** (3534) specializes in rather kinky custom designs in leather, suede, and fur. Prices are high, but how many places sell six-inch spike heels in large sizes? Leather items for very specific purposes are among the offerings at **The Pleasure Chest** (3143), a supermarket of erotica with paraphernalia to satisfy almost every sexual whim and accouterments for well-dressed fetishists—even candy underpants.

More conventional candy novelties—white chocolate swans, customized bonbons—can be found at **Martha's Candies** (3257 North Broadway), a longtime neighborhood fixture. Unlike most Chicago candymakers, Martha's caters to East Coast tastes with lots of dark chocolate and unusual items, such as chocolate-covered kumquats and ginger. Prices are comparable to Marshall Field's.

With a marble-topped Art Deco soda fountain, wall murals, and stuffed-animal displays, **Ideal Candies** (3311 North Clark Street) looks like a Norman Rockwell *Saturday Evening Post* cover. Peter Vasilakos, whose father opened the shop in 1937, makes all the candy on a single-burner stove in the back. Although he doesn't make the ice cream, this is a fine place to come for a hot-fudge sundae or delicious whipped hot chocolate. Soak in the ambiance and don't leave without some treats.

A reminder of the area's German heritage, **Rahmig's House of Fine Choc-olate** (3109 North Broadway) stocks a few candies but does a bigger business in decent cakes and pastries. **Fong's Fortune** (2850 North Clark Street), a bright, modern Chinese bakery, offers an impressive array of tea pastries ranging from hearty beef-curry puffs and barbecued pork buns to sweet custard tarts and fruit turnovers. You can eat them in the store, but the tables are uncomfortable and tea comes in bags. Fong's also makes party trays.

If you're planning a big bash, consult with Karen and Robert Smith at **Lisi's Hors d'Oeuvre Bakery** (954 West Diversey Parkway), and they'll come up with special treats. Quiches, pâtés, goodie-filled puff pastries, and all sorts of other delights are great just to nibble on, too. Quiche is also on the bill of fare at **Rolf's Pâtisserie** (621), as are croissant sandwiches, pasta and vegetable salads, ice creams, and pastries to take out or enjoy in the café with espresso.

On the forefront of the recent trend, **Pasta Sugo** (2852 North Broadway) makes fresh pasta and sauces—pesto, oil and garlic, Genovese, clam, and sev-eral more—to go. Cold pasta salad, an impressive assortment of imported meats and cheeses, bread, and lots of homemade antipasti provide the fixings for a pic-nic. Other prepared foods help round out a hot meal. The shop also whips up special orders for parties.

The Bread Shop (3400 North Halsted Street), a no-holds-barred natural-foods store and bakery, produces whole-grain breads, cakes, and cookies that to junk-food junkies might taste too good to be healthy. A success despite low-key, counter-culture predilections, the shop has expanded over time, adding or-ganically grown produce, bulk grains and flours, additive-free honeys, and a deli section.

For a taste of a genuine, New York-style, 1950s coffeehouse, check out **Caffé Pergolesi** (3404 North Halsted Street). Chess games, patrons absorbed in esoteric conversations, indifferent coffees, and a variety of hot chocolates—cin-namon, rum, brandy—create an atmosphere that makes you wonder if Jack Ker-ouac's ghost might drop in. A menu of mostly vegetarian soups, omelettes, sand-wiches, and salads, and exhibits of local artists lighten the intensity. Cheerfully eccentric, Pergolesi is closed on Friday and brunch is served on weekdays as well as Sunday.

A more visible neighborhood institution looks like a Germanic castle left over from a movie set. Once a restaurant on the itinerary of every tourist, the old Ivan-hoe, with its baronial dining hall, bar with presiding magician, and spooky cata-combs, has been converted to the flagship store of the **Chalet Wine and Cheese** chain (3000 North Clark Street). The main floor is devoted to a huge selection of wines, cheeses, and gourmet foods, while the catacombs serve as a wine cellar for the more prestigious vintages, a wine-tasting area, and customer wine-storage space. The adjacent theater has been renovated to house independent productions, touring shows, and transfers from smaller theaters.

Many people don't know that **Kenessey Gourmets Internationale** (Hotel Belmont, 403 West Belmont Avenue) has a downstairs; there you can find lots of imported wines, beers, cheeses, and gourmet foods. Part of the space is a wine-cellar-like dining area serving European open-faced sandwiches throughout the day and a Continental menu at dinner. Best of all, you can select any wine from the bins and enjoy it at a table for a slight surcharge. Upstairs is Kenessey's pastry shop with scores of Austro-Hungarian goodies to take out or eat at tables—espresso and cappuccino, too. They may be the most expensive pastries in town, but the napoléons are sublime.

Tango (3172 North Sheridan Road), across the hotel lobby from Kenessey's, is the neighborhood's most elegant restaurant. Although the seafood offerings aren't always up to the highest standards, potato skins are the city's best, service is friendly, and the austere décor and well-chosen artwork are extraordinary.

Dimly lit and romantic, **The Paradise Café** (3352 North Broadway) was a very "in" spot for a while. Unfortunately, a change in ownership affected the food adversely and staples, such as fresh fish, roast duck, and sautéed veal, are only adequate. Soups, salads, and other light fare are on the daytime café menu; the wine bar is a nice place to relax over dessert and coffee—or wine by the glass.

Although the menu on any given night is limited to three items out of a repertoire of some 25 different entrées, **Genesee Depot** (3736 North Broadway) has a strong local following. The menu is not especially daring—stuffed pork chops and chicken Kiev are long-time favorites—but most dishes are well prepared. The homey, plant- and antique-filled room, great desserts, and reasonable prices keep people coming back, despite frequent waits for tables.

New Town's cosmopolitan streets are checkered with ethnic dining spots. **The Casbah** (514 West Diversey Parkway), Chicago's finest Armenian restaurant, offers beorak (filo pastry filled with a lamb and spice mixture), kibbeh (raw lamb and bulgur wheat), nicely spiced kebabs, and unusual fish preparations. Owner Varouj Vartanian also serves couscous, a treat that fits nicely with the room's North African décor. Less exotic but equally popular, **La Crêperie** (2845 North Clark Street) slathers buckwheat crêpes with hearty meat, seafood, or vegetable-and-cheese fillings for entrées. Fruits or chocolate grace the lighter wheat-flour dessert crêpes. No reservations; so the romantic, bistrolike ambiance is overwhelmed by Sunday brunch crowds. Crowds also flock to **Ann Sather** (925 West Belmont Avenue) for inexpensive food with a Swedish flavor. Some of that flavor has faded since Sather sold the restaurant, but you'll still find fruit soup, potato sausage, and Swedish meatballs on the menu of this crisp and bright community institution.

You don't have to be Argentinian to enjoy the hearty grilled meats at **Buenos Aires** (2856 North Clark Street), but a gaucho-sized appetite helps. Chicken, beef asado (garlicky short ribs), and sweetbreads are among the entrées that come in portions so large that what doesn't fit on your plate is kept warm on tableside grills. **La Paella** (2920 North Clark Street) presents the more sophisticated cuisine of Spain. Besides the rice-seafood-and-chicken mélange that is the restaurant's namesake, expect to find duck with mangoes and a variety of seafood specialties. It's all presented in a comfortable Iberian setting with muted guitar music from the tape deck. **Boca del Rio** (917 West Belmont Avenue) serves some of the city's best Mexican-style seafood—cocktails, soups, snapper a la Veracruzana, shrimp with garlic—in simple cantina surroundings.

The community has always had a sizable Japanese population and a number of good Japanese restaurants, including the highly regarded **Matsuya** (3469 North Clark Street). Seafood specials are the trump card at this clean, spare storefront. The chef's daily trip to the market may have yielded trout, butterfish, or sea pike for teriyaki-style treatment; scallops or tuna could wind up in a tempura. Meat and poultry also find their way onto the moderately priced menu. Everybody's happy at **Happi Sushi** (3346 North Clark Street), especially customers lucky enough to find seats at the counter where, in a flurry of flashing knives, chefs slice up fresh raw fish for sushi and sashimi presentations that are works of art. (Take-out orders get the same careful attention to appearance.) An imaginative, larger-than-usual choice of appetizers lets you nibble while watching the show. If you haven't worked up the nerve for raw fish, you'll find happiness in the well-prepared tempuras or sukiyaki.

Star Market (3349 North Clark Street), a small, impeccable grocery, carries clear-eyed fish, crisp vegetables, and all the staples and seasonings for Japanese home cooking. For more exotic efforts, cross the street to **Arirang** (3330), the neighborhood's largest Oriental grocery. Though the owner is Korean, the store stocks meats, fish, produce, staples, canned goods, and a full line of fairly priced utensils for every style of Asian cooking.

A few places offer more than food. Lettuce Entertain You's **Lawrence of Oregano** (662 West Diversey Parkway) moves show biz from the menu to the stage with weekend acts that warble pop-folk and Broadway melodies. An Italian accent pervades the kitchen's generally tasty offerings, but the real star is the salad bar. The chef plays a supporting role at **Deni's Den** (2941 North Clark Street), a boisterous, Mediterranean-style, white-walled Greek cabaret. Top billing goes to Vasilios Gaitanos, who leads his splendid musicians in the best of Greek popular and patriotic music. Excitement peaks after 11 p.m. when half the patrons start dancing. Drinks are a bit expensive, but there's no cover or minimum.

Other night life is plentiful, varied, and exciting. The neighborhood is home to several theater companies and scores of bars, both straight and gay. Though few are "singles bars" per se—unless you've a really great story about your astrological sign, breaking the ice is difficult—live entertainment at some contributes to a congenial atmosphere. **The Piano Man** (3801 North Clark Street), in a one-time neighborhood tavern, hosts some of Chicago's most promising young blues and jazz artists and retains that comfortable corner-saloon feeling. Small and somewhat seedy, **His 'n' Hers** (944 West Addison Street) draws gays and straights alike with an eclectic parade of performers. Well-known, seldom-heard, and yet-to-be-discovered blues, folk, comedy, and cabaret acts pocket the weekend cover.

Places with entertainment spring up and close down regularly, but **Cross-Currents** (3206 North Wilton Avenue) may typify New Town at its best. Located in an old Swedish temperance hall, it is an enthusiastic effort to create a focus for community activities and a forum for the exchange of ideas. The cabaret theater has hosted original musicals and stand-up comics, as well as black, Hispanic, feminist, and experimental productions; the **Joseph Holmes Dance Theatre** studios and school are on the second floor *(see Dance)*. Meeting rooms are booked solid by groups ranging from supporters of solidarity with El Salvador to the Belmont Avenue Business Association; and the handsome bar-café is a fine place for meaningful discussions over drinks or pastries and espresso.

Interesting places

Jane Addams Center Hull House Association
3212 N. Broadway
549-1631
The first outpost of Hull House offers swimming, a senior center, day care, and classes in photography and ceramics.

*Alta Vista Terrace
1054 West between Byron and Grace Sts.

*Anshe Emet Synagogue
Pine Grove and Grace St.
281-1423
Conservative congregation, founded 1873, has worshipped here since 1926. Alfred Alschuler designed the Georgian-style building.

*Brewster Apartments
2800 N. Pine Grove Ave.

*Broadway United Methodist Church
Broadway and Buckingham
281-9548, 348-2679

Helen L. Kellogg Houses
2946, 2952, 2960 N. Lake Shore Drive West
Designated city landmarks in 1981, these three stately mansions are nonetheless scheduled for demolition.

*Lake View Presbyterian Church
Addison St. and Broadway
281-2655

Link's Hall
3435 N. Sheffield Ave.
472-3441
Old German hall now houses a naprapath, the IWW, a mime, the Chicago Women's Health Center, and a performance space.

"A Mural for a New World"
West wall, Parish of the Holy
Covenant
925 W. Diversey Pkwy.
*Hopeful, humanistic;
by Martinez and Weber,
1973, for the Chicago
Mural Group.*

***Our Lady of
Mt. Carmel Church**
Belmont Ave. and Orchard
525-0453

***St. Peter's
Episcopal Church**
Belmont and Broadway
525-0844

**Salvation Army School
for Officer Training**
700 W. Brompton Ave.
975-2400
*Located in the Joseph E. Tilt
mansion, designed in 1904
by Holabird and Roche.*

*Temple Sholom
Lake Shore and Stratford
525-4707

*Wrigley Field
Clark and Addison Sts.
281-5050

Shopping
and services

The Alley
2900 N. Broadway
525-3180
*Records and tapes, T-
shirts, smoking accesso-
ries, cards, and gifts.*

**American Youth
Hostels, Inc.**
3712 N. Clark St.
327-8114
*No longer just for young
people, membership gets
you entry to hostels here
and abroad. Skiing and
biking trips.*

*Apropos
3315 N. Broadway
528-2130

Art Furniture Shop
3516 N. Clark St.
472-6800
*Restoration of antique
furniture.*

Art Resource Studio
2931-33 N. Clark St.
477-7062
*Art classes, using found
objects, for kids ages
4 to 16.*

Atlantis Bedrooms
2935 N. Broadway
281-9210
*Elaborate brass, water,
and platform bed set-ups;
brass coatracks and
other furnishings.*

Aunt Edie's Glass
3339 N. Halsted St.
528-1617
*Nicely displayed 20th-
century glassware at mod-
erate prices. Good place to
round out a set.*

Banana Moon
554 W. Diversey Pkwy.
525-8080
*High-quality clothing and
accessories for kids; some
from France, some hand
crafted, most unusual or
unique.*

*Barbara's Bookstore
2907 N. Broadway
477-0411

*Blake
614 W. Belmont Ave.
477-3364

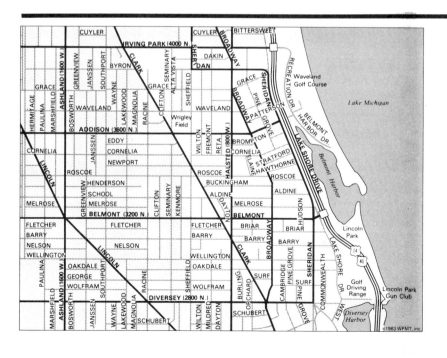

Bob's in Newtown
2810 N. Clark St.
883-1123
One of the largest selections of magazines and hard-to-find periodicals.

Bon Ton Chicago
2929 N. Broadway
935-0027
Large men's store with designer clothing.

Born Beautiful
3206 N. Broadway
549-6770
Friendly shop with designer clothes for kids.

*Brewster Antiques Mall
500 W. Diversey Pkwy.
327-8666

H. Brian Convertible Sofas
2840 N. Halsted St.
281-7650
Enormous selection of convertibles, both their own and name brands, at discount prices. Price guarantee; unusually rapid, free delivery. Other locations.

Buckingham Bike Shop, Ltd.
3332 N. Broadway
525-9660
Fine shop caters to professionals and "Sunday cyclists" with bikes by Fuji, Nishiki, Trek, and others; Campagnolo and Suntour accessories. Competent repair work; competitive prices.

*The Century
2828 N. Clark St.
929-8100

Chicago Blues
2926 N. Broadway
477-9020
The Italian look reigns supreme at this classy men's store.

*Chicago Fine Arts
3521 N. Halsted St.
929-2988

Chicago Folklore Center
3341 N. Halsted St.
935-2774
Builds and repairs acoustic and electric instruments. Warranty station for C. F. Martin guitars, among others.

*Chicago Ltd.
The Century, 1st level
2828 N. Clark St.
929-6900

*Chicago Ltd. for Her
The Century, 1st level
2828 N. Clark St.
528-8182

Chicago Tattooing Co.
922 W. Belmont Ave.
528-6969
Huge selection, including fancy Oriental numbers. You might have to wait in a line of recruits from Great Lakes, but a pinball machine helps pass the time.

*Conrads Leather House
3147 N. Broadway
348-8581

*The Contemporary Quilt
2863 N. Clark St.
528-0360

Divine Idea
2959 N. Clark St.
975-0909
Vintage 1940s to '60s clothing, some never worn.

Double Happiness
907 W. Belmont Ave.
929-1122
Gifts, books, and toys from China.

*East West Books
506 W. Diversey Pkwy.
525-5157

*Elle
3435 N. Broadway
327-2145

*Europa Bookstore
3229 N. Clark St.
929-1836

Fabrile Gallery
2945 N. Broadway
929-7471
Fine art glass and some porcelain.

Joseph W. Fell, Ltd.
3221 N. Clark St.
549-6076
Very fine antique Oriental rugs. Appointments.

Floral Designs Inc.
3021 N. Southport Ave.
528-9800
Imaginative florist's greenhouse. Other retail outlets.

The Flower Cart, Inc.
3819 N. Broadway
477-7755
Custom-made flower arrangements, fine silver and crystal, jewelry, and other pretty things.

Formerly Yours, Ltd.
3443 N. Halsted St.
248-7766
General collection of antiques with some especially nice Art Deco pieces and a good stock of Roseville art pottery.

Frame Factory-Chicago
760 W. Waveland Ave.
929-8930
Warehouse stocks 40,000 frames at discount prices. Custom framing, too.

Graphic Expectations
757 W. Diversey Pkwy.
871-0957
Good poster shop specializes in film, theater, and dance. Framing.

*The Great Ace
2818 N. Broadway
348-0705

*The Great Frame Up
2905 N. Broadway
549-3927

*Great Showing Machine
3534 N. Broadway
248-0566

The Green Thumb
3336 N. Clark St.
248-8111
All the plants are fresh as a daisy in this pleasant shop.

*The Greenhouse on Buckingham
745 W. Buckingham Pl.
248-0044

Greetings
560 W. Diversey Pkwy.
935-0875
Scads of zippy greetings; novelties, too.

*Hammock House
3201 N. Halsted St.
549-2232

He Who Eats Mud
3247 N. Broadway
525-0616
High-tech lights alternating with colorful umbrellas decorate this trendy shop. Cards and stationery, jewelry, art glass, toys, posters, dinnerware, silk flowers, and lots of other neat stuff.

International Antiques
2907 N. Clark St.
528-4602
Large shop features European furniture, much of it imported from Scotland.

Japan Books and Records
3345 N. Clark St.
248-4114
The name says it all.

*Josie's
3323 N. Broadway
871-3750

*Jovanna Ltd.
3441 N. Broadway
975-0303

*Kiyo's Oriental Gifts
2831 N. Clark St.
935-0619

Lake Shore Furniture
934 W. Roscoe St.
327-0972, 271-5702
Cluttered antiques shop with many used religious articles—chalices, monstrances, censers, and votive-candle stands.

Light & Space Design
3324 N. Halsted St.
883-9800
Designers of neon, interiors, and accessories. If you've lusted after a neon hot dog (with glowing mustard), this is the place to find it. Some stock; they'll work with you to realize your gaseous fantasy.

Madame X
3339 N. Clark St.
327-3372
Cozy salon in back of a dance studio carries lovely, offbeat women's clothing and accessories by Chicago designers; a charming place to relax over a cappuccino.

Mansfield Picture Framing
2950 N. Clark St.
472-1820
Some interesting old prints.

Miller Piano Works
3800 N. Clark St.
549-6528
Ex-journalist David Miller and genetics Ph.D. Morris Fiddler rebuild and restore pianos, especially players. Concert tuning.

Mrs. Peel's
3221 N. Clark, 2nd floor
281-4761
Designer Judy Fell makes au courant clothes for professional women. Appointments suggested.

*Natural Selection
711 W. Belmont Ave.
477-0203

The Oblisk
3405 N. Broadway
477-1545
Behind classy display windows are perfect-for-the-étagère gifts: leaded-crystal vases, brass bookends, small statues, and the like.

*Occult Bookstore
3230 N. Clark St.
281-0599
Call about performances in the theater.

Offshore Marine
901 W. Irving Park Rd.
549-4446
Boating paraphernalia and instruction; boardsailing a specialty.

Les Parfums Shoppe
3017 N. Broadway
935-0543
Perfumes and colognes for both sexes; cosmetics and some gifts.

Pier 1 Imports
651 W. Diversey Pkwy.
871-1558
Fiber rugs, metalwork, baskets, china, glassware, and bamboo furniture. Some bargains, especially on smaller stuff.

Pinter's Violin Shop
3804 N. Clark St.
248-6536
Pinter, who apprenticed in Hungary, repairs bowing instruments for musicians from all over the country.

*The Pleasure Chest, Ltd.
3143 N. Broadway
525-7151

Plump Pudding
2854 N. Clark St.
975-4222
California, Chicago, and New York fashions—mostly sportswear—for women sized 38 to 46. Good selection of lingerie.

*Poster Plus
2906 N. Broadway
549-2822
Also at 210 S. Michigan.

*Roan Galleries
3457 N. Halsted St.
935-9093

*Scandinavian Design
548 W. Diversey Pkwy.
248-8229

Silver Moon
3337 N. Halsted St.
883-0222
Fine vintage clothing from the turn of the century to the early '50s.

Southport Studio
3323 N. Clark St.
871-2274
Makes, repairs, and restores stained glass.

*Sportmart
3134 N. Clark St.
871-8500
Other locations.

Sports Arena
The Century, 2nd level
2828 N. Clark St.
975-0055
Oodles of souvenirs of all your favorite out-of-town, major-league teams.

Lou Stein's on Diversey
440 W. Diversey Pkwy.
348-2141
Vintage and new clothing with few bargains. Silks, furs, funky styles; good for browsing.

Stuff 'n' Such
3249 N. Broadway
248-7000
Gay men's boutique.

J. Toguri Mercantile Co.
851 W. Belmont Ave.
929-3500
Old standby for Japanese products—cookware, china, gifts, and some foods.

*Traffick
3313 N. Broadway
549-1502

*Victorian House Antiques
806 W. Belmont Ave.
348-8561

Waldenbooks
616 W. Diversey Pkwy.
549-3792
Branch of national chain.

Warpworks
3117 N. Broadway
248-5225
Small fabric gallery features imported silk-screen prints.

*Weaving Workshop
3352 N. Halsted St.
929-5776

Wheel & Deal
3515 N. Halsted St.
871-7639
Mostly small stuff— magazines, postcards, glassware. They deal in "icons to eyesores" and the fun comes in bargaining your eyesores for theirs.

Yesterday
1143 W. Addison St.
248-8087
A long fly from Wrigley Field, Tom Boyle's cluttered shop holds a treasure trove of old baseball cards and scorecards. Movie posters, 19th-century newspapers, magazines.

Ziggurat
3420 N. Halsted St.
327-7787
Excellent collection of clothing and decorative pieces from the '20s and '30s; some furniture.

Foodstuffs

*Arirang Supermarket
3330 N. Clark St.
549-3948

*The Bread Shop
3400 N. Halsted St.
528-8108
Baking classes.

Coffee and Tea Exchange
3300 N. Broadway
528-2241
Excellent coffees, including their delightful special blend, roasted on the premises and ground for you at very good prices.

*Fong's Fortune
2850 N. Clark St.
348-5150

*Ideal Candies
3311 N. Clark St.
327-2880

*The Ivanhoe Chalet Wine and Cheese Shop
3000 N. Clark St.
935-9400

*Kenessey Gourmets Internationale
403 W. Belmont Ave.
929-7500

*Lisi's Hors d'Oeuvre Bakery
954 W. Diversey Pkwy.
327-3455

*Martha's Candies
3257 N. Broadway
248-8733

The Mousserie
3145 N. Halsted St.
348-8700
Delicious mousse pies in flavors from Amaretto to white chocolate. Brownies and cheesecake, cakes and cookies, too. All frozen for carry-out.

*Pasta Sugo
2852 N. Broadway
327-8866

*Rahmig's House of Fine Chocolates
3109 N. Broadway
525-8338

Rainbow Grocery
946 W. Wellington Ave.
929-1400
One of the best stocked and most knowledgeable natural-foods markets.

*Rolf's Pâtisserie
621 W. Diversey Pkwy.
883-0660

Small Planet Catering
3757 N. Sheffield Ave.
549-8200
Vegetarian and natural foods for parties.

*Something's Brewing
The Century, 6th level
2828 N. Clark St.
871-7475

*Star Market
3349 N. Clark St.
472-0599

La Union Panaderia
3919 N. Sheridan Rd.
525-0445
Good-sized Mexican bakery where you wander among shelves of baked goods, picking and choosing from the pastries and cookies.

Dining and drinking

Bangkok Restaurant
3525 N. Halsted St.
327-2870
One of the first Thai restaurants in the city has become the most Americanized. Brunch buffet on weekends.

Ben's
3200 N. Lake Shore Dr.
528-0700
Good value, careful presentation, handsome setting, and a large Continental menu offering few surprises.

Bento
3328 N. Clark St.
975-5959
Reminiscent of Chinese storefronts, this friendly spot is named after the elegant Japanese packed lunch. Good food; great ginger ice cream.

*Boca del Rio
917 W. Belmont Ave.
281-6698

*Buenos Aires
2856 N. Clark St.
549-3633

*Caffé Pergolesi
3404 N. Halsted St.
472-8602

*The Casbah
514 W. Diversey Pkwy.
935-7570

*La Crêperie
2845 N. Clark St.
528-9050
You can watch the chef make the crêpes here and buy them unfilled by the dozen to take out. Lovely outdoor patio.

Far East Restaurant
510 W. Diversey Pkwy.
935-6550
Better-than-average Cantonese food. Everything on the menu's also to go.

Garfinkel's
2918 N. Clark St.
281-6500
The food doesn't measure up to the flash of the room's New York ambiance. Nice place to relax over a drink.

Gaslight Corner
2860 N. Halsted St.
348-2288
Great brats, reubens, and hamburgers in a friendly neighborhood tavern.

*Genesee Depot
3736 N. Broadway
528-6990

*Happi Sushi
3346 N. Clark St.
528-1225

El Jardin
3335 N. Clark St.
528-6775
Mexican food, a lot of warmth, and a tiny garden.

Jorge's
666 W. Diversey Pkwy.
281-3353
Amenities make up for unexceptional Mexican food. Past the steam table is an indoor patio and a guitarist.

Korea House
3301 N. Clark St.
348-3480
Very good food, excellent service. Condiments on lacquered trays and a well-appointed room put this near the top of its class.

*Lawrence of Oregano
662 W. Diversey Pkwy.
871-1916

Charlie Lui's
3805 N. Clark St.
929-3969
Good Mandarin and Szechwan food; bright and cheery.

*Matsuya
3469 N. Clark St.
248-2677

Medici on Surf
2850 N. Sheridan Rd.
929-7300
North Side outpost of a long-time Hyde Park fixture serves deep-dish pizza, burgers, pastas, and light fare in handsome surroundings. Espresso and cappuccino, too.

Nakayoshi Sushi Restaurant
919 W. Belmont Ave.
929-9333
Good, cheap sushi to take out or eat at a few tables in a woody storefront.

*La Paella
2920 N. Clark St.
528-0757

*The Paradise Café
3352 N. Broadway
348-8454
Free parking.

*Ann Sather
925 W. Belmont Ave.
348-2378

*Tango
3172 N. Sheridan Rd.
935-0350

*Victorian House Restaurant
800 W. Belmont Ave.
327-4500

Wickline's Restaurant
3335 N. Halsted St.
525-4415
Creative soups, salads, quiches, and splendid desserts at moderate prices in California-style casual setting. Don't miss the bread pudding.

Entertainment

Broadway Limited
3132 N. Broadway
935-3070
Very popular, mostly gay disco with the latest sounds and lots of mirrors.

*CrossCurrents
3206 N. Wilton Ave.
472-7884, 472-7778

*Deni's Den
2941 N. Clark St.
348-8888

The Ginger Man Tavern
3740 N. Clark St.
549-2050
Handsome hangout for off-Loop theater people has cabaret entertainment.

*His 'n' Hers
944 W. Addison St.
935-1210
Weekend cover and minimum.

*Joseph Holmes Dance Theatre
3206 N. Wilton Ave.
975-3505
(See Dance)

The Organic Theater Company
3319 N. Clark St.
327-5588
(See Theater)

Paradise Island
2848 N. Broadway
871-4200
The owners want this nightclub to be Chicago's Studio 54. Several rooms; five bars, two dance floors, live entertainment, light food, a private club, and surprises.

*The Piano Man
3801 N. Clark St.
348-8948
Music nightly; cover varies.

Stages Music Hall
3730 N. Clark St.
549-0203
Reggae, rock, jazz, and more, by out-of-town and local groups, are on the bill at this one-time theater with a wonderfully ornate stage.

Steppenwolf Theatre Company
2851 N. Halsted St.
472-4141
(See Theater)

Tuts
959 W. Belmont Ave.
477-3365
Even the el trains can't drown out the sounds at this 2nd-floor mecca for national and local New Wave, Motown, blues, and jazz.

The Wild Hare and Singing Armadillo Frog Sanctuary—A Tavern
3530 N. Clark St.
327-0800
Reggae seven nights a week.

Lakeview

Lakeview is waking up. The cash and hype that converted DePaul to an urban showcase and transformed Belmont Harbor into "swinging New Town" nibble at the neighborhood's edges. Hip refugees from the lakefront's astronomical rents rub shoulders with Latinos, Indians, Orientals, and Gypsies on the east. Artists and performance groups have snapped up some bargain-priced spaces, and on the west, astute antiques dealers have given a dying stretch of stores new life.

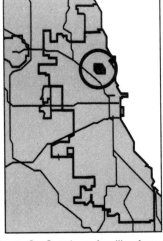

But there is a Lakeview that's untouched by this sophistication. Unlike many inner-city regional business bastions, the old-line shopping centers at Lincoln-Belmont-Ashland and Lincoln-Irving Park-Damen remain healthy, thanks to an infusion of main-line vitality from a new generation of merchants. "Roscoe Village" and parts of Lincoln Avenue are reminiscent of the neighborhood's solidly German days. On Sundays, families from the last century's narrow, wooden row houses still fill towering churches.

Lakeview's main drag, Lincoln Avenue, traces an old Indian and fur-trapper trail to the Green Bay and Fox River portages. Farms flanked "Little Fort Road" by the mid-19th century. The fields and greenhouses of the early Luxemburger and German settlers fed nearby Chicago and the Budlong sauerkraut-pickle works. A bit later, local clay pits supplied many of the bricks used to repair the Chicago Fire's ravages.

Because it was outside the city's stringent, post-Fire building codes, Lakeview boomed in the 1880s and '90s. Large landowners (including Chicago's first mayor, William B. Ogden, governor-to-be and labor supporter John P. Altgeld, and McCormick Seminary benefactor Mike Diversey) subdivided their holdings or sold them outright to developers. Big-time real estate operator S. E. Gross platted the triangle of land at Lincoln and Wellington Avenues in 1881. (A would-be author, Gross squandered much of his fortune in a protracted lawsuit charging Edmond Rostand with lifting the plot for *Chantecler* from his novel *The Merchant Prince of Cornville.*)

When the Redemptorist fathers from Old Town's St. Michael established a mission in 1882 across from Gross's subdivision, it "lay in the midst of corn fields, vegetable gardens, and clay-holes." By the time they laid the cornerstone for the magnificent **St. Alphonsus Church** (Wellington and Southport Avenues) in

1889, the surrounding land had been filled in with rows of narrow, wood-frame, peaked-roofed houses, occasionally interrupted by a brick one. Lakeview was annexed to Chicago the same year, and Lincoln Avenue became the Hauptgasse of the city's German community.

During the same period, many of the early wheelwrights and wagon makers who had served Little Fort Road's travelers adapted to increased urbanization by building furniture. Some, like Heinrich Birren and Christian Krauspe, were also casketmakers and undertakers—a lucrative sideline. Funeral parlors run by their descendants are still in the community. For others, furniture making led to furniture retailing and, until the late 1950s, the Lincoln-Belmont shopping area had the largest concentration of furniture stores outside the Loop.

Those elegant emporiums have given way to credit and chain outlets, but Wieboldt's department store, in Lakeview's 200-shop commercial core, still maintains a separate furniture annex. **Peerless Rug and Linoleum Co.** (3028 North Lincoln Avenue) stocks just about everything to put under furniture: vinyl, parquet, slate, and quarry tiles; wall-to-wall carpeting; area rugs and mill ends; and a surprising variety of fine rugs (Oriental, Chinese, American Indian, and designer carpets). An excellent catalogue is available by mail, and the semiannual sales offer some dramatic price cuts.

H. C. Struve opened the area's first dry goods store in 1904 but, with remarkable prescience, sold out to Goldblatt's in 1929. Lincoln-Belmont's lower-priced department store anchor closed in 1981, but dozens of stores peddle everything from old-line, going-to-church outfits to jeans, T-shirts, inexpensive sportswear, and trendy Latino duds. The clothing and shoe chain stores look the same from neighborhood to neighborhood, but **Schreck Army Navy Surplus** (3100 North Lincoln Avenue) is one of a kind. The cavernous wholesale/retail warehouse is crammed to the rafters with enough battle-chic goodies to outfit a small army. Parkas, jackets, and coats jam the racks; tables are buried under head-high piles of pants, shirts, sweaters, gloves, and socks—a quartermaster's olive-drab dream from a dozen countries. Prices aren't low, but there's nothing drab about the quality.

If you like furniture with the patina of age, check out the nearby antiques shops. **Lincoln Avenue Antiques** (2954) is the best of the lot. Prices may be a bit high, but knowledgeable owner Gary Gist's large stock of mostly turn-of-the-century furniture in oak, maple, walnut, and cherry is tops. A good selection of leaded-glass lamp shades complements the collection.

The city's golden oak El Dorado is on Belmont Avenue between Ravenswood and Western Avenues. More than a score of dealers sell everything from vintage American and European furniture, wicker, and accessories to Depression-era kitchen gadgets, knickknacks, and collectibles, plus antique store fixtures and slot and pinball machines. Hours are unpredictable, but almost all the stores are open on weekends. Merely seeing the rehab jobs that have been done on some of the century-old buildings is a pleasure.

Working the entire strip could take days, but if you have only hours, several stores are musts. **Eaton Place Antiques** (1951) displays nicely refinished Victorian and turn-of-the-century furniture and a few smaller antiques in virtual room settings. The shop also provides complete restoration services. **The Good Old Days** (2138) stocks similar furniture, perhaps in greater profusion, as well as stained glass, brass chandeliers and floor lamps, crystal, jewelry, old radios, and some smaller collectibles. Prices are reasonable, and the store has been beautifully redone. For golden oak, cherry, walnut, and mahogany perfectly refinished to a high glow and priced to match, check out **Cokes Antiques** (2129). The tables, dressers, and iceboxes couldn't have looked as good from the factory. An overwhelming assortment of collectibles for tops of tables, dressers, and shelves can be found at the cluttered **Addie's Attic** (2306): Depression glass, badges, jewelry, dishes and vintage kitchenware—all modestly priced. **Frantz Antiques** (2323) is the antithesis: Carefully chosen pieces are shown with gallerylike precision (and prices) in a lovingly renovated building. The spare selection includes hand-refinished furniture, a bit of jewelry, a Victorian gown or two, and antique textiles.

The Leather Works (2057) specializes in revitalizing old leather. Besides being one of the few places in the city that cleans, repairs, reupholsters, and redyes leather furniture, the shop also revives old hide and other clothing that most cleaners won't touch, restores luggage and riding gear, and, generally, does wonders with almost anything made of leather.

If you've picked up a great stained-glass window with a cracked panel, consider taking it to **Drehobl Brothers Art Glass Co.** (2847 North Lincoln Avenue), the city's oldest family-owned art-glass business. Frank Drehobl started the firm in 1919. His son and other family members custom make stained- and beveled-glass windows for commercial customers and individuals, and they work magic on old stained glass from all over the country, including pieces created decades ago by the company. Samples of Drehobl's work can be seen in museum collections, at Anshe Emet Synagogue (3760 North Pine Grove Avenue), and in the "interior sky-dome" of Wieboldt's State Street store.

Moldering old paintings find new life at Zivko Zic's **Lincoln Gallery** (3107 North Lincoln Avenue). A courtly gentleman, Zic studied medicine in Rome after his family fled postwar Yugoslavia, but gave that up to enroll in the Accademia di Belle Arti. His strong, boldly brushed paintings drew acclaim in Argentina (where he had a joint show with Henry Moore) during a 14-year wait for U.S. immigration papers. Since arriving in Chicago in 1962, Zic has been framing and restoring art, while selling his own work throughout the country. Don't be misled by the sign in the window advertising music boxes: That's his wife's sideline.

The **Anhalt Book Store** (1710 West Belmont Avenue), another multifaceted shop, is a link with Lakeview's past. The Fornberg family has been selling German books here since 1928; as a result of reduced demand they have added bookbinding and picture framing.

Many delicatessens, bakeries, and restaurants dotting the area also recall its Germanic heyday. Canny German-food lovers flock from afar to **Kuhn's Delicatessen** (3053 North Lincoln Avenue), a venerable Deutsche Supermarkt with aisles of tinned goods, packaged puddings, luxurious jams, chocolates, cookies, liquors, wines, beers, and other imported delicacies, as well as breads from half a dozen bakeries. The women bustling behind the city's best-stocked, Germanic deli counters unerringly greet English-speaking customers in English, Teutonic ones in German. They patiently guide novices through a landscape of cheeses, salads, prepared meats and fish, a score of wursts, and a dozen varieties of ham including lachsschinken, which resembles lox. Prices aren't low, and everything from sülzkotelett—pork chop and egg glistening in aspic—to chunks of unsalted butter hacked from a pale yellow, farm-fresh mound is top quality. Take a number for the deli counter and browse until your turn comes—on busy Saturdays, as long as a half hour.

Kuhn's carries some pastries, but **Dinkel's Bakery** (3329 North Lincoln Avenue) overflows with breads of all sorts, rolls, outstanding butter cookies (Mexican as well as German), tortes, great cheesecake, sinfully rich whipped-cream creations, and superb stollen and fruitcake. Mornings, this large, family-run store serves free coffee so you can enjoy the goodies on the spot (no tables, though).

In addition to homemade sausages, the **Paulina Meat Market** (3352 North Paulina Street) offers one of Chicago's best selections of meats. Skilled, helpful butchers not only cut to order, but also fill the display cases with specialty cuts that reflect cooking trends. But expect to wait: The shop gets crowded and some customers discuss each purchase as if they were buying a sculpture. In the shadow of St. Alphonsus, the half-timbered **Zum Deutschen Eck** (2924 North Southport Avenue) serves hearty (though not outstanding) fare at reasonable prices. At this multiroomed spot, the joviality peaks on weekends when live music and community singing create a happy din, which makes the food taste just about perfect. Costumed waitresses and weekend entertainment are also attractions at **Schwaben Stube** (3500 North Lincoln Avenue), a standby with solid "continental" food: sauerbraten and spätzle, pork shank with sauerkraut, wienerschnitzel, and roast duck. If you want to test the limits of *gemütlichkeit,* try **Math Igler's Casino** (1627 West Melrose Street) where the food is forgettable, but the unashamedly corny entertainment (including singing waiters) is carried out with great style.

The pace is slower in "Roscoe Village," a few blocks from Lincoln Avenue's bustle. This broad, semicommercial, four-block stretch of Roscoe Street west of Damen Avenue seems frozen in time. The **Riverview Nostalgia Shop** (2040) is devoted to the memory of that lost, but not unmourned, nearby landmark. Until it was demolished in 1967, Riverview Amusement Park was the world's largest— 70 acres of roller coasters, fun houses, kiddy rides, midway booths, and side shows. It all started in 1903 when a hunter, William Schmidt, acquired an abandoned clay pit along the Chicago River, where he and fellow nimrods were accustomed to wander, and opened Schuetzen Park. Picnic tables and a few little rides for children were added in 1905 to amuse the riflemen's families, and the name was changed to Riverview Sharpshooter's Park. When a fanciful carousel was delivered three years later, Riverview Amusement Park was born.

The **Black Forest Meat Market** (2002) conjures up the past with jars and tins of imported delicacies stacked on old-fashioned wood shelves over meat counters bursting with Bela Mohapp's own smoked hams, bacon, sausages, sublime salamis, and wondrous wursts (try the goose liver). The accommodating butchers trim the meat with a care that would win plaudits from the American Heart Association. Other businesses on the strip include several taverns; a couple of card stores and beauty parlors; a music school; two small curio shops; the **Schleswig-Holsteiner Sängerbund** (2044), a private club with public Tuesday-night bingo; **Europa House** (2125), a restaurant-bar with modestly priced German food and nightly organ music; and **Heck's Bakery** (2038), which offers ordinary pastries but usually has inexpensive Black Forest cakes on hand.

Better sweets can be found in the heart of Belmont Avenue's antiques-store row at **Phillip's Butter Kist Bakery** (1955 West Belmont Avenue). This 1950s-looking shop makes excellent Austrian pastries, melt-in-your-mouth butter cookies and pound cake, tasty breads, and the usual Danishes and cakes. The oak bread cabinets in the ma-and-pa **Reynen's Bakery** (3056 North Southport Avenue) were probably antiques when the present owner's family opened the shop in 1936. Everything—the coarse pumpernickel, butter cookies, and sweet rolls— looks like someone's grandmother baked it.

Another old-line spot on Southport Avenue is part of a shopping strip that grew up around the Ravenswood el stop. Locals hang out and talk soccer at the **Hansa Inn** (3356), a very German bar with an adjoining lunch restaurant and a summer beer garden. Mixed in with several other restaurants and taverns are the usual convenience stores, a nice bookshop, and the **Music Box Theatre** (3733), which shows Arabic films on weekends.

The street marks a subtle but real division. To the east, homes—many delightful, stone-fronted Victorians—owed development more to the el than to Lincoln Avenue. A large Swedish community centered around Belmont Avenue was one of many ethnic enclaves that made this section cosmopolitan. The area remains polyglot today, but the names have changed. The 1000 block of Belmont Avenue hosts an Indian supermarket with a restaurant annex, an Hispanic bakery serving Cuban sandwiches, an aikido academy, and a Philippine trading company store as large as the nearby Polk Brothers. The 1883 Gothic Trinity Lutheran Church (Seminary and Barry Avenues), one of half a dozen Protestant churches built in the same period within a block or two, is now the **Church of the Valley,** a Spanish Assembly of God congregation. The streetscape's a bit seedy but a change is in the offing.

Two taverns a few blocks apart tell the whole story. **Leo's Southport Lanes** (3325 North Southport Avenue) sports Black Forest décor in a taproom with Arian-nymph murals over the bar and an adjoining four-lane bowling alley, the last one in the city with human pinsetters. A similar, old, Schlitz-built bar, on the other hand, caters to the new Lakeview. **Gaspars** (3159 North Southport Avenue) was into New Wave for awhile, but now the spare clubroom features an intriguing pastiche of folk, jazz, and rock—both national and local acts.

Affluent sophisticates from nearby Lincoln Park and New Town support many more retrofitted Lakeview performance spaces. **The Theatre Building** (1225 West Belmont Avenue), a strikingly renovated chocolate warehouse with three theaters, hosts many companies. The **MoMing Dance and Arts Center** (1034 West Barry Avenue) occupies the old Trinity Lutheran School. The **New Haven Playhouse Company** (2956 North Racine Avenue), an acting school and theater, has revitalized an old storefront. Rehabbers saying "Lakeview is hot!" are right.

Interesting places

Belmont Bowl
1637 W. Belmont Ave.
Closed. This rococo-façaded building was originally the Balaban & Katz Belmont Theater. Plans are afoot to turn it into a shopping mall.

"Central Lakeview Tapestry," mural
Southeast corner, Kenmore and Belmont Aves.
A project of Esther Charbit and the Chicago Mural Group. Larger-than-life faces smile in the spirit of brotherhood.

*Church of the Valley
Seminary and Barry Aves.
525-4254

"Herstory," mural
Underpass, Addison St. and Lincoln Ave.
Anna Marie Coveny directed this bicentennial project celebrating women in U. S. history. Well preserved, surprisingly free of graffiti.

Lane Technical High School
2501 W. Addison St.
935-7205
Until 1971 a boys-only school, the Board of Education's Lane enjoys a solid academic reputation, especially in math and science, and is a tough, no-nonsense place with a strong school spirit. Constructed in 1934; WPA murals grace the assembly hall's entrance and fire curtain, the library, and the cafeteria.

Lincoln Ave. and George St. wholesale district
At 2900 N. Lincoln Ave.
Swift and Armour were part of this meat and poultry wholesaling area during its heyday in the '20s. Of the remaining firms, only George Street Packing Co. (2933 N. Lincoln Ave., 248-5960) sells retail—5- to 6-lb. boxes of frozen steaks, patties, pork chops, etc., at lower-than-store prices.

Lincoln Turners Gymnasium
1019 W. Diversey Pkwy.
248-1682
Originally the Turnverein Lincoln, a German gymnastic club.

*St. Alphonsus Church
Wellington and Southport
525-0709
Façade, stairs, and veranda of blue Bedford rock seem timeless, but the church was gutted by fire in 1939, and the interior and sidewalls had to be completely rebuilt. Still served by Redemptorist fathers, many of whom are now Irish, "St. Al's" has German Mass Sundays. The adjoining Athenaeum Theater has been leased by a variety of performance groups.

St. Benedict Church
Irving Park Rd. and Leavitt
588-6484
Established in 1901, this was the last parish in the neighborhood that could be termed German. A grand church.

*Schleswig-Holsteiner Sängerbund
2044 W. Roscoe St.
348-9765

Sheil Park
3505 N. Southport Ave.
929-3070
Modern field house without any park to speak of. Full schedule of activities includes drama and music.

Shopping and services

*Anhalt Book Store
1710 W. Belmont Ave.
472-1880

Bookman's Corner
3454 N. Southport Ave.
929-8298
Good selection of used, nonfiction books; much art, architecture.

Chicago Music Company
3530 N. Lincoln Ave.
472-1023
Sells and repairs musical instruments—particularly guitars, drums, and keyboards. Also sells lots of accessories and gives lessons.

Chicago Stripper
2965 N. Lincoln Ave.
477-8776
Expert furniture stripping in a lovingly restored frame building.

Darkroom Aids
3449 N. Lincoln Ave.
248-4301
More used photographic equipment than just about anywhere. New stuff, too. Several hundred old cameras (not for sale) line the hallway—a real museum.

Discovery Center
2930 N. Lincoln Ave.
348-8120
Classes in calligraphy, yoga, photography, and anything else that comes up when they match a competent instructor with interested students.

*Drehobl Brothers Art Glass Co.
2847 N. Lincoln Ave.
281-2022

Floral Designs Inc.
3021 N. Southport Ave.
528-9800
Greenhouse and one of the firm's three retail outlets. Sophisticated floral arrangements.

Fran's Miniatures
3831 N. Lincoln Ave.
525-1770
Craftsman-built dollhouses and kits, as well as lots of tiny furnishings.

Emma Goldman Women's Health Center
2114 W. Belmont Ave.
528-4310
A self-help clinic and referral service for women.

Kazi Publications
1215 W. Belmont Ave.
327-7598
Islamic books; also has Middle Eastern art objects and clothing.

Lava-Simplex International
1650 W. Irving Park Rd.
528-6000
The factory store sells everything the company makes at discount prices: Lava Lites (remember them?), Waves (blue liquid in a motorized box), Infinity Boxes (lighted boxes with a rotating tunnel that looks endless).

The Learning Exchange
2940 N. Lincoln Ave.
549-8383
Not-for-profit educational and recreational telephone referral service matches students with teachers of 6,000 subjects.

*The Leather Works
2057 W. Belmont Ave.
871-1863

*Lincoln Gallery
3107 N. Lincoln Ave.
248-3647

Merz Bros. Apothecary
2921 N. Lincoln Ave.
525-0184
A Deutsche Apotheke dispensing proprietary medicines since 1875.

Midwest Aikido Center
3943 N. Lincoln Ave.
477-0123
The aikido martial art of Morihei Ueshiba, taught and demonstrated by Akira Tohei.

Monastery Hill Bindery Ernst Hertzberg and Sons
1751 W. Belmont Ave.
525-4126
More than a century old, this firm leather binds books, restores old ones, and specializes in paper and book conservation for universities and libraries. Leather-bound dictionaries and blank books in stock.

Northern Golf Ball Co.
2350 W. Roscoe St.
472-1760
Everything for the golfer at 15%-20% off list price. Lots of used golf balls and top-brand new ones.

*Peerless Rug and Linoleum Co.
3028 N. Lincoln Ave.
525-4876

The Philippine World
1051 W. Belmont Ave.
248-5100
A huge store with loads of wicker, rattan, bentwood, carved and inlaid-wood furniture (mostly for living and dining rooms) from Victorian-style to modern. Also has baskets, wood bowls, carvings, purses and shoes, and a food section.

Plowshares
1216 W. Diversey Pkwy.
281-9040
Not-for-profit shop sells handcrafted items, mostly from Third World countries.

Prescott Reed Manufacturing Co.
1840 W. Irving Park Rd.
935-6870
Manufactures reeds, also repairs reed instruments, and carries a full line of harmonicas.

Roosevelt Chair & Supply Co.
1717 W. Belmont Ave.
248-3700
Rent everything you need for parties.

Rose Records
3259 N. Ashland Ave.
528-8827
Just about everything, including salsa, reggae, comedy, and nostalgia.

*Schreck Army Navy Surplus
3100 N. Lincoln Ave.
477-0112

Tom Tooley Graphics
3100 N. Southport Ave.
871-3138
Imaginative graphic artist tackles any job, including customizing motorcycle gas tanks.

Victor-Ace
1300 W. Barry Ave.
348-7777
Hand washes fine linens and drapes.

Wooden Music Co.
3824 N. Lincoln Ave.
472-7250
Sells and repairs guitars and other stringed instruments.

Shopping and services: Antiques

*Addie's Attic
2306 W. Belmont Ave.
525-8497

Antique Store Fixtures and Display
1900 W. Belmont Ave.
281-6495
Just what the name implies.

Belmont Antique Gallery
2310 W. Belmont Ave.
248-6366
Buy where the dealers buy. A jumble of furniture, mostly from the 1920s and '30s.

By Gone Treasures
1919 W. Belmont Ave.
549-2388
Sparse, well-chosen selection of collectibles, glassware, and dishes, plus a small room of costumes.

*Cokes Antiques
2129 W. Belmont Ave.
935-1200

The Cradle
2252 W. Belmont Ave.
528-4515
Small store crowded with 20th-century collectibles: Depression glass, kitchenware, a bit of vintage clothing, and more.

*Eaton Place Antiques
1951 W. Belmont Ave.
281-3231

*Frantz Antiques
2323 W. Belmont Ave.
327-6676

*The Good Old Days
2138 W. Belmont Ave.
472-8837

Harlon's Antiques
3058 N. Lincoln Ave.
327-3407
Small, cluttered, and fun to poke around in.

Kismet Vintage Clothing
2934 N. Lincoln Ave.
528-4497
Cluttered as an Oriental bazaar, with clothes and accessories from the '30s to the early '50s, most in the class of thrift-store finds.

*Lincoln Avenue Antiques
2954 N. Lincoln Ave.
477-6180

Miscellania
1800 W. Belmont Ave.
348-9647
All sorts of stuff from the '20s to the '40s. Always has something useless you can't live without. Reasonable prices.

Modern Art
2217 W. Belmont Ave.
975-4088
Good source for chrome accessories, super clocks, and radios; some furniture and other Art Deco collectibles.

On Belmont Antiques
1903 W. Belmont Ave.
248-4822
Refinished turn-of-the-century and later oak furniture; some smaller stuff. Lots of brass and architectural fixtures. Stripping, refinishing, and brass and copper polishing, too.

Penny Lane Antiques
2343 W. Belmont Ave.
929-3444
"Antique Coin Operated Machines and Misc. Antiques." This says it all.

The Renovation Source
3512 N. Southport Ave.
327-1250
A warehouse of mostly wood architectural pieces: mantels, doors, stair railings, lavatory pedestals, and some reproductions, including tin ceilings. Stuff sold as is (some has been stripped). Also an architectural firm.

*Riverview Nostalgia Shop
2040 W. Roscoe St.
871-1542
Riverview, world's fair, and transportation memorabilia. Ralph Lopez also gives Riverview lectures. Open weekday evenings and Saturday.

Studio V
2908 N. Lincoln Ave.
528-9816
Large, handsome, exposed-brick-and-tin-ceiling store. Men's and women's vintage clothing, much like that at Kismet. Also Art Deco and decorative pieces.

Task Force Militaria
2341 W. Belmont Ave.
477-7096
Domestic and foreign uniforms, medals, and other military memorabilia.

The Wicker Witch of Chicago
2146 W. Belmont Ave.
528-5550
Wicker and other antiques in good condition in a lovely store which rents to photographers and also does wicker repairs.

Foodstuffs

Alexis Chocolate Shop
1631 W. Belmont Ave.
281-4141
A tiny store with a small selection of inexpertly hand-dipped chocolates, good fudge, and "taffy" apples.

*Black Forest Meat Market
2002 W. Roscoe St.
348-3660

*Dinkel's Bakery
3329 N. Lincoln Ave.
281-7300

*Heck's Bakery
2038 W. Roscoe St.
472-1812
Also at 4006 N. Lincoln Ave.

India Gifts and Foods
1031 W. Belmont Ave.
348-4393
Good selection of Indian foodstuffs, including large sweets counter; records and tapes; sari fabrics (mostly polyester), Madras prints; and a bit of giftware. Not too clean.

George L. Jewell Catering
1110 W. Belmont Ave.
935-6316
Well-known caterer creates individualized menus for the "beautiful people."

*Kuhn's Delicatessen
3053 N. Lincoln Ave.
525-9019, 525-4595
Another branch: Deerbrook Mall, Lake-Cook and Waukegan Rds., Deerfield.

Latin American Bakery
1010 W. Belmont Ave.
477-2320
Hispanic bakery serves Cuban sandwiches at its lunch counter.

Meyer Import Delicatessen
3306 N. Lincoln Ave.
281-8979
A smaller version of Kuhn's.

Oriental Store of Chicago
1804 W. Irving Park Rd.
348-0222
A large, supermarket-type operation providing groceries to the Filipino community.

*Paulina Meat Market
3352 N. Paulina St.
248-6272

*Phillip's Butter Kist Bakery
1955 W. Belmont Ave.
281-4150

Reliable Liquors
3066 N. Lincoln Ave.
935-0505
A huge store with a very good selection of German, Yugoslavian, and Hungarian wines. Loads of liqueurs and brandies, some open for tasting.

*Reynen's Bakery
3056 N. Southport Ave.
281-9532

Ziggy's Meat Market
1839 W. Irving Park Rd.
935-1840
Serbian homemade sausages, smoked meats, fresh kajmak (a cheesy-buttery spread), and imported ajvar (red pepper relish). There's still a small Serbian community in Lakeview.

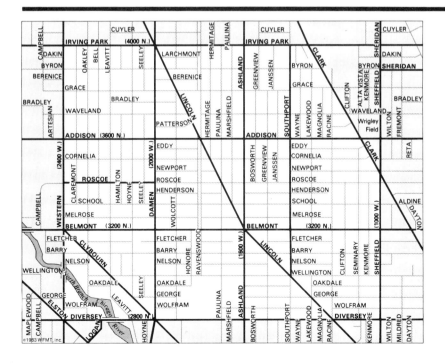

©1983 WFMT, Inc.

Dining and drinking

Cozy Cafe #1
2819 N. Lincoln Ave.
549-9374
Cozy Cafe #3
1846 W. Belmont Ave.
525-9731
North Side slicks learn down-home tricks with biscuits, grits, and red-eye gravy at these greasy spoons.

*Europa House
2125 W. Roscoe St.
528-2562

Garden of Happiness
3450 N. Lincoln Ave.
348-2120
A large place offering Korean, Japanese, and Mandarin specialties. Stick with Korean and ask for menu translation to sample the more exotic dishes. Several "teahouses"; music and dancing in one room.

Gordana's
2007 W. Irving Park Rd.
935-7044
A demure, slightly expensive Yugoslavian spot.

*Hansa Inn
3356 N. Southport Ave.
248-7276

House of Hunan
3150 N. Lincoln, 2nd floor
327-0427
Different owners and lower quality than House of Hunan on Michigan Ave.

*Math Igler's Casino
1627 W. Melrose St.
935-2000

Leona's Pizzeria
3215 N. Sheffield Ave.
327-8861
Small, New York-chic-looking spot serves thin-crust and pan pizza, sandwiches, Italian specialties, ribs, and chicken.

Moti Mahal Restaurant
1033 W. Belmont Ave.
348-4392
Part of India Gifts and Foods. Squalid, inexpensive spot invites take-out business. A good idea.

Old Serbian Village
1841 W. Irving Park Rd.
935-1840
The meats from Ziggy's next door, which owns the place, are transformed into ražnjići ćevapcici, and other treats.

Pops for Champagne
2934 N. Sheffield Ave.
472-1000
Classy wine bar pours an impressive array of the bubbly and serves appetizers and desserts.

Resi's Bierstube
2034 W. Irving Park Rd.
472-1749
Enjoy 48 imported beers—many of them German, including four Weissbiers—in a beer garden with real trees and grape vines or in a bar decorated with military paraphernalia. A fine way to wash down German food.

*Schwaben Stube
3500 N. Lincoln Ave.
528-1142

Sheffield's
3258 N. Sheffield Ave.
281-4978
Zippy, new-Lakeview-style neighborhood tavern with a woody, late-'30s backbar, recorded jazz, and an outdoor beer garden in summer.

Thai Villa
3811 N. Lincoln Ave.
472-9478
A few Vietnamese offerings along with the better-known Thai fare.

*Zum Deutschen Eck
2924 N. Southport Ave.
525-8389

Entertainment

Asi es Colombia
3910 N. Lincoln Ave.
348-7444
Food is only fair; entertainment is spectacular if you like Latin jazz; dancing. See if you remember how to do the bossa nova or tango.

Clearwater Saloon
3447 N. Lincoln Ave.
935-6545
A friendly, down-home spot where country rock is the standard fare; occasional forays into bluegrass.

*Gaspars
3159 N. Southport Ave.
871-6680
Entertainment almost every night; dancing in the back room; and a fine juke box in the bar.

*Leo's Southport Lanes
3325 N. Southport Ave.
472-1601

Mr. Kiley's
1125 W. Belmont Ave.
No phone
Freewheeling country-rock place with a 4-a.m. license.

*MoMing Dance and Arts Center
1034 W. Barry Ave.
472-9894
(See Dance)

*Music Box Theatre
3733 N. Southport Ave.
871-2235

*New Haven Playhouse Co.
2956 N. Racine Ave.
327-5550
Acting classes on three tracks for casual dabblers, aspiring thespians, and professionals. Several productions a year.

Schulein's
2100 W. Irving Park Rd.
478-2100
Chicago memorabilia cover the walls of this former speakeasy, a handsome, woody tavern and restaurant with a fine backbar and white linens. Four generations of Schuleins have amused patrons with card tricks and other magic. The present practitioners prove nightly that the hand is quicker than the eye.

*The Theatre Building
1225 W. Belmont Ave.
327-5252
Home of Pary Productions and the Performance Community; host to other companies. (See Theater.)

Lincoln Square

Lincoln Square is best known as Chicago's new Greektown, successor to the bulldozed Halsted Street original, but the blaze of Hellenic signs doesn't tell the whole story. Eastern European food stores and restaurants dot the streets; a varied Oriental presence includes more than a smattering of Korean enterprises; and vestiges of a Teutonic heyday still line Lincoln Avenue.

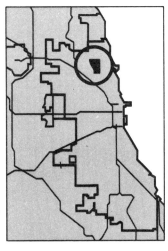

"Reflections of Ravenswood" (off Leland and Western Avenues, near the el station), a bold, naïve mural, catalogues the community's 125-year history in a splash of symbols: farmers and fruitstands, a brickworks and a church, a tram and an omnibus, Riverview Amusement Park and the Krause Music Store, the 1956 Lincoln statue and the pylon marking the recent shopping-mall treatment of Lincoln Avenue between the mural and statue.

The images seem so familiar because the neighborhood shares a common history with many of Chicago's once-upon-a-time suburbs. German families from Old Town pushed northward along Lincoln Avenue into Lakeview Township after the Fire. Some established St. Alphonsus parish on Wrightwood; others settled around Irving Park Road, building St. Benedict; and yet more eventually founded **St. Matthias** (Ainslie Street and Claremont Avenue) in 1887. While the present red-brick basilica was dedicated in 1916, the original frame church wasn't built in the wilderness, but rather in a Swedish and Luxemburger agricultural settlement known, after an early resident, as Bowmanville. As this German community grew, the general area's focus shifted to Lawrence and Western Avenues from the nearby, earlier suburb of Ravenswood, a subdivision laid out by the Ravenswood Land Company in 1868 and served by a Chicago and North Western station at Wilson Avenue.

Immigration transformed the farms, greenhouses, and brickworks into a neighborhood of frame houses and cottages of modest scale compared to the grander homes of adjoining Ravenswood. When annexed to Chicago in 1893, the community was heavily residential. By the time streetcars began rumbling down Lincoln, Lawrence, and Damen Avenues in 1900, these routes were commercial arteries. Completion of the Ravenswood elevated in 1907 solidly welded the area to 20th-century Chicago but, since then, the streetscape has changed slowly. No rush of high-rise construction disrupted the essentially family charac-

ter of the neighborhood; three-flats and small apartment buildings filled in occasional blocks instead. Always overshadowed by the more vibrant Lakeview
and Uptown shopping strips, all-dressed-up-with-no-place-to-go Lincoln/West-
ern escaped booms and busts.

Little of the present-day lakefront sophistication penetrates Lincoln Square.
From the Sears, Roebuck and Company department store at Wolcott Avenue to
the cluster of Greek emporiums at Western Avenue, Lawrence Avenue is an
unremarkable neighborhood shopping street, notable only for the many auto-
parts stores and body shops that herald Western Avenue's car-lot row. Damen
Avenue's spotty commercial strips abut lovely Queen Anne houses, offering little
more than a few groceries, bakeries, taverns, and secondhand/collectibles
shops. Beyond the ethnic enclaves, only a few special retailers demand attention.

The city's oldest pet shop, **Vahle's Bird Store** (4710 North Damen Avenue),
started in New York City in 1866 and moved here in the 1890s. A colorful flurry
of canaries, parakeets, parrots, macaws, finches, and cockatoos chirps and
squawks away in this wonderful aviary, much to the consternation of the mouse
and hampster populations. (The fish don't seem to mind.)

You've probably seen some of John Prater's strong, California-feeling,
macramé wallhangings in restaurants such as Mel Markon's. Although he works
mostly with natural fibers, his **Macramé Workshop** (2215 West Lawrence Avenue) also stocks a broad range of synthetic rope, as well as all the necessary ac-
coutrements, accessories, and books. Prater gives lessons that help the neo-
phyte knotter tie into his craft, and his for-sale finished works provide inspiration.

Set back from the street, the two-story **Griffins & Gargoyles** (2140 West
Lawrence Avenue) is easy to miss, but don't. The neighborhood's classiest antiques store is crammed with American and European period furniture including
lots of case pieces, armoires, dining sets, and smaller items, too, priced to reflect
the collection's quality. While much of the furniture at **Penn-Dutchman Antiques** (4912 North Western Avenue) is nothing special, every drawer in every
dresser, sideboard, and highboy hides some collectible treasure. A flea market's worth of old photographs, magazines, other paper ephemera, badges, jewelry, dishes, glassware, kitchen gadgets, and more lines the walls in all four
rooms, jams display counters, and clutters tables. Plan on spending at least an
hour to look at everything.

Lincoln Avenue is the place to find Teutonic portables. German books and
magazines, beer steins, bric-a-brac, and all the paraphernalia to make a recreation room a rathskeller fill **Schmid Imports** (4606), and Heinz Holz's **Lincoln
Music Center** (4613) can make it sound like one. The city's largest selection of
German, Swiss, and Austrian records runs from current pop hits to classical and
folk music.

For eatables and potables, head to **Delicatessen Meyer** (4750). This crowded, Old World-like shop stocks more than 50 varieties of sausages; baked hams,
pork, and beef; homemade leberkäse, a smooth veal meat loaf sometimes laced
with mushrooms or bacon; prepared seasonal salads such as herring (winter)
and noodle (summer); cheeses; honeys; jams; imported tinned foods; German
wines and liquors; even toiletries. **North Star Bakery** (4545) sells only bread—
but what bread! The kommisbrot, bauernbrot, and pumpernickel are the real
things, served by better German restaurants. Time your visit right, and they'll be
hot from the oven.

Pastries laden with chocolate, butter cream torte slices, fruit-topped squares,
beautiful cakes, and delicious butter cookies are all irresistible at the **European
Pastry Shop** (4701), an inviting bakery made more cheery by several tables
where you can linger over coffee and goodies and soak up the European atmosphere. Only zither music and Orson Welles lurking in the shadows are missing

from **Lutz's Continental Café and Pastry Shop** (2458 West Montrose Avenue). Behind the city's best-stocked German bakery is a trim dining room, but the real treat is the tranquil, plant-filled, walled patio. On summer evenings, this is the perfect place to enjoy a light meal, the tortes—rich and sweet in the Austro-German style—and *kaffee mit schlag,* all served on individual trays set with lovely china. The sandwiches are okay, but avoid the ladies'-lunch hot food.

For more substantial fare, try **Heidelberger Fass** (4300 North Lincoln Avenue). The extensive menu offers thick kasseler ribs, wiener rostbraten, sauerbraten, schnitzels, several sausages, fish, and an occasional roast-goose special. Bountiful dinners include relishes, soup, salad, and trimmings. Costumed waitresses and a pleasant din punctuated by timely announcements from the many cuckoo clocks make the cozy, artifact-filled rooms very festive. Not as atmospheric, **Hogen's** (4560) and **Treffpunkt** (4743) have shorter menus, but these neighborhood spots can't be beat for values like a lunch-time bratwurst washed down with a German beer. Like many local taverns, Treffpunkt has live music some evenings.

There's a time-forgotten quality about the German businesses in the Lincoln Square mall, but the Greek community, anchored by **St. Demetrios Greek Orthodox Church** (Winona Street and Washtenaw Avenue), shouts with a newcomer's vigor. A modest basilica-type structure built in 1928, the church contains some interesting iconography, but its real strength lies in the community center, library, and 500-student Solon Greek School, modern additions that wrap around the building and keep old traditions alive. The complex is a magnet for immigrants, and even those who have left the neighborhood return every summer for the parish festival. (*See Annual Events.*)

Along Lawrence Avenue, Greek shop signs, old women in black, and men palavering in coffeehouses provide Mediterranean spice, and mural-decorated restaurants beckon customers with promises of succulent lamb, aromatic red snapper, and flaming cheese. The call has been heeded by so many that **Family House** (2421) expanded several times to keep up with the demand for their fresh seafood, complimentary appetizers, and modest prices on a full range of Greek specialties. The décor is a pastiche of plastic arbors and hunting-lodge accouterments, and the large place is still crowded on weekends. At **Grecian Psistaria** (2412), the menu is weighted towards traditional lamb dishes. When musicians take the stage nightly, forget about intimate conversation.

Off the beaten path, **Lindos** (5035 North Lincoln Avenue) serves Greektown's best food in its most sedate atmosphere. Everything from cooked-rare-as-ordered lamb chops and fresh red snapper to stewlike beef stifado is terrific, and service is competent and friendly. For a full-blown floor show complete with belly dancers, head to **The Athens** (4726 North Western Avenue) but be warned that the Greek entrées are a couple of bucks more here than at most places (and usually not as good), and a bottle of Retsina might set you back $20!

Naturally, all the ingredients for preparing a Greek meal at home are available nearby. In addition to a good selection of olives and cheeses, the **West Meat Market** (2549 West Lawrence Avenue) sells almost every part of the lamb except the wool. Lamb heads stare up from display cases, surrounded by chops, shanks, breasts, livers, kidneys, and brains. **John's Import Foods** (2611) not only carries a full line of Greek staples but also Italian and Arabic ones, especially condiments and spices. Shop here for couscous mix, bashmatti rice, tahini, and rosewater. The little **Psarpoula Fish House** (4755 North Rockwell Street) is the place to go for most of the fish used in Greek cooking, including sea bass, squid, octopus, and shrimp. The selection is best on Mondays, Wednesdays, and Fridays. **Tom's Delicatessen and Bakery** (2612 West Lawrence Avenue) stocks some of everything: wines and liquors, cold cuts, cheeses, other standard deli fare, and Greek breads—the same great ones that once came from a hole-in-the-wall bakery a couple of doors away. Rotisseried lambs, pigs, and chickens are available on weekends.

Satisfy a sweet tooth at **Akropol Pastry Shop** (2601) where the Tiravolos brothers turn out masterful wedding and birthday cakes. Also fine are the kourabiedes (butter cookies with crushed almonds), melomakarona (honey cookies with walnuts and cinnamon), and honey-drenched baklava. Akropol even carries dough for do-it-yourselfers.

For Eastern European goodies with a reassuring homemade look, head to **Tomas Bakery** (4054 North Lincoln Avenue). Everything from bread to cookies is first-rate. The whipped-cream creations are out of this world, and the napoléons will take you back to the Old Country. Continue the culinary trip with Magyar delights from the marvelous **European Sausage House** (4361): debreceni sausage, diszno sagt (head cheese), and paprikas szalona (garlicky, cured pork jaw). The shop also carries robust Hungarian sweet and hot paprikas (worlds better than the common Spanish variety), prune or apricot lekvar (a kind of preserve), and strudel from the Bon Ton.

Shopping for sausages in Lincoln Square is a treat. **Michael Fless Homemade Sausage** (4452 North Western Avenue) produces a dazzling array of wursts and smoked meats, mostly German-style, but some Hungarian and Serbian. The Serbian selection is better at **George's Delicatessen** (1964 West Lawrence Avenue). The store is a ready link to the homeland with sausages,

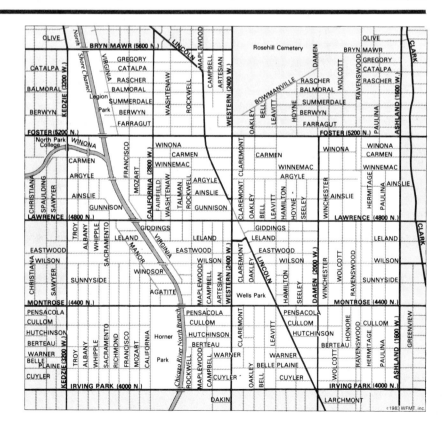

smoked meats, fresh kajmak (a spread that looks and tastes like a mix of butter and cream cheese), imported ajvar (a vinegary red-pepper relish), and Yugoslavian wines.

Prices are a bit high for basic Serbian dishes at **Miomir's Serbian Club** (2255 West Lawrence Avenue), but the entertainment and Miomir's irrepressible personality make up for them. Gypsy fiddlers, Cossack baritones, and an array of instrumentalists are orchestrated by the host into a rollicking floor show. When he snaps his fingers at the band and calls out "tango," you know he's about to ask the prettiest woman in the room to dance.

New Oriental restaurants seem to open in the area every week, and several are topnotch. The off-putting, garish décor at the huge **New Korea House** (4050 North Lincoln Avenue) belies some of the best Korean food in town. Generous portions of all the standards—bul gogi, galbi, and chop chae—are joined by outstanding fish and seafood; modestly priced full dinners come with a rainbow of condiments and garnishes. **Cho Sun Ok Steak House** (4200 North Lincoln Avenue) began as a greasy spoon, but the owners found that more and more customers were ordering Korean dishes hidden on the hot-dog-and-hamburger menu, so they decided to go with the flow. Everything's Korean and Chinese now, even if the place isn't really a steak house.

For Thai food that compromises little for timid Western palates, try **Rosded** (2308 West Leland Avenue). The large menu is cryptic and the helpful staff struggles with English, but almost everything is delicious. Be sure to try the fried mussels. Carefully prepared Thai dishes from an exceptionally lengthy menu can also be had at the **Thai Room** (4022 North Western Avenue), a friendly, family-run storefront restaurant.

Lincoln Square's restaurants and shops may not be fancy, but they're fun. Find a parking space near Lawrence and Western Avenues, or take public transportation, and go exploring.

Interesting places

Dankhaus
4740 N. Western Ave.
561-9181
A branch of the German-American National Congress houses a hall, meeting rooms, a library, and the offices of Amerika-Woche newspaper.

Frederick H. Hild Regional Library
4544 N. Lincoln Ave.
728-8652, TDD 728-2062
Constructed in 1929, this handsome Art Deco building offers special services for the deaf. Check out Secondhand Prose, the basement bookshop, for bargains. (See Libraries.)

Krause Music Store
4611 N. Lincoln Ave.
Now the Arntzen-Coleman Funeral Home. The façade was Louis Sullivan's last commission. The lavish ornamentation almost overwhelms the small building.

Lincoln, the Friendly Neighbor, sculpture
Lincoln Square, Lincoln and Lawrence Aves.
Erected in 1956, Avard Fairbanks's sculpture is inscribed "Free society is not, and shall not be, a failure." Also in the square is an ornate, cherub-adorned street lamp like those used on the Lombard Bridge in Hamburg, Germany, since 1869.

*"Reflections of Ravenswood," mural
4662 N. Lincoln Ave., north wall

*St. Demetrios Greek Orthodox Church
Winona and Washtenaw
561-5992

*St. Matthias Church
Ainslie and Claremont
561-6020

Shopping and services

Attica
2527 W. Lawrence Ave.
271-3374
Lavish Greek wedding and christening gowns.

Chinese Linens
2607 W. Lawrence Ave.
334-6682
Embroidered table linens from China at reasonable prices. Also at 3211 N. Central Ave.

Circle Studio
5600 N. Western Ave.
275-5454
*Topnotch stained-glass
work shows a flair for
fantasy.*

Dr. Michael's Products
5109 N. Western Ave.
271-7738
*Herbs, roots, and medicinal
botanicals since 1928.*

**Eastwood True Value
Hardware Store**
4655 N. Lincoln Ave.
769-6206
*Basic neighborhood hard-
ware shop that carries a
large stock of imported
kitchen gadgets.*

European Import Corner
2316 W. Leland Ave.
561-8281
*High-quality fancy dinner-
ware and cut crystal from
Germany, good stock of
German magazines, and
assorted gift items.*

5-7-9 Shops Outlet Store
4949 N. Western Ave.
561-5795
*Travel a little out of the way
for big savings.*

*Griffins & Gargoyles
2140 W. Lawrence Ave.
769-1255, odd hours

Jazz Record Mart
4243 N. Lincoln Ave.
528-8834
*Branch of the much larger
Grand Ave. store (see North
of the River) but still has
every important Chicago
blues artist, and a thoughtful pick of jazz and blues
classics. If you're there
around 7 p.m. on a Friday,
you might be lucky enough
to get invited to see the
screening of one of Bob
Koester's great collection of
jazz movies.*

Kaufmann Costumes
5117 N. Western Ave.
561-7529
*All sorts of costumes rent-
ed; make-up and wigs, too.*

Lincoln Flower and Gift
4064 N. Lincoln Ave.
525-1640
*Bonsai and orchids are
specialties at this shop,
which does a big business
in flower baskets
for Oriental-restaurant
openings.*

*Lincoln Music Center
4613 N. Lincoln Ave.
561-4151

*Macramé Workshop
2215 W. Lawrence Ave.
561-4499

Magic, Inc.
5082 N. Lincoln Ave.
334-2855
*Chat with the magicians
who hang around the shop
or take some lessons so you
can work the tricks that are
sold here. Magicians and
clowns are available for
kids' parties.*

Henry A. W. Mundt
4143 N. Lincoln Ave.
935-5115
*Howard Mundt learned
cabinet making from his
dad, Henry, in the '30s. With
his wife, Linda, he repairs
and restores old furniture
and makes new pieces.*

Pacific Enterprises, Inc.
4626 N. Lincoln Ave.
334-3044
*This Korean firm imports
kimonos from China
and florid, embroidered,
synthetic fabrics and bed
linens from Korea.*

Panellinion Imports
2411 W. Lawrence Ave.
784-7066
*Amid the books and usual
touristy stuff such as worry
beads, you can find some
nice pottery and metalwork
museum reproductions.*

***Penn-Dutchman
Antiques**
4912 N. Western Ave.
271-2208

*Schmid Imports
4606 N. Lincoln Ave.
561-2871

*Vahle's Bird Store
4710 N. Damen Ave.
271-1623
Cats and dogs, too.

**Wanke Brothers
Taxidermy Studio**
4539 N. Lincoln Ave.
728-1440
*William Wanke has been in
the business more than 50
years; he just does birds
and fish now.*

Foodstuffs

*Akropol Pastry Shop
2601 W. Lawrence Ave.
878-0205

Berwyn Fisheries
5300 N. Lincoln Ave.
561-3445
*Sells fresh, fried, and its
own smoked fish; will
smoke your fish, too.*

Charlanne's Pastry Shop
1822 W. Montrose Ave.
561-9239
*Ordinary sweet rolls; very
good breads. Cakes, too.*

*Delicatessen Meyer
4750 N. Lincoln Ave.
561-3377

**Doshi Grocery and
Coin Enterprises**
2207 W. Montrose Ave.
463-2111
*The sign says it all: "Foods
from the Indian Sub-
Continent. We buy gold and
silver rings, coins, etc."*

*European Pastry Shop
4701 N. Lincoln Ave.
769-2220

***European Sausage
House**
4361 N. Lincoln Ave.
472-9645
Whole pigs available.

Farmers' Market
Lawrence and Oakley Aves.
744-6426
*This city-sponsored
produce market was a
smash hit its first few years
at this location.*

***Michael Fless
Homemade Sausage**
4452 N. Western Ave.
478-5443
*Biggest selection on Thurs-
days and Fridays.*

*George's Delicatessen
1964 W. Lawrence Ave.
728-6333

Greek Town Food and Bakery
2707 W. Lawrence Ave.
784-0700
Produce, staples, condiments for Greek cooking.

Hellas Pastry Shop
2627 W. Lawrence Ave.
271-7500
Mirror image of the Akropol.

*John's Import Foods
2611 W. Lawrence Ave.
561-5200

Korea Market
2606 W. Lawrence Ave.
989-0200
One of the largest.

*North Star Bakery
4545 N. Lincoln Ave.
561-9858

*Psarpoula Fish House
4755 N. Rockwell St.
728-5415

*Tomas Bakery
4054 N. Lincoln Ave.
472-6401

*Tom's Delicatessen and Bakery
2612 W. Lawrence Ave.
784-2431

Treasure Island
2540 W. Lawrence Ave.
271-8711
This branch of the chain carries the largest selection of Greek and Middle Eastern products along with the usual topnotch produce.

Wein Haus
4314 N. Lincoln Ave.
267-5431
Good selection of German and Eastern European wines plus glassware and gifts.

*West Meat Market
2549 W. Lawrence Ave.
769-4956

Dining and drinking

The Bake Shop Café
2310 W. Leland Ave.
334-1347
A ban on smoking and a menu of sandwiches, salads, and herbal teas make you feel virtuous— until you indulge in a sensuously rich pastry.

*Cho Sun Ok Steak House
4200 N. Lincoln Ave.
549-5555, 348-9409

Delphi Food Market and Restaurant
2655 W. Lawrence Ave.
271-0660 (market),
878-4917 (restaurant)
A reminder of the days when many Greek restaurants were in side rooms of groceries. Unremarkable food is made up for by a pleasant atmosphere.

*Family House
2421 W. Lawrence Ave.
334-7411

Gin Go Gae
5433 N. Lincoln Ave.
334-3895
Popular with Koreans, this neighborhood spot serves excellent food.

*Grecian Psistaria
2412 W. Lawrence Ave.
728-6308

*Heidelberger Fass
4300 N. Lincoln Ave.
478-2486

*Hogen's
4560 N. Lincoln Ave.
334-9406

The Hungarian Restaurant
5062 N. Lincoln Ave.
334-4850
Small dining room in front of a bar offers so-so versions of Hungarian standards, surprises like good liver or sausage, and holiday specials such as rabbit paprikash. Excellent strudel.

*Lindos Restaurant
5035 N. Lincoln Ave.
878-1115
Live music most nights after 9 p.m.

*Lutz's Continental Café and Pastry Shop
2458 W. Montrose Ave.
478-7785
The bakery sells candy, too, and wonderful marzipan figures at Christmas.

Mabuhay
2124 W. Lawrence Ave.
275-3688
Filipino food, a cuisine that's unusual but not overly spicy. Live music for dancing, too.

*New Korea House
4050 N. Lincoln Ave.
935-3350

Roong-Petch
1828 W. Montrose Ave.
989-0818
Small storefront restaurant serves good Thai food.

*Rosded
2308 W. Leland Ave.
334-9055

*Thai Room
4022 N. Western Ave.
539-6150

*Treffpunkt
4743 N. Lincoln Ave.
784-9296

Entertainment

*The Athens
4726 N. Western Ave.
878-1150

The King's Manor
2122 W. Lawrence Ave.
275-8400
Minstrels and jesters entertain while "servingwenches" deliver the barbecued ribs and Cornish game hens to revelers at the Manor's re-creations of medieval feasts. Wednesday through Sunday, two seatings Saturday.

*Miomir's Serbian Club
2255 W. Lawrence Ave.
784-2111

New York Lounge
5151 N. Lincoln Ave.
334-8953
This friendly, neighborhood bar is a hangout for magicians; all the bartenders are practitioners.

Uptown

Studs Terkel calls Uptown "the United Nations of the have-nots." Uptown has more than its share of the poor and the dispossessed, including one of Chicago's highest concentrations of the elderly. There's a halfway house, a convalescent home, a residential treatment center, or some other social-service agency on almost every block. The people—American Indians, Japanese, East Indians, blacks, Vietnamese, Mexicans, Chinese, Cubans—sometimes squabble, sometimes work together in their effort to make Uptown livable.

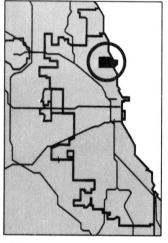

Uptown also has its share of haves. Elegant homes line Hutchinson Street and Castlewood Terrace; high-rise apartments dominate the skyline along Marine Drive; well-kept houses and small apartment buildings typify East Ravenswood, west of Clark Street. The people who live in these areas resent Uptown's bad press. They also hope that this time, finally, the much-talked-about rebirth of the community will become reality.

Nobody really expects the neighborhood to return to the glory it enjoyed when it was the most prosperous section of Lake View Township. Even after annexation in 1899, Uptown continued to attract the well-to-do. Proximity to the lake and excellent transportation triggered construction of elegant homes and luxurious apartments, many of which remain—some sadly deteriorated, some in fine condition.

The houses on **Castlewood Terrace** and **Hutchinson Street** are among the finest. Castlewood, conveniently near the old Essanay movie studios, attracted residents like Mary Pickford, Wallace Beery, and Francis X. Bushman, functioning, for a time, as Chicago's Beverly Hills. Hutchinson Street, originally called Kenesaw Terrace, was developed by merchant John C. Scales in the 1890s. The first mansion was his own (840 West Hutchinson Street), a Queen Anne gem designed in 1894 by George W. Maher, one of America's great architects. Maher's growth is mirrored by the Lake House (826), which shows his vision of Prairie architecture, and the Seymour House (817), where that vision is combined with European influences. The residences at 750 and 839 are also attributed to him. The other houses on the street and in the immediate neighborhood, now protected by landmark designation, provide such rich examples of period design that they are a museum of Chicago's grand turn-of-the-century residential architecture.

As Uptown's population grew in the early 20th century, new housing was built to accommodate the influx of Irish and Jews, joining the Germans and Swedes who settled earlier. High property values dictated apartment construction, and in the 1920s, tall apartment houses, residential hotels, and courtyard buildings filled the blocks closest to the lake. To the west, **Graceland Cemetery** (Clark Street and Irving Park Road) and **St. Boniface Cemetery** (4901 North Clark Street) dominated the high ground and raised a barrier to rapid residential expansion. Even today, the areas west of Clark Street have a lower population density with more single-family homes and small apartment buildings.

A burgeoning population, mostly well-off, and convenient transportation made Uptown a shopping area that, by the 1920s, challenged the Loop in elegance and variety of merchandise. The original Wilson el station was designed by Frank Lloyd Wright in 1909 and included a shopping arcade. It was demolished in 1923 and replaced with a once-handsome example of Beaux-Arts grandeur that has lost most of its ornamentation. In 1915, Loren Miller, sensing the neighborhood could be a real rival to downtown, helped give it an identity by dubbing his fancy dry-goods emporium The Uptown Store. Uptown held its own through the '20s as the area around Sheridan Road and Wilson Avenue bloomed into one of the city's most desirable office and retail locations. Today, a few buildings remain as reminders, notably the Renaissance-inspired **McJunkin Block** (4550 North Broadway), the Kemper Insurance Building (4750 North Sheridan Road), now the **Ecumenical Institute of Chicago,** and a marvelously rococo building at 4707 North Broadway. The Goldblatt's that was in the old Uptown Store has folded, and the rest of the area is given over to rowdy bars, a tattoo parlor, wig shops, and a cluster of discount stores.

During its heyday, Uptown also challenged the Loop as an entertainment center. The **Green Mill Lounge** (4802 North Broadway) started out as a roadhouse; by 1910 it had blossomed as the Green Mill Gardens, with a lantern-lit outdoor dancing and drinking area on the site of the present Uptown Theater; headliners included Sophie Tucker and Al Jolson. No headliners today, but the Green Mill still offers nightly entertainment—usually a piano player assisted by the customers' off-key vocalizations. This well-run bar is worth a stop, if only to admire the remnants of past glories.

Before flinty-eyed financiers took over, the **Bank of Chicago** (1050 West Wilson Avenue) was the Standard Vaudeville Theatre. A major stop on the circuit until vaudeville gave way to movies, it closed its doors in the early '20s. Many of the movies that killed vaudeville were made in Uptown. For ten years Chicago reigned as the film capital of America, largely because of **Essanay Studios** (1345 West Argyle Street), founded by George K. Spoor and "Bronco Billy" Anderson in 1907. Greats such as Ben Turpin, Francis X. Bushman, Gloria Swanson, and Charlie Chaplin starred in the movies that were cranked out at Essanay's 16-acre lot.

The Little Tramp's image flickered across a mighty screen at the **Uptown Theater** (4816 North Broadway). Covering an entire block and seating more than 4,000, this Balaban & Katz beauty brought a Spanish castle to Uptown, magnified by architects Rapp and Rapp's lens that made everything larger than life. The furnishings were as florid as those in any American theater, the mechanical facilities the most modern. Six feet of air space between the inner and outer walls shielded patrons from any hint of street noise. In the 1970s, hard times hit the Uptown and most of the fixtures were sold off. After a stint with Spanish-language films and occasional rock concerts, it closed in 1982. The **Riviera Theatre** (4746 North Racine Avenue), another one-time Balaban & Katz house, screens exploitation films; the old Sheridan is now the **Teatro El Palacio** (4040 North Sheridan Road), showing Spanish-language features; and the Lakeside now houses the

Columbia College Dance Center (4730 North Sheridan Road).
For many people, entertainment in Uptown meant dancing at the **Aragon Ballroom** (1106 West Lawrence Avenue). Greek immigrants Andrew and William Karzas started their careers in America with a South Side nickelodeon in 1907; by 1922 they had done well enough to open the elegant Trianon Ballroom at 62nd Street and Cottage Grove Avenue; and, in 1926, they capped it all by creating the Aragon. The building's Moorish design owed more to Hollywood than to Iberia, but its lavish ornamentation fit Uptown's flush feeling. Huge crowds came to dance to the nation's top bands in an atmosphere that was romantic, yet as tightly controlled as a church social—worlds apart from the rock concerts that are staples of today's Aragon.

The 1920s glitter helped spawn today's grimy Uptown. Housing pressure in the trendy neighborhood led owners of less successful apartment houses to break up large flats, and single people replaced many families. As entertainment attracted larger crowds, honky-tonks sprang up, especially around the el station, giving the area an unsavory reputation. In the '30s, with new construction killed by the Depression, Uptown wore around the edges. The war years brought heavier demand for housing—even sleeping rooms—and conversion accelerated.

Cheap rents and a glut of rooms made Uptown a port of entry for immigrants to Chicago after the war. Southern whites from Kentucky, Tennessee, and West Virginia, unused to urban ways, crowded into a small part of a city that had little love for "hillbillies." In the 1960s, they were joined by American Indians encouraged to leave the reservation by the Federal government. Blacks, many displaced by urban renewal of their old neighborhoods, arrived in increasing numbers. (Uptown has had an all-black block, Winthrop Street between Leland and Wilson Avenues, since the '20s, when servants lived there.) Crowding, poverty, and people who were "different" made most Chicagoans shun the community and attracted an army of social strategists. Uptown became one of the most-studied and least-loved neighborhoods in the country.

Uptown is still a port of entry, now for East Indians and Southeast Asians. Problems of housing, schools, and jobs remain—but there's a growing feeling that diversity might be a virtue. The radical '60s bred the Rainbow Coalition, a local community organization whose logo was a blend of colors. Some of today's community groups still work toward that goal.

Argyle Street (5000 North), east of Broadway, serves as a laboratory for that dream. A decade ago a group of Chinese businessmen, led by restaurateur Jimmy Wong, tried to create a new Chinatown here. They were only partly successful. Several Cantonese restaurants opened, including **King's** (1109 West Argyle Street), the "oldest and finest," with nice preparation of all the old standbys. **Sanford Chinese American Groceries** (1125) sells roast duck and barbecued pork on Saturdays and Sundays, and stocks a full line of Chinese food products. The **Phoenix Bakery** (1133) offers duck and pork daily, as well as a nice assortment of fresh-baked Chinese pastries, meat buns, and "Chinese tamales"—pork, salty egg yolk, and bean paste wrapped in bamboo leaves.

Vietnamese are outstripping the Chinese on Argyle Street. A large Vietnamese clothing and gift shop parades a modernized façade, while **Viet Hoa Plaza** (1110), one of many groceries serving the neighborhood's sizable Southeast Asian population, is a medley of sights and smells that bowl over even veteran Oriental-food shoppers. The language barrier is a problem here, as it is at Vietnamese restaurants such as the seedy looking **Saigon Restaurant** (1104), where menu translations only hint at what you can expect, and the servers' explanations tend to be inscrutable. The delicious and unusual food makes eating here a rewarding adventure. On weekends, you can try bu nhung dam mot phan, a Vietnamese fondue. Goi cuon, an unusual cold appetizer of shrimp, rice, scallions, and more wrapped in a rice "paper" pancake, is available every day. Better yet, bring a lot of people, let your eyes wander, and point. Dubbing Argyle a second Chinatown didn't bring back its old commercial vitality. The opening of the Vietnamese shops provided a shot in the arm, but hasn't triggered a resurgence. What may is the growing recognition by business people that they are a rather special group. Modene Dawson, a black woman who worked many years for the Small Business Administration, turns out intricately designed cakes—they taste as wonderful as they look—at **Modene's Ice Cream & Cake Shop** (1052 West Argyle Street). Foremost Liquors is owned by a family of Albanian immigrants. Biscuits and gravy, served up by an engineer trained in Yugoslavia, draws people to Coffee Sam's. Al Esquitin, a Spanish-American from Texas, runs New Star Foods with his Japanese wife and Chinese partner. Together with their Greek, Mexican, and Irish colleagues, they formed Argyle International to call attention to this amazingly diverse street. The city is involved in upgrading the streetscape, easing parking problems, and beefing up police protection. For now, Argyle's still pretty rough—you should be careful where you park and walk at night—but things are definitely getting better.

Argyle Street is the showcase, but Indian groceries, taco stands, and other signs of Uptown's diversity are everywhere. **Kamdar Imports** (5024 North Broadway) advertises "Saris, Spices, and Sweets." It delivers three stores' worth. One will make up a sari from your choice of materials lining the walls in bolts, and also has Indian gifts and records; spices, staples, and condiments packed by Kamdar out of bulk shipments from Kenya and India fill another; the sweet shop's exotic, milk-based, rose-water-perfumed desserts round out the picture.

Plenty of spices flavor the Spanish soups and casseroles at **Costa Brava** (4006 North Broadway), a pleasant storefront with a menu and décor that speak of the sea. Paella is the house specialty, but the seafood chowder is the real bargain. Steaks, several chicken dishes, and even kid in wine sauce attract fish haters. As much a bar as a restaurant, **Copacabana** (4005), just across the street, is so Cuban that the menu can pose problems for those whose Spanish isn't working. The staff may need some prodding, but they'll help you choose from the seafood, beef, or pork—lots of pork—selections. Naïve paintings of scenes from Cuban history cover one wall, the coffee packs a Havana wallop, and the music from the too-loud juke box aims at the regulars, so don't expect to be pampered.

Uptown's Japanese population grew rapidly after World War Two. While the **Buddhist Temple of Chicago** (1151 West Leland Avenue) attracts a multiracial congregation, the form of Buddhism practiced is traditional. Classes in calligraphy, tea ceremonies, and martial arts are open to all, but they, too, reflect centuries-old rituals. The Temple's summer festival (*see Annual Events*) draws people from all over the city to see those rituals and to sample Japanese food. That food's available year-round at **Azuma Sukiyaki House** (5120 North Broadway), possibly Chicago's oldest Japanese restaurant. The building is a charmer, teahouses offer privacy, but the food is so-so. **Shiroma Imports** (1134 West Argyle Street) sells fine Oriental gifts and artwork, mostly Japanese.

This generation of American Indians has been around Uptown a short time, even though their ancestors held the original deed. But despite their urban problems, they retain a stubborn pride. They display that pride once a year at the American Indian Pow Wow (*see Annual Events*) sponsored by the **American Indian Center** (1630 West Wilson Avenue), a social-service agency. Beadwork, silver and turquoise jewelry, rugs, pottery, paintings, and Indian records demonstrate pride in tradition, and they're all available at the **American Indian Gift Store** (1756 West Wilson Avenue). This is the real stuff, not Fred Harvey gift-shop knock-offs.

Some of the Indian pride has rubbed off. From the balcony of an apartment on Sheridan Road hangs a banner proclaiming "We love you, Uptown." It's not a rehabbed building. There's excitement in the air; everyone's talking about Uptown being on the way up. The question is who decides which direction is up.

Interesting places

All Saints Episcopal Church
Hermitage and Wilson
561-0111
Delightful church, one of the few examples of Carpenter's Gothic used in religious architecture, recently celebrated its centenary.

*American Indian Center
1630 W. Wilson Ave.
275-5871

*Bank of Chicago
1050 W. Wilson Ave.
271-8000

*Buddhist Temple of Chicago
1151 W. Leland Ave.
334-4661

*Castlewood Terrace
4862 North between Sheridan Rd. and Marine Dr.

Combined Insurance Company of America
5050 N. Broadway
275-8000
W. Clement Stone can look out his window and see people practice positive mental attitudes.

*Ecumenical Institute of Chicago
4750 N. Sheridan Rd.
769-5635
Kemper Insurance donated its one-time headquarters building to the Institute to use as an international training center.

*Essanay Studios
1345 W. Argyle St.
Soundstages are used for making films, television programs, and commercials. The building's occupants include Lukas-Lippert Productions and Essanay Studio & Lighting Co., Inc., which rents commercial lighting equipment. The Spanish Episcopal Service, a community agency, sponsors adult-education classes, concerts, and theatrical productions on the premises.

*Graceland Cemetery
4001 N. Clark St.
525-1105
Established in 1860, the cemetery took on much of its present character through the careful planning of landscape architect Ossian Simonds, who also helped design Lincoln Park. The tombs were designed by distinguished architects. Getty Tomb, the work of Louis Sullivan, is an official Chicago landmark. Sullivan himself is buried here, along with famous colleagues Daniel Burnham, Ludwig Mies van der Rohe, and Howard Van Doren Shaw. Two important sculptures by Lorado Taft, Eternal Silence (or the Statue of Death) and The Crusader, are also found here. An excellent guidebook to Graceland by Barbara Lanctot is available through the Chicago Architecture Foundation, 326-1393.

Hip Sing Association
1123 W. Argyle St.
334-6537
A Chinese business and benevolent society.

*Hutchinson Street
4232 North between Marine Dr. and Hazel St.
A description of the Hutchinson District has been published by the Commission on Chicago Historical and Architectural Landmarks, 744-3200.

Japanese American Service Committee Mural
North wall, 4427 N. Clark St.
275-7212
A powerful mural showing the difficulties experienced by earlier generations of Japanese in America and expressing the hope that the Sansei, the third generation, can live in a world where all people live and work together.

Lakeview High School
4015 N. Ashland Ave.
281-1684
The main section of this fortresslike building was built in 1889; some excellent stained glass.

Lakeview Post Office
1343 W. Irving Park Rd.
327-2932
Harry Sternberg's mural, "Chicago—Epic of a Great City," was completed in 1938.

*McJunkin Block
4550 N. Broadway

Our Lady of Lourdes Church
Leland and Ashland Aves.
561-2141
When this Spanish-influenced church was dedicated in 1910, it stood on the southeastern corner. The widening of Ashland forced the move of the entire structure across the street. The move allowed the church to be separated into two sections so an addition could be inserted.

Pensacola Place
Montrose Ave. and Hazel
Architect Stanley Tigerman's design shows his willingness to experiment with new forms, especially when compared to his Mies-influenced Boardwalk (4343 N. Clarendon).

Peoples Church
941 W. Lawrence Ave.
784-6633
This church, built in 1926 as the Uptown Temple, has seating for 1,700 worshipers. But, when Dr. Preston Bradley, one of Chicago's great preachers, delivered his sermons, crowds spilled out onto the sidewalks and listened over loudspeakers.

*St. Boniface Cemetery
4901 N. Clark St.
561-2995
Founded in 1863 by German Catholics. The grounds include a monument to German Civil War volunteers, the graves of distinguished church architect Henry Schlacks and songwriter Paul Dresser ("On the Banks of the Wabash"), and the burial plots of numerous German societies.

St. Mary of the Lake Church
Sheridan Rd. and Buena
472-3711
Henry Schlacks patterned his design after St. Paul Outside the Walls and St. Mary Major in Rome. The elegant stained-glass windows were designed by the Royal Bavarian Art Institute of Munich.

Harry S. Truman College
1145 W. Wilson Ave.
878-1700
The full impact on the community of this Chicago City College has still not been felt.

Uptown Baptist Church
Sheridan Rd. and Wilson
784-2922
Services in Spanish, Cambodian, Vietnamese, Hmong, and English. A sign atop the tower proclaims to all of Uptown that "Christ Died for Our Sins."

Uptown Post Office
4850 N. Broadway
561-8916
Henry Varnum Poor's 1943 ceramic-tile murals honor Carl Sandburg and Louis Sullivan. Magnificent stone eagles out front.

*Uptown Theater
4816 N. Broadway

Shopping and services

All Nations Moped
5051 N. Clark St.
878-0797
Claims to be the largest moped dealership in the Midwest.

*American Indian Gift Store
1756 W. Wilson Ave.
769-1170

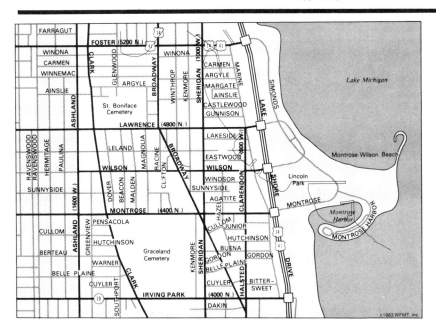

The Book Box
4812 N. Broadway
334-5311
The selection of used books, mostly paperbacks, isn't impressive, but there's a fair stock of left-wing and radical periodicals.

Frank's Live Bait and Sports
1437 W. Montrose Ave.
549-0631
Bait and fishing supplies—including smelt nets—for anglers heading to try their luck at Montrose Harbor.

Howard Art Galleries
5100-08 N. Broadway
271-7100
Periodic auctions with an Atlantic City-boardwalk flair. Lots of estate jewelry and Orientalia. Some of the pieces here are not on consignment, but owned by the establishment, so the auctioneer really works on the prices. On the other hand, that means they can be purchased between sales. An adjoining showroom offers Oriental and Persian carpets at wholesale prices.

S. W. Lewis Orchestral Horns
1770 W. Berteau Ave.
348-1112
Makes and repairs French horns for Chicago Symphony Orchestra musicians, among others.

Loomcraft Textiles
4898 N. Clark St.
275-1414
Enormous collection of upholstery fabrics at discount prices.

Monitor Formal Wear
1422 W. Wilson Ave.
561-0573
The place to go if you want to rent one of those magnificently flamboyant tuxes you see at Mexican weddings.

New World Resource Center
1476 W. Irving Park Rd.
348-3370
A reminder of the turbulent '60s, New World sponsors programs and workshops dealing with emerging nations—all with an anti-colonialist, anti-imperialist bent. Good selection of left-wing books and periodicals.

Pepper's Waterbeds
4405 N. Clark St.
275-0330
The usual. Other locations.

Pete's Tattoo Studio
4408 N. Broadway
989-4077
Talk it over with friends first.

*Shiroma Imports
1134 W. Argyle St.
561-5794

Soolim Ltd.
4625 N. Clark St.
728-6266
Korean herb shop offers an herbal weight-loss program.

Wood As New
4511 N. Clark St.
275-4511
Furniture stripping and refinishing.

Foodstuffs

Asia Oriental Foods
5000 N. Broadway
271-3535
Good-sized store carrying foods from throughout the Orient.

Casa Hernandez
4409 N. Sheridan Rd.
784-0398
Like its twin in Rogers Park, an excellent full-service Hispanic supermarket.

Clark Fish Market
4609 N. Clark St.
334-3348
Tidy Korean fish house with a small grocery next door.

India Grocers
5010 N. Sheridan Rd.
334-3351
They import and package spices and staples.

J & M Kosher Meat Market
1009 W. Argyle St.
561-4550
A reminder of the days when Argyle St. was solidly Jewish.

*Kamdar Imports
5024 N. Broadway
878-2525

*Modene's Ice Cream & Cake Shop
1052 W. Argyle St.
989-0060
Also at 312 S. Dearborn St.

*Phoenix Bakery
1133 W. Argyle St.
878-5833

*Sanford Chinese American Groceries Inc.
1125 W. Argyle St.
784-0088

Song Quang Company
1058-60 W. Argyle St.
271-4523
The grocery handles specialties for the neighborhood's Vietnamese. Also Vietnamese books and tapes; small restaurant is part of the shop.

Thailand Plaza
1135 W. Argyle St.
728-1199
Not for Thais only: They happily supply specialties for Chinese, Vietnamese, Cambodians, Laotians, Koreans, and Japanese.

*Viet Hoa Plaza
1110 W. Argyle St.
334-1028

Dining and drinking

*Azuma Sukiyaki
5120 N. Broadway
561-2448

Chinese Lantern
1046½ W. Argyle St.
769-3900
Cantonese with some Filipino dishes, including pansit and fried crabmeat kok.

*Copacabana
4005 N. Broadway
883-1212, 883-0220

*Costa Brava
4006 N. Broadway
472-5322

Dolphin Restaurant
4631 N. Clark St.
784-4114
*Typical Korean fare with
some Chinese selections.
Tableside gas rings let
you try your hand at
the cooking.*

**Jim Dowling's
Hobson's Oyster Bar**
5101 N. Clark St.
271-0400
*Unpretentious spot for
freshly shucked oysters at
the bar, or sit at a table for
more elaborate seafood
offerings.*

Ha Miên Restaurant
4944 N. Sheridan Rd.
728-9594
*Good, very inexpensive
Vietnamese food.*

*King's
1109 W. Argyle St.
878-8385

*Saigon Restaurant
1104 W. Argyle St.
275-8691

Siam Café
4654 N. Sheridan Rd.
989-0157
*Crowded hole-in-the-wall
serves outstanding Thai
food at low prices.*

Song Quang Restaurant
1058-60 W. Argyle St.
271-4523
*Attached to Song Quang
Company; serves Viet-
namese and Chinese food.*

Zephyr Ice Cream Shop
1777 W. Wilson Ave.
728-6070
*Extremely stylish Art Deco
restaurant and ice-cream
parlor. The food is indifferent, the menu too cute, but
the ice-cream concoctions
are good and the place
is fun.*

Entertainment

*Aragon Ballroom
1106 W. Lawrence Ave.
561-9500
*The Aragon's last hurrah as
a ballroom came in 1955
when 8,900 people
jammed in for Lawrence
Welk, although today it is
used for Latin American
and disco dances as well as
rock concerts.*

***Columbia College
Dance Center**
4730 N. Sheridan Rd.
271-7804
(See Dance)

*Green Mill Lounge
4802 N. Broadway
878-5552

*Riviera Theatre
4746 N. Racine Ave.
561-5049

*Teatro El Palacio
4040 N. Sheridan Rd.
528-8578
*The menorahs on the mar-
ble façade are reminders of
Anshe Emet Synagogue,
whose congregation used
the old Sheridan Theatre as
an auditorium in the '50s.*

**United Skates
of America Inc.**
(formerly Rainbo Gardens)
4836 N. Clark St.
271-6200
*Lavish, well-run roller rink
where the music is more often disco than waltzes.
Rentals and a pro shop, too.
An entertainment center for
most of the 20th century, the
building was the Moulin
Rouge dance hall and café
in the teens, Mann's Rainbo Gardens Magnificent in
the '20s, the French Casino
in 1934, and Mike Todd's
Million Dollar Ballroom (a
theater-restaurant) in 1939.
In the '50s, millions of
Americans watched
televised wrestling from the
Rainbo Gardens. Later, it
housed ice skating, bowl-
ing, kids' hockey leagues,
and rock concerts.*

The grandeur that was Aragon

Edgewater

Modern lakefront high-rises with names like "Malibu," "Surfside Condominiums," and "Hollywood Towers" and amenities like enclosed shopping malls, swimming pools, and putting greens are heirs to Edgewater's tradition of elegance. In the 1920s, the flamboyant, pink, rococo Edgewater Beach Hotel (5349 North Sheridan Road, demolished) was a popular, de luxe resort, and the equally pink but more sedate **Edgewater Beach Apartments** (5555 North Sheridan Road) was one of Chicago's most sought after co-ops. A string of Prairie School-influenced mansions separated them from the Edgewater Golf Course (Sheridan Road and Devon Avenue, now part of the Loyola University campus), where "Chick" Evans taught prominent Chicagoans the finer points of the game. Edgewater epitomized the good life of the period.

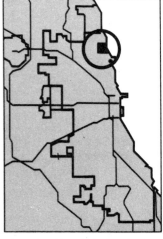

The good life was what developer John L. Cochran had in mind when he began to subdivide lakefront marshes and farmlands north of Foster Avenue in the late 19th century. Cochran gave the streets he platted names of stops along the Pennsylvania Railroad's main line out of Philadelphia—Bryn Mawr, Berwyn, Ardmore. After the extension of the elevated from Wilson Avenue to Evanston in 1907, the area east of Broadway blossomed with courtyard apartment buildings, fine single-family homes, and residential hotels. Lakefront land prices jumped from $200 a frontage foot in 1910 to $3,000 in 1929.

To serve the burgeoning population, churches sprang up at a rate that would have dumfounded medieval cathedral-builders. **Bethany Evangelical Lutheran Church** (Thorndale and Magnolia Avenues) was one of several Protestant churches built in the century's first decade. The small Prairie-style Tudor building now houses the Rogers Park Montessori School; the present church, a beautiful example of Prairie-style Gothic, faced with the same red brick, was added in 1913. The expansion of the Episcopal **Church of the Atonement** (Kenmore and Ardmore Avenues) incorporated part of the original 1888 building in a handsome Romanesque structure with heavy stonework and fine stained glass.

The spirit of prosperity in the 1920s encouraged lavish adornments. The parishioners of the Italian Romanesque **Edgewater Presbyterian Church** (Kenmore and Bryn Mawr Avenues) hired one of the country's master woodcarvers, John O. Torell of Palatine, to create the interior decoration. Beautiful stained-glass windows from Munich, now valued at more than $1 million, enhance **St. Gertrude's Church** (Glenwood and Granville Avenues). At **St. Ita's Church** (Broadway and Catalpa Avenue), architect Henry Schlacks drew heavily on the examples of the church of Brou and the Chartres cathedral to design a masterpiece whose tower, with its delicate tracery, still dominates the neighborhood's skyline.

The residential boom filled the area west of Broadway with three-flats and solid, middle-class houses. Two of the most architecturally interesting examples are the **Walter Burley Griffin houses** at 5917 and 5921 North Magnolia Avenue. The substantial, two-story homes in the Lakewood/Balmoral neighborhood (Lakewood, Balmoral, and Wayne Avenues between Foster and Bryn Mawr Avenues) display a variety of Chicago styles and are reminders of Cochran's dream of a suburb in the city.

Unlike Lakewood/Balmoral, other sections of Edgewater have fallen prey to common urban ills. Demand for housing during and after World War Two caused massive conversions to sleeping rooms and efficiency apartments; single-family houses were razed to make way for that bane of the 1960s, the four-plus-one; and many solid, older apartment buildings deteriorated under absentee landlords. However, recent condominium conversions and rehabilitation of buildings for moderate and low-income rental hold promise for a brighter future.

Despite the affluence lakefront condominiums represent, Edgewater's shops are quite ordinary. Convenience stores cluster around the el stops, particularly at Bryn Mawr and Granville Avenues. Supermarkets and auto dealerships and their satellites dominate Broadway, and Clark Street's broad reaches north of Ridge Avenue offer little to the visitor.

There are a few exceptions, some dating back to the neighborhood's palmier days. The thoughtfully chosen women's wear at **Avenue Fashions** (1042 West Bryn Mawr Avenue) attracts customers from all over the city and suburbs. **Leon Beloian Rug Company Inc.** (6243 North Broadway) has been dealing in fine floor coverings since the area's first luxury housing went up. It carries new and used Oriental carpets ranging from about $2,500 for a room-sized Indian rug to tens of thousands for a rare Persian. **Smith's Clock Shop** (6217 North Broadway), a local fixture for more than 40 years, repairs fine wall and standing clocks and always has a fascinating assortment of timepieces on hand. **Admiral Music Company,** also known as The Piano Gallery (5951 North Clark Street), moved to Edgewater after decades in Logan Square. It doesn't look like much from the outside, but at least two dozen restored instruments are always on the sales floor. The pianos are completely rebuilt from the soundboard up and then carefully refinished by a couple of skilled craftsmen in the back room. A Steinway concert grand that costs $27,000 when new might be found here reconditioned for $16,000. Less expensive pianos, player pianos, and organs are also available, or Admiral will rebuild yours for about three grand.

Edgewater's most popular restaurant is probably Lettuce Entertain You's **Jonathan's Seafood** (5419 North Sheridan Road). The ambiance is high-rise modern and the seafood buffet offers more than 50 items. **Wing Hoe** (5356 North Sheridan Road), across the street, did better when it was a Jewish Romanian steak house and the Edgewater Beach Hotel stood where Jonathan's is now. The atmosphere is faded and the food unreconstructed Cantonese. You can make a more interesting Oriental meal by shopping at the **Siam Market** (1131 West Berwyn Avenue), which carries Vietnamese, Cambodian, and Laotian specialties as well as more common staples. **Tacos & Things** (5551 North Broadway) doesn't have a grocery like its sister on Webster Avenue, but you can enjoy the same Mexican and Cuban fare in clean, airy surroundings. The Peruvian prix fixe dinners at Alberto and Linda Asturrizaga's **El Inca** (6221 North Broadway), a small storefront next to the Devon Theatre, are good, but no match for those served by his brother at Piqueo (5427 North Clark Street).

The Broadway-Granville Avenue intersection is one of Edgewater's nightlife centers. The bars have "clever" names, occasional entertainment, and, except for **The Pumping Company** (6157 North Broadway) with its penny game machines, handsome bar, and friendly bartenders, little neighborhood feeling. However, one of the city's best and cheapest movie theaters is nearby. The **Devon** (6225 North Broadway) bounces between second-run and revival films but almost always screens something interesting.

When Cochran was subdividing lakefront marshes, Scandinavians were settling the ridge above. Most were Swedish and, as early as 1904, the Svenska Lutherska Ebenezer Kyrkan, or **Ebenezer Lutheran Church** (Foster Avenue and Paulina Street), provided the focus for Andersonville. Swedish halls, clubs, restaurants, and taverns lined Clark Street and Foster Avenue.

But Andersonville is no longer a solidly Scandinavian enclave. The changes that accelerated after World War Two continue to this day. The old Verdandi Club (5015 North Clark Street) is now **Man's Country Chicago,** baths serving the gay community. The **Calo Theater** (5404 North Clark Street), with its romantic, terra-cotta frieze over the arched doorway, houses a carpet store. Next door, **The Swedish Tobacco Shop** (5400 North Clark Street) is in an extraordinarily fanciful, white terra-cotta-covered building. Swedish is heard less and less in the taverns, even though they still serve glögg in winter.

Since 1964 when the city officially designated the neighborhood Andersonville USA, there has been a conscious effort to slow the rate of change. For example, each Christmas *God Jul* signs decorate the lampposts, and many shops bear banners proclaiming *Välkommen*. All this may be veneer, but it helps make strolling and shopping more pleasant.

Don't be surprised to see a log cabin-like façade on the **Swedish American Museum** (5248 North Clark Street; *see Museums*): The Swedes are credited with the log cabin's invention. For more Nordic handiwork, visit the **Swedish Style Gift Shop** (5309 North Clark Street), which is not as elegant as the Sweden Shop in North Park, but carries some nice crystal and metal work, as well as the usual run of curios. The **Swedish Style Knit Shop** (5301 North Clark Street) sells Rya and knit rugs plus patterns and materials to create your own needlework.

If you want to put together an authentic smörgåsbord, the cheerful **Wikstrom's Delicatessen** (5247 North Clark Street) has lots of luncheon meats, hand-sliced smoked salmon, Scandinavian cheeses, homemade potato sausage, limpa bread, lingonberries and other jarred and tinned specialties, rye crackers, salads, herring, and more. You can sip free coffee while you shop; get sandwiches to eat at the few tables or take out; and arrange for catering services. Across the street, **Erickson's Delicatessen and Fish Market** (5250 North Clark Street) has no tables but offers an equally wide selection of Swedish specialties, including herring prepared many ways, yellow-pea soup, wonderful potato salad, and glögg mix. More potato sausage can be had at **Tip Top Meat Shop** (5224 North Clark Street), a high-quality neighborhood butcher shop with a Scandinavian accent. The **Swedish Bakery** (5348 North Clark Street)—the sign still says Bjuhr's—carries excellent coffee cakes, cookies, sweet rolls, miniature pastries, and Swedish-style napoleons to round out the meal.

Smörgåsbord, with something of a Greek-American influence, is often available at **Villa Sweden** (5207 North Clark Street), an unpretentious and homey restaurant. Locals and those who have left the neighborhood keep coming back to this Andersonville landmark for fruit soup, meatballs, salmon, and a variety of good, standard dishes. **Svea** (5236 North Clark Street), a combination lunch counter-dining room, is a popular place for Swedish pancakes, open-face sandwiches, and neighborhood gossip.

The changes that have taken place bring variety to Clark Street: Korean and Thai restaurants; a Filipino grocery; ethnic nightclubs; and **Piqueo** (5427), Chicago's oldest Peruvian restaurant, owned by Moises, the eldest of the Asturriza-ga brothers. The Middle Eastern presence is also growing. **Bethlehem Restaurant** (5815), one of the city's most popular Arabic spots, serves a wide selection of regional dishes (including terrific felafel) at affordable prices. The Lebanese Faraj family's **Beirut Restaurant** (5204) offers unusual boiled and stuffed specialties, as well as more typical lamb dishes. Honey-laced baklava and other exotic pastries make a perfect finish to a meal. And the Assyrian-owned **Atour Food Importers** (5406) bristles with shelves of Middle Eastern delicacies and barrels of pistachio nuts and other tempting treats. Andersonville USA has become a true melting pot.

Interesting places

*Bethany Evangelical Lutheran Church
Thorndale and Magnolia
561-9159

*Calo Theater
5404 N. Clark St.

*Church of the Atonement
Kenmore and Ardmore
271-2727

*Ebenezer Lutheran Church
Foster Ave. and Paulina St.
561-8496

*Edgewater Beach Apartments
5555 N. Sheridan Rd.

*Edgewater Presbyterian Church
Kenmore and Bryn Mawr
561-4748

Emanuel Congregation
Thorndale and Sheridan
561-5173
1953 temple is beautifully set on the lakefront.

*Walter Burley Griffin houses
5917 and 5921 N. Magnolia

Rosehill Cemetery
5800 N. Ravenswood Ave.
561-5940
Although not as famous as Graceland, this cemetery still has a great deal of interest. The gates, designed by Water Tower architect W. W. Boyington, are an official Chicago landmark. Civil War burial plots, the soaring memorial to one-time mayor "Long John" Wentworth, and a monument to George S. Bangs, designer of the first railway mail car, are worth seeking out. A dozen other mayors, Charles G. Dawes, A. Montgomery Ward, John G. Shedd, Richard Sears, and Frances Willard are among the notables buried here. Stop at the office near the main gate for more information.

St. Andrew's Greek Orthodox Church
Sheridan and Hollywood
334-4515
Watch for the sign inviting the whole city to its huge annual picnic.

*St. Gertrude's Church
Glenwood and Granville
764-3621
A sign on the door says "Ring rectory doorbell to see the church." Do it.

*St. Ita's Church
Broadway and Catalpa
561-5343

*Swedish American Museum
5248 N. Clark St.
728-8111
(See Museums)

Shopping and services

*Admiral Music Co.
5951 N. Clark St.
271-4400

*Avenue Fashions
1042 W. Bryn Mawr Ave.
784-2277

*Leon Beloian Rug Co. Inc.
6243 N. Broadway
743-5700

The Book Mark
1515 W. Foster Ave.
275-4022
Small, eclectic shop with mostly newer hardbacks. You might want to chat with the owner about treasure hunting and even buy one of the treasure maps.

Charlie's Penny Candy Store
5622 N. Clark St.
No phone
Your basic school store with candies that will set you back at least two cents.

Chicago Recycle Shop
5308 N. Clark St.
878-8525
A cavernous space filled with old clothing, furniture, and just about anything else imaginable. Fun to browse, but wear old clothes. The largest, by far, of several resale shops in Andersonville.

East West Markets Exchange
5533 N. Broadway
878-7711
Uniforms, books, and equipment for practitioners of martial arts.

Hebard Storage Warehouses Inc.
6331 N. Broadway
764-0282
Warehouse foreclosure sales every Saturday.

Hollywood Antiques Too
5657-59 N. Clark St.
275-0747
Three storefronts crammed with furniture, dishes and glassware, jewelry, knick-knacks, and all sorts of little collectibles.

*Man's Country Chicago Inc.
5015 N. Clark St.
878-2069

Maritza Arts and Gifts
5221 N. Clark St.
334-0332
A classy shop with good Scandinavian wood carvings, crystal, china, and curios.

Mr. Video Movies
5916 N. Clark St.
271-4343
Videocassettes of movies sold, rented, swapped.

Robin's Studio
1482 W. Summerdale Ave.
769-2475
Works in fiber—macramé, weaving, wrapping—by Robin Whitespear, who claims to be a Jewish Indian.

Ruth's Antiques
5303 N. Clark St.
271-4438
A small and pleasant shop with a flag of Sweden in the window. Offerings include an excellent collection of miniatures.

*Smith's Clock Shop
6217 N. Broadway
262-6151

*Swedish Style Gift Shop
5309 N. Clark St.
561-6859

*Swedish Style Knit Shop
5301 N. Clark St.
561-3471

*The Swedish Tobacco Shop
5400 N. Clark St.
334-0368
Snuff, too—that most Swedish of "vices."

A. Zakarian Tapes and Records
6323 N. Clark St.
761-3332
Armenian, Assyrian, Turkish, Kurdish, and Arabic records and tapes. Middle Eastern drum lessons, too.

Foodstuffs

*Atour Food Importers
5406 N Clark St.
334-8040

Carl's Quality Market
5557 N. Clark St.
561-5855
Excellent meats; imported Scandinavian delicacies.

*Erickson's Delicatessen and Fish Market
5250 N. Clark St.
561-5634

Furuya and Company
5358 N. Clark St.
561-0887
Sukiyaki meat, fish for sushi, fresh produce, frozen specialties, advice. Sushi and chicken teriyaki Saturday mornings.

Let Them Eat Cake Pastry Shop Inc.
1701 W. Foster Ave.
728-4040
Good selection of pastries that are lovely to look at, delicious to taste, never cloying. Baking done here for several locations.

Nelson's Bakery
5222 N. Clark St.
561-5494
Breads, cookies, Scandinavian pastries, and not-to-be-missed raisin-and-cinnamon coffee cake.

Pan American Supermarket
5647 N. Clark St.
275-7474
A large selection of Cuban specialties among the usual run of Latin produce and groceries. They also make up Cuban sandwiches.

Philhouse
5430 N. Clark St.
784-1176
Magnet for the Filipino community offers fresh, dried, and frozen fish in mind-boggling variety (with smells to match), as well as spices, staples, and some produce. Live crabs most days.

*Siam Market
1131 W. Berwyn Ave.
989-7177

*Swedish Bakery
5348 N. Clark St.
561-8919

*Tip Top Meat Shop
5224 N. Clark St.
561-2072

*Wikstrom's Delicatessen A-Scandinavian American Catering
5247 N. Clark St.
878-0601, 275-6100

Dining and drinking

*Beirut Restaurant
5204 N. Clark St.
769-1250

*Bethlehem Restaurant
5815 N. Clark St.
769-0717

Carson's— The Place for Ribs
5970 N. Ridge Ave.
271-4000
Always crowded with diners anxious to try the ribs that Chicago picked as the best in the city. If you'd rather not put up with the usually long wait, they've an efficient carry-out service.

Chop Chae House
5668 N. Clark St.
784-7381
An unprepossessing storefront with excellent, authentically hot, Korean fare.

Felice's Round Table
5721 N. Clark St.
769-0606
The food's nothing special, but this place opened in 1899 and the interior hasn't changed much since then. Beautiful beveled glass, tin ceiling, dark woodwork.

Gaylord India
Kabob Corner
5440 N. Sheridan Rd.
334-5393
Northern branch of near-Loop Gaylord India. The location, a seedy motel, might put you off.

House of Sweden
5314 N. Clark St.
334-8757
Typical Swedish menu in crinkly-clean restaurant.

*El Inca
6221 N. Broadway
262-7077

*Jonathan's Seafood
5419 N. Sheridan Rd.
878-1846

Moody's Pub
5910 N. Broadway
275-2696
Good Chicago pub-style hamburgers. Pleasant outdoor dining and drinking.

*Piqueo
5427 N. Clark St.
769-0455

*The Pumping Company
6157 N. Broadway
743-7994

Seoul House
5346 N. Clark St.
728-6756
Presentation isn't the most artful, but the Korean food is among the tastiest.

Simon's Tavern
5210 N. Clark St.
(no phone)
Glögg in season at this quintessential Swedish bar.

*Svea
5236 N. Clark St.
334-9619

*Tacos & Things
5551 N.Broadway
878-7743

Thai Restaurant
5143 N. Clark St.
334-5757
One of Chicago's first Thai restaurants is a good value, though the food has been overshadowed by others.

*Villa Sweden
5207 N. Clark St.
334-1883

*Wing Hoe
5356 N. Sheridan Rd.
275-4550

Zazoo's Foods
and Delicatessen
1355 W. Foster Ave.
561-7277
Delicatessen is an afterthought in this trendy spot decorated with stylized animal drawings and sculpture. The menu is standard New Town "gourmet," but you can be served in an attractive indoor arbor.

Entertainment

Benchley's
6232 N. Broadway
973-6565
Jazz musicians every night.

Coconuts
5320 N. Sheridan Rd.
275-2222
Crowded club draws everyone from gays to greasers with everything from jazz to disco. Has a dance floor with a sophisticated sound system, three indoor bars and two on the patios, and a cheap buffet Tues.-Thurs.

*Devon Theater
6225 N. Broadway
743-1924

On Broadway Chicago
5246 N. Broadway
878-0202, 878-0203
Big bar and concert room attracts singles with rock, blues, rhythm and blues, reggae and jazz fusion. Outstanding sound system.

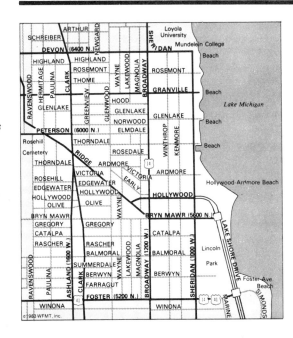

Rogers Park

Rogers Park has always been a staging area, a way station for those bound upward and elsewhere. Its earliest inhabitants were the Indians, who hunted here and roamed the natural trails formed after Lake Michigan rolled back to reveal a tall ridge—now Ridge Boulevard. They moved north of the Indian Boundary Line (today's Rogers Avenue) in 1816, ceding the land to the south and opening the way for later homesteading in this region. The settlers, many of them European truck farmers trying to make their first bankrolls in this country, included Phillip Rogers (after whom the community is named) and Patrick Touhy (whose name is now that of a thoroughfare). Both men became major developers here between 1840 and 1870.

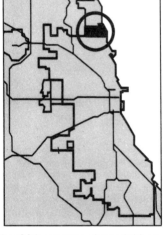

Although the fields of West Rogers Park (originally called West Ridge) didn't begin to sprout suburbanlike bungalows until well into the 20th century, the neighborhood east of Ridge Boulevard exploded with the coming of the el in 1907. The Irish, joining German landed gentry and tradesmen near the lakefront, built **St. Ignatius Church** (Glenwood and Loyola Avenues), a 1917 Jesuit landmark designed by Henry J. Schlacks after the Gesú, the order's mother church in Rome. By the 1920s, area Jews had founded **Congregation B'nai Zion** (Pratt Boulevard and Greenview Avenue)—Chicago's first Conservative congregation—and **Temple Mizpah** (now the Korean United Presbyterian Church; Morse Avenue and Ashland Boulevard)—the North Side's first Reform congregation—challenging the Germans as the neighborhood's largest ethnic group and, by mid-century, surpassing them.

Rogers Park's population quadrupled between 1910 and 1920, then doubled again in the next decade. The area was transformed by an apartment and residential-hotel building boom. Many of the elegant, pre-World War Two three-flats and fine court buildings remain; a sizable number are condominiums. Scattered among them are 1960s-vintage low-rises. The most desirable of the older buildings may be east of Sheridan Road by the lake, but the streetscape is much the same all the way west to Ridge Boulevard. The beautifully maintained **Casa Bonita Apartments** (7340-50) are an exercise in Moorish splendor that stops just short of being garish.

Spacious apartments, convenient transportation to the Loop, and the string of beaches on Lake Michigan remain East Rogers Park's lures today, while the faces of the residents continue to change. There are still many Jews, a number of them recent arrivals from the Soviet Union, but current denizens also include East Indians, Chinese, Koreans, Latinos, and lots of college students.

Loyola University (6545 North Sheridan Road) dominates the southern end of East Rogers Park. The campus buildings are a mixture of turn-of-the-century red brick (Loyola was chartered in 1909) and modern concrete and glass. Adjacent is **Mundelein College** (6363 North Sheridan Road), a Catholic women's school in a masonry skyscraper that is listed on the National Register of Historic Places. Construction began on the Art Moderne building with its Art Deco detailing in 1929, just three days after the stock market crash that ended Rogers Park's building boom.

The campuses and students strolling the streets lend a college-town flavor to parts of the neighborhood. Sheridan Road is lined with pizza parlors and other inexpensive restaurants, clothing shops, secondhand stores, an army-surplus spot, and a brightly lit pool hall. The largest and most intriguing of several bookstores in the area is **Project 1999 Gallery, Cafe & Bookstore** (6544 North Sheridan Road). Half of the second-story shop is a maze of passageways and floor-to-ceiling shelves jammed with worn but readable hardcovers and paperbacks, some of which may have been peddled by students eager for pocket money. The collection is particularly strong in European literature and history. Owner Eduard Vidmar converted the space across the hall to a café and gallery where you can enjoy espresso, coffees, teas, and light snacks amid exhibits of paintings and photographs by local artists.

The Morse Avenue elevated stop leads to the heart of a multifaceted shopping area. For example, the stock, shop signs, and conversations at the **European Delicatessen** (1339 West Morse Avenue) testify to the new Russian presence. One half of the store is filled with glass, brass, and wooden wares from the U.S.S.R.; the other has enticing twist breads, fish, and meats. Nearby, **Perry's Prime Meats** (7011 North Glenwood Avenue) has been selling prime aged steaks, specialty cuts, and homemade breakfast sausages for decades. **Prem Mark Natural Foods** (1527 West Morse Avenue), an attractive natural-foods market, has everything from frozen organic meats, fresh produce, bulk grains, honey, and coffee (grind your own in the store) to trail mixes and a full line of natural cosmetics.

If you're hooked on healthy foods—even if you've always shunned "health food"—**Heartland Cafe** (7000 North Glenwood Avenue) is a real treat. Salads with yogurt dressing and hearty soups with corn bread precede economically priced chicken, fresh fish, quiche, and vegetarian dinners. Sandwiches, omelettes, and more than 30 natural juices are also on the menu. Jazz, folk, or classical musicians hold forth on the makeshift stage some evenings and during weekend brunches.

But the choice spot for entertainment is the **No Exit Café & Gallery** (7001), a relaxed, honest-to-goodness coffeehouse. Besides the coffees, teas, and pastries, the best local and national folk musicians are the principal fare, although the stage is surrendered for jazz or classical music on some evenings and on weekend afternoons. There are even occasional poetry readings.

Morse Avenue also has interesting little shops. **Camelot Shoe Company** (1501) is a factory outlet for women's shoes and boots, with stock changing periodically. **Leonard's Juvenile** (1550) is crammed with clothes for toddlers and youngsters, most at bargain prices. A block north is **Liesl's Sample Shop** (1409 West Lunt Avenue), offering stylish women's dresses, suits, and separates at a touted 20 to 30 percent below suggested retail prices.

Low rents, a cosmopolitan aura, and a sense of community have attracted a variety of artisans. Sol Kaniuk turns out a glass menagerie of animals and birds, delicate ships, miniatures for dollhouses, and vases at **Creative Glassblowing** (1445 West Morse Avenue). Stoneware and porcelain pots, jars, bowls, dinnerware, and mugs made by several artists are sold at **Chicago Clay Feat** (1405 West Lunt Avenue), a studio and gallery. And jazz and classical musicians from all over the country visit **Peterson Musical Instrument** (7003 North Glenwood Avenue) to have Tom Peterson repair their horns, to buy a new one, or just to talk.

For fine stringed instruments, musicians travel north to the Howard Street el stop and stroll east to **Fritz Reuter and Sons** (1565). The original Fritz—he established the firm in 1921 to create fine violins, violas, and cellos—isn't around any more, but his two sons, Fritz Jr. and Gunther, carry on the craft. Gunther is reputedly the most prolific master violin maker in the U.S., having created 100 in Europe before making nearly 200 more instruments in this country. In addition to selling fine instruments, the Reuters repair and rent all types of violins. When they opened this shop in 1964, a touch of class returned to an area that has seen turbulent swings.

"Germania," the little residential enclave south of Calvary Cemetery, was originally part of Evanston, but, because isolation precluded effective delivery of that suburb's services, the voters chose annexation to Chicago in 1915. Prosperity in the 1920s brought a spate of fairly elegant houses and apartment buildings to Juneway and Jonquil Terraces as well as fashionable shops and a movie palace to Howard Street. Post-World War Two neglect earned this decaying section an unattractive tag—The Jungle. Today, however, massive public and private apartment-rehabilitation efforts augur a rosier future. In fact, in the mid-1970s, the **Wisdom Bridge Theatre** (1559 West Howard Street) opened in the neighborhood, signaling the climb back to respectability. The remodeled house hosts first-rate productions (they have captured about two dozen Joseph Jefferson Awards) that regularly draw sell-out crowds (*see Theater*).

Although still marred by sleazy bars, greasy spoons, and dubious thrift stores, this end of Howard Street also has its noteworthy shops. A classy, eclectic assortment of antiques, jewelry, and vintage clothing crowds one section of **Lost Eras** (1517), while the other sets forth an eye-popping assortment of Art Deco. **Sherwyn's Health Food Shops** (1511) carries a huge selection of additive-free foodstuffs, everything from goat's milk and organically grown rice to carob syrup and salt-free pretzels.

For much of its length, Howard Street separates Rogers Park from Evanston. The plethora of taverns on the Chicago side of the street is a legacy of Evanston's efforts to keep Prohibition alive well into the 1970s. But Howard Street also has worthwhile eateries, including **Edwardo's Pizza** (1937)—try spinach-stuffed pie—and **Charlie Lui's** (2741), a lavishly decorated Mandarin and Szechwan spot serving such seductive delicacies as princess chicken, asparagus-abalone casserole, and smoked tea duck.

The makings for Mandarin fare—or for Cantonese, Korean, Japanese, Filipino, or any Asiatic cuisine you favor—may be found at the **Oriental Food Market** (2801 West Howard Street). The store sells all the staples, from ginger and dried seaweed to sesame buns, rice sticks, and X-rated fortune cookies. Chu-Yen and Pansy Luke, the friendly and helpful owners, also teach Oriental cooking and sell or rent woks, steamers, Mongolian hot pots, and other utensils. At the triangular intersection of Clark, Rogers, and Jarvis, you can round out your diet with a visit to the **Rogers Park Fruit Market.** Enclosed and in the midst of the city, it still seems like a roadside vegetable stand, setting forth a broad array of produce, from lettuce and tomatoes to papaya and guava.

Across the street is Rogers Park's most inventive sandwich shop. **Capt'n Nemo's Submarine Sandwiches** (7637 North Clark Street) slathers layers of meats, cheeses, eggs, and vegetables onto French bread and serves up a half-sandwich that will satiate any but the hungriest trencherman. For the take-out crowd, homemade soup (free sample) is sold by the cup to the gallon, and sandwiches by length: Partygivers may order them two to six feet long (a foot serves six to eight, costs about $10). Prices at **Affy Tapple** (7110) can be a bargain if you buy their factory seconds—those which are undersized, unevenly coated, or with broken sticks.

In addition to its snack shops, convenience stores, and services, Clark Street harbors several antiques stores. One is **Yesterday, Today & Tomorrow** (7046), a shop dealing in movie posters, baseball cards, and comic books. Another find, **Kenneth L. Gustafson Antiques and Books** (6962), has a sizable section devoted to Civil War history and Lincoln lore. The shop is a jumble and you have to paw around, occasionally moving a cat, to get at what you want. Gustafson himself is a treat—a seeming curmudgeon with a rollicking sense of humor, doing precisely what he enjoys.

The shops of West Rogers Park exhibit the same eclectic air, with perhaps even more diversity. Stroll down its main commercial street, Devon Avenue. Within a two-block stretch, signs beckon you to purchase gyros and knishes, blue jeans and saris, antique brass beds and mezuzahs. The thoroughfare throbs with life and is a Babel of tongues. Amid the crush of everyday shops are specialists (some closed on Saturdays) that cater to the neighborhood's particular needs.

The **Mid-West Fish Market** (2948) smokes its own whitefish and sable, and it will grind fresh fillets for gefilte fish. Great homemade hot dogs, bologna, salami, and other smoked meats highlight the offerings at **Hungarian Sausage and Delicatessen** (2613). Complete a brunch-buying trip by joining the number-clutching crowds at **Leonard's Bakery** (2651) or at **Gitel's Bakery** (2745) for chale, almond rings, and, seasonally, hamantaschen. You can stock up on Indian foods at **International Foods and Emporium** (2537), an importer's retail outlet. And **Taj Sari Palace** (2553), one of the largest and classiest East Indian clothiers, displays a mind-boggling assortment of diaphanous fabrics, some precut to sari length.

The restaurant scene is even more varied. Russian immigrants have opened several dining spots, among them **Kalinka** (2842), a Ukrainian-run storefront that features delicious charcoal-grilled marinated chicken and shashlik served on skewers. At **Kavkaz Restaurant & Club** (6405 North Claremont Avenue), the generally excellent food is Georgian—a cuisine similar to Armenian or Middle Eastern and touted as the Soviet Union's best. Live music and dancing on weekends make the atmosphere quite festive. **The Bagel** (3000 West Devon Avenue) dishes up dinner just like Bubbe used to make. Try the gefilte-fish-stuffed whitefish. One of the oldest Thai places in the city, **Bangkok House** (2544) remains a good value (shrimp with bai ka pao is outstanding), while **Dae Ho** (2741) serves notable mandoo and sweet-and-sour red snapper, as well as Korean palate scorchers. **Family Corner** (2901) offers Kashmiri-style fare in a former Italian restaurant, which may account for the Himalayan-style vegetarian pizza; **Satkar's** (2240) Indian menu is exclusively vegetarian. **Standard India** (2546) displays a colorful array of sweets and has a wide selection of well-prepared dishes from the subcontinent; don't miss the "snacks and appetizers." A good place to take kids for burgers, ribs, ice-cream treats, and other American dishes of middling to good quality is **Sally's Stage** (6335 North Western Avenue), where "The Mighty Barton" theater organ (from the Nortown Theatre across the street) merrily toots, whistles, jangles, and clangs in accompaniment to amateur and near-amateur performers.

Western Avenue bisects the community, and between Peterson and Touhy

Avenues, it's largely lined with a clutch of car lots that limits other commercial enterprises. Farther north, **Direct Auctioneers** (7232) is worth a visit for its celebrated Sunday sales, which can yield almost anything. Auctions of fine arts and museum-quality antiques are seldom found at this gigantic, rather insalubrious former garage. But frequent sales offer enough run-of-the-mill 19th- and 20th-century furniture, furnishings, tableware, and collectibles to stock a dozen antiques stores. There are no catalogues, but each lot is numbered, and bidders who've obtained a bidding paddle by making a refundable deposit get some bargains. On the other hand, "estate and storage" auctions provide the best buys and most convivial gatherings. Mountains of unnumbered box lots are put on the block to sell for pittances; a liquor case filled with shoes, bedding, books, or dishes may go for as little as $5; an entire apartment might be furnished for $300. Bring lots of cash to these sales: Only long-time buyers get credit.

Off Western Avenue is one of Chicago's most fortuitously positioned residential enclaves, the **Park Castle Condominium** (2416-58 West Greenleaf Avenue) and the **Park Gables Apartments** (2438-84 West Estes Avenue). Developer Irvin Blietz lavished both buildings' interiors with swimming pools—Park

Interesting places

Angel Guardian Center
2001 W. Devon Ave.
973-6000
Originally Angel Guardian Orphanage, founded by Germans in 1865 to serve Civil War orphans, the grounds are now owned by Catholic Charities of Chicago and house a social service complex. Facilities include a senior citizens' center; Misericordia North, a retarded children's home; a learning center; and a large gymnasium where the Chicago Bulls and Chicago Sting practice when they're in town. Don't miss the striking red-brick church, designed by Henry J. Schlacks and built in 1905.

*Casa Bonita Apartments
7340-50 N. Ridge Blvd.

Cobbler's Mall
1330 W. Morse Ave.
764-5906
This small shopping mall is a nice reuse of a building that once housed a theater, then a synagogue.

*Congregation B'nai Zion
Pratt Blvd. and Greenview
465-2161

Cook County Federal Savings and Loan
2720 W. Devon Ave.
761-2700
The building is a replica of Independence Hall, and the commitment to patriotism is carried out by plaques inset on the façade and a statue of "the fighting Yank."

Granada Theatre
6427 N. Sheridan Rd.
No phone
This masterpiece of movie-palace Moorish architecture was built by the Marks Brothers in 1923 to present stage shows; Balaban & Katz bought it in 1932 and converted it to a movie house; today it features occasional rock concerts.

Bernard Horwich Jewish Community Center
3003 W. Touhy Ave.
761-9100
A center for cultural events, the building also houses recreational facilities, including a pool and gym.

*Indian Boundary Park
2500 W. Lunt Ave.
764-7648

*Loyola University
6525 N. Sheridan Rd.
274-3000
Don't miss the Martin D'Arcy Gallery of Art (see Museums).

*Mundelein College
6363 N. Sheridan Rd.
262-8100

*Park Castle Condominium
2416-58 W. Greenleaf Ave.
973-0760

*Park Gables Apartments
2438-84 W. Estes Ave.
No phone

*St. Ignatius Church
Glenwood and Loyola
764-5936

*Temple Mizpah
(now the Korean United Presbyterian Church)
Morse Ave. and Ashland
465-3377

Thillens Stadium
Devon and Kedzie Aves.
743-5140
866-7044 (events)
The check-cashing firm donated this playing field to the community as a setting for all sorts of organizational fund-raisers, including, occasionally, donkey baseball (yes, the players ride donkeys).

*Warren Park
2045 W. Pratt Ave.
973-0620

Gables's bedecked in Turkish trappings, Park Castle's with a rustic waterfall. Formal gardens and fountains grace the courtyards, which open onto one of the city's most delightful green swaths, **Indian Boundary Park** (2500 West Lunt Avenue). The name recalls the pioneer-days' treaty, but the lovely space has everything an urban park should: a Tudor field house, benches beneath shade trees, tennis courts, playgrounds, a migratory-waterfowl pool, and a vest-pocket zoo—with sadly cramped bears, deer, goats, and more comfortable, smaller wildlife—all provided on a rotating basis by the Lincoln Park Zoo.

Warren Park, along Pratt Avenue between Western and Damen Avenues, doesn't have Indian Boundary Park's charm, but it does represent a victory for the neighborhood. Formerly a private golf club, the land almost fell into the hands of condominium developers eager to turn the huge green space into high-rises. After a public outcry, the Chicago Park District acquired the property, converting it to public use with a nine-hole golf course, five baseball fields, four basketball courts, three playlots, tennis courts, and a toboggan hill. There are winding pathways for biking, jogging, and cross-country skiing. A field house with a gym and an indoor/outdoor swimming pool is planned.

Shopping and services

Bais Stam
6343 N. California Ave.
973-1311
This traditional Jewish bookstore also is the workplace of Yochanan Nathan, a sofer, whose tasks include verifying the ritual scrolls.

Bargain Inn
7069 N. Glenwood Ave.
338-4495
Recycled children's clothing.

Bob's in Rogers Park
6360 N. Broadway
743-1444
Thousands of magazines from all over the world.

Brown Beaver Antiques
2600 W. Devon Ave.
338-7372, 869-5589
Rooms full of antique brass beds with (according to the management) nary a reproduction among them.

*Camelot Shoe Co.
1501 W. Morse Ave.
465-4488

*Chicago Clay Feat
1405 W. Lunt Ave.
262-2522

Chicago Hebrew Bookstore
2942 W. Devon Ave.
973-6636
Religious reading matter, prayer shawls, mezuzahs, ceremonial goblets.

Coren's Rod & Reel Service
6424 N. Western Ave.
743-2980
Has everything you need to make your own fishing rod and reel. Also custom builds, repairs, and handles mail orders (catalogue available). Note the colorful terra-cotta tilework on the Art Deco building.

*Creative Glassblowing
1445 W. Morse Ave.
764-1164

Cut-Rate Toys
2424 W. Devon Ave.
743-3822
Quality toys at economical prices. Frequent sales make for even better bargains.

*Direct Auctioneers
7232 N. Western Ave.
465-3300

Dress It Up
6979 N. Sheridan Rd.
761-6673
Vintage clothes, some never worn, from the Victorian era to the '50s.

Erehwon Mountain Supply
1252 W. Devon Ave.
262-0516
A super stock of camping and hiking equipment and books. Gives knowledgeable answers to questions. Also in Niles.

Everybody's Bookstore
2120 W. Devon Ave.
764-0929
Comics, old magazines, bubble-gum cards, used books—all in a jumble.

The Frame Gallery
2925 W. Touhy Ave.
973-3888
Donald Leman restores antique clocks and frames; he also does framing.

Guitar Asylum
6975 N. Sheridan Rd.
262-6011
Discounts on new Gibsons and one of the city's largest collections of used ones (mostly electric) for sale.

*Kenneth L. Gustafson Antiques and Books
6962 N. Clark St.
761-0904

Dining and drinking

Astoria Restaurant
2340 W. Devon Ave.
761-5050
Decent Russian food in a baronial, though faded, dining room with elaborately set tables. Dance band on weekends.

*The Bagel
3000 W. Devon Ave.
764-3377
Braille menus.

*Bangkok House
2544 W. Devon Ave.
338-5948

Cafe Hanegev
6407 N. California Ave.
761-8222
Storefront restaurant with good Israeli food, excellent salads. Crowded on Sunday with family groups ordering kosher burgers.

*Capt'n Nemo's Submarine Sandwiches
7367 N. Clark St.
973-0570

La Choza Restaurant
7630 N. Paulina St.
465-9401
Always crowded, despite its location on a shabby street. Relatively inexpensive Mexican dishes in Mexican mess-hall atmosphere.

*Dae Ho
2741 W. Devon Ave.
274-8499

*Edwardo's Pizza
1937 W. Howard St.
761-7040

*Family Corner India Restaurant
2901 W. Devon Ave.
262-2854

Fluky's
6821 N. Western Ave.
274-3652
Drive-in-type operation for state-of-the-art Chicago hot dogs.

Constructing the massive earth fill for the Howard Street El, 1916

Glenway Inn
1401 W. Devon Ave.
743-2208
Hearty American fare, with occasional offerings of corned beef and cabbage as a gesture to the Auld Sod. Irish decorations surround the bar, where old-timers reminisce about the days when East Rogers Park was crowded with Irish taverns.

Golden Bull
7308 N. Rogers Ave.
764-1436
Wild-game dishes (some require 24-hour notice) are a big attraction at this Hungarian spot, which also serves all the standards. Beer garden in summer. Moderately priced, but not cheap.

Hamilton's Pizza & Pub
6341 N. Broadway
764-8133
Pizza is the specialty in this pleasant hangout for Mundelein students.

*Heartland Cafe
7000 N. Glenwood Ave.
465-8005
Outdoor tables in summer.

Jim's Deli
6574 N. Sheridan Rd.
764-3354
Breakfasts and cheesecakes are specialties at this student hangout. Lots of take-outs, too.

*Kalinka Restaurant
2842 W. Devon Ave.
465-5675

*Kavkaz Restaurant & Club
6405 N. Claremont Ave.
338-1316

*Charlie Lui's Restaurant
2741 W. Howard St.
465-5252

My Place For?
7545 N. Clark St.
262-5767
A busy Greek restaurant that features fresh seafood. A good value.

Poolgogi Steak House
1334 W. Morse Ave.
761-1366
Korean standards; some Chinese and Japanese dishes; many omelettes available before 5 p.m.

Ruthie's
7011 N. Western Ave.
743-3333
Good ribs and steaks; everything else varies in quality.

*Satkar Vegetarian Restaurant
2240 W. Devon Ave.
274-1300

*Standard India
2546 W. Devon Ave.
274-4175

Troyka
6352 N. Broadway
338-4440
Entertainment, dancing, and good food make this a popular rendezvous for recent Russian immigrants.

Entertainment

Adelphi Theater
7074 N. Clark St.
764-3656
Neighborhood movie house screens second runs and revivals at low prices.

Biddy Mulligan's
7644 N. Sheridan Rd.
761-6532
Big names in blues, as well as some rockabilly, R & B, jazz, and soul. Music almost every night; cover varies.

Campus Room Inc.
6550 N. Sheridan Rd.
743-0438
Large, well-run pool hall, also has pinball and video games.

Club C.O.D.
1201 W. Devon Ave.
743-3020
New Wave and hard-core punk; national acts on weekends, locals during the week. Cover varies.

The Commons Theatre Center
6443 N. Sheridan Rd.
465-3030
Lovely little theater in a converted dance studio on the 2nd floor of the Granada Theatre Building (see Theater).

400 Theater
6746 N. Sheridan Rd.
761-1700
Imaginative booking policy makes this an interesting movie theater.

Minstrel's
6465 N. Sheridan Rd.
262-6230
Local blues, country, and jazz entertainers nightly in this crowded room.

Misfits
6459 N. Sheridan Rd.
465-4063
Up-and-coming out-of-towners as well as the best Chicago groups make this a must for New Wave fans. Decent sound system; cover varies.

*No Exit Café and Gallery
7001 N. Glenwood Ave.
743-3355

*Sally's Stage
6335 N. Western Ave.
764-0990

*Wisdom Bridge Theatre
1559 W. Howard St.
743-6442
(See Theater)

India Sari Palace
2534 W. Devon Ave.
338-2127
Saris, jewelry, perfumes, and other Indian imports.

Kid's Stuff
7017 N. Glenwood Ave.
764-9760
New and used toys, used furniture, and equipment.

*Leonard's Juvenile Shop
1550 W. Morse Ave.
262-0386

*Liesl's Sample Shop
1409 W. Lunt Ave.
764-1130

*Lost Eras Antiques
1517 W. Howard St.
764-7400

More By Far
6926 N. Glenwood Ave.
973-6070
Small contemporary gallery features fine arts and selected handcrafts by dozens of artists, including sterling silver sculptures (sailboats, trees, etc.) and jewelry by Frank A. Rosa.

Natural Rhythm Futon Co.
1947 W. Howard St.
338-3600
Doug Martin makes Americanized versions of Japanese futons (mattresses) you can sleep on or roll up and use as sofas. Lots of cover fabrics to choose from; pillows, too.

Olga Imports
6410 N. Western Ave.
465-6026
Peruvian imports, including alpaca capes and rugs, jewelry, metalwork, and ceramics.

*Peterson Musical Instrument
7003 N. Glenwood Ave.
973-0342

*Project 1999 Gallery, Cafe & Bookstore
6544 N. Sheridan Rd.
743-6685

*Fritz Reuter and Sons Violins
1565 W. Howard St.
764-2766

Rogers Park Book Store
1422 W. Morse Ave.
262-3765
A large, no-frills shop with good collections in architecture, Chicago history, Judaica. New and used.

Schwartz-Rosenblum
2906-08 W. Devon Ave.
338-3919
Good source for Judaica—books and gifts.

Simonas Shoe Repair
6948 N. Glenwood Ave.
No phone
Shoes and boots, from the staid to the outlandish, made to order and repaired.

Studio Sew Sew
7023 N. Glenwood Ave.
338-7914
Original clothing designs and reconstructions.

*Taj Sari Palace
2553 W. Devon Ave.
338-0177

*Yesterday, Today &Tomorrow
7046 N. Clark St.
743-7185

Foodstuffs

*Affy Tapple
7110 N. Clark St.
338-1100

Casa Hernandez
6978 N. Clark St.
743-2525
Full-service supermercado with Mexican and Central American staples.

Cheesecakes by JR
2841 W. Howard St.
465-6733
Janet Rosing's cheese-cakes are available at finer restaurants, such as the Chestnut Street Grill, and at this retail shop, where they're sold whole and by the slice in a variety of flavors. Discounts on seconds.

*European Delicatessen
1339 W. Morse Ave.
338-5560

*Gitel's Bakery
2745 W. Devon Ave.
262-3701

*Hungarian Sausage and Delicatessen
2613 W. Devon Ave.
973-5991
Hot deli carry-outs, too.

*International Foods and Emporium
2537 W. Devon Ave.
465-8382

*Leonard's Bakery
2651 W. Devon Ave.
743-0318

*Mid-West Fish Market
2948 W. Devon Ave.
764-8115

New York Kosher Sausage Corp.
2900 W. Devon Ave.
743-1664
Queen Esther poultry, Sinai sausages, Vita herring, Manischewitz matzo, and more.

*Oriental Food Market and Cooking School
2801 W. Howard St.
274-2826
Catering, too.

*Perry's Prime Meats
7011 N. Glenwood Ave.
465-3702

*Prem Mark Natural Foods
1527 W. Morse Ave.
465-6200

*Rogers Park Fruit Market
7401 N. Clark St.
262-3663

Romanian Kosher Sausage Co.
7200 N. Clark St.
761-4141
Makes sausages, smoked meats, deli products.

Shaevitz Kosher Meat & Sausage
2907 W. Devon Ave.
743-9481
A neighborhood butcher shop with a wide selection.

*Sherwyn's Health Food Shops
1511 W. Howard St.
761-1380
Also at 645 W. Diversey.

Swiss Pastries
7016 N. Western Ave.
465-5335
Fancy pastries, tortes, and petit-four assortments.

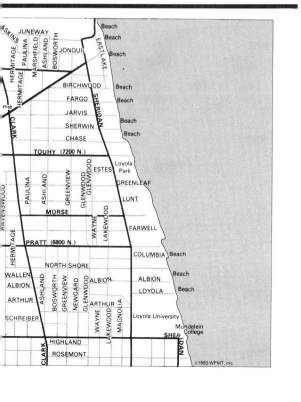

Albany Park

Across the river from "Greektown," Lawrence Avenue is ablaze with store signs in Korean, Greek, Arabic, and Spanish, proclaiming Albany Park one of Chicago's ethnically diverse communities. Hebrew, among others, is in evidence, too. As late as the fifties, this was one of the city's largest Jewish settlements. Although rapid population shifts brought problems and left scars, this neighborhood that has seen so many changes in the last 75 years is a treasure trove of the unexpected.

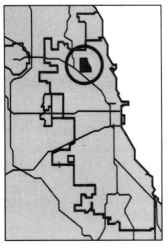

Unlike communities east of the river that were largely developed before they were annexed by Chicago, Albany Park and its environs became part of the city while still mostly farmland. Except for a couple of racetracks, there was little reason for anyone to make the journey along plank roads from more populated areas. Then, in a compressed version of the history of many neighborhoods, transit moguls bought up the land and laid tracks to fill it. With the Lawrence Avenue streetcar (1896), the Ravenswood el (1907), and the Kedzie trolley (1908), tidy profits were turned by Charles T. Yerkes, DeLancey Louderback (who named the community after his New York home town), and Clarence Buckingham (whose money built the downtown fountain). Subdivisions sprouted bungalows, and a spate of apartment building in the 1920s completed the area's physical development.

During the same decade, an exodus of mostly Reform Jews from North Lawndale transformed what had been a predominantly German and Scandinavian section. Throughout the Depression, their Conservative and Orthodox brethren followed, and by 1945, Jewish residents totaled nearly 35,000. Then, as the most upwardly mobile families moved on to North Park, Rogers Park, and Skokie, the process repeated itself. By 1964, the Jewish population had dropped to 17,000 and, by 1980, few remained.

Little recalls the neighborhood's Jewish heyday. **Kaufman's Bagel Bakery** (4411 North Kedzie Avenue), perhaps the best-known shop, stocks lovely breads and cakes and a good selection of some of Chicago's best hot-from-the-oven bagels. More than half a century old, **Simon Brothers Bakery** (3548 West Lawrence Avenue) is a source for traditional holiday sweets as well as breads and rolls, which can also be sampled at such restaurants as Carson's, The Palm, and Gene Sage's spots. **Rosen's Finer Foods** (3419) sells appropriate accompaniments, such as lox and schmaltz herring, while **Ada's Famous Deli** (4407 North Kedzie Avenue) is a local favorite for corned beef and dill pickles. The city's only retail, kosher, live-poultry outlet, **R. L. Odes Live Kosher Poultry Market** (4741), carries eggs and chickens, ducks, geese, and turkeys.

Of the few Orthodox synagogues that remain, most are small and worn. The oldest, **Congregation A Chay Bais Itzchok** (Drake and Leland Avenues), built in 1917, looks older than its years. The neighborhood's largest synagogue, constructed the same year, served the Northwest Side's biggest Reform congregation for decades, but in 1981, Temple Beth Israel followed its members to Skokie; and the stately building became the **First Korean Methodist Church of America** (Bernard and Ainslie Streets).

Many of the shop windows that bore flowing Hebrew letters now display geometric Korean characters. Koreans make up about 15 percent of Albany Park's population and have achieved a commanding presence. Some observers refer to them as "today's Jews" because of their devotion to hard work, education, and their religion. Diligent shop owners, they helped stabilize commercial sections once on the verge of collapse; their children are driving up test-score levels in area schools; their conversion of old synagogues to Korean churches is bringing an institutional balance to the once-sagging neighborhood.

Korean enterprises along Lawrence Avenue range from physicians and lawyers to herb shops and tae kwon do studios. You can get kung fu shoes and suits plus more usual equipment at **Olympic Sporting Goods** (3247), while **Y. S. Fashions** (3437) is the home of custom-made women's clothing designed by Yun Jung Ho. **Asiana & Co.** (3312) and the **House of Asian Treasure** (3222) stock unexpected lines of clothing and accessories (Bally of Switzerland, Christian Dior) for locals and Oriental tourists, as well as more customary gifts such as tea sets. Asiana also offers a large selection of ornate Korean furniture. The **Chicago Christian Book Center** (3830) satisfies the needs of the soul with Korean devotional aids.

For lots of Oriental foodstuffs, including meats, produce, and fish, visit **East West Foods** (3810). The **St. Louis Fish Market** (3537) is a good choice for sea bass, snapper, shrimp, and, bowing to history, smoked fish and herring. To sample Korean-style seafood at its best, head to **Villa Garden** (3553 West Montrose Avenue), a surprisingly pleasant room behind an inauspicious façade. Oysters and squid are specialties, preparations are authentically hot, and dinners come with a dizzying array of pickles and garnishes. In plainer surroundings, **Doh Soon Ne** (3220 West Lawrence Avenue) also offers carefully prepared, generously apportioned Korean dinners. Try the bibim naeng myun (cold noodles with meat in red-pepper sauce); it can't be beat. Nearby, Thais run the popular **Thai Little Home Café** (3125), which serves blisteringly spicy fare and is easy on the pocketbook.

Ironically, around Kedzie and Lawrence Avenues, at the heart of a section once solidly Jewish, an Arab community is developing as increasing numbers of Palestinians, Iraqis, Syrians, and Lebanese lend a new flavor to the area. **Alia Imports** (3136 West Lawrence Avenue) offers Arabic records and tapes, Middle Eastern metalwork, and "belly-dancing uniforms." Across the street, **Saba Meat and Grocery** (3139) has a fine selection of dates, pine nuts, spices, and such exotica as lamb livers. Much the same assortment is available at the **Holy Land Bakery and Grocery** (4806 North Kedzie Avenue) with the addition of fresh pita and sweets. These are supplied in large part by **Feyrous Pastry** (3450 West Lawrence Avenue), a lovely bakery that produces pastries and cookies sold over the counter and at Middle Eastern food stores and restaurants all over the city.

You can get ingredients to make Greek food at **International Foods** (4724 North Kedzie Avenue), a large supermarket with lots of specialty items and a staggering variety of tinned, stoned-ground coffees. The **International Bakery** (4742) sets forth freshly baked Greek breads, baklava, and filo dough, while **Andy's Fruit Ranch** (4725) bustles seven days a week with a cross section of the neighborhood's denizens picking out exotic produce. The gyros, souvlaki, and other lamb dishes at **Vrahos Restaurant** (3256 West Lawrence Avenue) are good any time, but live Greek music on Saturday nights is the big draw.

Yugoslavia is represented by **D.S.D. Delicatessen** (3818 West Lawrence Avenue) with its smoked meats, homemade sausage, and barbecued pigs and lambs. Affordable Hungarian meals compensate for the lack of atmosphere at **Magyar Csarda** (3724 West Montrose Avenue), an old-line neighborhood tavern. For tasty schnitzel, goulash, and strudel in a pleasant storefront eatery, try **Hungarian Delights** (3510 West Irving Park Road).

Other ethnic pleasures include the pastas at **Cas & Lou's Italian Restaurant** (3457 West Irving Park Road), delicious soups and Polish daily specials at the **Forum Restaurant** (3158 West Montrose Avenue), and the intriguing cuisine at **Rio's** (4611 North Kedzie Avenue), the city's first Portuguese restaurant. Here, for a modest sum, you can sample duck casserole accented by spicy sausage, chicken African-style, caldeirada (a piquant seafood medley), and other unfamiliar delights at white-clothed tables set with handsome dishes and fresh flowers. Some Brazilian food can be had from time to time, too. In keeping with Iberian custom, the room fills up very late on weekends, and impromptu entertainment sometimes replaces recorded Portuguese music.

Not all the area's attractions are steeped in ethnicity, however. **Archery Sales and Service** (3542 West Lawrence Avenue) features a fine-feathered selection and a 20-yard-long indoor range, as well as instruction. Along Irving Park Road's mostly uninteresting, broad reaches, a few stores stand out. The **Adams Factory Shoe Outlet** (3655) sells brand-name, factory overstocks and slight seconds of men's, women's, and kids' shoes at 10 to 50 percent off list price. **Tobacconist, Inc.** (4001 North Monticello Avenue) is an old-fashioned smoke shop where the proprietor will repair your favorite briar or blend a personal tobacco mixture. And at the elegant-looking **Antique Doll Hospital** (3110 West Irving Park Road), Edith Garney, D.D. (for Doll Doctor) restores, repairs, and sells antique and celebrity dolls for collectors and doll fanciers.

North Park, Albany Park's younger neighbor, enjoys less of the excitement that recent immigration brings, but it more actively recalls the entire area's Scandinavian history. **Sweden Shop** (3304 West Foster Avenue), spread over several rooms, overflows with reminders of this heritage: Royal Copenhagen porcelain, Orrefors crystal, Jensen pewter, Cornwall clocks, jewelry from Lapland, Båstad clogs, woodcarvings, candles, and other handicrafts. A community fixture since 1948, the shop publishes an 86-page catalogue.

College campuses, greenswards, and tree-lined streets emphasize North Park's differences from its neighbor to the south. The compact campus of **North Park College and Theological Seminary** (5125 North Spaulding Avenue) epitomizes the small-town feel. Founded in 1891 in Minneapolis by first-generation Swedish Americans and owned by the Evangelical Covenant Church of America, the school soon moved to the banks of the North Branch of the Chicago River where the Budlong Cucumber Farm once lay. It retains a traditional flavor, and Old Main, the 1894 central building, is listed on the National Register of Historic Places and is being restored. North Park College is known for its music department, whose dozens of public events include an annual Orchestra Hall concert. The basketball team's no slouch either.

In stark contrast, the modern buildings on **Northeastern Illinois University's** 67-acre campus (5500 North St. Louis Avenue) belie the school's age. Older than North Park College, the 10,000-student commuter school was founded in Englewood in 1867 as the Cook County Normal School—the state's first teacher-training institution. Later known as the Chicago Teachers College, it became part of the state university system in 1967.

Public resources at Northeastern include music, dance, and theatrical performances. The long-running hit *Do Black Patent Leather Shoes Really Reflect Up?* was first staged here; Ensemble Español is a resident dance company (*see Dance*); and the Jazz Ensemble toured Poland. The free Creative Writing Center offers budding authors criticism from published ones; the Popular Culture Resource Center, Dr. J. Fred MacDonald's baby, boasts his collection of comics, tapes, scripts, records, and other Americana from the 1930s through the '60s; the Biology Department owns and operates conducted tours of the Gensburg-Markham Prairie, one of Illinois's last virgin prairies. In addition, a Mini-U offers more than 100 noncredit courses, ranging from ballet to how to become a real-estate agent; and the city's only free Motorcycle Safety Program even provides a training cycle.

Backing on Northeastern is the 126-acre **Bohemian National Cemetery** (5255 North Pulaski Road), site of the Tomáš Masaryk Mausoleum and Mayor Anton Cermak's tomb. (Cermak was killed during a supposed assassination attempt on President-elect Franklin D. Roosevelt, to whom he is reputed to have said: "I'm glad it was me instead of you.") Just across Pulaski Road, the 80-acre, nonsectarian **Montrose Cemetery** (5400) has sections devoted to Japanese and Serbians, with stones carved in characteristic letterforms, and a memorial to the 1903 Iroquois Theater fire victims.

The grounds of the former Municipal Tuberculosis Sanitarium stretch along Pulaski Road from Bryn Mawr to Peterson Avenues, a reminder that, until World War Two, North Park was out in the country. Harry Chaddick's plans to replace the obsolete facility with a mammoth shopping center occasioned such vociferous neighborhood resistance that City Hall, at first enthusiastic, backed off. Today **North Park Village,** it contains a city health-care facility, special schools, housing and a community center for the elderly, Peterson Park (named for the nurseryman from whom the site was originally purchased), a nature preserve, and a very active nature center (which operates the city's only nature trails). New construction and rehabilitation of the handsome old buildings are still underway, but this is already a fine example of successful adaptive reuse.

Unlike North Park, which is one-fourth green space, Albany Park isn't blessed with much open land. But **Ravenswood Manor,** a residential enclave between Lawrence and Montrose Avenues, from the river to Sacramento Avenue, has an almost small-town ambiance with towering shade trees and large, single-family houses of brick and stucco. And **Horner Park** (2741 West Montrose Avenue) anchors the neighborhood's southeastern border, providing 52 acres of uninterrupted grass and trees, running from Montrose Avenue to Irving Park Road. The park is laced with jogging and bike paths, tennis courts, and ball fields; it even has an honest-to-goodness hill.

Interesting places

Albany Plaza Sculpture Garden
Kimball and Lawrence
267-7300
To foster local interest in sculpture, the Albany Bank and Trust Company rents pieces from Chicago artists.

Bohemian Home for the Aged
5061 N. Pulaski Rd.
588-1220
Founded by Bohemian freethinkers in 1894 as Bohemian Orphanage and Old People's Home.

*Bohemian National Cemetery
5255 N. Pulaski Rd.
539-8442

*Congregation A Chay Bais Itzchok
Drake and Leland Aves.
478-6416

***First Korean
Methodist Church
of America**
Bernard and Ainslie Sts.
463-2742

*Horner Park
2741 W. Montrose Ave.
267-2444

**Lakeside Evangelical
Church**
Lawndale and Wilson
463-4900
Once the Albany Park He-
brew Congregation, the
community's largest Con-
servative congregation, this
imposing building now
houses a Korean church.

*Montrose Cemetery
5400 N. Pulaski Rd.
478-5400

***North Park College
and Theological
Seminary**
5125 N. Spaulding Ave.
583-2700

*North Park Village
Pulaski to Central Park,
Bryn Mawr to Peterson
583-8970

***Northeastern Illinois
University**
5500 N. St. Louis Ave.
583-4050
Creative Writing Center: ext.
8129; Popular Culture
Resource Center: ext. 8364;
Gensburg-Markham Prai-
rie tour information: ext.
702; Mini-U: ext. 392; Motorcycle Safety Program:
ext. 457.

**Our Lady of Mercy
Church**
Troy and Montrose
588-2620
Completed in 1961.
Topped with a statue of the
Virgin, the brilliant gold
dome towers over sur-
rounding buildings. The
Italian-marble altar is
modeled on that at St.
Peter's in Rome.

*Ravenswood Manor
Lawrence to Montrose,
North Branch Chicago River
to Sacramento Ave.

*Space Junction of
Energy, sculpture*
Ravenswood el terminal
Kimball and Lawrence
Jerald Jacquard's abstract,
welded steel-plate piece,
painted industrial orange,
was the first artwork to be installed in a CTA facility. The
$1-million station was con-
structed in 1974.

Shopping
and services

Ada Furniture Co.
3622 W. Lawrence Ave.
784-6000
Good selection of used
furniture and brass beds.

***Adams Factory
Shoe Outlet**
3655-59 W. Irving Park Rd.
539-4120

*Alia Imports
3136 W. Lawrence Ave.
588-8969

Am Vets Thrift Store
3309 W. Lawrence Ave.
388-7800
A huge selection of used
clothing in a converted supermarket. Rack after
color-coded rack of shirts
and blouses for $1.50 each,
winter jackets for $8, house-
hold utensils for small
change.

*Antique Doll Hospital
3110 W. Irving Park Rd.
478-7554

***Archery Sales
and Service**
3542 W. Lawrence Ave.
588-2077

Artiques
3352 W. Foster Ave.
588-3585
An orderly shop with a nice
selection of Victorian and
American pieces at affordable prices.

*Asiana & Co.
3312 W. Lawrence Ave.
539-6666

C. W. Beu Floral Co.
4445 N. Pulaski Rd.
478-0091
A neighborhood fixture
since telephone numbers
were two digits, this family-
run florist in a sprawling
Deco building has three
greenhouses with plants of
all sorts, flats and garden
supplies, and related gifts.

**Brown's Bird Hospital
and Pet Shop**
3924 W. Lawrence Ave.
478-8200
Sales of and services for
feathered friends.

***Chicago Christian
Book Center**
3830 W. Lawrence Ave.
588-0577

**Council for Jewish
Elderly Resale Shop**
3503 W. Lawrence Ave.
583-5118
Classic thrift shop with an
added attraction—recently
published hardcover books
at a buck each.

Covenant Press
3200 W. Foster Ave.
478-4676
Bookstore of publishers for
the Evangelical Covenant
Church of America.

Gnostic Association
3760 W. Lawrence Ave.
478-5484
Books and classes, in
Spanish and English,
dealing with philosophy, art,
and the like.

**Harriet's Variety
and Department Store**
3444 W. Lawrence Ave.
463-4329
Old-time emporium sells
clothes, toys, etc.

*House of Asian Treasure
3222 W. Lawrence Ave.
463-2662

'K' Butsudans
5207 N. Kimball Ave.
463-3800
Specializes in Buddhist altars and accessories for them.

Olden Goodies
4808 N. Bernard St.
463-1450
Charming little antiques shop with a nice collection of dishes and glassware.

*Olympic Sporting Goods
3247 W. Lawrence Ave.
588-2811

Onyx Gallery
3235 W. Bryn Mawr Ave.
583-8835
Large selection of onyx carvings. Other gifts, too.

The Painted Lady Antiques, Inc.
3742 W. Irving Park Rd.
583-5116
Multiroom shop is great for browsing; whole rooms are devoted to kitchenware, crystal and porcelain, and the like.

Scriptorium Bookbinding
2656 W. Montrose Ave.
539-8495
Scott Kellar hand makes and restores fine book bindings.

*Sweden Shop
3304 W. Foster Ave.
478-0327

*Tobacconist, Inc.
4001 N. Monticello Ave.
463-8468

U-Myung Herbs
3435 W. Lawrence Ave.
478-8475
Korean herbalist and acupuncturist.

*Y. S. Fashions
3437 W. Lawrence Ave.
588-5815

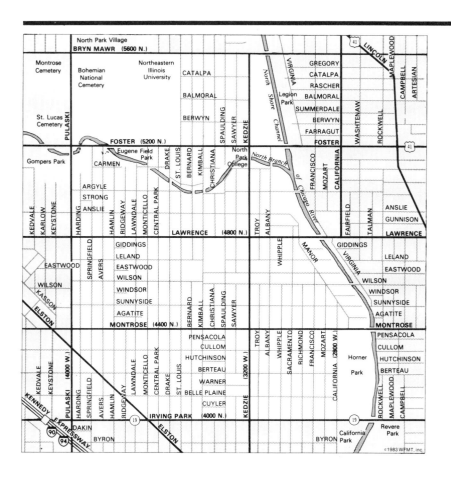

Foodstuffs

*Ada's Famous Deli
4407 N. Kedzie Ave.
539-5363
*Also in Lake Cook Plaza,
Deerfield.*

*Andy's Fruit Ranch
4725 N. Kedzie Ave.
583-2322

Beil's Bakery
4229 W. Montrose Ave.
725-0021
*A bit out of the neighbor-
hood, this large German
bakery is a local landmark.*

**Bob's Gift
Fruit Basket Market**
3610 W. Lawrence Ave.
463-2306
*Fresh fruit and a large
choice of wicker baskets.*

The Candy Tree
3323 W. Foster Ave.
478-1103
*Cards, gifts, and candies;
rich, homemade fudge.*

*D.S.D. Delicatessen
3818 W. Lawrence Ave.
539-1499

*East West Foods, Inc.
3810 W. Lawrence Ave.
267-8810

*Feyrous Pastry
3450 W. Lawrence Ave.
478-4230

Greco's Pastry Shop
3254 W. Montrose Ave.
478-7431
*You're greeted by the
aromas of freshly baked
Italian bread, cookies,
and cannoli.*

**Ed Hobfoll Kosher
Meats and Poultry**
3550 W. Lawrence Ave.
588-6778
*One of the few remaining
Jewish butchers in the area.*

***Holy Land Bakery
and Grocery**
4806 N. Kedzie Ave.
588-3306

*International Bakery
4742 N. Kedzie Ave.
583-7500

*International Foods
4724 N. Kedzie Ave.
478-8643

*Kaufman's Bagel Bakery
4411 N. Kedzie Ave.
267-1680
Also in Skokie.

Kum Ho Oriental Grocery
4606 N. Kedzie Ave.
539-3122
*Also carries a line of Orien-
tal cooking utensils.*

Lily's Bakery
4205 W. Lawrence Ave.
777-7377
*Offers baked, filled Chinese
buns as well as American
pastries.*

***R. L. Odes Live Kosher
Poultry Market**
4741 N. Kedzie Ave.
539-4685

Olga's Delicatessen
3209 W. Irving Park Rd.
539-8038
*A small deli selling wursts,
imported candies, German
toiletries.*

La Playa Food Store
4662 N. Kedzie Ave.
463-2484
*A Latin supermarket with a
good selection of meats,
produce, and spices.*

*Rosen's Finer Foods
3419 W. Lawrence Ave.
588-2756

*Saba Meat and Grocery
3139 W. Lawrence Ave.
583-3077

*St. Louis Fish Market
3537 W. Lawrence Ave.
478-4424

*Simon Brothers Bakery
3548 W. Lawrence Ave.
267-5005

Dining
and drinking

***Cas & Lou's
Italian Restaurant**
3457 W. Irving Park Rd.
588-8445

*Doh Soon Ne
3220 W. Lawrence Ave.
267-3050

*Forum Restaurant
3156 W. Montrose Ave.
267-9320

Glenshesk Public House
4102 N. Kedzie Ave.
267-1755
*Friendly tavern has Irish en-
tertainment on weekends.*

***Hungarian Delights
Restaurant**
3510 W. Irving Park Rd.
463-9875

*Magyar Csarda
3724 W. Montrose Ave.
588-9219

The Red Star Inn
4179 W. Irving Park Rd.
286-7788
*Urban-renewed landmark
transplanted with new owners to a modern brick
building. Offers a German-
American, mid-price-range
menu and bargain, all-you-
can-eat, daily specials.
Special packages include
brunch or buffet dinner and
bus rides to Chicago Bears
games; free beer on bus.*

*Rio's Restaurant
4611 N. Kedzie Ave.
588-1212
*Adjoining Portuguese
rôtisserie.*

*Thai Little Home Café
3125 W. Lawrence Ave.
478-3944

*Villa Garden
3553 W. Montrose Ave.
583-0126

*Vrahos Restaurant
3256 W. Lawrence Ave.
583-2688

Near Northwest Side

Terra incognita to most tourists, suburbanites, and lakefront sophisticates, West Town, Wicker Park, and Logan Square were once very much a part of the city's mainstream. Milwaukee Avenue—in turn a footpath, plank road, mainline streetcar route, and still a quintessential Chicago shopping strip—is the gateway to these wonderfully diverse neighborhoods. Each has contributed a thread to the city's tapestry, but a trip along the miles-long thoroughfare does more than trace Chicago's history. A vibrant Hispanic community flourishes where Poles, Germans, and Scandinavians once reigned, and eager rehabbers compete for buildings in elegant enclaves amid the welter of working-class streets.

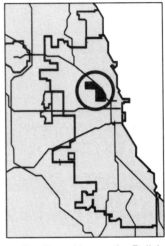

The tangled Division-Ashland-Milwaukee intersection, where the Polski Kiosk stocks newspapers and periodicals from the Old Country, is the heart of West Town. Through World War Two, this was the Polish downtown—the commercial hub for the largest concentration of Poles outside of Warsaw. Many of the signs are now in Spanish and gaudy modern storefronts mar handsome old buildings, but in good weather merchandise still spills out onto the sidewalks. Inexpensive clothing and shoe stores, myriad *supermercados* and taco joints, and scores of credit-furniture, linoleum, and linens outlets share the business streets with a few reminders of the past.

Business may be slow at the musty **A. S. Wegrzyn Books and Religious Articles** (1164 North Milwaukee Avenue) compared to the days when the shop's founder published Polish-language dream-interpretation books, tarot cards, and a monthly humor magazine, but **Dr. Michael's Herb Center** (1223) is still doing well. With an eye to changing times, the store has added ginseng, kelp, and health foods to Polonia's finest stock of traditional remedies. And an old-fashioned, gleaming white, former sausage shop, which might have become a theme restaurant in New Town, is now **Sea Merchants** (1456). Sausages are still on hand, but the real treat is the store's own line of smoked fish.

Even stronger links to another age are the **Polish Museum of America** (984)—the country's largest ethnic collection (*see Museums*)—and the neighborhood's magnificent churches. Many of these rococo monuments can be seen from the Kennedy Expressway, which sliced through Polonia nearly three decades ago. Approaching them on foot, however, brings home their dominance in the community and their special role in its history.

Blessed in 1881, **St. Stanislaus Kostka** (Noble Street and Evergreen Avenue) is the oldest of the grand Polish churches. Patrick Charles Keely, who also designed Holy Name Cathedral, was the architect of this Italian Renaissance masterpiece. Inside, under the dome of the altar, Tadeusz Zukotynski's painting, *The Triumph of Christ,* looms large in the immense central nave. Keely may have designed the building, but Father Vincent Barzynski determined the course of the city's oldest Polish parish in the late 19th century. Under his leadership, St. Stanislaus became the world's largest Polish parish. In 1893, its priests performed more than 2,000 baptisms and officiated at 1,000 funerals. Father Barzynski was also instrumental in founding schools, developing the Polish Roman Catholic Union, and starting a Polish daily newspaper.

In the mid-1870s, a group of dissidents formed Holy Trinity parish, triggering a 20-year dispute ended only by the intercession of the Vatican's delegate to the United States. Completed in 1906, **Holy Trinity Roman Catholic Church** (Noble and Division Streets) rivals St. Stanislaus in grandeur. William Krieg finished the design of Washington architect Olszewski (known as Von Herbulis), which may account for the building's mixture of neoclassical and baroque architecture. The church's open design was attained by using iron construction in the vaults, eliminating the need for internal supporting columns. Irena Lorentowicz's stained-glass windows, installed in 1955, highlight the open spaces.

Perhaps most beautiful of all, **St. Mary of the Angels Church** (Hermitage Avenue and Cortland Street) has been called the finest example of Roman Renaissance architecture in America. Begun in 1911 and completed nine years later, the 2,000-seat church was designed by Henry J. Schlacks and reminds some people of St. Peter's in Rome.

Churches are also the keystones of Ukrainian Village, another West Town ethnic community. Dedicated in 1915, **St. Nicholas Ukrainian Catholic Cathedral** (Oakley Boulevard and Rice Street) was modeled on the Basilica of St. Sophia in Kiev, although only 13 of the original's 32 copper-clad domes were incorporated in the Chicago version. Rich in mosaics and iconography, the interior has a brilliance rarely found in Western churches. When St. Nicholas switched to the Gregorian calendar, a rift between older congregants and more recent immigrants led to the formation of a new parish in 1973. At the conservative **Sts. Volodymyr and Olha Ukrainian Catholic Church** (Oakley Boulevard and Superior Street), the old (Julian) calendar is maintained. The building's gilded Byzantine domes are set off by a colorful, two-story-high mural on the façade.

A city landmark, the neighborhood's most striking church is Louis Sullivan's 1901 **Holy Trinity Orthodox Cathedral** (Leavitt Street and Haddon Avenue), a triumphant blend of mysticism and functionalism. The intimate, stucco-covered building is loosely based on wooden octagon-on-a-square churches familiar to the original parishioners—rural Byelorussians, Carpathians, and Ukrainians. The lavishly stenciled polychrome interior contrasts dramatically with Sullivan's restrained, geometric ornamentation around the eaves, doors, and windows. As at other local Ukrainian churches, coffee and cakes are served after the services.

Chicago Avenue, roughly between Western and Hoyne Avenues, is the community's main artery. The **Ukrainian Institute of Modern Art** (2320), in an old store building intriguingly modernized by Stanley Tigerman, is well worth a visit. Regular shows feature paintings, sculptures, and avant-garde works by contemporary artists, most of Ukrainian extraction. Along with the churches, the museum hosts community events heralded by Cyrillic-lettered posters cluttering local store windows. The **Ukrainian National Museum** (2453), open only on Sundays (or by appointment), fills a 19th-century townhouse with a collection of historic documents and photos, costumes, and folk art (*see Museums*).

Dyes, instruction books, and tips on where to learn how to make marvelous, traditional Ukrainian Easter eggs can be found at the **Ukrainian-American Publishing Company** (2315), along with records, other books, and gifts. Stroll down the street to **Delta Import Company** (2242) for a nice selection of finished eggs, ceramics, jewelry, fabrics, linens, and Czechoslovakian crystal. The shop also ships parcels to the Soviet Union and carries a large stock of blue jeans—much sought-after status symbols in Eastern Europe.

Stylized folk murals in a cheery dining room behind the bar at **Sak's Ukrainian Village Restaurant** (2301) set the stage for a taste of the Old World. Borscht is always available, as are Ukrainian sausages, cabbage rolls, and chicken Kiev. Be sure to try cheese-filled dessert crêpes topped with whipped or sour cream. Behind a chic, modern façade, **Galāns Ukrainian Café** (2212) brings together the old and the new. Besides Ukrainian specialties (more at lunch than at dinner), the menu offers German, Rumanian, and American dishes. Lovely tortes, pâtés, vareniky (filled dumplings), and other delights are also available at a deli-pastry take-out counter. The ambiance and prices are more like those in Lincoln Park than in Ukrainian Village.

East of Ukrainian Village, on both Chicago Avenue and depressed, depressing Division Street, Hispanic stores have supplanted most of the Polish ones. Try **Restaurant Tecalitlan** (1814 West Chicago Avenue) for fresh-fruit drinks and a wide variety of tacos that will make you forsake pallid Tex-Mex ones. Along with the long loaves for which it is named, **La Baguette Bakery** (1438) stocks a full range of dry and cookielike Mexican pastries, French storefront billing notwithstanding. **Las Villas Bakery** (1959 West Division Street), on the other hand, specializes in fancy refrigerated pastries and cakes. Flan (caramel custard), available in square pieces, can save a summer hostess lots of bother. Close to the vestiges of an old Italian neighborhood on Grand Avenue, the **Gonnella Baking Company's** outlet store (2002 West Erie Street) sells fresh-from-the-oven bread until midnight seven days a week; after then you can buy right in the plant. Older Chicago-style bungalows and ornate apartment buildings that rival Pilsen's for fanciful bays and decoration line the side streets. Beer-drinkers lounging on stoops and rowdy adolescents give the streets a sinister air that the reasonably discreet visitor can probably ignore.

In the Wicker Park community, many of the homes also date from the immediate post-Fire period, but here builders let their imaginations run rampant for a middle- and upper-class clientele. Spurned by the lakefront Anglo-Saxon, Protestant establishment as parvenus, German beer barons, packers, and merchants settled near the park, at that time a beautiful pleasure ground with a large swan pond. They were soon joined by their less wealthy countrymen (including the four Haymarket martyrs) and by Scandinavians who built more modest dwellings. Today **Wicker Park** (Damen Avenue and Schiller Street) has basketball and softball facilities instead of a pond, but the environs are again some of the city's hottest real estate.

Elegant brick and stone mansions in a delightful range of styles stand lovingly restored in this National Historic District, nominated as "a major survival of the 19th-century city." Along Pierce Avenue, massive stone houses with classic columns and arches face Victorian Gothic ones highlighted by intricate gingerbread on porches and entranceways. The steamboat-Gothic, Swiss-chalet Runge House (2138) served as the Polish Consulate in the 1930s. Once, famous Polish pianist Ignace Paderewski entranced a crowd of thousands with a recital played from the broad porch.

A delicate, wrought-iron fence surrounds two magnificent, early mansions on Hoyne Avenue. Set well back on a spacious lot, the John Raap House (1407) is a sprawling, three-story, red-brick, French Empire beauty with an adjoining coach house. Next door (1417), the Italianate home built in 1879 for furniture manufacturer Carl Warnecke boasts a lovely gazebo. The 1906 Romanesque **Wicker Park Lutheran Church** (Hoyne Avenue and Le Moyne Street) was built for a parish established in 1870 with stone salvaged from a Levee whorehouse. When queried about the seeming impropriety, the pastor is said to have replied, "It has served the Devil long enough. Let it now serve God." The World War One cannon nestled amid the ivy in front of 1558 is a reminder that the brick Victorian was once an American Legion post. It is one of the neighborhood's oldest houses, built in 1878 for C. Herman Plautz, one-time City Treasurer.

St. Paul's Evangelical Lutheran Church (North Avenue and Leavitt Street) dates from 1892, although the parish is almost a decade older. The stained-glass windows and interior woodcarvings are worth a look. Take Leavitt Street across North Avenue to hard-to-find Caton Street's proud brace of 1890s mansions, including real-estate developer Ole Thorpe's Romanesque home (2156). Houses like these command $300,000-and-up asking prices when they reach the market. However, most of the homes along Wicker Park's streets are smaller, workers' dwellings built after the Logan Square elevated reached the neighborhood in 1895. The Wicker Park Greening Festival (and house tour) allows glimpses of some of the more lavish interiors (*see Annual Events*). An architectural tour of the neighborhood should also include the marble-and-terrazzo lobby of the striking, Art Deco **Northwest Tower Building** (1608 North Milwaukee Avenue), hailed in 1929 for taking the skyscraper out of the Loop. The building has stood empty for years, but new owners have embarked on an ambitious renovation plan.

New ownership is revitalizing another Wicker Park landmark, the **Luxor Baths** (2039 West North Avenue). Built in 1923 as the North Avenue Bath House, this institution served an endless stream of immigrants in the European tradition and was a popular stopping place for traveling "drummers." There were private sleeping cubicles on the third floor, and the steam rooms, pool, restaurant, and lounge areas made it a sort of poor man's club. Over the years, the ornate terracotta façade got grimy, the building decayed, and the third floor earned a well-deserved unsavory reputation. But a pair of enterprising lawyers bought the operation in 1980, betting on Wicker Park's increasing acceptability. Men enjoy the facilities—Russian (normal humidity heat), Turkish (wet heat), and sauna (dry heat) rooms; a pool; and an exercise room with Nautilus equipment—for a daily fee or yearly membership. All day Wednesday and some hours on other days are reserved for women. Patronizing the second-floor bar and deli—chicken soup and skirt steak are popular choices—doesn't require paying an admission charge, but since attire even here is very informal, sex discrimination applies. The facilities may be rented for private parties.

Although a recent undertaking, **Orlofski Homemade Sausage and Delicatessen** (1658 North Damen Avenue) harkens back to the neighborhood's old days. The small, spotless shop offers 40 types of wursts and smoked meats, plus pierogi, stuffed cabbage, and imported delicacies. The Orlof brothers (one a butcher, the other a contractor) even stretched their name to make this old-fashioned place sound more authentic.

Margie's Candies (1960 North Western Avenue), in the Poulos family for 65 years, dares dieters with fudge, heavenly hash, and other homemade goodies, which cram cases topped with stuffed animals. But the real treat is custom-formulated, 18 percent butterfat ice cream. Lounge in one of the booths lining the odd-shaped store's periphery while a concoction, perhaps even the gargantuan $8 "world's largest sundae," is created behind the old-fashioned soda fountain. A mere 55 cents buys a cone big enough for a meal, and Margie makes passable sandwiches, too.

Milwaukee Avenue is a gray stretch of small factories, auto-parts outlets, secondhand stores, modest restaurants, and fading businesses from Orlofski's to Margie's and beyond, all the way to its intersection with Kedzie and Logan Boulevards. Vitality returns north of this grand traffic circle, which surrounds the Illinois Statehood Centennial Monument, a towering, gleaming white, eagle-topped column erected in 1918. Even here, however, most of the stores are the common, neighborhood-shopping-strip variety until Milwaukee Avenue enters Avondale, the new Polonia, north of Diversey Avenue.

Logan Square may lack intriguing shops, but the neighborhood was conceived on a sweeping scale unknown to the rest of the North Side. Crisscrossed by grand residential streets, it is the northern terminus of Chicago's matchless park-linking boulevard system. Kedzie and Logan, once dubbed "the boulevards of millionaires," and Palmer and Humboldt Boulevards, offer a picture of pre-Depression gentility. Although occasional homes, such as the George Maher-designed John Rath House (2703 West Logan Boulevard), stand out, the streetscape depends not so much on individual mansions as in Wicker Park, but on the panoramas.

Strikingly set at the head of Logan Boulevard, one of the city's widest, the **Norwegian Lutheran Memorial Church** (Logan and Kedzie Boulevards) is a red-brick charmer. Built in 1912 as the Minnekirken, the church still has only one English service a month, even though the community hasn't been a Norwegian bastion for years. The congregants come from all over the metropolitan area for services and for activities at the **Norway Center** (2350 North Kedzie Boulevard), a 1917 building that would look at home on the banks of a fjord. A few blocks south of the center, Kedzie Boulevard runs into Palmer Square, another charming, once Norwegian, parkway.

Logan Square's Scandinavian heyday was short. By the 1920s, Eastern Europeans, particularly Poles, added to the neighborhood's diversity, and more recently, Hispanics have settled here in great numbers. Decay on the humbler side streets spread to the broad ways, where mansions and huge apartments were broken up into smaller units. Telltale rusting cars litter some of the streets, but today Logan Square is one of those strange communities that is simultaneously on its way up and on its way down. Rehabbers are claiming some buildings, while less affluent newcomers are making do in meaner housing. In any case, this is a lovely area for a drive. Who knows? You might find that perfect house and join the boosters.

Interesting places

Bucktown
Bounded roughly by Bloomingdale, Western, and the Kennedy Expwy. *This old Polish working-class neighborhood had a rough reputation. Nobody's come up with a better explanation for the nickname than that many families kept goats, and male goats are called bucks.*

*Holy Trinity Orthodox Cathedral
Leavitt St. and Haddon Ave.
486-6064

*Holy Trinity Roman Catholic Church
Noble and Division Sts.
489-4140

*Northwest Tower Building
1608 N. Milwaukee Ave.

Northwestern University Settlement
1400 W. Augusta Blvd.
278-7471
Established in 1891, and still active, it was the city's first infant-welfare station and first portable children's day hospital. The building was designed by Allen and Irving Pond in what was then called English Domestic style.

*Norway Center
2350 N. Kedzie Blvd.
227-9759

*Norwegian Lutheran Memorial Church
(Minnekirken)
Logan and Kedzie Blvds.
252-7335

Old Wicker Park Committee
1527 N. Wicker Park Ave.
342-1966
Write for Nicholas H. Sommers's excellent $2 guide to Wicker Park houses.

*Polish Museum of America
984 N. Milwaukee Ave.
384-3352
(See Museums)

Polish Roman Catholic Union of America
984 N. Milwaukee Ave.
278-3210
National headquarters of the fraternal and benevolent society.

St. Boniface Church
Noble and Chestnut Sts.
666-4268
Originally a German parish, but by 1895, the church was the center for Chicago's Kashubes, German-speaking Pomeranians who are closely related to Poles. The present building was dedicated in 1903.

St. John Berchmans Church
Logan and Maplewood
486-4300
This Romanesque structure, dedicated in 1906, once was the center of Chicago's Belgian community, and dedication ceremonies were spoken in Flemish, French, and English.

*St. Mary of the Angels Church
Hermitage and Cortland
278-2644

*St. Nicholas Ukrainian Catholic Cathedral
Oakley Blvd. and Rice St.
276-4537

*St. Paul's Evangelical Lutheran Church
North Ave. and Leavitt St.
486-6244

*St. Stanislaus Kostka
Noble and Evergreen
278-2470

*Sts. Volodymyr and Olha Ukrainian Catholic Church
Oakley and Superior
829-5209

*Ukrainian Institute of Modern Art
2320 W. Chicago Ave.
227-5522
(See Museums)

***Ukrainian
National Museum**
2453 W. Chicago Ave.
276-6565
(See Museums)

*Wicker Park
1500 N. Wicker Park Ave.
276-1723

***Wicker Park
Lutheran Church**
Hoyne Ave. and Le Moyne
276-0263

Shopping
and services

Am Vets Thrift Store
2032 N. Milwaukee Ave.
388-7800
*Biggest and perhaps best of
the Am Vets resale stores,
with a broad selection,
some of which is funky.*

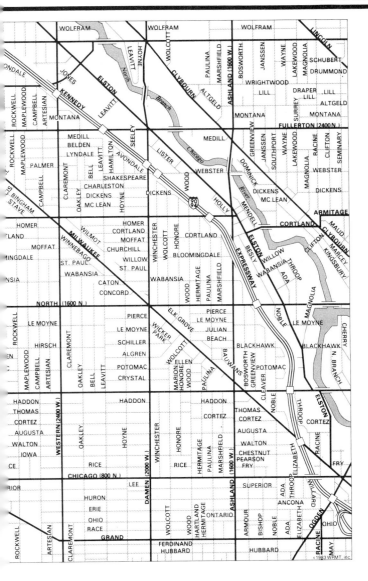

LOGAN SQUARE

Animal Kingdom
2980 N. Milwaukee Ave.
227-4444
Louie the lion and Clipper the dalmatian share a cage at this wonderful pet store/minizoo that sells out-of-the-ordinary and not always well-suited pets—monkeys, raccoons, foxes, rare birds. Also has cats, dogs, and loads of supplies.

J & D Brauner—
The Butcher Block
1735 N. Ashland Ave.
276-1770
Butcher-block tables, counters, etc. Custom work, too. Other locations.

Casa Central
2635 N. Kedzie Ave.
276-0500
Principal social-service agency for Logan Square's Hispanic population.

*Delta Import Co.
2242 W. Chicago Ave.
235-7788

Division St. Russian
Turkish Baths
1916 W. Division St.
384-9671
Old baths that haven't been spiffed up. They were portrayed in Saul Bellow's Humboldt's Gift.

*Dr. Michael's
Herb Center
1223 N. Milwaukee Ave.
276-7186

Edward Eggler
Leather Findings
1116 N. Milwaukee Ave.
486-4214
The sign of the cow hangs over the door, and the display of leather-working tools in the window is worthy of a museum. Edward Eggler sells everything needed for making or repairing shoes. He also makes leather specialty items, from aprons to holsters for Chicago cops.

Guild Clothing Mart
2427 N. Milwaukee Ave.
235-3733
Very low prices; surplus brand-name clothes.

Ikona Religious Art
and Bookstore
2208 W. Chicago Ave.
276-2040
Ukrainian religious articles and books in Ukrainian make this shop feel a bit too mystical for easy browsing, but some of the objects are quite beautiful.

Little Max's Shoes
1536 W. Chicago Ave.
421-8435
More than 50 years old, this business specializes in large and extra-wide women's shoes and wide-calfed boots. Also does custom work.

*Luxor Baths
2039 W. North Ave.
486-0234

Northwestern Pharmacy
1576 N. Milwaukee Ave.
486-0987
Open 24 hours a day.

Palatine Draperies, Inc.
1326 N. Milwaukee Ave.
276-6260
European-style goose-down comforters in a variety of tickings, including imported, high-thread-count cambric, are sold in stock sizes or are custom made. The shop looks like any of the cheap curtain/sheet stores on the strip.

Polonia Book Store
2886 N. Milwaukee Ave.
489-2554
What may be the largest Polish book shop in the country stocks books in Polish (lots of literature) and ones translated to English, as well as records, maps, cards, gifts, and Polish-language newspapers. Also a publishing house.

Sam Serota & Sons
1815 N. Milwaukee Ave.
276-7332
The store has been selling plumbing fixtures here so long that it's a fixture in the neighborhood. New goods, of course, but you may also find an old cast-iron bathtub in stock. Also at 2450 N. Milwaukee Ave.

Stauropegion Bookstore
2226 W. Chicago Ave.
276-0774
New and old, religious, art, and other books in Ukrainian and English. Also sells cards, sundries, and Smith-Corona typewriters with Cyrillic keys.

*Ukrainian-American
Publishing Co.
2315 W. Chicago Ave.
276-6373

Oscar Wastyn Cycles
2221 N. Milwaukee Ave.
384-8999
The store has been selling and repairing bicycles for more than 70 years. A meeting place for those interested in bike racing, including the Schwinn Lakeshore Wheelmen.

*A. S. Wegrzyn Books
and Religious Articles
1164 N. Milwaukee Ave.
276-1416

Ed Woehl Photo Supplies
1800 N. Honore St.
276-2280
From the outside it looks like a junk store, but inside there's a treasure of old cameras, stereopticons, and other photography-related items. Woehl also repairs cameras.

W.P.A.
1539 N. Damen Ave.
278-9724
Wicker Park gallery of environmental art mounts about ten shows a year, many featuring Chicago artists.

Zeller's Textile Co.
1723 W. Chicago Ave.
666-3985
This old Polish fabric and clothing store carries hundreds of babushkas.

Zirka Children's Fashions
2310 W. Chicago Ave.
772-8235
Nice line of youngsters' clothes, with some items showing the influence of Ukrainian folk costumes.

Foodstuffs

Alliance Poultry Farms
1636 W. Chicago Ave.
829-1458
Typically scruffy live-poultry store carries chickens, guinea hens, and rabbits, as well as fresh chicken and goose fat. Muscovy ducks are in stock occasionally.

Ann's Bakery
2158 W. Chicago Ave.
384-5562
Cakes and pastries are ordinary, but the thick-crust, light, Ukrainian rye bread is out of this world.

Augusta Bakery
901 N. Ashland Ave.
486-1017
Retail outlet of a big wholesale bakery that sells to Polish delis, etc. More good rye bread.

*La Baguette Bakery
1438 W. Chicago Ave.
421-2971

The Bulk Food Store
525 N. Ada St.
733-4253
Perhaps the nicest source for whole grains, raw honey, dried fruits, fresh peanut butter, and all that good stuff. One of five retail outlets of a big wholesaler (the others are suburban), so prices are low.

Caesar's Polish Deli
901 N. Damen Ave.
486-6190
More than half a century old, this gleaming grocery store and deli sells fine salads, naleśniki (crêpes), pierogi with a variety of fillings, and much more.

D'Amato's Bakery
1124 W. Grand Ave.
733-5456
Great Italian bread in all sorts of old-fashioned shapes in an Old World bakery that also carries cookies and a few pastries. They'll sell you uncooked pizza dough, too.

Economy Baked Goods
1452 N. Milwaukee Ave.
No phone
Day-old bread and rolls, coffee cakes for as low as 30¢ a package; pita bread may set you back $1 for 3 bags.

Europe Meat Market
1650 W. North Ave.
278-5329
A small Serbian butcher shop with exceptional sausages and kajmak also bakes lambs and pigs to order.

Gnatek Sausage Shop
1722 W. Chicago Ave.
226-5146
A nice Polish sausage shop.

*Gonnella Baking Co.
2002 W. Erie St.
733-2020

*Margie's Candies
1960 N. Western Ave.
384-1035

Marianao Food Market
3101 W. Armitage Ave.
278-4533
Bustling grocery does a big business in Cuban-style sandwiches. Try the steak.

Max's Fresh Fish Market
1472 N. Milwaukee Ave.
278-9127
Most of the smoked and fresh fish is the sort that appeals to European tastes (herring, whitefish, smelt), though some varieties are stocked for Hispanics. Fried fish and shrimp to go.

Michal's Delicatessen
1012 N. Western Ave.
486-0684
Fine old-fashioned deli with great oak fixtures stocks homemade sausages and makes up sandwiches.

*Orlofski Homemade Sausage and Delicatessen
1658 N. Damen Ave.
772-0969

St. Stanislaus Kostka's Boys Choir, Easter, 1942

*Sea Merchants
1456 N. Milwaukee Ave.
227-0600

S. N. A. Nut Co.
1350 W. Grand Ave.
421-2800
Raw and roasted nuts at
reasonable prices.

**Sunshine Bakery
and Delicatessen**
1238 N. Milwaukee Ave.
235-7808
Scrumptious Polish cook-
ies, strudels, and breads.
Polish and Hungarian
canned and bottled goods
and jams.

*Las Villas Bakery
1959 W. Division St.
278-3380
Other locations.

Dining
and drinking

Busy Bee Restaurant
1546 N. Damen Ave.
772-4433
Always-busy place serves
hearty Polish food and is a
hive of Wicker Park
business and social activity.

Café Du Liban
1001 N. Western Ave.
384-3153
Stunning décor (including
blue recessed lighting and
Deco bas-reliefs), good
Lebanese food, "Ameri-
can" and Arabic music, and
a belly dancer make this a
worthwhile stop.

Casa Aranda
1436 N. Ashland Ave.
342-9066
Unusual dishes—veal
cooked in a banana leaf,
bacon rind in green tomato
sauce—highlight the varied
menu at this spacious, airy
cantina. Lots of nice
touches.

Como Inn
546 N. Milwaukee Ave.
421-5222
Italian institution serves a
very broad menu in a
labyrinth of rooms ranging
from rococo to high-tech.
Sidewalk café in summer.

Father & Son Pizza
2475 N. Milwaukee Ave.
252-2620
Thin-, medium-, and thick-
crust pizza to eat here or to
take out.

*Galāns Ukrainian Café
2212 W. Chicago Ave.
384-7793

La Lechonera
2529 N. Milwaukee Ave.
772-6266
A large, clean Cuban res-
taurant with a menu that lists
about 100 items, ranging
from blue-plate specials at
less than $4 to paella for two
at $19. Fish specialties in-
clude snapper, kingfish,
and squid. Bring the kids.

Lindo Mexico
2607 N. Milwaukee Ave.
227-7252
A pleasant spot serving
Mexican food, with a slight
bow to American tastes.

El Mexicano
3137 W. Logan Blvd.
772-0441
Very broad menu offers intriguing house specialties
and Puerto Rican dishes, as
well as fair renditions of
Mexican standards. Pleas-
ant décor; good service;
overamplified guitarist most
evenings.

Orbit Restaurant
2948-54 N. Milwaukee Ave.
342-1515
Enjoy a very wide range of
Polish specialties at reasonable prices in the coffee
shop or in the more formal
dining room. Cocktail
lounge; live entertainment;
banquet facilities.

Ostioneria Playa Azul #3
821 N. Ashland Ave.
243-9244
Like its sister restaurants on
18th St. and 47th St., #3
serves good seafood
dishes. Shellfish cocktails
are a nice appetizer.

*Restaurant Tecalitlan
1814 W. Chicago Ave.
384-4285

***Sak's Ukrainian
Village Restaurant**
2301 W. Chicago Ave.
278-4445

Slodkowski's
1219 N. Milwaukee Ave.
486-6458
A wonderful old Polish cafeteria, where old-timers sit
and kibbitz after they've
finished their sausages,
stuffed cabbage, or roast
pork. Evokes a strong community feeling.

El Tacuchito Restaurant
2323 W. Chicago Ave.
342-4037
Outstanding Mexican sea-
food (snapper with garlic,
ceviche, soup) and solid
renditions of standards in a
muraled storefront spot.

Tania's Restaurant
2659 N. Milwaukee Ave.
235-7120
Friendly place at the back of
a supermarket offers Cuban
specialties (try seafood or
sandwiches) as well as
Mexican fare. Piano music
in the bar.

Entertainment

The Artful Dodger Pub
1516 N. Milwaukee Ave.
252-9665
Trendy drinking spot for the
new Wicker Park crowd is a
good place to catch folk,
blues, and rock acts most
nights.

**Old Belgrade
Restaurant and Lounge**
3245 W. Fullerton Ave.
486-3698
Mediocre food, except for
fine cevapcici, but the live
Serbian music most nights
is entertaining.

The Puppet Place
1656 W. Cortland St.
278-1600
(See Theater)

Sahara Restaurant
3304 W. Fullerton Ave.
772-6964
Turkish and Arabic music
on weekends; excellent
belly dancer.

Oak Park/River Forest/Forest Park

"Wright makes might" in Oak Park. The world's largest collection of Frank Lloyd Wright buildings—25—has long been the village's strongest draw. But there's more to Oak Park than that. Prairie School landmarks share the broad, tree-lined streets with Italianate, neo-classical, Victorian, and Queen Anne mansions, and some striking modern structures are interspersed among them.

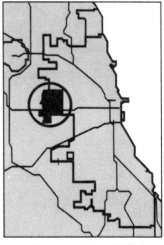

Although the building stock is a great source of pride, locals are working hard to dispel the misconception that Oak Park is nothing more than a museum of the last hundred years' architectural development. Antiques stores and crafts studios abound; a few trendy shops spruce up the Oak Park Mall, created in the mid-1970s to enliven the moribund central shopping district. The introduction of on-premise liquor sales seems to have given birth to several interesting restaurants in what was once a culinary wasteland. "Swinging Oak Park" may never become a glib catch phrase, but the village is catching up with the last quarter of the 20th century after a strange 50-year hiatus.

Oak Park is also wrestling successfully with the problems of race relations. A housing board works to encourage integration rather than block-by-block racial change and resegregation. It has even become fashionable for young couples to move to Oak Park, halting a population decline in the 1950s.

Like Hyde Park and Evanston, Oak Park is about ten miles from the Loop, and its history is linked to railroads. In 1848, the area (then called Harlem) was the destination of the very first train from Chicago (on the Galena and Chicago Union line), but development didn't really take off until the Chicago and North Western built a station here in 1872. Although it never caught up with Hyde Park and Evanston, which had commuter service a bit earlier, Oak Park prospered until the Depression. Then, lacking the attractions of a lakefront location and a major university, the village stagnated through the 1950s.

This lack of growth may have been fortuitous, since it undoubtedly saved many older buildings from redevelopment. Between Harlem and Ridgeland Avenues and Madison and Division Streets, almost every block is worth a look, even though all but two Wright buildings are in the **Oak Park Historic District,** which starts just north of Lake Street. The **Oak Park Visitors Center** (158 North Forest Avenue) is a good place to begin a tour. Here you'll find a ten-minute introductory slide show, an annotated street map, a variety of helpful pamphlets, and recorded self-guided tours. A conducted tour that covers the historic district and includes visits to Unity Temple and the Frank Lloyd Wright Home and Studio begins at the center on Saturdays at 2 p.m. (on Sundays, it starts at Unity Temple). The home, studio, and temple are also open to visitors not taking this tour (call 848-1978 for hours). A spring open-house tour (*see Annual Events*) provides an opportunity to see the interiors of some private homes. Paul Sprague's *Guide to Frank Lloyd Wright and Prairie School Architecture in Oak Park* ($3.50), available at the center and at many shops in the village, is an excellent introduction to Wright and his local contemporaries—among them George Maher, Robert Spencer, E. E. Roberts, Tallmadge and Watson, John S. Van Bergen—who rejected traditional styles to create an architectural vocabulary that was uniquely American and in tune with the prairie's flatness. Strong planes, angularity, stark stylized ornament, and flat or low-pitched hip roofs that combine to reduce spaces to their basic, geometric shapes characterize their style.

Because he designed them for himself, **Wright's Home and Studio** (951 Chicago Avenue) are perhaps the most personal statements of his theories; however, they also grew organically over time to reflect the changing needs of his family. Built in 1889 when Wright was 22, the house was extensively renovated in 1895 to expand the kitchen/dining room, where the architect installed the first furniture he designed. A second-story, barrel-vaulted playroom with a Giannini mural of the Arabian Nights was also added. The octagonal, two-story studio was built in 1898 to accommodate Wright's flourishing practice and is more typically "Wrightian," with art-glass windows and plain geometric shapes. Before leaving the Home and Studio, check out the Ginkgo Tree Bookshop, which has an excellent selection of books on Wright and Prairie School architecture, as well as gifts and memorabilia, for sale.

Designed in 1905, the starkly geometric **Unity Temple** (Lake Street at Kenilworth Avenue) is a showpiece of Wright's Prairie School vocabulary. Despite the massive concrete exterior, it is intimate and inviting inside. Geometric wood ornamentation leads the eye towards the pulpit and up to the skylights and clerestory windows.

Wright's contemporary, George Maher, known for his many houses in Chicago's Hutchinson Street District, designed the **Farson-Mills House** (217 South Home Avenue) and its furniture. Built in 1897 and set on spacious grounds (now a public park), this formal mansion houses a senior-citizens' center and the Historical Society of Oak Park and River Forest museum. Displays include local historical memorabilia and pictures of early Oak Park by pioneer photographer Philander Barclay. The village's literary links are noted by plaques in front of Ernest Hemingway's birthplace (339 North Oak Park Avenue), his boyhood home (600 North Kenilworth Avenue), and the house where Edgar Rice Burroughs knocked off several of his Tarzan novels (700 North Linden Avenue).

Architectural innovation is flourishing again in Oak Park. Besides designing the ultramodern **Oak Park Village Hall** (1 Village Hall Plaza) in 1975, Harry Weese has helped create Euclid Place (Lake Street and East Avenue), a group of modern townhouses that surrounds the old Bishop Quarter Boy's School, which now houses the **Bishop Quarter Artists Co-op,** a gymnastics/dance school, and offices of the **Festival Theatre.** Just west of the townhouses, Weese built a new rendition of Wright's Francisco Terrace and, in true Oak Park fashion, incorporated the arch and terra-cotta trim rescued from the Chicago original when it was demolished.

John Vinci supervised the return of the village's only major Prairie School commercial building to its original appearance. E. E. Roberts designed the 1908 Second Scoville Building (Oak Park Avenue and Lake Street) for shops on the ground floor with professional space and a Masonic temple above, but for years Oak Parkers knew it as the Gilmore Building (after its largest tenant, a department store that closed in the early 1970s). The project included restoration of an impressive central staircase, railings, and bronze work, and re-creation of a magnificent glass entrance canopy. The building's owner, the Industrial Fire & Casualty Insurance Company, occupies **Scoville Square's** third floor; shops are on the street level. One of the most exciting is the **Beggars Market** (133 North Oak Park Avenue), which carries an eye-catching mix of antiques and fine contemporary American crafts, new art glass, unusual kids' stuff (super wood toys), delicate Chinese paper cutouts, old and new silver jewelry, French milled soaps, and more. The stock changes frequently, and such things as antique clothing are sold almost as soon as they come into the store.

The Second Scoville Building and its Dutch Colonial predecessor across the street mark Oak Park's turn-of-the-century downtown, but over the years, the major shopping focus moved west toward Harlem Avenue. Between these two commercial centers, Lake Street has several handsome old churches; the **Oak Park Public Library** (834), designed by Holabird and Root in 1964; the 1933 Art Deco **Oak Park Post Office** (901) with a mural-decorated, two-story lobby; and the delightful, little **Scoville Park,** graced by a reconstruction of a fountain Wright designed with River Forest sculptor Richard Bock.

More than 100 stores and occasional free entertainment make the **Oak Park Mall** a good place to begin a shopping tour. Unlike the latest vertical shopping centers or sprawling suburban ones, the mall is not enclosed; however, the old Montgomery Ward building is being revamped as the Galleria, a small indoor mall with several shops and restaurants. The handsome, Art Deco **Marshall Field's** that anchors the Lake Street axis of the mall is a twin of the one in Evanston and sells a bit of everything.

Amid the usual shoe, sportswear, and jeans stores, **Bogarts** (1117 Lake Street) offers trendy to avant-garde men's wear in a slick-looking space. The clothes are casual or positively sporty; the look is very European. **Jean Sherman** (118 North Marion Street) is the chic equivalent for women. A touch of Oak Street in Oak Park, the shop features the latest natural-fabric sportswear, separates, and suits by European (especially Mondi of West Germany) and American designers. Shoes by Joan & David, colorful socks and stockings, whimsical jewelry, hair ornaments, small leather goods, bright nylon bags, some outlandish surprises, and cosmetics round out the collection. For high-quality conservative clothing, locals turn to **Spaulding's for Men and Women** (106-110). Of a dozen places specializing in jewelry, a branch of **The Peacock** (1024 Lake Street) has a big gold selection, as well as lots of gauzy dresses, blouses, skirts, and quilted jackets imported from India. Kids can have a field day at the **Fantasy Factory** (125 North Marion Street), a spacious, beautifully arranged shop that not only stocks loads of good, popularly priced children's clothing, but is also a kind of mini mall. Sections are devoted to party supplies (one tenant provides clowns and storytellers for parties), toys and games, and the like; special programs keep an activities area hopping.

At the **Creative Workshop** (1024 North Boulevard), Tom Cameron makes leather goods that range from such everyday items as jackets, hats, belts, purses, and wallets to suits for rock stars. Although most of his own leather works are custom ordered, about 20 percent of the crowded store's stock is also Cameron's; the rest comes from manufacturers of good enough quality for him to guarantee it for a year. The Creative Workshop rode high on the Western wear craze, selling lots of leather and straw cowboy hats with fancy bands and feathers, hand-tooled belts, and elaborate buckles. The shop also offers custom-made sandals, sheepskin slippers and mittens, handmade and production-line silver and jewelry, and, of all things, electronic synthesizers.

Essence (169 North Marion Street) has all the natural cosmetics, scented soaps, oils, and lotions to give your skin a healthy outdoor look. They come from companies like Crabtree & Evelyn, Caswell-Massey, and Potter & Moore, or are the Berlinskis' own private-label goods. Quality personal-care necessities, such as natural-bristle hair- and toothbrushes and sable make-up brushes, are also available, as are potpourris and custom-made feathered hats.

For fantastic feathered eye masks, mirrors surrounded by peacock feathers, and pheasant-feathered giant eggs, head to **Alphabet Soup** (134 North Marion or 1107 Lake Streets). An eclectic assortment of goodies runs the gamut from jewelry (carnelian, malachite, enamel, silver) and unusual cloisonné items (shoe horns, eyeglass cases, whistles, magnifying glasses, change purses on silk cords) to lifestyle furniture, furnishings, Oriental objêts d'art, baskets, brass, and glassware.

Henry Kochman at **Columbia Artcraft, Ltd.** (1022 North Boulevard) has been lighting up people's lives since 1934. He and his wife Madeline create lamps out of exotic imported materials as well as anything their customers bring them: musical instruments, military hats, seashells, fire call boxes, even lox and bagel sandwiches. They also restore lamps and china and are one of the few Chicago area outlets for hand-sewn shades. Fixtures they've designed include the mushroomlike millefiori ones at Le Perroquet.

Although Oak Park's chain and department stores are in or near the mall, some of the village's most intriguing shops are in clusters further afield. Marion Street, just south of the el, is a friendly, neighborhood strip with a used-books store, the **Lamar Theater** (120), which shows Indian-language films, a cream-and-green Art Deco barbershop that seems frozen in time, and an antiques shop or two. Just a few blocks east, Oak Park Avenue offers several more antiques stores selling everything from the beautifully refinished golden oak at **Spoon River Antiques** (179 South) to vintage clothing and accessories at **Memory Lane Vintage Clothing** (159 South).

Further south on Oak Park Avenue, the village made the best of a bad deal by renaming the shopping strip centered at Harrison Street the Eisenhower Shopping Center, after the expressway that bisected the area. Here, the cooperative **Oak Park Women's Exchange** (839) carries handicrafts by more than 100 local men and women: knitted goods, kids' stuff, ceramics, embroidery, quilts, needlepoint, toys, lots of pillows. Prices are reasonable, and a special-order catalogue facilitates personalized gift buying. **Prism Art Glass** (906) has stained-glass supplies (the glass selection is excellent), patterns, tools, and instruction books. Finished windows hanging in the store provide inspiration, but if you don't have the energy to do it yourself, owners Dick Bullard and Sally Carter turn out beautiful custom-made stained glass at the studio next door (908). The owners of the **Expressions Gallery Graphics Workshop** (907) specialize in four types of print making: lithography, etching, silk screen, and relief. They not only run the studio and gallery, but also provide classes and rent press time to artists.

Gerhart Schmeltekopf, at **The Early Music Center** (1045 Garfield Street), makes replicas of instruments used before 1750: harpsichords, clavichords, psalteries, rebecs, sackbuts, krumhorns. He also sells kits, stocks lots of recorders, and repairs and rebuilds harpsichords. A professional trombone and tuba player, Schmeltekopf got into the instrument business indirectly when he built his bride a harpsichord. He started with kits, but now also designs instruments based on museum pieces. Most are custom ordered and cost $2,000 to $7,000. His early-music ensemble plays parties and private concerts and offers occasional public series.

Allan Day, who learned the piano business from his father, has been operating **The Muse Piano Workshop** (225 Harrison Street) for more than 12 years. He and a small staff completely rebuild and refinish pianos—mostly antiques—and offer them for resale. They will also tune your "88" or rebuild it from the sound board up for about $3,000. Because of painstaking quality control at every stage, Day claims the result is a piano better than new in many ways. He and a partner have also started a school to teach the trade.

The Muse Piano Workshop is one of the more interesting stores on the Harrison Street commercial strip centered around Lombard Avenue. Others include Indian food stores, a batik gallery, a couple of antiques shops, an Italian deli, and a Mexican restaurant. Adversely affected by the Eisenhower Expressway, the area is now the scene of both private and public restoration guided by a strong neighborhood association. Landscaping and façade decorations enliven Harrison's diffuse aura, and efforts are being made to encourage conversion of underutilized wholesale spaces to more vibrant retail operations. The renovation of an older six-flat (107), with a stripped-to-the-brick, skylighted hallway art gallery, typifies efforts to improve urban living conditions.

Other noteworthy places are sprinkled amid everyday commercial enterprises on most of Oak Park's major shopping streets. On Lake Street, **The Treasure Chest** (734) carries dollhouses by Lawbre, American Craft, and Batrie, as well as Houseworks, Inc. trim and a good selection of miniature furniture and accessories. Although dollhouses are great for those who would like a full-sized Oak Park home but can't afford one, the decision to buy shouldn't be made lightly because a finished dollhouse can go for as much as $2,000—unfurnished! For more affordable kids' stuff, check out the used toys and books at **Short Stuff Revue** (723); racks of used and new children's togs (some samples, some seconds) are also reasonably priced. **Guitar Fun** (400) has an unusually large stock of sheet music and "how to" books, in addition to guitars.

Antiques stores dot the east and west ends of Chicago Avenue, and just off the strip, the glittering **Sunrise Art Glass Studio** (429 North Marion Street) restores antique glass and makes new windows and lighting fixtures. North Avenue, the dividing line between Oak Park and Chicago, is lined with offices and stores of every kind, including a big **Pier 1 Imports** (6311).

Overshadowed by Oak Park (and known mainly to newspaper readers as the stomping ground of Tony Accardo and other Mafia chieftains), River Forest remains today what it has always been: an upper-class residential area with large homes on spacious lots and virtually no commercial development except on peripheral through streets. Early growth was centered south of Chicago Avenue because of proximity to the commuter station and patterns of large land holdings. After World War One, the scattered housing north of Chicago Avenue was filled in with palatial homes. The tract north of Division Street developed last. Like the nabobs of Chicago's Kenwood, wealthy River Foresters had no use for the hurly-burly of shops and were willing and able to resist the blandishments of modern subdividers and developers.

While the early houses are Italianate, the irregularly shaped **River Forest Historic District** in the center of the village—separated from Oak Park's by just two blocks—contains six Wright houses, as well as many by his contemporaries, both in the Prairie School idiom and in the medieval and classical revival styles that became fashionable in the 1920s. Before exploring, pick up a copy of *A Guidebook to the Architecture of River Forest,* edited by Jeanette S. Fields, available locally or at the ArchiCenter and The Art Institute of Chicago.

Driving around River Forest under tall elms shading the streets and broad lawns is a tranquil pleasure. Be sure not to miss the magnificent **William Winslow House** at 515 Auvergne Place, a little, hidden street behind brick gateposts off Lake Street at the village's western edge. Winslow's firm produced the ornamental metalwork for the façade of Adler and Sullivan's Carson Pirie Scott & Co. building and the elevator grilles for Wright's remodeling of The Rookery. This house, Wright's first important independent commission after he left Adler and Sullivan, betrays their influence in its massiveness, use of rounded arches, and applied naturalistic ornament. Edgewood Place, just east of Auvergne Place, sports a superb group of Prairie School homes including the Japanese-style William Drummond House (559), designed by Guenzel and Drummond in 1910; Wright's look-of-thatched-cottage Chauncey Williams House (530); and his Isabel Roberts House (603), built for the daughter of one of the architect's early benefactors. Homes of River Forest's early prominent citizens are also here—the David C. Thatcher House (511), built around 1858, and that of his son George (543)—and on nearby streets, especially Keystone Avenue.

Follow Edgewood Place to Thatcher Avenue and continue north to the **Trailside Museum** (738) on the edge of the forest preserve. One of the village's earliest surviving homes, it was built by A. J. Hoffman in 1874. Four years later, he established the River Forest Young Ladies' Seminary in the house; in 1881, he converted it to a home for boys from broken homes. In 1917, the house and grounds became part of a forest preserve; the museum opened in 1932. Most of it is given over to a small zoo for indigenous forest preserve animals, birds, and fish.

River Forest isn't all grand houses, however. Smaller residences dot most streets, and the 700 block of William Street is lined with 46 modest, Prairie School-related dwellings—the largest collection of its kind around. **Rosary College** (7900 Division Street), established in 1918, looks just like a small-town, Gothic college campus should. Many Chicago librarians are alumni of the nationally known Library School. Rosary, along with Smith College, initiated the Junior Year Abroad, and the school maintains a graduate fine arts campus in Florence, Italy. The River Forest campus art gallery exhibits works by students, faculty, alumni, and community residents. Most of the concerts and dramatic productions are open to the public. Don't miss Henri Azaz's Architectural Wall on the West Campus. Originally in Chicago's Sherman House, the 70-ton sculptural wall traces Chicago's architectural history from 1836 to 1965.

The Prairie School played hooky in Forest Park, and this lower-middle-class community looks like many of Chicago's working-class neighborhoods. Oak Park and River Forest are so closely linked architecturally and socially that they share a high school and historical society, but Forest Park's connection with its more affluent neighbors is based on liquor. River Forest is dry, as was Oak Park until recently, so the Forest Park package stores and taverns do a brisk business. In addition to the usual neighborhood stores and a couple of antiques shops along Madison Street west of Harlem Avenue, one specialty store attracts customers from all over the western suburbs and Chicago. The **Archery Custom Shop** (7240 Madison Street) is run by internationally known bowman Donald Schram and his wife. Filled with Schram's hunting trophies, the shop has the largest selection of bows in the metropolitan area and two in-store professional ranges. Schram fits his customers carefully, manufactures arrows, and gives lessons and hunting tips.

A mile south as the arrow flies, **Dewey's Sandwich Shop** (7209 Roosevelt Road) dates back about 40 years, and this little white-tiled spot's chopped steak meal-on-a-bun is a local legend. The onion-and-spice-laden half-pound patty's taste stays with you for hours. Memories of the brew at **Chicago's Original Bishop's Famous Chili** (7220), a branch of the famous Chicago operation, also linger on.

Giannotti's (7711 Roosevelt Road) dominates Forest Park's Italian-restaurant field. Loyal fans fill the huge, free-standing building for generous portions of pasta, seafood, and other specialties at reasonable prices. Massive "fiesta dinners" for three or more are multicourse eating orgies. Some of the same dishes are served at Forest Park's oldest restaurant, **Otto's Cafe** (7212 Washington Street). Founded in 1890 as a roadside watering hole, Otto's has grown with the village, pushing out the trim white house to add more and more seating. Besides the Italian entrées, Otto's offers German food—reflecting the ethnic mix of the community.

Oak Park's dining scene is more varied. **Chung's Japanese Steak House** (507 Madison Street) serves the only teppanyaki steak, shrimp, and chicken for miles around. At **Erik's Danish Delicatessen** (107 North Oak Park Avenue), you can enjoy sandwiches, light meals, ice-cream treats, and other goodies in the large, gardeny-looking dining area or pick up the ingredients for a Danish picnic at the retail counter. **Kwality India** (954 Lake Street)—spoken aloud, the name says it all—has a glass partition that allows you to see the tandoori chef turn out chicken, lamb, and fish, as well as nan, one of the eight breads on the menu. Vegetarian entrées are reasonably priced, as are South Indian specialties such as dosai—large filled crêpes served with soupy lentils. Combination plates provide

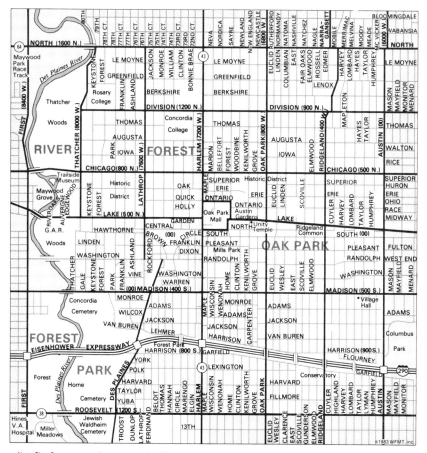

Note: River Forest street numbers are an extension of Chicago's. Forest Park uses the Chicago system on E-W streets, but numbers N-S streets south from Central Ave. Oak Park uses Austin Blvd. as a base for E-W numbering. The elevated track between North and South Blvds. is the base line for addresses on N-S streets.

an opportunity to taste many dishes, and the carefully translated menu is a real plus.

Seafood provides another Oak Park dining option at a spot that opened after the liquor laws were relaxed. **Philander's** (1120 Pleasant Street), Oak Park's finest restaurant, is a slick operation. The turn-of-the-century décor is muted wood and brass; the help is plentiful and well trained; chef Chlumsky has a talent for seafood and values freshness with an uncharacteristic zeal, by Midwestern standards. Simply prepared, generously portioned entrées are in the $12 range.

Zuppa's (189 North Marion Street), a high-tech, SoHo-looking place with a cutesy menu, has salads, crêpes, omelettes, sandwiches, etc. Stick to the simple choices for safety, or just order espresso and dessert and enjoy the décor. The **Bohemian Crown Restaurant** (7249 Lake Street, River Forest), a surprisingly handsome, 1950s "Early American" room just west of the mall, is the antithesis of Zuppa's: nothing trendy here, just competently prepared, complete dinners for about $5, à la Berwyn.

No matter where you dine in the area, save room for an ice-cream cone, soda, or sundae at the famous **Petersen Ice Cream** (1100 Chicago Avenue). Better yet, head to **Al Gelato** (7434 West North Avenue) in nearby Elmwood Park for velvety, Italian-style ambrosia—dozens of flavors of almost 24 percent butterfat ice cream made with imported flavorings that taste like real fruits, nuts, etc. Taste a few for free, then settle down with a favorite and an espresso in the little café or get a cone to go. The tab is high but worth every dollar.

Unless otherwise indicated, all addresses are in Oak Park.

Interesting places

Altenheim
7824 Madison St.,
Forest Park
366-2206
When the original, European-looking building opened in 1885, it was one of the first nonprofit homes for the German elderly in the country and functioned as a farm. Residents grew vegetables, raised and cured pigs, and maintained an apple orchard (destroyed by the addition of the most recent building in 1968). The home has grown considerably over the years and now accepts all nationalities and denominations. Residents still plant their own small vegetable gardens.

Ascension Church
East Ave. and Van Buren St.
848-2703
A handsome graystone, Mediterranean-Byzantine, 1929 building with a large statue of Jesus atop the dome; ceiling murals of the Passions painted in muted colors; two magnificently carved confessionals; an impressive altar; and striking, high-relief, cast bronze Stations of the Cross.

*Bishop Quarter Artists Co-op
605 Lake St.
383-9785
Enter from the rear of the building off the alley. More than half a dozen artists have studios here.

Calvary Memorial Church
Lake St. between Kenilworth and Forest Aves.
386-3900
Designed by W. G. Williamson and built in 1902 as the First Presbyterian Church of Oak Park. The stone is red granite from Wisconsin. The congregation's original frame church, built in 1883, was moved to the back of the lot when this one was constructed. First Presbyterian merged with First Congregational in 1975 to become First United and moved half a block away in 1979.

Concordia College
7400 Augusta St.,
River Forest
771-8300
A 1,000-student Missouri Synod college.

*Farson-Mills House
Historical Society of Oak Park and River Forest
217 S. Home Ave.
848-6755
Open Fri., Sun., 2-4 p.m. and by appointment; free.

First United Church of Oak Park
Lake St. and Kenilworth
386-5215
Designed by Norman S. Patton and built as the First Congregational Church in 1918. Modeled on chapels at Oxford and Cambridge and graced by beautiful stained-glass windows, the church houses relics that include a column from Boston's Old North Church and a stone tablet thought to be from the Church of the Sepulcher.

Forest Home Cemetery
863 S. Des Plaines Ave.,
Forest Park
366-1900
The area was once a Potawatomi burial ground. German Waldheim (now a part of Forest Home) was incorporated in 1875. Best known for Albert Weinert's monument to the Haymarket martyrs, depicting Justice placing a laurel wreath on the head of a fallen worker, a scene suggested by a verse of La Marseillaise. Each year, on the Sunday closest to May 4, red roses are placed at the monument, opposite the cemetery's chapel. At her request, Emma Goldman was buried nearby.

Jewish Waldheim Cemetery
1800 S. Harlem Ave.,
Forest Park
366-4100; tours 366-4541
More than 300 congregations, lodges, and other organizations are represented in one of the country's largest Jewish cemeteries. Each group owns a section with a little roadway; some date back to the 1870s. The Balaban & Katz mausoleum is here, as is the grave of Michael Todd.

Medical Arts Building
715 Lake St.
An Art Deco gem designed by Roy Hotchkiss and built in 1929. Los Angeles comes to Oak Park!

Mills Park
Home Ave. and Pleasant
The annual spring art fair—Art in the Park—is here.

Oak Park Conservatory
621 Garfield St.
386-4700
Saved from the wrecking ball by a few determined preservationists. The central tropical house has a fish pool; the fern house, a good variety of temperate-zone plants; and the desert house features a smell-and-touch herb garden. Horticulturist on duty Mon., 2-4 p.m., to answer questions and to help solve your plant problems.

*Oak Park Historic District
Bounded roughly by Lake St., Marion St., Division St., and Ridgeland Ave.

*Oak Park Mall
1040 Lake St.
383-4145 (office)

*Oak Park Post Office
901 Lake St.
848-7900

*Oak Park Public Library
834 Lake St.
383-8200
Special collections on local history and on hometown boys Frank Lloyd Wright and Ernest Hemingway.

*Oak Park Village Hall
1 Village Hall Plaza
(135 Madison St.)
383-6400

*Oak Park Visitors Center
158 N. Forest Ave.
848-1978
Open Mar. 1-Nov. 30. Conducted neighborhood tours: $3.

Park District of Forest Park
7501 Harrison St.,
Forest Park
366-7500
The park and the Tudor-style community center were built by the WPA between 1936 and 1938. Houses one of the finest west-suburban pools.

Pilgrim Congregational Church
Scoville Ave. and Lake St.
848-5860
Oak Park's oldest church building was constructed in 1889. The shingle-style church survived the lightning that struck down taller-steepled ones on the open prairie.

Ridgeland Common
415 Lake St.
383-6400, ext. 210
Winter ice skating with rentals, warm-up area, refreshments, etc. The Oak Park Department of Parks and Recreation offers a busy schedule of activities.

River Forest Community Center
414 Jackson Ave.
771-5820
A private, nonprofit equivalent of a park district field house. The River Forest Centennial Commission's guide to the historic district is sold here.

*River Forest Historic District
Bounded roughly by Lake St., the Des Plaines River, Chicago Ave., and Harlem

*Rosary College
7900 Division St.,
River Forest
366-2490

St. Edmund Church
Oak Park Ave. and Pleasant
848-4417
The low, intricately ribbed vault is elaborately painted, and the marble altar elaborately carved. The church's school is modeled on the Palais de Justice at Rouen.

*Scoville Park
Lake St. and Oak Park Ave.
Site of summer craft fair.

*Scoville Square
Oak Park Ave. and Lake St.

*Trailside Museum of Natural History
738 Thatcher Ave.,
River Forest
366-6530
Reservations required for groups.

Unless otherwise indicated, all addresses are in Oak Park.

***Unity Temple
(Unitarian Universalist
Church in Oak Park)**
Lake St. at Kenilworth Ave.
848-6225
Tours: $3.

*William Winslow House
515 Auvergne Pl.,
River Forest

***Frank Lloyd Wright
Home and Studio**
951 Chicago Ave.
848-1976
Tours: $3.

Shopping
and services

*Archery Custom Shop
7240 Madison St.,
Forest Park
366-4864

The Barn Door
7349 Madison St.,
Forest Park
771-2988
*Antiques, 1920s and '30s
furniture, primitive tools,
kitchen stuff, hard-to-find
large items. Don and Gloria
Young hold auctions five or
six times a year.*

*Beggars Market
133 N. Oak Park Ave.
848-9740

A Child's Place
163 S. Oak Park Ave.
524-0550
*Good selection of educa-
tional toys and records.*

Crown Books
7119 W. North Ave.
848-8822
*Loads of new books and
magazines at discount
prices. Other locations.*

Daffy-Down-Dilly
1116 Chicago Ave.
848-2293
*Brass, silver, crystal, and
other gift items, plus wom-
en's clothing.*

Owen Davies Bookseller
200 Harrison St.
848-1186
*Pictures of trains, street-
cars, and airplanes dot the
walls of this store, which
may be the country's old-
est one specializing in railroading and maritime
history. Has books, old
timetables, travel folders
dating from the late 19th
and early 20th centuries,
maps, and back issues of
railroad magazines. Fic-
tion, history, travel, biography, and some military
history are also in stock.
Thomas Bullard gets hard-
to-find, new railroading
books from all over the
world and publishes free
catalogues.*

*The Early Music Center
1045 Garfield St.
848-1020, 848-5406

***Expressions Gallery
Graphics Workshop**
907 S. Oak Park Ave.
386-0020

Freelance
129 S. Oak Park Ave.
386-7262
*Handcrafted, fairly main-
line gifts.*

The Furniture Recycler
7605 Madison St.,
Forest Park
771-2020, 383-8574
*Repairs, hand-strips, and
refinishes antique furniture.*

*Guitar Fun, Inc.
400 Lake St.
848-5222

Gunzo's Sports Center
7706 Madison St.,
River Forest
771-8666
*"Gunzo's the Name,
Hockey's my Game." Pros
patronize the place for the
large stock of hockey gear.*

House of Teak
101 S. Oak Park Ave.
524-0361
*Scandinavian furniture
and accessories.*

Joyce Klein
177 S. Oak Park Ave.
386-6564
*Antiques and books,
especially early kids' ones.*

The Learning Circus
300 Madison St.
848-8855
*Educational resource cen-
ter offers lots of materials
and activities.*

Left Bank Bookstall
104 S. Oak Park Ave.
383-4700
*A nifty used-books store
that sometimes has
poetry readings.*

***Memory Lane
Vintage Clothing**
159 S. Oak Park Ave.
386-2072
*Velvet 1920s party clothes,
day dresses, jewelry, and
much more in comfortable
surroundings.*

***The Muse Piano
Workshop**
225 Harrison St.
383-0195

**Merle Norman
Cosmetic Studio**
169 S. Oak Park Ave.
386-1360
*Carries a custom line of
hypoallergenic cosmetics
you can sample at the
make-up bar.*

***Oak Park
Women's Exchange**
839 S. Oak Park Ave.
848-4693

Peaches
7123 W. North Ave.
383-5505
*A gigantic record store with
tons of rock. The large cut-
out section is arranged by
type of music, including
many classical selections.*

*Pier 1 Imports
6311 W. North Ave.
383-1523
All the usual.

*Prism Art Glass Inc.
906-908 S. Oak Park Ave.
524-1452

*Short Stuff Revue
723 Lake St.
524-0043

Siri-Lak Galleries
11 Harrison St.
386-4936
Modern batiks from Sri Lanka—wall hangings of every size, shirts, and wrap-around dresses (some in silk)—display the bold colors and dramatic designs of a vibrant folk art. Evenings and weekends.

*Spoon River Antiques
179 S. Oak Park Ave.
383-5234

*Sunrise Art Glass Studio
429 N. Marion St.
587-0096

Toby House Antique Center
137 S. Oak Park Ave.
848-2882
Orientalia, art and cut glass, formal furniture, and other high-class stuff.

*The Treasure Chest
734 Lake St.
848-5300

Shopping and services: Oak Park Mall

*Alphabet Soup
1107 Lake St.
848-0301
134 N. Marion St.
848-2708

Animal Faire, Ltd.
1036 Lake St.
386-4440
Nice assortment of high-quality toys and games.

Barbara's Bookstore
121 N. Marion St.
848-9140
A good selection of periodicals and books from small presses at this branch of the Chicago shop.

Bishop's Magic Shop, Inc.
1105 Westgate St.
386-0854
Small shop has lots of tricks to light up your friends' eyes.

*Bogarts
1117 Lake St.
524-0442

*Columbia Artcraft, Ltd.
1022 North Blvd.
383-4819

*Creative Workshop
1024 North Blvd.
524-9891

*Essence
169 N. Marion St.
848-7999

*Fantasy Factory
1025 N. Marion St.
848-6616

Kroch's & Brentano's
1028 Lake St.
848-9003
A large store with K & B's usual good selection.

*Marshall Field's
1144 Lake St.
386-3600

*The Peacock
1024 Lake St.
386-5556

Royal Flush Bath Shops, Inc.
1122 Lake St.
383-2940
Bed and bath bargains in the back room. Other locations.

*Jean Sherman
118 N. Marion St.
848-0842

Oak Park Avenue prior to World War II

Unless otherwise indicated, all addresses are in Oak Park.

*Spaulding's for Men and Women
106-110 N. Marion St.
386-1802, 383-1300

Foodstuffs

Carnovale Italian Deli
411 Harrison St.
383-9400
Pasta and sauces to heat and eat, four varieties of sausages made famous on Taylor St., all the usual Italian goodies, cheeses, and fresh fish, too. Sandwiches and pizza to go.

Daniel's Bakery
7413 Madison St.,
Forest Park
771-1627
Good pastries and breads in a charming shop with half a dozen checked-clothed tables, polished wood floors, and an old-fashioned tin ceiling.

Milano Sausage Shop
6039 W. North Ave.
386-9657
The wonderful smells of homemade Italian sausages—mild and spicy—fill this small grocery. They are made in a large kitchen in back, as are raviolis and other treats. (Peek in through the window.) Lots of Taylor St.-style sandwiches to go, too.

Oak Park Wine Merchants
165 N. Marion St.
383-4485
Oak Park's first wine and beer store. Excellent collection includes many California boutique wines and French choices; some older vintages.

Welsch's Bakery
7625 Lake St.,
River Forest
366-1041
7332 Madison St.,
Forest Park
366-3669
You can sit down in both shops to enjoy coffee and decent pastries.

The Wine Lover
115 N. Oak Park Ave.
848-6436
High-tech shop in a Victorian building specializes in moderately priced California, Italian, Spanish, and Hungarian wines.

Dining and drinking

*Al Gelato
7434 W. North Ave.,
Elmwood Park
453-9737

*Bohemian Crown Restaurant
7249 Lake St.,
River Forest
366-8140

Chez Polonaise
144 S. Oak Park Ave.
386-1596
Modestly priced Polish meals; excellent soups.

*Chicago's Original Bishop's Famous Chili
7220 Roosevelt Rd.,
Forest Park
366-4421

Chinese Tea House
6248 W. North Ave.,
Chicago
237-3073
One of the city's oldest Mandarin restaurants; fair food.

*Chung's Japanese Steak House
507 Madison St.
383-1460

*Dewey's Sandwich Shop
7209 Roosevelt Rd.,
Forest Park
366-9721

*Erik's Danish Delicatessen
107 N. Oak Park Ave.
848-8805

*Giannotti's
7711 Roosevelt Rd.,
Forest Park
366-1199

*Kwality India Restaurant
954 Lake St.
848-1710

La Maison de Bon Bon
7353 Madison St.,
Forest Park
366-0775
Food with a French flair, ice-cream creations, and candies (French crèmes are famous) in pleasant surroundings.

La Majada
226 Harrison St.
848-8838
Popular with locals, but the food is ordinary.

*Otto's Cafe
7212 Washington St.,
Forest Park
366-0298

*Petersen Ice Cream
1100 Chicago Ave.
386-6131
Sandwiches and other food, too. Neat old-fashioned touches (extra seltzer served on the side for sodas, ample pitchers of hot fudge for sundaes) at this busy, multiroom spot. Ice-cream cones and hand-packed pints, etc., to go in a separate room.

*Philander's Oak Park
1120 Pleasant St.
848-4250
Early evening piano-bar entertainment.

*Zuppa's
189 N. Marion St.
386-1230

Entertainment

*Festival Theatre
Austin Gardens,
Forest Ave. at Lake St.
605 Lake St. (office)
524-2050
Summer Shakespeare in the park (see Theater).

Lake Theatre
1020 Lake St. (in the mall)
848-9088
Family-oriented films; inexpensive.

*Lamar Theater
120 S. Marion St.
383-4024
Some Indian films shown with English subtitles.

Evanston

When he stepped ashore at Grosse Point bluff in 1674, Père Marquette looked around and labeled the land worthless. Today, it's our most cosmopolitan suburb.

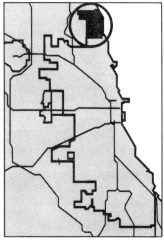

Although Evanston is just 30 minutes from the Loop and is linked to Chicago by history, commerce, and the CTA, it often seems worlds apart. Studded with stately homes and mansions, enlivened by the youthful exuberance of a Big Ten university, and replete with shops worth a special trip, Evanston has a distinctive ambiance that's heightened by its small-town way of doing things.

An expensive spraying program preserves a canopy of elms over many of the streets, and a spirited citizens' campaign saved Thomas Tallmadge's quaint 1920s street-lamp standards from the scrap heap. A pioneer desegregation program in the nationally respected school system continued a tradition of concern dating back to Underground Railroad days. And for 120 years, this headquarters city of the Woman's Christian Temperance Union was at the vanguard of the antisaloon movement.

Ironically, the town's first permanent building was a tavern constructed in 1836 near Chicago on Ridge Avenue—then the Green Bay Trail. Within a few years, the area, dubbed Ridgeville, was a cluster of farmers' houses, a few shops, and another saloon or two. But both the name and the taverns were short-lived after **Northwestern University** purchased 379 acres of lakefront land and shaped the town's growth. A unique state charter that still sparks litigation gave the school unusual freedom from real-estate taxes and the right to exclude liquor sales within four miles of the campus. Northwestern platted much of the area; it donated land for churches, schools, and parks; it gave the town a *raison d'être;* and it bestowed upon the village the name of its president and founder, John Evans.

The three-story frame structure that opened its doors to ten scholars in 1855 has grown to a 162-building mix of architectural styles serving almost 10,000 students. Gothic stone towers blend with neoclassical colonnades and contrast with the stark planes and bronze-tinted glass of modern concrete halls. Because buildings buried deep inside the campus bear Sheridan Road addresses, finding your way around can be difficult. Daily tours begin at the **Crown Center Office of Admissions** (633 Clark Street). You can pick up maps here or at the **Norris University Center** (1999 Sheridan Road), which houses the university's main bookstore. It also has the Dittmar Gallery, where art on display is sometimes for sale, an auditorium used for films and other activities, a cafeteria, and the Cone Zone (concourse), where some say you can get the best ice-cream cones in town.

Several newer campus attractions are **Pick-Staiger Concert Hall** (1977 Sheridan Road), a facility acclaimed for its acoustics and sight lines; the **Theatre and Interpretation Center** (1979), home of four stages; and the adjacent **Mary and Leigh Block Gallery** (1967). Also, be sure to see the **Shakespeare Garden,** just south of the Technological Institute (2145 Sheridan Road). The formal garden with roses, rosemary, and other plants mentioned in the Bard's works is a traditional student trysting spot. Two-thirds of Northwestern's students are undergraduates and most live on campus, a sizable number in fraternity and sorority houses.

The university owns many of the handsome old homes near the campus, but the grandest by far is the mansion left by Charles Gates Dawes, vice president under Coolidge, to house an historical museum. The **Evanston Historical Society** (225 Greenwood Street) maintains much of the 1894, 28-room, turreted château as a testimonial to a lost lifestyle. The spacious library and terrace overlook the lake, and the elegant dining room has a musicians' loft. Exhibits include Victorian-era clothing and toys, Indian artifacts, and Evanston and Dawes memorabilia. Christmastime brings turn-of-the-century decorations (*see Museums*). The house is a perfect jumping-off spot for an Evanston architectural tour because its magnificent wood-paneled interior is accessible and the gift shop sells informative, inexpensive booklets published by the Evanston Planning Department. Buy *Evanston Architecture; A Sampler of Self-Guided Tours* and use it to see some of the country's finest domestic architecture.

In general, the most spectacular homes are north of Main Street between the lakefront and Ridge Avenue. The earliest are Italianate, Queen Anne, and Victorian Gothic. A prime example of the last, the frame **Willard House** (1730 Chicago Avenue) with carved bargeboard lining its eaves, was built in 1865 and, like the Dawes mansion, is a National Historic Landmark. Famous educator and temperance leader Frances Willard called her 17-room home a "rest cottage" and lived here until her death in 1898. Nine rooms are open to the public: Five are fitted out with Willard's furniture and furnishings; four contain a temperance-history museum. The house is on the grounds of the W.C.T.U. national headquarters, which has a predictably extensive library on alcohol and drug abuse.

By the turn of the century, the genteel suburb attracted a wealthy clientele for many of the Midwest's finest architects, who worked in an imposing variety of styles. A short walk along Forest Avenue provides a delightful overview. Tallmadge and Watson designed the 1908 Prairie School beauty at 1000; Ernest Mayo built the Tudor one at 1025 two years later. The massive brick mansion wrought for meat packer Oscar Mayer (1030) contrasts with the work of popular local architect J. T. W. Jennings (1043). Harvey L. Page created the neoclassical masterpiece at 1047 just one year later than Beers, Clay, and Dutton's 1896 French châteaux at 1100 and 1101. Stroll over to Judson Avenue to see Ernest Mayo's 1894 Tudor (1110); a classic early Italianate (1028), once a tannery and then home of pioneer settler John Clough; and Walter Burley Griffin's monumental Carter House (1024). Hinman and Michigan Avenues are also well worth touring, as are Sheridan Road and Lake Shore Boulevard.

Explore the Prairie School's variety west of Ridge Avenue. Thomas Tallmadge, Evanston's first plan commission chairman, and his partner Vernon Watson were responsible for the modest homes at 1120, 1239, and 1335 Asbury Avenue; Pond & Pond for 1410. Myron Hunt is thought to be the architect of the sprawling, hip-roofed structure built as an inn at 1300 Davis Street. Evanstonian Dwight Perkins's affection for a tall Prairie can be seen at 1416 Elinor Place and at

1415, once the home of Harold Ickes. George Maher's use of massive symmetry is typified by 1583 Ashland Avenue, while Walter Burley Griffin's Comstock Houses (1631 Ashland Avenue and 1416 Church Street) are archetypal examples of his work. Frank Lloyd Wright's sole Evanston commission is at 2420 Harrison Street.

Evanston's churches—there are more than 60 of them—also display touches of the masters. Tallmadge and Watson's **First Congregational Church** (Hinman Avenue and Lake Street) is one of the finest Georgian churches in the Midwest. They also worked with Ralph Adams Cram on the **First United Methodist Church** (Hinman Avenue and Church Street) to create a striking English Gothic limestone building with superb carved oak and stained glass gracing the interior. Daniel Burnham not only built lakefront mansions in the community for himself and his children; he also designed the lovely, 1894 Romanesque **First Presbyterian Church** (Chicago Avenue and Lake Street) with fine wood carvings in the sanctuary. **Emmanuel United Methodist Church** (Oak Avenue and Greenwood Street) is one of John Root's last works. The low, red-sandstone building with a massive tower is reminiscent of Root's St. Gabriel in Canaryville. The marble altars in Evanstonian Holabird and Roche's **St. Mark's Episcopal Church** (Ridge Avenue and Grove Street), with its castlelike tower, and in S. A. Jennings's rough limestone **St. Mary Church** (Oak Avenue and Lake Street), designed for Evanston's oldest Catholic parish, are alone sufficient reasons for a visit.

Concerts are regular features at several churches, but one of Evanston's major cultural focuses is in a building designed as a school by Burnham in 1892. The **Noyes Cultural Arts Center** (927 Noyes Street) sponsors arts, crafts, and dance classes and provides facilities for a branch of the **Old Town School of Folk Music,** which gives classes and performances, as well as for **Piven Theatre Workshop** programs. The **North Light Repertory Company** (2300 Green Bay Road) presents a thoroughly professional theater season in another decommissioned school, and the **Practical Theatre Company** (703 Howard Street) concentrates on improvisation and new plays at its storefront location (*see Theater*). Year-round comedy, drama, and musical productions at Northwestern's Theatre and Interpretation Center offer a chance to see tomorrow's stars of stage, screen, and television (Charlton Heston and Peter Strauss are among the alumni), and other on-campus favorites include the annual Waa-Mu Show. Northwestern also schedules scores of concerts a year—everything from chamber works to jazz. Student and faculty performances are free, but tickets must be purchased in advance for artists the caliber of Julian Bream, Murray Perahia, or the Roger Wagner Chorale. The **Evanston Symphony Orchestra,** directed by the Chicago Symphony's principal cellist, Frank Miller, presents a four-concert season at Evanston Township High School (1600 Dodge Avenue). The National College of Education, one of the nation's oldest and most respected teachers' colleges, hosts moderately priced demonstrations, concerts, and performances by professionals such as pianist Jeffrey Siegel and Gus Giordano Jazz Dance Chicago at the **Weinstein Center for the Performing Arts** (2840 Sheridan Road).

Kendall College (2408 Orrington Avenue), a small, private school, houses a little-known resource: the **Mitchell Indian Museum.** More than 1,000 tools, weapons, baskets, musical instruments, weavings, and hide paintings; many outstanding examples of beadwork; and more from Indians in five geographic areas are displayed more or less chronologically (3000 B.C. to the present). A teaching room, arranged geographically, provides kids with the opportunity to touch and hold some objects. One of the newest jewels on Evanston's fine arts scene, the **Terra Museum of American Art** (2600 Central Park Avenue), is in a handsomely renovated, multilevel space. Although the museum is small, the permanent collection (strong on American Impressionists) and imaginative, beautifully displayed visiting exhibitions are worth seeing (*see Museums*).

To experience the bucolic charms often pictured in paintings at the Terra Museum, visit **Ladd Arboretum**—23 acres of grounds running alongside McCormick Boulevard, which also houses the **Evanston Ecology Center** (2024 McCormick Boulevard)—or **Lighthouse Landing Park** (2535 Sheridan Road). Completed in 1873, the 113-foot-tall Grosse Point Light Station (the climb is only for the hearty, but the glassed-in top offers a different perspective on Evanston's homes, tree-shaded streets, and relationship to the Loop's towers 12 miles away) is a highlight of the park, which also includes a nature center, a maritime museum, keeper's quarters, and a center for natural landscaping. (*See Museums.*)

Other Evanston parks feature a variety of activities, among them indoor skating at the **Robert Crown Ice Center** (1701 Main Street), pedal boating at Lovelace Park (Grosse Point Road and Thayer Street), and winter skiing and tobogganing at James Park (Oakton Street and Dodge Avenue), where "Mount Trashmore" (built primarily of refuse) forms the area's tallest slopes. The town's 4½-mile lakefront is almost half parkland, with an excellent blacktopped path for bikers and runners winding through the entire green strip. Five public beaches dot the shore; to use them in the summer, you need to buy a season token or to pay a $3 daily charge. Tokens are available at the **Evanston Civic Center** (2100 Ridge Avenue) as are *News Source* and the Evanston Arts Council's *Cultural Calendar*. Both publications can also be received by mail and, between them, most public activities in town are noted.

Unlike bedroom suburbs, Evanston also has a real downtown. Department stores and specialty shops spread out from the Davis Street stations of the CTA and Chicago and North Western Railway. (The tracks diverge here, forming the elongated "Y" that splits the town.) For years, the area between the campus and church-bordered Raymond Park looked like an idealized movie set, right down to the ornate centennial casting in Fountain Square. The gentry shopped decorously at the lovely Art Deco **Marshall Field's** (1700 Sherman Avenue)—a twin to Oak Park's—and then took tea at Cooley's Cupboard, a restaurant behind counters of sweets. Evenings, college kids on a post-big-game date snuggled in the elegant room's commodious booths to share a banana split.

Since the 1950s, however, the picture has altered considerably. Evanston has aggressively courted change to avoid the decimation central business districts often experience from shopping-mall competition. A modern concrete fountain replaced the quaint old one, and Cooley's gave way to an insurance company. Liberalization of the town's restrictive building height ordinance has sparked office-tower construction. The shopping scene has been reinvigorated.

The department stores may not challenge the Loop's or Skokie's Old Orchard's for size, but shopping here is usually a leisurely pleasure and parking is plentiful. The situation can change during special events, such as the annual Midwest Crafts Festival, the Fountain Square Arts Festival, and the World's Largest Garage Sale, when hundreds of entrepreneurs fill the multilevel city parking garage with every imaginable treasure (*see Annual Events*), or on Saturdays during the **Farmers' Market** season.

Specialty shops are Evanston's big attraction. There are dozens of all kinds downtown, and each of the shopping strips along the el-stop streets has a special flavor. Misnamed Central Street is a haven for antiques and used-books stores. Main Street and the nearby Washington Street-Custer Avenue cluster offer more antiques, trendy clothes, and handmade goods. Dempster Street has a vague, 1960s counterculture aura. West of the tracks, Davis Street combines a busy overflow from downtown with the neighborhood service shops that dot all the strips. The mix of shops gives some legitimacy to the proposition that most Evanstonians dress in preppy garb or gauzy Indian-style clothes as they work on needlepoint, play musical instruments, or read books in their antiques-and-craftsware-filled homes.

The ceramics, glass, wood, metal, and textile works that fill every nook, cranny, and the floor-to-ceiling display-window shelves at the large **Mindscape Gallery** (1521 Sherman Avenue) transcend the rubric "crafts." A constant delight, the ever-expanding gallery represents 350 of the country's most talented artists. Many are ceramists making simple raku-fired vases, fanciful animal grotesqueries, sophisticated bas-relief sculptures, and more. Beautifully polished wooden accessories, gorgeous glassware and stained glass, arresting bronzes, and dramatic soft sculptures also compete for attention.

Exhibits of paintings and sculptures change frequently at **Grove Street Galleries** (921 Grove Street); the **Botti Studio of Architectural Arts** (919), which shares the half-block-long building, excels at creating and restoring stained-glass windows. Credits include work at the Chicago Public Library, Roosevelt University, and a Greek Orthodox church in New York; the firm also builds and restores architectural metalwork, sculptures, and mosaics. There is a small sales area with ready-made glass pieces and supplies for the do-it-yourselfer.

Peggie Robinson Design (1514 Sherman Avenue) is one of several shops specializing in original gold and silver jewelry. Smoothly sculptured, classy pieces often feature naturalistic patterns, such as necklaces of lithe leaves or bracelets and pendants of picture agate and jasper. Prices are quite reasonable, even for custom work. The precious-metal and stone jewelry at the slightly zippier **Calf & Dragon** (507 Davis Street) has a more organic, hammered look.

Adornments at **The Mexican Shop** (801 Dempster Street) range from exotic, handcrafted African bracelets and heavy beadwork to with-it plastic combs, funky jewelry, and crazy sunglasses—perfect accents to the varied collection of ethnic attire. A steady stream of co-eds and others committed to the natural look browse for peasant skirts and tapestry tops, as well as styled-for-Americans dresses, made from handwoven Guatemalan fabrics; batik, embroidered, and cutwork Indonesian dresses and separates; Indian prints; Oriental kimonos; and antique, embroidered Syrian dresses. There are also less dramatic clothes like comfortable cotton pants and shirts for both men and women. Although similar, if less distinguished, togs fill half of Evanston's casual clothing stores, the Mexican Shop also has unusual household accouterments—Latin American tin lamps, pottery, and hundred-year-old statues of saints; Bedouin saddlebags; unique fabrics; and more.

In a more practical vein, the huge **Practical Tiger** (1629 Chicago Avenue) sells lifestyle and unpainted furniture, trendy accessories, and an enormous selection of stoneware dishes. Other types of tableware, gourmet galley goodies, graphics, and a sale corner round out the picture. **The Corner Store** (1511 Chicago Avenue) has a smaller collection of contemporary furniture, but stocks more kitchenware and lamps.

If your lifestyle is minimalist, or if you just want your back to stop aching, head to **Natural Design** (809 Dempster Street). Tara Pearl sells *futons* (Japanese cotton-batting mattresses), *zabutons* (floor pillows), and buckwheat-hull-filled neck pillows, as well as yoga mats and cotton kimonos. The multiroom **Dynasty Shop** (2644 Green Bay Road) is jammed with top-quality, fairly restrained antiques and reproductions from the Orient, including lots of furniture, Korean chests, embroidered pillows, occasional boxes, and cloisonné; ivory and stone carvings; Japanese hibachi jardinières; and painted scrolls and screens. Collectors won't want to miss the antique-porcelain decorator pieces and dishes. In general, prices are fair, and discounts are offered "to the trade."

The United States can't equal the Orient for native antiquities, but **Harvey An-**

tiques (1231 Chicago Avenue) takes a good stab at it with an enviable selection of 18th- and 19th-century American furniture (some of it museum quality), antique jewelry, and folk arts ranging from baskets to quilts. The English antiques at the **Original Crost Furniture Store** (1004 Emerson Street) are more recent, but the big, rambling building is filled with container-loads of the furniture—washstands, armoires, dressers, dining-room sets, desks—and all the usual smaller items. The owners frequently have carefully authenticated museum pieces, do restoration work, and, with wonderful incongruity, also sell name-brand bedding.

A turn-of-the-century, Chicago North Shore and Milwaukee interurban trolley car sets the stage at **Mike's Trolley Car Antiques** (1937 Central Street). The dimly lit, jammed-to-a-jumble store is an endless bounty of oak furniture, Victoriana, and American collectibles such as buttons and advertising signs. Mike's is one of a half-dozen antiques stores worth seeing in the few blocks that feature several used-books shops and **Hogeye Music** (1920). Only a few of the guitars here are antiques, but the store sells everything a folk musician needs. It also offers lessons, makes and repairs instruments, and has weekend miniconcerts and workshops of down-home music. The shop's mascot is a red, old-fashioned, coin-operated child's rocking hog that beats mechanical bulls hands down.

Hidden behind Main Street's main-line shops and cut off from spiritual brethren on the other side of the rail embankment, the Washington Street-Custer Avenue merchants work hard to promote their fertile antiques-and-crafts stomping ground. The annual Custer's Last Stand, a pleasant street fair that reflects the shops' diversity (*see Annual Events*), and the sobriquet "Washington Square" are fruits of their labors. The continually changing scene is always worth a visit.

Ken Young Antiques (703 Washington Street) sprang from former camera salesman Young's passion for vintage pocket watches; it wound up a prime source for antique timepieces, jewelry, and objêts d'art. Next door, **Penny Arcade Antiques** (705) specializes in old coin-operated machines—test your grip, play pinball, view "bathing beauties" as you turn a crank—as well as nostalgia: baseball cards, campaign buttons, and advertising paraphernalia. The double store even has a decorative bas-relief rescued from the front gate of Riverview.

Washington Square's craft shops include **Off the Hoof** (838 Custer Avenue). In this spare, high-ceilinged, exposed-brick showroom, Gerry Morris displays his remarkable leatherwork. You'll find the expected (belts, purses, cases, wallets, custom-made sandals) plus unusual small boxes—all expertly crafted from heavy, oak-tanned hides. Some are enhanced by exquisite, Art Nouveau-like motifs, carved and hand-painted. The shop also sells striking, handcrafted belt buckles from all over the country.

Two Main Street stores rival anything Chicago has to offer. **Good's of Evanston** (714) stocks a wealth of artists' supplies and a strong selection of custom frames for the finished products. **Vogue Fabrics** (718) is even more amazing. The immense textile supermarket offers one of the Midwest's largest arrays of materials: a whole room of designer fabrics, luxurious silks, and hard-to-find novelties like rayon Hawaiian prints (all at good prices); several others of upholstery and drapery yard goods and accouterments; and yet another of patterns and findings. Of course, huge assortments of cottons, wools, and synthetics are also on hand.

Tom Thumb Hobby & Craft Center (1026 Davis Street) covers just about every hobby and craft except sewing. You'll find supplies for macramé, beading, candlemaking, rug hooking, and Christmas ornament making in one half of the gigantic store; the other is jammed with every kind of model kit, remote-control and free-traveling planes, gliders, boats, rockets, trains, and slot cars. There's even a large slot-car-racing track.

The biggest surprise among Evanston's stores may be the venerable

Chandler's (630 Davis Street). Established in 1895 in the town's oldest commercial structure, the business expanded in the 1920s into an elegant, five-story building that wraps around the original store. There's a huge stock of new and used books in the basement, art and office supplies on the main floor, and Boy Scout gear on the mezzanine. The second-floor "Student Co-op" bursts with Evanston and Northwestern University-proud T-shirts and other memorabilia. The upper floors have utilitarian office furniture and one of the Midwest's largest stamp and coin departments. Get on the mailing list to keep abreast of the monthly stamp auctions (which accept private consignments). Chandler's antebellum ambiance is the perfect foil for the activity that's transforming downtown.

A nice part of the change is the quantum leap Evanston dining has taken since the 1972 legalization of liquor-by-the-drink in restaurants. Now, choices range from haute cuisine to ethnic, the number of eateries keeps increasing, and the most inviting are conveniently located downtown.

One of the Chicago area's best country-French restaurants is **Café Provençal** (1625 Hinman Avenue), a cozy place with a small menu, fresh flowers, and a classical harpist. Haute cuisine can be had at **La Mirabelle** (Orrington Hotel, 1710 Orrington Avenue), run by Dominique and Fritzie Beauchard, formerly of Chicago's Ritz-Carlton Hotel. The restaurant is one of the last viable components of the Orrington, Evanston's grand dame of hostelries and host to thousands of families visiting their NU-student relatives over the years. The hotel filed a bankruptcy petition in 1980, and most of its street-level shops are vacant.

Lettuce Entertain You Enterprises is represented by **Fritz, That's It!** (1615 Chicago Avenue), where the salad bar, funky drinks, and a good Sunday brunch compensate for the long waits (no reservations are accepted). Fresh fish, clever specials, the salad bar, and pleasant help make **The Keg** (810 Grove Street) the best of the obligatory rough-cut-cedar-stained-glass-and-lots-of-plants college places.

The **Budapest Cafe** (505 Main Street) specializes in Austro-Hungarian fare and serves the pastries that distinguished the owners' original restaurant, State Street's Bon Ton. The **Pine Yard** (924 Church Street) has the area's best Chinese food, and it's mostly Mandarin. At the tiny **Daruma** (2903 Central Street), Japanese specialties (try the tempura) are generously apportioned, attractively served, and reasonably priced. On weekdays, the dinner crush at Evanston's popularly priced restaurants is in full swing by 6 p.m. Plan to go either before or after the just-off-the-train-from-the-Loop crowd, and import your own booze from outside town for the unlicensed spots.

Interesting places

Baha'i House of Worship
Linden Ave. and Sheridan, Wilmette
256-4400
Thirty years of technical difficulties hindered translating Louis Bourgeois's bell-shaped, lacy-walled, Oriental-looking masterpiece into concrete and steel. The 1953 structure is deservedly on the National Register of Historic Places.

Byer Museum of the Arts
1700 Hinman Ave.
866-6600
Opened in 1982; restored building is on the National Register of Historic Places. (See Museums.)

Calvary Cemetery
301 Chicago Ave.
864-3050
Founded in 1859, the oldest cemetery operated by the Chicago archdiocese has many ornate and imaginative monuments—firemen's hats (for those lost in the line of duty), a baseball (for a fallen player), a shelf of books (for members of a printers' union)—and is the resting place of four Chicago mayors and scores of other notables, e.g. names like Cudahy, Comiskey, and Cuneo.

***Robert Crown
Ice Center**
1701 Main St.
328-9400

***Emmanuel United
Methodist Church**
Oak Ave. and Greenwood
864-9637

Evanston Art Center
2603 Sheridan Rd.
475-5300
*Housed in a lakefront mansion in Lighthouse Landing
Park and surrounded by
Jens Jensen landscaping,
the center offers workshops and has several exhibit galleries.*

*Evanston Civic Center
2100 Ridge Ave.
328-2100

***Evanston
Ecology Center**
2024 McCormick Blvd.
864-5181
*Home of the Evanston Environmental Association
and resource center on the
environment and conservation. Solar and windpowered energy demonstration projects, too. (See
Museums.)*

***Evanston
Historical Society**
225 Greenwood St.
475-3410
*Sponsors an annual house
walk. (See Museums.)*

Evanston Public Library
1703 Orrington Ave.
866-0300
*The main branch of one of
Illinois's oldest public library systems hosts classical music recitals, a film
series, and theatrical productions. Collection is
strong on art.*

***First Congregational
Church**
Hinman Ave. and Lake St.
864-8332

***First Presbyterian
Church**
Chicago Ave. and Lake St.
864-1472

***First United
Methodist Church**
Hinman Ave. and Church
864-6181

*Ladd Arboretum
2024 McCormick Blvd.
864-5181
(See Museums)

***Lighthouse
Landing Park**
2535 Sheridan Rd.
864-5198
*Weekend afternoon tours,
May through October.
(See Museums.)*

Merrick Rose Garden
Oak Ave. and Lake St.
*More than 1,000 rosebushes representing 83
varieties. The 1876 fountain was moved here from
Fountain Square, center of
downtown Evanston.*

*Mitchell Indian Museum
Kendall College
2408 Orrington Ave.
866-1395
(See Museums)

***Noyes Cultural
Arts Center**
927 Noyes St.
491-0266

***St. Mark's
Episcopal Church**
Ridge Ave. and Grove St.
864-4806

*St. Mary Church
Oak Ave. and Lake St.
864-0333

***Terra Museum
of American Art**
2600 Central Park Ave.
328-3400
(See Museums)

***Weinstein Center
for the Performing Arts**
National College
of Education
2840 Sheridan Rd.
256-5150
(See Music)

*Willard House
1730 Chicago Ave.
864-1397
(See Museums)

Interesting places: Northwestern University

***Mary and Leigh Block
Gallery**
1967 Sheridan Rd.
492-5209
*Exhibits of various arts and
crafts change every five to
six weeks. (See Museums.)*

***Crown Center
Office of Admissions**
633 Clark St.
492-7271
*Campus tours daily at
2 p.m. during school
year, weekdays 1 p.m.
in summer.*

Dearborn Observatory
2131 Sheridan Rd.
492-3173
(See Museums)

Dyche Stadium
1501 Central St.
492-7070
*Built in 1926, the home of
the Wildcats (football) seats
more than 49,000. Track
and soccer, too.*

*Norris University Center
1999 Sheridan Rd.
492-5400

***Pick-Staiger
Concert Hall**
1977 Sheridan Rd.
492-5441

*Shakespeare Garden
South of Technological Institute, 2145 Sheridan Rd.

***Theatre and
Interpretation Center**
1979 Sheridan Rd.
492-7282

Shopping and services

Abraham's Books
805 Chicago Ave.
475-1777
*General used-books shop
also has rare and out-of-print works.*

Arabesque
825 Chicago Ave.
864-2618
Trim, woody shop with very stylish, European-looking women's clothing at moderate prices.

The Athenaeum
1814 Central St.
475-0990
Used books—especially art, literature, literary criticism, and regional American history.

Audio Consultants
1014 Davis St.
864-9565
One of the city's, if not the country's, finest stereo stores. Owner Simon Zreczny stocks topnotch equipment in all price ranges (not just for audiophiles), stays abreast of the best, and devotes the utmost attention to personal service. No sale is final until you're satisfied, after which there's a five-year guarantee on parts, three years on labor.

Roberta Balfanz Hawaiian Shop
1630 Orrington Ave.
864-7709
Women's dresses, blouses, accessories, cosmetics, even fragrances from the islands. Men's Hawaiian shirts, too.

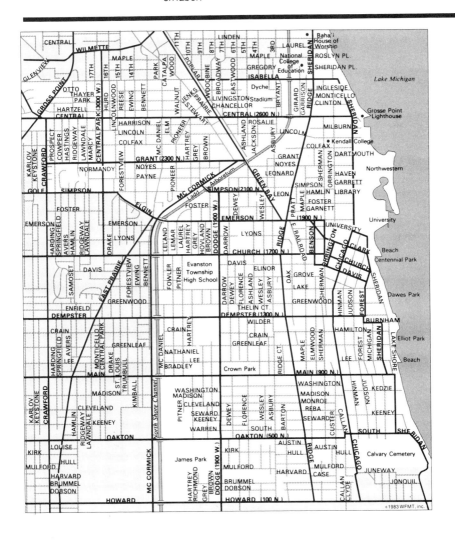

**Richard S. Barnes
& Co. Books**
821 Foster St.
869-2272
Used books include sets, quality editions, art, literature, Americana, and lots of history in this cluttered shop "decorated" with bookbinding equipment and historical pictures.

***Botti Studio
of Architectural Arts**
919 Grove St.
869-5933

Brannen Woodwinds
908 Hinman Ave.
866-7576
Repairs woodwinds for symphony and student musicians from all over the country.

*Calf & Dragon
507 Davis St.
328-3128

Campfitters Ltd.
924 Davis St.
864-1940
Camping gear and clothing store with a separate cross-country ski shop.

*Chandler's, Inc.
630 Davis St.
475-7200
Other locations.

**Chicago-Main
Compleat Newsstand**
Chicago Ave. at Main St.
864-2727
Corner newsstand-shop crammed with out-of-town newspapers, every imaginable magazine, and paperback books.

The China Bazaar
1024-26 Emerson St.
328-2000
Discount room at importers H. Wittur & Co. sells discontinued lines, close-outs, and some seconds of Continental china and crystal (much of it from West Germany) at half price or less.

**Chinese Cultural
Academy**
608 Dempster St.
869-0554
Teaches not only tai chi chuan and other martial arts but also Chinese calligraphy, painting, literature, and more.

Classic Artists
2904 Central St.
869-0090
A good source for vocal, choral, and organ music, both sacred and secular.

*The Corner Store
1511 Chicago Ave.
475-0036

**Dave's "Down to Earth"
Rock Shop**
1312 Chicago Ave.
866-7374
A truly wonderful collection of minerals, geodes, fossils, and other fine specimens. Some lapidary equipment, scrimshaw, and jewelry made from polished stones, too.

Designs in Bloom Ltd.
743 Main St.
869-5580
Custom-designed silk floral arrangements, loose flowers, and plants.

EPIcenter
1612 Central St.
475-2161
Adults and kids learn to use home computers. Free sample lesson.

Evanston Seed & Bulb Co.
1640 Maple Ave.
864-2050
Old-fashioned little shop.

Good Children St eet
842 Custer Ave.
869-5980
Outlet for Susan Langworthy's business making colorful, appliquéd overalls and jumpers for kids. Knit goods by her sister, too. Some items sold at wholesale.

*Good's of Evanston
714 Main St.
864-0001

Great Expectations
911 Foster St.
864-3881
Old-style, maze like bookstore with comfortable chairs adjacent to each section and library ladders to reach high shelves; specializes in philosophy and economics. Knowledgeable proprietor Truman Metzel is a provocative conversationalist and holds philosophy club meetings.

*Grove Street Galleries
921 Grove St.
866-7341

Gustafson's, Inc.
1510 Sherman Ave.
866-9700
"Everything for the hearth's desire." No fireplaces.

Herdrich's Variety
2100 Central St.
864-6706
Neat, old-fashioned five-and-dime—with somewhat higher prices.

*Hogeye Music
1920 Central St.
475-0260

Jewellery Chez Faye
1909 Central St.
869-6788
Handsome shop with antique, new, and custom-made baubles.

Kaehler Luggage Shop
1421 Sherman Ave.
328-0744
All the big names—Hartmann, Skyway, American Tourister, Lark, Samsonite—and gifts. Also in Highland Park.

Karlson Kitchens
1815 Central St.
491-1300
Top-of-the-line cabinetry and appliances including Poggenpohl; some handsome accessories, such as cutting boards and cookbook racks.

Kennedy's Bookshop
1911 Central St.
864-4449
Good general used-books store usually has interesting items, such as turn-of-the-century children's books and old pamphlets.

Khaki
1245 Chicago Ave.
869-8090
Practical, durable, trendy casual wear for men and women. Also in Winnetka.

Kroch's & Brentano's
1711 Sherman Ave.
328-7220
Excellent branch of top-flight chain.

Lekotek
613 Dempster St.
328-0001
The country's first toy-lending library for handi-capped children takes a therapeutic approach and provides a parent-support network. By appointment.

Ruth McCulloch Shops
527 Davis St.
475-6161
Women's designer clothes "for town and country," from classic casuals to mother-of-the-bride chif-fons. Also in Northbrook Ct.

*Marshall Field's
1700 Sherman Ave.
475-6600
Graham, Anderson, Probst & White, 1929.

*The Mexican Shop
801 Dempster St.
475-8665

*Mindscape Gallery
1521 Sherman Ave.
864-2660

Mostly Handmade
508 Main St.
864-0845
Handcrafted toys, jewelry, soft sculptures, rugs, quilts, etc., by local and out-of-town artists. No pottery or glassware.

Mud Pies
2012 Central St.
869-9191
Good selection of kids' clothing; some toys; pad-ded play pit for the little ones.

Murphy's Fit
518 Main St.
869-4101
A hundred kinds of athletic shoes (running ones a spe-cialty) and related clothing for men, women, and chil-dren. Attention to proper fit extends to encouraging customers to test the shoes they've selected, before buying.

*Natural Design
809 Dempster St.
864-1002
Also at 607 W. Belmont Ave., Chicago.

Neville-Sargent Gallery
509 Main St.
328-9395
An old main-line gallery.

*Off the Hoof
838 Custer Ave.
864-4830

*Old Town School of Folk Music
927 Noyes St.
864-6664

The Percussion Shop
822 Custer Ave.
864-2997
Drums of all sorts, cym-bals, and unusual percus-sion instruments. Drum lessons and repairs.

The Pot Shop
604 Dempster St.
864-7778
Nicely glazed, lead-free, dishwasher-safe dinner-ware like you see at art fairs. Classes include unlimited studio time.

*Practical Tiger
1629 Chicago Ave.
869-8234

Private Lives
1504 Sherman Ave.
869-8920
Excellent bed-and-bath shop with enormous selec-tion has full design and cus-tomizing services.

The Rams
828 Custer Ave.
866-7960
One of many boutiques in town with lots of gauzy In-dian dresses and jewelry. Also in Wilmette.

*Peggie Robinson Design
1514 Sherman Ave.
475-2121

Paul Rohe & Sons, Booksellers
2002 Central St.
866-7555
Good, used-books store.

The Salzburg Shop
1601 Chicago Ave.
328-8441
Small shop with a mix of clothing, print yard goods from Austria, and carved-wood knickknacks.

The Saxophone Shop, Ltd.
918 Noyes St.
491-0075
Sells and repairs . . . you guessed it!

Scandinavian Design
1527 Chicago Ave.
869-6100
Attractive branch of a chain specializing in Danish-modern furniture, lamps, rya rugs, and accessories.

Scandinavian Design Warehouse Store
2510 Green Bay Rd.
491-1583
Surplus, discontinued, and some damaged items at substantial savings.

The Shepherd's Harvest
1925 Central St.
491-1353
Homey shop with hand-somely displayed natural fibers and yarns for weav-ing, crocheting, and knit-ting; looms, too. Weaving and spinning classes. Stu-dents may rent looms.

The Sound Post
1239 Chicago Ave.
866-6866
General music store fea-tures guitars, keyboards, PA systems. The Sound Post School of Music across the street (1240; 491-6220) gives lessons in guitar, piano, woodwinds— just about anything.

Thorpe Furs
1506 Sherman Ave.
328-3333
Fine Evanston furrier dating back to 1890 stocks the latest in winter warmers for men, women, and children. Also in Water Tower Place and Northbrook Court.

Tokyo Shop Inc.
1006 Church St.
864-3638
Enormous store with loads of Japanese dishes, tea sets, and novelties.

*Tom Thumb Hobby & Craft Center
1026 Davis St.
869-9575

Turin Bike Shop
1027 Davis St.
864-7660
Good, full-service bike shop.

*Vogue Fabrics
718-32 Main St.
864-9600

Mary Walter
1 American Plaza
475-6644
Thoughtfully selected suits, separates, and accessories for the career woman at moderate prices.

Wild Goose Chase Quilt Gallery
526 Dempster St.
328-1808
Excellent selection of antique quilts (ones by the Amish are particularly fine) and some new ones. Classes; you bring supplies.

Windy City Soot Suckers
869-5658
Dennis and Connie Conroy, dressed in traditional top-hat garb, will sweep your chimneys clean.

Windy City Tub Works Ltd.
Windy City WesternWear
1240 Chicago Ave.
864-1221
Hot tubs, Jacuzzis, spas, saunas, and all the accessories. Also Western wear.

Shopping and services: Antiques

Antiques of Evanston
912 Chicago Ave.
869-3555
Art glass and fine pottery to Fiesta ware.

Sarah Bustle Antiques
1701 Central St.
869-7290
Specializes in Victorian through Art Deco lighting fixtures, glassware and dishes, jewelry, and furniture.

Chicago Art Galleries Inc.
1633 Chicago Ave.
475-6960
Mostly ornate antiques sold, bought, and auctioned off (every six to eight weeks) at this large place.

*The Dynasty Shop Inc.
2644 Green Bay Rd.
864-2495

Fond Memories
826 Custer Ave.
864-0666
Golden oak galore and more.

*Harvey Antiques
1231 Chicago Ave.
866-6766

Hiltie's
1733 Central St.
492-1001
Refinished furniture and restoration services.

*Mike's Trolley Car Antiques
1937 Central St.
864-1188

Miscellanea
1310½ Chicago Ave.
328-1551
Loads of very wearable vintage clothing and accessories.

North Evanston Resale
1706 Central St.
869-6681
Not a resale shop, but the refinished oak furniture is reasonably priced. Collectibles, too.

*Original Crost Furniture Store
1004-06 Emerson St.
864-0189, 864-2550
Exclusive line of antique reproductions, too.

*Penny Arcade Antiques
705 Washington St.
475-4800

Tin Pan Alley
709 Washington St.
491-1200
Twentieth-century Americana—advertising signs, buttons, gadgets, mechanical figures, commemoratives, machines— and more.

F. B. Turnip & Co.
2566 Prairie Ave.
869-4894
Small shop crowded with lamps and other Victorian through Deco lighting fixtures, plus jewelry and oddities. Electrical repairs, rewiring, and brass polishing. Nice owner.

*Ken Young Antiques
703 Washington St.
869-6670

Foodstuffs

Bennison's Bakery
1000 Davis St.
328-9434
Excellent selection of very tasty, modestly priced breads and pastries. Also in Wilmette.

Evanston Sea Foods
719 Main St.
475-4890
Nice neighborhood Scandinavian deli and fish store with lots of tinned goods (especially fish and soups), homemade herring, and some cheeses.

*Farmers' Market
Maple Ave. between Clark and University Sts.
Farmers bring in their freshest on Saturdays, from late June through early fall.

Green Earth Natural Foods
2545 Prairie Ave.
864-8949
Very large, very complete natural-foods store.

Maier's Bakery & Pastry Shoppe
706 Main St.
475-6565
A favorite with locals for a broad assortment of decent breads, pastries, cakes.

The Oak Street Market
1615 Oak Ave.
864-0330
Large gourmet/health market.

Orchid Food & Flower Shop
610 Davis St.
328-6200
Small grocery specializes in fancy fruit baskets and fresh-cut flowers.

Ratzer's Catering Service
705 Main St.
864-2879
Full-service caterer sells homemade soups and hearty American sandwiches at lunchtime.

Tag's Bakery
2010 Central St.
328-1200
Another good bakery. Delicious cookies and very friendly owners.

Dining and drinking

Blind Faith Café
800 Dempster St.
328-6875
Vegetarian and natural foods at low prices. Pick up orders at kitchen and bus own dishes, so no tipping. Live music on weekends.

*Budapest Cafe
505 Main St.
491-0333

*Café Provençal
1625 Hinman Ave.
475-2233
A big winner in Chicago magazine's annual readers' poll.

Carmen's of Evanston
1600 Orrington Ave.
328-6131
Topnotch pizzeria even serves a stuffed pie for one.

*Daruma Restaurant
2903 Central St.
864-6633

Dr. Jazz Ice Cream Parlor
913 Chicago Ave.
328-9795
Ice-cream creations are served in a charming red-brick storefront fitted out with booths from Chicago's 1924 Sweetland Confectionery and even nicer Art Nouveau ones and a back-bar from the 1913 Austin Sweet Shop. Nickelodeon, silent movies.

Famous Deli & Pub
501 Davis St.
328-5252
Deli food in zippy surroundings.

Firehouse No. 2
750 Chicago Ave.
328-1234
Imaginative sandwiches and dinners, served in an interesting, comfortable atmosphere. Live entertainment some nights.

*Fritz, That's It!
1615 Chicago Ave.
866-8506

*The Keg
810 Grove St.
866-7780

Leslee's
1 American Plaza
328-8304
Striking décor, eclectic menu; food quality varies; good selection of affordable wines by the glass, carafe, or bottle.

*La Mirabelle
Orrington Hotel
1710 Orrington Ave.
864-8700
Some of the haute cuisine dishes are excellent; others are inconsistent.

*Pine Yard Chinese Restaurant
924 Church St.
475-4940

Pradhans
514 Main St.
491-1145
Handsome place serves imaginative, inexpensive vegetarian food. Nice salad bar; Al Gelato's ice cream. No liquor or smoking.

J. K. Sweets
720½ Clark St.
864-3073
Peacock's ice cream, giant cookies, and croissants in a little college-hangout-type shop with a few tables.

Swensen's Ice Cream Factory
1724 Orrington Ave.
869-7420
Okay ice-cream concoctions but not as good as California Swensen's. Sandwiches, too.

Yesterday's
1850 Sherman Ave.
864-8464
A campus hangout with excellent barbecued ribs, sandwiches, full meals.

Entertainment

See also: Interesting places (Evanston Public Library, Northwestern University, Noyes Cultural Arts Center, Weinstein Center for the Performing Arts) and Shopping and services (Hogeye Music, Old Town School of Folk Music)

*Evanston Symphony Orchestra
P.O. Box 778,
Evanston, IL 60204
965-2440
Concerts are Friday evenings. Tickets: $5 each; $14 season's subscription.

Fountain Square Concerts
Sherman and Orrington
328-2100
Jazz, blues, folk, etc., most Fridays at noon mid-June through late July.

Gus Giordano Jazz Dance Chicago
Gus Giordano Dance Center
614 Davis St.
866-9442, 251-4434
(See Dance)

*North Light Repertory Company
2300 Green Bay Rd.
869-7278
(See Theater)

*Piven Theatre Workshop
927 Noyes St.
866-6597
(See Theater)

Practical Theatre Company
703 Howard St.
328-4151
(See Theater)

The Spot
827 Foster St.
869-2800
College hangout has live music some nights. Pizza, Mexican food, ribs, etc. Big pinball room.

Varsity Theatre
1710 Sherman Ave.
864-8900
Double-feature film revivals; bill changes every two or three days.

Parks and Boulevards

Chicago's official motto, *Urbs in Horto*—City in a Garden—was ironic hyperbole when it was adopted in 1837, but the Chicago Park District motto, *Hortus in Urbe,* tells the story today. Most of the lake shore is devoted to parks, and the city's western edge is ringed with forest preserves. A once-grand boulevard system links a chain of inland parks designed by some of the country's foremost landscape artists around the turn of the century. Hundreds of small neighborhood parks and playlots dot the map. Recreational facilities range from old-fashioned croquet and horseshoe courts to a trendy obstacle fitness course and a roller rink.

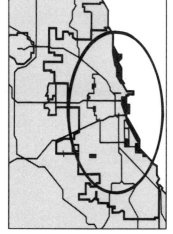

Chicago spends about $200 million a year to keep it all going. The budgeting process is as arcane and closed as can legally be arranged. A substantial body of opinion believes the money is spent more to build patronage empires than to benefit the parks. Federal grants are passed up to avoid tiresome restrictions, and the legal set-up of the park district deprives Chicago of millions of revenue-sharing dollars.

Even something as simple as park refreshments has political overtones. Two clout-heavy corporations held a no-bid monopoly on park concessions for decades, and served awful pap. After years of fruitless rage, citizens' groups finally got the bidding opened up, and a consortium led by Herman Berghoff, Sue Gin, Richard Lelko, and Leon Finney, Jr. won the contract for the North and South Side lakefront parks. Now quiche, ribs, Perrier water, Chicago-style Italian beef and pizza, yogurt, and fresh fruits widen the culinary expectations of hot-dog-and-soda-pop-weaned parkgoers.

The parks are also an ideological battleground for the competing claims of pastoralists and the more athletically inclined. The large parks were designed to be tranquil pleasure gardens, respites from city pressures, as much as centers of activity. This balancing act has been precarious. Since the Depression, the Chicago Park District itself has been the most powerful opponent of the grass-and-tree lovers. Politically connected commissioners have parted with greenery for roads, parking lots, an exposition hall, even an airport.

Grant Park

But for a happy accident 150 years ago, Chicago's lakefront would be much like its industry-laden river banks. When land along the proposed Lake Michigan–Mississippi River canal was platted, the canal commissioners designated the east side of Michigan Avenue, from Madison Street to Roosevelt Road, "Public Ground—A Common to Remain Forever Open, Clear and Free of Buildings or other Obstructions." After the Fort Dearborn Reservation was dismantled, the public land was extended north to Randolph Street.

The impoverished, young city never developed "Lake Park" and accepted an Illinois Central Railroad offer in 1851 to build a breakfront-trestle in the lake between 22nd and Randolph Streets. Although the deal seemed reasonable at the time, Chicago's first big lakefront blunder embroiled the city in a 60-year legal battle with the railroad over ownership of the space between the tracks and the old shoreline as it was gradually landfilled. Starting in 1890, wealthy mail-order merchant Montgomery Ward conducted a 20-year war in the courts to keep Lake Park "Open, Clear and Free," which earned him an "anti-progress" label rather than public gratitude. His efforts were generally successful, although the Art Institute slipped by him, and the Field Museum of Natural History was placed just outside the park's original borders to escape his ire.

The World's Columbian Exposition provided a vehicle to finish Jackson Park and engendered a wave of civic pride, which led to the Chicago Plan—a comprehensive blueprint for a better city. Conceived by Daniel "Make No Little Plans" Burnham, the fair's manager, the determinedly neoclassical and fanatically symmetrical scheme envisioned a universe of improvements, building on the existing park and boulevard system. Although many of the projects came to naught, Roosevelt Road was widened; Wacker Drive displaced the South Water Market; a bridge was built over the river at Michigan Avenue and the street widened to the north, opening the North Side to intense development; and one of a chain of proposed islands was constructed, as was one of two massive piers—Navy Pier.

By the 1933 Century of Progress fair, Edward H. Bennett's Grant Park design was a reality. **The Field Museum of Natural History** opened in 1920 and was followed by the rest of the world-famous cultural complex. (*See Museums.*) The 280-foot **Clarence Buckingham Fountain,** a rococo structure flanked by rose gardens and illuminated by an intricate, computer-operated light show, dates from 1927. The Holabird and Roche **Soldier Field** was completed in time to accommodate the 250,000 who packed the stands for the 1926 World Eucharistic Congress. A crowd of 145,000 saw the Dempsey-Tunney long count here, but the stadium isn't ideal for most sports, although the Bears make do. In his last years, Mayor Daley pushed through a multimillion-dollar renovation of the underutilized facility, which hosts a variety of events from soccer to rock concerts, so it and the acres of parking lots will be around for some time.

The handsome, octagonal, domed **Shedd Aquarium,** across Lake Shore Drive from the Field Museum, was finished in 1929 and has undergone extensive renovation. Further east stands the beautiful pink-marble **Adler Planetarium.** The 1930, 12-sided building housed the United States's first sky projection system (replaced in recent years with the latest version); a subterranean expansion provides additional space for the astrological museum's displays, activities, and a "moonscape" cafeteria.

In the late 1970s, the decaying 1932 band shell north of the Field Museum started yet another open-space preservation battle. The park district wanted to tear up two square blocks of park for a concert complex accommodating 20,000 people, but was thwarted when a few Michigan Avenue property owners refused to give their legally required consent. Since no permanent building can be constructed in the park without the unanimous consent of adjacent property owners, the park district effected a compromise. The **James C. Petrillo Music Shell** behind the Art Institute is a "temporary structure" that can be dismantled after the summer Grant Park Concert Series. Naturally, it stands year-round; the old band shell was destroyed.

Over the years, the **Art Institute** itself has spread way beyond its original boundaries. The collection is so magnificent that the sprawl is hard to resent, but the institution's many wings, the art school addition, and the **Goodman Theatre** cover a huge block of land off Michigan Avenue.

The park commissioners added to the park's landscaped space in 1979, a rare occurrence. For years, a 2,700-car parking lot marred Grant Park north of Madison Street, but construction of the **Richard J. Daley Bicentennial Plaza** has roofed the space over (with some difficulty—the roof collapsed). Besides 12 lighted tennis courts, there's a skating rink (ice in winter, roller in summer), cross-country skiing in January and February, and field house activities all year.

Although the Daley Plaza recreation facilities were welcome additions, Grant Park has always been more than a cultural oasis. On warm days, office workers picnic everywhere. From Memorial Day to Labor Day, tourists and residents crowd around Buckingham Fountain to watch the grand light show. On Venetian Night in mid-August, traffic comes to a standstill while the regatta of floats passes along the harbor's banks, and the fireworks finale is one of the city's most impressive. (Another is the Independence Day show.) Concerts fill the park with music and people four evenings a week from the end of June to the end of August. The park hosts the Taste of Chicago in July, the world's largest free jazz festival for a week in early September, and a summer art show. (*See Annual Events; Music.*)

Burnham Park

The city's Lake Front Ordinance of 1919 called for a connecting link between Grant and Jackson Parks. Named Burnham Park, it occupies landfill east of the I.C. tracks from Roosevelt Road to 56th Street, and Northerly Island. When banker Charles Dawes, his brother Rufus, and Chicago Plan Commission president James Simpson came up with the idea of a world's fair honoring Chicago's 100th anniversary, the raw landfill was the natural spot. There was even an historical precedent: The World's Columbian Exposition had filled Jackson Park 40 years earlier.

The theme of the Century of Progress was man's mastery of nature, and the sleek Art Deco buildings were monuments to functionalism. They were also harbingers of the park's future. After the fair, it was all downhill for Burnham Park; only the southernmost portion adjoining Jackson Park was sympathetically developed. In this section, the famous **Promontory Point** (55th Street and the lake) is an example of what the park could have been.

The Century of Progress's financial success led Mayor Edward J. Kelly to suggest a year-round amusement park for Northerly Island and a giant exposition hall on the mainland across the lagoon. In 1934, Chicago's 22 park boards were consolidated into one highly politicized body, and the new Chicago Park District heartily endorsed Kelly's plans. Although pastoralists screamed, the Illinois Legislature passed a bill allowing the Chicago Park District to devote ten percent of its space to expositions and fairs. The impecunious city couldn't float the amusement-park plan, and Northerly Island lay fallow until **Meigs Field** was constructed in 1947. The airport idea had been tacked onto the amusement-park concept and may have scuttled hoped-for Federal funds in the 1930s, but aviation enthusiast Merrill C. Meigs, publisher of the *Chicago Herald & Examiner* and the *Chicago American,* resurrected it and provided the necessary clout.

Another Chicago publisher spearheaded the next Burnham Park land grab. With the Chicago Plan in ruins, Robert R. McCormick of the *Chicago Tribune* had little trouble proselytizing a lakefront convention hall. With *The Tribune's* considerable political power behind it and with Mayor Daley's blessings, the project easily sailed over myriad objections and lawsuits. The hideous first McCormick Place opened in 1958 and quickly fulfilled its opponents' worst fears. After it burned nine years later, **McCormick Place** (23rd Street and South Lake Shore Drive) unfortunately rose again, consuming acres of irreplaceable lakefront. Distant from hotels and restaurants, the hall is the site of some of the nation's largest trade shows and the giant, public auto show in late February (*see Annual Events*). The Arie Crown Theatre hosts Broadway-musical road companies and, occasionally, touring ballets, operas, and orchestras (*see Theater*). Several smaller theaters, including the financially troubled Playhouse, share the southern half of the building with the Arie Crown. The underground parking lot is a block away from the public spaces. For all the activity it supports, McCormick Place is far from a model of intelligent parkland use. A long stretch of Burnham Park to the south of it is still unlandscaped.

Jackson and Washington Parks

Burnham and Grant Parks have been continually besieged by commercial and political empire builders, but Jackson Park, along Hyde Park's lakefront, owes its very existence to the forces that have threatened them. Paul Cornell, Hyde Park's founder, saw the advantages of a city-supported park at the edge of his property holdings and in 1867 lobbied in Springfield for the creation of a South Park Board modeled on New York's system. Land deals were struck and he got his bill, but a required referendum failed. During the next session, in 1869, he returned to the capital with an even more ambitious scheme—that three park boards be created, with control of the city's parks segmented by the branches of the Chicago River. The bill, which also provided for a boulevard system, passed and gained popular approval.

Plans for Jackson and Washington Parks, with their connecting link, Midway Plaisance, were drawn by the firm of Olmsted and Vaux. The extensive lagoon systems and the Midway's connecting canal reflected Frederick Law Olmsted's belief that the parks should recognize Lake Michigan's presence. They were also to serve as drainage for the marshy soil and were to be surrounded by carefully landscaped gardens and wilderness areas.

Land was acquired, but true to the Chicago spirit, costs overran the $75,000 budget by $3,425,000. Work had started on Washington Park when the Chicago Fire destroyed the blueprints and interrupted the project. After the Fire, architect H. W. S. Cleveland pared the plans (the Midway would never be flooded), and the northern half of Washington Park opened in 1874. Chicago was enthralled. Thousands came to roam and enjoy one of the largest expanses of grass in the system. Ten years later, the wealthy drove along the park's elegant carriageways to the nearby Washington Park Race Track, a private preserve where the American Derby boasted the country's largest purse.

Washington Park exhausted the South Park Board's funds, so the selection of Jackson Park as the site of the 1893 World's Columbian Exposition was a godsend. Olmsted returned to design the fairgrounds. More lagoons, gardens, and rare plantings sprouted to frame the wildly successful "White City's" magnificent neoclassical buildings, which transformed Lake Michigan's marshy shores into a fairyland that amazed millions of visitors. After the fair closed, Jackson Park was gradually converted to parkland along the lines suggested by Olmsted. Although demands for organized recreation brought dozens of facilities to the park, some of the bucolic character remained. The fair's Fine Art Palace housed the Field Columbian Museum until the Grant Park building opened. It then entered a period of decay until rescued as Julius Rosenwald's **Museum of Science and Industry** (*see Museums*), which draws four million visitors a year. The park system's first golf course—18 short holes—was built in 1900 along Jackson Park's southern edge, and the lagoons became boat harbors.

Through the Depression, the war years, and the complacent 1950s, much of the park's beauty was allowed to decay. The park district's army of patronage workers couldn't maintain the lawns and plantings formerly tended by trained experts. On the **Wooded Island,** a Columbian Exposition legacy, for example, the Japanese garden became overgrown, and the famed Ho-O-Den palace, the fair's Japanese pavilion, burned. Fortunately, the garden has been nicely restored, though not to its original glory.

But for the repeated protests of neighborhood groups, Lake Shore Drive would have been widened to eight lanes through Jackson Park. As it is, cars dominate the park's northern edge, particularly around the Museum of Science and Industry, and whiz perilously close to the 57th Street beach. Hyde Parkers in the know swim off the rocks at "The Point" (55th Street). The bathing pavilion at the 63rd Street beach is sadly deteriorated.

Except for modern structures on its periphery and general neglect, Washington Park probably resembles Olmsted's plans for the South Park's twin jewels more closely than Jackson Park. It has no attraction to equal the Museum of Science and Industry, although the **DuSable Museum of African American History** (*see Museums*) occupies the old South Parks Administration Building—a dollhouse version of the Jackson Park museum. The sunken plot in front of the DuSable has been turned into a sculpture garden by the museum. Burnham's firm also designed the refectory that stands near a WPA swimming pool and a modern field house.

The post-1930 system-wide decay was exacerbated in Washington Park by racial change in the surrounding neighborhood. The lagoons are overgrown, the formal gardens shadows of the past. Although frayed on the edges, the park's not unused. Summer weekends, Washington Park is alive with families barbecuing. Cricket and soccer games draw West Indians (and others) from all over the South Side to the open meadow.

Between the two parks, the Midway Plaisance might have been a sculpture garden if Lorado Taft, whose studio overlooked it, had had his way and the money had materialized. Taft's **Fountain of Time,** one of Chicago's largest and loveliest classical monuments, was unveiled in 1922 on the Midway's west end, just inside Washington Park. The opening lines of Henry Austin Dobson's *The Paradox of Time*—"Time goes, you say? Ah no! / Alas, Time stays, we go."—inspired the sculpture. The shrouded figure of Father Time leans on his staff surveying a mass of humanity—about 100 figures—across a reflecting pool.

Taft planned his *Creation* for the Midway's east end, but Albin Polášek's **Tomáš Masaryk Monument,** a much-ridiculed work with a trouble-laden history, stands here instead. Czechoslovakia's first president is represented by a knight. Polášek started the sculpture at the Art Institute, but World War Two diverted all metals from artistic endeavors. Since Chicago's foundries didn't reopen after the war, he had to complete the piece in New York. When it was erected, the general scorn was typified by a critic calling it "Paul Bunyan with whiskers."

John Dyfverman's statue of **Carl von Linné,** a copy of Johannes Kjellberg's sculpture in the royal gardens at Stockholm, is between the two (just west of University Avenue). Moved from Lincoln Park in 1976, it depicts the Swedish botanist in the costume he reputedly donned to roam his native countryside. Four magnificent allegorical figures representing the branches of science, which were vandalized in Lincoln Park, have not been restored and replaced by the Swedish

Bicentennial Commission. The University of Chicago, which lines the Midway, offers many more sculptures and dozens of other sights. (*See Hyde Park/ Kenwood.*)

South Parks Boulevards

To capture the ambiance of the South Parks and the neighborhoods that surround them, tour the splendid boulevards. This drive takes about an hour and passes some of the South Side's finest old homes, as well as some appalling decay. Keep your car doors locked.

Exit South Shore Drive at 31st Street and head west, skirting **Michael Reese Hospital and Medical Center.** The modern buildings to the right are the Prairie Shores apartments and, to the left, Lake Meadows—late 1950s private urban-renewal projects designed to create an integrated, middle-class, inner-city community. (South Commons, a more comfortably scaled development at Michigan Avenue and 26th Street, comes closer to attaining this goal.) The **Olivet Baptist Church** (King Drive and 31st Street), built in 1875, was the only building to survive the massive "slum clearance" for the complex.

One block west of the church, take Calumet Avenue south to the **Robert W. Roloson Houses** (3213-19). Official Chicago landmarks, these 1894, Frank Lloyd Wright, Tudor-revival townhouses are typical of the Douglas community's elegance at the turn of the century.

The **Pilgrim Missionary Baptist Church** (Indiana Avenue and 33rd Street), two blocks west, is also a city landmark and is on the National Register of Historic Places. Built as Temple K.A.M., it was designed by Dankmar Adler, the son of the congregation's first rabbi, and his partner Louis Sullivan. The massive stone structure has a dramatically pitched wooden roof and was lavished with gilt and stained-glass windows, retained when the Baptists bought the building in 1921 and made it one of the country's strongest black churches.

Backtrack to King Drive and travel south past the sad remains of a once-glorious neighborhood to the black-doughboy-crowned **Victory Monument** at 35th Street. Turn east and proceed to the **Douglas Tomb State Memorial** (35th Street and Lake Park Avenue). Leonard Volk's 1881 heroic, nine-foot-nine-inch bronze of the Little Giant faces the lake from the neighborhood that was once his estate. Beneath the statue are four allegorical figures: Illinois, Justice, History, and Eloquence. Inside the tomb, the marble sarcophagus is inscribed: "Tell my children to obey the laws and uphold the Constitution." The little state park is lovingly maintained by a resident caretaker; it is a CTA Culture Bus stop.

Just north of the monument is **Groveland Park,** a private plaisance off Cottage Grove Avenue at 33rd Place. Established in 1855 on Douglas's farm, the park was once an upper-class enclave. All the houses on the north side, including H. H. Richardson's Morton (salt) mansion, were demolished for the planned expansion of Chicago Memorial Hospital when Lake Meadows was developed. The hospital deal fell through, and after a series of legal maneuvers, a private developer built townhouses. The southern edge of this charming park still retains older homes, the grandest of which is the easternmost one (633 Groveland Park) built in 1888. The ruins of a second, similar park lie just to the south.

Take Cottage Grove Avenue to Oakwood Boulevard—named for its once-fine stand of oaks—and head west back to King Drive, past three 19th-century churches and the **Northeastern Illinois University Center for Inner City Studies** (700 East Oakwood Boulevard), formerly the Abraham Lincoln Center. Founded by Reverend Jenkin Lloyd Jones to foster interracial, national, and religious harmony, the 1905 red-brick building was designed by his nephew, Frank Lloyd Wright, and has a WPA mural inside.

James J. Egan designed the late 1890s, French Romanesque **Holy Angels Church** (Oakwood Boulevard between Langley and Vincennes Avenues) for an Irish congregation. From the Celtic-cross-topped spire to the Notre Dame-like entranceway, the spacious, barrel-vaulted building is a visual treat. *In situ* high reliefs adorn the façade, rich figures of saints the windows, intricate carving the marble altar and oak interior trim. The elementary school is one of the best in the black community.

The **Metropolitan Community Church** (King Drive and 41st Street) is an 1889 Solon S. Beman, Richardson Romanesque building. Formerly the First Presbyterian Church, it sports a magnificent interior with an E. M. Skinner pipe organ dominating the west wall. Alfred S. Alschuler designed the neoclassical, graystone **Mt. Pisgah Missionary Baptist Church** (King Drive and 46th Street) for the Chicago Sinai Congregation in 1909 when the Grand Boulevard neighborhood was one of the city's most desirable Jewish communities.

The first owners of the **Melissia Ann Elam Home** (4726 South King Drive) may well have been Chicago Sinai congregants. Simon L. Marks built the châteauesque home, designed by Henry L. Newhouse, in 1903. His sons changed the spelling of their name and achieved some notoriety in the movies. The house has been used as a home for girls since the mid-1930s, when several similar institutions dotted what was called Bronzeville, the center of Chicago's black community. The house is a city landmark, and the booklet published by the Commission on Chicago Historical and Architectural Landmarks describes the luxurious interior so evocatively that no one could fail to mourn what the area's empty lots represent.

The **George Washington Monument** at 51st Street stares down King Drive toward the distant doughboy. This statue, which represents our country's father taking command of the army at Cambridge, is a replica of a casting given to the people of France. It toured the Buffalo and the St. Louis world's fairs before the Daniel Chester French figure astride an E. C. Potter horse was raised on a Charles McKim pedestal at the entrance to Washington Park.

At this point, you can continue through Washington Park's drives and on to Jackson Park via the Midway, or leave Washington Park at Drexel Square after a sweeping circle past most of the park's points of interest. Elegant townhouses and early apartment buildings face the square on the south; it is dominated by the neighborhood's oldest sculpture, Henry Munger's 1882 **Drexel Square Fountain** with banker Francis Drexel on an ornate base with allegorical figures.

Drexel Boulevard is a copy of King Drive: a broad, even more extravagantly landscaped parkway that was once lined with opulent homes, most of which are gone. Many on King Drive were replaced by public housing of assorted quality, starting in the 1930s. On Drexel Boulevard, whole blocks of mansions fell to middle-class apartment buildings in the 1920s, most of which are now gutted or demolished. The area from 51st Street to Oakwood Boulevard is a crying indictment of the city's housing policies and a mute reminder of the forces that transformed the neighborhood.

Operation P.U.S.H. (Drexel Boulevard and 50th Street) was the home of K.A.M. for 50 years after the congregation left Indiana Avenue. Newhouse and Bernham designed the gray neoclassical building, and Todros Geller did the main sanctuary's stained glass. Reverend Jesse Jackson frequently addresses the problems of Chicago's black community from the pulpit. **"A Time to Unite"** (Drexel Boulevard and 41st Street) also speaks to neighborhood residents' frustrations. Painted on a viaduct, which once supported the Stockyards–Kenwood el, the work is bold, almost expressionistic.

The **Grant Memorial A.M.E. Church** (Drexel Boulevard between 40th and 41st Streets) was built in 1897 as Chicago's First Church of Christ, Scientist. Architect Solon S. Beman modeled the Bedford stone building on the Columbian Exposition's Fine Art Palace. James Renwick's 1888 **New Testament Missionary Baptist Church** (Drexel Boulevard and 40th Street), on the other hand, is a massive pile of stone, an eclectic castle with a huge corner tower/entrance. The striking interior is rich with wood; the stained-glass windows are in disrepair. Oakwood Boulevard leads to a Lake Shore Drive interchange.

West Parks

Douglas, Garfield, and Humboldt Parks are the Chicago Park District's stepchildren—a Cinderella story in reverse. Along with their connecting boulevards, they were the old West Park Board's crowning glory, equal in every way to Jackson and Washington Parks. Conceived along 19th-century guidelines, their very form is anathema to the park district's current activities orientation. The gyms in elegant old field houses are too small for regulation basketball, relatively few playing fields serve many teams, and classical sculptures don't support patronage jobs. Besides, since they're surrounded by minority neighborhoods, there has been little pressure until very recently to keep them up or to make improvements.

Perceived as unsafe, the West Parks elicit little casual use. Few strollers or joggers trace the winding paths, and benches by flower gardens attract almost no pigeon feeders or sun-bathers. During the week in warm weather, they come alive with kids when schools let out. On weekends, Douglas Park is jammed with people and cars. The home of Latin-American soccer in Chicago, the park's lawns are filled with players, observers, and picnickers. Weekend baseball and softball are big in Douglas and Humboldt Parks, while Garfield hosts weekly concerts at the bandstand, as well as sports activities.

The 1869 law that created the South Park Board also set up the West Park Board. Local developers were eager to sell some of their holdings for parks, removing the parcels from their tax bills and increasing the value of their remaining land. The state legislature extended Chicago's boundaries to Pulaski Road, ostensibly to place the proposed system entirely inside the city. Coincidentally, this expansion also brought sought-after city services. (Nothing much ever changes in Chicago politics.)

The 1870s were spent acquiring land and laying out the boulevard system. William Le Baron Jenney was retained to supervise conversion of the arid, treeless prairie into wooded gardens. Although far from fully landscaped, the parks opened by 1880. O. R. DuBois succeeded Jenney as West Park architect and continued his work, but the parks didn't really become beautiful until Jens Jensen's tenure at the beginning of this century.

Under the self-taught genius's guidance, the three parks flowered with formal gardens and rustic walkways. At Humboldt, for example, Jensen installed a rose garden with three pergolas designed by Schmidt, Garden, and Martin; and he redesigned the lagoon with a half-mile miniature replica of the Rock River. Boating pavilions/refectories were built in all the West Parks (now gone or unused), as was the **Garfield Park Conservatory** (300 North Central Park Avenue). The huge, seldom-visited conservatory dwarfs Lincoln Park's and shares its familiar schedule of shows. More than 5,000 varieties of plants include orchids, ferns, succulents, and economically valuable flora. Don't miss the two Lorado Taft marble figures—**Pastoral** and **Idyl**—at the entrance to the Palm House.

The West Parks got another shot in the arm during the mid-1920s. Michaelson and Rognstad designed magnificent combination field-and-boat houses in unique styles; the grounds were spruced up, and the system entered the Depression shiny-bright, basking under the reflected glow of the new Garfield Park Administration Building's (now the **Garfield Park Field House,** 100

North Central Park Drive) golden dome. Sitting on an artificial hill flanked by boating lagoons, this Spanish baroque fantasy (the grandest of the 1926-27 buildings) was lavished with exterior ornament, murals, and a marble-clad central rotunda. The West Park Board moved its administrative offices from Union Park to the building, and the Art Institute opened a branch gallery there. Now it has the usual field-house activities and a Department of Health Neighborhood Center (a "VD clinic").

The 1920s beautification was the West Parks' last hurrah. After consolidation in 1934, park district resources were funneled into lakefront parks and, later, into smaller neighborhood ones. In the 1950s, when the park district traded control of the boulevard system with the city for hundreds of playlots, the process continued. Even boating was discontinued in the West Parks. With any luck, the 1980 renovation of the Garfield Park Field House and recent Federal grants will arrest the slide and improve the future.

West Parks Boulevards

The deterioration of the surrounding neighborhoods paralleled that of the parks. Although none of the connecting boulevards ever equaled the South Side's opulence, those on the northern end of the system—Humboldt, Palmer, Kedzie, and Logan Boulevards—were quite grand. Built up in the first part of this century, they are still mostly intact and offer some delightful vistas and attractions. (*See Near Northwest Side.*)

The central part of the system—between Humboldt and Douglas Parks—was encircled by middle-class communities until the Depression, but has fared poorly since. Lawndale, for example, was heavily Jewish by 1910. It was not genteel like the communities surrounding Grand (King Drive) and Drexel Boulevards, but rather a scrappy neighborhood filled with on-the-way-up families. Institutions central to the Jewish way of life lined Douglas Boulevard. The Jewish Peoples Institute (3500) boasted classes, gyms, club and lounge rooms, a theater, a library, and an anthropological museum, as well as a kosher restaurant—the Blintzes Inn. The institute fielded a tough basketball team that competed successfully with taller teams throughout the city. The Hebrew Theological College was just across St. Louis Avenue. Both buildings are now part of the **Julius Hays Hess Public School.**

One of the grandest synagogues, Temple Anshe Kanesses Israel, now the **Friendship Baptist Church** (Douglas Boulevard and Homan Avenue), was designed by Jacob Aroner and E. S. Somers. The 1913 curved-pediment building combines Byzantine and Moorish influences with a form based on 19th-century European synagogues. Striking lions guard the stained-glass windows.

Jews remained through the Depression; almost a dozen temples are today black Baptist churches. Many of the boulevard's houses and three-flats have disappeared, leaving only gaping vacant lots. North of Douglas Park, a thriving Hispanic community has converted Cermak Road to a virtual duplicate of 18th Street in Pilsen, with similar street life and stores.

A drive on the West Side boulevards south of Douglas Park is uninviting. The West Park Board tried to control construction and to encourage the wealthy to build mansions like those on Drexel Boulevard and King Drive, but it failed. The draw of the lakefront and the North Side was just too great. Although Marshall, 24th, California, and 31st Boulevards eventually hook up with Washington Park via Garfield Boulevard (55th Street), the route passes mostly railroad yards, industrial wastelands, factories, and institutions such as the **Cook County Department of Corrections** complex, relieved only by monuments at little squares where it takes a turn. The trip probably isn't worth the effort, but it's interesting to take once—if it happens to be a convenient way to get to a desirable destination.

Lincoln Park

In the United States, New York's Central Park is usually touted as the model urban park. The Olmsted and Vaux masterpiece seems to have everything: pastoral tranquility, cultural attractions, startlingly beautiful topography, grand architecture, and the bustle of thousands of people playing, walking, running, rowing, sleeping, viewing, meeting, eating, even drinking. Although hemmed in on all sides by towering buildings, the 880-acre park feels huge, removed from the hustle of the surrounding streets. Chicagoans with a confirmed Second City complex mourn our deprivation—no Central Park—but on anything but the most literal level, they're misled. To thousands of savvy North Siders, Lincoln Park *is* the central park, bigger and, in some ways, better than New York's.

Zoo for zoo, tennis court for tennis court, statue for statue, meadow for meadow, garden for garden, Lincoln Park holds its own. In addition, our park offers something New York's can't hope to offer: the lakefront. From North to Hollywood Avenues, Lake Michigan's waters define Lincoln Park. Sandy beaches break the rock-lined shore, two boat harbors pinch the land to impossibly narrow waists, and a third is formed by a crooked finger of land reaching out from the Montrose Avenue peninsula.

But people, not things, make the comparison between the two parks natural. Lincoln Park is populated from dawn to dusk seven days a week, particularly when the weather's nice. The youthful lifestyle that makes New Town, Lakeview, DePaul, and Lincoln Park 24-hour-a-day neighborhoods also makes for lots of daylight leisure. Actors, artists, waiters (sometimes all in one person) share the park with moms minding kids. In the early morning and after work, joggers trod the cinder paths where horses once trotted. Because there's always someone around, Lincoln Park is as safe as anywhere in the city; the biggest dangers are from errant frisbees or unscooped poodle poop.

On summer weekends, Lincoln Park is a circus. The weekday crowd is joined by 9-to-5ers, families from all over the city, and an endless stream of adolescents, particularly at the beaches. Each bathing area has a particular personality. Fullerton Avenue Beach attracts the young professionals from the hip lakefront neighborhoods; the strip south of Belmont Avenue is a gathering place for gays. Montrose Avenue Beach is a bit tough and menacing. The drives and parking lots to the west have a well-deserved reputation as a drug supermarket. Foster and Hollywood Beaches are primarily working-class-family spots. The shiplike **North Avenue Beach House** and nearby **Chess Pavilion** draw a mixed crowd—part Old Town eclectic, part Cabrini-Green, and part Gold Coast glitter—but the best body-watching spot in the city is probably the Oak Street Beach. It's packed with stews and their male fellow-travelers seeking the perfect tan—or ten.

After the beaches, the park's biggest attraction is probably the **Lincoln Park Zoo** (2200 North Cannon Drive). It isn't large, but a renovation program is transforming it from a dour place with neurotic animals pacing pathetic pens to a more humane facility. The 1976 Great Ape House, designed by Dan Brenner, is an example of what zoo architecture can be. Partially subterranean to minimize its visual impact, the structure provides spacious habitats for the apes behind a winding, glass-walled passageway. The apiary, big-cat outdoor habitats, sea-lion pool and central mall, Crown-Field Center, outdoor large-mammal habitat, and hoofed-animal area make the zoo grounds more confusing than ever. Get a map from the information center along its main axis (Webster Avenue), and don't miss the eerie reptile house. The delightful **Farm in the Zoo** is just south of the main campus on Stockton Drive, and the Prairie School-inspired **Zoo Rookery,** a rock-and-lagoon-graced bird sanctuary, is just to the north along Cannon Drive (enter on Fullerton Avenue). It's a nice, low-key place to relax.

The **Lincoln Park Conservatory** (Fullerton Avenue and Stockton Drive) is much smaller and more crowded than Garfield Park's, but some ancient specimens grow in the oldest hall, built in 1891. There are five halls in all, and four annual shows—azaleas (February and March), Easter (April), mums (November), Christmas (December and January). Lincoln Park's finest formal garden stretches for a block in front of the conservatory, past the **Storks at Play Fountain**, sculpted by Augustus Saint-Gaudens and Frederick MacMonnies in 1887. The Grandmothers' Garden and the Rock Garden are nearby.

About 20 other sculptures in individual natural settings are scattered throughout Lincoln Park between Diversey Parkway and North Avenue. The Friends of the Parks booklet *Have You Talked to Lincoln lately?* by Cindy Mitchell and Joyce Bolinger elaborates on them. Friends of the Parks's interest in sculpture extends beyond print to action. The group donated the **Ellsworth Kelly** 36-foot curve of steel rising from the ground at Fullerton Avenue and Cannon Drive.

Café Brauer (2021 North Stockton Drive), overlooking the North Pond, is itself a work of art. Dwight Perkins designed the 1908 Prairie School refectory/boathouse as an elegant restaurant. The formal second-floor dining room is enhanced by two huge leaded-glass chandeliers and mosaics of park scenes; it leads to open-air patios atop the building's wings. Until Prohibition killed liquor sales, Café Brauer was one of the city's most delightful spots. The beauty of the setting helped the restaurant limp through the Depression until World War Two. In recent years, it has been reduced to a cafeteria, but rejuvenation plans are in the works, and Café Brauer may find new life as an elegant Lincoln Park Cafe.

Another vestige of the past is nearby on the park's edge: The **Chicago Academy of Sciences** (2001 North Clark Street). Dedicated to exploring Illinois's natural history, since the 1890s it has occupied the Patton and Fisher Italian Renaissance building donated by Mathew L. Laflin. The displays are limited. The **Chicago Historical Society** (Clark Street at North Avenue) is as vital as the Academy of Sciences is stodgy. The Chicago area's history is vividly portrayed through art, artifacts, and special exhibits. It's a great place for kids, and has an outstanding research library, too. (*See Museums; Libraries.*)

Lincoln Park's history explains why all of its cultural institutions are clustered south of Fullerton Avenue. The park grew north along the lake in sections, just like the city. In 1864, the City Council decreed that a park should replace the city burial ground at North Avenue, after a campaign by Dr. John H. Rauch warning of the cemetery's menace to public health. The bodies in half the graveyard were carted to new cemeteries, and in 1869, the area came under the control of the Lincoln Park Board, which hired Swain Nelson to landscape it on the English-garden model. The second half of the 120-acre cemetery was acquired in 1871. For 50 years, development was concentrated in this section, providing homes for the institutions that have grown to dominate what was once an open Victorian park. Later, landfills were created under a more sports-and-activities-oriented management; so Lincoln Park is almost two separate parks, joined by a common name and lakefront.

Other Parks

Columbus Park (500 South Central Avenue) was Jens Jensen's most representative work. The land on the city's western edge was acquired by the West Park Board in 1911. Six years later, Jensen's landscaping, using only indigenous plants to symbolize the Illinois prairie, was unveiled. With it, he hoped to stimulate meditation as well as bodily recreation. Today much of his work is gone. The lagoon, which once ran the length of the park, is more than half filled in, and the bluffs on its edge are leveled. Handsome stable and recreation buildings have been remodeled as recreational facilities to supplement those in the elegant

Chatten and Hammond refectory.

Marquette Park was one of the West Park Board's last major projects. The WPA executed much of the grounds. Half the park is given over to a nine-hole golf course. There's a lovely rose garden at the southwest corner, and the undistinguished field house (6700 South Kedzie Avenue), which was once a golf shelter, has all the usual park district programs. Local Lithuanians can be found playing soccer on weekends.

Besides the giants, the Chicago Park District runs hundreds of other operations. About ten field houses in the system were designed by D. H. Burnham and Company in 1904-05. The oldest, McKinley Park's, predates any in the country. Many of the more interesting parks are covered in chapters devoted to the neighborhoods they're in. Here are a few more:

• Auburn Park (406 West Winneconna Parkway)—A stream runs through the eight-and-a-half-acre-long, narrow park and is crossed by several rustic stone bridges. Some nice 1920s houses line the northern edge. A hidden treasure.

• California Park (3843 North California Avenue) has the only indoor sports arena in the system.

• Fuller Park (331 West 45th Street)—The field house was built in 1915 from Edward H. Bennett's design. It is constructed entirely of interesting patterned and textured concrete.

• Hamilton Park (513 West 72nd Street) has a nice Art Deco field house.

• Harrison Park (1824 South Wood Street)—Facilities include a boat building shop.

• Portage Park (4100 North Long Avenue)—The Olympic-size swimming pool is used for tournaments.

• Pulaski Park (1419 West Blackhawk Street)—William Zimmerman's magnificent Prairie School-Tudor field house dwarfs the park and stands in striking contrast to the surrounding neighborhood's rococo churches. A classical mural graces the assembly hall's proscenium, although the rest of a series has been painted over. Very full schedule of activities, two large gyms, and a pool.

• Rainbow Park and Beach (South 75th Street and the lake)—The site of racial rumbles in the 1950s and of a hideous water-filtration plant.

• Riverview Park (River's east bank, north of Belmont Avenue)—Owned by the city, not the park district. Rare access to the river with a path for strolling and an exercise course.

• Shedd Park (3660 West 23rd Street)—William Drummond's 1917 Prairie School field house takes up most of this tiny, hard-to-find park.

• Sheridan Park (910 South Aberdeen Street) has a modern, $4 million field house with an indoor pool.

• Welles Park (2333 West Sunnyside Avenue)—The model of a neighborhood park with 40 acres and lots of activities. Surprise: It's in Chicago Park District Superintendent Ed Kelly's ward!

See the appropriate chapters for these neighborhood parks: Calumet Park (*Southeast Side*), Davis Square Park (*Back of the Yards*), South Shore Country Club (*South Shore*), Indian Boundary Park—a real gem with a little zoo (*Rogers Park*), Palmer Park (*Pullman*), Peterson Park—formerly part of the Municipal Tuberculosis Sanitarium (*Albany Park*), Sherman Park (*Back of the Yards*), Union Park (*Near West Side*).

The park system's diversity results from cycles of development, each reflecting the time's conditions and fashions. Today, we are on an upswing. The Chicago Park District's hegemony is loosening up, and citizens' groups are as likely to gain a sympathetic ear as real-estate developers and monument builders. The bureaucracy's inclinations may still favor construction, but other voices are being heard.

The Cook County Forest Preserve's 65,000 acres wrap a green ring around Chicago. Eighty percent of the land is kept in a natural state for hiking, biking, horseback riding, boating, skiing, and picnicking (groups of more than 15 require permits). The remainder hosts myriad recreational facilities from eight golf courses to 16 toboggan slides. Besides the 10,000-acre Palos division (the most scenic), most of the holdings trace rivers: North Branch Chicago River and Skokie River, Des Plaines River, and Salk Creek. The Forest Preserve's waters are among the world's most heavily fished; largemouth bass, bluegill, and northern pike are stocked. Seventeen million people visit the system each year, with the North Branch division getting the heaviest use. The district publishes lots of very helpful maps and pamphlets listing recreational facilities, biking and riding trails, fishing areas and depth soundings, picnic grounds and trails, and more. These and further information are available at each of the nine division headquarters and from the Forest Preserve General Headquarters, 536 North Harlem Avenue, River Forest; 261-8400.

Grant Park

*Adler Planetarium
1300 S. Lake Shore Dr.
322-0304, 322-0300
Twelve cascading pools lined with mosaic zodiac symbols, installed for the Century of Progress Exhibition, were destroyed in the 1973 underground expansion. The new entrance looks like it should lead to a subway. The encircling road offers superb Loop skyline vistas. (See Museums.)

*Art Institute of Chicago
Michigan Ave. at Adams St.
443-3500, 443-3600
(See Museums.)

*Buckingham Fountain
Foot of Congress Dr.
Modeled on the Latona Fountain in Versailles—only much bigger. During the summer, sightseeing boats load passengers across Lake Shore Dr. for moonlight cruises. Be careful: The crosswalk is marked, but there's no signal and some motorists are distracted by the light show.

Columbia Yacht Club
Washington and the lake
943-3342
A permanently docked ship: The only one of the many private, lakefront yacht clubs of sympathetic design and visual interest.

Christopher Columbus Monument
Columbus Dr. at Roosevelt
Sculpted by Carlo Brioschi and erected in 1933, this statue symbolizes aspects of Columbus's expedition that resulted in the discovery of America. During World War Two, people thought one of the pedestal relief carvings—the Roman symbol of strength and unity—looked like Mussolini and wanted it removed.

Congress Plaza
Congress and Michigan
The formal entrance to Grant Park is framed by Ivan Meštrović's equestrian Indians and Frederick Hibbard's bronze eagles.

Nicolaus Copernicus Monument
Achsah Bond Dr., just west of Adler Planetarium
The original statue of the Polish astronomer adorns the façade of the Staszic Palace Polish Academy of Sciences in Warsaw. Bronislaw Koniuszy's copy was erected in 1973. Soil from six locations connected with Copernicus's life is sealed in the base.

*Richard J. Daley Bicentennial Plaza
337 E. Randolph Dr.
294-4792
Skate for free or dancercise for a buck. Reserve tennis courts a day ahead.

East Monroe Underground Garage
350 E. Monroe Dr.
294-4740
Bargain, flat-rate, all-day parking. Meters on Columbus Dr. are cheaper, underground garages off Michigan Ave. more expensive.

*Field Museum of Natural History
Roosevelt Rd. and Lake Shore Dr.
922-9410
One of the world's largest marble buildings, designed by D. H. Burnham and Company. Limited free parking at north entrance. (See Museums.)

Fountain statues
North and south of Buckingham Fountain
Leonard Crunelle's charming statues (Crane Girl, Dove Girl, Turtle Boy, Fisher Boy) are virtually hidden in the rose gardens.

*Goodman Theatre
200 S. Columbus Dr.
443-3800
(See Theater)

*Hebe, sculpture
1100 S. Michigan Ave.
The Greek goddess of youth and cupbearer of the gods sculpted by Franz Machtl in the early 1890s surmounts a fountain.

Thaddeus Kościuszko Monument

Achsah Bond and Lake Shore Drs., west of Adler Planetarium

Alexander Chodinski's 1904 statue of this Polish, American Revolutionary War hero was moved from Humboldt Park.

Abraham Lincoln Monument

Congress Dr. between Michigan and Columbus

This highly acclaimed seated Lincoln is one of Augustus Saint-Gaudens's last works.

General John A. Logan Monument

900 S. Michigan in the park

Augustus Saint-Gaudens's 1897 statue of the Commander of the Grand Army of the Republic is atop one of Chicago's few hills—a small, manmade one at that.

*James C. Petrillo Music Shell

Jackson and Columbus
294-2420

A park commissioner and president of the Chicago Federation of Musicians, Petrillo instituted the Grant Park concerts on July 4, 1935. They are now held Wednesday, Friday, and Saturday at 8 p.m., and Sunday evenings at 7 p.m., from late June through the end of August.

*John G. Shedd Aquarium

1200 S. Lake Shore Dr.
939-2426
(See Museums)

*Soldier Field

425 E. McFetridge Dr.
294-2200

Spirit of the Lakes

South Wing of the Art Institute near Jackson Dr.

Lorado Taft's five classic maidens symbolize the Great Lakes. The highest (Lake Superior) spills the waters of her basin into the one held by Lake Michigan, who in turn empties hers into Huron, Erie, and Ontario.

Burnham Park

Burnham Administration Building

425 E. McFetridge Dr.
294-2200
Park district headquarters.

*McCormick Place-On-the-Lake

2300 S. Lake Shore Dr.
791-6000
This is the number for everything, including the theaters.

*Merrill C. Meigs Field

15th St. at Lake Michigan
744-4787

Scheduled to be parkland after the Century of Progress, Northerly Island is devoted to private aviation. Mayor Byrne's proclaimed intention to reclaim the space for parks ran afoul of long-term agreements with the Federal government. May be used as part of a 1992 World's Fair site. 10¢ observatory deck overlooks almost nothing.

*Promontory Point

55th St. at Lake Michigan

A favorite gathering place for Hyde Parkers—picnickers, sun-bathers, ballplayers, and musicians. The pedestrian tunnel leading to it is lined with lively graffiti. Keep a strong hold on your bicycle. The park can be unsafe at night.

David Wallach Fountain

55th St., on the Point side of the pedestrian tunnel

A bronze fawn, sculpted by Elisabeth Halestine (assistant to Lorado Taft), rests on a hexagonal marble pedestal, designed by her husband, Frederick Hibbard, and is equipped with a drinking fountain and a small pool for animals. David Wallach, who died in 1894, willed the interest accrued on a set sum to the park district for a fountain for "man and beast." The charming work cost $4,000 and was dedicated in 1939.

Jackson Park Washington Park Midway Plaisance

*DuSable Museum of African American History

740 E. 56th Pl.
947-0600
D. H. Burnham and Co.; 1904. (See Museums.)

*Fountain of Time

Washington Park, west of Cottage Grove Ave. facing Midway Plaisance

Jackson Park Driving Range

Hayes and Lake Shore Drs.

Bitterly fought by many Hyde Parkers, the range impinges on the park's bird sanctuary.

Jackson Park Field House

6401 S. Stony Island Ave.
643-6363

Built in the 1950s on the same plan as the Russell Square and Avalon Park field houses. Has basketball leagues, golf for senior citizens, and other programs.

General Richard L. Jones Armory

5200 S. Cottage Grove Ave.
288-8131

Solon S. Beman designed the Art Deco-ornamented National Guard armory, one of the largest.

Gotthold E. Lessing Monument

Washington Park, near 55th St. and Cottage Grove Ave.

Albin Polášek's 1930 statue of the dramatist and philosopher overlooks sunken gardens near the site of the park's long-gone conservatory.

*Carl von Linné, sculpture

Midway Plaisance, just west of University Ave.

*Tomáš Masaryk Monument

Midway Plaisance, east end

Midway Studios

6016 S. Ingleside Ave.
753-4821
Was Lorado Taft's studio. (See Hyde Park.)

*Museum of Science and Industry
57th St. and Lake Shore Dr.
684-1414
The only remaining building from the World's Columbian Exposition. "Lakeside Promenade" concerts on the south portico overlook the Jackson Park lagoon. Pedal boats for rent. (See Museums.)

La Rabida Children's Hospital and Research Center
65th St. at Lake Michigan
363-6700
Originally housed in a Columbian Exposition replica of the Spanish monastery where Columbus left his son when he sailed to the New World. The present buildings date from 1932, 1953, and 1959 and offer treatment to children with rheumatic, respiratory, and other chronic diseases.

The Refectory
Washington Park, Morgan Dr. just east of King Dr.
Now unused. Housed a delightful restaurant and the ice-cream factory for the South Parks.

The Republic, sculpture
Jackson Park, Richards and Hayes Drs.
A scaled-down replica (about two-thirds size—but still huge) of Daniel Chester French's sculpture, which stood in the Court of Honor at the World's Columbian Exposition.

Washington Park Drama Shop
5746 S. Cottage Grove Ave.
752-6577
Once a stable; now houses the park district's enormous costume collection and props for the extensive drama program. Nearby buildings contain a riggers shop, electrical equipment, and more.

Washington Park Field House
5531 S. King Dr.
684-6530
A modern building with a full schedule of activities for children and adults, senior citizens, and mentally retarded children that includes tennis, racquetball, handball; football and softball leagues; lapidary, ceramics, woodworking, and photography shops; sewing, macramé, and other arts and crafts; music, drama, and more.

Washington Park Open Forum
Just east of King Dr., south of 53rd St.
The successor to the famous "Bug Club," a daily open forum during the first two decades of this century, continues on weekend afternoons in good weather.

*Wooded Island
South of the Museum of Science and Industry
Teems with flora and fauna. Doug Anderson leads early-morning bird-watching walks spring through autumn (493-7058, weekdays between 5 and 6 p.m.), which start at the Clarence Darrow Memorial Bridge leading onto the island. (Darrow fans meet here once a year to commune with their hero.) Wooded Island Festival, the last Sunday in September, is a major community event. (See Annual Events.)

South Parks Boulevards

Corpus Christi Catholic Church
King Dr. and 49th St.
285-7720
Designed by Joe W. McCarthy and dedicated in 1916, the Italian Renaissance, Bedford limestone church was built for an Irish congregation. The interior has a magnificent coffered ceiling.

*Douglas Tomb State Memorial
35th St. and Lake Park Ave.
Chicago's oldest sculpted monument.

*Drexel Square Fountain
Drexel Sq. and Drexel Blvd.

*Melissia Ann Elam Home
4726 S. King Dr.
373-9745

*Grant Memorial A.M.E. Church
Drexel Blvd. between 40th and 41st Sts.
285-5819

*Groveland Park
Off Cottage Grove Ave. at 33rd Pl.

*Holy Angels Church
Oakwood Blvd. between Langley and Vincennes
624-5375

*Metropolitan Community Church
King Dr. and 41st St.
536-2046

*Mt. Pisgah Missionary Baptist Church
King Dr. and 46th St.
373-0070
John Singer Sargent's frieze of the prophets is copied in wood for the pulpit.

National Conference of Black Lawyers Community College of Law
4545 S. Drexel Blvd.
285-2600
The grand stone mansion was designed by Burnham and Root in the late 1880s for W. E. Hale.

*New Testament Missionary Baptist Church
Drexel Blvd. and 40th St.
536-0870
Originally South Congregational Church.

*Northeastern Illinois University Center for Inner City Studies
700 E. Oakwood Blvd.
268-7500
Topchevsky's 1940 casein-on-glass murals depict the "development of man."

*Olivet Baptist Church
King Dr. and 31st St.
842-1081
Originally the First Baptist Church. Organized in 1850, Olivet was one of Chicago's earliest black congregations and the parent church for many others in the area. The Gothic, yellow-stone building is a good example of 19th-century Protestant-church architecture.

*Operation P.U.S.H.
Drexel Blvd. and 50th St.
373-3366

*Pilgrim Missionary Baptist Church
Indiana Ave. and 33rd St.
842-5830

Provident Hospital
426 E. 51st St.
285-5300
Chicago's first black hospital.

*Michael Reese Hospital and Medical Center
2929 S. Ellis Ave.
791-2000
The main Ellis Ave. and 29th St. hospital was designed by Schmidt, Garden, and Erickson, opened in 1907, and is surrounded by a score of buildings. One of Chicago's major medical centers.

*Robert W. Roloson Houses
3213-19 S. Calumet Ave.
The Commission on Chicago Historical and Architectural Landmarks booklet describes them fully.

*"A Time to Unite," mural
Drexel Blvd. and 41st St.
Sponsored by the Chicago Mural Group and the Kenwood-Oakland Community Organization and painted in 1976 by Mitchell Canton, Justine De Van, and Calvin Jones.

*Victory Monument
King Dr. and 35th St.
Dedicated in 1927 to members of the Illinois National Guard 8th Infantry who died in France in W.W. I. Three heroic bronze figures around the shaft symbolize the glory and tragedy of war. The black doughboy overlooks what was the "Black Belt."

*George Washington Monument
King Dr. at 51st St.

West Parks

Norman J. Cornwall Memorial
Garfield Park, southwest corner of Jackson and Central Park
All that remains of the memorial to West Town soldiers and sailors who died in W.W. I is a lonely shaft. Four 2½-foot cannon shells and large chains connecting them to the obelisk are gone, as is "The Eternal Flame" the piece was dedicated as.

Douglas Park Field House
1401 S. Sacramento Dr.
521-3244
Designed by Michaelson and Rognstad in the Colonial Georgian style, the 1926 building is also a boathouse, but the boats are gone. Activities focus on training youths with baseball, basketball, and soccer clinics, as well as roller skating and other indoor sports and games. Twenty-four soccer teams, members of the Chicago Latin-American Soccer League, use three soccer fields; 18 baseball teams use three diamonds; and the basketball teams shine.

Douglas Park Garden Pergola
Sacramento Dr. and Ogden
Constructed of reinforced concrete, this classical structure overlooking formal gardens was designed by W. C. Zimmerman around 1910.

Garfield Park Bandstand
Just east of Hamlin Blvd. and Wilcox St.
The park's oldest surviving structure is a delightful, copper-roofed, Victorian fantasy called "Indian Saracenic" when J. L. Silsbee designed it. There were no concerts from 1939 to 1980, but park supervisor John Houston reinstituted them in summer. The bandstand can hold 100 musicians; bands, church choirs, gospel groups, and others perform.

*Garfield Park Conservatory
300 N. Central Park Ave.
533-1281
Modeled on Paxton's Great Conservatory at Chatsworth, England, and one of the world's largest when it was built by Hitchings & Co. in 1907. Was also the main propagating house for the West Parks. A touch-and-smell garden for the blind is just to the south.

*Garfield Park Field House
100 N. Central Park Dr.
826-3175
Four smaller domes surrounding the gold-leaf one have been removed. Full program includes gymnastics, arts and crafts, drama, modern dance, the usual sports, and roller skating (with music and refreshments).

Garfield Park Refectory/Boathouse
Off Washington and Hamlin
W. C. Zimmerman's 1907 Prairie School building is boarded up.

Garfield Park Water Court and Flower Garden
Madison St. between Woodward Dr. and Hamlin
Jens Jensen; 1907. The garden entrance is guarded by two monumental statues cast from World's Columbian Exposition originals. Daniel Chester French did the women, E. C. Potter the bulls they're leaning against.

Humboldt Park Field House
1400 N. Humboldt Dr.
276-0107
Designed by Michaelson and Rognstad in English Tudor style, the 1926 building overlooks one of the park's lagoons and is also a boathouse. Tiny gyms. No more boats. Programs include sports (notably boxing), table games, music, roller skating. There's also a woodworking shop.

Humboldt Park Pavilion
East of Humboldt Dr., south of the Field House
Hugh Garden's 1907 Prairie School beauty with three huge arches was a boat-landing and boat-storage area. Unused now, it and Garden's nearby light standards are in disrepair.

Humboldt Park Rose Garden
Humboldt Dr. and Division
Jens Jensen designed the garden; Schmidt, Garden, and Martin the three pergolas (there are more Garden light standards here); and Edward Kemeys the east entrance bisons. The originals of the sculptures won a medal at the World's Columbian Exposition and were recast in bronze for the park in 1911.

Humboldt Park Stable
Division St. and Humboldt
A fanciful, 1896 Germanic minicastle designed by Emil H. Frommann and Ernest Jebsen is used for storage.

*Pastoral and Idyl
Garfield Park Conservatory
Lorado Taft was particularly fond of these 1914 statues.

West Parks Boulevards— and a few detours

*Cook County Department of Corrections
26th St. and California Blvd.
376-9800
The huge complex includes the 1929, neoclassical, Indiana limestone Criminal Courts building designed by Eric E. Hall and a modern, college-dorm-style jail.

*Friendship Baptist Church
Douglas Blvd. and Homan
762-0382

Carter H. Harrison High School
2850 W. 24th Blvd.
277-1215
Huge yellow-brick building with rococo terra-cotta friezes was designed by A. F. Hussander in 1915.

*Julius Hays Hess Public School
3500 W. Douglas Blvd.
762-7746

Independence Boulevard Seventh Day Adventist Church
Independence and Polk
826-1447
Was Congregation Anshe Sholom, designed by Newhouse and Bernham and dedicated in 1926. Exquisite, Jewish liturgical stained glass over arched entrance.

Independence Square Fountain
Douglas and Independence Blvds.
The 15-foot pedestal of Charles J. Mulligan's charming granite-and-bronze fountain is shaped like the Liberty Bell. Around a central flag boy on top, children celebrating the 4th of July hold tubes that represent Roman candles. Unveiled on July 4, 1902, the sculpture is in disrepair.

Marquette Monument
Marshall and 24th Blvds.
Marquette, Joliet, and an Algonquin Indian sculpted by Hermon A. MacNeil. Also in very bad shape.

Our Lady of Sorrows Basilica
Jackson Blvd. and Albany
638-5800
Servite Fathers founded the parish in 1874. Completed in 1901, the magnificent church was elevated to the rank of basilica (the first in Illinois) by Pope Pius XII in 1956, primarily because the "Sorrowful Mother Novena" began here and spread to 2,000 other churches. The Renaissance-style interior, designed by William J. Brinkman, is richly adorned with marble, paintings by F. Giusti and others, and carvings. Descriptive pamphlets are available.

Presentation Catholic Church
Springfield Ave. and Polk
533-2820
Irish parish founded in 1898; joined by Italians in the 1930s and '40s; now all black. The 1903 Beaux Arts, graystone church is quite ornate. Lovely stained glass and painted ceiling.

St. Agatha Church
Douglas Blvd. and Kedzie
522-3050
Handsome but decaying French Romanesque church with a Byzantine dome; designed by Egan and Prindeville in 1904.

St. Casimir Church
Cermak Rd. and Whipple
521-8400
Parish founded in 1890 to serve a growing Polish population. The huge, octagonal, red-brick church with handsome wood altars and towering, pictoral stained glass was built in 1917. The community is now Spanish-speaking.

Sears, Roebuck and Co.
Centered at Homan Ave.
and Arthington St.
265-2500
When it opened in 1906, the mail-order distribution center in this huge complex was the largest business building in the world, with more than three million square feet of floor space—and it's a wood-frame structure! Sears's first retail store opened in the building in 1925. Opposite the administration building is a lovely park with a pergola.

Westinghouse Vocational High School
3301 W. Franklin Blvd.
638-0133
Schmidt, Garden, and Martin, 1922; one of the last major Prairie School buildings constructed in Chicago. Eagles perch atop paired brick piers on three sides of the central section.

Lincoln Park

John Peter Altgeld Monument
Southeast of Diversey Pkwy. at Stockton Dr.
Gutzon Borglum's statue of the Illinois governor who pardoned the Haymarket participants and was described by Vachel Lindsay as setting "himself tasks which took a lion's courage and a martyr's heart" was dedicated on Labor Day, 1915, by William Jennings Bryan.

*Café Brauer
2021 N. Stockton Dr.

Casting Pool
Fullerton and Stockton
Brush up on your fly casting.

*Chess Pavilion
North and Lake Shore Dr.
Play or kibbitz.

*Chicago Academy of Sciences
2001 N. Clark St.
549-0606
(See Museums)

*Chicago Historical Society
Clark St. at North Ave.
642-4600
(See Museums)

Cricket Hill
Near Wilson Ave.
and Simonds Dr.
Weekend rugby soccer.

Diversey Driving Range
Diversey Pkwy. and Lake Shore Dr. West
294-2274 (city-wide park district golf information)
Driving range and miniature golf course.

Eugene Field Memorial
Between Reptile House and Small Mammal House in the zoo
Edward McCarten's tribute to the Chicago poet, who spent many hours in the park, is often called Wynken, Blynken, and Nod *and depicts scenes and characters from Field's children's poems.*

Johan Wolfgang Von Goethe Monument
Stockton Dr. south of Diversey Pkwy.
Herman Hahn's symbolic statue makes the poet look better than he did in real life. Since it's dedicated to Goethe, the mastermind of the German people, W.W. II anti-German sentiment was for melting it into a bomb.

Ulysses S. Grant Monument
East side of South Pond
Can be seen from about 1900 N. Lake Shore Dr.
Just a year after it was dedicated in 1891, a bolt of lightning struck this statue and killed three picnickers.

Willie Green's Park Bait Shop
Montrose and Simonds
271-2838
Get your bait and tackle right in the park.

Alexander Hamilton Monument
Stockton Dr., south of Diversey Pkwy.
Commissioned by Kate Buckingham in the 1930s, the smallish figure in gold leaf on a large base wasn't erected until 1952.

*Ellsworth Kelly Sculpture
Northeast corner of Fullerton Ave. and Cannon Dr.
Dedicated to the "I Will" spirit and unveiled in late 1981.

David Kennison Boulder
Off Clark and Wisconsin
The oldest survivor of the Boston Tea Party was 115 when he died in 1852 and was buried somewhere near this boulder.

Kiva Ma Rolas, totem pole
Lake Shore Dr. at Addison
Brought to Chicago in 1929 from the Queen Charlotte Islands of British Columbia, this Haida Indian totem is carved with the legend of the steel-headed man and other stories relating to tribal history. Kolus, sister of the Thunderbird and the protectress of the tribe, clutches the tail of the killer whale on top.

Abraham Lincoln Monument
Stockton Dr. and North Ave.
Augustus Saint-Gaudens's 1887 standing Lincoln is the most famous sculpture in the park. The head, modeled from a life mask, and hands were done by Leonard Volk. Stanford White designed the setting and chair, a copy of one in an ancient Athenian theater. Lorado Taft called it "the greatest portrait statue in the United States."

*Lincoln Park Conservatory
Fullerton and Stockton Dr.
294-4770
The core buildings, including the lovely 1891 Palm House, were built to Joseph L. Silsbee's design in 1891. The modern front addition is totally unsympathetic.

Lincoln Park Field House and Cultural Arts Center
2045 N. Lincoln Park West
294-4750
Boxing and arts with many classes in lapidary and jewelry, drama, music, woodcraft, yoga, etc.

Lincoln Park Gun Club
Lake Shore Dr. and
Diversey Pkwy.
549-6490
Facilities are open (reluctantly) to the public, and the little metered parking lot is as close to the water as can be. No swimming, but you can watch the power boats going in and out of Diversey Harbor.

*Lincoln Park Zoological Gardens
2200 N. Cannon Dr.
294-4660
Dwight Perkins designed several of the older buildings, including the Lion House; Harry Weese did much of the work for the new mall. A nice zoo.

*Lincoln Park Zoo's Farm in the Zoo
Stockton Dr. just south of Armitage Ave.

Margate Field House
4931 N. Marine Dr.
561-9809
A full range of field-house activities; a basketball league plays in the full-size gym.

*North Avenue Beach House
North and Lake Shore Dr.
A boat on the prairie!

William Shakespeare Monument
Stockton Dr. and Belden
William Partridge's poetic rendering was first displayed at the Columbian Exposition and placed in Lincoln Park on April 23, 1894, an anniversary of the Bard's birth and death.

*Storks at Play Fountain
Stockton Dr. and Belden

Tennis Courts
Between Diversey Pkwy. and Belmont Ave., west of Lake Shore Dr.; east of Lake Shore Dr. near the Totem Pole; and at Wilson Ave. and Simonds Dr.

Theatre On The Lake
Fullerton Ave. and
Lake Shore Dr.
294-2375
The home of amateur summer stock was designed by Dwight Perkins as the Daily News Fresh Air Sanitarium. Much altered, it hosts the culmination of the park district's vast drama program. The best of the lot get a chance at the big time.

Waveland Golf Course
North of Irving Park Rd. east of Lake Shore Dr.
294-2274
The Tudor clubhouse looks like an English church, right down to the Wolford Chimes Belltower.

*The Zoo Rookery
Fullerton and Cannon Dr.
This lovely spot was designed by the park district's landscape architect's staff in 1936.

In what Frank Lloyd Wright called the world's finest park system, circa 1900

Museums

"We have boasted long enough of our grain elevators, our railroads, our trade. . . . Let us now have libraries, galleries of art, scientific museums, noble architecture and public parks. . . . Otherwise there is danger that Chicago will become merely a place where ambitious young men will come to make money . . . and then go elsewhere to enjoy it." So said the Chicago Historical Society's president in 1877, and no other injunction has been more heeded by Chicagoans, save for Daniel Burnham's "Make no little plans."

From limestone palaces to little ethnic collections, huge arboretums to vest-pocket nature centers, full-service establishments with every amenity to tiny efforts with limited appeal, the institutions listed here offer something for everyone. To make the most of your visit, keep a few ground rules in mind. All museums are more crowded on weekends. Zoos, botanical gardens, and other outdoor exhibits are subject to the weather's vicissitudes. Memberships available at many larger organizations confer benefits, such as free admissions and gift-shop discounts. Most museums, particularly ethnic ones, feature holiday festivities and activities tailored to kids. Remote or specialized collections may be open only on weekends or part of the year; some others have limited weekday hours. Consult a current issue of *Chicago* magazine or phone ahead for specifics on shows, hours, holiday closings, and lower admissions for children, students, and senior citizens.

KEY TO SYMBOLS

● Free admission at all times.

B Culture Bus service. One of the CTA's unlimited-ride specials stops nearby. Service operates Sundays and holidays from the Memorial Day weekend through the last Sunday of daylight-saving time in October.

C Classes. From an occasional lecture or demonstration to formal lessons.

F Food available. More than a candy machine, but not necessarily much more.

L Library. Anything from a collection of related periodicals to a major research-institution library. Advance permission is usually required.

P Parking. On-site space for autos, but not necessarily free or sufficient.

S Gift shop. Anything from a stand selling a few postcards to a full-scale store with souvenirs, books, etc.

T Reasonably convenient to public transportation.

W Wheelchair access. No architectural barriers; surfaces fairly smooth. A robust wheeler should be able to manage unaided, but call ahead for special needs and questions. Washrooms are not necessarily accessible.

X Performances and special events. Programs ranging from short films to concerts on a fairly regular basis.

Major assets

● **The Adler Planetarium**
1300 S. Lake Shore Dr.
322-0300
Sparked by German exam-

ples, Sears, Roebuck and Co. executive Max Adler funded this country's first planetarium (in recent years renovated and expanded). The astronomic museum

has one of the world's largest collections of antique stargazing instruments, a navigation display, huge photographs taken from space, and the new

Doane observatory with a 16-inch telescope for firsthand heavenly viewing. A Mark VI Zeiss planetarium projector uses light from a Chicago street-lamp bulb to paint pictures of the heavens on the Sky Theatre's dome (fee for sky shows). Mirror grinding and telescope construction are among the classes and workshops. Open late in summer. (See Parks and Boulevards.) PBTWFSCXL

The Art Institute of Chicago
Michigan Ave. at Adams St.
443-3600
Justly renowned for its medieval masterpieces and French Impressionists, Chicago's major art museum boasts treasures in every room. Modern painters such as Chagall, Picasso, Matisse, and Dubuffet are well represented, as are Chinese works from the last two dynasties. The photographic collection has few peers; an impressive array of graphics can be seen in the print and drawing galleries; and no one who has ever had, or wanted, a dollhouse should miss the Thorne Miniature Rooms. Special exhibits are always in progress. Oppressive crowds may blight superstar shows, but quieter ones are real pleasures. The biennial American Exhibition and the annual Exhibition by Artists of Chicago and Vicinity attract the cognoscenti.
Although the museum's connection with the Goodman Theatre and School of Drama has been severed, the art school flourishes in a dramatic new building on Columbus Dr. (which also provides wheelchair access to the building). Get your kids interested in art school by taking them to the fine Junior Museum.
Outstanding libraries, a terrific film center, free gallery talks, and lots of art books and prints in the gift

shop are additional attractions. The restaurants' food is only fair, but warm weather alfresco dining in McKinlock Court is so pleasant, who cares? $3 suggested; free Thurs. BTWFSCXL

Brookfield Zoo
8400 W. 31st. St.,
Brookfield
242-2630
Seeing the dozens of major exhibits on more than 200 acres in one day is an accomplishment. Lions, tigers, bears, monkeys, mountain sheep, and goats romp (or loll) in their craggy natural habitats (surrounded by moats); zebras, antelope, camels, bison, and rhinos roam outdoor ranges; birds soar in the Perching Bird House; reptiles slither about their dioramas; swans glide across a formal pool; king penguins keep cool in refrigerated indoor cases; African birds, primates, and a hippo survey intruders upon the steamy Tropic World (an indoor recreation of a rain forest); small nocturnal, carnivorous cats haunt habitats in the Predator Ecology Exhibit (guided tours only); a Tasmanian devil holds forth in the show-bizzy Australia House; dolphins delight crowds at the Seven Seas Panorama; new zoo babies join domestic animals and tamer wild species in the ever-popular Children's Zoo, which features many demonstrations. (Fees for some exhibits and shows.) For an overview, take the narrow-gauge railway around the zoo's periphery or the Motor Safari guided tour. Audio tours with a staff member and free volunteer guides are also available. Pick up the Brookfield Guide and don't miss the bookstore (on the bird plaza) with more than 4,000 titles. $2; free Tues. PTWFSCX

Chicago Historical Society
Clark St. at North Ave.
642-4600
A fine permanent collection devoted to American, Illinois, and Chicago history includes items as diverse as the Santa Maria's anchor, John Brown's Bible, the Pioneer (Chicago's first locomotive), and a large selection of American folk art. A sizable exhibit documents Lincoln's life through dioramas, paintings, furniture, artifacts, and manuscripts. World's Columbian Exposition and Century of Progress memorabilia, Chicago Fire dioramas, period rooms, and early photographs of the city are among the Chicago materials; and the Illinois Pioneer Life Gallery provides a setting for volunteers' demonstrations of frontier household arts. Copies of all the First Ladies' Inaugural gowns as well as finery from Chicago's society dames form a fraction of the extensive costume holdings. Special exhibits, such as old-fashioned toys (at Christmastime), puppets, Art Deco, and other nostalgia, are sheer delights. The outstanding library is a must for anyone interested in Chicago history (see Libraries), and the annual An Old-Fashioned Fourth of July Celebration gives patriotism a good name. Usually uncrowded. $1; free Mon. BTWSCXL

• **Chicago Public Library Cultural Center**
78 E. Washington St.
269-2820
744-6630 (events)
This Greco-Italian Renaissance masterpiece lavished with marble, mosaics, and Tiffany glass was almost demolished when the library's central collection burst its seams, but wiser heads prevailed. Besides the library's fine arts, lan-

guage and literature, au-
dio-visual, popular, children's, and special collections (see Libraries), the
building has several exhibit
areas including the Grand
Army of the Republic
Memorial Hall, a testimony
to passions long subsided.
Friends of the Chicago
Public Library conduct
tours of the building (269-
2922), and innumerable
free concerts, films, lectures, and art shows make it
a must. BTW (Randolph St.)
SCXL

Field Museum of Natural History

Roosevelt Rd. and
Lake Shore Dr.
922-9410
Harry Weese's 1970s
renovation of the magnificent building heralded the
formerly staid institution's
revitalization plan, epitomized by the King Tut exhibition, possibly a bigger
draw than all the Field's
previous shows combined.
A new emphasis on the an-
thropology department (the
museum's other traditional
divisions are botany,
geology, and zoology) has
rationalized shows previ-
ously considered to be the
province of the Art Institute.
Beautifully mounted ex-
hibits, such as The Great
Bronze Age of China, focus
on other cultures through
their artworks.
  Of course, the grand,
marble-clad Stanley Field
Hall still has the famous
fighting African bull
elephants and the first free-
standing Gorgosaurus
dinosaur. There are also
halls of animal dioramas,
plant models, and ethno-
logical displays (don't miss
the one on American Indi-
ans), as well as the Hall of
Gems, the Egyptian Hall
with its walk-through tombs,
the Hall of Chinese Jades,

and the Maritime Peoples of
the Arctic and Northwest
Coast exhibit, which in-
cludes some of the
museum's founding arti-
facts from the World's
Columbian Exposition.
Even with 20 acres of floor
space, the museum can
display less than one percent of its holdings; scholars use the balance for
research. Special in-house
shows, such as the 1979
Feather Arts, are real treats.
The museum also offers
many excellent films, lectures, concerts, and
programs for kids. (See
Parks and Boulevards.) $2;
free Fri. PBTWFSCXL

• Lincoln Park Zoo

2200 N. Cannon Dr.
294-4660
(See Parks and Boule-
vards.) PBTWFSCXL

Museum of Contemporary Art

237 E. Ontario St.
280-2660
Dedicated to the "untried
and controversial," MCA
functions much like a huge
gallery, mounting one major
show after another, in-
troducing Chicagoans to
new works of neon, paper,
video, geometric, mono-
chromatic, op, pop, and just
plain odd art. It also exhibits well-known Chicago and
other artists and presents
lectures, demonstrations,
performances, films, and
seminars.
  The remarkable redesign
of an old bakery building
and the striking renovation
of an adjoining brownstone
annex reflect the museum's
avant-garde approach to
art, although some may
sympathize with Christo's
erstwhile draping of the
buildings with tarpaulins.
$2; free Tues. BTWFSCX

• Museum of Science and Industry

57th St. and Lake Shore Dr.
684-1414
More than four million people each year flock to Chicago's most popular tourist
attraction to push buttons,
pull cranks, and flip levers
that animate displays of
everything from basic
physics to state-of-the-art
technology. Bus fleets dis-
gorge hordes of kids who
noisily pack the informative,
sometimes smug, exhibits
financed by trade associations, government agen-
cies, and industrial giants. A
coal mine, the only German
submarine captured on the
high seas, and a 16-foot-tall
heart you can walk through
are also crowd-pleasers.
  Quiet corners are remi-
niscent of the Smithsonian,
with historic planes, bicycles, autos, and more. Yesterday's Main Street is complete with a silent-movie
theater, an ice-cream
parlor, and an old-time photographer's studio for
souvenirs. Colleen Moore's
Fairy Castle and the huge
model-train set-up are kids'
fantasies come true.
  The museum mounts lots
of special shows; some are
quite hip, others, such as
Christmas Around the
World, are traditions.
Programs include lectures,
demonstrations, work-
shops, films, festivals, and
field trips. PBTWFSCXL

• Oriental Institute Museum

University of Chicago
1155 E. 58th St.
753-2475
In addition to mummies and
the famous 40-ton winged
bull that once guarded the
entrance to the palace of
King Sargon II of Khor-
sabad, this research institution has Sumerian sculpture
unrivaled outside of Iraq,

Ripley's Believe It or Not Museum

1500 N. Wells St.
337-6077
Do you believe a 6,057-dime model of the White House, a sugar replica of Cleopatra's barge, a gruesome torture chamber? Do you care? $3. TS

• Sisters of St. Casimir Lithuanian Cultural Museum

2601 W. Marquette Rd.
776-1324
Lithuanian folk arts, textiles, costumes, maps, modern paintings, and several cases of amber in four rooms. Thirty-one costumed dolls portray a charming wedding. By appointment. PTSCL

• David and Alfred Smart Gallery

University of Chicago
5550 S. Greenwood Ave.
753-2121
Overshadowed by the Art Institute of Chicago, the Smart would be big time in a smaller city. The permanent collection is strong on 19th- and 20th-century sculpture, Oriental and European art of every period, and 20th-century painting. A growing decorative-arts department boasts the dining-room suite from Wright's Robie House. Intelligent special shows usually explore a period, problem, or premise in depth and are accompanied by films, symposia, free noon-hour gallery talks, and expensive catalogues.

The handsome building, the first in the University of Chicago's Cochrane-Woods Art Center, was designed by Edward Larrabee Barnes with flexible, well-lit viewing spaces, but with little consideration for the handicapped. BTSCX

Maurice Spertus Museum of Judaica

618 S. Michigan Ave.
922-9012
Part of Spertus College, the Midwest's largest Jewish museum mounts extraordinary special exhibitions and maintains a permanent collection rich in decorative arts, both religious and temporal, Ashkenazi and Sephardic. Many objects, such as intricately wrought silver plates, cups, menorahs, and Torah covers, are grouped by holiday; others, for example, embroidered prayer shawls and calligraphic wedding contracts, are arranged thematically.

The moving Bernard and Rochelle Zell Holocaust Memorial, a terrifying reminder of Nazi atrocities, is permanently displayed on the first floor; small rotating exhibits are in a second-floor gallery. The Asher library is outstanding. (See Libraries.) $1.50; free Fri. BTWSCL

• Swedish American Museum of Chicago

5248 N. Clark St.
728-8111
Started as a bicentennial project to document Swedish contributions to American life, the log-cabin-fronted (Swedes built the country's first) museum houses tributes to Swedish Colonial and Revolutionary War heroes, paintings and photos, costumes, handicrafts, a model of Charles Lindbergh's The Spirit of St. Louis, Carl Sandburg memorabilia, and a photo of Gloria Swanson, who grew up in Andersonville. TWCL

Terra Museum of American Art

2600 Central Park Ave.,
Evanston
328-3400
One of the newest stars on the area's art scene is housed in an attractively renovated, trilevel building that can be faulted only for ignoring access for the handicapped. The infant permanent collection and intelligent shows are devoted to 19th- and early 20th-century American work. $1.50. TSCL

• Ukrainian Institute of Modern Art

2320 W. Chicago Ave.
227-5522
Several strip stores remodeled by Stanley Tigerman in the late 1970s house a permanent collection of paintings and sculptures by Ukrainian-American and Ukrainian-Canadian artists. Has six annual shows (two devoted to non-Ukrainians) that are sufficiently important to rate reviews in the art press. Concert series, literary evenings, and a children's art workshop serve the community. BTWSCXL

• Ukrainian National Museum

2453 W. Chicago Ave.
276-6565
Costumes, fine examples of embroidery, woodcarvings, decorated Easter eggs, folk implements, oil portraits, and other distinctive displays fill the upper two floors of an old brownstone and illustrate the Ukraine's diversity, although the substantial Jewish population isn't even mentioned. Many of the folk costumes and crafts exhibited probably haven't changed much since the Ukrainian Empire's heyday in the 10th century. The caretakers conduct visitors about with much obvious pride and little English. Open Sun., noon to 3 p.m., and by appointment. BTSCL

• John H. Vanderpoel Memorial Art Gallery

Beverly Art Center
2153 W. 111th St.
445-9616
(See Beverly Hills/Morgan Park.) PTWX

• Morton B. Weiss Museum of Judaica

K.A.M. Isaiah Israel Congregation
1100 E. Hyde Park Blvd.
924-1234
A fine collection strikingly displayed in a small room includes ceramics unearthed by Moyshe Dayan, illuminated parchment wedding contracts dating to 1492, potsherds from Masada, mezuzahs, Megillahs, exquisite spice boxes, and other items tracing the European and Asian roots of many American Jews, as well as memorabilia of Chicago's oldest congregation. The 1924 Byzantine temple, a city landmark, is a must-see. (See Hyde Park.) Ring bell at school entrance on Greenwood Ave. for admission. PT

Nature and science

AFTMA International Sports Fishing Museum

2625 Clearbrook Dr.,
Arlington Heights
364-4666
The lures here are the history of fishing equipment and reels of audio-visual presentations. If you're hooked on fishing, worm more information out of a guide or cast about in the reference library. $1. PWSCXL

• Argonne National Laboratory

9700 S. Cass Ave., 1 mile south of I-55, Lemont
972-2000
Two-weeks-in-advance reservations are required for the 3½-hour Saturday group tours, but individuals can join one by prior arrangement, if there's room. It includes an orientation talk, then a hike through some of the many labs. PFL

Cernan Earth and Space Theatre

Triton College
2000 5th Ave.,
River Grove
456-5815
This 60-seat, wrap-around-screen theater, named for a local astronaut, offers several programs, including "The Grand Canyon" and a rock/laser show, on a complex evenings-and-weekends time-and-rate schedule. Call ahead. PSX

• The Chicago Academy of Sciences

2001 N. Clark St.
549-0606
Chicago's oldest, and for some time stodgiest, scientific museum is undergoing extensive renovations, but the second-floor ecology-in-Chicago dioramas are open and worth a look. BTWSCXL

• Chicago Botanic Garden

Lake-Cook Rd.,
half a mile east of I-94,
Glencoe
835-5440
What was once swampland has been converted to a 300-acre botanic beauty. The grounds offer wildlife areas, as well as formal and vegetable gardens, lawn exhibits, Japanese gardens, and a nature path. A welter of exhibits, classes, and demonstrations are in the visitors center. Membership in the Chicago Horticultural Society, which manages the garden, includes a monthly newsletter with extensive listings of walks and talks of interest to gardeners. PTWFSCXL

Robert Crown Center for Health Education

21 Salt Creek Lane,
Hinsdale
325-1900
Formerly the Hinsdale Health Museum, this educational facility offers programs for children in four areas: general health, sex education, drug abuse, and environmental education. Adults may observe classes daily and/or see the exhibits from 2:30 p.m. to 4 p.m. (reservations required). Complex concepts are explained with sophisticated, animated displays, the most popular of which is the talking transparent woman. $1.25 for a 1-hr. program. PWSC

• Dearborn Observatory

2131 Sheridan Rd.,
Evanston
492-3173
On clear Friday evenings from April to October, with prior reservations, you can look through a Civil War-era 18½-inch refracting telescope. If clouds move in, the antique instrument and a film program are still worth the trip to this building tucked in a corner of Northwestern University's campus. PT

the country's only Dead Sea Scroll jar, and a fine Palestinian gallery. Because the museum is dedicated to archaeology, everyday objects are as important as great artworks. In the Egyptian wing, for example, the huge stone sculpture of King Tutankhamen (the institute cosponsored the landmark King Tut exhibit) is joined by furniture, jewelry, musical instruments, and even mummified food. Other highlights include a huge group of Mesopotamian cylinder seals, Megiddo ivories, and a reconstruction of the Ishtar gate, complete with original tile fragments.

Scholarly texts and photographs placing objects in their cultural contexts illuminate the displays; well-informed docents conduct frequent tours. Reinstallation of major exhibits has left the building's polychromed ceilings, carved stonework, and brass fixtures intact. Film-lectures accompany some special shows. Books, prints, and attractive jewelry reproductions for sale in the "Suq." BTW (call ahead) SCXL

John G. Shedd Aquarium
1200 S. Lake Shore Dr.
939-2426
More than 500 species of fish (5,000 specimens) from all over the world, as well as invertebrates, sea horses, seals, a few penguins, and a fresh-water dolphin inhabit the aquarium. Six galleries are devoted to tropical, temperate, and cold-, salt-, and fresh-water fish; Tributaries displays small tropical fish in Chinese settings; and the 90,000-gallon Coral Reef is a popular attraction, especially when divers, equipped with microphones to talk to the crowds, hand-feed the colorful Caribbean denizens. Free programs for kids (some for adults) are held in the Aquatic Science Center. $2; free Thurs. PBTWSCXL

Smaller and ethnic

Balzekas Museum of Lithuanian Culture
4012 S. Archer Ave.
847-2441
Easy to miss, were it not for Stanley Balzekas's auto showroom next door, the two-story, storefront museum glorifies a country that knew only a few years of modern-day political independence and hasn't had a really good decade since the 16th century. There's a wistful air about the War Memorial, Women's Guild, Philatelic, and Eminent Lithuanians Rooms, but the antique armor and weapons are high caliber, as are displays of amber, beads, finely crafted jewelry, and decorative objects. Some exhibits rotate; special ones include the results of the annual Easter-egg-decorating and straw-ornament-making classes. The museum sponsors many community activities. Children's exhibit, too. $1. TSCXL

• Mary and Leigh Block Gallery
Northwestern University
1967 Sheridan Rd.,
Evanston
492-5209
Opened in 1980, this large gallery exhibits everything from paintings and drawings to photography and decorative arts. Lively shows are often thematic and educational. The permanent collection (not on display) is particularly notable for Walter Burley Griffin's drawings. PTW

Byer Museum of the Arts
1700 Hinman Ave.,
Evanston
866-6600
Stephen and Barbara Byer's collections of paintings, sculpture, decorative arts, Orientalia, books and manuscripts, mineralogical specimens, and more formed the basis of this museum, which also mounts special shows; it is in a National Register building. $5. PTWCXL

• Czechoslovak Society of America Heritage Museum, Library & Archives
2701 S. Harlem Ave.,
Berwyn
795-5800
The oldest such fraternal organization in the country maintains a room of costumes, glassware, folk art, etc., as well as the library and archives, which are significant because many 19th-century local political and intellectual leaders were Czechs. PTW (call ahead) L

• Martin D'Arcy Gallery of Art
Cudahy Library
Loyola University
6525 N. Sheridan Rd.
274-3000, ext. 786
An exquisite collection of about 150 medieval, Renaissance, and Baroque pieces (1100-1700 A.D.) includes a carved, linden wood, silver-covered head of John the Baptist on a platter; a precious-stone-encrusted ebony jewel case; a rosary bead with tiny, carved Biblical scenes inside; a late 16th-century chest decorated with bizarre winged creatures, angels, and imps; a 14th-century gold chalice; and a sculpture of the scourging of Christ, made of silver, ebony, lapis lazuli, agate, and tiger-eye. Rev. Donald F. Rowe, founder and director of this little-known two-room museum, is a font of information about the objects and their history. PTW

DuSable Museum of African American History
740 E. 56th Pl.

947-0600

Highlights at the country's first black-history museum include Robert Witt Ames's massive carved-mahogany mural Freedom Now, the Robert B. Mayer Memorial Collection of African Art, and a good selection of black American pop-culture stuff. The museum sponsors activities for community youths, and a multimedia center houses a library and extensive collections of tapes, films, slides, and jazz recordings.

The old Washington Park Administration Building has been renovated; much of the main-floor space is given over to museum offices. The sunken sculpture garden is the site of the museum's summer art fair. 50¢. PBTSCXL

Fine Arts Research and Holographic Center Museum
1134 W. Washington Blvd.

226-1007

More than 40 holograms (three-dimensional, laser-created images) from around the world are on display. A short film and hard-to-grasp diagrams explain how they work. $1. TSCXL

• Freeport Art Museum
511 S. Liberty St.,
Freeport

815-235-9755

American Indian art, pottery, textiles, Oriental art, Art Nouveau, and minor Italian classics are displayed on a rotating basis and augmented by special shows, many of which showcase local artists. PS

• International Polka Association Polka Music Hall of Fame and Museum
4145 S. Kedzie Ave.

254-7771

Musical instruments once played by polka greats, sheet music, old polka records, pictures of famous polka bands, and plaques honoring polka personalities are included in this collection. Call ahead. TL

Italian American Sports Hall of Fame
7906 W. Grand Ave.,
Elmwood Park

452-4812

Exhibits as diverse as one of Mario Andretti's cars and Rocky Marciano's championship belt fill a former union hall, which also has a replica of a locker room. $1. PTWSCX

• Latvian Folk Art Museum
4146 N. Elston Ave.

588-2085

Small but charming collection in the Latvian Community Center is particularly strong on textiles. TL

• Ling Long Museum
2238 S. Wentworth Ave.

225-6181

Miniature dioramas in the back of a gift shop depict Chinese history and legend. (See Chinatown.) TWS

• Mitchell Indian Museum
Kendall College
2408 Orrington Ave.,
Evanston

866-1395

Splendid examples of beadwork, exquisite baskets, fine Navajo rugs, and photographs by Edward S. Curtis are among the highlights at this museum, which occupies two rooms and a hall on the lower level of Kendall College. Opened in 1977 to house the collection of John and Betty Mitchell, the museum also has tools, weapons, musical instru- ments, carvings, pottery, and jewelry representing Indians of five geographic regions from 3,000 B.C. to the present (although most items are late 19th and 20th century). Great for kids: There's even a table with objects to touch and to hold. PTCL

The Peace Museum
364 W. Erie St.

440-1860

The accolades that accompanied its opening in 1981 and the many donations to its collection suggest that this museum and resource center is dedicated to a theme whose time has come. Special exhibitions are thought-provoking and well mounted. $1. TSXL

• Polish Museum of America
984 N. Milwaukee Ave.

384-3352

Exhibits from the 1939 New York World's Fair's Polish Pavilion trapped in this country by the outbreak of World War Two formed the nucleus of the country's largest ethnic museum, which occupies three floors of the Polish Roman Catholic Union building. Diverse displays include military memorabilia, a carved-salt icon and other religious art, drawings, costumes, and, of course, an Easter-egg collection and other folk art. The central rotunda is painted with WPA-like murals and mounted with plaques detailing Polish scientific accomplishments. A separate Paderewski room and an art gallery are opened on request. The library houses thousands of books, periodicals, maps, photos, manuscripts, recordings, slides, films, clippings, and genealogical materials. PBTSL

• **Evanston Ecology Center**
2024 McCormick Blvd.,
Evanston
864-5181
In Ladd Arboretum, the headquarters of the Evanston Environmental Association is set up to demonstrate ecologically sound, energy-conserving techniques. See the introductory slide show, get the self-guided-tour pamphlet that explains the building's solar- and wind-energy systems, and stop by the Energy Information Center to use reference materials or to pick up free booklets on energy efficiency and conservation. The staff is happy to answer questions.
PTWSCXL

• **Fermilab**
Kirk Rd. and Pine St.,
Batavia
840-3000
A self-guided tour includes a 15th-floor view of the accelerator ring and the 640 acres of restored prairie it encloses, as well as an orientation film. Swans, ducks, and buffalo roam the grounds! PWFSCL

• **Garfield Park Conservatory**
300 N. Central Park Ave.
533-1281
(See Parks and Boulevards.) PBT

• **International Museum of Surgical Sciences and Hall of Fame**
1524 N. Lake Shore Dr.
642-3632
Dozens of rooms on four floors of a mansion modeled on a Versailles building trace medical history thematically and geographically through authentic surgical instruments, paintings, sculptures, and more. A ground-floor 1873 apothecary shop is outfitted with paraphernalia from America's medical past.
PBTCL

• **Hillary S. Jurica Memorial Biology Museum**
Science Center
Illinois Benedictine College
5700 College Rd.,
Lisle
968-7270
Numerous bird, insect, and mammal specimens are exhibited with minerals, fossils, flora, and fauna collected by the late biologist and educator. By appointment. PW

• **Ladd Arboretum**
2024 McCormick Blvd.,
Evanston
864-5181
The 23 acres along the North Shore Channel are divided between natural settings (including a bird sanctuary) and formal gardens, such as the Rotary International Friendship Garden. Hiking trails and bike paths crisscross the grounds. The Evanston Ecology Center (see above) can answer questions about the arboretum. PT

Lighthouse Landing Park
2535 Sheridan Rd.,
Evanston
864-5181, 864-5198
Tours of the 113-foot-tall Grosse Point Light Station, built by the U. S. government in 1873 and used until 1935, are on weekend afternoons, May through October. A nature center contains stuffed native wildlife, rocks and fossils, an ecology pond, and other local fauna and flora, while a small maritime museum documents Grosse Point passersby, from canoes to steamships. On the site of former Jens Jensen landscaping, the park's Center for Natural Landscaping project includes a prairie garden, woodland wildflowers, and dune plantings. Donation requested. PT

• **Lincoln Park Conservatory**
2400 N. Stockton Dr.
294-4770
(See Parks and Boulevards.) BT

Lizzadro Museum of Lapidary Art
220 Cottage Hill Ave.,
Elmhurst
833-1616
One of the country's finest collections of carved jade and gemstones is housed in this pleasant, modern museum with a 1,300-lb. hunk-of-jade doorstop. Treasures include a huge Chinese screen, a Last Supper carved of ivory, faceted gems, and shimmering semiprecious stones. Naturally, the lapidary art is explained, too. 50¢; free Fri. PTWSXL

Morton Arboretum
Ill. 53 north of Ill. 5,
Lisle
968-0074
About eight miles of road and 30 miles of trails cross 1,500 acres, which constitute an outdoor museum of woody plants from around the world, with wildlife sanctuaries, cultivated gardens, and prairie. Attend an orientation slide show and buy a trail guide at the visitors center to maximize efficiency. The only surviving portion of Joy Morton's mansion, the library wing, makes up part of the Thornhill Conference Center; the Founder's Room is full of Morton-family photos and memorabilia. The Sterling Morton Library, designed by Harry Weese and opened in 1963 (see Libraries), usually has rare nature books on display. There's a plant clinic, too. The restaurant serves the arboretum's homemade ice cream. $2 per carload.
PTWFSCXL

• **Oak Park Conservatory**
621 Garfield St.,
Oak Park
386-4700
*(See Oak Park/River
Forest/Forest Park.)* TCL

• **Telephony Museum**
225 W. Randolph St.
727-2994
*Around the corner from Illinois's first telephone
exchange, Ma Bell tells the
telephone story with displays ranging from the
earliest instruments to
tomorrow's, and tosses in
some corporate hype. The
adjoining Telephone Center
also has displays, continuous TV shows in the Bell
Theater, and an art gallery.*
TW

• **Trailside Museum
of Natural History**
738 Thatcher Ave.,
River Forest
366-6530
(See Oak Park/River Forest/Forest Park.) T

History
and nostalgia

*In addition to the following,
some Chicago neighborhoods have historical
societies, as do many suburbs. They usually occupy
delightful older houses and
keep limited schedules.
Check* Chicago *magazine
for occasional listings of
them; or call information for
the town in question.*

• **Jane Addams' Hull
House and Dining Hall**
800 S. Halsted St.
996-2793
(See Near West Side.) BTXL

Boone's Buggies Ltd.
2238 W. 167th St.,
Markham
596-3120
*Antique cars on display
(and for sale) include a
1915 Ford touring car, a
1929 Pierce Arrow, a 1932
Auburn roadster, Model-A
Fords, and the like. Sold "as
is" but "run good." $2.* PW

**The Bradford Museum of
Collector's Plates**
9333 N. Milwaukee Ave.,
Niles
966-2770
*More than 1,000 of the most
actively traded collector's
plates are on display with
current market prices. The
earliest example is an 1895
Bing and Grondahl. The
gallery's staff answers
questions about the hobby.
The inside-garden restaurant is a surprise. $2; free
Sat.* PTWF

• **Cantigny**
1 S. 151 Winfield Rd.,
Wheaton
668-5161
Chicago Tribune *publisher
Col. Robert R. McCormick
left his 500-acre country estate as a park. Take the
guided tour of his grandfather Joseph Medill's 1896
Georgian mansion, attend a
Sunday chamber concert in
the library (reservations required), roam the woods
and gardens, or visit the 1st
Division Museum (McCormick served in World
War One)—a push-button-diorama, sound-and-light
paean to the glories of war.*
PWCXL

**Chicago Historical
Antique Auto Museum**
3200 Skokie Valley Rd.,
Highland Park
433-4400
*The 55-car collection
includes novelties (Elvis
Presley's limo) and classics. An indoor miniature
golf course and a pinball arcade adjoin the museum.
$3.* PWS

• **DuPage County
Historical Museum**
102 E. Wesley St.,
Wheaton
682-7343
*Designed by Charles S.
Frost as the Adams
Memorial Library, this 1891
Romanesque limestone
building now houses a
collection heavy on military
memorabilia and local period domesticity. A massive
model-railroad layout in the
basement includes much of
the route of the Chicago and
North Western, for which
Frost designed many stations, among them the ill-fated Loop building.* TSCXL

**The Evanston
Historical Society**
225 Greenwood St.,
Evanston
475-3410
*The 28-room Romanesque
château of Charles Gates
Dawes, banker, philanthropist, Nobel Peace Prize
winner, and public servant
(including Vice President
under Coolidge), boasts a
Jacobean great hall, a
Tudor dining room, and a
magnificent Renaissance library. Besides the house itself, there are Dawes and
Evanston memorabilia, plus
the historical society's excellent library devoted to
local subjects and authors.
You can buy inexpensive
guides to Evanston architecture here. 50¢; free Fri.*
TSL

Fagan's Antique and Classic Car Museum
162nd St. and Western, Markham
264-6342
See 30 old autos, carriages, sleighs, antique bicycles, and a 19th-century store, barbershop, and dining room for one price. $2. PTW

Fox River Trolley Museum (R.E.L.I.C.)
Ill. 31 on the south edge of South Elgin
697-4676, 357-4653
Ride Chicago Aurora & Elgin or Chicago North Shore & Milwaukee interurban electric cars, an open-bench streetcar from Rio de Janeiro, or an old elevated car along 1½ miles of track that traces the Fox River and was once part of the interurban line between Aurora and Elgin. A few more cars are on display, and an Electric Railroad Fair in late June or early July features a flea market, slides, movies, and food. Open mid-May to Oct. $1.50. PS

Glessner House
1800 S. Prairie Ave.
326-1393
Owned by the Chicago Architecture Foundation, Chicago's only remaining H. H. Richardson building is the kingpin of the Prairie Avenue Historic District. Take the guided, one-hour tour of the massive Romanesque mansion to see the warm interior and courtyard behind the stern exterior, or attend special functions that recall the days when the city's movers and shakers made the area their home. $3. PBTSCX

Graue Mill and Museum
York and Spring Rds., Oak Brook
655-2090
This 150-year-old building on Salt Creek served as an Underground Railroad way station and is the state's last working gristmill. Tour the extensive Civil War-period rooms upstairs, then buy some cornmeal to test your favorite muffin recipe, and check out the foamy pollutants floating down the creek. May to Oct. 50¢. PSCX

The Great Lakes Naval and Maritime Museum
Navy Pier
600 E. Grand Ave.
884-6312
The U.S.S. Silversides (a W.W. II submarine) and the Rachel Carson (an operational research vessel, formerly a navy gunboat) form the backbone of this expanding museum. There are informative exhibits, and the store has a fine selection of maritime publications and some instruments. $2. PBTSC

Hartung's Automotive Museum
3623 W. Lake St., Glenview
724-4354
See more than 100 antique cars, trucks, tractors, and motorcycles, plus motoring ephemera (including a fine collection of license plates) and other antiques. By appointment or chance. Donation requested. PW

• Illinois–Michigan Canal Museum
803 S. State St., Lockport
815-838-5080
Exhibits trace the history of the canal and of Will County. The 1830s building originally housed canal commission offices and the canal master's residence; some rooms are fitted out with representative furnishings. Don't miss the nearby Pioneer Settlement, more than a dozen restored buildings (some moved from elsewhere) reflecting early settlers' lives. PSL

Illinois Railway Museum
Olson Rd., 1 mile east of Union
262-2266, 815-923-2488
More than 150 locomotives and streetcars are displayed at this outdoor museum. Several run on a couple of miles of track through farmland. Trips take 15 to 20 minutes; passengers load at an 1851 Galena & Chicago Union depot moved from Marengo, Illinois. There's a separate streetcar track, too. Closed winter. Call for schedule. $3.50. PFSCL

Naper Settlement
201 W. Porter Ave., Naperville
420-6015
Williamsburg-style recreation of a Northern Illinois town circa 1831 to 1885 has about 20 historic buildings, including a reconstruction of Fort Payne. Costumed "residents" add to the ambiance. May to Oct. $3. PTSCXL

*Raymond F. Neuzil Memorial Sherlock Holmes Collection
Library
Illinois Benedictine College
5700 College Rd., Lisle
968-7270
Unravel the sleuth of Baker Street's legend in a room of books, video tapes, and memorabilia. By appointment. PWL

- **Printers Row
Printing Museum**
715 S. Dearborn St.
987-1059
*Nostalgic collection of
printing ephemera and
working presses in a 19th-
century setting is open
weekends. Custom and
stock invitations, stationery,
and cards from antique
typefaces are sold.* TSC

**Seven Acres Antique
Village Museum**
8512 S. Union Rd.,
Union
815-923-2214
*This is an entire afternoon's
nostalgia glut: military
memorabilia, 1890s shops,
an "Old West" street, the
gallows built for the Haymarket rioters, Edison artifacts, and the world's
largest collection of antique
phonographs. $3.* PWFSXL

The Time Museum
7801 E. State St.,
Rockford
815-398-6000
*The largest museum in the
world devoted exclusively
to timekeeping devices
from every period and
place. The 2,000-plus item
collection includes everything from 15th-century
B.C. water clocks to up-to-
the-minute atomic clocks.
Don't miss the early English
pocket sundial, the opu-
lently decorated Renais-
sance clocks, or fantastic
astronomical models. The
passing of each hour brings
a remarkable display. If time
passes you by while you're
watching the clocks, don't
worry. The museum, locat-
ed in the Clock Tower Inn at
the intersection of I-90 and
Business 20, is a 90-mile
trip from the Loop via I-90,
but time flies when you're
anticipating fun. $2.50.*
PWFS

**Victory World War II
Aircraft Museum**
Gilmore Rd., 2 miles north
of Ill. 176,
Mundelein
949-9595
*About 15 as-is planes are
displayed on the tarmac.
The hangar shelters parts,
sections, and memorabilia.
Don't miss the intact kami-
kaze. How many could
there be? $2.* PWSXL

**Volo Antique Auto
Museum & Village**
Ill. 120, half a mile west of
U.S. 12, Volo
815-385-3644
*This nostalgia treasure-
trove includes a 70-auto
display, a carriage
museum, old bicycles and
popcorn machines, a pet
farm, a general store, a
"Street of Yesteryear," and
a 1930s arcade, plus weekend comedy-classic
screenings. $3.25.* PWFSX

Widow Clarke House
1855 S. Indiana Ave.
326-1393
*Built in 1836 and moved
south around the time of the
Chicago Fire, the city's
oldest building was
returned to within a few
blocks of its original location
in 1977. Chicago's only surviving Greek revival house
and a rare example of post-
and-beam construction, it
has been beautifully
restored and furnished to
reflect the life and times of
the Clarke family (1830s to
1850s). Like Glessner
House, it is a city landmark
and part of the Prairie Avenue Historic District. $3.*
BTW

- **Willard House**
1730 Chicago Ave.,
Evanston
864-1396
*Famous educator, suf-
fragette, and temperance
leader Frances E. Willard
lived in the 1865 Victorian
Gothic house she called her
"rest cottage" until her
death in 1898. Several
carefully preserved rooms
show her furniture and furnishings, as well as those of
her family and long-time
companion Anna Gordon.
Others are devoted to temperance history and
memorabilia. The house is
on the grounds of the na-
tional headquarters of the
Woman's Christian Tem-
perance Union, which
maintains an extensive library on alcohol and drug
abuse and provides chatty
guides for the one-hour
house tour.* TS

**Frank Lloyd Wright
Home and Studio**
951 Chicago Ave.,
Oak Park
848-1976
*(See Oak Park/River
Forest/Forest Park) $3.*
TSCL

• free   **B** Culture Bus   **C** classes   **F** food   **L** library   **P** parking   **S** gift shop   **T** public
transportation   **W** wheelchair access   **X** performances

Galleries

More than ever, Chicagoans are interested in art—buying it, talking about it, creating it. In the last dozen years, the gallery scene has developed to the point that few close and new ones open every year. Dealers from New York and Europe fall over each other to show at the Chicago International Art Exposition (*see Annual Events*). Interest in Chicago artists grows as the likes of Richard Hunt, Roger Brown, Ellen Lanyon, and John Henry move toward international reputations. All this encourages more and more artists to stay here to work, giving Chicago art a new excitement and diversity.

Haunting the galleries is the best way to stay *au courant,* and doing so is convenient because they're clustered in fairly coherent groups. Recently a flurry of openings in lofts north of the Loop has started to change the situation. *Chicago* magazine columnist Henry Hanson called the loft area SuHu (for Superior and Huron Streets), noting its similarity to Manhattan's SoHo (south of Houston Street)—but in the lofts, as elsewhere in Chicago galleries, there is a mostly healthy feeling that this is Chicago, not an imitation of New York.

The prestigious showrooms on and near Michigan Avenue may not forge new paths, but they do muster the masters, both old and soon to be. Ontario Street's galleries form the Museum of Contemporary Art's aureole; they reflect the best current trends and don't shy from controversy. On Ontario Street, collectors shop for still-affordable works by artists with soaring reputations. Exciting if uneven exhibits of young artists fill the cooperatives and other galleries clustered around Hubbard Street, west of State Street. Recognition begins here, and a good eye can spot tomorrow's stars.

Don't be intimidated by art galleries: They're just retail outlets, much like fashionable boutiques. Check *Chicago* for the month's most interesting shows, then browse and talk to the staffs—most are friendly and helpful. Or take one of Art Safari Tours' Saturday-morning walks (343 Florence Avenue, Evanston; 328-4377). Show enough interest and you may end up on the mailing lists for openings (usually Friday nights), joining the wine-sipping crowds for a taste of Chicago's increasingly active art scene.

In town

Aiko's Art Materials Import
714 N. Wabash Ave.
943-0745
This Japanese art-supply shop frequently has shows of woodblock and silk-screen prints, ceramics, and more.

The Alaska Shop
104 E. Oak St.
943-3393
Canadian and Alaskan native arts, including prints and soapstone carvings. Also in Lake Forest.

American West
2110 N. Halsted St.
871-0400
Paintings and graphics by contemporary Southwestern artists.

ARC Gallery
6 W. Hubbard St.
266-7607
*Cooperative gallery found-
ed by women artists has
consistently exciting shows
that typify the youthful, exuberant Hubbard Street
gallery scene. Excellent
work features large installations. The ARC Founda-
tion brings local artists and
critics in for free-swinging
lecture-discussions.*

Art Rental and Sales Gallery of the Woman's Board of The Art Institute of Chicago
Michigan Ave. at Adams St.
443-3503
*Doesn't mount shows, but
all the works (generally safe,
middle-of-the-road art) are
by artists who live within a
130-mile radius of Chicago.
Renting enables you to live
with a piece of art before
you decide to buy it; rental
fees can be applied to purchase price.*

Artemisia Gallery
9 W. Hubbard St.
751-2016
*As youthful and adven-
turous as ARC (also was
founded as a women's gal-
lery). Lectures and other
educational activities.*

Artists Guild of Chicago
664 N. Michigan, Suite 720
951-8252
*Professional organization
for fine and commercial artists mounts shows at various Chicago-area galler-
ies. Exhibits include works
by nonmembers.*

Arts Club of Chicago
109 E. Ontario St.
787-3997
*Don't be intimidated be-
cause this is a private club;
visitors are welcome, and
the shows are thoughtfully
selected. Mainstream to
avant-garde; many big
names.*

Balkin Fine Arts
425 N. Clark St.
321-9010
*Exhibits young artists in all
media and maintains a large
inventory of prints and
drawings.*

Jacques Baruch Gallery
900 N. Michigan Ave.
944-3377
*Shows in this baronial
space lean toward Middle-
European artists with em-
phasis on giant wall hangings and photography.*

Mary Bell Galleries
10 W. Hubbard St.
642-0202
*Seemingly adventuresome
gallery is establishing a nice
track record with contem-
porary work from all over
the country.*

Benjamin-Beattie Galleries, Ltd.
900 N. Michigan Ave.
337-1343
*Specializes in 19th- and
20th-century American
graphics and American
Scene Prints. Excellent
source for small pieces, especially sculpture, if you're
beginning to collect
seriously.*

Bernal Gallery
612 N. Michigan Ave.
943-1147
*A tilt toward the avant-
garde; frequent shows by
young Chicagoans. Limited
hours.*

Roy Boyd Gallery
215 W. Superior St.
642-1606
*Boyd's young artists veer
toward the avant-garde, but
never quite collide with it.
Good place to get your feet
wet if you're interested in
abstract art, particularly
sculpture.*

Campanile Galleries
200 S. Michigan Ave.
663-3885
*Good, solid, conservative
gallery. Nice 19th-century
landscapes and portraits
and rich holdings of early
20th-century American
painters.*

Merrill Chase Galleries
835 N. Michigan Ave.
337-6600
*Mass-market art with ex-
citement coming only from
offerings of minor works by
very, very big names.
Curated graphics shows are
generally quite solid. Other
locations.*

Jan Cicero Gallery
437 N. Clark St.
644-5374
*Excellent shows, heavy on
Chicagoans, from a gallery
owner dedicated to helping
her young artists. Good
place to check out trends on
the local art scene.*

Columbia College Galleries
600 S. Michigan Ave.
663-1600, ext. 600
*Good, nicely displayed
shows, especially photog-
raphy, in a very well laid-
out space.*

ConStruct
101 N. Wacker, Suite 235
853-1125
*Marvelous showcase for
big, outdoor pieces by such
sculptors as Mark di
Suvero, John Henry, Linda
Howard, Jerry Peart,
Charles Ginnever, and
Kenneth Snellson.*

Contemporary Art Workshop
542 W. Grant Pl.
525-9624
*Provides studios for
promising artists in all
media. Mounts monthly
shows by artists from all
over the Midwest.*

Dart Gallery
155 E. Ohio St.
787-6366
*The cutting edge of New
York art along with some of
Chicago's most innovative
artists; uncompromisingly
avant-garde.*

Marianne Deson Gallery
340 W. Huron St.
787-0005
*Experimental, advanced,
challenging art—much of it
by Chicagoans—that still
manages to be accessible.*

Distelheim Galleries
1030 N. State St.
642-5570
Contemporary American painting and sculpture includes works by School of Paris painters.

Dobrick Gallery
216 E. Ontario St.
337-2002
Well-chosen, broad range of mostly one-of-a-kind works by up-and-coming and established artists.

Linda Einfeld, Inc.
620 N. Michigan Ave.
951-0309
Excellent gallery of traditional art of Africa, Oceania, and the Americas.

Exhibit A
233 E. Ontario St.
944-1748
Specializes in contemporary ceramics by established artists.

Fairweather Hardin Gallery
101 E. Ontario St.
642-0007
One of the city's oldest galleries; mostly middle-of-the-road, some avant-garde, but all tasteful work by established artists.

Joseph Faulkner– Main Street Galleries
620 N. Michigan Ave.
787-3301
Old, established gallery with few shows, not many sculptures or big canvases, but an impressive selection of prints, drawings, and watercolors by internationally known artists.

Wally Findlay Galleries
814 N. Michigan Ave.
649-1500
Light, fluffy paintings (many Impressionistic). High sales volume, despite being virtually ignored by the art press. Laid out like a museum.

Frumkin & Struve Gallery
309 W. Superior St.
787-0563
First-rate, intelligent shows by vanguard artists. Gallery recently has been showing a lot of architectural work—an exciting development on the local scene.

Galeries d'Art International
299 E. Ontario St.
664-2848
First North American branch of a Paris-based gallery exhibits high-quality paintings and graphics by Frenchmen and also by Americans who've been working in Europe.

Galerija
744 N. Wells St.
280-1149
Photography, paintings, and sculpture by artists from the Lithuanian community. Some folk art.

Galleries Maurice Sternberg
612 N. Michigan Ave.
642-1700
Very eclectic, very busy gallery with some surprising goodies among a lot of run-of-the-mill 19th- and 20th-century paintings and drawings.

Gilman Galleries
277 E. Ontario St.
337-6262
Handsome space with eclectic, mainstream art. Shows are often whimsical.

Richard Gray Gallery
620 N. Michigan Ave.
642-8877
One of Chicago's finest: solid record of support for newer artists; imaginative showings of established painters and sculptors. Prints and primitives, too.

Grayson Gallery
356 W. Huron St.
266-1336
Large, newer gallery has good shows of modern and contemporary painting and sculpture, as well as of ancient and primitive art.

Guildhall Galleries
132 E. Delaware Pl.
787-2132
Mostly unadventurous, decorative paintings and sculpture at fair prices.

Hammer & Hammer American Folk Art
620 N. Michigan Ave.
266-8512
Sculpture, textiles, paintings, drawings, and decorative arts from the 18th to 20th century.

Hokin Gallery
210 W. Superior St.
266-1211
Sets no trends, but shows big names in contemporary painting and sculpture. Also carries primitive art.

B.C. Holland, Inc.
222 W. Superior St.
664-5000
No longer mounts shows but does have super collections of 20th-century paintings, classical antiquities, antique textiles, ethnographic objêts d'art, and other objects reflecting a very broad cultural and stylistic range and the owner's extraordinary taste. By appointment only.

Joy Horwich Gallery
226 E. Ontario St.
787-7486
Very contemporary, very eclectic, very hard to categorize—except that many of the artists have an eye for the fanciful.

Edwynn Houk Gallery
233 E. Ontario St.
943-0698
Excellent photography gallery features works from 1900 to 1950.

Hyde Park Art Center
1701 E. 53rd St.
324-5520
Frequent shows with a long record of spotting the most innovative work by Chicago artists. Excellent classes.

Illinois Arts Council Gallery
111 N. Wabash Ave.
793-6750
Juried shows by some of Illinois's best artists—well known or about to be.

Indian Tree Gallery
233 E. Ontario St.
642-1607
Pottery, weavings, baskets, beadwork, and jewelry by native Americans.

R. S. Johnson International
645 N. Michigan Ave.
943-1661
Fine exhibitions of 19th-and 20th-century European and American prints, drawings, paintings, and sculpture, as well as of old master (c. 1450-1800) prints and drawings.

Kelmscott Gallery
410 S. Michigan Ave.
461-9188
Delightful gallery in the Fine Arts Building focuses on 19th- and 20th-century British and American architecture (especially Frank Lloyd Wright), prints, drawings, decorative arts, and photography.

Douglas Kenyon, Inc.
155 E. Ohio St.
642-5300
Very tasteful, high-quality gallery deals mostly in photography. Prints and Audubons, too.

Phyllis Kind Gallery
226 E. Ontario St.
642-6302
Not only has Kind shown consistent support for Chicago artists, she's the only local gallery owner to carry the word to New York by opening a branch in SoHo. One of the liveliest galleries.

Klein Gallery
356 W. Huron St.
787-0400
A fairly new gallery in a large, airy space that is perfect for showing big paintings and sculpture by up-and-coming younger American (and some Mexican) artists. Emphasis is on modern works that play with texture and perception.

Landfall Gallery
215 W. Superior St.
787-6844
Jack and Ethel Lemon own both this gallery, which specializes in shows of paintings, sculpture, and drawings, and the renowned Landfall Press, which publishes lithographs and etchings.

R. H. Love Galleries
100 E. Ohio St.
664-9620
Has always been strong in American Impressionists, which recently have been "hot." The gallery for 19th-century American art.

Nancy Lurie Gallery
1632 N. La Salle St.
337-2882
Off the beaten track, this fine gallery has a stable of exciting young Chicago artists, most of whom are innovative, all of whom are worth watching.

Peter Miller Gallery
356 W. Huron St.
951-0252
Miller is a hard worker who presents shows that are advanced but accessible, solid but not challenging.

Mongerson Gallery
620 N. Michigan Ave.
943-2354
Focuses on high-quality American West art by the likes of Frederic Remington and Charles Russell. Contemporary works, too.

N.A.M.E. Gallery
9 W. Hubbard St.
467-6550
One of the oldest alternative galleries in the city fits nicely into the Hubbard Street milieu with eye-popping shows and an exciting series of poetry readings, experimental music, and performance art.

Phyllis Needlman Gallery
216 E. Ontario St.
951-8660
Eclectic, contemporary works.

Everett Oehlschlaeger Galleries
107 E. Oak St.
787-6779
Features older, established artists with romantic visions. A nice selection of Chicago realists, too.

Jack O'Grady Galleries
333 N. Michigan Ave.
726-9833
O'Grady runs one of the biggest graphics studios in the nation. He also puts on some great shows, often of commercial illustrators stretching their wings.

Les Primitifs
2038 N. Clark St.
528-5200
Mind-boggling array of Oceanic and African ethnographic art.

Roger Ramsay Gallery
620 N. Michigan Ave.
337-4678
Specializes in a broad range of smaller works on paper—watercolors, pastels, drawings, collages.

Randolph Street Gallery
756 N. Milwaukee Ave.
243-7717
A newer gallery with a solid commitment to Chicago art, most of it avant-garde.

Renaissance Society at the University of Chicago
5811 S. Ellis Ave.
962-8670
Don't let the name fool you: Since 1915, the RS has been showing the best in contemporary art. Splendid exhibits at the Bergman Gallery are presented with care and intelligence. Don't miss the Art for Young Collectors Sale in late November (see Annual Events).

Rizzoli International Bookstore Gallery
835 N. Michigan Ave.
642-3500
Eclectic showings of prints, paintings, and sculpture on the mezzanine of the outstanding bookshop.

Betsy Rosenfield Gallery
212 W. Superior St.
787-8020
Rapidly becoming one of the city's best contemporary galleries. Paintings, sculpture, etc., by a wide variety of distinctive artists, with an emphasis on works in glass.

Dorothy Rosenthal Gallery
233 E. Ontario St.
664-3224
Interesting artists, most with big reputations, working in graphics, painting, and sculpture.

St. Albus Fine Arts
620 N. Michigan Ave.
337-3282
American and European paintings and prints from the 18th to early 20th century, with a few forays into Art Nouveau and Art Deco decorative arts.

School of the Art Institute Gallery
Columbus Dr. and Jackson
443-3703
Good, interesting shows, often by students or alumni.

Sheffield Gallery
1970 N. Dayton St.
883-8848
Interesting, but not very challenging, works by young artists, many of whom have links to the School of the Art Institute.

South Side Community Art Center
3831 S. Michigan Ave.
373-8666
Work of local and national black artists.

Samuel Stein Fine Arts
620 N. Michigan Ave.
337-1782
Prints, with occasional paintings or sculpture, by the biggest and most fashionable names. No discoveries.

van Straaten Gallery
361 W. Superior St.
642-2900
Probably the best place for starting, or filling out, a collection of prints. Wide range, great selection, and fair prices.

Paul Waggoner Gallery
111 E. Oak St.
664-9384
Exhibits a great variety of contemporary American and ethnic works. Shows in the coach house (rear) feature Haitian Naïve art; roof sculpture garden.

Worthington Gallery
233 E. Ontario St.
266-2424
Masterful showings of 20th-century European artists, especially German Expressionists. The gallery is eclectic enough to also exhibit some young artists.

W.P.A. Gallery
1539 N. Damen Ave.
278-9724
"Environmental art," much of it by Chicagoans.

Michael Wyman Gallery
233 E. Ontario St.
787-3961
Long-time dealer in traditional primitive art, particularly African.

Young Hoffman Gallery
215 W. Superior St.
951-8828
Imaginative shows of avant-garde work—some of it accessible, some of it hard to decipher.

Zaks Gallery
620 N. Michigan Ave.
943-8440
Painting and sculpture, much of it by Chicagoans, in a gallery that demonstrates real concern for its artists.

Zolla/Lieberman Gallery
356 W. Huron St.
944-1990
One of the largest galleries in the city, often filled by excellent shows of paintings and sculpture from around the world. Eclectic and innovative; a few artists have been discovered here.

Suburban

Eva Cohon Gallery Ltd.
474 Central Ave.,
Highland Park
432-7310
You'll often find nationally and internationally known artists showing at this fine gallery.

Countryside Art Center
408 N. Vail St.,
Arlington Heights
253-3005
Frequent shows of palatable, accessible art. Classes, too.

Evanston Art Center
2603 Sheridan Rd.,
Evanston
475-5300
Marvelous place with five galleries—one for photography, one for crafts, one sales and rental—exhibits exciting young artists and more established ones.

Neville–Sargent Galleries
509 Main St.,
Evanston
328-9395
Nice shows of middle-of-the-road art, much of it by Chicagoans.

Siri-Lak Galleries
11 W. Harrison St.,
Oak Park
386-4936
Arts and crafts of Sri Lanka, formerly Ceylon.

Squash Blossom
1888 First St.,
Highland Park
432-3280
American Indian art.

Yolanda Fine Arts
542 Lincoln Ave.,
Winnetka
441-5557
Twentieth-century American and international folk paintings (Naïves) and some prints.

Libraries

Libraries are a little-understood resource. To many, they are mere book warehouses—regulation-bound bastions of dusty tradition ruled by stern, bespectacled spinsters. Even putting this Hollywood stereotype aside, few people realize how exciting and accessible they are.

Public systems, including Chicago's maligned one, variously offer books, magazines, sheet music, records, video tapes, artworks, even toys. Add great research libraries, much-lauded specialized collections, and hundreds of institutional and corporate ones, and the question becomes not what materials are available, but who has them and how to get your hands on them?

Illinois Libraries and Information Centers (1981), a detailed reference guide available at most libraries, can help with the "who," as can any librarian. As to the "how," most public libraries in the state offer reciprocal borrowing privileges. A card from one enables you to use any, though computer requirements may necessitate the formality of additional cards. But traveling from library to library in search of a tome isn't necessary. The interlibrary loan system will bring requested material to you from virtually anywhere in the state, including the University of Illinois Library in Champaign/Urbana (the country's fifth largest) and many hard-to-access private collections.

Prolonged research projects, however, usually require the hands-on access provided by Infopass. Essentially a formalized letter of introduction, Infopass facilitates reference use of specific areas of a specialized collection, but not wide-range browsing. Both Infopass and interlibrary loans fill requests through a tiered structure that directs users first to public institutions and then as a last resort, to certain private ones. Indeed, librarians dispense these privileges only after exhausting their own systems' resources.

KEY TO SYMBOLS

C Circulating. Books may be borrowed, though the privilege may be restricted to persons affiliated with the institution or to interlibrary loan. Unless indicated, the library is for reference use only.

O Open stacks. Patrons have access to the book shelves, though not necessarily to all of them.

P Parking. Off-street, on-site space, but not necessarily free or sufficient.

R Telephone reference. Questions answered over the phone, though often only on a limited basis.

T Reasonably convenient to public transportation.

W Wheelchair accessible. No architectural barriers; surfaces reasonably smooth. A robust wheeler should be able to manage unaided, but call ahead with special needs and questions.

X Performances. Anything from short films to chamber concerts on a fairly regular basis.

Chicago Public Library

When the 1871 Chicago Fire destroyed the Chicago Library Association's 30,000-volume collection, the British sent several thousand books, many autographed by their illustrious donors, as a partial replacement. The Chicago Public Library was established in 1872 to administer the collection, temporarily housed in an old water tank. After outgrowing several other locations, it was moved in 1897 to Shepley, Rutan and Coolidge's magnificent new building, replete with splendid mosaics and stained-glass domes designed by Louis Tiffany. Seventy-seven years later, the ever-growing main collection was transferred—again temporarily—to the Mandel-Lear Building, and its former home was renovated as the CPL Cultural Center. Current plans call for a 1984 move to the former Goldblatt's store on the State Street Mall.

It seems everyone has a horror story about the CPL: broken machines, missing titles, inadequate assistance. Despite problems, the system is improving and can be a convenient resource. The Telephone Information Center (269-2800) provides quick reference on hundreds of subjects; the Spanish Information Center (269-2940) does the same and also offers social-service information. Almost 80 branch libraries (a few are discussed in neighborhood chapters), including two regional ones, supplement the Central Library and the Cultural Center. They vary in size and quality, but many have local-history and foreign-language materials reflecting the neighborhood; some offer special programs, particularly for kids. Chicago residents and members of reciprocating libraries can obtain CPL cards on the spot by presenting two I.D.s to any CPL librarian. Pick up a copy of the descriptive pamphlet for useful information and phone numbers.

Central Library
425 N. Michigan Ave.
269-2900
Five major divisions account for most of the holdings: Government Publications (CPL is a congressionally designated depository for U.S. government materials); Social Science and History (a good resource for genealogists); Education and Philosophy; General Information Services (including periodicals and a fine selection of foreign and domestic newspapers); and Business, Science, and Technology. This last division excels with complete specifications and drawings of all U.S. patents, a computer-assisted reference center, career-information sources, and microfilms of corporate disclosures filed with the Securities and Exchange Commission, as well as full runs of all major business journals. Data banks.
TWCOR

Cultural Center
78 E. Washington St.
269-2900
Besides myriad cultural activities, this wonderful building is home to the system's Audiovisual Center (films, tapes, cassettes, records), Popular Library (current fiction and nonfiction, some periodicals), Thomas Hughes Children's Library, Fine Arts Division (art and music), and Literature and Language Division. Special collections include Civil War materials (artifacts as well as printed matter), rare books (many by Chicago authors), the CPL archives, Chicago theater arts, graphic arts, the Chicago Fire, material from the World's Columbian Exposition and Century of Progress, and holdings on freedom of the press. TW (Randolph St. ramp) XCOR

Chicago Library System
Services for the Blind and Physically Handicapped/
Illinois Regional Library for the Blind and Physically Handicapped
1055 W. Roosevelt Rd.
738-9200, 738-9210
Located in the colorful Roosevelt branch specially designed for the handicapped, the Chicago service has records and cassettes of general-library holdings, machines for listening to them, and a selection of Braille books; the IRL distributes them state-wide. Free services include the mailing of books, cassettes, and machines to users' homes. Some classes. PTWCOR

Frederick H. Hild Regional Library
4544 N. Lincoln Ave.
728-8652, TDD 728-2062
Though a new building is under construction, this one is an outstanding example of institutional Art Deco. The city's only phone-reference service for the deaf, a circulating telecaption

decoder, and the Ravenswood-Lakeview Historical Association collection are among the noteworthy features. Secondhand Prose, a basement bookshop, sells very cheaply CPL discards and patron-donated books. TCOR

Carter G. Woodson Regional Library
9525 S. Halsted St.
881-6900
Comfortable, modern building, with a two-story atrium and monthly art exhibits, houses the 40,000-volume Vivian G. Harsh Collection of Afro-American History and Literature (reference use only). The country's second-largest public-library collection of its kind

includes scores of periodicals, partial or complete runs of hundreds of Afro-American newspapers from the mid-19th century to the present (on microfilm), original manuscripts by such authors as Richard Wright and Langston Hughes, the Illinois Writers Project's pamphlet and clipping file on The Negro in Illinois, graphics, tapes, and much more. PTWXCOR

Major research libraries

In 1895, Chicago's three largest libraries agreed to avoid duplication by dividing knowledge into thirds. The John Crerar Library took science, the Newberry Library history and the humanities, and the Chicago Public Library pleasure reading and instruction. While the CPL has expanded its scope, the other two have become internationally known in their fields. Although the Newberry Library, John Crerar Library, and the major university libraries restrict public access to reference use, they provide boundless research opportunities.

Center for Research Libraries
6050 S. Kenwood Ave.
955-4545
Almost 200, mostly university, libraries nationwide (including all those listed below except The Newberry Library) store rare and rarely used materials here. Add purchases, exchanges, and gifts, and the collection numbers about three million volumes (hard copy, microfiche, microfilm). Just a few of the highlights are complete transcripts and tapes of the Nuremberg War Trials, a comprehensive collection of doctoral dissertations from all over the world (except the U.S. and Canada), current catalogues of all four-year colleges and universities in the U.S. and Canada, lesser-known newspapers from foreign countries, and a sea of state-government documents from all of the 50 states. Though the emphasis is on social science,

the sciences, and technology, there are also extensive holdings on European and American literature and culture—for example, copies of every extant book, pamphlet, and broadside published in this country from 1639 to 1800. PTWC (interlibrary loan only) O

The John Crerar Library
35 W. 33rd St.
225-2526
Science, technology, engineering, and medicine are the purview of this reference library, which has particularly strong collections on the history of science and medicine and extensive periodical holdings, including foreign publications. The National Translations Center is located here and is the country's main depository and information center for unpublished translations into English of materials on the natural, physical, medical, and social sciences. It has 300,000 articles, patents,

reports, etc., translated from 40 languages; and its data banks show the availability of 450,000 more. Research, for a fee, is one of many services the library provides. Located in the same building as the Illinois Institute of Technology's Kemper Library, Crerar is scheduled for a 1984 move to a new building on the University of Chicago campus. PTW (call ahead) C (members only) OR

DePaul University Library
2323 N. Seminary Ave.
321-7939
Lewis Center Library
DePaul University
25 E. Jackson Blvd.
321-7619
Special collections on Irish studies, Dickens, and Napoleon highlight the liberal-arts holdings at the Lincoln Park campus, while finance, investment, and accounting are the strengths of the business-oriented downtown library. TW (call ahead) COR

C circulating   **O** open stacks   **P** parking   **R** phone reference   **T** public transportation
W wheelchair access   **X** performances

Cudahy Memorial Library
Loyola University
6525 N. Sheridan Rd.
274-3000, ext. 791

Julia Deal Lewis Library
Loyola University
820 N. Michigan Ave.
670-2875
The general collection plus special ones on theology and Latin America are at Cudahy, in the northeast corner of the main campus. The Water Tower campus library focuses on business, education, and social work.
P *(main campus only)*
TWCOR

The Newberry Library
60 W. Walton St.
943-9090
The stately 1893 building, designed by Henry Ives Cobb, faces Washington Square—better known as Bughouse Square. The collection (1.4 million volumes) covers Western civilization from the Middle Ages to the 20th century, with emphasis on history and the humanities. Four special-collection research centers focus on the history of cartography, international family- and community-history records, American Indian history, and Renaissance studies. Outstanding exhibits are drawn mostly from Newberry's rich holdings, which include five million manuscripts and

60,000 maps. Users must register and present identification to be admitted to the reading rooms. A new adjacent bookstack building was completed in 1982. Extensive adult-education program plus seminars and colloquia. Fine bookshop is strong on genealogical and book-conservation materials (the library's facilities are renowned). TR

Northwestern University Library
1935 Sheridan Rd.,
Evanston
492-7658
The modern, three-tower, main building houses the Melville J. Herskovits Library of African Studies (more than 80,000 volumes), U.S. government documents and publications of the United Nations, maps, reference works, and the social sciences and humanities holdings. The original, ivy-covered Deering Library (entered through the main library) has the transportation collection, as well as special ones on modern movements in art and literature, women's studies, underground newspapers, and 20th-century little magazines. There are separate libraries for mathematics, science and engineering, and the like. PTCO

Joseph L. Regenstein Library
University of Chicago
1100 E. 57th St.
962-7874
The city's largest library has more than four million books and 30,000 periodicals. Many and varied rare-book and special collections include Lincolniana, the papers of Enrico Fermi, the Rosenberger Library of Judaica, the Encyclopaedia Britannica Historical Collection of Books for Children, the Goodspeed Collection of New Testament Manuscripts, and the Harriet Monroe Modern Poetry Collection. Access is difficult and an Infopass is required; research privileges are granted to outside scholars mostly on a fee basis. PTWCOR

University of Illinois at Chicago Library
801 S. Morgan St.
996-2726
Special collections include maps, U.S. government documents, labor archives, women's history, and the Jane Addams Memorial Collection on social welfare in Chicago (located in Hull House). PTWCOR

Specialized Collections

Most museums have libraries (*see Museums*), as do many foundations, corporations, organizations, and government agencies. Here are some of the more interesting ones.

The Adler Planetarium
1300 S. Lake Shore Dr.
322-0304
Astronomy and space, including NASA materials. Call ahead. PTWOR

Norman Asher and Helen Asher Library
Spertus College of Judaica
618 S. Michigan, 5th floor
922-9012, ext. 50
One of the Midwest's largest Judaica collections has

Rabbinica, Jewish history, Bible commentary, Hebrew and Yiddish literature, and Jewish literature in English. Publications and documents from Israel, Holocaust literature, the Chicago Jewish Archives, and the Badona Spertus Art Library of Judaica are among the special collections.
TWCOR

Central States Institute of Addiction
120 W. Huron St.
266-6100
Excellent collection on drug and alcohol addiction; some on counseling. It also has materials in Spanish, as well as a film library.
TWCOR

Chicago Board of Education Library

Bureau of Libraries
228 N. La Salle, Room 846
641-4105
This library has all Board of Education curriculum guides, proceedings, and reports since the mid-1800s, Chicago public-school histories, as well as other materials on elementary and secondary education. It is also a depository for publications put out by ERIC (Education Resources Information Center). TWO

Chicago Board of Trade Library
141 W. Jackson Blvd.
435-3552
Has materials on futures trading, commodity exchanges, and finance; government documents relating to agriculture and commerce; Board of Trade statistical annuals from 1958. TWR

Chicago Historical Society
Clark St. at North Ave., 3rd floor
642-4600
Books, manuscripts, and 500,000 photos on Chicago and Illinois history, the Civil War, and Abraham Lincoln; special collection of architectural drawings; records and manuscripts from Chicago organizations and prominent citizens. TWR

Chicago Transit Authority Library
Merchandise Mart Plaza, Room 450
664-7200
Public transit and urban transportation. Infopass necessary, or phone ahead. TWO

Cook County Law Library
2900 Richard J. Daley Ctr.
443-5423
Federal law, the laws of the 50 states, business laws for trade with Western Europe and Japan, Latin Ameri-

can law, and international law. Materials on laws of the Americas in the original languages; foreign-law librarian on staff; large collection of legal periodicals and texts. Several branches. TWO

Donors Forum of Chicago
208 S. La Salle, Room 600
726-4882
Philanthropy and private-funding collection includes foundation directories, grant lists, tax returns, and annual reports; files on nonprofit Chicago organizations; information on corporate giving; material on how to write a grant proposal. Sessions on proposal writing and seminars are given. TO

Environmental Information Library
Illinois Department of Energy and Natural Resources
309 W. Washington St., 3rd floor
793-3870
Illinois's central environmental library. Technical works on air, water, solid wastes, and noise pollution; energy, environmental law and health, land-use planning. State- and federal-government documents. TCOR

Field Museum of Natural History
Roosevelt Rd. at Lake Shore Dr., 3rd floor
922-9410, ext. 282
Anthropology, botany, geology, zoology, archaeology, paleontology, and materials on the Far East. The Mary W. Runnells Rare Book Room has notable holdings on ornithology, ichthyology, and Oriental languages. No admission charge for library use; get pass from guard at the north entrance. PTWR

Latino Institute Information and Referral Center
55 W. Jackson, Suite 940
663-3603
Bilingual materials on Latinos: dissertations, census figures, social-service referral listings. TWOR

Library of International Relations
666 N. Lake Shore Dr., 11th floor
787-7928
Though somewhat disorganized, the country's only open-to-the-public library specializing in international relations has many materials unavailable elsewhere. Resources in about 45 languages (strong in South African and Indian); documents from world organizations such as the UN and the EEC. Seminars. PTWR

McLean Library
Institute for Psychoanalysis
180 N. Michigan, 23rd floor
726-6300
Basic collection on psychology and psychoanalysis. TWC (members only) OR

Merriam Center Library
Charles E. Merriam Center for Public Administration
1313 E. 60th St.
947-2162
Urban planning, public works, public administration, and housing and redevelopment. Data bank; classes. TOR

Midwest Women's Center Library
53 W. Jackson, Room 1015
663-4163
A clearinghouse on women's issues—law, employment, pregnancy, abuse. Directories of women's organizations; issues file; referral service. TWCOR

C circulating   **O** open stacks   **P** parking   **R** phone reference   **T** public transportation
W wheelchair access   **X** performances

Sterling Morton Library
Morton Arboretum
Ill. 53 north of Ill. 5, Lisle
968-0074
Botany, horticulture, land-
scape architecture, con-
servation, and natural
history. Excellent rare-book
and Jens Jensen collec-
tions. Reading garden.
PXCOR

Municipal Reference
Library
City Hall, Room 1004
121 N. La Salle St.
744-4992
Main strengths are city gov-
ernment and planning, pub-
lic administration, and law
enforcement. Collects all
published Chicago docu-
ments; has by-precinct
results for all local elec-
tions since 1892; and main-
tains an excellent newspa-
per-clipping file. TWR

National Safety Council
Library
444 N. Michigan, 25th floor
527-4800, ext. 312
One of the world's largest li-
braries on accident pre-
vention and occupational
and traffic safety. TWR

North Park Village
Nature Center Library
5801 N. Pulaski Rd.
583-8970
Books and periodicals on
ornithology, environmental
education, and the ecology
of the Midwest. PT

Northeastern Illinois
Planning Commission
Library
400 W. Madison St.,
Concourse
454-0400
Census statistics, public
laws, housing, transporta-
tion, land use, and the
history of urban planning.
Call ahead. TWR

Office for Senior Citizens
and the Handicapped
Information and
Document Center
180 N. La Salle, 5th floor
744-7304
Information on programs
and services; collection on
aging and rehabilitation.
TWR

Olcott Library and
Research Center
The Theosophical Society
of America
1926 N. Main St.,
Wheaton
668-1571
Eastern and comparative

religions, science and
philosophy, astrology, and
occultism. POR

Oriental Institute
Research Archives
1155 E. 58th St.
753-2650
Archaeology, history,
linguistics, art, and archi-
tecture of the Ancient Near
East. A large periodical
collection, and many mono-
graphs on excavations.
TOR

Ryerson and Burnham
Libraries
The Art Institute of Chicago
Michigan Ave. at Adams St.
443-3666
One of the country's best
general collections on art,
art history, and architec-
ture (particularly Midwest-
ern). Extensive periodical,
catalogue, and mono-
graph holdings. Nonmem-
bers need an Infopass and
must pay museum admis-
sion. TW

United Way of Metropoli-
tan Chicago Library
72 W. Adams, Room 1733
263-1756
Child welfare, the elderly,
and social services and
management. TOR

U.S. Government Libraries

While many government departments maintain libraries of their own publications,
those listed here have more.

General Services
Administration Federal
Archives and Record
Center
7358 S. Pulaski Rd.
353-0160
Semi-active and permanent
federal records from Mid-
western states. Especially
useful for genealogists:
census manuscripts, Revo-
lutionary and Civil War rec-
ords, papers on Indian af-
fairs, naturalization records,
and Port of New York
passenger-arrival lists
dating from 1820. No print-
ed government docu-
ments. By appointment.
PTOR

U.S. Army Corps of
Engineers, North Central
Division Library
536 S. Clark, Room 346
353-5038
Civil engineering, dams,
waterways, ecology,
energy, navigation, public
works. Call ahead. TWCOR

U.S. Department of
Commerce ITA Library
55 E. Monroe, Room 1406
353-4450
Domestic and international
commerce including
census statistics for the en-
tire country, statistics on
economics, industrial pro-
duction projections, and in-

formation on foreign
manufacturing. TWO

U.S. Environmental
Protection Agency
Library
230 S. Dearborn St.,
Room 1420
353-2022
Mostly technical materials
on the subject. TWCOR

Music

The Chicago Symphony Orchestra and Lyric Opera command international plaudits, while myriad less-famous groups spread the classical light throughout the city and suburbs. But Chicago's musical pre-eminence extends to every genre. Our blues musicians created and nurtured a unique art form; jazz is enjoying a resurgence; folk clubs really thrive here; and the sounds of everything from accordions to zithers throb in countless ethnic taverns. Since bars and clubs provide the forum for most nonclassical performances, neighborhood imperatives dictate most booking policies, and covers or minimums range from nothing to hear "nobodies" to big bucks for big names. More detailed discussions of the clubs can be found in the neighborhood chapters. (*See Index under Clubs.*)

Loud, powerful, sometimes brutal: Blues are Chicago's music. Yet some of our internationally known blues makers are little-known at home because they usually play for mostly black audiences in South and West Side clubs. Only the Checkerboard Lounge (423 East 43rd Street, 373-5948), where Buddy Guy and Junior Wells regularly hold court, and Theresa's (4801 South Indiana Avenue, 285-2744), where local and touring stars often sit in with the driving house band, attract significant numbers of white customers. The street scene suggests extreme caution, but inside these clubs it's cool. While in the area, try the soul food at Gladys' Luncheonette (4527 South Indiana, 548-6848), a local highlight.

The faint-hearted can fill their blues quotas in less threatening DePaul and environs, where such clubs as B.L.U.E.S. (2519 North Halsted Street, 528-1012) and the Wise Fools Pub (2270 North Lincoln Avenue, 929-1510) are interspersed with the city's best folk-music spots. Holsteins (2464 North Lincoln Avenue, 327-3331), for example, isn't a dairy bar but a folk-performer-owned club with an enviable sound system, an admirable music environment, and an estimable booking policy. You can also see noted and notable folk acts in somewhat less comfortable surroundings at The Earl of Old Town (1615 North Wells Street, 642-5206). Both places are steady supporters of Chicago singer-songwriters.

Folkies aren't hard drinkers, so booze and banjos needn't mix. A delightful, old-fashioned coffeehouse, the No Exit Café & Gallery (7001 North Glenwood Avenue, 743-3355) serves up a fine array of performers along with coffees, teas, and pastries. Concerts, sing-alongs, and other mostly traditional music celebrations beguile at the Old Town School of Folk Music (909 West Armitage Avenue, 525-7472 and 927 Noyes Street, Evanston, 864-6664) and at Hogeye Music (1920 Central Street, Evanston, 475-0260) throughout the year, while the winter University of Chicago Folk Festival is a bargain-priced frozen folk follies. (*See Annual Events.*)

Most of the bars that jumped on the country-Western bandwagon are substituting bang for twang as they mosey toward country-rock or just return to rock. But the Sundowners' old-line Nashville sound continues to draw Chicagoans and conventioneers to the RR Ranch (56 West Randolph Street, 263-8207), a peripatetic Loop landmark. Other remaining country-Western spots cater mainly to neighborhood crowds, as do the run-of-the-mill rock clubs.

At hundreds of watering holes from the heart of the city to the superboonies, weekends bring out beer-drinking locals ready to boogie to main-line rock bands with no future but lots of volume. In heavily ethnic neighborhoods, the corner tap's entertainment may lean toward national favorites or, for the upscale, piano-bar Perry Como-style artists. In the city's night-life districts, rock clubs embrace the *au courant,* be it New Wave, reggae, or. . . .

Rock, pop, and country stars play sports stadia, convention halls, and faded movie palaces, any place that will accommodate monster crowds. Sight lines are often terrible, the sound system as bad, amenities few, and safety debatable, but that doesn't deter the mostly adolescent fans from fighting for tickets. Far better to seek the headliners at the Park West (322 West Armitage Avenue, 929-5959), one of the country's handsomest concert clubs and, in many ways, the legitimate heir to the London House/Mr. Kelly's mantle.

Rush Street's famous nightclubs may be only a fond memory, but the area remains the center for jazz, although jazz bars now dot the city, and hotel lounge acts are as likely to be gentle jazz as soft rock or pap pop. Two premier spots, however, are downtown. Touring stars shine at Rick's Café Americain (Holiday Inn, 644 North Lake Shore Drive, 943-9200) and at Joe Segal's Jazz Showcase (Blackstone Hotel, 636 South Michigan Avenue, 427-4300). The late-summer Chicago Jazz Festival, the world's largest free jazz celebration, brings nationally known artists to town for a week of music with more than 20 Chicago groups. ChicagoFest, a heavily policed, bargain-priced, music mob scene, boasts everything from main-stage superstars to respected recording artists, plus food from dozens of restaurants. (*See Annual Events.*) Various ethnic and neighborhood festivals add to the summer music offerings, too.

Our wealth of musical performances has one very real drawback: Keeping track of what's going on isn't easy. The most complete listings appear monthly in *Chicago,* with weekly updates on classical music during the WFMT (98.7 FM) "Music in Chicago" program. The Bulletin Board on the station's "The Midnight Special," Saturday night's wildly eclectic mix of folk music, comedy, and whatnot, provides up-to-date information for simpatico clubs. Friday and Sunday entertainment listings in the daily newspapers may reflect last-minute changes, and the *Reader,* a free weekly, has deep club/bar coverage.

For more details than the mass media is likely to offer, get a copy of *Come for to Sing* (281-4234). This quarterly publication covers the Midwest folk scene through interviews, commentary, club news, and reviews; and it puts out an annual guide to folk-music resources. The same phone number also reaches Aural Tradition, traditional-music impresarios and newsletter publishers. *Grass Clippings* is the monthly newsletter of the Chicago Area Bluegrass Music and Pickin' Society (274-7333).

The Jazz Institute of Chicago (664-4069), which also coordinates the Chicago Jazz Festival, has a newsletter and maintains a Jazz Hot Line (666-1881). Founding member Bob Koester, of the Jazz Record Mart, is a mine of jazz and blues information, as well as of records. For news, interviews, and commentary, *Living Blues* (281-3385) can't be beat. The *Illinois Entertainer* (298-9333), a free monthly found at bars and music stores, is tireless in its coverage of the pop and rock scene.

Classical

If your thoughts on classical music in Chicago begin and end with the Chicago Symphony Orchestra or the Lyric Opera, you're overlooking a lot. This is one of the most musically active cities in the world, with an enormous reservoir of talented musicians and countless opportunities to hear them perform. All year long, indoors and out, a dizzying array of concerts provides music to satisfy any taste, whether for Renaissance madrigals or for the most challenging modern scores. With everything from organ recitals in neighborhood churches to touring superstars in recital at the Auditorium Theatre, finding time even to sample the riches creates pleasant problems.

Skimming the city's classical *crème de la crème* can be costly, even with the savings offered by subscription series, but affordable options abound. Less-than-top-ranked groups performing in halls and churches around town typically command one-half to two-thirds the price of the downtown front-runners. Most school and conservatory concerts are free or inexpensive. On Sundays, you can hear some mighty organ and choral works in churches for a prayer.

Choral groups

Apollo Chorus of Chicago
427-5620
Dr. William J. Peterman, music director and conductor, leads more than 200 voices in mostly sacred music, continuing a tradition that began in 1872. Major performances are a December Messiah and one or more large choral works in spring at Orchestra Hall, and a concert of shorter pieces at St. Peter's Church, 110 W. Madison St.

Chicago Baroque Ensemble
383-4742
Victor Hildner brings together 16 professional singers and instrumentalists to re-create original baroque performance practices. The repertoire includes hundreds of pieces. Four programs a year, some with baroque dancers.

Chicago Chamber Choir
St. Pauls United Church of Christ
655 W. Fullerton Pkwy.
929-1649
George Estevez leads his 40-voice choir in seldom-heard music of all periods, providing the city with some real musical treats. Four subscription concerts.

Chicago Children's Choir
324-8300
Now in its 27th year with founding director Christopher Moore, this marvelous organization involves 450 children in various stages of choral training. The 130-voice senior group tours extensively but is always in town for Christmas concerts and a spring gala, usually in Hyde Park.

Chicago Monteverdi Singers
621-9494, 524-2117
Eight professional singers, accompanied by players of period instruments, cover vocal literature from late Renaissance to early baroque in programs that mix well-known and little-known works. Director Robert Holst does some transcriptions, so there's always something new to the ear. Several subscription concerts at the Church of Our Saviour, 530 W. Fullerton Pkwy.; other performances around town.

Classic Chorales
328-8440
Three groups, really: the Classic Chorale, the Classic Chamber Singers, and the Classic Children's Chorale. The Classic Chorale, 70 voices directed by Lee Jacobson, performs works from Bach to Samuel Barber with occasional forays into jazz and Broadway tunes. Northern suburbs and Chicago.

Do-It-Yourself *Messiah*
726-0484
Margaret Hillis conducts the orchestra and you in this popular event. Orchestra Hall fills with joyful voices at two sing-alongs in December. The much-sought-after, free tickets are distributed by Talman Home Federal Savings and Loan, 72 E. Randolph St., Chicago 60601. Requests must include a stamped, self-addressed envelope, and those postmarked before November 15 are not honored.

William Ferris Chorale
236-3466
Director William Ferris is a composer who celebrates other living composers in concert. The repertoire of the 55-voice chorus also includes works dating to the Renaissance. Three major concerts a year at the Cathedral of St. James, 65 E. Huron St., with other appearances throughout the city. Tours extensively.

Music of the Baroque
461-9541
Thomas Wikman's superb singers and musicians perform works from the 15th to the 18th centuries, but feel most at home in the 17th century and are justifiably famed for their interpretations of the great oratorios and Passions. The orchestra also does splendidly with instrumental works. Five programs a year in each of four series: Hyde Park, Evanston, Near North, and the western suburbs.

The Oriana Singers
275-5291
William Chin directs this small chorus in everything from madrigals to recent compositions. Four-program subscription series at Chicago and Evanston locations; other concerts, too.

Rockefeller Chapel Choir
5850 S. Woodlawn Ave.
753-3383
One of the best things about Rodney Wynkoop's 25-voice professional choir is that you can hear it free at 11 a.m. Sunday services throughout the academic year. Wynkoop and assistant choir director David Beaubien conduct the smaller chancel choir at 9 a.m. Tickets for the subscription series, which includes a Christmastime Messiah, can be purchased at the University of Chicago box office or at Ticketron.

Ensembles

Bach Society Musicians
Glencoe Union Church
263 Park Ave.,
Glencoe
432-4458
Nancy Humphrey is music director and harpsichordist for this group specializing in solos, trios, and sonatas by J. S. Bach (the season opens with a "Bachanalia") and his contemporaries. Five concerts a year.

Chamber Consortium
943-1955
Violinist Arnold Roth, cellist Barbara Haffner, and pianist Andrea Swan, the core musicians, are joined by topnotch guest artists in programs of chamber music of all eras. Especially notable is the Consortium's policy of honoring living composers-in-residence at each concert and playing selections of their works, many of them premières. The group is exciting in concept, and performances are splendid. Three to four concerts are in the subscription series.

Chicago Brass Quintet
465-2780
Since 1962, five players from major Chicago orchestras have presented the best in music for brass, as well as their own transcriptions. Programs touch everything from Renaissance works to commissioned contemporary pieces. Three-concert subscription series are at St. Pauls United Church of Christ, 655 W. Fullerton Pkwy., and at the Unitarian Universalist Church (Unity Temple), 875 Lake St., Oak Park. The group also appears around the city and tours nationally.

Chicago Chamber Brass
461-1929
Two trumpets, a trombone, a French horn, and a tuba combine in sparkling renditions of Renaissance dances, contemporary conundrums, and everything in between. The group makes summer appearances at plazas and parks, performs about town year-round, tours, and offers winter subscription series at four locations (in Hyde Park, Evanston, Oak Park, and North of the River).

The Chicago Ensemble
271-3810
About a dozen musicians belong to this group. The striking juxtaposition of works (some of which are commissioned) from an eclectic repertoire provides unique musical excitement at their concerts. Five or six members perform at each of five concerts in the subscription series, held from January to June in Hyde Park, Evanston, River Forest, and Aurora.

Chicago Soundings
472-3002
Twentieth-century solo and chamber music makes up the repertoire of these splendid musicians. Performances range from piano solos to works for small ensemble. Home base is the Ukrainian Institute of Modern Art, 2320 W. Chicago Ave., but you also can hear them in Hyde Park and on the North Side.

Contemporary Chamber Players of the University of Chicago
962-8068
Since the mid-1960s, composer Ralph Shapey's fine group has championed 20th-century music, especially works by living composers and those ignored by the establishment. The spring Fromm Music Foundation concert is always an important musical event. Free concerts at Mandel Hall, 5706 S. University Ave.

Early Music Celebration
848-5406
Gerhart Schmeltekopf directs this small group in baroque, medieval, and Renaissance music played on replicas of period instruments. Singers occasionally join in for performances at various Chicago and Oak Park locations.

The Harwood Early Music Ensemble
775-6696
John Nygro's nine musicians present carefully researched, entertaining, medieval and Renaissance selections, using replicas of original instruments and appropriate vocal styles. Explanatory narratives and literary readings augment some performances. Five-concert subscription series at three locations: the Loop, Hyde Park, North Shore.

Sheffield Winds
337-7180
The 11 players, with occasional guest artists, model themselves after 17th-century small-wind ensembles, but perform music of all eras, including frequent world premières and commissioned works. Performances throughout the area and subscription concerts in central Chicago, Hyde Park, and the North Shore.

Vermeer Quartet
815-753-1450
Violinists Shmuel Ashkenasi and Pierre Menard, violist Bernard Zaslav, and cellist Marc Johnson are in residence at Northern Illinois University, but the school sponsors four Chicago concerts at the Goodman Theatre, 200 S. Columbus Dr.

Opera companies

Chicago Opera Theater
Athenaeum Theatre
2936 N. Southport Ave.
663-0555
Artistic director Alan Stone founded the company in 1973, and it has been delighting Chicagoans with operas in English ever since. Productions range from classics like Mozart's Cosí Fan Tutte to Chicago premières of contemporary works such as Robert Kurka's The Good Soldier Schweik. Robert Frisbie has conducted brilliantly since COT's founding; and Frank Galati and Michael Maggio, two names familiar to Chicago stage audiences, have lent their talents to the staging of several productions. Three operas a season.

Hinsdale Opera Theater
Hinsdale Central
Auditorium
55th and Grant Sts.,
Hinsdale
323-8989
Young singers from all over America appear in productions by this company, which deserves to be better known. Each season, they try to do one standard, one neglected work, and a contemporary opera (all in English). Nancy Hotchkiss is general manager and Pier Giorgio Calabria is resident conductor.

Light Opera Works
Cahn Auditorium
Northwestern University
600 Emerson St.,
Evanston
869-6300
This new company's repertoire includes comic opera, operetta (lots of Gilbert and Sullivan), and operettalike American musicals, all sung in English. Philip Kraus is artistic director; musical chores are handled by Barney Jones. (Not affiliated with Northwestern University.)

Lithuanian Opera Company
Maria High School
6727 S. California Ave.
471-1424
Since 1956, this company has been doing a grand job of producing grand opera in Lithuanian. They've done everything from the war horses to American premières of rarities like Ponchielli's I Lituani. Usually three performances of one opera a year.

Lyric Opera of Chicago
Civic Opera House
20 N. Wacker Dr.
332-2244
A civic treasure, the Lyric enters a new era as Ardis Krainik takes over managerial duties of the late Carol Fox. Whatever changes that brings, it's a good bet that Lyric will remain one of the hottest tickets in town, especially when Pavarotti is singing. Real opera lovers should invest in a subscription for the September-to-December season. As an extra treat, Lyric has added a spring production, bringing us something frothy as a reward for enduring Chicago's winter.

Orchestras

American Chamber Symphony
236-7347
Music from the 18th century to the present—including an impressive number of American premières— makes up the repertoire of this ensemble of 35 exceptional musicians. Robert Frisbie conducts the four subscription programs, which feature outstanding soloists, and takes the group touring here and abroad. The Chicago base is the Civic Theatre, 20 N. Wacker Dr.

Chicago Chamber Orchestra
922-5570
Dieter Kober's group has been presenting delightful free concerts of well-known and seldom-heard works since 1952. Frequent appearances from winter through spring, at the Museum of Science and Industry, 57th St. and Lake Shore Dr., and at the Chicago Public Library Cultural Center, 78 E. Washington St., are capped in May by the Blair Memorial Concert, featuring major soloists, at the Cathedral of St. James, 65 E. Huron St. There's an annual performance of American music at the Chicago Historical Society, Clark St. at North Ave.; and summer Lakeside Promenades begin at south portico of the Museum of Science and Industry with Handel's complete Water Music.

Chicago String Ensemble
St. Pauls United Church of Christ
655 W. Fullerton Pkwy.
880-5255
Alan Heatherington's 20 to 22 musicians give splendid performances of string-orchestra literature of all periods. Four subscription concerts.

Chicago Symphonic Wind Ensemble
631-5800
Large-scale and chamber works for winds by master composers share space with "obscure marches from 1880 to 1930" on the programs of Truman College's resident ensemble. Music director Lloyd Vincent Byczek takes the 35-member group to various concert halls during the regular season and, in summer, leads them in park and plaza pops programs.

Chicago Symphony Orchestra
Orchestra Hall
220 S. Michigan Ave.
435-8111, 435-8122
The CSO is Chicago's world-championship team. Single tickets for subscription concerts—especially those conducted by music director Sir Georg Solti, or ones featuring Margaret Hillis's superb chorus—are often difficult to come by (sometimes, returned tickets are available on the night of a performance); watch Chicago for dates of nonsubscription events and university nights.

Civic Orchestra of Chicago
Orchestra Hall
220 S. Michigan Ave.
435-8158, 435-8159
The hundred or so musicians in this 60-year-old "training orchestra" of the Chicago Symphony present some of the finest concerts in the area. Principal conductor Gordon Peters puts together distinctive programs, placing more emphasis on 20th-century works and American music than is usual for the Civic's home auditorium.

Evanston Symphony Orchestra
Evanston Township High School Auditorium
1600 Dodge Ave.,
Evanston
965-2440
Founded in 1945, this 90-member community orchestra gives four concerts annually. Principal CSO cellist Frank Miller conducts; various groups pitch in for choral works.

Friends of Mozart Society
962-8068
Conductor Mark Prentiss leads this chamber orchestra through the works of Mozart, Haydn, and other composers of the classical period. Four to six concerts a year in Hyde Park, with guest soloists at most.

Lake Forest Symphony
Drake Theater
Barat College
700 E. Westleigh Rd.,
Lake Forest
295-2135
Seventy musicians and a community chorus perform throughout the year under the direction of Chicago Symphony coconcertmaster Victor Aitay. The parent Lake Forest Symphony Association also sponsors a youth orchestra and maintains vigorous musical education and outreach programs.

Orchestra of Illinois
263-3786
Musicians for the Lyric Opera have put together America's only self-governed orchestra. Between 60 and 80 of them do everything from keeping the American Ballet Theatre on its toes to playing popular concerts for conventions. They get down to their own business with a spring concert series held in three locations. Holiday pops concerts in the Loop.

Sinfonia Musicale
Pick-Staiger Concert Hall
1977 Sheridan Rd.,
Evanston
869-4844
Music director Barry Faldner selects lesser known works of major composers and major compositions by new talents, many of them commissioned by the Sinfonia or winners of an annual competition. Well-known and up-and-coming soloists frequently appear with the 60 musicians, all members of the Chicago Symphony or Lyric Opera orchestras. Three-concert subscription series.

Festivals and series

Allied Arts Association Concerts
Orchestra Hall
220 S. Michigan Ave.
782-6094
The season includes single attractions and several series, which bring in everything from the London Symphony Orchestra and Andrés Segovia to Egyptian musicians and dancers, carrying on the tradition established by the late Harry Zelzer, one of the last of the great impresarios.

Auditorium Theatre Council Concerts
70 E. Congress Pkwy.
922-2110, 922-6634
Musical offerings in these series range from major orchestras to solo recitals, all gaining immeasurably from the wonderful acoustics in this gorgeous concert hall.

Bach Week in Evanston
St. Luke's Episcopal Church
939 Hinman Ave., Evanston
475-3630
For a couple of weeks (usually around the second week) in May, music director Richard Webster gathers members of the Chicago Symphony and other talented musicians for performances of the orchestral, choral, chamber, and vocal works of J. S. Bach and his contemporaries.

Chamber Music Council of Chicago
World Playhouse
410 S. Michigan Ave.
663-1628
As the Fine Arts Music Foundation, the Council served chiefly as sponsor of concerts by the Milwaukee-based Fine Arts Quartet. All that's changed: The Council now presents six or more subscription-series performances by top international chamber musicians playing a repertoire from Mozart to Bartók. There's also a new emphasis on educational activities, with workshops, open rehearsals, and more.

The Chicago Academy of Early Music
328-2310
L'estro armonico, a baroque chamber ensemble, and Concentus Musicus Chicago, a full baroque orchestra, under artistic director Kenneth Dorsch, perform on original instruments and authentic replicas. Topflight soloists join in the programs, many featuring Chicago premières. At Church of the Ascension, 1133 N. La Salle St., and in the western suburbs.

Contemporary Concerts
Fullerton Hall
Art Institute of Chicago
Michigan Ave. at Adams St.
328-5714
Unflinchingly avant-garde, Contemporary Concerts brings to Chicago top interpreters of the works of living composers. Three to five concerts a year.

Grant Park Concerts
James C. Petrillo Music Shell, Grant Park
294-2420
Since 1935, Chicagoans have enjoyed free concerts in the city's front yard. The topnotch Grant Park Symphony and Chorus are led by some of the world's most promising conductors in programs ranging from pops to concert opera and ballet. The pre-Fourth of July concert and the elaborate fireworks display that follows draw enormous crowds. Late June until September: Wed., Fri., and Sat. at 8 p.m.; Sun. at 7 p.m. Four Thurs. noon concerts are also scheduled.

Dame Myra Hess Concerts
Preston Bradley Hall
CPL Cultural Center
78 E. Washington St.
744-6630
An outstanding free series provides exposure and performance experience for young musicians from around the world. Occasionally, established artists are invited also. Every Wed. at 12:15, except Christmas and New Year's weeks. Supported by Talman Home Federal Savings and Loan and broadcast live on WFMT (98.7).

Mostly Music
924-2550
More than 70 concerts feature young as well as established artists. From fall through spring, weekly lunchtime concerts of vocal and instrumental music of all periods bring shoppers and office workers to First Chicago Center, Dearborn and Adams Sts.; and performances of chamber music in homes and in other intimate settings are a great success in Hyde Park–Kenwood, the western suburbs, and on the North Side and the North Shore. In summer, you can hear outdoor lunchtime concerts at Michael Reese Hospital, 2929 S. Ellis. Special events, too.

Pick-Staiger Concert Hall Series

1977 Sheridan Rd.,
Evanston
492-5441
Northwestern University's music school fills this 1,000-seat auditorium with glorious music from fall to late spring. The Performing Arts Series holds a traditional line-up of orchestras, chamber groups, and soloists; other series lean toward contemporary music, up-and-coming artists, and specialized programs.

Ravinia Festival

728-4642 (May to Sept.),
782-9696 (winter)
Ravinia is more than just the bucolic summer home of the Chicago Symphony: There are visiting orchestras, chamber music ensembles, soloists, pop artists, dance companies, master classes, and young people's programs. Music director James Levine, who shares the podium with distinguished guest conductors, always schedules some big pieces—concert operas or choral works—to cap the season. Special buses (728-4642) and Park 'N' Ride facilities (432-3325) help get you there and back; several dining facilities (432-7550). Ravinia Park is in Highland Park; take the Edens Expwy. to Lake-Cook Rd. exit and go east.

University of Chicago Department of Music

Mandel Hall
5706 S. University Ave.
962-8484
The Early Music and Chamber Music series bring notable artists to a nicely renovated hall.

Weinstein Center for the Performing Arts

National College of Education
2840 Sheridan Rd.,
Evanston
256-5150, ext. 255,
256-5216, ext. 284
Chicago-based ensembles, soloists, dance companies, theater groups, and more are booked into this well-equipped hall. Pianist Jeffrey Siegel gives four concerts yearly. The season usually runs from fall to early summer; most performances are on weekends.

Colleges and conservatories

Chicago is blessed with some of the nation's finest music schools, and we all reap the benefits of their low-priced (often free) offerings of everything from student recitals to full operas. Bands, orchestras, choruses, and ensembles play everything from ancient instruments to electronic gewgaws throughout the academic year in some of the area's finest concert halls. Faculty groups, such as Northwestern University's Eckstein String Quartet and Ralph Shapey's Contemporary Chamber Players of the University of Chicago, rank with the best professional ensembles, and there are students who'll make you happy to be able to say "I heard them when. . . ." Look beyond the schools' big-name performance series and you'll be rewarded.

American Conservatory of Music

116 S. Michigan Ave.
263-4161

Chicago Musical College of Roosevelt University

430 S. Michigan Ave.
341-3780

DePaul University School of Music

804 W. Belden Ave.
321-7760

Northwestern University School of Music

711 Elgin Rd.,
Evanston
492-7575

University of Chicago Department of Music

5845 S. Ellis Ave.,
(enter from quadrangle)
962-8484

Dance

You have to stay on your toes to keep up with dance in Chicago. While extravaganzas like Geraldine Freund's International Dance Festival highlight visiting artists, new companies have sprung up locally at a remarkable rate in the past five years. Because very few have performance spaces of their own, the dance scene is less organized than the theatrical one. But it's almost as impressive. Major local and visiting groups play the big houses (*see Theater*), MoMing Dance & Arts Center, and the Columbia College Dance Center; dozens of others dance at schools, parks, plazas, museums, festivals, city-sponsored events such as ChicagoFest—anywhere and any time they can. For details and reviews, see *Chicago* magazine, the *Reader,* and the dailies, or call the Chicago Council on Fine Arts (dial F-I-N-E-A-R-T).

Ballet and modern

Small, mostly modern-dance troupes are flourishing artistically, but money and space problems continue to plague them and the many important independent choreographers. Virtually all of the companies discussed here offer classes or run full-fledged schools, both to further their art and to raise funds for performances. Chicago Dance Arts Coalition, an organization formed to promote dance in Chicago, may improve this sometimes chaotic and discouraging situation. (Contact Tim Anstett at MoMing for more information about Chicago Dance.)

Akasha & Company
c/o Laura Wade,
3047 N. Kenmore Ave.
475-8118, 871-5385
Five dancers formed this company in 1979 to present pieces by local choreographers, such as Maggie Kast, Fury Gold, Poonie Dodson, Sharon Jackman, and Kate Kuper. Varied repertoire.

American Dance Center School and Ballet Co.
22413 Governors Hwy.,
Richton Park
747-4969
Started about a decade ago to upgrade south-suburban cultural life, the company performs the classics; original ballets; jazz, tap,

spirituals, and modern dance; and the Christmas-time Hansel and Gretel ballet, presented with guest artists at a 1,300-seat Chicago Heights auditorium. The core group of eight is augmented by several dozen dancers for most productions. Classes for kids, adults, and aspiring professionals (some for college credit) are held at the center and at suburban park districts.

Amundson Arts Academy, Inc.
6400 N. Artesian Ave.
465-4800
This performing-arts school's children's troupe does tap and musical com-

edy, and the adult company can do everything from chorus lines to ballet.

Arve Connection Dance Company
1016 N. Dearborn St.
337-6543
This high-energy, kinetic, quick-moving, 11-member company, started in 1977, is fascinating to watch and popular with audiences. Company founder and dancer, Richard Arve, choreographs a repertoire that ranges from Naja—an East Indian cobra dance for three men —to Currents— an abstract piece for the full company done to the music of Pink Floyd. Arve is also head of the modern-dance

department at the Ruth Page Foundation School of Dance and has studios in Crestwood and Calumet City. The company tours nationally.

Chicago City Ballet
223 W. Erie St.
943-1315
After several years as the Ballet School of Lyric Opera, CCB was established in 1980 as the city's much-needed resident professional ballet company. Twenty-six dancers strong, it presented its inaugural season at the Auditorium Theatre in June, 1981. Under Maria Tallchief's artistic direction, CCB maintains a long-standing association with George Balanchine, using his choreography and drawing guest artists from the New York City Ballet. Assistant artistic director Paul Mejia and others also choreograph for the company. Now financially on its feet, the group tours the Midwest extensively, performs about town, continues to dance with Lyric Opera, and provides professional training for young dancers.

Chicago Contemporary Dance Theatre
5320 S. University Ave.
643-8916
After running a company and school through the 1970s, Maggie Kast now concentrates on developing and dancing her own works and collaborating with other artists. Her background in ballet and the Graham technique is reflected in rather intellectual pieces.

Chicago Dance Medium
Dancespace
410 S. Michigan, Room 833
939-0181
Known mostly for their work in grade schools as part of Young Audiences, Inc., Rosemary Doolas and her dancers present both abstract and dramatic modern works. Doolas and Fred DeVore develop most

of the pieces, but other Chicago choreographers also are showcased. Dance-space, their studio, functions as a school and hosts some concerts.

Chicago Repertory Dance Ensemble
CrossCurrents
3206 N. Wilton Ave.
327-7777, 871-8180
Under the artistic direction of Tara Mitton, about a dozen top Chicago dancers from various companies get together three times a year to present works by well-known local and out-of-town choreographers.

Concert Dance, Inc.
2400 N. Lake View Ave.
472-8692
Venetia Chakos Stifler founded this ten-dancer company in 1979 and choreographs most of its works. The modern-dance repertoire includes a wide variety of styles that combine to produce a beautiful whole. Fugues, a signature piece that captures the essence of Bach's Art of the Fugue, is a fine example of the technique.

Dancycle
1000 W. 20th Pl.
226-2990
Four independent choreographers—Jan Bartoszek, Carrie Stern, Kathleen Maltese, and Jean Parisi—pool their talents for administrative and promotional chores. They also collaborate with each other and with performance artists (musicians, painters, sculptors, poets) to produce modern dances that range from traditional to very experimental. Performances can be seen at their studio, MoMing, Link's Hall, galleries such as N.A.M.E., and other locations.

Pros Arts Studio operates from the same address and from an art studio at 910 W. 19th St. (829-0766). This community organization teaches visual and performing arts and maintains a

traveling exhibit of paintings, sculptures, and drawings by students and professionals. It also teaches the art of clowning.

Gus Giordano Jazz Dance Chicago
311 3rd St.,
Wilmette
251-4434
Gus Giordano Dance Center
614 Davis St.,
Evanston
866-9442
Gus Giordano's brand of jazz dance is big, accessible, highly theatrical, involves a lot of torso and arm movement, and has "punch." From Ragtime to Rock, a lecture-demo tracing the evolution of jazz dance, augments the regular repertoire and is presented at schools, parks, etc. The huge, four-studio Dance Center accommodates more than 1,000 students—from amateurs to aspiring professionals—and hosts some concerts. Giordano's ten-dancer company tours nationally and internationally.

Margot Grimmer American Dance Co.
442 Central Ave.,
Highland Park
835-2556, 433-1350
Whether presenting a whole era of history danced to coordinating slides or a rousing rock ballet, Margot Grimmer's choreography features many multimedia effects. A knock-out dancer, she performs with the company and also runs a school.

Joel Hall Dancers
New School for the Performing Arts
410 S. Michigan, Suite 300
663-3618
Jazz dance is the mainstay of this 15-member troupe whose repertoire includes modern-dance and ballet pieces by Hall and other choreographers. Some works combine dance and drama; others make state-

ments about urban life. Often seen at the Francis Parker School, the company also began a "metropolitan touring program" in 1982 to bring Hall-style jazz dance to area schools.

Joseph Holmes Dance Theatre
CrossCurrents
3206 N. Wilton Ave.
975-3505
Ballet, modern dance based on the Graham technique, jazz, blues, spirituals, dance drama, and African dance are all part of the repertoire of this 16-member company whose signature piece may be Sunday Go To Meetin'. Holmes (who also dances with the troupe) does all the choreography for the group, which performs throughout the city and the Midwest. Their "Chance to Dance" program provides an opportunity for interested youths to sign up for two free months of special instruction after seeing a lecture-demonstration-performance presented at schools, community centers, boys' clubs, etc.

Hubbard Street Dance Company
218 S. Wabash, 3rd floor
663-0853
In just a few years, Lou Conte's ten-member company has become the darling of the Chicago dance world with an easily accessible blend of ballet, show, and jazz dance. Uniquely American dance forms, set to Broadway and popular melodies, are performed with great theatrical flair by talented, highly trained, always "together" dancers. The combination is a sure-fire hit. The Lou Conte Dance Studio offers ballet, jazz, and tap classes for beginners as well as for professionals.

Link's Hall Studio
3435 N. Sheffield Ave.
281-0824
Dancers-choreographers

Carol Bobrow, Bob Eisen, and Charlie Vernon share this space for rehearsals, performances (solo and collaborative), and recitals by other artists. The facility can be rented by outside groups.

Lynda Martha Dance Co.
1116 Maple Ave.,
Evanston
864-2830
Director of modern dance at Gus Giordano's studio and a teacher at UIC, Lynda Martha started her own modern-dance company in 1979. Her contemporary, jazz-influenced, high-energy, angular style is exemplified in City Suite. *The eight dancers rehearse and sometimes perform at the Gus Giordano Dance Center, at universities, and elsewhere.*

Masi Ballet Chicago Inc.
5153 N. Ashland Ave.
989-7100
Started in 1980, this 12-member company presents classical and original ballets. The school, for kids through professionals, boasts a beautiful studio.

MoMing Dance & Arts Center
1034 W. Barry Ave.
472-9894
A Chicago-dance mainstay and innovative force, MoMing provides space for and coproduces programs by local and out-of-town dancers and troupes, mimes, multimedia performers, and more. Something new and interesting can be seen almost every weekend year-round, and MoMing has helped gain recognition for many fine choreographers who might otherwise have remained unknown. The center's art gallery hosts shows by local, Midwestern, and national artists; the school offers a full range of dance classes, with a special dance program for kids 4-14. Although MoMing has no resident dance company, several faculty

members—Jan Erkert, Jan Bartoszek, Jackie Radis, Amy Osgood—are independent choreographers worth watching. They frequently develop and perform pieces at the center.

Mordine & Company
Columbia College
Dance Center
4730 N. Sheridan Rd.
271-7804
Increasingly important to Chicago dance since its inception in 1969, the CCDC provides one of the few prime performance spaces, scheduling more than 50 events a year from October through May. The small resident company, started at the same time by Shirley Mordine, has been getting stronger every year and, unlike most, develops pieces through experimentation and improvisation. Mordine does most of the choreography but also commissions guest artists to create for the group. Works performed often tell a story—some humorously, some seriously, but frequently to an original score. They are also characterized by controlled spontaneity. The company tours nationally and internationally, performs regularly at the center, and offers a full range of public classes.

Nana Solbrig & The Chicago Moving Company
Chicago Dance Center
2433 N. Lincoln Ave.
929-7416
Formerly a repertory company, CMC produced some beautiful works such as Bill Evans's For Betty *and Martin Kravitz's* The Holy Fire. *Nana Solbrig, who started the group in 1972, has changed its name and now focuses on her own choreography. Based on José Limon's technique, her style is smooth and flowing, sometimes almost lyrical. The Chicago Dance Center is a rehearsal space for the six to ten dancers and a school.*

Folk and ethnic

There are hundreds of folk and ethnic dance companies in Chicago. This small sampling includes the thoroughly professional (Ensemble Español), the intensely ethnic (Polish Highlanders), and Americans who simply enjoy folk dancing (International Dancers). Folk Dance Leadership Council representative Sanna Longden (328-7793) can provide information on additional groups and can steer you to recreational ones to join.

Balkanske Igre Ensemble
(The Chicago Balkan
Dance Ensemble)
18548 Morris Ave.,
Homewood
799-2486
*More than 20 dancers, sing-
ers, and musicians from the
metropolitan-Chicago area
make up this 1964 offshoot
of the International Folk
Dancers at the University of
Chicago. With the occa-
sional help of Richard Crum
and other experts, they
research and choreograph
traditional dances of
Eastern Europe and, by
special requests, those of
Italy and Israel.*

Carol Crisostomo Philip-
pine Dance Company
7734 S. County Line Rd.,
Burr Ridge
887-1257
*Crisostomo's group was
formed in 1974 and now
has a repertoire of 25
Filipino dances. Elaborate,
authentic costumes and
props create especially colorful performances.*

Dennehy Irish Dancers
10608 S. Lockwood Ave.,
Oak Lawn
636-8241
*Dennis Dennehy teaches
nearly a hundred students,
the best of whom perform
Irish step dances at festivals
and functions around town.*

Ensemble Español
5500 N. St. Louis Ave.
583-4050, ext. 443
*The exciting classical,
regional, and flamenco
dances of Spain are the
domain of Northeastern Illinois University's resident
company, started in 1976.
Founder and director Libby
Komaiko Fleming choreo-
graphs for her troupe of half
a dozen dancers and sev-
eral apprentices, and they
are sometimes joined by
guest artists, such as Maria
Alba, William Carter, Nana
Lorca, and Lola Montes.
Besides touring extensively and mounting series for
kids and adults at the university, the company hosts
the summer American
Spanish Dance Festival—a
two-week extravaganza of
performances, workshops,
and seminars.*

Ethnic Theatre of Near
Eastern Dance
Ridgeville Community
Center
908 Seward St.,
Evanston
869-5640
*This small troupe performs
traditional and regional folk
dances of the Middle East,
as well as stylized, modern
Egyptian ones (the most familiar of which is cabaret-
style belly dancing).
Classes, too.*

Hromovytsia
2255 W. Chicago Ave.
252-9366, 628-1398
*Sts. Volodymyr and Olha
Ukrainian Catholic Church
sponsors this acclaimed
troupe of 23 young
dancers. They choreograph
and perform traditional,
regional, and stylized-for-
the-stage dances of the
Ukraine in beautifully embroidered, elaborate
costumes made by the
community.*

International Dancers
c/o George Davis,
1025 E. 50th St.
268-4856
*Since the mid-1960s, this
group of from 12 to 20
dancers has been per-
forming folk dances from all
regions of the world.*

Midwest Minyo Group
Midwest Buddhist Temple
435 W. Menomonee St.
943-7801
*Once a year, Tamotsu Mat-
suda comes from Japan to
teach the group traditional,
regional Japanese folk
dances he has learned
visiting villages at home.
They perform the dances at
the temple's summer Obon
and Ginza festivals and
elsewhere.*

Muntu Dance Theatre
704 E. 51st St.
548-0268
*A baker's dozen of dancers
and nine musicians stage
traditional and contem-
porary West African
dances, most of which are
choreographed by Alyo
Tolbert. Purification Ritual,
a progressive interpretation
of an end-of-the-year
ceremony, characterizes
the work of the troupe.
Muntu was formed in 1972.*

Najwa Dance Corps
414 W. Goethe St.
664-7943, 921-4722
Kabiring to Now, a dance-story that traces the history of blacks from the 1600s in Africa to the American present and includes African, West Indian, and American (tap, jazz, ballet, and modern) segments, typifies the repertoire of this company, which aims to be a "living archive of dance" reflecting the Afro-American experience. Najwa I choreographs for both the 15-dancer, eight-musician group, which began in the mid-1970s, and the younger corps of dancers-in-training.

New Metro Dancers
2757 W. Le Moyne St.
484-6128
About a dozen dancers, under the direction of Joe Shramovich, perform traditional Ukrainian, Byelorussian, and Moldavian dances.

Nitzanim Israeli Folk Dance Troupe
2341 Meadow Dr. South, Wilmette
251-2676
Six couples demonstrate a variety of Israeli folk dances, which have been choreographed and embellished for the stage. Director Phil Moss also conducts recreational folk-dancing sessions on Thurs. evenings at Northwestern University.

Opa
1315 Elizabeth Lane, Glenview
724-7241
Sponsored by the Greek Heritage Society, Opa specializes in regional dances of the Greek mainland, mountains, and islands.

Polish Highlanders Alliance
3035 W. 51st St.
778-1414
Two Tatra mountaineers' dances—the goralski and the zbojnicki (for men only)—are the mainstays of three groups—Hyrni, Podhale, Harnasie—each representing a town, village, or parish in Poland. However, since each dancer has an individual style, the diversity is considerable. Costumes made in Poland highlight very authentic performances.

Rabai Hungarian Folk Dance Ensemble
4422 W. Bryn Mawr Ave.
736-8427
About 20 Hungarian immigrants and first-generation Americans present choreographed versions of remarkably diverse Hungarian village folk dances in authentic costumes as varied as the repertoire. Group rehearsals and a class for youngsters are in Hungarian. Directed by Karoly and Eva Nemeth.

Julian Swain Dance Theater
813 W. Sunnyside St.
271-5781
The oldest (1969) company dedicated to expressing the Afro-American experience through ballet, modern, jazz, blues, and ethnic forms has toured nationally and internationally, danced with the Joffrey Ballet in Chicago, and appeared in the film, The Blues Brothers. Swain does most of the choreography for the 23 dancers whose most familiar piece may be The Village, a suite of African dances informal enough to be presented on street corners.

Ukraina
American Ukrainian Youth Association
2457 W. Chicago Ave.
486-4204
A company of 54 re-creates traditional and character Ukrainian dances combining original choreography with a few innovations. The AUYA also maintains a choir, a children's chorus, a brass band, a trio of singers, and a dance school.

Wesoly Lud
c/o Lorie Rose Gorny, Polish Roman Catholic Union of America
984 N. Milwaukee Ave.
278-3210
More than a dozen Polish folk dances, choreographed for the stage by Misia Bencik, make up the repertoire of the 24 "happy folk" dancers. Sponsored by the Polish Roman Catholic Union.

Western Jamaica Folk Dance Co.
4241 W. Washington Blvd.
722-8333
This company of 15 West Indian and American dancers was formed in Jamaica in 1972 and has been touring the United States for several years with folklore pieces that incorporate the legends and history of Jamaica. The troupe and school are sponsored by the Episcopal Urban Center.

Theater

A decade ago, theater in Chicago meant the Goodman, road shows at a few downtown houses, half a dozen dinner playhouses, community troupes, and a handful of struggling off-Loop groups. Saying there's been a dramatic explosion since then isn't being theatrical. Fueled by a liberalized fire code, government grants, and a wellspring of creative energy, scores of professional and semiprofessional off-Loop theaters opened during the 1970s. More than a few resulted from college-days collaborations of directors, designers, actors, and playwrights—fruitful shades of Mickey Rooney's "I've got an idea: Let's put on a show!"

The successes of the best helped beget others, and although some companies fold for lack of space or funds, new ones continue to emerge. Synergy sustains the renaissance. Not only do theaters share resources; the very existence of so many keeps a pool of talent in Chicago, contributes to ever-increasing audiences, prompts private financial backing, and makes drama criticism a growth industry.

In autumn, the Joseph Jefferson Awards Committee honors excellence in local professional theater with Chicago's equivalent of the Tony Awards. Established in 1968 and named for Joseph Jefferson III, a member of the first professional company to play Chicago in 1837, the 40-member committee also maintains a noncompetitive Citations Wing to recognize achievements by non-Equity (*i.e.,* nonunion) groups.

Some theaters offer four- to six-play subscription seasons that run from around October through June; others feature open-ended engagements and/or operate year-round. Established companies usually perform Wednesday or Thursday through Sunday; smaller ones, only on weekends. Some have no space of their own and play wherever and whenever they can. The League of Chicago Theaters, a theatrical umbrella organization, maintains the HOT TIX booth (west side of State Street between Madison and Monroe Streets; 977-1755), which sells half-price, day-of-performance tickets to theater, music, and dance events throughout the Chicago area.

These listings are, of necessity, partial, excluding most college and community groups, city arts activities, the Chicago Park District's extensive drama programs, and the growing number of comedy troupes. For up-to-date information and reviews of current shows, consult *Chicago* magazine, the *Reader,* and the daily newspapers.

Houses

Unless otherwise indicated, these theaters have proscenium-arch stages.

Arie Crown Theatre
McCormick Place
23rd St. and Lake Shore Dr.
791-6000

Big Broadway musicals (usually road companies with big stars; occasionally try-outs on their way to the

Big Apple) are the mainstay of this 4,312-seat house with limited visibility from any but the first 15 or so rows. Static-ridden, tinny-sounding body microphones and often inadequately rehearsed orchestras make bad acoustics worse, but the 1981 production of Sweeney Todd proved that the theater has possibilities. Visiting ballets, operas, acrobats, and others sometimes play here. The Chicago Tribune Charities' annual production of The Nutcracker does, too.

Athenaeum Theatre
2936 N. Southport Ave.
935-6860, 525-0709
St. Alphonsus Church owns this medium-sized theater (with a wonderfully painted fire curtain) and rents it out to the Chicago Opera Theater and various other performing groups. Acoustics are best in the center of the balcony.

Auditorium Theatre
70 E. Congress Pkwy.
922-2110
Adler and Sullivan's magnificent, 4,000-seat theater houses all types of entertainment—The Peking Opera, folk ballets from foreign countries, Fiddler on the Roof. Bring your opera glasses and Dramamine for the balconies! (See also Music; South of the River.)

Blackstone Theatre
60 E. Balbo Ave.
977-1700
Because Broadway comedies and dramas are not as big draws as musicals, the Shubert organization books them into this relatively small (1,400-seat), but beautifully ornate, 1910 house.

Civic Theatre
20 N. Wacker Dr.
346-0270
The Art Deco minimasterpiece (906 seats) at the north end of Samuel Insull's magnum opus is seldom used, but is a wonderful space for medium-sized shows. (For the Civic Opera House, home of Lyric Opera of Chicago, see Music.)

Drury Lane Theatre Water Tower Place
175 E. Chestnut St.
266-0500
Like all the Drury Lanes (and ex-Drury Lanes), this is theater-in-the-square with ostentatious red décor. An inadequate pitch sometimes makes seeing the stage difficult. Shows range from star vehicles to original musicals (risked for the first time in 1981). Successful off-Loop plays sometimes transfer here.

11th Street Theatre
62 E. 11th St.
663-9465
This 530-seat theater is used primarily for Columbia College's increasingly noteworthy productions. With a renovation job, it could be a fine space.

Ivanhoe Theater
750 W. Wellington Ave.
975-7171
Once part of Chicago's premier dinner-theater (but shuttered for some time), this auditorium has been revamped (with 395 seats and a three-quarter-thrust stage) to house touring off-Broadway-type shows, transfers from smaller off-Loop theaters, and independent productions. Bar; wheelchair seating.

The Playhouse
McCormick Place
23rd St. and Lake Shore Dr.
791-6000
Underutilized 872-seat theater-in-the-square hosts plays (and an occasional musical) with or without big-name stars. Buffet dinner in the lobby for some shows.

Shubert Theatre
22 W. Monroe St.
977-1700
Showplace for Broadway musicals such as Chorus Line and Evita, the opulent, 2,000-plus-seat theater began as a vaudeville house in 1906. Pick your seats carefully, avoiding pillars and the second balcony.

Studebaker Theatre
418 S. Michigan Ave.
Often dark, the comfortable, 1,200-seat house has been Michigan Ave.'s white elephant. When in operation, it houses touring plays and small-scale musicals.

Victoria Theater
3145 N. Sheffield Ave.
883-0008
After many years and many uses, "The Vic," built in 1912, is being restored as a 1,400-seat theater (complete with orchestra pit and huge fly loft) to accommodate performances by students in the fledgling, in-house school of performing and variety arts, outside groups, and concerts.

World Playhouse
410 S. Michigan Ave.
922-5101
The 1898 Fine Arts Building's Music Hall (see South of the River) booked recitals, concerts, lectures, and plays until becoming a cinema in 1933. Falling on hard times decades later, it closed in 1972. It was refurbished along original lines and reopened as a legitimate theater in 1980. With 585 seats, it is an ideal compromise between small off-Loop houses and large downtown ones. Presently home to Travel Light Productions (see below).

Major theater groups

Unless otherwise noted, these theaters seat 150 to 200 persons, and the stages are more or less three-quarter thrust.

Apollo Theater Center
2540 N. Lincoln Ave.
935-6100
The handsome, 330-seat theater with a striking lobby was the first, all-new commercial house spawned by the 1970's off-Loop movement. The policy of presenting premières and musical revues that aim for mass appeal and financial success has been virtually supplanted by the practice of bringing in proven moneymakers from elsewhere. Part of the Apollo Group, a fledgling but vast commercial enterprise. Poor sight lines from the sides. Although the building is new, it lacks wheelchair access.

Body Politic Theatre
2261 N. Lincoln Ave.
871-3000, 348-7901
The granddaddy of off-Loop theaters moved to Lincoln Ave. in 1969 and almost closed because of financial problems in 1980. Reprieved, it mounts a varied subscription season in the revamped 182-seat upstairs theater and sometimes rents the space to other groups, continuing the policy of hosting outside companies that brought in the first production of the Organic Theater's Warp! and Paul Sills's Dream Theater in the early '70s. BP productions range from duds to delights; some, such as Alan Gross's Lunching and Steve Wade's Banjo Dancing, have gone on to long runs elsewhere. BP offers community outreach programs, has a lobby art gallery, and sponsors an annual street fair.

Court Theatre
5535 S. Ellis Ave.
962-7300, 962-7005
Completed in late 1981, CT's splendid, 250-seat theater with state-of-the-art light, sound, and stage facilities makes an ideal home for the resident professional company's topnotch productions of established plays. Five-play subscription series during the school year. Court's outdoor summer season of classics has been trimmed, but at least one show is presented in the lovely Hutchinson Court (5706 S. University Ave.). Also at the University Ave. address, Court Studio productions alternate between the intimate, 124-seat New Theatre and the third-floor, less adequate Reynolds Club. Wheelchair seating at the Ellis Ave. theater.

Goodman Theatre
200 S. Columbus Dr.
443-3800, TDD 443-3820
A gift to The Art Institute of Chicago from the parents of Kenneth Sawyer Goodman, a dramatist-poet who died in World War One, Chicago's resident regional theater has been producing a wide range of classical and contemporary plays for more than half a century. Under Gregory Mosher's artistic direction, the last few main-stage seasons have brought intriguing shows, as well as a few extraordinary duds. The annual A Christmas Carol is always a hit. With lots of leg room for the 683 seats, a proscenium-arch stage, and excellent sight lines, the theater is a delight. The 135-seat studio houses experimental or developing productions and special events, such as visits by the Kuklapolitans. Goodman offers study guides and extensive program notes; a wide range of adult-education classes, lectures, and workshops; braille programs, signed performances, special

parking, and other facilities to make the theater accessible to the handicapped. Ingrid's, a restaurant in the rehearsal room, is open for a before-theater buffet. Goodman School of Drama is now part of DePaul University, and Goodman/DePaul Children's Theatre shows are staged at the theater.

Organic Theater Company
3319 N. Clark St.
327-5588
Artistic director Stuart Gordon calls the Organic "the theater that never ceases to amaze." Since 1970, the company has been bombarding audiences with productions filled with special effects, action-packed world premières, revivals of its own works, and original adaptations of nondramatic material, such as Bleacher Bums and the three-part, sci-fi epic Warp! Taking its name from Stanislavsky's organic process of theater, the ensemble often works closely with Chicago writers to develop plays, for example, the 1974 first professional production of David Mamet's Sexual Perversity in Chicago. The Organic moved to the Buckingham Theater on Clark St. in 1981, creating a 250-seat house that is a perfect arena for its brand of theater. In addition, a 50-seat cabaret showcases local groups.

Second City
1616 N. Wells St.
337-3992
Chicago's venerable comedic institution got its start in Hyde Park bars and has been holding forth on Wells St. for more than two decades. The litany of famous alumni is mind-boggling, and some terrific performers still tread the boards. Nowadays, the troupe mounts one or two new revues a year: a series of set skits, the funniest of which

are often the songs. There is very little improvisation, except, perhaps, in the free routine-development sessions following regular shows some evenings. Second City also has a rollicking children's theater (929-6288), with plenty of improvisation and audience participation to delight adults, too, and a touring company.

Steppenwolf Theatre Company

2851 N. Halsted St.
472-4141
Steppenwolf has become one of the city's best companies in just seven years. It is also one of the few true ensembles of actors, playwrights, directors, and designers; and it chooses plays—classics, new ones, neglected ones—suited to the considerable talents of the young group. Outstanding productions like Waiting for Lefty, Say Goodnight, Gracie, and Balm in Gilead have drawn raves from critics and audiences alike. In addition to an almost year-round season, Steppenwolf offers late-night shows and classes.

Travel Light Productions

World Playhouse
410 S. Michigan Ave.
922-5101
Michael Cullen began TL as a pub-touring troupe with $52 and ten volunteers in 1974. After several years at the Theatre Building mounting 1940s and '50s revivals and bringing in such hits as Say Goodnight, Gracie and Gretchen Cryer's I'm Getting My Act Together and Taking It on the Road, TL has become an independent producing organization, in addition to one staging its own shows at the 585-seat, proscenium-stage World.

Victory Gardens Theater

2257 N. Lincoln Ave.
871-3000, 549-5788
Started in 1974 to stem the flow of professional talent from Chicago, each season the VG stages at least four premières (often by Chicago playwrights), as well as interesting revivals. Noteworthy new plays have included Jeffrey Sweet's Porch and Ties. Productions usually are first-rate, although some scripts have needed more polish. VG bought the downstairs half of the Body Politic building in 1981; the revamped 195-seat main-stage theater is quite comfortable. Shows in the 50- to 75-seat studio space are varied, some showcasing the talents of students enrolled in a full program of theater classes. The free Readers Theater (alternate Sun. nights) provides a forum for the development of new works by local playwrights. Wheelchair accessible; braille programs; signed performances.

Wisdom Bridge Theatre

1559 W. Howard St.
743-6442
Founded in 1974 by actor-playwright David Beaird and named for a painting, this Far North Side theater is off the beaten path but always worth the trip. Under Robert Falls's artistic direction, it has achieved great success with fine productions that range from classics to contemporary plays. In 1981, the second floor was completely renovated, a proscenium-arch stage installed, the seating of the house increased to 196, and the lobby nicely decorated. What was once a fire inspector's nightmare now looks as established as can be. Classes geared to working professionals are available (743-4172).

Others around town

Absolute Theatre Company

3224 N. Clark St.
883-1699, 871-3754
After a bang-up start with Holy Ghosts in 1981, Warner Crocker's group opened this small theater in 1982 to present proven and new plays, children's theater, and some late-night shows.

Amistad Productions

2138 E. 75th St.
734-0383
A professional black theater-company-in-the-making eschews domestic melodrama in favor of off-beat pieces with broader appeal. Proficient actors.

Atrium Theater

3544 N. Clark St.
975-7711
Productions of new plays and musicals by members of the Playwrights' Center help local authors develop their works. Evening play readings are open to the public and sometimes lead to productions. Playwriting classes; actors' workshop and lab; kids' theater.

Beacon St. Playhouse

4520 N. Beacon St.
561-7300
Under the artistic direction of well-known Chicago actor and playwright William J. Norris, this theater produces classics from all periods. The comfortable, 175-seat, three-quarter-round house has steep rises and good sight lines.

Black Arts Celebration (BAC)

39 S. La Salle, Suite 825
663-9580
Education through entertainment: This community organization produces plays (as well as radio, slide, and video shows) about social problems. Performances given throughout the city and suburbs.

Black Ensemble Theater Corporation

1655 N. Burling St.
751-0263

Started in 1975, actress Jackie Taylor's group (probably best known for A Black Musical) presents plays reflecting the black experience. Taylor is one of the driving forces behind black theater in Chicago.

Black Visions Theatre Company

Parkway Community House
500 E. 67th St.
493-1305 (after 5 p.m.)

Black community theater stages plays by blacks, about blacks, with blacks, and for blacks in a 120-seat theater.

Blackbird Theatre

5845 N. Broadway
248-3434

Having gotten off to an intriguing start with experimental productions in 1982, this group continues to focus on new scripts. The largish theater is also available for rent by other companies.

Blackstreet U.S.A. Puppet Theatre

223 W. Washington St., 4th floor
372-0543

Former Kungsholm Miniature Grand Opera puppeteer Gary Jones's innovative theater combines mime, puppetry, and dance. Exquisite, handmade, three-foot-tall puppets, attached to their always-visible puppeteers by slender metal rods, perform everything from Broadway musicals to jazz ballets and Jones's original fairy tales. As much for adults as for kids, the shows can be seen in the large loft on Fri. and Sat. nights, except when the group is on tour.

Chicago City Theatre Company

410 S. Michigan, 4th floor
663-3618

Dedicated to creating a thoroughly integrated, language-oriented theater, the resident company stages low-budget, more-inventive-than-good productions that run the gamut from classics to evenings of one-acts and poetry. Sixty-nine discarded seats from the Blackstone Theater were used to furnish the small room with a proscenium-arch stage at one end. Shallow rises; only fair sight lines. CCTC is affiliated with the Joel Hall Dancers and the New School for the Performing Arts. Groups can arrange to discuss plays with the actors before or after performances.

Chicago Comedy Showcase

1055 W. Diversey Pkwy.
348-1101

Sit on the church's pews to see comedy groups, stand-up comedians, jugglers, magicians, and more. Bring your own refreshments.

Chicago Premiere Society

c/o Kingsley Day,
420 W. Melrose St.
477-9075

They don't have their own theater, but Philip LaZebnik and Kingsley Day, who write rather bizarre musicals, are the Chicago Premiere Society. Their Byrne, Baby, Byrne "packed them in" at Zanies (1548 N. Wells St.) for more than two years, and their other inventions can be seen at various locations.

Chicago Theatre Company

2850 N. Clark St.
935-4945

Though predominantly black, Charles Finister's company aims to attract a mixed audience with classic and experimental plays. It may be best known for Jefferson Award-winning productions of Athol Fugard's Boesman and Lena and Leroi Jones's Dutchman. Workshops and staged readings, too.

City Lit Theater Company

2520 N. Lincoln Ave.
935-1429

Started by Arnold Aprill, David Dillon, and Lorell Wyatt in 1979, this company presents concert readings and full-stage productions of adaptations of literature, original works, and scripts by language-oriented playwrights.

The Commons Theatre Center

6443 N. Sheridan Rd.
465-3030

Actors Judith Easton and Michael Nowak and playwright Kathleen Thompson created CTC in 1980, converting a 2nd-floor studio in the Granada Theatre building into a little theater with an airy art-gallery lobby. Produces new plays and a few musicals, which tend to be witty and humane.

The Company

2856 N. Halsted St.
283-8483

Small ensemble (whose members all studied together) focuses on new plays and adaptations of nondramatic material.

Equity Library Theatre of Chicago
360 N. Michigan Ave., Room 1401
641-0393
Started in 1952 to provide exposure for Actors' Equity (the theatrical union) members, ELT showcases their talents in staged readings, excerpts, and short plays, and conducts workshops for professionals at a minimal cost. Free performances are at the CPL Cultural Center and branch libraries.

E.T.A. Creative Arts Foundation
7558 S. Chicago Ave.
752-3955
Both a school and a company, this group produces plays and musicals that speak to the black experience. Readers' theater, too.

Facets Performance Ensemble
1517 W. Fullerton Ave.
281-9075
Branch of Facets Multimedia. The avant-garde troupe trains intensively and produces unusual, evocative, poetic pieces, such as The Book of Lear, *developed in the Sahara desert, and* Macondo, *developed in the Colombian jungle.*

Free Shakespeare Company
1608 N. Wells St.
337-1025
Lively ensemble applies improvisational and experimental techniques to a repertory of Shakespeare and other classics.

Free Street Theater
620 W. Belmont Ave.
880-5151
Using a showmobile, FST brings musical skits with messages to parks, shopping centers, schools, and almost anywhere else. Audience participation is a big part of the show. Free Street Too, an ensemble of actors who are over 65 years old, performs separately and with FST.

The Huron Theater
1608 N. Wells St.
266-7055
Young company, that's worth watching, concentrates on intelligent productions of contemporary and new works (some by its members) that might otherwise not be performed. Late-night shows, too.

Imagination Theater
7535 N. Washtenaw Ave.
262-4292
Founded in 1966, Eunice Joffe and Blanche Stein's group develops educational-participatory programs geared to elementary-school children, senior adults, and the handicapped.

Kuumba Professional Theatre
72 E. 11th St.
461-9000
Val Gray Ward started Kuumba in 1968 to further the black liberation struggle through art controlled entirely by blacks. Besides pioneering a free-form Ritual Theatre, the group has produced numerous plays by celebrated and less-known authors to educate blacks about black experiences. The quality of the shows varies, but Kuumba is one of the most established of the city's many black theatrical troupes. Classes and community programs, too. Performances are at 218 S. Wabash Ave.

LaMont Zeno Theatre
1512 S. Pulaski Rd.
277-9582
Stages a variety of black plays, some of them unusual and fascinating. Located at the Better Boys Foundation, LaMont Zeno also hosts productions by other companies, maintains an art gallery, and runs a children's theater.

Latino Chicago Theater Company
953 W. Grace St.
929-3184
Started by the Victory Gardens Theater in 1979 with a grant from CBS, the city's first professional Latin-American theater company is now independent, maintains several ensembles, tours throughout the city, and performs at its own space. Traditional and original plays about the Latin-American experience here and in Latin America are performed in Spanish, English, and bilingually. Scripts are sometimes weak, but the productions are usually redeeming. Classes, too.

Lavage Theatre Company
3430 N. Elaine Pl.
883-1689
Produces new experimental plays, many by artistic director Bob Dodd, at various locations.

National Marionette Company
The Puppet Parlor
5301 N. Damen Ave.
774-2919, 989-0308
Ralph Kipniss, his staff, and more than 1,000 handmade, beautifully costumed puppets, ranging from 28 inches to 8 feet tall, present everything from classics and fairy tales to adult nightclub shows. Weekend performances (by reservation) and workshops. They also spend part of their time on the road.

New Broadway Theatre
3212 N. Broadway
472-4488
Mounts Chicago premières (with local talent) of shows that have been successful in New York or Los Angeles.

New Concept Theatre
5143 S. Harper Ave.
288-4233
Marcus Nelson's group presents new plays, some by Nelson himself, in the basement of St. Paul and the Redeemer Church, 4945 S. Dorchester Ave. Aims for a mixed audience.

New Haven Playhouse Company
2956 N. Racine Ave.
327-5550
Secessionists from St. Nicholas's faculty started this school in late 1980 and offer classes for kids, amateurs, aspiring professionals, and actors who want to sharpen their skills. A professional ensemble produces mostly modern plays, sometimes quite stunningly.

Old Town Players
c/o Frank Carioti,
503 W. Aldine Ave.
645-0145
Chicago's oldest community theater began in 1933 and, between 1967 and 1981, staged more than 50 shows, ranging from classics to contemporary plays and musicals, at a North Park Ave. church. OTP lost its lease in 1981 and hopes to build a community center for the performing arts at the intersection of North, Ogden, and Larrabee.

Pary Production Company
1225 W. Belmont Ave.
327-5252, 248-8151
In its small Theatre Building space, Pary produces new and avant-garde plays that probably wouldn't otherwise be seen.

Pegasus Players
Edgewater Presbyterian Church
1020 W. Bryn Mawr Ave.,
2nd floor
271-2638
This outgrowth of teacher Arlene Crewdson's college drama classes presents six productions a year—classics, original musicals, and new works by Chicago playwrights—in a cozy, 90-seat theater. More enthusiasm than polish, but open auditions turn up some good actors. Hosts ethnic dance and theater groups, maintains a touring troupe, and offers classes for kids and adults.

Performance Community
1225 W. Belmont Ave.
327-5252, 929-7367
Originally the nationally touring Dinglefest Theatre Company, Byron Schaffer, Jr.'s group found a permanent home in an old warehouse in 1976 and converted it to the Theatre Building: three theaters, a gallery, and offices. PC produces only new plays, frequently working with the playwrights on their development, and solicits audience response in post-performance discussions. Most of the plays need a lot more development, but productions are generally okay.

Performers Arena
Theatre Shoppe
2636 N. Lincoln Ave.
929-6288
Storefront theater offers workshops in improvisation and produces mostly new and experimental works, some of which feature improvisational techniques and workshop students.

Philbin's Little Theatre
4541 W. Peterson Ave.
777-5394
Children and teen-agers at this theater and ballet school perform musicals, comedies, and dramas in the 130-seat theater.

Prop. Thtr. Cor.
3443 N. Lincoln Ave.
248-6986
Offbeat company of about 15 members produces old and new plays (often with political overtones) in repertory at a tiny storefront theater. Some highs, some lows. Late-night performances, too.

The Puppet Place
1656 W. Cortland St.
278-1600
With a cast of hundreds at its disposal, the Puppet Place has been delighting children and adults since 1970 with adaptations of well-known stories, combining mime, dance, puppetry, opera, drama, and music. It also offers classes, apprenticeships, workshops, and touring shows. Antique and foreign puppets are on display in the storefront theater. Reservations suggested.

Remains Theatre
1034 W. Barry Ave.
549-7725
Formed in 1979, this dedicated company of actors and tech people has experienced a meteoric rise by presenting Chicago premières of unusual, experimental plays, which most established groups won't touch. Productions are challenging and thought-provoking.

Shakespeare Festival of Chicago
1118 W. Pratt Ave.
761-3707
This ensemble (with guest artists) performs Shakespeare and other classics at various locations.

Theatre First
Athenaeum Theater
2936 N. Southport Ave.
792-2226, 528-7507
This all-volunteer, completely self-supporting group, formed in 1956, mounts three quite credible shows (plays and musicals) a year. Inexpensive tickets.

Suburban and outlying

American Players Theatre
Route 3, Spring Green, Wis.
608-588-7401
Started in 1980, this ambitious, very professional company under the artistic direction of Randall Duk Kim is working its way through Shakespeare's plays chronologically, presenting three to six plays in revolving repertory from June through early October each year. Other classics, too. Charming outdoor setting; mosquito-repellent towelettes are issued with programs.

Candlelight Dinner Playhouse
5620 S. Harlem Ave., Summit
496-3000

William Pullinsi, with his mother and grandfather, began the country's first dinner theater in 1959, and the present building, with the first dinner-theater elevator stage, opened in 1964. Rather small, it makes choreography for the major musical revivals difficult. About four shows a year (12-week runs) feature Chicago-area talent and are fairly standard dinner-theater fare. Show-only tickets available for many performances.

Centre East
7701 N. Lincoln Ave., Skokie
673-6300

Saved from the bulldozer by local residents, this 1,240-seat house with a proscenium-arch stage offers subscription series that bring in a variety of plays, as well as dance and musical attractions. The theater also is rented to outside groups, as are rehearsal spaces, and other artistic facilities.

Chateau Louise Playhouse
Ill. 31, West Dundee
426-8000

Resort theater books comedies with big-name stars and, quite frequently, the Second City's second-string troupe. The 500-seat house is equipped with cocktail tables (and serves drinks) for that cabaret atmosphere.

Chicagoland Theatrical Troupe
8708 Ridgeway Ave., Skokie
674-1959

Young people from all over the Chicago area perform two Broadway musicals a year at Centre East, 7701 N. Lincoln Ave., Skokie. Some are so talented they go on to Broadway. The group started in 1973 as a Chicago Board of Education program and was picked up by a group of teachers when the board dropped it three years later.

Drake Theatre Repertory
Drake Theatre
Barat College
700 Westleigh Rd., Lake Forest
295-2620

Although affiliated with the college, this is a professional theater, not a student one, that does summer productions of classics, both old and new.

The Drama Group
330 W. 202nd St., Chicago Heights
755-3444

One of the country's oldest continuously operating community theaters (more than 50 years) stages three "commercial," family-oriented shows at Bloom Township High School and three studio shows at its own theater each year. Open auditions; completely amateur.

Drury Lane South
2500 W. 95th St., Evergreen Park
779-4000

South Side, red-plush home of star vehicles. For information about periodic children's theater here and at the McCormick Place Playhouse, call 274-7881.

Festival Theatre
605 Lake St., Oak Park
524-2050

Shakespeare and other classics are the mainstays of this group, which started in 1975 to present the Bard outdoors. Summer shows at Austin Gardens (Forest Ave. at Lake St.) are quite good, but traffic noise necessitates microphones that function imperfectly and seem inappropriate in an outdoor setting. Bring a picnic and insect repellent.

Forum Theatre
5620 S. Harlem Ave., Summit
496-3000

This 423-seat theater adjacent to the Candlelight Dinner Playhouse is, perhaps, best known for its long-playing (several years) production of John Powers's Do Black Patent Leather Shoes Really Reflect Up?

Illinois Theatre Center
400 Lakewood Blvd., Park Forest
481-3510

From the basement of the Park Forest Library, this professional theater presents a six-play main-stage season (everything from Neil Simon to Sam Shepard), four or five workshop productions, three children's theater ones, three Summerfest shows, and a free outdoor Shakespeare festival. The center also offers classes, a summer program for kids, discussion groups, and more.

Marriott's Lincolnshire Theatre
Ill. 21 (Milwaukee Ave.), Lincolnshire
634-0200

Productions of major musicals with Chicago-area performers at what was originally the Drury Lane North are usually quite decent. Dinner packages with the hotel are available.

The Next Theatre Co.
Noyes Cultural Arts Center
927 Noyes St.,
Evanston
475-1875
*Started by Brian Finn and
Harriet Spizziri in 1981,
NTC is developing a fine
track record with modern
classics and contemporary
plays.*

North Light
Repertory Company
2300 Green Bay Rd.,
Evanston
869-7278
*Well-balanced five-play
seasons draw subscribers
from all over the city and the
North Shore to a 298-seat
auditorium in a former
grade school. Each year
brings comedy, tragedy,
mystery, plays that were hits
off-Broadway, and one new
work. In between regular
productions, the "Satellite
Season" offers staged
readings of three new plays.*

Opus Mime Ensemble
551 Custer Ave.,
Evanston
491-9709
*A stylistic cross between
the Peking Opera and the
Pilobolus Dance Theatre,
Scott Shepherd's small
troupe presents mimed versions of myths, legends,
poems, and folk ballads.
Gymnastics are the prime
source of imagery, with
masks and some symbolic
props.*

Paramount Arts Centre
11 E. Galena Blvd.,
Aurora
896-6666, 896-7676
*Broadway musicals, groups
such as the Guthrie Theater,
classical music including
the Chicago Symphony
Orchestra, country-West-
ern stars, and film classics
are all on tap at this glorious
Art Deco theater, which was
once a movie palace and is
now on the National
Register of Historic Places.*

Pheasant Run Theatre
Ill. 64, St. Charles
261-7943
*The play selection is more
interesting and the productions are better than one
would expect at this 349-
seat dinner theater. Nonetheless, local actors who
seem brilliant at in-town
theaters may come off as
only good out here.*

Piven Theatre Workshop
Noyes Cultural Arts Center
927 Noyes St.,
Evanston
866-6597
*Theater games and scene
study through improvisation
are the backbone of Byrne
and Joyce Piven's work-
shops. The company, made
up of professional actors
and workshop students,
specializes in a unique
brand of story theater, using
great works of literature
such as Chekhov's stories.
The Young People's (high-
school age) and Junior
(junior-high) Companies
apply similar techniques to
Greek myths, American
tales, and so forth. Byrne
Piven is a well-known, excellent actor.*

Practical Theatre
Company
703 Howard St.,
Evanston
1608 N. Wells St.
328-4151
*Started by Northwestern
University graduates in
1979, this creative, energetic group presents new
and seldom-produced
plays at its 40-seat Evanston storefront and rollicking,
improvisational revues at a
cabaret in Old Town's Piper's Alley.*

Shady Lane
Farm Playhouse
U.S. 20, Marengo
815-568-7218
*More than 40 years of Neil
Simon-style comedies in a
barn theater!*

Theatre of the Deaf
8207 Crawford Ave.,
Skokie, Ill. 60076
*For-profit touring company,
composed of the deaf and
the hearing, advocates
museum-program ac-
cessibility by presenting
signed and spoken lec-
tures, plays, and improvisations at museums all over
the Midwest. Workshops
available for groups.*

Theatre of
Western Springs
Hillgrove and Hampton,
Western Springs
246-3380
*More than 50 years old, this
community theater is known
for high-quality produc-
tions of light comedies and
serious contemporary
plays. Auditions aren't
open: aspiring actors, who
must be season-ticket holders, have to participate in
studio workshops from
which all the roles are cast.
Children's theater, too.*

Woodstock Music
Theatre Festival
Woodstock Opera House
121 Van Buren St.,
Woodstock
815-338-5300
*This group presents new
and innovative musicals
during the summer at the
charming, restored, turn-of-
the-century opera house,
which is comfortably small
and offers good sight lines
from most seats. Before the
show, browse at the an-
tiques shops, stroll around
Woodstock's central
square, and listen to the
town band.*

Sports

From the sidelines

Until the 1981 Sting triumph, no present-day Chicago professional team had garnered a major title since the Bears clinched the 1963 National Football Championship! Yet, despite a record recommending a shift of allegiances to quilting bees and flower shows, Chicago remains one of the nation's best sports towns. Every major professional sport is contested here, and fledgling gladiators stage bargain-priced battles in school gyms and stadiums year-round.

Baseball

Chicago Cubs
Wrigley Field
1060 W. Addison St.
248-7900
Ivy-covered outfield walls, a manually operated scoreboard, and seating that puts fans on top of the action make Wrigley Field the country's most charming ballpark, but the National League team has been held together with bale rope and chewing gum for years. The poor bedraggled Cubs play all their home games in the pitiless glare of the sun, where they can't hide their mediocrity, because the Wrigley family wouldn't spring for lights or decent players. The late 1981 conveyance to the moneyed Tribune Company, however, may signal a rejuvenation, although pressure is strong to keep the North Side the country's last holdout against night games. TW (call ahead) F

Chicago White Sox
Comiskey Park
324 W. 35th St.
924-1000
When baseball was the all-American game, Chicagoans asked strangers whether they were Cubs or Sox fans before inquiring about such trivialities as ethnicity, religion, or politics. Such die-hards still exist, but now more fans follow fortune's flip-flops from North to South Side and back. Current ownership isn't afraid to spend money in the free-agent market and on the farm system. So far, the result has been a team that looks better on paper than on the field. For many Chicago fans, that's enough. Although ancient, Comiskey Park features a state-of-the-art scoreboard and a picnic area. With the team's recent improvement, good tickets are sometimes hard to get; buy them in advance for important games. TWF

Basketball

Chicago Bulls
Chicago Stadium
1800 W. Madison St.
346-1122
Previously plagued with front-office problems, the Bulls are approaching respectability, although the cavernous home stadium is in an unsafe neighborhood, cheap seats are far from the play, beer is overpriced, and the hot dogs defy decorous description. For important contests, buy tickets well in advance from the box office or from Ticketron. PTW (call ahead) F

Football

Chicago Bears
Soldier Field
425 McFetridge Dr.
663-5408
Fans speak wistfully of the 1963 championship as a once-in-a-lifetime happenstance, but the Bears are improving. They might even be willing to experiment with such alien concepts as the forward pass to go with Walter Payton's brilliant running. The days when disputes over season tickets could throw estates into probate are gone, but paying a hefty surcharge to a downtown broker is still often the only way to get a seat in this wind-swept classical arena more suited to Christians-vs.-lions contests. With the departure of P. K. Wrigley, George Halas is the last of the old-line curmudgeons left in Chicago sports. PTW (call ahead) F

Chicago Blitz
Soldier Field
425 E. McFetridge Dr.
670-0100
There's a new kid on the block. George Allen, George Halas's old nemesis, heads up Chicago's entry in the new United States Football League and would like nothing more than to steal some of Papa Bear's thunder. Quality of play in the 12 team league won't measure up to the NFL but should be more wide-open in the style of the old American Football League. The season runs from early March to early July—a fact already noted by football nuts who, in the past, became comatose after Super Bowl Sunday.

Chicago Lions
Triton College Stadium
2000 Fifth Ave.,
River Grove
637-8993
The equivalent of a baseball AAA team, the Northern States Football League's 11 are unabashedly semipro. PTWF

Lincolnwood Chargers
Niles West
High School Stadium
Oakton at Edens Expwy.,
Skokie
274-4063
A 1982 addition to the Northern States Football League. PTWF

Golf

Butler National Golf Club
2900 York Rd.,
Oak Brook
539-4600
The Western Open, one of the oldest tournaments on the American tour, is usually played on this difficult course the first weekend in July. PWF

Hockey

Chicago Black Hawks
Chicago Stadium
1800 W. Madison St.
733-5300
Expansion teams have bypassed the Hawks, once the city's proudest franchise. A new coach and some promising rookies may help turn the clock back to those palmier days. Until then, good seats are fairly easy to come by. PTF

Horse racing

Arlington Park Race Track
Euclid Ave. and Wilke Rd.,
Arlington Heights
775-7800,
255-4200 (suburbs)
The Budweiser Million, the world's richest race, symbolizes the larger purses and improved backstretch conditions attracting better stables to local tracks. Only thoroughbreds race here, the classiest of the lot. Good number of races on turf. PTWF

Balmoral Park
Ill. 1 and Elmscourt Lane,
Crete
568-5700
The state dispenses racing dates with a parsimonious hand, eliminating competition between tracks, in theory to guarantee the public coffers' enrichment. Balmoral's distance from the other parks has won it year-round dates, with trotters running in winter, thoroughbreds in summer. PWF

Hawthorne Race Course
3501 S. Laramie Ave.,
Cicero
652-9400
Racing, a very popular early diversion, fostered outlying development, but Chicago outlawed the tracks in a fit of 19th-century morality. Naturally, the city limits were soon lined with tracks. Three remain after the spectacular Washington Park fire. A harness meet usually follows autumn's thoroughbreds here. PTW (call ahead) F

Maywood Park
North and 5th Aves.,
Maywood
626-4816
Strictly trotters; mostly in winter. PTWF

Sportsman's Park
3301 S. Laramie Ave.,
Cicero
242-1121
Prime summer harness dates after a long spring thoroughbred meet. PTWF

Polo

Oak Brook Polo Club
1000 Oak Brook Rd.,
Oak Brook
654-3060
On Wed., Fri., and Sun., from May to Oct., the beautiful people gather to watch outdoor tournament play. All the trappings, like tailgate parties, too. PF

Soccer

Chicago Sting
558-5425
World-class players made the 1981 North American Soccer League champions a consistent power. Lately, they've been suffering a brown-out. The summer outdoor season is split between Wrigley Field and Comiskey Park. For the winter season, the team hides from the elements in the Chicago Stadium. PTW (call ahead) F

National Soccer League
275-2850
Games between these tightly knit, ethnically organized teams enliven various public parks (and nearby bars afterward) on warm weekends. Indoor play, too.

Tennis

Chicago Aces
Richard J. Daley
Bicentennial Plaza
337 E. Randolph Dr.
787-0606
The fledgling Aces represent the latest effort at bringing team tennis to Chicago. Men's and women's singles, men's and women's doubles, and mixed doubles make up each night's card. PT

Vehicle racing

Santa Fe Speedway
9100 S. Wolf Rd.,
near Willow Springs
839-1050
Stock cars burn up the track on warm weekend evenings. PWF

U.S. 30 Drag Strip
U.S. 30, 2 miles east of I-65,
Merrillville, Ind.
874-0700, 219-942-7142
The drags scream every clement Sun., March through May, and on Wed., Fri., and Sun., June through Oct. PWF

College and university

DePaul University
Alumni Hall
1011 W. Belden Ave.
321-8010
For the last few seasons, the Blue Demons have given Chicago basketball fans something to cheer about as the team piled up victories until tournament time. Still, it's been fun riding the roller coaster with legendary coach Ray Meyer. The frenzy has obscured the winning seasons of almost every other DePaul varsity team. Tickets for the men's basketball games, held at the Rosemont Horizon, are scarce. PTF

Loyola University
Alumni Gymnasium
6525 N. Sheridan Rd.
274-1211,
274-3000, ext. 381
Although the Ramblers play consistently exciting basketball (some games are at the Rosemont Horizon), they labor in the Blue Demons' shadow. Even less attention is paid to Loyola's nationally ranked water-polo squad, a promising soccer side, or strong women's basketball and volleyball teams. PTF

North Park College
Gymnasium
Foster and Kedzie Aves.
583-2700, ext. 230
The Vikings nailed down three straight NCAA Division III basketball championships. In general, this Albany Park college plays with spirit, free from big-time pressures. PTF

Northwestern University
Dyche Stadium/
McGaw Hall
1501 Center St.,
Evanston
492-7070, 492-7503
If an athletic department shakeup changes the Wildcats' traditional spot as doormat for Big Ten basketball and football squads, the last easily obtainable tickets to see teams such as Michigan and Ohio State will disappear. NU fields a respectable track team, excellent field hockey and women's basketball teams, and the only local women's lacrosse side. PTWF

University of Chicago
Henry Crown Field House
5550 S. University Ave.
753-4431, 962-8364
The Monsters of the Midway are muggers now, and old castellated Stagg Field, sight of so many Maroon victories and cradle of the nuclear age, has been replaced with a demure, modern facility west of the field house. Today, football is played for fun, not fame, and the same holds true for cricket, crew, rugby, and all the other league or club activities. The U. of C. Track Club, a private organization open to nonstudents, is home to some of America's most talented competitors. T

University of Illinois at Chicago
UIC Pavilion
1140 W. Harrison St.
996-0460
With this new facility and NCAA Division I status in all major sports, UIC enters the big time. The tough hockey team keeps up with the likes of Wisconsin, and the gymnasts do well in the Windy City Gymnastics Meet, a national event they host each Nov. Less prestigious events are held at the Physical Education Building, 901 W. Roosevelt Rd. PTWF

F food   **P** parking   **T** public transportation   **W** wheelchair access

Joining in

The lake, parks, and forest preserves offer Chicagoans unrivaled athletic opportunities. Although the **Chicago Park District,** or **CPD** (294-2493), does little to encourage the simple enjoyment of nature, it pulls out all the stops for less pastoral endeavors, providing equipment, instruction, and team/league management. The **Cook County Forest Preserve,** or **CCFP** (261-8400, suburbs 366-9420), maintains sports grounds, but most of this green belt encircling the city is open space reminiscent of state parks. It's also free from the anachronistic "sports, the slum kids' salvation" syndrome that seems to be the guiding light of the Chicago Park District. Many of the larger suburbs also offer a very wide range of activities open to locals and nonresidents. Publicly owned facilities are the least expensive to use, but are often determinedly egalitarian, as are many charitable operations such as YMCAs and neighborhood clubs. The sheer number of programs and activities they offer is staggering, however, and they warrant exploration.

Fine-tuned bodies are "in," sweat has become chic, and an industry has evolved to cash in on the phenomenon. Health and racquet clubs service thousands of people who swore they would never take communal showers after college. They are also social centers—urban country clubs. Their suburban counterparts, bastions of golf, tennis, and cocktails, continue to flourish. Unlike at health clubs, however, membership usually involves more than merely buying in. The ultimate athletic/social exclusivity remains the old-boy clubs, such as the Illinois Athletic, Chicago Athletic, and Standard.

Fraternities devoted to almost any arcane athletic activity also abound. Some are just loose groups using public spaces; others are highly organized and have substantial physical plants. Sports-equipment stores (*see* Index or Yellow Pages) often have facilities of some sort and are frequently fonts of information. Associations dedicated to the well-being of a specific sport are usually eager to help you get involved.

Archery

CPD *has indoor and outdoor ranges; so do many shops. For a list of area clubs and facilities, write to the* **Illinois Archery Association,** *506 E. Locust St., Chatham, Ill. 62629.*

Backgammon

Pickup games at countless watering holes; join the **Backgammon Club of Chicago** *(Valerie Valentine, 782-0142); or stop by* **Gammon's of Chicago,** *2715 W. Peterson Ave. (271-8877), for tournament and casual play (hourly fee), sets, lessons, and so forth.*

Badminton

The **Chicago Metropolitan Badminton Association** *(Jim Wigglesworth, 736-1072) coordinates local clubs.*

Ballooning

Ninety-minute, daylight hot-air rides cost about $200 for two passengers. Check the Yellow Pages *or write to the* **Northeastern Illinois Balloon Association,** *Box 349, Deerfield, Ill. 60015, for information on rides and races.*

Baseball

Reserve a diamond for your own big game by calling the specific park well in advance; **CPD** *(294-2325) also has league information.*

Basketball

Every playground, school yard, and neighborhood club has a budding Mark Aguirre; the **CPD** *has an organized program.*

Bicycle racing

The **United States Cycling Federation** *(Jim Rossi, 889-3903) uses the bike track in* **Meadowhill Park,** *Maple Ave. and Waukegan Rd., Northbrook (291-2960), Thurs. evenings. On Fri. there is open stock racing from mid-May through late summer.*

Bicycling

A marked bike path traces most of Chicago's lakefront, and there are paths in the forest preserves. City-street bike-route markings should be ignored. The **Northeastern Illinois Planning Commission** *(454-0400) offers a six-county, bike-touring map package for $3;* **American Youth Hostels** *(327-8114) and the* **Sierra Club** *(431-0158) sponsor biking trips.*

Turin Bike Shop *(864-7660) keeps track of area touring and racing events.*

Billiards and pool

Most of the city's old-fashioned poolrooms have disappeared, as have their replacements, "family billiard centers." There's still plenty of action in neighborhood taverns, though, and tournaments at the **Illinois Billiard Club,** *2435 W. 71st St. (737-6655).*

Bird watching

The best source of information is the **Chicago Audubon Society** *(671-6446). For a recorded sightings message, call 675-8466; to turn stool pigeon after sighting a rare bird, phone 673-4295.*

Boardsailing

Lake Michigan is usually too calm for surfing and too rough for water skiing (which is expensive and requires a two-man boat crew), but it's fine for this increasingly popular sport, which has already swept Europe. **Midwest Boardsailing Unlimited,** *901 W. Irving Park Rd. (549-1199), provides instruction and equipment.*

Boating

The **U.S. Coast Guard Auxiliary** *(Elaine Hofer, 564-8262) offers classroom instruction in power boating and sailing, navigation, and water safety.* **American Youth Hostels** *(327-8114) conducts in-water sailing classes. The CPD's* **Rainbow Fleet** *(294-2320) gives you hands-on experience with small sailboats.* **CPD** *maintains boat-launching ramps at several harbors (launching any craft at other than designated sites is illegal) and dispenses harbor moorings with a scandal-tainted hand. The yacht clubs in public parks are private, as are the key-card*

controlled parking lots next to the harbors. How odd. Most of the **CCFP** waters prohibit motors. How nice.

Bowling

Join the company team, or see the Yellow Pages for a lane near you. Several are open 24 hours a day. The **CPD** *maintains greens for lawn bowling and bocci ball.*

Boxing

The **CPD** *(Bill Shay, 294-4766) offers all levels of instruction in the manly art at 24 field houses. The* **Catholic Youth Organization** *(421-8046) has several coaches and has been sponsoring contests since 1930. Both groups' championship bouts, along with the Chicago Tribune Charities'* **Golden Gloves Tournament** *(222-4300), are the best amateur action in town.*

Bridge

Call the **Chicago Contract Bridge Association** *(271-0133) for information on play and lessons.*

Canoeing

Rent or buy canoes, kayaks, racing shells, materials for building your own, car carriers, books, etc., and tap Ralph Frese's store of knowledge at the **Chicagoland Canoe Base,** *4019 N. Narragansett Ave. (777-1489). The* **Illinois Travel Information Center** *(793-2094) can tell you where to use all the gear;* **American Youth Hostels** *(327-8114) and the* **Sierra Club** *(431-0158) organize trips.*

Chess

Casual play during summer daylight hours at the **Lincoln Park Chess Pavilion** *near North Ave. Chess clubs (see Index or Yellow Pages) offer both casual and tournament play; the* **Illinois Chess Association** *(Helen Warren, 246-6665) has information on clubs and tournaments. The city's more intellectual (or pretentious) bars and coffeehouses also have boards.*

Cricket

You'll find wickets in several city and suburban parks. Call the **U.S. Cricket Association** *(Owen Murray, 721-2973) for more information.*

Darts

Look for telltale holes in the wall in your favorite tavern. (Irish and hip bars are the best bet.)

Fencing

The **United States Fencing Association** *(Joe Folker, 248-6785, 286-8824) organizes meets and tournaments. Both the* **Chicago Fencing Club** *(Sven Ahlstrom, 475-7344) and the* **Illinois Fencers Club** *(Erwin Guttman, 835-1888) give classes. The* **Discovery Center,** *2930 N. Lincoln Ave. (348-8120), has a complete program.*

Fishing

The **Illinois Department of Conservation** *(793-2070) publishes a booklet listing fishing areas, regulations, and tips, and sells the $7.50 annual license required for anglers over 16 years old. The* **CCFP** *also publishes a guide to fishing its waters. The* **CPD** *lagoons and lakefront fishing sites are open from Apr. to mid-Nov. (to mid-May for smelt). Bait shops (see Index or Yellow Pages) sell licenses, too.*

Football

*The **CPD** sponsors neighborhood league play. Several macho bars field tough touch teams.*

Gō

*Saturdays are the best time to catch masters of this ancient Japanese game of strategy at the **Chicago Gō Club** (588-8869).*

Golf

*Senior citizens and juniors pay reduced greens fees at the five **CPD** (294-2274) courses (only Jackson Park has 18 holes) and at the six 18-hole and two 9-hole **CCFP** courses. Many large suburbs also have courses. The Chicagoland Golf Course Guide, available at bookstores, evaluates more than 20. Naturally, the best are at country clubs, and although the Chicago Tribune regularly runs a list of those that welcome daily players, the very best are never open to nonmembers.*

Gymnastics

*Classes offered by the **CPD** vary in quality by field house. Many suburban park districts and YMCAs also give lessons. For information on scores of clubs and classes, send a stamped, self-addressed envelope to the **U.S. Gymnastics Federation Women's Committee for the State of Illinois,** c/o Viv Navratil, 8609 West 144th Pl., Orland Park, Ill. 60462, and indicate the level of instruction you want.*

Handball

*With 12 courts, the **Lattof YMCA,** 300 E. Northwest Hwy., Des Plaines (296-3376) is one of the best public facilities. Many health clubs also have courts. The **Chicago Metro Handball League** (Dick Sleeper, 927-3009), the city's largest league, fields about 30 teams. The **U.S. Handball Association** (Bob Peters, 673-4000) keeps a schedule of events in the area.*

Hiking

*During the summer and fall, experienced naturalists, biologists, and curators from the **Field Museum of Natural History** (922-9410, ext. 363) lead adults and families in one-day, weekend Kroc Environmental Field Trips to nearby nature preserves. **American Youth Hostels** (327-8114) and the **Sierra Club** (431-0158) also organize hikes. For information about the many trails in state parks, call the **Illinois Travel Information Center** (793-2094).*

Horseback riding

*Rent a mount (and buy the required license) at one of the private stables (see Yellow Pages) bordering the **CCFP's** 150 miles of year-round trails.*

Hunting

*Get the straight poop from the **Illinois Department of Conservation** (793-2070).*

Hurling

***Irish Imports** (637-3800) will tell you where to catch this rough-and-tumble Gaelic game.*

Ice hockey

*Get league information from the **Amateur Hockey Association of the United States** (William Peluse, 279-8658).*

Ice skating

*Almost every good-sized park district has a year-round rink and programs; there are a few private ones (see Yellow Pages). When the weather's right, you can skate outdoors at many flooded park meadows and at the **Richard J. Daley Bicentennial Plaza** (294-4792) in Grant Park, where you can rent skates.*

Judo/martial arts

*Judo is taught at many YMCAs and clubs. The **Chicago Judo Blackbelt Association** (Henry Okamura, 761-7027) sponsors tournaments and can recommend schools. Esoteric philosophic differences and economic self-interest make any blanket organization for other martial arts unthinkable. Karate, tae kwon do, and kung fu—all very aggressive fighting techniques—attract macho types. If a school offers contact karate and insists on a contract, forget it. Aikido and t'ai chi ch'uan are more meditative disciplines with systems of formalized exercises that have self-defense implications. For each of these, check the Yellow Pages, sample a lesson, and talk to students to find a comfortable spot.*

Mountain climbing

*Illinois has no mountains, but you can do some clambering at Starved Rock State Park and the Mississippi Palisades, and at Devil's Lake, Wis. The **Sierra Club** (431-0158) organizes climbs and provides some instruction, as does the **Chicago Mountaineering Club** (Judy Demkowicz, 863-5394), which also maintains a library on the subject and conducts monthly programs.*

Orienteering

It's not a Chinese martial art, but the pedestrian equivalent of sports-car rallies. The **Chicago Area Orienteering Club** (Richard Gaylord, 964-5634) offers activities for all skill levels. Basics are taught at **Indiana Dunes National Lakeshore** (Dave Zahller, 219-926-7561).

Parachuting

Update your insurance, then check the Yellow Pages.

Racquetball and squash

Park districts, YMCAs, and private clubs all have courts. The **Illinois State Racquetball Association** (Alan Shetzer, 371-7616) and the **Illinois Squash Racquets Association** (Jim Maguire, 726-2840, ext. 268) have information on tournaments.

Roller skating

The **Richard J. Daley Bicentennial Plaza** (294-4792) has outdoor skating in summer. Check the Yellow Pages for indoor rinks.

Rugby

The **Chicago Area Rugby Football Union** (Chuck Riley, 377-3103) fields 14 men's teams. Women should contact the **Chicago Women's Rugby Club** (Denise Uveges, 477-9736).

Running

Marathoners can get the low-down on events, clinics, races, and clubs from the **Chicago Area Runners' Association** (828-0524).

Scuba diving

YMCAs have instruction and conditioning sessions, as do most shops (see Yellow Pages). They are all good spots to hook up with other divers and to find out about outings.

Shooting

The **Lincoln Park Gun Club** (549-6490) welcomes nonmembers for trap and skeet shooting, but requires that everyone have an Illinois Firearm Owner Identification Card. So, too, will conscientious owners of the many suburban gun shops (see Yellow Pages) before they sell you arms or ammo, or let you use their ranges. They all have application blanks. The **Illinois State Rifle Association** (341-0432) has more information.

Skiing

Illinois is mostly too flat for Alpine, but forest preserves and park districts maintain cross-country trails and a few have compacted-trash-based downhill slopes. Cross-country lessons with equipment are available right in the Loop at the **Richard J. Daley Bicentennial Plaza** (294-4792). **American Youth Hostels** (327-8114) and the **Sierra Club** (431-0158) organize outings. The **Illinois Travel Information Center** (793-2094) and the **Chicago Metropolitan Ski Council** (P.O. Box 7926, Chicago, Ill. 60608) have suggestions, too, as do most ski shops (see Yellow Pages).

Snowmobiling

The **CCFP** (261-8400) has a list of designated areas that may be used if you have a permit. Dealers (see Yellow Pages) have more tips, and the **Illinois Association of Snowmobile Clubs** (Ron Hambly, 815-436-8688) will help you hook up with like-minded folks.

Soaring

Sailplane instruction, rental, and demonstration at **Hinckley Soaring** (815-286-7200).

Soccer

Not only can you see games at lots of parks, the **Illinois Soccer Association** (271-5416) has information on teams, leagues, and how you can join.

Softball

Sixteen-inch softball is as much a Chicago institution as deep-dish pizza, and it's played nowhere else. The **CPD** organizes summer leagues in the parks. Traditionally, some of the best games are at Clarendon Park, 4501 N. Clarendon Ave., and at Grant Park, where 16 diamonds are in almost constant use after work and on weekends. The **Amateur Softball Association** in Aurora (Ferris Reid, 892-0269) covers all types, including alien 12- and 14-inch softball games that are played with gloves, for cryin' out loud.

Sports car racing

The **Chicago Region Sports Car Club of America** (728-4466) keeps tabs on races, rallies, and meetings.

Square dancing

Get the lowdown on the hoe down from the **Metropolitan Chicago Association of Square Dancers** (437-5270) or the Yellow Pages.

Swimming

The **CPD** (294-2333) supervises the city's beaches and public pools with a heavy hand and gives lessons. Also check YMCAs, JCCs, and private health clubs. Most suburban facilities can be used on a daily-fee basis. Best of all, make friends with someone who has a pool.

Table tennis

Check out YMCAs, etc. For clubs see the Yellow Pages.

Tennis

The **CPD's** poorly maintained courts are usually crowded, but many are lighted for evening play; lessons are available (294-2312, 294-4790). Suburban park districts do better, but the best courts (and the most expensive) are at country and racquetball clubs. The **Chicago District Tennis Association** (834-3727) sponsors leagues and tournaments at all levels of play.

Tobogganing

The **CCFP** has five areas. Two runs at the **James Park Winter Sports Complex,** Oakton St. near Dodge Ave. (869-8111), are operated by the **Evanston Recreation Department** (328-2100, ext. 2395).

Volleyball

Every park, neighborhood club, and YMCA has courts. The regional office of the **U. S. Volleyball Association** (297-3815) keeps tabs on league play and tournaments.

Weightlifting

Few are the gyms without some iron to pump. Naturally, chic Nautilus equipment is found in private facilities, and dumbbells at the free ones.

Wheelchair sports

Contact **Chicagoland Wheelchair Sports,** c/o Bruce Karr, 1433 Coventry Rd., Schaumburg, Ill. 60195 (289-0200 or 490-1555), for information on activities.

"Gentlemen, start your pedals." The big race, 1901

Annual Events

"To everything there is a season." In Chicago that means more than flags waving on the Fourth of July, special exhibits at museums on holidays, or the change of perennials at conservatories. Indoors or outdoors, from the Loop to the sticks, *someone* is always staging *something*. These listings cover established events and some impulses, all of them vulnerable to the vagaries of time and fortune. Current information is best found monthly in *Chicago* and in the newspapers' weekend editions. A phone call is the best protection against disappointment. Compulsive planners might want free calendars of events from the **Illinois Department of Conservation** (annual *Preservation Calendar),* the **Illinois Office of Tourism** (semiannual *Calendar of Events*), the **Chicago Association of Commerce and Industry** (bimonthly Chicago-area *Headline Events*), or the **Chicago Council on Fine Arts** (monthly *Calendar of Events*). Many universities, theaters, museums, etc. publish calendars; most will put interested parties on their mailing lists. Although there is an admission charge for many events, the charge at festivities held on Chicago streets is actually a voluntary donation.

Frequently cited sites

The Adler Planetarium
1300 S. Lake Shore Dr.
322-0300

Arlington Park Exposition Center
Arlington Park Race Track
Euclid and Wilke Rds.,
Arlington Heights
255-4300, 775-7800

Brookfield Zoo
8400 W. 31st St.,
Brookfield
242-2630

Clarence Buckingham Fountain
Grant Park
Congress and Columbus

Chicago Public Library Cultural Center
78 E. Washington St.
744-6630

Chicago Stadium
1800 W. Madison St.
733-5300

Evanston Art Center
2603 Sheridan Rd.,
Evanston
475-5300

Grant Park
Lakefront east of the Loop

International Amphitheatre
4220 S. Halsted St.
927-5580

McCormick Place-On-the-Lake
23rd St. and Lake Shore Dr.
791-7000

Museum of Science and Industry
57th St. and Lake Shore Dr.
684-1414

Navy Pier
Lakefront at Grand Ave.

Old Orchard Shopping Center
Skokie Blvd. and Golf Rd.,
Skokie
674-7070

Rosemont Horizon
6920 N. Mannheim Rd.,
Rosemont
635-6600

Winnetka Community House
620 Lincoln Ave.,
Winnetka
446-0537

January

Forget the winter chill with vacation thoughts: Visit the sporting-goods shows and indoor tennis tournaments. But don't miss the mayor's annual speech: "We're doing a great job plowing the streets."

Chicago Boat, Sports & RV Show: *Celebrities and entertainment enliven the Midwest's biggest. Early Jan. McCormick Place. 836-4777.*

Chicago Challenge of Champions: *Men's international pro-tennis stars. Rosemont Horizon. 635-9800.*

Chicago Fishing, Vacation, and Sports Show: *Enough literature to last until the ponds thaw. Arlington Park Exposition Center. 963-4810.*

Chinese New Year: *Chinatown festivities; also specialties served at Chinese restaurants citywide (see Chicago). Sometimes falls in Feb. 225-0234.*

The Jazz Fair: *An evening of jazz bands, jazz films, and more. Last Mon. Blackstone Hotel, 636 S. Michigan Ave. 664-4069.*

University of Chicago Folk Festival: *Many of the musicians are making their first Chicago appearances. Last weekend. Concerts at Mandel Hall, 5706 S. University Ave. Free workshops and hootenannies at Ida Noyes Hall, 1212 E. 59th St. 753-3567, 753-3591.*

February

Cabin-fever time. The snow's getting dirty and nobody can figure out what's closed on which President's birthday.

Black History Month: *Special programs and exhibits throughout the city, particularly at the Chicago Public Library Cultural Center; DuSable Museum of African American History, 740 E. 56th Pl. 947-0600; and the Museum of Science and Industry.*

Chicago Auto Show: *The world's largest and best attended. Nine days from late Feb. to early Mar. McCormick Place. 693-6630.*

Chicago Sports Show: *The area's oldest sporting exposition has lots of entertainment. International Amphitheatre.*

Elmhurst College's Mid-West College Jazz Festival: *Big-name artists give critiques, hold clinics, and sit in with the school's band during the final concert of this invitational competition. Last full weekend. 190 Prospect Rd., Elmhurst. 279-4100.*

Golden Gloves Tournament: *Chicago Tribune Charities sponsors these amateur bouts. Late Feb. to early Mar. Rosemont Horizon. 222-4300.*

Harlem Globetrotters: *See the big guys at the Chicago Stadium.*

Lincoln State Cat Club Show: *Third weekend. International Amphitheatre. 530-8808.*

Loop Alive: *A mayoral fest to banish downtown's winter doldrums. Has bargain-priced live entertainment. 644-7430.*

RV, Camping and Travel Show: *Retailers stir up wanderlust. Arlington Park Exposition Center. 934-8300 (Bill Kerwin).*

Silver Skates Derby: *Illinois's best speed skaters have vied in these events for more than 60 years. McFetridge Sports Arena, 3845 N. California Ave. 478-0210.*

Speed and Custom Car Show: *Enough chrome to dazzle. International Amphitheatre.*

Virginia Slims of Chicago: *These champions of women's tennis have come a long way, baby. International Amphitheatre. 787-0606.*

March

Circus lions and Pascal lambs (some years) verify the proverb. Sap rises in man and maple. Wait out winter at an antiques show.

America's Largest and Finest Antiques Show: *And modest, too! Also in Oct. Arlington Park Exposition Center. 219-367-2341.*

Chicago Antiques and Collectors' Show: Hobbies Magazine's big show. Also in Nov. The Conrad Hilton, 720 S. Michigan Ave. 939-4767.

City House: *Exhibits and advice on everything from minor repairs to full-scale restorations. McCormick Place West/Donnelley Hall, 23rd St. and King Dr. 644-7430.*

Ice Capades: *World champions trip the ice fantastic. Mid-Mar. Chicago Stadium.*

International Kennel Club Dog Show: *Lots of classy canines. Thirteenth weekend of the year. International Amphitheatre.*

Medinah Shrine Circus: *Three weeks of aerialists, clowns, and wild animals. Proceeds benefit the Shriners Crippled Children's Hospital. Medinah Temple, 600 N. Wabash Ave. 642-9300.*

Midwest Boat and Resort Show: *Last of the season. Arlington Park Exposition Center.*

St. Joseph's Day: *Some Italian churches and restaurants (and some Polish ones) set out feasts in honor of the patron saint of the poor. Mar. 19.*

St. Patrick's Day: *The Chicago River is dyed green, the Irish and near-Irish parade through the Loop, and politicos jockey for position on the reviewing stand. Whiskey flows like water at Hibernian pubs. 263-6621.*

Salute to Chicago Fashion: *Exhibits, workshops, fashion shows, and a chance to meet designers. Chicago Public Library Cultural Center.*

South Suburban Builders Association Home Show: *Learn about the latest innovations in the home-building industry. Ford City Shopping Center, 7601 S. Cicero Ave. 460-6600.*

Winnetka Antiques Show: *Dealers are carefully chosen for this sale, which helps to finance the center's activities. Winnetka Community House.*

Women's History Week: *Programs presented throughout the city. Held the week in which International Women's Day falls. 922-8530.*

April

Spring has come when smelt fishermen line the lakefront and fans line up for opening day at the ballparks. There's a basketful of Easter-egg exhibits, and taxes are due (get that crucial postmark right up to midnight at Chicago's Main Post Office).

Brookfield Zoo Easter Parade and Bonnet Contest: *Easter Sunday.*

Energy & Home Improvement Fair: *Arlington Park Exposition Center. 329-1191.*

Hispanic Festival of the Arts: *Early Apr. Museum of Science and Industry.*

The Lambs' Giant Easter Egg Hunt: *The festivities make a visit to this worthy center for mentally retarded adults even more heartwarming. Easter Sat. I-94 and Ill. 176, Libertyville. 362-4636.*

National Sports and Fitness Expo: *Exhibits, seminars, and more on everything from body-building to soccer. McCormick Place. 441-7536.*

O'Hare National Antiques Show: *A good show. Also in Aug. O'Hare Exposition Center, 5600 N. River Rd., Rosemont. 441-7530.*

May

This may be the city's best month. It's house-tour time, and the gardens are beautiful. Park districts host amateur ice extravaganzas. On Memorial Day weekend, the beaches are opened and Buckingham Fountain comes to life, signaling the start of summer. Take a weekday off to enjoy the city before the kids are out of school and the mosquitoes are out in full force.

American Indian Center Arts and Crafts Exposition: *Exhibits, dances, fashions, food. Mother's Day weekend. 1630 W. Wilson Ave. 275-5871.*

Art in the Park: *Third Sunday. Mills Park at Home and Pleasant Aves., Oak Park. 383-6400, ext. 210.*

Aurora Historic Preservation Week: *Usually includes free walking tours of residential neighborhoods. 892-8811, ext. 267.*

Beverly Hills/Morgan Park Annual Home Tour: *One of the area's largest tours buses visitors from house to house while promoting the "Village in the City." 233-3100.*

Beverly Hills/Morgan Park Memorial Day Parade: *Kicks off at 10 a.m. from 110th St. and Longwood Dr. Some of the city's few real hills challenge runners in the 9 a.m. 10,000-meter Historic Ridge Run. 233-3100.*

Brandeis Used-Book Sale: *300,000-volume, nine-day tent event with first-day admission charge and closing-day deep price cuts. Opens or closes Memorial Day weekend. Edens Plaza Shopping Center, Edens Expwy. and Lake Ave., Wilmette. 251-0690.*

Chicago Circus Parade: *Treat the family to elephants, calliopes, and antique circus wagons that come to Michigan Ave. from Baraboo, Wis. Near Memorial Day. 644-7430.*

Chicago International Art Exposition: *More than 100 galleries from around the world display excellent work. Navy Pier. 787-6858.*

Coho Fishing Derby: *150,000 anglers try for prizes. Chicago Park District waters. 536-4900 (Richard Kehn), 294-2493.*

EvansFest: *Activities for Northwestern University students, townies, and everyone else. 328-1500.*

Evanston Historical Society House Walk: *Self-guided walk ends with a reception at the Dawes mansion. Buy tickets in advance. 225 Greenwood St., Evanston. 475-3410.*

Festival of the Arts: *Several weeks of music, dance, theater, and art on the University of Chicago campus. 753-3591.*

The Great Art Robbery: *Art and antiques bargains. Evanston Art Center.*

Greek-American Parade Commemorating Greek Independence and Culture: *Bouzouki through the Loop. 580-0111.*

Historic Preservation Week: *First full week. 922-1742.*

Hyde Park and Kenwood House Tours: *Ancona Montessori School sponsors a self-guided, ten-house walk. 924-2356.*

Kite Derby: *James Park, Dodge Ave. and Oakton St., Evanston. 328-2100, ext. 2395.*

Lill Street Studios Spring Show and Sale: *Good cross section of ceramics. 1021 W. Lill Ave. 477-0701.*

Lombard Lilac Festival: *Parade, carnival, ice-cream social, and more old-fashioned fun amid lots of lilac bushes and tulips. Lilacia Park, 150 S. Park Ave., Lombard. 627-1281.*

Midnight Tour of the Windy City: *Thousands of motorcyclists take to the highways and byways after 11 p.m. 629-1579.*

Midwest Bookhunters' Book Fair: *Collectible and out-of-print books, maps, and prints. 232-6383.*

Midwest Craft Festival: *The North Shore Art League sponsors this outstanding show. Old Orchard Shopping Center. 446-2870.*

Norwegian Independence Day Parade: *Closest Sat. to May 17. Downtown Park Ridge. 545-0606.*

La Nuit de Fantaisie: *An important social event for the benefit of the Art Institute's school. The $100-a-plate dinner also includes cocktails and a chance to bid on such dreams as a week-long yacht cruise or lunch with Mike Royko at the Billy Goat   443-3765.*

Poland's Constitution Day Parade: *Loop parade; other nationalities participate. First Sat. 286-0500.*

Wellington-Oakdale Old Glory Marching Society Memorial Day Parade: *"Everybody marches; nobody watches" this homegrown operation that leaves from Wellington and Pine Grove Aves. at 11 a.m. 327-4924.*

Women's Career Convention: *Leigh Communications. 951-7600.*

World's Largest Rummage Sale: *Winnetka Community House.*

Wright Plus: *Tour ten Prairie School buildings. Buy tickets in advance from the Oak Park Tour Center, 951 Chicago Ave., Oak Park 60302. 848-1976.*

June

Fests alfresco in parks, plazas, churchyards, and streets; ethnic, neighborhood, community, and art fairs compete for your weekends. Batons rise at Grant Park and Ravinia (see the splendid picnics!); produce beckons at farmers' markets.

Austin-Schock District Walking Tour: *Includes interiors of seven to ten homes in an elegant enclave revived by preservationists. 626-6572.*

Beverly Art Center Art Fair and Festival: *Juried. Third weekend. 2153 W. 111th St. 445-3838.*

Body Politic Festival of the Arts: *The theater sponsors this happy street fair along the 2200 block of Lincoln Ave. First weekend. 348-7901.*

Cherry Blossom Festival: *Two days of Japanese dances, tea ceremonies, food, and martial-arts displays. Chicago Botanic Garden, Lake-Cook Rd., east of I-94, Glencoe. 835-5440.*

Chicago Feis: *A day of Irish dance (and music) competition. DuPage County Fair Grounds, 2015 Manchester Rd., Wheaton. 763-1956.*

Craft Fair: *Scoville Park, Oak Park Ave. and Lake St., Oak Park. 383-6400, ext. 210.*

Custer's Annual Last Stand: *Sidewalk sale of antiques, arts, and crafts around Evanston's Washington St./Custer Ave. shops. Usually on the last weekend. 328-5657.*

A Day in Our Village: *Festivities throughout Oak Park. 383-6400, ext. 266.*

Des Plaines Art Guild's Invitational Art Fair: *Last Sun. Downtown Des Plaines. 824-1925.*

57th Street Art Fair: *The Midwest's oldest outdoor art fair. (Scarcity of juried spaces has spawned a nearby "community" fair.) First weekend. Kimbark Ave. and 57th St. 644-5800.*

Fountain Square Arts Festival: *Artists from around the country vie for 135 spots at this excellent fair. Performing arts, too. Orrington Ave. and Church St., Evanston. 328-1500.*

Galena's June Open House and Victorian Tea: *Tour homes and the historical museum; see real hills along the Mississippi! Second full weekend. 815-777-0203.*

Gay Pride Week: *Culminates in a parade starting at Addison and Halsted Sts. on June's last Sun. 348-8243.*

Haeger Potteries Tent Sale: *Truckloads of bargains, plants from Florida, and refreshments. 7 Maiden Lane, East Dundee. 426-3441.*

Junefest: *Different theme each year; exhibits, sales, food. K.A.M. Isaiah Israel Congregation, 1100 E. Hyde Park Blvd. 924-1234.*

Lake Forest Academy Antiques Show: *One of the country's best. Lake Forest Academy/Ferry Hall, 1500 W. Kennedy Rd., Lake Forest. 234-3045.*

Lighthouse Landing Rendezvous: *On the Sat. nearest to the summer solstice, celebrate with crafts, food, and entertainment at Lighthouse Landing Park, 2535 Sheridan Rd., Evanston. 864-5181, 864-5198.*

Lockport Old Canal Days: *The town's tribute to its raison d'être. Third weekend. Ill. 171 and Ill. 7. 815-838-3357.*

Logan Square Summer Celebration: *The usual activities, plus double-decker bus rides, a foot race, and a bike race. Logan, Palmer, and Kedzie Blvds. 384-1703.*

Mid-American Canoe Race: *1,000 canoes ply 22 miles of the Fox River from South Elgin to Aurora. First Sun. 897-0516.*

Midsummer Festival: *Ethnic food, crafts, and entertainment in Andersonville on the weekend closest to the summer solstice, an important event in winterbound Sweden. Clark St. at Catalpa Ave. 769-0222.*

Joe Naper Day: *Craft demonstrations, entertainment, and more re-create the atmosphere of a 19th-century village. Sun. after Father's Day. Naper Settlement, 201 W. Porter Ave., Naperville. 355-4141.*

Old Town Art Fair: *The Midwest's oldest juried outdoor fair boasts a good auction and a lovely garden walk. Second weekend. Orleans St. and Lincoln Park West. 337-1938.*

Park West Antiques Fair: *Charming. First weekend. The alley north of Fullerton Pkwy., west of Clark St. 477-5100.*

Puerto Rican Day Parade: *Loop parade and impromptu horn-honking in the barrios. 935-7103, 486-5354.*

San Juan Day Celebration: *Logan Square Boys and Girls Club. 3228 W. Palmer St. 342-8800.*

Sand Castle Competition:
You'll want to photograph
the astonishing results
architects and talented
amateurs achieve with
such humble clay. First Sat.
North Ave. Beach.
663-4111.

Senior Citizens' Picnic:
Buckingham Fountain.
744-4016, TDD 744-6777.

**South Holland Wooden
Shoe Festival:** About the
only reminder of this suburb's early roots (besides its
name). Thornton Com-
munity College, U.S. 6 at
State St. 841-7110.

SummerDance: Local
groups perform throughout
the city all summer.
744-3315.

Swedish Days: A balloon
race, a worm race, quilting
and rosemaling demonstra-
tions, and more. Down-
town Geneva. 232-6060.

Winnetka Children's Fair:
Clowns, rides, games, etc.,
on the Village Green. Second Fri. and Sat. Green Bay
Road and Elm St., Win-
netka. 446-4432.

WLS Run for the Zoo: 8.9
miles along the lakefront.
First Sun. 984-0890.

July

Fireworks and festivals for the Fourth, culinary pyrotechnics for the fourteenth
(Bastille Day), church carnivals, and county fairs; lots of family fun.

Air & Water Show:
Aerobatics and other
events, on and over the
lake. Fourth weekend. Lake
Shore Park, Chicago Ave.
294-2493.

**American Spanish Dance
Festival:** Guest artists join
Ensemble Español for con-
certs, seminars, and special
events at Northeastern Illinois University, 5500 N. St.
Louis Ave. 583-4050, ext.
443.

**ARCO/Jesse Owens
Games:** Regional finals of
local track-and-field meets.
Finalists compete in the Los
Angeles Championships.
Hanson Stadium, 5501 W.
Fullerton Ave. 744-5829.

**Arlington Heights Festival
Frontier Days:** Five days of
fun and games with a Fourth
of July fireworks display at
Arlington Park Race Track.
Recreation Park, 500 E.
Minor St., Arlington
Heights. 640-2596.

Bastille Day: French restaurants throughout the city
and suburbs offer special
menus and other treats (see
Chicago). The Alliance
Française-Maison Fran-
çaise de Chicago cospon-
sors several days of fun.
337-1070.

Chicago Comicon: Not a
local Communist con-
spiracy, but a comic-book
convention and swap meet.
Third weekend. Americana
Congress Hotel, 520 S.
Michigan Ave. 743-4493,
274-1832.

**Chicago to Mackinac
Island Yacht Race:** Third
Sat. 861-7777.

Chinatown Summer Fest:
Lion dancers and more.
Cermak Rd. and Wentworth
Ave. 225-0234.

City Child in Summer:
Films and other educational
entertainment. Chicago
Public Library Cultural
Center.

**Country Fair for City
Folks:** Future Farmers of
America, Four-H Club
members, and others give
city folks a look at farm life.
Lincoln Park, south of the
lagoon. 744-5829.

Dearborn Garden Walk:
Sunday stroll on Dearborn
St. and on adjoining side
streets between Division St.
and North Ave. Sometimes
in Aug. North Dearborn Association, P.O. Box 10521,
Chicago 60610.

**Dolton Volunteer Fire De-
partment Fourth of July
Celebration:** Almost a
week of carnival games and
rides recalls a simpler age;
includes a parade and one
of the southern suburbs'
nicest fireworks displays on
the Fourth. Dolton Park,
147th St. and Evers Ave.
849-2145.

Duneland Folk Festival:
Interpretive displays and
programs at the Westches-
ter Library (Chesterton,
Ind.; 219-926-7697)
precede a weekend of
traditional music, crafts,
and foods at two historic
sites in the Indiana Dunes
National Lakeshore, U.S.
20 and Mineral Springs Rd.,
Porter, Ind. 219-926-7561.

DuPage County Fair:
Everything from a horse
show to apple-pie judging.
Last full weekend. Man-
chester and County Farm
Rds., Wheaton. 668-6636.

**DuSable Museum Arts &
Crafts Festival:** In the
sunken garden. 740 E. 56th
Pl. 947-0600.

**La Fête de France à
Facets:** Films, food, wine,
dancing, and other delights
for Francophiles. Sat.
before Bastille Day. Facets
Multimedia Center, 1517 W.
Fullerton Ave. 281-4114,
281-9075.

Andy Frain Softball Tournament: *A week of evening competition between the best Chicago and suburban Class A teams. Clarendon Park, 4501 N. Clarendon Ave. 561-1274.*

Illiana Bluegrass Festival: *Third weekend. Pine Lake, Exchange and Old Monee Rds. Park Forest South. 534-6451.*

Independence Day Concert and Fireworks: *Spectacular fireworks over the harbor follow a special July 3 Grant Park Symphony concert. Draws huge crowds. 744-3315.*

Jazz Comes Home: *Local and national blues, gospel, and reggae groups, too. Several weekends. South Shore Country Club, 7059 S. South Shore Dr. 667-2540.*

Kane County Fair and Industrial Exposition: *Kane County Fairgrounds, Randall Rd., St. Charles. 584-6926.*

King Richard's Faire: *"Renaissance" crafts, foods, and entertainment on a pleasant wooded site just over the Wisconsin state line. From the Fourth of July weekend through mid-Aug. 12420 128th St., Kenosha, Wis. Exit I-94 at Russell Rd. 689-2800, 414-396-4385.*

Lake County Fair: *Includes tractor pulls, rodeos, and other contests. Lake County Fairgrounds, Ill. 120 and U.S. 45, Grayslake. 223-5192.*

Mid-America Benefit Horse Festival: *A show, precision drills, and equine arts and crafts. For the Northeastern Illinois Special Olympics. Kane County Fairgrounds, Randall Rd., St. Charles. 584-9412, 741-8063.*

Natsu Matsuri: *Cultural exhibits and demonstrations, martial arts, Japanese games, and lots of good food. First weekend. Buddhist Temple of Chicago, 1151 W. Leland Ave. 334-4661.*

The North Lincoln Avenue Association Street Fair: *Arts and crafts; lots of entertainment. Third weekend. 2400 and 2500 blocks of Lincoln Ave. 549-1177.*

Obon Festival: *Lovely folk dances and music. Second Sat. Midwest Buddhist Temple, 435 W. Menomonee St. 943-7801.*

An Old-Fashioned Fourth of July Celebration: *Oratory and band music. ·Chicago Historical Society, Clark St. at North Ave. 642-4600.*

Our Lady of Mt. Carmel Festival: *A week of Italian food and entertainment precedes an outdoor Mass and procession through the streets on the third Sun. 1101 N. 23rd Ave., Melrose Park. 344-4140.*

St. Andrew's Picnic and Folk Festival: *Greek food, rides, Greek dances, and games. Second Sun. Sheridan Rd. and Hollywood Ave. 334-4515.*

Sheffield Garden Walk: *Self-guided tour of this National Historic District includes beautiful gardens and lots of garage sales. Starts at Sheffield and Webster Aves. Fourth weekend. 642-9420, 477-5100.*

Space Day: *Special guests and exhibits celebrate man's landing on the moon (July 20, 1969). Adler Planetarium.*

Taste of Chicago: *On the Fourth of July weekend, Grant Park turns into a giant outdoor café as scores of local restaurants sell bite-sized samples of their specialties to hungry hordes. 644-7430.*

Western Open Golf Championship: *Top pros on a very tough course. Butler National Golf Club, 2900 York Rd., Oak Brook. 539-4600.*

World's Largest Garage Sale: *Fills a municipal parking facility. Last full weekend. Sherman Ave. and Davis St., Evanston. 328-1500.*

August

Hardly a day passes without a sea of music fans surging to a major event along downtown's lakefront, as cool breezes mix with hot licks far into the night.

Arts and Crafts Festival: *Juried. Dawes Park, Church St. and Sheridan Rd., Evanston. 328-2100, ext. 2395.*

Bud Billiken Day Parade: *A huge parade from 35th St. and King Dr. to Washington Park. Second Sat. 225-2400.*

Bonsai Show: *Chicago Botanic Garden, Lake-Cook Rd., east of I-94. 835-5440.*

Buckingham Fountain Art Fair: *Winners of local city-sponsored competitions.* 744-5829.

Budweiser Million: *A week of equestrian events culminates in America's richest race on the last Sun. Arlington Park Race Track.*

ChicagoFest: *Crowds seethe up and down Navy Pier for 12 days of rock, blues, jazz, and country music; rivers of beer; endless street food; rivers of beer; tamer entertainment for seniors and kids; and rivers of beer. Monster pop stars play to thousands more imbibers from a stage in front of the Pier. Lots of music for the price, but not for the faint of heart, particularly on evenings and weekends. Use mass transit.* 644-7430.

Chicago Jazz Festival: *Not only is this week-long, world-class fest free, but Grant Park is dry and everything's more laid back than at ChicagoFest. Follows the Grant Park Symphony season; varies from late Aug. to early Sept.* 744-3315.

Dance for a Dollar at MoMing: *Several weekend programs showcase more than 20 Chicago companies and choreographers. Admission is only a buck.* 1034 W. Barry Ave. 472-9894.

Festa Italiana: *Food and frolic. Last weekend.* Navy Pier. 372-6788.

Fiesta del Sol: *Hispanic street fair.* Blue Island Ave. and 18th St. 666-2663.

Ginza Holiday: *It's not Tokyo, but. . . . Third weekend.* Midwest Buddhist Temple, 435 W. Menomonee St. 943-7801.

Gold Coast Art Fair: *About 600 artists participate; the swarming crowds turn Rush St. traffic into a nightmare. Third weekend. Centered at Walton St.*

Irish Family Days: *Our Lady's Day of the Harvest celebration held on the weekend closest to the 15th.* Hawthorne Park, 3500 S. Cicero Ave. 939-0899.

Lithuanian Plaza Festival: *Ethnic food, folk dancing, and more.* Lithuanian Plaza Ct. (69th St.) and California Ave. 434-3800.

McHenry County Fair: *First Wed. to Sun.* Country Club Rd. and Ill. 47, Woodstock. 815-338-5315.

Old Orchard Classic Car Show: *Not just old or collectors' cars, but 40 true, mint-condition classics.* Old Orchard Shopping Center. 673-6800.

St. Demetrios Church Festival: *Four days of Greek food, music, and dancing.* 2727 W. Winona St. 561-5992.

Venetian Night: *How many times can you spot the mayor's name on the fanciful, illuminated floats in the aquatic parade that drifts by Grant Park's harborfront? Great fireworks.* 744-3315.

The Wicker Park Greening Festival: *Neighborhood fair and house tour centers around the park. Third weekend.* Damen Ave. and Schiller St. 342-1966.

Will County Fair: *Last weekend.* Wilmington Rd., one mile east of I-57, Peotone. 258-3266, 258-3354.

September

Labor Day signals summer's end and school's beginning. The theater season takes off, and the social whirl begins. Were it not for the bad-luck Bears, this might be a perfect month.

ALS Mammoth Music Mart: *Charity tent sale of new and used pianos, stereos, records, tapes, sheet music, and memorabilia.* Old Orchard Shopping Center. 673-6800.

America's Marathon/ Chicago: *This 7,000-competitor run along the lakefront and through the neighborhoods benefits the Chicago Boys Clubs.* 951-0660.

Boul-Mich Bike Rally: *International champs pedal 25-mile and 50-mile races around Grant Park. Labor Day.* 939-0897.

Chicago International Antiquarian Book Fair: *Rare, out-of-print, and collectible books, maps, and prints.* 432-3690.

Des Plaines Art Guild Art Fair: *Exhibits by members.* Des Plaines Library, Graceland and Thacker Aves. 824-1925.

Dinosaur Days: *Explore the myths and realities, learn how bones are preserved, and play pin the bone on the dinosaur.* Field Museum of Natural History, Lake Shore Dr. and Roosevelt Rd. 922-9410.

Evanston Historical Society Flea Market: *Collectibles, antiques, and books. Last Sat.* 225 Greenwood St., Evanston. 475-3410.

Fiesta de la Villita: *Labor Day weekend.* 26th St. and Kostner Ave. 521-5387, 762-3468.

Frankfort Fall Festival: *Arts and crafts, antiques, a carnival, wagon tours, and food enliven a charming century-old town on Labor Day weekend.* 815-469-3356.

Hinsdale Antiques Show and Sale: *Interesting, eclectic show. Hinsdale Community House, 415 W. 8th St., Hinsdale. 323-7500.*

Junior League of Chicago Gazebo: *About 30 mostly out-of-town dealers sell gifts. Saddle & Cycle Club, 900 W. Foster Ave. 664-4462.*

La Salle Drive Association House and Garden Walk: *Ten homes and the Germania Club. 337-1725 (Chuck Straus).*

Lyric Opera of Chicago Opening Night: *Benefit performance followed by a socially important ball at The Conrad Hilton. 346-6111.*

Mexican Independence Day Parade: *Horsemen, bands, and floats parade through the Loop. Closest Sat. to Sept. 16. 674-5838.*

Music Bowl-Illinois: *More than 30 high-school marching bands from Illinois, Indiana, and Michigan compete for a shot at the nationals and at the Orange Bowl Parade. Soldier Field, McFetridge and Lake Shore Drs. 372-7090.*

Old Orchard Art Festival: *One of the most important juried fairs. Coordinated by the North Shore Art League. Old Orchard Shopping Center. 673-6800.*

Rush-Presbyterian-St. Luke's Fashion Show: *Celebs (and others) model designer clothes for charity. Medinah Temple, 600 N. Wabash Ave. 226-1125.*

Steuben Day Parade: *United German-American Societies of Chicago march through the Loop. Third Sat. 478-7915 (Karl Laschet).*

Taste of Polonia: *Entertainment and eats. Labor Day weekend. Copernicus Cultural & Civic Center, 5216 W. Lawrence Ave. 777-8898.*

Tour of Historic Galena Homes: *Five of them; market and melodrama, too. Last full weekend. 815-777-0203.*

Village Art Fair: *All media; juried. First Sun. after Labor Day. Holley Court parking lot, near Marion and Lake Sts., Oak Park.*

Wellington-Oakdale Old Glory Marching Society Labor Day Parade: *A reprise of the Memorial Day celebration steps off at 11 a.m. from Wellington and Pine Grove Aves. 327-4924.*

Wooded Island Festival: *A laid-back fair on the refurbished World's Columbian Exposition greensward. Jackson Park, 59th St. and Stony Island Ave. 288-8343.*

October

Illinois Arts Week occasions a wealth of special programs, the Chicago Symphony Orchestra season begins, and the Jeff Awards honor the best in local theater. For the young at heart, the circus visits town!

Brookfield Zoo Halloween Party: *Fun for kids. Come in costume. Sat. before Halloween. 242-2630.*

Chicago Fire Party: *Everyone who's anyone on the local folk-music scene turns up at this all-night bash, one of three such annual benefits (others in Feb. and June) for the Old Town School of Folk Music, 909 W. Armitage Ave. 525-7793.*

Chicago Ski Show: *Manufacturers' exhibits and demonstrations. Arlington Park Exposition Center.*

Children's Science Book Fair: *The Museum of Science and Industry brings together the latest children's science books and many of their authors. Late Oct. 684-1414.*

Columbus Day Parade: *The Italian-American community celebrates with a parade through the Loop. 372-6788.*

Come for to Sing Benefit: *The best local folk musicians join forces with national stars for the country's pre-eminent folk-music magazine. Three days late Oct. Holsteins, 2464 N. Lincoln Ave. 327-3331.*

Halloween Pet Costume Party: *Prizes for the best costumes; treats for all contenders. Outside the Park View Pet Shop, 2222 N. Clark St. 549-2031.*

Historic Pullman House Tour: *Self-guided walk on the second weekend begins at the Historic Pullman Center, 614 E. 113th St. 660-1276, 785-8181.*

International Houby Festival: *Arts and crafts, a race, a talent contest, and lots of Bohemian food in a week-long celebration of the mushroom. Culminates in a parade on the Sunday before Columbus Day. In Cicero and in Berwyn, mostly on Cermak Rd. 863-2104, 863-8979.*

Joseph Jefferson Awards: Never mind that you don't know who J.J. was; the gala drama-awards ceremony is usually televised and is followed by a dinner-dance. Open to all by ticket. 630-0027.

Pilsen East Artists' Open House: View their works and tour some of the picturesque studios. The 800 block of W. 19th St., the 700 block of W. 18th St., and the 1800 block of S. Halsted St. 738-0786.

Ringling Bros. and Barnum & Bailey Circus: Still "The Greatest Show on Earth." Mid-Oct. through Nov. Opens at the Rosemont Horizon; finishes at the International Amphitheatre.

The Carl Sandburg Literary Arts Ball: The Chicago Public Library Cultural Center is a fitting setting for luminaries to honor local writers. 269-2922.

Scottish Fair: Films, pipers, dancers, imports for sale, food, and readings of Bobby Burns's poetry. Winnetka Community House. 825-6189 (Donald Munn).

World's Second Largest Rummage Sale: Worth the trip just to see the church. Christ Church, Maple and Oak Sts., Winnetka. 446-2850, 446-4484.

November

Not even a misanthrope can deny the holiday season's cheer. As the leaves change color and fall, the curtains rise on downtown store-window displays and at a mind-boggling array of Christmas programs. Have you hugged your furnace today?

Jane Addams Center Open House: Hull House affiliate shows off the work of a modern settlement house, and there's plenty of inexpensive ethnic food. First weekend. 3212 N. Broadway. 549-1631.

Art for Young Collectors Sale: Affordably priced, good art—paintings, graphics, sculpture—draws crowds. Renaissance Society at the University of Chicago, Cobb Hall, 5811 S. Ellis Ave. 962-8670.

Chicago Christmas Parade: Santa Claus and dozens of huge balloons parade down the State Street Mall. Sun. after Thanksgiving. 744-3315.

Chicago International Film Festival: Cinema/Chicago screens dozens of new films, retrospectives, and animations at several movie houses. Occasional talks by film-making greats. First Fri. and continues for two or three weeks. 644-3400.

Chicago International Folk Fair: Ethnic communities show off their traditional music, foods, and crafts. McCormick Place West/Donnelley Hall, 23rd St. and King Dr. 744-3315.

Christmas Around the World: Lovely decorated trees, ethnic entertainment, and foods. Third week of Nov. through early Jan. Museum of Science and Industry.

A Christmas Carol: Goodman Theatre's lavish production draws bigger raves every year. Late Nov. through Dec. 200 S. Columbus Dr. 443-3800.

Disney's World on Ice: World-class figure skaters and production numbers featuring Mickey and the whole gang. Some years it's Ice Follies/Holiday on Ice. Two weeks starting the Tues. before Thanksgiving. Chicago Stadium.

Evanston Art Center Holiday Market: Day after Thanksgiving to Christmas.

Excellence in Woodworking Exhibition: Products, supplies, and experts. Hyatt Regency Chicago, 151 E. Wacker Dr. 823-2151.

The Lambs' Old-Fashioned Christmas: Nice gifts in the decorated shops; live-animal Nativity tableau. Day after Thanksgiving to Dec. 24. Handicrafts gift bazaar second weekend in Nov. I-94 and Ill. 176, Libertyville. 362-4636.

Latke-Hamentash Symposium: U. of C. types debate the relative merits of potato pancakes and poppy-seed pastries at Ida Noyes Hall, 1212 E. 59th St. Afterwards everyone retires to Hillel House, 5715 S. Woodlawn Ave., to make an empirical study of the problem. Who can question the relevance of a classical education? Tues. before Thanksgiving. 752-1127.

Old Town Triangle Association Holiday Market: Most of the artworks are less than $50 and are by Old Town Art Fair artists. Gourmet foods, too. Mid-Nov. to mid-Dec. 1816 N. Wells St. 337-1938.

Skokie Valley Skating Club Exhibition and Competition Preview: *Club members who've qualified to compete in the Upper Great Lakes Championships perform with guest stars. One of the better amateur shows. Sometimes in Oct. Centennial Park Ice Rink, 2300 Old Glenview Rd., Wilmette. 256-6100.*

University of Chicago International Folk Dance Festival: *Mandel Hall concerts and Ida Noyes Hall workshops. First weekend. 5706 S. University Ave. 753-3591.*

Windy City Gymnastics Meet: *America's best gymnasts compete; men on the weekend before Thanksgiving, women in Jan. University of Illinois at Chicago Pavilion, 1140 W. Harrison St. 996-2772.*

December

Holiday shoppers make the Loop look as it did when it was *the* place to shop. Almost every choral group in town is doing the *Messiah.* Museums and historic villages have special displays. Ethnic stores offer special gifts, ethnic bakeries and delis sell seasonal foods, and ethnic churches have a special charm. Buy a battery, antifreeze, and snow tires, and curse the darkness. But take heart: Summer's only six months away.

American Indian Center Pow-Wow: *Arts and crafts, food, entertainment, and competition dancers from all over the continent. Navy Pier. 275-5871.*

Brookfield Zoo's Christmas Party: *Brunch with Santa and the elves at the Safari Lodge, followed by a party at the Children's Zoo. Bring a stocking (if you've been good). Sun. before Christmas. 242-2630.*

Caroling to the Animals: *Bring a bit of holiday cheer to a penguin. Sun. before Christmas. Lincoln Park Zoo, Stockton Dr. and Webster Ave. 935-6700.*

Chicago Antiques Show: *A Stratford Manor show that benefits the Chicago City Ballet. Expocenter/ Chicago, 350 N. Orleans St. 441-7530.*

Crystal Ball: *Many consider this Michael Reese Hospital benefit to be the social event of the season. Second Sat. By invitation (but prospective supporters can easily get one). 791-3115.*

Do-It-Yourself Messiah: *Margaret Hillis conducts the orchestra, soloists, and you in two Orchestra Hall performances the week before Christmas. 726-0484. For free tickets, send a stamped self-addressed envelope to the sponsor, Talman Home Federal, 72 E. Randolph St., Chicago 60601, after Nov. 15.*

Gold Coast Kennel Club Dog Show: *Largest east of California. Expocenter/ Chicago, 350 N. Orleans St. 664-4664.*

Midwest Potters' Guild Exhibition and Sale: *1236 Sherman Ave., Evanston. 475-9697.*

The Nutcracker: *Proud, camera-toting parents of the young dancers punctuate Ruth Page's choreography with flashes of brilliance. Well, it's for charity and the kids will like it. Arie Crown Theatre, 23rd St. and Lake Shore Dr. 791-6000.*

The Nutcracker on Ice: *Robert Crown Ice Center, 1701 Main St., Evanston. 328-9400.*

Randolph Street Gallery Annual Artists' Christmas Store: *Many innovative, inexpensive, and offbeat gifts are sold at this benefit for the nonprofit gallery. Two weeks before Christmas. 756 N. Milwaukee Ave. 243-7717.*

WFMT's New Year's Eve Midnight Special: *A delightful mixture of by-request favorites and live performances by local and visiting folkies runs through the night. Many fans stay at home to listen rather than braving the cold for some dull party. (98.7 FM.)*

Phone Numbers

Ma Bell's got your number. In fact, because she's got just about every number, Chicago's collection of phone books is frustrating and cumbersome to use. To help you through times of stress and frustration in a more convenient manner, we've compiled this list of potentially useful numbers of social, governmental, and charitable agencies. Some are manned around the clock; others are not. Many numbers serve the metropolitan area or the entire state; those of city agencies refer specifically to Chicago.

Who do you call when . . .

. . . you have a medical or life-threatening emergency

Police dept.; fire dept.
911
Also free fire dept. ambulance to nearest hospital.

Rush-Presbyterian-St. Luke's Poison Control Center
942-5969

U.S. Coast Guard Search and Rescue
Chicago   353-0378
North Shore   251-0185

Chicago Dental Society
726-4321

Chicago Veterinary Emergency Services, Ltd.
281-7110

. . . you have an emotional emergency

Community Referral Service
322-0580

Metro-Help
929-5150

Evanston Hospital Crisis Intervention and Referral Service
492-6500

Parental Stress Services
463-0390
Adult callers only.

. . . you have any kind of housing emergency

Chicago Dept. of Neighborhoods
744-5000, TDD 744-8599

. . . you're suddenly out in the cold

Salvation Army Emergency Lodge
275-9383

Red Cross Disaster Service
440-2000

. . . you need medical or emotional aid

Alcoholics Anonymous
346-1475
Counseling services.

Chicago Alcoholic Treatment Center
254-3680
Clinical help.

Chicago Medical Society
670-2550
Referral service.

Gamblers Anonymous
346-1588
Counseling services.

Overeaters Anonymous
922-7676
Counseling for the obese.

Gay Horizons
929-4357
Referrals and counseling for gays.

Howard Brown Clinic
871-5777
Testing and treatment of sexually transmitted diseases; particularly for gays.

Chicago Dental Society
726-4076
Nonemergency referrals.

American Cancer Society
372-0471
Support and referrals.

South Side Women's Health Service
667-5505
Low-cost pregnancy testing.

WICCA (Women in Crisis Can Act)
528-3303
Women's crisis intervention and referral service.

HERS (Health Evaluation and Referral Service)
248-0166
Women's health referrals.

Biracial Family Network
288-2253
Counseling and support for parents and children.

Planned Parenthood
322-4240
Clinics, referrals, counseling services.

Visiting Nurses Assn.
663-1810
In-home care.

Chicago Memorial Assn.
939-0678
Arrangements made for low-cost funerals.

Chicago Hearing Society
332-6850, TDD 782-0796
Hearing aids and testing; classes for hearing-impaired people.

Family Service Bureau
939-1300
Domestic-problem referrals.

Service for the Aged
324-1600
Referrals and counseling.

Access Living
649-7404, TDD 649-8593
Advocacy and counseling for handicapped people.

. . . you need legal aid

Chicago Bar Assn.
332-1111
Referral service.

Legal Aid Bureau
922-5625
For low-income clients.

. . . you need language aid

Language Bank
332-1460
Volunteers translate 24 hours a day.

. . . you need traveler's aid

Travelers and Immigrants Aid
435-4500

. . . you need red tape unsnarled

Federal Information Center
353-4242

State of Illinois Building
793-3500

Governor's Office of Interagency Cooperation
793-2754

Cook County Office of Inquiry and Information
443-3390

Chicago Dept. of Neighborhoods
744-5000, TDD 744-8599
Operators at 744-5000 will relay your messages to any TDD in the city.

. . . you want to be a good samaritan

Voluntary Action Center
782-2870

Red Cross
440-2161
Blood-donor information.

. . . Fido needs help, too

Anti-Cruelty Society
644-8338

Animal Welfare League
Chicago   667-0088
Chicago Ridge   636-8586

. . . there's a dead skunk in the middle of the road

Chicago Dept. of Neighborhoods
744-5000
Removal of dead animals.

. . . your car seems to have left without you

Chicago Police Dept.
744-4000
Auto towing.

. . . you wish that car would go away

Chicago Police Dept.
744-5512
Abandoned-auto removal.

. . . you've been held up by a crooked parking meter

Chicago Police Dept.
744-4815
To report malfunctions (and to void tickets).

. . . you have questions about tickets and your rights

Cook County Courts
Moving violations 443-6080
Parking violations 443-4590

. . . you want to report fire hazards

Chicago Fire Prevention Bureau
744-4762

. . . you want to report building-code violations

Chicago Dept. of Inspectional Services
744-3420

. . . you're tired of cursing the darkness

Chicago Dept. of Neighborhoods
744-5000
To report streetlights out.

Who do you call when . . .

. . . there's a swimming pool where your garage had been

Chicago Dept. of Neighborhoods
744-5000
To report water leaks.

. . . you just went through a free car wash

Chicago Dept. of Water
744-7038
To report open fire hydrants.

. . . your pet eggplant is sick

Garfield Park Conservatory
533-1281
Plant information.

. . . the shrub just ate your dog

Chicago Bureau of Forestry
744-4383

. . . the air just ate your shrub

Environmental complaints
Chicago   744-3210
Cook County   865-6165
Illinois   345-9780
United States   353-2650

. . . the butter is blue

Food and Drug Administration
353-7840

. . . your nose is red

Abbott Laboratories
761-6750
Pollen counts (Aug. to Oct.).

. . . your FM has CB, and AT&T is on your TV

Federal Communications Commission
353-0195

. . . you think you've just been sold the Michigan Avenue Bridge

Chicago Dept. of Consumer Services
744-4091

Illinois Attorney General's Consumer Protection Division
English   793-3580
Spanish   793-5638

Cook County State's Attorney's Consumer Fraud Division
443-8425

Better Business Bureau
346-3313

U.S. Postal Inspection Service
886-2820
Mail fraud investigations.

. . . you *have* been sold the Michigan Avenue Bridge!

Mike Royko
321-2198

. . . you think you paid too much

Consumer Price Index Hotline
353-1883

. . . somebody's trying to sell you insurance on it

Illinois Dept. of Insurance
793-2427

. . . your tax bill includes the bridge

Cook County Assessor
443-7550
Taxpayers' queries.

. . . you want to buy at auction next time

Chicago Police Dept.
744-6224

U.S. Customs Service
353-4516

U.S. Postal Service
886-2420

. . . you want to know what they're saying behind your back

Trans Union Credit Information Co.
645-6008

TRW Credit Data
981-0296

. . . you learn that they're right

Family Financial Counseling
939-1250
Management advice, sliding fee.

. . . you need to learn how to do it yourself

Learning Exchange
549-8383
Teacher referral service.

. . . you want to learn how to undo it yourself

Pro-Se Divorce Project
567-5715

. . . it's neither a bird, a plane, nor Superman

Center for UFO Studies
491-6666

. . . you want to turn in a baddie

Illinois Central Registry for Child Abuse and Neglect Child Abuse Hotline
800-252-2873

Chicago Fire Prevention Bureau Arson Hotline
744-4762

U.S. Drug Enforcement Administration
353-7875

Chicago Crime Commission
372-0101

Chicago Commission on Animal Care and Control
247-5400

Chicago Police Dept. Office of Professional Standards
744-6307

. . . you want to keep out a baddie

Chicago Police Dept. Preventive Programs Division
744-5490

. . . you want to hear everybody talk about it

National Weather Service forecasts
Local   976-1212
Traveler's   298-1413
Pilot briefings 686-2156

. . . you need to know

League of Women Voters
236-0315
Information on public officials.

U.S. Census Bureau Library
353-0980
Demographic figures.

Chicago Public Library Information Center
English   269-2800
Spanish   269-2940

"Dial-It" Time of day
976-1616

Illinois Bell Customers' Name and Address Bureau
796-9600
Reverse directory for phone numbers.

"Dial-It" Sports
976-1313
Recent scores.

. . . you want to send it

U.S. Postal Service
ZIP Codes   886-2590
Information   886-2420

United Parcel Service
920-2900
Pick-up and drop-off information.

. . . you want to go

Amtrak
800-572-2419, 558-1075

RTA and CTA
800-972-7000, 836-7000,
TDD 836-4949
Commuter information.

Illinois Tollway conditions
Chicago no.   242-3620
Suburban no.   654-2200

Illinois Office of Tourism
800-252-8987

U.S. State Dept. Passport Agency
353-5426
Passport and visa information.

U.S. Customs Service
353-6115

Chicago Dept. of Health
744-4340
Inoculation information.

. . . you want to stay

Greater Chicago Hotel & Motel Association
236-3473
Room rates and availability.

. . . you want to dine out without leaving home

Dinner at Your Door, Inc.
348-DINE

Gourmet-O-Gram
433-5131

. . . you want a show

Curtain Call
977-1755
Ticket availability.

Black Theater Alliance Hotline
288-SOUL

Jazz Hotline
666-1881

Chicago Council on Fine Arts
FINE-ART
Cultural events information.

Visitors' Eventline
225-2323

ArchiCenter
782-1776
Architectural tours information.

. . . you just want to play

Cook County Forest Preserves
261-8400

Chicago Park District
Information   294-2200
Tennis   294-4790
Ice skating   294-2314
Golf   294-2274

Illinois Dept. of Conservation Outdoor Line
793-2588
Hunting, fishing, boating information.

. . . you only want to listen

Tel-Med
670-3670

DIAL-PET
342-5738

DIAL-LAW
644-0800

Dial-a-Poem Chicago
346-3478

Dial-a-Story
943-2166
Bible stories for children.

Dial-a-Prayer
332-6080, 736-1166

Dial-an-Atheist
772-8822

Sherman Skolnick's "Hotline News"
731-1100

Call Ann Landers
976-1919

"Dial-It" Santa Claus
976-2525

Singles Activities Hotline
271-1200

Chicago Audubon Society Bird Alert
675-8466

Illinois Bell "Dial-It" directory
976-3636

. . . you want to hear everybody talk about it

Chicagoland Association of Barbershop (quartet) Chapters Hotline
661-1215

University of Chicago Activities Hotline
753-2150

Index

Gray, Richard, Gallery, 137, 159, 336
Gray Line of Chicago, 16
Grayslake, 18
Grayson Gallery, 336
Great Ace, The, 212, 218
Great Art Robbery, 378
Great Chicago Fire (1871). See Chicago Fire
Great Expectations, 300
Great Frame Up, 212, 218
Great Lakes Hot Tubs, 163
Great Lakes Jewelry, 162
Great Lakes Naval & Maritime Museum, 152, 332
Great Showing Machine, 213, 218
Grecian Psistaria, 233, 237
Greco's Pastry Shop, 268
Greek-Amer. Ind. & Culture Parade, 378
Greek Islands, 56, 64
Greektown, 56. See also New Greektown
Greek Town Food & Bakery, 237
Green, 181, 185
Green Bay Road, 187
Green Bay Trail, 291
Greene, Thomas E., 183
Green Earth Natural Foods, 302
Greenhouse on Buckingham, 213, 218
Greenhouse Unlimited, 201, 204
Green Mill Gardens, 239
Green Mill Lounge, 239, 245
Green's, Willie, Park Bait Shop, 321
Greenstone Church, 120, 121
Green Things, 127
Green Thumb, The, 218
Greetings, 218
Greifenstein's Pharmacy, 78
Greyhound Bus Lines, 15
Griffin, Walter Burley, 124, 126, 292, 293
Griffin, Walter Burley, Houses, 247, 249
Griffin, Walter Burley, Place, 124, 126
Griffins & Gargoyles, 232, 236
Grimmer, Margot, American Dance Co., 354
Groceries, ethnic. Arirang Supermkt., 216, 220; Asia Oriental Foods, 244; Athens Groc., 56, 63; Atour Food Imp., 249, 250; Borsini's Food Mart, 63; Caesar's Polish Deli, 277; Carmen's Italian Foods, 96; Carnovale Italian Deli, 290; Casa del Pueblo, La, 68; Casa Hernandez, 244, 257; Conte di Savoia, 54, 63; D & M Foods & Liquors, 115, 118; Delphi Food Mkt. & Rest., 237; Dong Kee, 71, 72; Doshi Groc. &

Coin, 236; Eastern Bakery & Groc., 93, 96; East West Foods, 263, 268; Furuya, 250; Golden Country, 71, 73; Greek Town Food & Bakery, 237; Holy Land Bakery & Groc., 263, 268; India Gifts & Foods, 229; India Grocers, 244; Intl. Foods (Greek), 263, 268; Intl. Foods & Emporium (Indian), 255, 259; John's Imp. Foods, 233, 237; Kamdar Imp., 241, 244; Korea Mkt., 237; Kuhn's Delicatessen, 224, 229; Kum Ho Oriental Groc., 268; Lucca Packing, 63; Meyer Imp. Delicatessen, 229; Milano Sausage Shop, 290; New Quon Wah, 71, 73; New Star Foods, 241; Oriental Food Mkt. & Cooking Sch., 254, 259; Oriental Store of Chicago, 229; Pan American Supermkt., 250; Parama Food & Liquors, 97; Philhouse, 250; Philippine World, 227; Playa Food Store, La, 268; Plaza Blanco, 68; R.C. Philippine Trading Corp., 64; Saba Meat & Groc., 263, 268; Sanford Chinese Amer. Groc., 240, 244; Siam Mkt., 247, 250; Song Quang Co., 244; Star Mkt., 216, 220; Sun Chong Lung, 71, 73; Thailand Plaza, 244; Tom's Delicatessen & Bakery, 233, 237; Viet Hoa Plaza, 240, 244; Wah May, 71, 73. See also Delicatessens
Gross, S.E., 210, 222
Grosse Point bluff, 291
Grosse Point Light Station, 294, 330
Groveland Park, 309, 318
Grover, Oliver D., 104
Grove St. Galleries, 295, 300
Grunts, R.J., 192, 198
Gruta, La, 171
GuadalaHarry's, 171
Guardian Angel Day Nursery & Home for Working Women, 80
Gucci, 135, 158
Guenzel & Drummond, 284
Guerin, Jules, 142
Guild Books, 202, 204
Guild Clothing Mart, 276
Guild for the Blind Boutique, 48
Guildhall Galleries, 336
Guitar Asylum, 257
Guitar Center, 125, 127
Guitar Fun, Inc., 283, 288
Gunzo's Sports Ctr., 288
Gurnee, 18
Gustafson, Kenneth L., Antiques & Books, 255, 257
Gustafson's, Inc., 300

Gymnastics, 372

H

Häagen Dazs, 166
Haas, Richard, 144, 177
Habitat Interiors, 204
Haeger Potteries Tent Sale, 379
Hahn, Herman, 321
Halestine, Elisabeth, 317
Hall, Eric E., 320
Hall, Joel, Dancers, 354, 362
Halloween Pet Costume Party, 383
Hal's Bakery, 87
Halsted, Ann, House, 194
Halsted St. antiques stores, 201
Halsted St. Fish Mkt., 202, 207
Hamburger Hamlet, 147, 170
Ha Mien Restaurant, 245
Hamill & Barker, 137, 159
Hamilton, Alexander, Monument, 321
Hamilton Park, 315
Hamilton's Pizza & Pub, 261
Hammer & Hammer Amer. Folk Art, 336
Hammock House, 213, 218
Hammond, Ind., 115
Hana East Jap. Steak House, 169
Hancock, John, Obs., 151
Handball, 372
Handle With Care, 180, 185
Handmoor, 24, 46
Hands of Peace (Azaz), 40
Handy Candy Fruit & Nut Co., 49
Hangge Uppe, The, 173
Hanig's, 158
Hansa Inn, 225, 230
Hanson, Wayne, 183
Hanzel Galleries, 32, 48
Happi Sushi, 215, 221
Happy Garden Bakery, 71, 73
Hardscrabble, 74
Harlem (Ill.), 279
Harlem Globetrotters, 376
Harlon's Antiques, 228
Harper, William Rainey, 104, 124
Harper Court, 101, 106
Harper Court Sports, 102, 106
Harper Lights, 102, 106
Harper Square, 106
Harriet's Variety & Dept. Store, 266
Harrington Inst. of Interior Design, 31, 43
Harrison, Carter H., 58
Harrison, Carter H., High School, 320
Harrison Park, 315
Harrison Street, 283
Harris Theater, 37, 41
Harry and the Bear, 208
Harry's Café, 150, 173
Harsh, Vivian G., Coll. of Afro-Amer. History & Literature, 341

Notes

Notes

Notes

Notes

Notes

Notes

Notes

Notes

Notes